Progressiveness and Conservatism

New Babylon

Studies in the Social Sciences

25

Mouton Publishers · The Hague · Paris · New York

Progressiveness and Conservatism

The Fundamental Dimensions
of Ideological Controversy
and Their Relationship to Social Class

C. P. MIDDENDORP
Steinmetz Archives

Mouton Publishers · The Hague · Paris · New York

This publication has been made possible by a grant of the Netherlands
Organization for the Advancement of Pure Research (ZWO)

ISBN: 90-279-7724-0

© 1978 Mouton Publishers, The Hague, The Netherlands

Printed in Great Britain by Ebenezer Baylis and Son Ltd
The Trinity Press, Worcester, and London.

To Lideweij

Preface

I owe quite a lot to the many people who have helped me design the present study, collect the data, and carry out the analyses.

In more or less chronological order, I would like to thank Prof. Dr. H. M. Jolles for his help in the earliest stages of the present project, in particular the application for a grant to the Netherlands Organization for the Advancement of Pure Research ZWO in 1968. His immediate agreement and enthusiastic reaction to my proposal to carry out a study on 'progressiveness' and 'conservatism' for a doctoral thesis has continually provided confidence in the fruitfulness of the undertaking. In the later stages of this project, he has been tolerant enough to leave me free to mess around in my own way. I also thank him for his comments on the preliminary final draft.

My first confrontation with the subject was during my graduate study in social psychology at the University of Amsterdam, when I did a secondary analysis on the study called 'Marriage and the Family', which was stored at the Steinmetz Institute (at present the Steinmetz Archives), in order to test Reiss' (1967) theory that the relationship between social class and premarital sexual permissiveness would be positive in liberals (progressives) but negative in conservatives (see Middendorp et. al., 1970). Dr. Wim Koomen and Drs. Wim Brinkman have stimulated my interest in the subject and have generally been excellent teachers during my graduate years.

I thank Prof. Dr. J. Goudsblom for having accepted me as a staff member at the Sociological Seminar in 1968 (a period of half a year in which I could start studying the literature), and the Netherlands Organization for the Advancement of Pure Research ZWO for having accepted me as a research fellow from 1969 to 1971, and for having made possible the survey among the general population in 1970 and among M.P.'s in 1971.

The secondary analyses of the many studies in the archives of the Steinmetz Institute were carried out in 1969. I thank Dr. Harm 't Hart and Ho Yam Jok for their assistance in making these studies available, and Peter Haringhuizen for carrying out the many factor analyses and scaling procedures at the X8-computer of the Mathematical Center, Amsterdam.

The data collection for the mass survey was carried out by the fieldwork staff of Makrotest NV; I have collaborated in a pleasant way with Jan Ligthart in designing the sample.

The analyses have all been carried out at the Mathematical Center at Amsterdam. I thank Hans van Vliet, Frank van Dijk and Babs van Rij for the work they have done on this study. Very useful advice on the application of Jöreskog's method of factor analysis and the subsequent measurements of the factors has been obtained from Drs. Wim van Nooten and, in reporting on this method, by Jan Rijvordt of the Mathematical Center.

The earliest analyses for this study were carried out by my present colleague Pim Hazewindus, who in later stages was again very helpful in carrying out some additional analyses. I also thank H. Verheyden (Psychological Laboratory, University of Amsterdam) and Lucienne Storm (Technical Center of the Faculty of the Social Sciences, University of Amsterdam) for assistance in carrying out the MINISSA-analysis.

I thank the Royal Netherlands Academy of Arts and Sciences for having given me permission for one 'study-day' a week from 1971 to 1976 in order to work on this thesis. Stanley Morales and Henriette Middendorp typed preliminary drafts, and the final manuscript was excellently typed by Marja van Oostveen.

This final version was inspired by the critical remarks of Prof. Dr. R. J. Mokken. To the extent that the present report is readable at all, this is mainly due to his detailed suggestions to improve the 'form' of the manuscript. I also thank him and Prof. Dr. A. Hoogerwerf for their criticisms on the content of the study; their comments have eliminated many errors. Hoogerwerf's by now classical study of 1964 has been very helpful to get a hold on the subject. Last but not least, I thank Dr. W. Koomen for his comments on this study.

The English has been very conscientiously corrected by Marilyn Audoire and the final draft by Bill Senger. Marjan de Groot has been very helpful in making the indices.

Finally, I thank my parents for their continuous support in many ways.   C. P. MIDDENDORP

Contents

List of Tables and Figures

Tables

PART ONE

*Towards the Ideal Type Model of
Conservatism as an Ideology*

CHAPTER 1

Introduction

The major aim of the present study is to define and conceptualize (i.e., operationalize and assess empirically) the progressive-conservative antithesis in the Dutch population. This will yield what might be called fundamental dimensions of ideological controversy.

The major questions that have to be answered are: (a) how can we *define* such an abstract and much-used construct like the progressive-conservative antithesis, (b) how can we *operationalize* it, and (c) will there be *one* ideological progressive-conservative antithesis (i.e. a *uni*-dimensional one) for the Dutch population or will progressiveness and conservatism be constructs indicating a *multi*dimensional domain of ideological controversy? An additional and somewhat complicating question is: will the progressive-conservative antithesis have the same meaning for the population at large and for a political elite of members of parliament, or is the antithesis, as has sometimes been maintained, just an elitist phenomenon with a completely different meaning, or no meaning at all, for the general population?

In this study the definition of the progressive-conservative antithesis will be attempted through the construction of an 'ideal type conceptual model' (however awkward or pretentious this expression may be) of *conservative ideology.*

The operationalization of this construct will be attempted at both an *abstract* philosophical level (by means of bipolar items, partly covering the model of the construct) and at the *attitude* level (a large number of attitudes will be derived from the model).

Both operationalizations will be tested for uni- or multidimensionality in the *general population* and in what will be called the '*strategic elite*' of M.P.'s.

A second aim of the present study is to relate the dimensions of ideological controversy that will be found in the Dutch population to the variable of *social class*, the phenomenon intimately related to that of ideology (this will be discussed in Chapter 4). By means of a procedure of 'systematic exploration', the construction of a *theory* on the relationship between these 2 phenomena will be attempted starting with the relationship between social class and a socio-economic *left-right* dimension. So, theory-*construction* rather than the testing of a number of hypotheses will be the aim of the study at this stage. At the very least, a *basis* for (further) theory-construction, so much needed in the social sciences, will be obtained.

General background to the study. The terms progressive and conservative are in widespread use; yet, although a considerable amount of research has been done, there seems to be little consensus as to their meaning [1].

In the present study this apparent antithesis will be defined and conceptualized in a somewhat broader and more fundamental manner than has been done so far: a 'model' of conservatism as an ideology will therefore be constructed [2].

It is common knowledge that originally conservatism was the name given to a body of thought or a political and social philosophy which arose in Europe towards the end of the 18th and at the beginning of the 19th century as a reaction to 18th century rationalism, Enlightenment philosophy and the French Revolution (see e.g. Mannheim, 1953: 79) [3]. The term 'progressiveness' does not have such a philosophical background. From this fact among others may stem the confusion regarding the meaning of the progressive-conservative antithesis (see also Chapman, 1960: 30).

To begin with, there seems to be *terminological* confusion. Although the word progressiveness is sometimes used in the United States and England to indicate a stand that is opposed to conservatism, this is far from common [4]. In the U.S., positions opposed to conservatism are mostly indicated by *liberalism* and sometimes by *radicalism*; in England *radicalism* is the most common term [5]. So the possibility exists that terms such as progressive, liberal and conservative have different meanings in different countries. And to some extent this is true. This is one reason why the model of conservatism that is to be constructed will have 'ideal type' characteristics in order to obtain a more general meaning [6].

Another source of confusion may be found in the relationship of progressiveness-conservatism to other general antitheses, for example, the *left-right* antithesis. Sometimes this is defined as being more or less *identical* to the progressive-conservative continuum (see e.g. Campbell et al., 1960: 193; Mannheim, 1953; Hoogerwerf, 1964: 53). Others define progressiveness and conservatism as *positions* on a left-right continuum (see e.g. Wolfe, 1923; Adorno et al., 1950: 152; Rossiter, 1962; Couwenberg, 1960).

Rossiter (1962: 11-14) distinguishes from left to right: revolutionary radicalism, radicalism, liberalism, conservatism, standpattism, reaction and revolutionary reaction. Here liberalism and conservatism are seen as moderate positions, which can hardly be differentiated. Although not opposed to change (this would be 'standpattism'), the conservative is here mainly distinguished from the liberal by his *mood*, which is, for example, somewhat more sceptical as regards human nature and the possibilities of reform. Sometimes communism is defined as representing the extreme left, and fascism the extreme right. This raises serious doubts as to the *unidimensionality* of the left-right antithesis since both extremes have an important common characteristic: they represent totalitarian, undemocratic ideologies [7].

Yet others consider progressiveness-conservatism as a *subdimension* within a broader left-right antithesis (see e.g. Lipschits, 1969).

Authoritarianism-egalitarianism is another continuum which appears similar to the left-right and progressive-conservative dimensions. The concept of authoritarianism has been derived (at least in part) from fascist ideology but has been presented as a fundamental personality characteristic (see Adorno et al., 1950). It has been pointed out that fascism and conservatism have much in common, and a positive relationship between measures of authoritarianism and conservatism has been found in empirical research (see Adorno et al., 1950: 262-265; Barker, 1963: 66-70). However, the concept of authoritarianism as measured by the F-scale has been criticized for limiting itself to the assessment of *right-wing* authoritarianism only, and for not taking into account *left-wing* authoritarianism. Rokeach (1960) has attempted to conceptualize *general* authoritarianism, which he termed *dogmatism*. In short, there seems to be a domain of concepts related to progressiveness and conservatism, but the nature of the relationship is unclear.

In *empirical research*, we find that further terminological confusion is still possible. Progressiveness and conservatism are mostly conceptualized here at the *attitude* level (i.e. measured by means of attitude scales). Within various fields there are various types of progressive-conservative attitudes, which are often labeled quite differently. Sometimes they are brought together under the broader heading of progressiveness-conservatism (see e.g. Anderson et al., 1965; Lenski, 1961;

Ferdinand, 1964). More often, however, such attitudes are studied separately.

In the field of *politics*, the rather well-known distinction between economic and non-economic conservatism is found (see e.g. Lipset 1963; O'Kane, 1970). In the economic sub-field there is not as much differentiation in terminology. Politico-economic or socio-economic conservatism are frequently-used terms. In addition, labels like 'attitude towards the welfare state' and 'attitude to government interference' are also used. In the non-economic field there is a greater variety of labels, e.g. nationalism vs. internationalism, attitude to civil liberties, democratic attitudes, humanitarianism, tolerance, etc.

In still other fields there are also various labels indicating attitudes that seem to belong to the progressive-conservative domain: in the field of *religion*, there is religious fundamentalism or orthodoxy; in that of *marriage and the family* traditionalism (e.g. the Traditional Family Ideology scale; Huffman and Levinson, 1950) and conventionality [8]

What seems essential is that the progressive-conservative antithesis can obviously be approached at 2 levels: at an *'abstract'* level: as a social and political philosophy or ideology (which arose in Europe as a reaction to the French Revolution (see e.g. Burke, 1790, and Mannheim, 1953), and at a *concrete* level, i.e. at the attitude-level, as is mostly the case in empirical research. There is terminological confusion at both levels, and in addition there are problems of definition.

Definition. At the attitude level, conservatism, that is at least semantically, appears to refer to an attitude *opposed to change*. Progressiveness, on the other hand, does *not* seem to point to an attitude in *favor of change*, rather, the very concept of progressiveness immediately poses the question: *which type of change can be considered as progressive*? The use of a simple time-dimension would be unsatisfactory in this instance, as it would imply that every change towards an unprecedented situation would constitute progress, and any change towards an earlier situation, 'regress'.

So, if one considers progressiveness against conservatism from the perspective of 'attitude to change', the possibility of regressive or reactionary change (as opposed to progressive change) poses the question: according to which *criteria* can it be decided whether change is progressive or reactionary? The establishment of such criteria is one of the major objectives of the present study [9]. Once such criteria have been established, the notion of 'attitude to change' becomes less important: *attitudinal positions can then be described in terms of the found criteria. In the present study, an attempt will be made to derive such criteria from a definition of conservatism as an ideology by way of the construction of an ideal type model* [10].

This is one way in which both 'levels of approach' towards the progressive-conservative antithesis will be combined: the philosophical level will be used to define the more specific domain of progressive-conservative attitudes.

Historical developments. A major problem is that many *variations* in conservative thought have manifested themselves historically. When the term was introduced in 1818 in France by Chateaubriand (see his journal *Le Conservateur*), it was rapidly adopted by many movements and groups in Western Europe which were opposed to the French Revolution and the ideas of the Enlightenment. The most notable common aim of these groups lay in their desire to preserve the old order (see e.g. Chapman, 1960: 29–31; Von Klemperer, 1968: 17). There were, however, substantial differences between Burkean conservatism in England (pragmatic and developmental), German romantic conservatism (with strong nationalistic and authoritarian tendencies) and French conservatism (which had a strong religious, i.e. Roman Catholic, bias and reactionary tendencies).

Conservatism has been regarded as *conscious traditionalism* (Mannheim, 1953: 95, 98). Thus, it is not surprising that variations in conservative thought reflect the socio-cultural and political situation from which it arose (see e.g. Freund, 1955: 10–11).

Moreover, when once in existence, conservatism *remains* sensitive to social developments mainly in 2 ways: (1) it tends to *accept* developments which seem inevitable, irreversible or which at least in retrospect, appear to have developed naturally; and (2), it tends to develop *new variations* aiming to legitimize the established order when new ideas and movements arise which seem to threaten that order.

The construction of an ideal type of conservatism will therefore not be very simple. Some even deny that conservatism incorporates any principles or that it constitutes a body of thought capable of delineation [11]. Others, on the other hand, find it comparatively easy to list the conservative principles [12].

Progressiveness has not manifested itself as an ideology under that name. Historically, 2 mainstreams of progressive ideology have manifested themselves: *liberalism* and *socialism*. These progressive ideologies have often been, and sometimes still are, quite strongly opposed to each other.

In the first half of the 19th century, conservatism was in *theory* opposed to the ideas of the Enlightenment and the French Revolution;

only in political *practice*, it opposed classical liberalism. In the European context, both classical liberalism and conservatism, by means of such processes as outlined above, became more and more integrated in their common opposition to the rise of socialism. (This will be discussed in more detail in Chapter 4.)

Findings of empirical research. In empirical research, we find that there is conflicting evidence as to the question of the *dimensionality* of the progressive-conservative antithesis: is there one general antithesis or are there various dimensions (and if so: how many and of which nature) that are more or less independent of each other? Although it was already found in an early study that "the individual does not tend to be consistently progressive or conservative" (Reed, 1927), in early factor-analytic studies on the structure of social attitudes, *general* factors were found which were labeled radicalism (or liberalism) vs. conservatism (see e.g. Thurstone, 1934; Eysenck, 1947, 1954). In the early days, the construction of liberalism-conservatism 'tests' also suggested unidimensionality (see e.g. Lentz, 1938; Hartmann, 1938). A general factor was also found in more recent studies by e.g. Comrey and Newmeyer (1965) and Wilson, ed., (1974).

Two-dimensionality has been strongly suggested by the work of Smith (1948 a,b) in terms of economic vs. non economic liberalism-conservatism. This distinction was taken up later by e.g. Lipset (1963) and O'Kane (1970). Another 2-dimensional structure has repeatedly been found by Kerlinger (1967, 1968, 1970, 1972) in terms of separate liberalism and conservatism factors.

Apart from the paper mentioned previously (see Reed, 1927), evidence in favor of multidimensionality in terms either of an unspecified number of dimensions or of at least more than 2, has been presented by e.g. Kerr (1952), Lenski (1961) and Anderson et al. (1965).

Finally, political research in the late 1950's and early 1960's indicates a complete lack of structured opinions on liberal-conservative issues, at least in the general public of the U.S. (see e.g. Campbell et al., 1960; Converse, 1964; McClosky, 1964). As an (abstract) ideological continuum, liberalism-conservatism only appeared meaningful to a few 'ideologues' and political elites such as congressmen. This would mean that only in such groups would there be sufficiently high correlations among opinions on various liberal-conservative issues to legitimize the postulation of the existence of a unidimensional liberal-conservative antithesis.

This proposition has not remained unchallenged (see Kerlinger, 1967, 1968, 1972; Axelrod, 1967; Luttbeg, 1968; Brown, 1970) and recently

Nie (1974) presented evidence that the lack of structured beliefs in the American public, as far as the liberal-conservative continuum was concerned, was perhaps a phenomenon of the period of the 1950's and early 1960's. Particularly after 1964, a dramatic increase in the correlations among various liberal-conservative opinions has become apparent.

An interesting specification of the matter of consistency of opinion relating to the level of *abstraction* of such opinions may also be mentioned. Prothro and Grigg (1960) and McClosky (1964) show that there may be consensus on *abstract principles* (i.e. of liberal democracy) in the general public but that such consensus is often lacking *on specific applications* of such principles. Free and Cantril (1967: 32) note that many people are *operational liberals* (i.e. favor liberal policies when presented in concrete, specific terms) but *ideological conservatives* (i.e. agree with general, abstract conservative principles). Mann (1970) and Merelman (1969) both argue that this situation may characterize the working class.

The research evidence introduced above is difficult to evaluate due to the variations in the samples used and in the analytical techniques applied. As a preliminary remark it may be stated that what is particularly lacking in many studies is a clear *criterion* (or criteria) guiding the researcher in the selection of items to be included in the design. How to arrive at such criteria constitutes an important problem which many researchers have not even attempted to tackle [13].

The confusing and conflicting results of empirical research on progressiveness-conservatism may have been discouraging to many social scientists. After Adorno et al.'s presentation of the F-scale in 1950 and their relative lack of success in constructing a politico-economic conservatism (PEC) scale, research in this field in the 1950's was dominated by studies on the nature of authoritarianism and the matter of response-sets. As mentioned above, fresh evidence on the irrelevance of liberalism-conservatism to the general public became available in the early 1960's.

Hence, although since the Second World War there has been an enormous increase in empirical research, relatively few studies on progressiveness-conservatism have been carried out. The possible general background to this phenomenon may be sketched as follows:

1. The experience of *fascism* brought with it an interest in and concern about the *anti-democratic potential at the personality level* in Western societies (often termed 'liberal democracies'). This was one factor which increased the interest in a concept such as authoritarianism (as a personality trait) and studies of the degree of consensus on liberal democratic principles and the prerequisites for liberal

democracy in general (see e.g. Hacker, 1957; Bachrach, 1962).

2. The desire for order and harmony, for cooperation and consensus after the war years was reflected on the one hand by an interest in phenomena such as anomia and alienation, on the other by the predominance of sociological theories postulating such a state of affairs (i.e. a consensus on basic values) as 'natural', thus denying the existence of fundamental social conflict and ideological controversy (e.g. Parsonian structural functionalism, Parsons, 1964). A movement like the *New Conservatism* in the U.S., which turned to classical conservative notions such as tradition and moral values, hierarchy and authority, may also have stemmed from this desire for order and harmony (see e.g. Kirk, 1954; Viereck, 1962).

3. The experience of *communism* during the Cold War probably turned the attention of researchers towards concepts such as general authoritarianism and dogmatism (i.e. Rokeach, 1960).

4. Both the experiences of communism and fascism provoked a general *distrust in ideology*, defined as a general abstract scheme or blueprint, interpreting society as a whole and postulating ideas to substantially improve the world or create a utopia. In addition, among the old 19th century ideologies (liberalism, socialism and conservatism) consensus appeared to have been reached on major political issues, and on the necessity of piecemeal reform; hence the postulation of the 'end of ideology' (see e.g. Lipset, 1963; Bell, 1965).

5. A distrust of general abstract ideas may have caused an increase in more limited research-designs, both in the sense of more limited conceptualizations of e.g. attitudes within specific fields and in 'theories of the middle range' (see Merton, 1957). The former is expressed in the numerous separate studies on opinions and attitudes which had formerly been conceptualized as part of the broader liberal-conservative antithesis [14].

If the situation outlined above has indeed been true during the 1950's and early 1960's, the situation in the late 1960's and early 1970's is certainly quite different. The experience of the Second World War has been replaced (especially for the younger generation) by that of the war in Vietnam (see e.g. Kenniston, 1968; Van Benthem van den Berg, 1969). There is a growing interest in ideology [15] which is related to the realization that fundamental conflict and ideological controversy exist alongside harmony and possibly consensus on some basic values. It has also been realized that basic values may underlie the many attitudes studied (see e.g. Rokeach 1968, 1973) in the same way that attitudes themselves underlie specific beliefs (see e.g. Green, 1959: 336). In this situation it seems increasingly relevant to again consider the *general* progressive-conservative antithesis as a central object of social research.

In summary, a major objective of the study is the development of one or more criteria (a) to distinguish between progressive and conservative opinions and attitudes, and (b) to delineate the progressive-conservative domain. The position taken is that such criteria may be derived from an *ideal type model of conservative ideology*, to be constructed out of the many empirical and historical manifestations of conservative philosophy. (This conceptual model will be a theoretical concept or construct, designed with the aim of approximating as closely as possible to the ideal type of conservative ideology.)

There are 2 levels of discourse on progressiveness vs. conservatism. One is at a philosophical level, the other is at the level of attitudes and opinions and is concerned with the empirical structure of such opinions. It is the confusion between these 2 levels and their relative lack of integration [16] which seems to be the main cause for the relatively unsatisfactory state of affairs regarding research-findings on the nature of the progressive-conservative antithesis today. In the present study, such an integration between both approaches will be attempted. *Conservatism* as an ideology, which has developed in Western Europe since the beginnings of the 19th century, is taken as the means or starting-point by which to approach the progressive-conservative antithesis at the philosophical level, since *progressiveness* 'as such' has not manifested itself here.

The aims of the present study, then, are the following:

(a) to define the (*theoretical*) *construct* of conservative ideology in an ideal type way, out of the many 'empirical' forms and discussions as they are found in the literature. This will result in a systematic outline of the elements of conservative thought, which are mutually related, at least partly, in a logical and/or deductive way. To the extent that this will in fact prove to be the case, we may speak of the conceptual *model* of conservatism.

(b) to investigate whether conservatism in fact constitutes an ideology in the sense that *basic values* underlie its various elements, i.e. give unity to conservative thought. These values — which in fact will be found — will serve as criteria to define the domain of progressive-conservative *attitudes* in various fields like politics, religion, the family.

(c) to *operationalize* the model of conservatism at 2 levels of 'abstraction': (1) at the level of the elements in the theoretical construct — this will be called the *abstract* level and (2) at the attitude level (see (b) above); this will be called the *concrete* or *specific* level. This distinction seems interesting in view of the research evidence cited above, suggesting that people's reactions to abstract notions can be quite different to, or even inconsistent with their reactions to specific 'applications' of such notions.

(d) to assess the *dimensionality* of both operationalized forms of the theoretical concept in 2 sampled universes: (1) the *Dutch population* (also indicated by terms such as 'the general public', 'the mass public' or simply 'the mass') and (2) *members of the Second Chamber of parliament* — M.P.'s — also indicated by the terms 'elite' or 'strategic elite' [17]. Although there has been assembled some evidence (i.e. Nie, 1974) that through the increasing salience of politics in the 1960's, the liberal-conservative antithesis in the U.S. has now also appeared at the mass level, it is still possible that such constructs, as abstract dimensions, are only elitist phenomena, hardly reflected at all in the general public (see e.g. Converse, 1964).

We will first see whether the progressive-conservative antithesis as a theoretical — perhaps also elitist — phenomenon will have some meaning for the general public at the *abstract* level (see (c) above). Subsequently, the structure of this theoretical antithesis will be assessed in some semi-elites like the highly educated and the politically involved, in anticipation of the assessment for the elite of M.P.'s.

Then we will go *back* to the mass-level and *down* to the attitude level and subsequently integrate abstract dimensions with attitudinal ones into what will be called *ideological dimensions*. The structure of the ideological domain will then be assessed in a similar way for semi-elites and the strategic elite of M.P.'s.

(e) to provide at least a *framework for theory-construction* around the major dimensions of ideological controversy which will — indeed — be found at the mass level. This will be attempted by means of a process of *systematic exploration* of the data at hand (i.e. the ideological dimensions and many other variables which have been brought into the design of the study). Not all of these variables have been conceptualized as carefully as the ideological dimensions; still, the results of this analysis should not be considered as only of 'exploratory' value (i.e. in the sense of De Groot, 1961: 54–57).

Given the nature of the sample and the conceptualization of the major variables, these results, though not predicted by way of a series of hypotheses (this is technically impossible as long as we do not know the nature of the ideological dimensions), appear to be meaningful in themselves and can form a starting-point for theory-

construction. This does not mean that there are no 'deductive moments' in systematic exploration (therefore, this process may also be called 'inductive-deductive'): at certain stages during the process, one may attempt to construct and test causal models, for example.

In the social sciences, pure deduction (i.e. the testing of hypotheses, still considered as the ideal of the scientific process in most methodological handbooks) is not always possible (i.e. there is no theory available to be tested), and not always necessary (e.g. when the sample allows generalization of results to a meaningful universe and when concepts are carefully constructed). However, this ideal could be approached to a larger extent when more *continuity* in social research is reached, i.e. by means of secondary analysis and replication (see Middendorp, 1976c).

Outline of the book. The general methodology of the present study will be outlined in more detail in *Chapter 2*. In particular the definition and conceptualization of complex constructs such as conservative ideology and the process of systematic exploration, in order to provide a framework for theory-construction around such constructs, will be discussed.

Previous research will be critically examined in *Chapter 3*, especially from the perspective of the 'ideal' construct-definition and the conceptualization (i.e. operationalization and empirical assessment) of constructs, as outlined in Chapter 2.

Chapter 4 starts with a discussion on the concept of ideology and gives a rough historical outline of the major ideological developments in Western Europe in the past 2 centuries. This leads to a presentation of the 'ideal type model' of the construct of conservative ideology, which will then be 'analyzed' for underlying values which will serve as criteria in the construction of progressive-conservative attitude-scales.

Chapter 5 deals with the operationalizations of the model of conservative ideology. As indicated above, conservatism will be operationalized in 2 ways (see point c). Previous Dutch surveys of the mid-sixties have been secondarily analyzed in order to provide a basis for the construction of progressive-conservative attitude-scales.

In *Chapter 6*, the operationalizations of conservative ideology will be empirically assessed as outlined above (point d): this will be called Type-1 analysis.

In *Chapter 7* the development of a framework for theory-construction will be attempted around the major dimensions of ideological controversy (point e), especially around the relationship between *social class* and the politico-economic progressiveness-conservatism dimension which has been called the *left-right* dimension. This type of analysis will be called Type-2 analysis. The construction and measurement of the many other variables which have been used in this analysis (i.e. background variables, personality variables, personal history variables and situational variables) will also be presented. Again some previous surveys have been secondarily analyzed in order to obtain a basis for the operationalization of variables.

Finally, *Chapter 8* will discuss and summarize the major findings.

NOTES ON CHAPTER 1

1. Some evidence of confusion or sheer ignorance regarding the meaning of the terms 'progressive' and 'conservative' in the Dutch population is given by Stapel (1971: 205-206). Earlier, Stapel (1968: 39) had found that the terms 'left' and 'right' are also unclear: 35% of the population could not give any description. The terms are mostly seen as 'communist-socialist' vs. 'capitalist' or 'christian' vs. 'non-christian'.
2. Concepts like model and ideology, which are rather loosely introduced here, will of course be discussed later, in particular the concept of ideology. A general indication of what is meant by a model of conservatism is given by e.g. Neumann (in: Von Klemperer, 1968: x, xvii) and Von Klemperer (1968: 12, 20).
3. This matter will be further discussed in Chapter 4.
4. See, however, e.g. Newcomb (1943); Gouldner (1946); Bremner (1953); McCoy (1956); Wilson (1959); Harrison (1967); Rogin (1968), and Hartz (1955: 229-234). Grimes (1956: 735) notes that until the 1930's, liberals in the U.S. tended to equate 'classical economics' with liberalism. 'Real' liberals had to use the term 'progressive'.
5. The terms progressive and conservative will be used throughout the present study, also when referring to studies in which the terms 'liberal' or 'radical' are used in preference to 'progressive'.
6. The nature of the concept of ideal type will be gone into later. Here, the word is used to indicate that the model aimed at should 'embrace' most of the 'empirical manifestations' (i.e. incorporate most of the elements present in such manifestations) of conservatism (see Neumann, in Von Klemperer, 1968: x, xvii; Hempel, 1965: 169).
7. Of course, this is a very rough indication of the common characteristics of fascism and communism, which gained popularity in the 1950's and early 1960's (i.e. during the Cold War).
8. The many studies that deal specifically with such concepts will not be discussed in the present study (see Chapter 3).
9. In the Netherlands this position has been taken by Hoogerwerf (1964: 30-35); Lipschits, however, again defines progressive and conservative in terms of 'attitude towards the status quo' (1969: 44-47). This is also the case in many early American studies (see Chapter 3).
10. This does not mean, of course, that criteria defining progressive vs. conservative positions have not been previously established or that those criteria would be unacceptable in every case. But what has generally been

lacking is an analysis at the philosophical level *legitimizing* the choice of such criteria. Hoogerwerf's analysis (1964: 28–29, 39–52, especially 40–44, 48–51) is an exception but is not totally satisfactory: as the author himself admits, the criterion of equality is not the *only* one underlying progressive-conservative positions. Hoogerwerf's study will be discussed further in Chapter 3.

11. See e.g. Von Klemperer (1968: 17); Mühlenfeld (1952: 179–180); Wilson (1941: 29–30); Freund (1955: 10–11).
12. Huntington (1957: 469) relates this characteristic to the *positional* nature of conservatism. Of course, such lists do not constitute 'models', as will become evident in Chapter 4. Examples are given by Kirk (1954: 7–8); Rossiter (1962: 64–66); Hearnshaw (1933: 22ff); McClosky (1958: 30–31); Kendall and Carey (1964: 418–419), and many others. Some will be presented later (Chapter 4). Mannheim (1953: 77–79) adopts a position between that of those who find it difficult or impossible to discern conservative principles, and that of those who find it relatively easy. He attempts to delineate the *basic intentions* behind conservative thought. Such basic intentions can be derived from a model of conservatism, in order to identify progressive-conservative opinions and attitudes.
13. One rarely finds a researcher who is concerned about the fact of whether the interpretation of his findings in terms of radicalism-conservatism is allowed (see e.g. Thurstone, 1934; Sanai, 1950, 1951), or about how items should be selected (see e.g. Pollack, 1943; Adorno et al., 1950; Ferdinand, 1964; Kerlinger, 1972).
14. E.g. attitudes like nationalism, civil rights, religious orthodoxy. Chapter 3 will show that as far as conceptualization is concerned, early studies of social attitudes were often designed in a much broader way than most recent studies. This has resulted in the existence of numerous attitude scales as summarized in e.g. Robinson et al. (1968, 1969).
15. Note the New Left (in the Netherlands: 'Nieuw Links') and New Radicalism movements in the U.S. and in Western Europe; as against the Radical Right. See Kroes (1974); Lynd (1969); Lasch (1965); Glazer (1968) and the discussion on the 'New Radicalism' in *Partisan Review*, (1965); see also Bell, ed. (1964); Waxman (1969).
16. In the only attempt to construct a scale for 'classical conservatism' (items derived from general notions of conservatism as a body of thought; McClosky, 1958), this approach has not been integrated with measurements on the attitude level.
17. The term is from Barnes (1966).

CHAPTER 2

On Methodology

2.1. INTRODUCTION

In this chapter, we will try to outline the general methodology behind the present approach to the progressive-conservative controversy, which has been indicated in the introductory chapter.

From this introductory outline, it is clear that there are 2 major issues which will concern us here:

(a) procedures of the definition and conceptualization (i.e. operationalization and empirical assessment) of complex constructs;

(b) procedures of systematic exploration, including both inductive and deductive moments (as opposed to the testing of sets of explicit formulated hypotheses), providing a framework for theory-construction.

Both issues are intimately related (see e.g. Stinchcombe, 1968: 41ff; Hempel, 1952: 1–2; 28, 47). It is often noted, for example, that the definition and conceptualization of constructs should be fruitful ground for the development of *theories*, rather than being based only on *operational* considerations (see Blalock and Blalock, 1968: 6–9; Dumont and Wilson, 1967: 994).

Problems of definition and conceptualization of constructs are, of course, often discussed in textbooks. However, these discussions are frequently presented in general terms and sometimes tend towards superficiality [1]. Insufficient attention has been paid to matters such as the degree of *complexity* of constructs, the various levels of *abstraction* at which the construct may be operationalized, and the relationship between the empirical assessment of such constructs and the types of sample used. Matters such as ideal type oriented procedures in the process of constructing a model of a construct do not seem to have been adequately discussed in the literature until now [2]. These procedures will be outlined below.

Problems of theory construction have not been discussed very much in textbooks (as compared to procedures of hypothesis-testing) although it is generally recognized that there is a *lack of theories* in the social sciences, and therefore that it is of the utmost importance to begin constructing such theories (see e.g. De Groot, 1961: 316; Galtung, 1967: 451; Selltiz et al., 1963: 486ff). It is also generally recognized that research strategies which are not directed at the *testing* of hypotheses may nevertheless contribute to the *formulation* of hypotheses, which may then be tested in subsequent research [3]. However, such strategies have also mostly been outlined in insufficient detail. Therefore, it may be useful to describe these procedures here as well [4].

This discussion on methodological issues will provide us with a framework for critical discussion and evaluation of previous research.

2.2. DEFINITION AND CONCEPTUALIZATION OF COMPLEX CONSTRUCTS [5]

2.2.1. *The ideal type approach to the definition of complex constructs*

In construct-formation, it is essential that an attempt be made to determine the *boundaries* of the construct [6]. The more complex (e.g. comprehensive) the constructs are, the more vague and often emotional the manner in which they are actually used in everyday speech. Disputes as to the 'real' meaning of such constructs frequently arise.

The social scientist is confronted by a dilemma: should he continue using such constructs, or should he introduce new ones, devoid of confused popular usage?

In this situation, one should attempt to *clarify* the meaning of such a construct. The first step towards such a clarification could be by the construction of a model of the construct [7].

A construct constitutes a model to the extent that its elements are mutually related in a logical or deductive way. As a model, the (theoretical) construct is *represented* by its (operational) concept in empirical research. The process of construct formation or model construction may have both inductive and deductive moments [8]. In the case of conservatism, first, an inventory is made of as many characteristics of the construct as have been outlined by its adherents, opponents or students: this is the inductive stage (see e.g. Dumont and Wilson, 1967: 991). Second, the model itself is constructed deductively from such an inventory by 'creating' the construct's inner structure or logic: some characteristics are more fundamental than others, and the latter may be derived from the former. Still others may be derived from these less fundamental characteristics, and so on. A hierarchy of statements which are divided into sections, is thus created: this may be considered the *model* of the construct (see e.g. Hempel, 1952: 11).

In the case of an ideology like conservatism, it seems quite likely that a model, in this sense, of the construct will in fact prove to exist . . . if we aim at the construction of the ideal type of conservative ideology [9]. In the literature, we find many outlines of conservatism which do not have model characteristics: the elements are *not* hierarchically ordered, their mutual relationships are *not* made explicit and the elements are *not* clearly represented by the operational concept. (Such outlines will be called 'quasi-models'.)

If a model can indeed be derived from such quasi-models and other manifestations of conservatism (by a process as outlined above), this model may be considered the ideal type conservative ideology: a (theoretical) construct in which the elements which are *essential* to conservative thought are integrated and their mutual relationships made explicit. We expect something like this to exist behind the many 'empirical' forms found in the literature.

The concept of ideal type was first introduced by Weber (see e.g. 1949) [10], and has recently been discussed by Rogers (1969) and Hendricks and Breckinridge Peters (1973) [11]. As is well known, Weber did not define the ideal type rigorously; it is clear, however, that he did not consider it only in a *conceptual* way, but also saw it as a rational structure of action, opposed to, or only approaching 'irrational' reality (see Weber, 1968: 65, 169). Watkins (1952: 22–43), for example, distinguishes 2 ways in which Weber uses the term ideal type: (a) *holistic*, i.e., describing the essential traits of a (historical) situation as a whole, and (b) *individualistic*, i.e., where individual actors are placed in some simplified situation: 'Its premises are the form (but not the specific content) of the actors' dispositions, the state of their information and their relationships' (p.24).

In the present study, the ideal type is used in the sense described by Hendricks and Breckinridge Peters (1973: 35–36): 'If definitions, types operate to select material of importance by selecting categories of observation and must be judged on their clarity, inclusiveness and conciseness . . . The ideal type is, despite its utility in the formation of concepts, much more than a mere summary and classification of important phenomena: it is also a means of ordering that portion of reality which is of immediate concern to the social scientist'.

In the social sciences, there is a lack of (theoretical) constructs. Still, science can only progress if such constructs are used (see e.g. Willer and Webster, 1970). Moreover, insofar as constructs are used, they are often insufficiently defined i.e. no attempts at ideal type model construction are made. In addition to this, it has often been too readily accepted that operationalizations of constructs necessarily cover only *part* of their meaning (see note 1). Methodologists have become increasingly aware of this situation. Willer and Webster (1970), Dumont and Wilson (1967), Hempel (1965), DiRenzo (1968) and Blalock and Blalock (1968: 26) all argue, in different terms, for greater conceptual clarity and better definitions of constructs. This is exactly what is intended by the present attempt to define the construct of conservatism by way of an ideal type approach aiming at the construction of a model, which can then be used as a starting-point for the development of operational concepts [12].

Willer and Webster (1970: 754–755) describe the process of formulating constructs by means of 'abduction' as follows: 'In forming constructs, he [the researcher, CPM] should be guided by his knowledge of empirical reality, but he cannot be wholly dependent upon it. . . . Abduction is the progressive development and refining of a concept, beginning at the stage of an observable and ending with a well-defined, abstract theoretical construct, which is embedded in theoretical assertions . . . empirical studies can be used as tools for theory construction. Such research would begin with the description of observable relations . . . sets of observables which later may be subsumed under a common concept or common concepts . . . The major task at the first stage of the abductive process is to compile a list of observational assertions . . . The second stage in the abductive process is . . . to use that information to reformulate the concepts more generally'. In this sense, they maintain, the reformulation of concepts in the second stage of abduction should be intended to render them *less* complete reflections of the real world, for the more complete any reflection of the world is, the more temporary its accuracy, and hence, its theoretical value (see note 11: Becker, 1940: 52).

Possibly the best statement on the role of theoretical constructs has been given by Marx (1956: 117–122): ' . . . theoretical constructs may (1) give suggestions for empirical research, (2) be transformed into intervening variables . . . It is precisely this characteristic of enabling an investigator to be *beyond* present knowledge and not to be tied to currently orthodox formulations that helps to justify the usefulness of such hypothetical constructs as guides to experimentation' (see also Dumont and Wilson, 1967: 991).

This is precisely the aim of the present study: the 'hypothetical construct' of conservative ideology suggests empirical research through its operationalization and empirical assessment for various universes. On this basis, the construction of (empirical) variables is aimed at; these will be used in subsequent attempts to outline a framework for theory-construction.

Finally, the term 'model' suggests a unity and consistency in conservative thought which may not (even: never) be found in reality but which may come to the fore by means of the ideal type approach to construct formation. As many see it, the term 'ideology' also suggests consistency, brought about by central values underlying a number of (related) ideas [13]. This suggests that to the extent that conservatism constitutes an *ideology*, it also constitutes a *model*. Thus, once the model has been constructed, one should be able to derive those basic values from it, which can then be used in empirical research (see below).

In conclusion, the procedures through which a model of a construct is made constitute a time-consuming, complex and tricky process. Still, if one intends to lessen the confusion that exists at present about the meaning of constructs such as progressiveness and conservatism, the construction of models seems necessary.

2.2.2. Conceptualizing constructs

2.2.2.1. Operationalization. A construct may essentially be operationalized at 2 levels of abstraction:

(a) on an *abstract* level, through translation of the construct's elements into an operational form (*direct* operationalization) and
(b) on a *specific*, concrete level, within areas relevant to the construct. (This operationalization may be called '*indirect*': one in which, for example, specific opinions and attitudes are defined as belonging to the domain of the construct at a lower level of abstraction. This domain can be defined with the help of *criteria* derived from the construct. For example, in the case of ideologies, *central values*, underlying the ideological orientations, may be used as such criteria.)

Since it has often been shown, as noted above, that people's reaction to abstract, general statements can be quite different to or even inconsistent with their opinions on specific, concrete issues, a construct should essentially be operationalized at *both* levels of abstraction [14].

In direct operationalization, an attempt is made to 'translate' the elements of the construct into such a format as to render them appropriate for the universe sampled. Of course, for highly sophisticated samples, such translations may remain very close to the original formulations. For less sophisticated samples (e.g. samples from the general population) it may be necessary to deviate more from the original formulations and a number of elements may even prove incapable of being operationalized. When universes with various levels of sophistication are used in one research design, one should try to find the 'golden mean', a position which is acceptable to *most* respondents from *both* types of samples (see par. 2.2.2.2.).

An important auxiliary measure could be the use of *bipolarity* in item construction. In operationalizing the construct of conservatism, for example, it may in fact be helpful to less sophisticated respondents if the *opposite* position is made explicit. By offering 2 statements simultaneously (and their mutual relation of opposition) it is possible that more valid responses will generally be obtained. Especially in the case of rather abstract items, bipolarity is further advisable as a means of reducing possible tendencies to acquiesce in responding (see Berkowitz and Wolkon, 1964).

As indicated above, for the indirect operationalization of a construct, one should be able to derive criteria from it for the selection of more specific manifestations and implications. We will not go into the details of this tricky process here (see Chapter 4 and 5).

What, however, should be the level of abstraction of these specific elements? First, one may distinguish between items and scales. (In the case of constructs like ideologies, items will refer to opinions; scales will be attitude scales.) Items, however, may refer to specific, popular issues of the day, or, as the other extremes, to general, abstract notions.

Both extremes have to be rejected. Abstract items are a matter of the *directly* operationalized model, and the jump from highly abstract (e.g. ideological) orientations to the issues of the day seems to be dependent on too many other factors as well as the respondents' orientation along the more basic dimensions. Rather, items should reflect positions on more enduring, general issues. In other words, the level of abstraction of items should be the *attitude*-level [15]. (An attitude may simply be defined as a more or less general, positive or negative orientation towards some 'object', which expresses itself in a number of opinions regarding such an object) [16]. The attitude-*scale* is in fact the correct unit of measurement in assessing broader (e.g. ideological) dimensions. Attitude-scales constitute the level of abstraction between single items (which are a part of such an attitude) and (abstract) ideological dimensions. In using attitude-scales, specific item variance is reduced and the measurement thus becomes more reliable. The attitude-scale level is also best suited to *'pre-conceptualize'* a broad, ideological domain to some extent before one jumps from many attitude-items to general dimensions.

There is a plethora of attitude-scales available in the social sciences today. If it could be shown that by a procedure such as that sketched above, a relatively large number of such scales could be identified as aspects of more general constructs, a more parsimonious conceptualization such as this might lead to more satisfactory results as far as theoretical insight is concerned. Thus, in the present study, the construct of conservative ideology will be operationalized at an abstract, philosophical level as well as the attitude level.

2.2.2.2. Empirical assessment: the universes. There has been a tendency among social scientists to erroneously assume that a relationship between 2 variables either exists (and has some strength) or does not exist [17]. This, for example, has stimulated research aiming at explaining or interpreting relationships, or assessing their spuriousness, rather than research aiming to *specify* relationships (see e.g. Galtung, 1967: 410–412). When relations between variables (e.g. items indicating a concept) can in fact vary considerably from sample to sample, as seems to be the case, this means that in the social sciences empirical concepts (i.e. concepts describing characteristics of people) do not exist in any universal sense: they are relative to the sampled universe [18].

Of course, scales (i.e. concepts) are preferred which prove relatively insensitive to sampling variability, but when one does not have such concepts, the use of *standard* samples, drawn from a universe which may be used as a standard for comparisons between sub-samples, seems to be the only solution. For constructs which are relevant to 'all people', it seems a matter of course to develop concepts (i.e. measuring instruments) on the basis of *national cross-sectional* samples [19].

There is one problem, however: for many constructs there are certain groups for which they have a *special relevance*. One might consider which is the more fruitful to choose as a standard: the general public or that which might be termed a *'strategic elite'* (see Barnes, 1966: 520).

Since it has been shown in a number of studies that the structure of beliefs (e.g. the scalability of items, the dimensionality of scales) may be very different in the general population as compared to such elites (see e.g. Converse, 1964; McClosky, 1964), the solution of this dilemma is obvious: constructs should be empirically assessed in *both* the general public and in at least one of its strategic elites [20]. To identify the factors that might contribute to possible differences found between both universes, *sub-groups* from the general population may be investigated.

Thus, in the present study, both operationalizations of conservative ideology, as outlined above, will be empirically assessed in both the general public and in a strategic elite.

2.2.2.3. Empirical assessment: Type-1 analysis. For constructs like ideology (i.e. the progressive-conservative controversy) it is of course interesting in itself to compare operationalizations at 2 levels of abstraction and to empirically assess such operationalizations for the general public as well as for a 'strategic elite' like members of parliament.

Above, some methodological rationales for these procedures have been developed which indicate that such a design is somewhat more than just 'interesting': it is *necessary* to obtain a *complete* insight into the characteristics (i.e. the dimensionality and the nature of the — possible — dimensions) of complex constructs, e.g. the major domain of ideological controversy. In the next chapter it will be shown that the lack of such a full Type-1 analytical design in the conceptualization of conservative ideology (in addition to the lack of an ideal type model approach to the definition of this construct) has mainly yielded confusing and contradictory results.

Type-1 analysis, then, follows essentially a 2 × 2 design: the construct (i.e. the ideal type model of conservatism) is operationalized at an abstract and at a specific level and it is empirically assessed in the general population and in a strategic elite (see Table 2.1.).

Table 2.1. *The empirical assessment of a complex construct: the Type-1 analytical design*

UNIVERSES SAMPLED	THE IDEAL TYPE MODEL OF A CONSTRUCT	
	Operationalizations	
	Direct: translation of the construct's elements	*Indirect:* elements derived from the ideal type model by means of criteria
National cross-sectional (the general population)	1	3
A strategic elite	2	4

Furthermore, both operationalizations of a construct may, in some cases, be integrated into one design. It is clear then that Type-1 analysis may yield complex results. The matter that finally has to be discussed is the interpretation of these results.

2.2.2.4. *Type-1 analysis: interpretations of results.*

First, since a construct is by definition a theoretical phenomenon, one need not expect that in any of the conditions of its empirical assessment, as shown in Table 2.1., a bi-polar distribution will have to show up in order for the model to be accepted. The term 'ideal type' already suggests that 'in reality', on the basis of whatever operationalization, individuals showing all characteristics of the construct will hardly be found (and so will individuals showing *none* of the characteristics at all).

However, there should be *some* relationship between the construct and the results of its empirical assessment. *The definition of the construct and its operationalizations should be such that in the 2 types of sample that were distinguished, after proper analysis, well-interpretable structures will be found.*

A *unidimensional structure* will of course be most easily interpretable, with all, or the vast majority, of the items or scales in the operationalization of the construct, showing a substantial relationship to each other. This dimension can then be interpreted in terms of the construct itself, i.e. in the case of conservatism, one would call such a dimension the 'progressive-conservative' one.

It will be more difficult to interpret a *multidimensional* structure: this depends on the nature of the dimensions. One solution should be mentioned: if more than one criterion can be derived from the ideal type of the construct (in the case of an ideology: if more than one basic value would seem to underlie the ideological positions), and we would find a multidimensional structure, we would expect that the dimensions would somehow 'reflect' this postulated underlying structure, i.e. they should be interpretable in terms of it. Other solutions are possible, however, for example when dimensions can be interpreted in terms of well known ideological postures.

Of course, the meaning of a construct will be substantiated in case at least one of its empirical assessments would yield a unidimensional structure, which can be seen as evidence in favor of the 'model'-nature of its ideal type. If no such structure at all would result, it would be better to split-up the construct into 2 or more 'subconstructs'.

Results, however, may not unequivocally point to either *uni*dimensionality or *multi*dimensionality. It may be that in some or perhaps most of the empirical assessments, only partial structures emerge, or even no structure at all appears. In such cases, when there is an unclear or insufficient relationship between the construct in its operational forms and the results of its empirical assessment (or even no relationship at all), either the construct itself or its operationalizations or both should be rejected, or at least they should be seriously reconsidered and modified.

Thus, a construct is a *theory*: the empirical assessment of its operationalizations should yield well-interpretable results; at least in one case results should be interpretable in terms of the construct itself and thus confirm the construct as a model of mutually related elements (cf. Hempel, 1952; 39, Dumont and Wilson, 1967: 992, DiRenzo, 1968: 373–375).

In all 4 conditions in which a construct is empirically assessed (see Table 2.1.) results should yield useful instruments for further analysis, aiming at *theory-construction* around such instruments (dimensions, variables). (See e.g. DiRenzo, 1968: 268–269; Hempel, 1952: 18.) It is clear, then, that in case no unidimensional structure emerges, the multidimensional structure should be based on *theoretical* considerations and not upon (arbitrary) statistical ones, although the 'statistical dimensionality' may give hunches as to possible theoretical dimension which are as yet unmeasured, due to a lack of indicators tapping this dimension in the operationalization of the construct.

Assuming that Type-1 analysis has been rather successful, we will now turn to an outline of analytical procedures which could provide us with a framework for theory-construction around (one or more) dimensions found in the empirical assessment of a construct.

2.3. TOWARDS THEORY CONSTRUCTION BY MEANS OF 'SYSTEMATIC EXPLORATION': TYPE-2 ANALYSIS

2.3.1. Introduction

The ideal of theory construction still appears to be the formulation of a set of interrelated hypotheses to be tested on the basis of some empirical evidence (see e.g. De Groot, 1961; Kerlinger, 1969: 20–24, 360, 369; see also Glenn, 1973: 43; Rosenberg, 1968: 197–198, 238–239). This ideal is purely *deductive*. Though many authors stress the value of *interaction* between inductive and deductive procedures (see e.g. Riley et al., 1954; Merton, 1957; Lenski, 1966; Galtung, 1967; Glenn, 1973; Hyman, 1972), few so far seem to have developed a strategy that could be systematically followed. Rosenberg (1968; Ch. 8 and 9) and Galtung (1967: 390–426) seem to come nearest to a systematic outline of procedures as they are meant here. It seems that the deductive testing of hypotheses suits both a situation which does not (yet) exist in the social sciences, and a situation which no longer (needs to) exist(s).

With reference to the first situation, such deductive procedures presuppose the existence of *theories* which might be further developed or modified by formulating (and subsequently testing) *additional* or *alternative* hypotheses. It has already been noted above that there is a scarcity of such theories, a scarcity which may be partly due to the fact that little attention has been paid to theory-*construction* as compared to the testing of hypotheses on isolated observables, not included in general (theoretical) constructs (see e.g. Willer and Webster, 1970) [21].

With reference to the second situation, I'm referring to the procedures, outlined above, regarding construct-definition and conceptualization. When major constructs in a research-design are properly defined and conceptualized, the very need for the deductive testing of hypotheses and theories diminishes. The major arguments in favor of deductive procedures originate from a situation in which constructs are (a) insufficiently defined ('explicated'; see e.g. Dumont and Wilson, 1967), (b) consequently operationalized in a way which only partially covers their definition, and (c) empirically assessed on the basis of an 'ad hoc' sample.

In such a situation — even if either (a), (b) or (c) is true — , one is almost completely dependent on 'theory' or hypotheses since any *non*-predicted result could be *specific* for the definition, the operationalization or the sample (see e.g. De Groot, 1961: 56, 323; Kerlinger, 1969: 35, 360).

Consequently, when constructs are defined by means of (ideal type) models and conceptualized on the basis of proper operationalizations and samples, the need to start with hypotheses to be tested on the available data is removed: such data are meaningful 'in themselves' [22].

2.3.2. Procedures

We assume that the total design of a study has been 'rounded out' through the construction of a relatively large number of other variables ('independent' and 'intervening' variables; e.g. background variables, situational variables, personality variables, 'personal history' variables).

We also assume that by means of Type-1 analysis we have obtained at least 1 dimension (a well-interpretable concept) which is of major interest to the researcher, i.e. around which his further attempts at theory-construction will be centered. The choice of this dimension might be difficult or arbitrary if Type-1 analysis would yield various results in the 4 'tests' of the operationalized construct. To make this choice somewhat easier, we will assume that (a) we limit ourselves to results on the basis of the national cross-sectional sample, and (b) that both operationalizations of the construct could be integrated in one domain which will yield a certain dimensionality in the general public. We finally assume that a choice has to be made from among only a few major dimensions. The analysis, based on the 'mass-sample', could then proceed as follows [23]:

1. All variables in the design are related to each other. This constitutes the basic body of data to be worked with.

2. An *initial relationship* (between an independent and a dependent variable) is chosen. One of the concepts resulting from Type-1 analysis is, of course, involved in this relationship. The *choice* of this concept and the other variables to be related to it will never be completely objective (subjective interests of the researcher play a role), but some rationale may be available, which may be found in the nature of the variables and/or in the strength or weakness of their relationship.

   Type-2 analysis 'centers' around this relationship, which may first be 'analyzed' (e.g. broken down into its components — assuming that both variables in the initial relationship are scales or indices: this is called *component analysis*; see Rosenberg, 1968: 40ff) and subsequently be 'embedded' in relationships with other variables. Here we may proceed as follows:

3. Variables *similar* to the independent variable may be included in the analysis as potentially interpreting, explaining and/or perhaps specifying the original relationship (see Hyman, 1955; compare also Galtung, 1967: 479; Rosenberg, 1968). This may be called 'within-analysis'.

4. Variables *dissimilar* to the original independent one may subsequently be included in the analysis in order to try to further *interpret* or *explain* the original relationship, if possible by means of causal model construction (see e.g. Blalock and Blalock, 1968). (Of course, variables that are *potentially* interpreting or explaining can be identified by their relationships to the 2 variables in the initial relationship.) Causal model construction should proceed first by means of elaboration (to detect *specifications*) and could subsequently be continued and extended by using partial correlations. Finally, causal models may, in certain cases, be tested by way of path-analysis, i.e. when indeed some clear 'paths' have been detec-

ted [24]. Here then, systematic exploration, on the basis of inductive evidence, approaches deductive theory-testing. This may be called 'between-analysis'.

5. Those variables *not* included in the causal models (also called Type–2 models, to distinguish them from 'conceptual' Type–1 models) are considered as potentially *specifying* the relationship. This is the more purely inductive stage of systematic exploration, since there is usually no basis upon which it can be predicted whether a variable will specify a certain relationship or not. Still, specification is an important phenomenon: though the effects are sometimes difficult to 'interpret', results may be interesting and rewarding (see e.g. Galtung, 1967: 417; Rosenberg, 1968: Ch. 5 and 6).

6. Finally, *suppressor* or *clouding* variables may be introduced. Some relationships are weakened by the very existence of other variables in a social system. This is especially important in case one is intrigued by the weakness of a certain relationship, and consequently interested in factors that help to bring this weakness about.

The proto-type of a suppressor-variable is a variable which is positively related to one, and negatively related to the other variable of a *positive* relationship. This implies that when a relationship between 2 variables is negative, a suppressor is similarly (either positively or negatively) related to *both* variables. Finally, zero-relationships may prove to be positive relationships when controlled for a suppressor which is related in opposite ways to both variables involved, or they may prove to be negative relationships when controlled for a suppressor which is similarly related to both variables.

Where we will stand after these first 6 'rounds' of Type–2 analysis (these rounds do not constitute a 'logical' or 'best' order, but they are one possibility to 'clarify' a relationship) cannot be predicted. This depends on the variables in the original relationship and the other variables in the design. Component analysis, for example, could yield fascinating and stimulating results (i.e. when there would prove to be a systematic variation in the strengths of the relationships between the components) but could also prove completely uninteresting. The same applies to the phase where variables similar to the original independent variable will be drawn in. Causal model construction can be quite disappointing if no clear 'paths' can be detected. Specifications can be quite uninterpretable and suppressors may not be there at all.

So there is no guarantee that Type–2 analysis will yield real building-stones for the construction of a theory. However, it will provide a framework which is *potentially* useful for theory-construction. To the extent that results are disappointing, there is a need for continuity in social research. First, however, we will consider the possibilities to extend the original analysis after its first 6 phases.

2.3.3. Extensions

How to extend Type–2 analysis after the first 6 stages (if, at least, all 6 have been gone through) depends largely on the results obtained. There are 2 extensions which seem rather obvious: (a) *replace* one of the variables in the original relationship and start again, (b) *add* a third variable to the original two.

The first extension is especially self-evident when 2 conditions have been fulfilled: (1) the conceptualization of the construct has yielded more than one concept (e.g. a construct has proven to be multidimensional in the mass sample) and (2) another concept (i.e. dimension) has effected the original relationship in a substantial way. In this case, one could extend the analysis by replacing the original dependent variable (one dimension of the construct which has been found empirically) by this other dimension.

The second type of extension mentioned above can be gone into in case there is a third variable that can be seen as a dependent variable to *both* variables in the original relationship, and thus will not have been drawn into the analysis so far. In this manner, the 'depth' of the analysis could be increased.

These 2 extensions will in fact be carried out in the present study. Another possibility for extension, i.e. replacement of the original *independent* variable, will not be carried out: this would probably effect the theme of the analysis rather drastically and is a matter for secondary analysis.

Finally, one should of course try to integrate the various findings and raise them to a theoretical level. As has already been mentioned above, there is no guarantee that this will in fact prove to be possible. However, a *basis* for theory-construction will probably have been found. Theory-construction can be seen as a *process* which implies a substantial amount of *continuity* in social research. How to realize such continuity, and hence set in motion a process of theory-construction, by way of secondary analysis and replication of one or more original studies, will be outlined elsewhere [25].

2.4. SUMMARY

In this chapter we have attempted to give the rationales behind our approach to the progressive-conservative antithesis, which has already been outlined and summarized in the introductory chapter.

Very briefly, we will start with the development of an ideal type model of conservative ideology which will serve as the definition of this construct. The concepts of ideal type, model and ideology seem to be mutually related: the ideal type approach to the many 'empirical manifestations' of conservatism in the literature will yield a model of mutually related elements and to the extent that these mutual relationships come about by a common reference to underlying values, the model constitutes an ideology. These underlying values will then serve as criteria in the operationalization of the construct at lower levels of abstraction.

For the conceptualization of this construct, a 2 × 2 scheme has been developed. The construct will be operationalized as an abstract ideology or philosophy, as well as at the more specific (or: applied) level of social attitudes, derived from it by means of the above mentioned criteria. The operationalizations will be empirically assessed in both a sample from the general population and in a strategic elite. It has been maintained that this design is essential in order to come to grips with the nature of this broad domain of ideological controversy.

Finally, the need for development of theories has been noted. If Type-1 analysis according to the 2 × 2 scheme sketched above would yield, in the general population, one or more well-interpretable dimensions, as it is meant to do, we would like to know how these dimensions are related to other variables which have been brought into the design. One procedure to do this (Type-2 analysis) has been outlined. It depends on the determination of an initial relationship, which will then be 'clarified' and 'embedded' in other relationships. It is hoped that this procedure will at least provide us with a starting point for a process towards theory-construction.

Before we will carry out this program, an overview will be given of the vast research-tradition in this field. The studies will be mainly seen in the perspective of the ideal type model approach to the construct of conservative ideology and the Type-1 analytical approach which has been developed in this chapter. Some elements of these approaches will indeed be found in several studies but it will be seen that since they are neither fully developed nor integrated in one design, the results are not very impressive and often confusing and contradictory.

NOTES ON CHAPTER 2

1. In a well-known Dutch work on methodology (see De Groot, 1961: 67–70), *empirical* and *hypothetical* constructs are distinguished. Similarly, Blalock and Blalock (1968: 7) distinguish *operational* and *theoretical* concepts; Kerlinger (1969: 33ff) uses the terms 'operational' and 'constitutive'; Willer and Webster, 1967, refer to 'observables' vs. 'theoretical concepts'. De Groot (1961: 39–40) is in favor of 'freedom of conceptualization'. He notes (p.91) that concepts often have a surplus meaning in addition to the way in which they have been operationalized and that operationalizations may constitute rather arbitrary specifications of a concept. (Similar views are held by Blalock and Blalock, 1968: 11, who even welcome this situation 'in a young science', by Kerlinger, 1969: 35 and Hempel, 1952: 43, 1965: 137ff. For opposite views see e.g. DiRenzo, 1966: 268 and Dumont and Wilson, 1967.)
   De Groot (1961: 179–210) discusses how to proceed from concept to objective variable and how to select data for the testing of hypotheses, but not *how items in a measuring instrument should be selected* or *which types of universe should be sampled*. The problem of isomorphy is considered (pp. 233–236), but is *not* noted that scaling procedures over sets (domains) of items may yield different types of instruments for different samples (see e.g. Mokken, 1970). He seems to accept that constructs may be operationalized *differently* according to the aims of a particular study (p.261). Of course, the question of the validity of an instrument is considered, but how e.g. *content*-validity may be increased is not indicated (pp. 265–278, esp. 275; see also pp. 84–85; 120–124; 262). Galtung (1967) notes 2 types of procedure which may be used in constructing variables or dimensions: *intensive* procedures (based on the opinions of the investigator only) and *extensive* procedures (based on statistical criteria). Both should, of course, be combined (pp.80; 246), but the only mention of the process through which variables (items) can be selected to construct clusters (dimensions) is that it is a complicated one, about which little can be said (pp. 80–84). In discussing replication, it is noted that every concept may be measured by various indices (i.e. instruments, variables; pp. 441–442), a position which seems unacceptable.

2. See, however, the comments of Neumann (in: Von Klemperer, 1968: x, xvll) and the brief discussion on conceptual models in Riley et al. (1954: 13–16, 19). For the use of the concept of ideal type in the conceptualization of constructs, see e.g. Hempel (1965: 161–171). Though not discussed in terms of model-construction, Rokeach's (1960) conceptualization of the construct of dogmatism and Lenski's (1966) conceptualization of radicalism-conservatism may be considered as 'approaches' to what is meant (in this context) by ideal type oriented conceptual model-construction, or: ideal type construct-formation.

3. De Groot (1961: 54–57; 322–324) would term such research *exploratory*. He warns that findings which have not been hypothesized should be tested on *new* data. One reason is that what is found may be *specific* to the sample (p. 56). He finds such exploratory research only legitimate in a case where there is a broad field in which insufficient theory has been developed, and where there are many variables of unknown relevance; not an uncommon situation in the social sciences. The only technique mentioned here that

might be used is factor-analysis. Selltiz et al. (1959) seem much more positive regarding exploratory research (pp. 35; 39–40; 52; 492–499) as are e.g. Riley et al. (1954: 11–13); Merton (1957: 102–117) and Galtung (1967: 376; 390ff) (see also note 22).

4. The present study aims at laying the foundation of such theory-construction along lines sketched by Galtung (1967: 390–426 and 477–481) and Rosenberg (1968, esp. Chapters 8 and 9).

5. Although for the most part the discussion in the present chapter will be in general terms, it should be clear that in matters of conceptualization the focus will be on *certain* complex constructs, such as that of progressiveness vs. conservatism. There are, of course, many other types of complex constructs, for which other procedures of conceptualization will probably have to be followed.

6. This seems almost too obvious to state explicitly. That there is nevertheless an astonishing overlap of constructs (at the nominal level) and their concepts (i.e. measurement at the operational level) in the social sciences appears to be largely due to paying an insufficient amount of attention to the (often complicated) process of construct-formation and its subsequent conceptualization.

7. The concept of 'model' in general will not be discussed in any detail here.

8. Here the terms inductive and deductive are not used in any formal way i.e. referring to schools in the tradition of the philosophy of science. The process is similar to that which Willer and Webster (1970: 755) call the first and the second stages of the *abductive* process (see below). What is referred to here by 'model-construction' is indicated as 'explication' of the meaning of a concept by e.g. Hempel (1952: 2; 6–12) and Dumont and Wilson (1967: 990–991); the term 'explication' is drawn from Carnap.

9. It is quite surprising that the 2 notions of 'conceptual model' and 'ideal type' have been integrated so little, Hempel (1965: 161–171) comes closest, but also notes the infrequent use of ideal type constructs (p. 166). This may be due to confusion as to the notion of 'ideal type' (see below and e.g. Watkins, 1952).

10. Weber discusses the concept of 'ideal type' e.g. in "Wirtschaft und Gesellschaft" (1956; Chapter 1) and in "Gesammelte Aufsätze zur Wissenschaftslehre" (1951: 146–214; Die Objectivität sozialwissenschaftlicher und sozialpolitischer Erkenntniss, 1904) (see also note 12 below).

11. Parsons (1949: 601–610) has also discussed Weber's notion of ideal type. Some quotations may be enlightening: ". . . it is a construction of elements abstracted from the concrete, and put together to form a unified conceptual pattern . . . It is a Utopia . . . it is not a hypothesis in the sense that it is a proposition about concrete reality which is concretely verifiable (p. 603) . . . the element of abstract 'unreality' is essentially a consequence of the selectiveness of scientific interest. It is precisely the statement in outline form of the aspects of the concrete situation which are of interest for explanatory purposes. If the historical individual is to be capable of causal analysis it must be oversimplified; it must be reduced to what is essential, omitting the unimportant (p. 604) . . . Here the (conceptual) ideal type may actually concretely exist in the sense that the system of ideas is explicit in some one document . . . But this is not methodologically necessary" (p. 605).

Hendricks and Breckenridge Peters refer to an interesting remark made by Becker (1940: 52): "If construct and reality exactly correspond, you are in the morass of the particular, you are talking about *this* thing at *this* time in such a way that explicit comparison with anything else becomes virtually impossible".

12. An ideal type does *not* constitute a more or less *arbitrary* selection of elements extracted from reality for specific research (or explanatory) purposes or chosen on the basis of subjective interest, as seems to be suggested by Weber ((1905), (1920–1921); 1947: 31) and Parsons (see note 11). The attempt to construct an ideal type as fully and 'objectively' as possible may be made (see also Tellegen, 1968: 54–56).

13. The concept of ideology will be discussed later. For a fruitful approach to ideology from a research point of view and a consideration of possible underlying values, see Naess (1956: 172–198), Minar (1961: 325), and Hempel (1965: 169).

14. This phenomenon will be discussed in the next chapter. See e.g. Hartman (1936) and Stagner (1936a) for early observations, and Prothro and Grigg (1960), McClosky (1964) and Free and Cantril (1967) for later and more extensive evidence.

15. Compare e.g. Lentz (1938), McNemar (1946) and Kerlinger (1967). In many studies, as will be discussed in the next chapter, items referring to 'issues' (of the day) have nevertheless been used to assess the structure of beliefs along 'liberal-conservative' continua in the general public; see e.g. Converse (1964), McClosky (1964), Nie (1974).

16. There are numerous definitions of 'attitude'. They all seem to refer to an attitude as a latent variable underlying specific opinions on issues or social objects. (See e.g. Green, 1959: 335, Rokeach, 1968: 112.) It is clear, then, that attitudes may only be measured by *unidimensional* scales, the unidimensionality pointing to the dimension (i.e. attitude) underlying responses (in a sample) to attitude statements (i.e. opinions). This means that attitudes should be measured on the basis of e.g. factor-, cluster- or scalogram-analysis (see e.g. Kerlinger and Kaya, 1959; Kerlinger, 1967).

17. The idea seems rather widespread that, contrary to means and standard-deviations, *correlations* between variables are relatively insensitive to sampling variability (see Galtung, 1967: 52–54).

18. Mokken (1970) has stressed this point, which has consequences for the problem of isomorphy (see De Groot, 1961: 233–236). Several techniques of avoiding this dilemma have been developed, which are all unacceptable. One is what Galtung (1967: 77–78) refers to as the *intensive* procedure of index construction, to which Hoogerwerf (1968: 354) refers as 'theoretical unidimensionality'.

19. In general the most satisfactory definition of a standard-sample is that which is made on the basis of a culturally homogeneous universe, for which the concept is *relevant*. Mostly, although not always, a society may be considered as such a universe. For *special* variables, special sub-universes should, of course, be defined as standard: e.g. concepts may be standardized from national cross-sectional samples of young people, housewives, laborers, farmers, nurses, etc.

20. Of course, constructs may have more than one 'strategic elite' for which they have special relevance. Such elites need not be similar to each other.

21. I am referring here, of course, to theory-construction in terms of a system of explicitly formulated, testable hypotheses (see Galtung, 1967: 451–466), not to other types of 'theories': more loosely arranged suggestions as to relationships of various kinds of loosely defined constructs. Dumont and Wilson (1967: 987–990) make a distinction between 'implicit' and 'explicit' theories, with 'theory sketches' as an intermediate stage. Here, *explicit* theories are meant.

22. A 'weak point' in the approach is, of course, that a researcher may not be able to construct 'models' for *all* constructs he wishes to include in the design. Results have to be considered most tentatively for constructs defined and operationalized in a more or less 'ad hoc' manner. One task of *replication-research* is to increase the number of variables in the design for which models have been constructed. On the other hand, there are many important variables for which the construction of a model is not necessary, e.g. background variables such as age and sex; 'personal history' variables like social class of parents; and variables such as party preference and voting behavior (see e.g. Blalock and Blalock, 1968: 19).

   One of the main reasons why psychologists tend to be more oriented towards rigorous deductive theorizing than sociologists may be that psychologists aim at the formulation of *general* laws of human behavior. Sociologists, on the other hand, often have a special interest in certain categories or groups of people. It also seems true that psychologists, far more frequently than sociologists, work with constructs whose definition requires an 'ideal type model' approach, e.g. intelligence, anxiety, stress, neuroticism, self-evaluation. They often face a situation in which (a) no standard samples are available, and (b) models of their constructs are lacking (or: the meaning of their constructs is heavily disputed). Sociologists often find themselves in a situation in which (a) they are interested in a specific group, and (b) their variables may be defined and conceptualized relatively simply.

23. Type-2 analysis does not entail a rigid strategy; all kinds of variations are possible, partly dependent on the nature of the variables resulting from Type-1 analyses and on the nature and number of the other variables in the design. It is normally based on the mass sample only since the elite sample will often be (a) not a proper sample, and (b) too small to allow meaningful analyses. This need not necessarily be the case, however, so in some cases, Type-2 analysis could be carried out in an elite sample, parallel to a similar analysis in the mass sample.

24. There are a number of publications on this subject. Here, only a few are mentioned; see e.g. Blalock (1960, 1961, 1962a, b, 1964, 1965, 1969), Boudon (1965) and Simon (1961). On path-analysis, see e.g. Borgatta and Bohrnstedt (1969).

25. The present study has been replicated in 1975 (see Middendorp, 1976, b, d). On the general strategy of secondary analysis and replication with the aim to realize continuity in social research and the beginnings of systematic theory construction, see Middendorp (1976f).

CHAPTER 3

A Survey of Previous Research

3.1. INTRODUCTION AND GENERAL OVERVIEW

In this chapter, a survey will be given of previous empirical research on progressiveness-conservatism [1].

In terms of the methodological terminology introduced in the previous chapter, the emphasis in this survey will be on the definition of constructs like conservatism and on their conceptualization in Type-1 analysis. Progressiveness vs. conservatism has been defined and conceptualized in many different ways. However, no approach exists which could form the basis for a *replication* [2]. This does not mean that the present study is completely unique: rather, various types of approach used in previous research are further developed and integrated in the present study.

The research tradition in this field is extensive. It started in the 1920's and 1930's in America and, until shortly after the Second World War was dominated by psychologists and social psychologists (see e.g. Allport, 1929; Likert, 1932; Thurstone, 1934). Later, sociologists and political scientists made important contributions.

Research on progressiveness-conservatism has been intimately related to the earliest studies on *social attitudes* and to the question central to the beginnings of social psychology: *can attitudes (as hypothetical constructs underlying opinions) be measured?* (e.g. Thurstone, 1928, 1929). Another early dispute in social psychology centered around the *generality* or *specificity* of attitudes. Some researchers intercorrelated and factor-analyzed *specific* attitude scales (often of the Thurstone-type, such as attitudes towards evolution, birth control, war, capital punishment) in order to identify *general* or *primary* attitudes, which were sometimes interpreted in terms of radicalism-conservatism (see e.g. Thurstone, 1934; Carlsson, 1934).

In the early days, items were also combined into general scales or tests of radicalism-conservatism (see e.g. Vetter, 1930; Hunter, 1942; Harper, 1927; Hartmann, 1938; Lentz, 1935). Such 'tests' were sometimes later split into subscales which were then intercorrelated or factor-analyzed; the tests were often (though not always) found to be multi-dimensional (see Lentz, 1938; Vetter, 1947; Lorr, 1951; Rubin-Rabson, 1954).

Factor-analysis of intercorrelated *items* has not been typical of early American research; only one such study seems to have been made (see Hayes, 1939 a, b, c). This type of study is more typical of English researchers, especially Eysenck (1944, 1947, 1954) and Sanai (1950, 1951). Later, this tradition was also followed in the U.S. by e.g. Comrey and Newmeyer (1965) and Kerlinger (1958, 1961, 1967, 1970, 1972). The samples used in these studies were all from among students or a mixture of students and non-student groups, or they were 'analytical'. Cross-sectional samples, representative of the population of a country were very uncommon (see e.g. Hayes, 1939 for an exception).

In the early studies, researchers did not pay much attention to even the crudest forms of definition of a construct like conservatism. Items were often brought together in an intuitive manner, by using common sense-definitions or simplistic definitions in terms of 'attitude to change'. Only rarely is there some discussion as to whether the factors found could be interpreted in terms of radicalism-conservatism (see e.g. Sanai, 1950, 1951). This contrasts with the serious attempts of some researchers to define and conceptualize the ideology of fascism in the 1930's and 1940's (see Stagner, 1936 a,b; Edwards, 1941, 1944).

One reason may have been that in the U.S. the liberal-conservative antithesis developed a special and clear socio-economic twist during the depression of the 1930's (see Grimes, 1956: 639; Ladd, 1969: 9; Free and Cantril, 1967: 3; McClosky, 1964: 420). Liberals and conservatives became opposed to each other on issues such as the welfare state and government interference in economics (the free enterprise system; attitude to the role of big business and the power of the federal government). It is a little confusing to Europeans that the *conservatives* took the *classical liberal* stand on these matters (i.e. the position of classical economics) whereas *liberals* opposed that position (see Hartz, 1955). The meaning of the liberal-conservative antithesis, however, hardly needed further explanation (see Kerr, 1944; Newcomb, 1943; Hartmann, 1938). Other issues on which liberals (or rather radicals) and conservatives had been opposed (and which had been included in early factor-analytic studies and in the early 'tests' mentioned above) faded into the background.

It was not until the 1960's that those *non-economic* aspects again received due attention, although this time often only within the political field (see e.g. Lipset, 1963; Lenski, 1961; Ferdinand, 1964; Kelly and Chamblis, 1966; Campbell et al., 1960) [3]. Such studies (again) cast serious doubt on the unidimensionality of the liberal-conservative antithesis.

Further doubts about the very *meaningfulness* of the liberal-conservative antithesis arose among political scientists in the 1960's as a result of data obtained from cross-sectional national samples (see for example Campbell et al., 1960; Converse, 1964). This may have originated in the relative failure by the authors of *The Authoritarian Personality* (see Adorno et al., 1950; especially Levinson: 151–207) to construct a politico-economic conservatism (PEC) scale. They proclaimed '*the absence of a well developed and articulate political left and political right in contemporary America*' (Levinson, 1950: 159), a position which was probably accepted by many researchers during the 1950's. The fact that Adorno et al. compensated for the disappointing PEC-scale by their rather successful construction of measuring-instruments for personality syndromes such as authoritarianism (the F-scale) and ethnocentrism (the E-scale), in addition to the fact that there did not appear to be a relationship between political ideology and social class (see Levinson, 1950: 172; see also 186, note 9) may have increased the interest of researchers in *personality* and decreased their interest in *ideology* [4].

Somewhat paradoxically, in the same period in which the interest of researchers in matters of ideology almost disappeared, a new social philosophy arose in the U.S.: the *New Conservatism* (see e.g. Wilson, 1941, 1951, 1960; Viereck, 1949; Schlesinger, 1953; Meyer, 1964; Kirk, 1954, Brown, 1955). The influence of this movement is still visible today (see e.g. Du Bois Cook, 1973), but its influence on *research* has been very modest.

McClosky's (1958) attempt to define and conceptualize 'classical conservatism' seems to have been the only one inspired by the New Conservatives (who tended on the whole to return to Burke). McClosky's conceptualization of conservatism at this abstract, general level, approaching what is meant by *direct* operationalization of a construct, has remained isolated in the U.S. and has often been misinterpreted when used in subsequent research (see e.g. Campbell et al., 1960; Anderson et al., 1965; Middleton and Putney, 1963; Matthews and Prothro, 1966; Schoenberger, 1968). Although the 1958 study was not the first in which rather *abstract* items had been used to tap conservative positions (see the discussion on the PEC-scale below), it was the first and only study in which such items were more or less systematically derived from a definition (by way of a 'quasi-model' see Chapter 2: 2.2.1) of conservatism as an ideology.

A major contribution of political research in the early 1960's was that it again considered the distinction between *abstract* and *concrete* statements. This distinction was not new. In the 1930's Hartmann (1936: 351-352) had already noted that *'the masses seem to like socialism but to dislike socialists'*. He also noted discrepancies between party-preference and the respondent's position as far as *details* of party programs were concerned. Even earlier, Allport (1929: 229-233) had noted a similar inconsistency between radicalism, candidate preference and anti-socialist prejudice. Stagner (1936b: 451) had noted that 'Many conservatives are strongly opposed to fascism — as a certain kind of stereotype. They are not opposed to the ideas and principles which would make up a fascist program under a different name' [5]. In the early 1960's research centered around the *abstract* principles of *liberal democracy* vs. the *specific* applications of those principles (see Prothro and Grigg, 1960; McClosky, 1964; see also Free and Cantril, 1967; Selznick and Steinberg, 1968; Mann, 1970).

Another contribution made by political science in the 1960's was the systematic study of the consistency of the individual's position on various issues and the differential responses of subgroups from the general public (or elitist vs. mass samples) to items at various levels of abstraction. Prothro and Grigg (1960) investigated levels of consistency between abstract principles and the specific applications of such principles in people with different levels of education; McClosky et al. (1960) studied the consistency of opinions of congressmen as compared to their Republican and Democratic followers. Campbell et al. (1960) report the lack of consistency shown in the general public, at the scale-level, regarding specific and abstract liberalism-conservatism dimensions. Converse (1964) notes a greater consistency of opinions, also in terms of liberalism-conservatism, in political leaders vs. the general public. Finally, McClosky (1964) integrates such findings to some extent by working with both abstract and concrete statements on liberal democracy, and with political leaders vs. the electorate.

The somewhat simplistic notion that arises out of the above mentioned studies (that the public has *no consistent liberal-conservative or liberal-democratic ideology* and that the politically articulate show a *unidimensional ideological antithesis*) has been challenged by research in the late 1960's and early 1970's (see Axelrod, 1967; Luttbeg, 1968; Brown, 1970). Finally, Nie (1974) presents evidence in favor of a possible *synthesis* between the various positions: the lack of constraint in belief systems regarding liberal-conservative issues could have been particular to the period around and before 1960. Since 1964 especially, Nie finds a dramatic increase of consistency in the general public, pointing to the existence of one liberalism-conservatism antithesis.

This rough survey of the research tradition gives us an idea of where we stand at present. Previous research will now be systematically analyzed from 2 points of view:

(a) Definition of constructs: the ideal type model approach
(b) Conceptualization: operationalization and empirical assessment

3.2. DEFINITIONS OF PROGRESSIVENESS (LIBERALISM, RADICALISM) VS.
     CONSERVATISM

Many researchers do not use definitions at all. There are 2 traditions here. In one of them (see e.g. Harper, 1927; Vetter, 1930a), *judges* are used to indicate whether items express liberal or conservative positions. In the other, the field of social attitudes is covered by attitudes such as those towards evolution, capital punishment, birth control, war, etc. and the scales are intercorrelated and factor-analyzed. (See e.g. Thurstone, 1934; Carlsson, 1934; Ferguson, 1939, 1942.) This tradition, albeit somewhat modified, has continued in factor-analytic studies up to the present day: items to be factor-analyzed are brought together on an *intuitive* or commonsense basis (see e.g. Hayes, 1939; Eysenck, 1944, 1947, 1951, 1954; Sanai, 1950, 1951; Kerlinger, 1967, 1968; Comrey and Newmeyer, 1965) [6].

There is a third tradition of making rather easy, superficial definitions (which often are hardly recognizable in subsequent operationalizations). Such definitions are often in terms of attitude to change. Reed (1927: 49), for example, defines a progressive attitude as one that is '. . . favourable to change from the conditions, beliefs or sentiments generally prevalent in the past or the present'. Nevertheless, the questionnaire includes such items as: 'Is the able-bodied and mentally sound adult who does no useful work, and who lives on the income from inherited wealth, a social menace?' (p. 50). (See also Lentz, 1935; Hunter, 1942, 1951: 283-292.)

Many authors define radicalism/liberalism-conservatism in rather simple socio-economic terms, as discussed above. Hartmann (1936: 337), for example, defines radicalism as: 'support of a collectivist policy such as public ownership of national resources and the principal industries, extension of governmental functions in the field of social insurance, internationalism, etc. Conservatism was considered as any attitude tending to preserve the status quo, particularly those institutions maintaining the current methods of distributing wealth and power'. (See also e.g. Pace, 1939: 333–334; and Kerr, 1941: 6.) After failing to give an explicit definition in his original piece of research (Vetter, 1930a), Vetter does so later (regarding liberalism) in the somewhat broader terms of: 'favoring communistic wealth distribution, pagan or non-moralistic, individualistic and an inclination to try the new' (1947: 125).

Such simplistic definitions are understandable because when an attempt is made to define liberalism-conservatism somewhat more broadly and fundamentally, researchers often report serious difficulties.

In an early secondary analysis of studies in the field of market and opinion research, for example, Pollak (1943: 175–176) turns to Michels' (1931) conceptualization of conservatism as: 'either a tendency to maintain the status quo, regardless of what that may be, or a particular pattern of a philosophy of life which may best be characterized by a love of authority and tradition', and to Wilson (1941), one of the first so-called New Conservatives in the U.S., who maintains that conservatism mainly aims at a defence of *primary* elements in the social structure. In operationalizing conservatism, however, Pollak limits himself to Michels' first definition, since 'it seems to offer the best chance for an accurate classification of data because it is rather definite and does not give much leeway for divergent interpretations'.

Kerr (1952: 112) complains: 'Admittedly, the operational liberal-conservative frames of reference are not exactly identical when one field (e.g. political) of behaviors is compared with another (e.g. economic). But this is the fault of nature rather than psychology' (!).

After the Second World War, researchers became much more uncertain and confused about the meaning of the progressive-conservative antithesis: it became problematic.

This may be related to the experience of fascism and communism, the general distrust in ideology and a growing sense that fundamental ideological controversy had been overcome in modern post-industrial society, both among the population at large and amongst scholars (see Chapter 1, pp. 9–10).

This may also be reflected in research findings in the 1950's (which will be further discussed below) showing a lack of ideological structure in the population at large.

On the other hand, such a situation may be fruitful for fresh attempts at the definition of the construct, sometimes by means of attempts at the construction of a conceptual 'model', as is shown in the work of e.g. Levinson (1950), Ferdinand (1964), McClosky (1958) and Anderson et al. (1965) [7].

An early example of such a situation as sketched above is shown in some American studies on fascism in the 1930's and 1940's. Fascism as a social philosophy did not have a definite or even implicit meaning in the American context [8]. Nevertheless, many researchers felt that fascist ideas might also hold some appeal for the American public. This resulted in a pioneering approach to the ideology of fascism by Stagner (1936a, esp. 309–310) using a conceptual model approach based on a study of fascist literature. Stagner's study was later elaborated upon by Edwards (1941, 1944), whose scale anticipates Adorno et al.'s (1950) F-scale [9]. The latter scale deserves the term fascism-scale much less than the former ones. The F-scale was developed from the more limited perspective of anti-semitism and ethnocentrism generally, rather than from a systematic study of fascist ideology.

It was only gradually that the perspective of 'anti-democratic potential' emerged; a perspective which has been a central one for Edwards. It was possibly under the influence of authors like Maslow (1943) and Fromm (1942), that this potential became located at the *personality* level; earlier, it was considered solely as an *ideological* position. The F-scale lacks the conceptual model construction approach of Stagner and Edwards.

In his review of *The Authoritarian Personality*, Smith (1950) noted that 'In no single place in the volume, in fact, is there to be found a concise statement of the hypotheses underlying the entire undertaking'. As Christie (1954: 123) further notes: '. . . the underlying theory (is not) explicit enough to permit the testing of unequivocal specific hypotheses in further research'; a concise statement on the drawbacks of a lack of conceptual model construction for continuity in social research and accumulation of knowledge.

It is then, somewhat surprising to find that one of the authors of *The Authoritarian Personality* (Levinson, 1950: 151–207) presents one of the most interesting attempts to define the liberalism-conservatism antithesis by means of a conceptual (quasi-)model.

3.2.1. *Levinson's 'politico-economic-conservatism'*

The author explicitly states his perception of the problematic nature of the concepts: '. . . there exists today a great deal of ideological heterodoxy, not to speak of simple confusion . . .' (p. 152) and 'It is symptomatic of the present political situation that terms like 'liberalism' and 'conservatism' are given numerous definitions and are used as shibboleths rather than as aids in description or analysis. We have therefore tried to make our meanings as explicit as possible' (footnote 2).

An attempt is made to find some underlying and therefore more stable ideological trends which characterize liberalism and conservatism (p. 153).

The conservative characteristics are outlined as follows:

1. *'Support for the American status quo'*: 'idealizing' existing authority, accepting the inevitability of economic depression and attributing the reason for social problems to 'charlatans' with a liberal background.
2. *'Resistance to social change'*: the rationalization of the existing social order in terms of human nature, to which the existing evils in society are attributed.
3. *'Support for conservative values'*: support for practicality, ambition, upward class mobility and competitiveness. Poverty is seen as being caused by the innate stupidity of the poor rather than by the economic organization of society.
4. *Balance of power* between business, labor and government: the most confused aspect since, as the author notes: ' . . . "laissez-faire", originally a characteristic of liberalism, is nowadays called "conservatism" . . . Here, conservatism is taken to mean "traditional economic laissez-faire individualism". This implies the great prestige of "business" and the acceptance of unions only when their actual power is less than that of business. . . . Conservative ideology has traditionally urged that the economic functions of government be minimized. Fear of government power (like union power) is emphasized, and great concern is expressed for the freedom of the individual, particularly the individual businessman' (p. 156) [10].

Another interesting attempt at model-construction is McClosky's (1958) approach to classical conservatism.

3.2.2. McClosky's 'classical conservatism'

This author also frankly expresses his confusion regarding the meaning of liberalism and conservatism (pp. 27–29). He notes, for example, that liberalism and conservatism have reversed themselves on issues like government regulation of the economy (p. 27). Again, however, this confusion is a stimulus for an attempt at a more fundamental approach to the definition of the construct of conservatism to be made. This is done by turning to the *tradition of conservative thought.* Here, the 'New Conservatives' referred to above have been quite helpful in outlining this tradition. 'The political writings of Russell Kirk, Clinton Rossiter, John Hallowell, or Richard Weaver, of the refurbished Southern Agrarians like Donald Davidson, the poets of nostalgia like T. S. Eliot, or of magazines like *Measure,* the *National Review,* the *American Mercury,* and *Modern Age* — express with varying degrees of intensity and spiritual violence the principles and doctrines which have enjoyed currency among self-styled conservatives for generations. Thus . . . the outlook of conservatism has, like liberalism, remained fairly firm through recent centuries' (p. 28).

On this basis the attempt is made: ' . . . to extract from the tradition of self-styled conservative thought, and especially from the writings of Edmund Burke, a set of principles representing that tradition as fairly as possible' (p. 30).

An important limitation to this approach is introduced as follows: ' . . . we have tried to avoid attitudes or opinions that seemed to us situationally determined and which, for that reason, appear to be secondary and unstable correlates of liberal or conservative tendencies. Many attitudes that arise mainly from party or class affiliation fall into this category, e.g. attitudes toward *free enterprise, toward trade unions, toward expansion of government functions, toward the New Deal and its welfare measures, toward tariffs, farm support* and a number of similar issues that have featured prominently in political campaigns' (p. 30) (my emphasis; CPM).

The author finds 'astonishing agreement' among disciples and disinterested scholars on the following 'quintessential elements' of conservatism:
1. Man is a creature of appetite and will, 'governed more by emotion than by reason' (Kirk) in whom 'wickedness, unreason and the urge to violence lurk always behind the curtain of civilized behavior' (Rossiter). He is a fallen creature, doomed to imperfection, and inclined to license and anarchy.
2. Society is ruled by 'divine intent' (Kirk) and made legitimate by Providence and prescription. Religion 'is the foundation of civil society' (Huntington) and is man's ultimate defense against his own evil impulses.
3. Society is organic, plural, inordinately complex, the product of a long and painful evolution, embodying the accumulated wisdom of previous historical ages. There is a presumption in favor of whatever has survived the ordeal of history, and of any institution that has been tried and found to work.

4. Man's traditional inheritance is rich, grand, endlessly proliferated and mysterious, deserving of veneration and not to be cast away lightly in favor of the narrow uniformity preached by 'sophisters and calculators' (Burke). Theory is to be distrusted since reason, which gives rise to theory, is a deceptive, shallow and limited instrument.
5. Change must therefore be resisted and the injunction heeded that 'Unless it is necessary to change, it is necessary not to change' (Hearnshaw). Innovation 'is a devouring conflagration more often than it is a torch of progress' (Kirk).
6. Men are naturally unequal and society requires 'orders and classes' for the good of all. All efforts at leveling are futile and lead to despair (Kirk and Rossiter), for they violate the natural hierarchy and frustrate man's 'longing for leadership'. The superior classes must be allowed to differentiate themselves and to have a hand in the direction of the state, balancing the numerical superiority of the inferior classes.
7. Order, authority and community are the primary defence against the impulse to violence and anarchy. The superiority of duties over rights and the need to strengthen the stabilizing institutions of society, especially the church, the family and above all, private property (pp. 30–31) [11].

Like Levinson's quasi-model presented above, McClosky's model is somewhat hierarchical; note, for example, that point (1) is on human nature; points (2) and (3) are on the nature of society; point (4) is a mixture of the preceding points and points (5), (6) and (7) refer to the *relationship* between man and society. Certain sub-elements can be distinguished within the various elements, but these have not been arranged systematically.

A preliminary point of criticism may be that although McClosky mentions the special place of the value of '*private property*' in conservative ideology, at the same time he refuses to include notions on '*free enterprise*' and on the *role of government* in society because these notions would be overly linked to party or class affiliation (see above). It seems, however, that for American conservative ideology as well as for 19th century European conservatism (notably after 1850), the notions of free enterprise and limited government interference — especially in attempts at 'leveling'; see McClosky's 6th point — have taken a central place [12].

3.2.3. Other recent definitions

Lipset (1959: 485; 1963: 101–102) elaborates on the early pioneering work of Smith (1948, a, b, c) in making a distinction between *economic* and *noneconomic* liberalism-conservatism 'Economic liberalism refers to the conventional issues concerning redistribution of income, status and power among the classes . . . in non-economic terms (liberalism means) . . . to support, for example, civil liberties for political dissidents, civil rights for ethnic and racial minorities, internationalistic foreign policies . . .' (see also O'Kane, 1970; Mitchell, 1966). Lipset's study marks the rise of political science and its concomitant and more limited definitions and conceptualizations of the liberalism-conservatism antithesis.

Lenski (1961: 208–211), for example, albeit somewhat superficially, distinguishes 4 dimensions: (1), attitude towards the welfare state; (2), attitude towards freedom of speech; (3), racial attitudes; and (4), nationalism-internationalism.

Kelly and Chambliss (1966) also distinguish 4 dimensions in terms of 'welfare', civil liberties, civil rights and internationalism.

Concomitant with such 'multidimensional' definitions of (political) liberalism-conservatism, there are others which are in unidimensional terms. Campbell et al. (1960: 193–194) note, for example: 'Perhaps no abstraction of this genre (ideologies) has been used more frequently in the past century for political analysis than the concept of a liberal-conservative continuum — the 'right' and the 'left' of a political spectrum. The generality of this dimension makes it a powerful summary tool. Above the flux of specific issues lie a number of broad controversies regarding the appropriate posture of the national government toward other sectors of the social order . . .' They continue: 'Differences between liberal and conservative tend to focus on the degree in which the government should assume interest, responsibility and control over these sectors of endeavor'. What is liberal or conservative in this respect may depend on time and place however (see McClosky, 1958: 27), so that the authors' conclusion is one in terms of 'change': 'The viewpoint termed conservative may thereby become that which is reluctant to disturb the existing order of relationships, whether they be laissez faire or interventionist. The liberal viewpoint sees room for improvement in the product of social and political process through change in these relationships', a definition which does not seem satisfactory.

In many other studies this antithesis is only superficially defined (see Converse, 1964: 214–215; McClosky et al., 1960: 410, note 15, 420; Key, Jr., 1961: esp. 154–157, 163–184, 171–172; Hero Jr., 1969; Axelrod, 1967; Luttbeg, 1968; Brown, 1970 and Nie, 1974) [13]. For many political scientists, the liberal-conservative antithesis at the level of 'political issues' did not create too many problems of definition.

Not for all researchers are matters so (relatively) simple, however, Middleton and Putney (1963: 378–379), for example, both reject Levinson's PEC-scale ('such a scale may be of considerable utility for classifying people in regard to the substantive issues, but the broader significance of these may be problematic.') and McClosky's scale ('McClosky has developed a conservatism scale which taps an underlying conservatism in the personality structure, but is so far removed from particular political issues that many aspects of ideological variation are likely to be obscured') [14].

Wiley (1967: 143) finds that 'The notion of liberalism has its clearest meaning in the history of economic ideas and even here it is subject to dispute. When it is applied to political life it begins getting fuzzy. When it is applied to Protestantism it becomes little more than a vague analogy, and when applied to Catholicism it can mean almost anything'.

There are only few recent studies in which the definition of liberalism-conservatism is seriously discussed. Ferdinand (1964: 77), for example, does so from the *liberal* point of view, basing the definition of political liberalism on (limited) model construction from a study of the literature (see below par. 3.3.2.2.). Anderson et al. (1965: 189–192) approach conservative attitudes from the standpoint of the 'radical right' and distinguish 4 such attitudes: economic conservatism (the extent that the government should promote welfare policies for the benefits of needy individuals), belief in domestic communist threat, tolerance of expression (of atheist and socialist opinions) and internationalism (the radical right has been conducting a vigorous campaign against the United Nations).

Free and Cantril (1967: 1–4) give possibly the most concise statement of the changing meanings of liberalism and conservatism in America (see remarks by Levinson, 1950: 156; McClosky, 1958: 27–29; Campbell et al., 1960: 194; see also e.g. Hartz, 1955; Ladd, 1969; Chapter 1, esp. note 2; Smith, 1968). They first discuss 'old style' liberalism: 'At the economic and social level, liberalism as then defined was closely linked to laissez-faire. Private property was sanctified. Private enterprise was looked upon not only as a direct expression of economic freedom but as important also in facilitating political liberty. Particularly after the Civil War, the prevailing theories of social Darwinism held that competition, unimpeded by government, assured the survival of the fittest. Poverty was considered the result of inherent inferiorities. State intervention, by inhibiting the development of individual initiative and responsibility, was seen as stultifying the development of character and protecting the lazy, the inefficient, and the shiftless. These doctrines of 'liberalism' (old style), widely propagated by the stories of Horatio Alger, are what we mean by the *traditional American ideology*' (my emphasis; CPM).

This *liberalism*, however, has become *conservative*: 'By the middle of the 19th century, however, the doctrines of liberalism, as further developed by such men as Spencer and Sumner, were being used for exactly the opposite purpose: namely, by 'conservatives' to defend a new status quo. By this time, particularly after the Civil War, the business class was in the saddle and was fearful that, with the extension of suffrage, governments would prove too sensitive to the needs of the people and adopt dangerous working-class reforms. Thus, while the doctrines of liberalism remained essentially the same, they were taken over from the liberals by the conservatives, and the term 'liberalism' came to mean resistance to change and the rationalization of the status quo. For this reason we refer in this book to the traditional American ideology as conservative rather than liberal, despite its origins'.

They then describe the emergence of a new liberalism in the 20th century: 'As a practical matter, the new style liberals increasingly recognized the need for governmental action to protect the underprivileged. They favored strengthening the powers of government in the interest of the public welfare, with particular attention to social amelioration. They supported compulsory education, unemployment and old-age insurance, minimum wages, and the like as enlargements of, not restrictions on, individual liberty. Earlier, resort to government was condoned to advance economic development; now, the idea was to use government to promote social justice'.

They finally point to possibly a basic problem in defining (and conceptualizing), at an 'ideological' level, this modern liberal position in America [15]: ' . . . neither Roosevelt nor those who followed him ever evolved a *coherent philosophy of liberalism* (new style) to rationalize the programs they supported. The approach has tended to be based on "problem solving" in the light of social conscience, rather than on any ideological premise. In our survey, therefore, while we were able to ask questions about the traditional American ideology — "liberalism" old style — we were unable to unearth a sufficiently coherent body of ideological doctrine commonly accepted by the public to ask questions about "liberalism" new style'. This, however, yields interesting empirical results, which will be discussed below.

Finally, 2 recent approaches to the definition of progressiveness-conservatism should be mentioned [16], as well as 2 studies showing an interesting model-construction approach in a related field: that of 'liberal democracy' [17].

Kerlinger (1972) constructed a number of liberal conservative '*attitude referents*' (see Kerlinger, 1967) made on the basis of a study of 'systematic discussions' on liberalism and conservatism.

Wilson (1973) constructed a quasi-model (in a rather 'ad hoc' manner and clearly in the Eysenck tradition) of the 'ideal conservative', who combines religious fundamentalism, a positive attitude to pro-establishment politics, insistence on strict rules and punishments, militarism, ethnocentrism and intolerance of minority groups, preference for the conventional in art, clothing and institutions, an anti-hedonistic outlook and restriction of sexual behavior, opposition to scientific progress and superstition.

One of the first studies on liberal democracy is the one of Prothro and Grigg (1960: 276) who attempted to test the generally accepted hypothesis that consensus on fundamental liberal-democratic principles is essential to democracy. They assumed that 'we would find the anticipated agreement on the basic principles of democracy when they were put in a *highly abstract form*, but that consensus would not be found on *more concrete questions* involving the application of these principles' (p. 281) (my emphasis; CPM).

They then formulated a small, hierarchical quasi-model of fundamental principles of democracy: (a) the principle of democracy itself, (b) the principle of majority rule, (c) the principle of minority rights. The latter 2 principles are then put into both abstract and specific terms. Their expectations are generally borne out, which can be seen as the first modern confirmation of the older evidence that such distinctions between 'abstract' and 'specific' are important.

McClosky's study (1964) is an elaboration of that of Prothro and Grigg. A quasi-model of liberal democracy, consisting of 5 sections (see below) is derived from the principles of 'American democracy' which are outlined as follows: 'such concepts as consent, accountability, limited or constitutional government, representation, majority rule, minority rights, the principle of political opposition, freedom of thought, speech, press and assembly, equality of opportunity, religious toleration, equality before the law, the rights of juridical defense and individual self-determination over a broad range of personal affairs' (p. 363) [18].

The operationalizations of both quasi-models and the importance of the distinction between 'abstract notions' and 'specific opinions' which these studies indicate, will be discussed in par. 3.3.3.2 [19].

In summary, we have seen in this paragraph that although there is a large research tradition, only very few serious attempts to define the (theoretical) construct of the progressive-conservative antithesis have been undertaken. We have seen that in 2 outstanding cases — those of McClosky and Levinson — the notion of model construction seems to stand behind the attempts, but we have also seen that no real models have been obtained. The ideal type nature of such attempts at model-construction has at best been implicit sometimes (e.g. Wilson's 'ideal conservative' and McClosky's 'quintessential elements'). The same applies to the notion that the progressive-conservative antithesis is an ideological one, probably due to the fact that researchers are often ambivalent or uncertain as to the notion of ideology itself (e.g. McClosky, 1958: 28, 44; 1960: 423; 1964: 368, and Campbell et al., 1960: 203-204), which has hardly been defined and used at all in the context of American research.

In the next paragraph we will see how the various notions of progressiveness-conservatism have been operationalized and empirically assessed.

3.3. CONCEPTUALIZATIONS OF PROGRESSIVENESS (LIBERALISM, RADICALISM) VS. CONSERVATISM

In this paragraph we will investigate how the various definitions and quasi-models of liberalism-conservatism have been conceptualized (i.e. operationalized and empirically assessed).

First, attempts to construct *one* liberalism-conservatism scale will be discussed. Here the work of Levinson (1950) and McClosky (1958) will again be given special attention.

Second, studies in which the construction of *more than one* scale was attempted will be discussed. For the most part, the scales were intercorrelated and some insight into the dimensionality of liberalism-conservatism was obtained.

Third, a number of approaches which remained at the *single item level* will be also discussed. Here, early studies by Smith (1948 a, b) and more recent work by Lenski (1961), Converse (1964), Axelrod (1969) and Nie (1974) will be considered.

The *fourth* major approach to liberalism-conservatism (often very weak in conceptualization) is by (second-order) factor-analysis of single items. Here the work of e.g. Hayes (1939 a, b, c), Eysenck (1947, 1954, 1971), Kerlinger (e.g. 1967, 1972), Comrey and Newmeyer (1965) and Wilson (1973) will be discussed.

3.3.1. One scale

In the early days, items, sometimes constructed or selected with the help of a team of judges, were often combined into 'tests' of liberalism-conservatism (see e.g. Harper, 1927; Hartmann, 1936, 1938; Lentz,

1935; Hunter, 1942, 1951; Vetter, 1930a). Sometimes, subscales were distinguished within the broader scale (see Hunter, 1951; Murphy and Likert, 1938).

In this context, an interesting observation is made by Lentz (1938): 'Low intercorrelations between the separate fields of the trait of conservatism-radicalism may be due to the reliability of the so-called specific measure, as well as to the *specificity* of the continuum being measured' . . . 'Specific is a term which applies to *items*, in contrast to each other, much more than to groups of items' . . . 'the specificity of a single item cannot be used as an argument for the specificity of a trait such as conservatism' (pp. 542–544) [20].

It is not uncommon that such early test-batteries are later 'broken up' into subscales which are then intercorrelated and sometimes factor-analyzed. Vetter (1930a) constructed an original test-battery of 36 groups of 5 items, each one judged as to whether it reflects a radical, liberal, neutral, conservative or reactionary point of view [21].

In a secondary analysis of his own original work, Vetter (1947) re-scored the items in terms of a new theoretical perspective (see above, p. 30). This resulted in high intercorrelations for 4 pairs of 'opposed' categories, but there were also other high(er) correlations. However, the correlation-matrix was not fully or adequately interpreted.

This was carried out in a *tertiary* analysis by Lorr (1951), who factor-analyzed Vetter's (1947: 127) correlation-matrix and then obtained a clear 2-factor structure. Only in a tertiary analysis, more than 20 years after the original study, was an underlying structure finally identified . . . which proved to be similar to results obtained in other studies 20 years earlier. The analysis shows, by the way, that contrary to results obtained by Lentz (1938), the liberal-conservative antithesis is not unidimensional but 2-dimensional.

A similar procedure was carried out on a smaller scale by Rubin-Rabson (1954) using new data for re-analysis (i.e. in replication).

Many scales only refer to the politico-economic realm and in many cases no scaling procedures were carried out (see Centers, 1949; Case, 1952; Wright and Hicks, 1966; Nettler and Huffman, 1957). Selznick and Steinberg (1969), for example, used an index of 'ideological agreement with Goldwater' without scaling the items. A curious case is that of Newcombe's (1943: 19–20) reconceptualization of Stagner's (1936) fascism-scale in terms of 'political and economic progressivism': indeed, the items that discriminated best between high and low groups on Stagner's 'scale' are politico-economic in nature and refer to 'public relief, labor unions and the public role of private and corporate wealth' (see Newcombe, 1943: 20).

Two scales will now be discussed separately: Levinson's (1950) attempt to construct the PEC-scale and McClosky's (1958) construction of the 'classical conservatism' scale.

3.3.1.1. The PEC-scale. Levinson's (1950) attempts to construct the PEC-scale (see par. 3.2.1.) have not been very successful. Unlike the F-scale, the selected items do not correspond to the previously-defined 'sections' or 'dimensions' of the construct (see Levinson, 1950: 153–157) and there are both 'positive' and 'negative' items [22]. The reliability of the original 16-items form is .73, which is low compared to the reliabilities obtained for the other scales. The author's interpretation of this has already been mentioned: it is suggested that there is an absence of a well developed, articulate political left and right. Attempts to develop a better scale were all unsuccessful.

In the third form of the PEC-scale (Forms 45–40), there are only 5 items left (p. 169).

The results obtained may (partly) be explained by (a) the *broad definition* of politico-economic conservatism (see Hyman and Sheatsly, 73–74, who also correctly note a strong similarity in the content of some PEC- and F-scale items), (b) the probable *multi*dimensional nature of the domain covered by the items, (which could not be uncovered by the analytical technique used) and (c) the various levels of *abstraction* of the items (which, as we will see below, may evoke quite inconsistent responses).

These 3 factors and the fact that economic and non-economic conservatism tend to be inversely related to social class (see e.g. Smith, 1948) may explain findings that surprise the researcher, such as: 'Furthermore, the extreme liberals tended, as noted above, to agree even with some of the "conservative" items' (p. 161); 'Why do so many individuals who are otherwise conservative support increase in government activity?' (p. 162) [23]; 'For example, some workers are strongly pro-union and resentful of "bosses", yet at the same time are anti-Negro, anti-foreigner and conservative regarding many political issues' (p. 173).

In conclusion due to the way in which the PEC-scale has been constructed, serious confusion may arise as to the existence and nature of ideological dimensions and ideological controversy. Not only may one arrive at findings that seem highly anomalous, but one may also be tempted to try to interpret such findings. Such interpretations can be highly misleading, e.g. conclusions such as those on the lack of *organization* of political ideology (see above) and the following: 'The apparent contradiction may reflect something much more basic, namely a shift from traditional laissez-faire conservatism whose economic unit was the individual competitive business-man, to a new type of conservatism whose economic unit is organized big business' (p. 162). 'It seems safe to conclude that over-all class differences in political ideology are not extremely large' (p. 192).

3.3.1.2. The 'classical conservatism' scale. McClosky's (1958) attempt to construct a 'classical conservatism' scale has been more successful than Levinson's attempts to construct the PEC-scale. Forty-three items (unfortunately never published) were derived from the quasi-model presented earlier (see above, par. 3.2.2.) and submitted to a regional cross-sectional sample from Minnesota.

By way of cluster-analysis, a 9-item scale was constructed which included the following items:

1. I prefer the practical man anytime to the man of ideas.
2. If you start trying to change things very much, you usually make them worse.
3. If something grows up after a long time, there will always be much wisdom in it.
4. It is better to stick by what you have then to be trying new things you don't really know about.
5. We must respect the work of our forefathers and not think that we know better than they did.
6. A man does not really have much wisdom until he is well along in years.
7. No matter how we like to talk about it, political authority really comes not from us but from some higher power.
8. I'd want to know that something would really work before I'd be willing to take a chance on it.
9. All groups can live in harmony in this country, without changing the system in any way.

(From Robinson et al., 1968: 96).

Obviously, these scale items do not cover to any worthwhile extent the conservative principles that constitute McClosky's definition of conservatism. There is very little on the nature of society and nothing on the nature of man, the natural inequality of men, orders and classes, the community or the family, and in particular nothing on the subject of private property. On the other hand, there is an over-representation of items on 'change', while the relationship of item 6 to the 7 principles is not immediately clear [24].

Some evidence in favor of the validity of the scale is presented. From the negative relationship between conservatism and educational level, it may be inferred that conservatism and its concomitant personality characteristics (like submissiveness, pessimism, hostility, rigidity) are typical of the working class. But *within* the different levels of social class, the relationships between conservatism and the personality characteristics remain essentially the same (see pp. 43–44). The scale is not (strongly) related to party preference, self-description in terms of liberal-conservative and to attitudes on economic issues.

In summary, the conceptualization may be criticized on 4 points: (a) the items are not systematically derived from the quasi-model; (b) they are often put in too simplistic terms; (c) the scale does not sufficiently cover the domain indicated by the quasi-model and (d) the analysis is 'biased' towards unidimensionality and, inevitably, still rather primitive (cluster-analysis by hand; personal communication).

McClosky's study is still unique, both for America and Europe, but since it was inspired mainly by European notions of conservatism [25], the 'classical conservatism' scale has been misinterpreted by most American researchers who used it later. Evidence that the scale taps notions of conservatism that are more typically European than American has been given by Schoenberger (1968) who finds that members of the Conservative Party of New York State do not show the personality-characteristics that are, according to McClosky's study, typical for the conservative. His conservatives are only characterized by their strong opposition to the Welfare State, the regulatory role of government, and trade unions (p. 876).

Evidence of misinterpretation is given by Campbell et al. (1960: 210) who interpret a 6-item Guttman-scale (derived from McClosky's 9 items) as tapping a 'posture towards change'; Matthews and Prothro (1966: 526) who literally identify 'classical conservatism' with an attitude towards change; Anderson et al. (1965: 191–192) who refer to the scale as indicating 'human nature' conservatism and Middleton and Putney (1963: 379) who consider that it taps a basic personality variable.

3.3.2. Preconceptualized dimensions (scale level)

3.3.2.1. Early factor-analytic studies. In the early days of attitude-research many Thurstone-scales were constructed to measure attitudes towards *specific* 'objects' such as war, capital punishment, the law, divorce, patriotism. Later, some researchers (e.g. Thurstone, 1934, Carlson, 1934, Ferguson, 1939, etc.) set out to determine whether there were *general* attitudes *underlying* the various specific ones (see Eysenck, 1944: 209–215).

Thurstone (1934) found 2 factors: the first one was termed '*radicalism-*

conservatism', with high loadings for attitudes such as those in favor of evolution, birth control, divorce and communism, and negative loadings for attitudes towards the church, Sunday observance, belief in a personal god and patriotism. (As Thurstone remarks, this factor could also have been labeled 'religionism'.) The second factor was termed *'nationalism-internationalism'* (although 'patriotism' loads on the radicalism-factor).

In a similar way, Carlson (1934), intercorrelated 5 attitude scales and an intelligence-test and found 1 factor labeled 'intelligence' after rotation (with high loadings for attitudes towards communism and pacifism) and one labeled 'radicalism-conservatism' (with high positive loadings for 'communism' and negative ones for 'god' and 'prohibition').

Ferguson (1939) originally found 2 orthogonal factors called 'religionism' and 'humanitarianism', the first one being defined by scales which measure attitudes toward god, evolution and birth-control, the second one by attitudes toward capital punishment, the treatment of criminals, and war. A third factor, related to the other 2, was later found (see Ferguson, 1942) and labeled 'nationalism' (defined by attitudes toward patriotism, communism, law and censorship; 4 scales which were eliminated from the original set).

It is clear that in those early factor-analytic studies no clear or convincing structure of general attitudes was found.

3.3.2.2. Modern multidimensional approaches. Quinney's (1964), Wiley's (1967) and Schindeler and Hoffman's (1968) attempts to assess measures for religious vs. political liberalism-conservatism are not particularly sophisticated. All the studies mentioned approach political conservatism as if it were unidimensional; Quinney uses no scaling procedures (or else very obscure ones); Wiley and Schindeler and Hoffman use Likert-type procedures. Religious conservatism (orthodoxy, fundamentalism) is assessed by Quinney (1969: 374) on the basis of items such as on e.g. 'gambling', 'drinking' and 'card playing'; Wiley (1967, 144, note 4) includes 'internationalism' and 'tolerance' as well as 'welfare' items in the measurement of political liberalism; Schindeler and Hoffman include 8 statements on issues such as foreign aid, labor unions, freedom of speech and grounds for divorce (p. 437, note 21) [26].

Ferdinand (1964: 77) based his conceptualization of political liberalism on 3 'dimensions' frequently mentioned in the works of Ruggerio, Laski and Sabine (see above; par. 3.2.3.), but then met with serious difficulties in operationalizing these aspects: 'It was necessary to sharpen the focus of these attitudes considerably, since most Americans would probably endorse a general version of all three attitudes regardless of their political orientation' (p. 77) [27]. Accordingly, a humanitarian concern for underprivileged or disadvantaged groups was considered an index of the degree to which an individual was concerned with the inalienable rights of man; a self-conscious refusal to conform to social conventions was taken as an index of the degree to which an individual supported a secular and sometimes negative attitude toward the dominant social institutions; and finally, support for the view that it is the government's responsibility to care for those who cannot care for themselves was considered to be an index of the degree to which an individual was willing to utilize political institutions in perfecting the social and economic condition of man. These three attitudes were labeled 'humanitarianism', 'aconventionalism' and 'welfarism'. In a student-sample, 3- to 4-item scales were constructed for all 3 dimensions by means of cluster analysis [28]. The scales were validated by relating them to political party preference and self-designation either as being liberal, conservative or other. Results were positive in that all 3 scales seemed to be valid and interrelated, although 'humanitarianism' and 'aconventionalism' were only very moderately so.

Anderson et al. (1965) constructed scales for their 4 'conservative attitudes' (see par. 3.2.3.) using a regional quota-sample and cluster-analysis. The 4 dimensions were not highly intercorrelated, so according to the authors, the extreme radical right would probably not attract many followers. However, the correlations increased considerably for those highly involved in politics (p. 197).

A large number of studies in the 1960's and early 1970's were oriented toward the effects of *'status-inconsistency'* [29] and *social mobility* on political attitudes and partisan choice (see further Chapter 7). Very rarely, however, such effects have been assessed by liberalism-conservatism scales.

Kelly and Chambliss (1966) attempted to solve the dispute between Lenski (1954) and Kenkel (1956) as to the effects of status-inconsistency on political liberalism. Four Guttman-scales were constructed to tap the following dimensions of political liberalism: welfare, civil liberties, civil rights and internationalism [30]. The welfare-scale was only moderately related to the other political liberalism scales (average Gamma = .27) while the latter were far more strongly related to each other (average .51), thus confirming both the multidimensionality of political liberalism-conservatism and the value of the economic vs. non-economic distinction. The fact that social class is found to be a far better predictor of political liberalism (*negatively related to economic, and positively related to non-economic liberalism*) than status-inconsistency, raises doubts as to whether the latter concept 'contributes to the accumulation of knowledge in the social sciences' (p. 382). On the other hand, the concept of social class may, according to the authors, be time-worn and 'even smack of Marxism' (!). 'But if they [social class and ethnic background; CPM] are in fact the kinds of sociological variables that determine the behavior of men, then we should use them. Concepts like status consistency, status congruency, status crystallization and status integration unquestionably have a more sophisticated sound to them. But if we sacrifice substantive usefulness for sophisticated appearance, then our constribution to knowledge will be meager indeed' (p. 382), so the authors conclude.

O'Kane (1970) sets out to synthesize the conflicting evidence on the effects of (intergenerational) mobility on liberalism-conservatism by making a distinction between economic and non-economic liberalism. Two Likert-type scales were constructed [31] which were moderately positively related to each other (.29), thus again confirming the value of making the economic—non-economic distinction.

High upward-mobility potential was *positively* related to *non*-economic liberalism but *un*related to *economic* liberalism. Therefore it is concluded that economic attitudes are probably more stable than non-economic ones (p. 504): 'Perhaps, as the Marxist interpretation of social classes as economic entities would suggest, the individual's identity is far more dependent on economic positioning and socialization than on other factors. Consequently economic orientations provide a foundation for one's political-ideological framework . . .'

Two studies are of particular interest here, and will be discussed separately:

(a) 'The American Voter' (Campbell et al., 1960). Campbell et al. constructed 2 Guttman-type scales: one on *domestic social welfare* and the other on *internationalism*. Their experiences in constructing these scales and the interpretation of findings are of special importance. (On their conceptualization of liberalism-conservatism: see above par. 3.2.3.)

Of the 10 items on domestic welfare issues only 5 formed a satisfactory Guttman-scale whereas this was the case for 4 out of the 6 internationalism items. The results of the scaling procedures are taken as evidence of the existence of only a slight degree of structure in the attitudes of the mass electorate (p. 195). The fact that low income groups and Democrats are both in favor of *extending* government welfare policy and *reducing* taxes causes the researchers to interpret positions on the domestic welfare scale in terms of *primitive self-interest* rather than *ideology* (p. 205, note 26). Another indication of the *non-ideological* nature of the domestic welfare scale lies (according to the authors) in the fact that items which do *not* have an immediate and obvious link with self-interest do not 'scale'; for instance, items on the *role of business.*

Further evidence of the lack of ideology amongst the masses is suggested by the virtual lack of relationship between the domestic welfare scale, the internationalism scale and the 6-item Guttman-scale labeled 'posture toward change' which has been developed from McClosky's classical conservatism scale (see above).

However, the authors' interpretation of the domestic welfare scale in terms of primitive self-interest is open to question. The non-scalability of the tax-item (i.e. the fact that some people are in favor of tax-reduction *and* extension of the government's tasks; mainly Democrats and lower class people) might well be caused by the fact that these people are only in favor of tax-reduction *for themselves*, but *not* for higher income groups (see e.g. McClosky et al., 1960: 414). For lower income groups, self-interest and to be in favor of a more egalitarian income-distribution go hand in hand, but it is not immediately clear why in this case the latter point of view should no longer be considered as *ideological* [32].

Regarding the item on the role of business (the exact wording is not given), anomalies occur which are similar to those observed by Levinson (1950: 161, 162, 173) which have been noted earlier (par. 3.3.1.1.). They will be discussed below, since Free and Cantril (1967) have documented this particular anomaly rather well.

(b) 'The Political Beliefs of Americans (Free and Cantril, 1967). Free and Cantril set out to document the strong support (since the New Deal) of the American people for a number of specific government programs. In a national survey, a number of questions *directly* pertaining to such programs were asked and combined into what is termed the '*operational spectrum*'. In addition, a number of questions were asked on the *general role* of the federal government in relation to free enterprise and local communities. There were also some general questions on personal initiative and the causes of unemployment. These questions were combined into what is termed the '*ideological spectrum*'.

Whereas on the operational spectrum, a clear majority (60–70%) of the population is *liberal* (on the conceptualization of liberalism and the background for the distinction between the 2 spectra see par. 3.2.3.), on the ideological spectrum there are only a *small* minority (16%) who are (completely or predominantly) liberal: 50% are *conservative* and 34% are middle of the road (p. 32).

Of course, there is a correlation between both dimensions, but 23% of the population proves to be operationally liberal and ideologically conservative (p. 37). Ninety percent of those who are ideologically liberal are also operationally liberal, but only 26% of the ideological conservatives are also operational conservatives. Almost half of the ideological conservatives are operationally liberal [33].

This schizoid tendency in the American population may be called a state of 'false consciousness' (see e.g. Mann, 1970; Runciman, 1970: 213–223) in the sense that for many there is a complete lack of consistency between (abstract) principles and their specific applications (cf. Prothro and Grigg, 1960; McClosky, 1964). Such states of false consciousness are more frequent in the working class than in the upper class (see Free and Cantril, 1967: 37).

The authors conclude that: 'The generally conservative stance at the ideological level indicates that the liberal trend of policies and programs that has characterized the American scene much of the time since the early days of Franklin Roosevelt's New Deal has little secure underlying foundation in any ideological consensus . . . As a Massachusetts business executive saw the problem: 'I am afraid that we are too frightened of the word socialism, and that there will be a reaction to programs to help people because people misunderstand this as socialism' (pp. 39–40, see also pp. 174–181). Similar observations have been made earlier and in other contexts. It may now be useful to consider some of these studies somewhat further.

3.3.3. *Differential reactions to abstract ideas vs. specific opinions and attitudes*

3.3.3.1. Early evidence. An anti-socialist 'prejudice' among the American people was already observed in 1929 (Allport, pp. 229–233). In 1936 Hartmann (pp. 351–352) notes: '. . . there appears to be a clear-cut discrepancy between what most American citizens want and the political channels through which they normally seek to attain it. The parties which are committed to the establishment of a collectivist society and the "economy of abundance" (which the bulk of the voters evidently want *when the details of such a program are presented*) [my emphasis; CPM] are the very ones to whose names an attitude of hostility or indifference is most marked . . . Briefly stated: the masses seem to like "socialism" but to dislike "socialists".'

This phenomenon is not confined to socialism or socialism-implying labels and specific opinions. It has been extensively documented that the term 'fascism' is almost always rejected, but that many people still accept fascist principles *when not labeled as such* (see e.g. Raskin and Cook, 1938: 205; Stagner, 1936b: 451; Edwards, 1944: 314).

Those early results may now be generalized to some extent. We have seen that many people may not only reject the term 'socialism', they in fact adhere (at least in America) to the prevailing 'classical liberal' (i.e. *conservative*) ideology while accepting 'modern liberal' policies. Similarly, there is not only a tendency for people to reject the fascist label, but they accept general democratic slogans much more readily than democratic principles in specific terms, as we will see below.

3.3.3.2. Studies on liberal democracy.

As indicated above, Prothro and Grigg (1960) outlined principles of liberal democracy both in abstract and specific terms and found consensus on the former type of principles but dissensus on their specific applications. Obviously, there are a large number of people who endorse abstract slogans of liberal-democracy, but who hold undemocratic views on their particular applications. Since educational level is shown to be a major factor in contributing to 'consistency', most inconsistency appears in the uneducated and the lower classes.

McClosky (1964) used both an elite sample (congressmen) and a national cross-sectional sample. Liberal democratic ideology is conceptualized into the following sections (see above): I, *Principles*, such as on (a) 'rules of the game' and (b) 'free speech' and II, *Specific applications* of the principles of (c) 'free speech' and (d) 'procedural rights'. Finally, there is a specific section on beliefs in economic, social and political equality (d). The operationalization of (i.e. the items in) many of these sections seems rather dubious, however. 'Rules of the game', for example, contains many items which plainly express a *tough* point of view, or even '*dogmatism*', e.g. 'Almost any unfairness or brutality may have to be justified when some great purpose is being carried out' (see Rokeach, 1960: 74, item 7). Other items express e.g. cynical points of view regarding politicians. In both the elite and the mass, there are broad majorities here favoring the 'democratic principles', though less so in the electorate than in the elite. There are also broad majorities in both groups who agree on the general principles of freedom of speech and opinion. Most agreement is reached on an item such as, 'No matter what a person's political beliefs are, he is entitled to the same legal rights and protection as anyone else'.

As expected, there is much less agreement on the specific applications of these principles, especially in the electorate. Here, for example, there is a majority opinion *against* the right to teach foreign ideas in schools. But even the majority of the elite (56% as compared to 76% of the electorate) agree that, 'Any person who hides behind the laws when he is questioned about his activities does not deserve much consideration'. In short, there are substantial minorities in the electorate (*not* in the elite) who are *against* the specific applications of free speech and procedural rights as listed by McClosky. These results are in agreement with those of Prothro and Grigg.

Given the interesting results on the specific applications of *equality*, it is to be regretted that operationalizations are again doubtful in this area. *Political* equality deals mainly with cynicism regarding the (intellectual) capacities of the common man; *social* and *ethnic* equality deals with racist attitudes and *economic* equality with typical domestic welfare issues and contains items such as, 'There will always be poverty, so get used to it'. The level of abstraction of the items varies rather extensively.

The resulting picture is mixed. The elite is rather divided in its opinion on political equality, but still less cynical about the common man than the electorate. Both samples are strongly divided in their opinions on the social and ethnic items, with no clear anti-egalitarian bias in the electorate. *Economically, the electorate is clearly more egalitarian*, '. . . a result strongly, though not exclusively influenced by the pronounced economic conservatism of the Republican leaders in the sample' (p. 367; compare McClosky et al., 1960: 423) [34]. It is concluded that: (p. 368) '. . . both the public and its leaders are uncertain and ambivalent about equality. The reason, I suspect, lies partly in the fact that the egalitarian aspects of democratic theory have been less adequately thought through than other aspects, and partly in the complications connected with the concept itself . . . Another complication lies in the diffuse and variegated nature of the concept, a result of its application to at least four separate domains: political (*e.g.* universal suffrage), legal (*e.g.* equality before the law), economic (*e.g.* equal distribution of property or opportunity), and moral (*e.g.* every man's right to be treated as an end and not as a means). Accompanying these are the confusions which result from the common failure to distinguish equality as a *fact* from equality as a *norm*'.

In short, however, the conclusion should be that economic equality is *not* a constituent part of liberal democratic ideology; hence McClosky's incorporation of this principle seems highly doubtful (see note 18). In his general outline of 'American democracy' (1964: 363), there is no reference to it either. (See also Lipsitz, 1970: 165–166, and Lipsitz, 1966: 1000–1.) Nevertheless, the study suggests 2 important things. First, it confirms rather extensively that many people tend to react differentially (and thus in an *inconsistent* manner) to items of various degrees of abstraction (i.e. general principles and their specific applications); second, that the elite is more consistent in this respect than the mass electorate.

3.3.4. Analyses at the item level: intercorrelations

Approaches to liberalism-conservatism by (intercorrelating) single items are relatively rare, but have nevertheless resulted in influential studies such as Smith's (1948, a, b, c) and Converse's (1964).

Smith's (1948) studies are among the first based on national cross-sectional samples. In one study he concludes that: 'Liberals as defined by non-economic or interclass values (e.g. endorsement of civil liberties, and internationalism, opposition to prohibition) were found to be better informed and educated than the conservatives. On the other hand, liberals as defined by approval of certain politico-economic proposals (e.g. more power for labor in the government, government ownership of the banks, increased unemployment compensation) tended to be poorer informed and educated than the conservatives' '. . . The liberals on non-economic issues tended to be economically well-off people; the politico-economic liberals were drawn heavily from the poorer respondents'. (1948a: 65). The negative relationship between politico-economic liberalism and level of information is contrary to a large body of research-findings on college students, in which the opposite relationship was found (see Kerr, 1944; Murphy and Likert, 1938; Newcomb, 1943). In the interpretation of those findings, the 'functional' nature of attitudes to the satisfaction of wants is stressed (see Smith, 1948a: 77-79) [35]. Lipset (1959) extends these findings to the notion of *working class authoritarianism* which will not be discussed here (see Chapters 6 and 7 and e.g. Lipsitz, 1965; McKenzie and Silver, 1968; Miller and Riesman, 1961; Parkin, 1967).

Lenski (1961: 208-211), as outlined above, makes a distinction between attitudes toward the welfare state, freedom of speech, racial minorities and internationalism, and finds that these attitudes are not strongly interrelated. It is again found that the working class is liberal as far as the welfare state issues are concerned, but conservative on other counts: 'The limited liberalism of the working class appears to be basically an expression of the spirit of selfseeking . . . the liberalism of the middle classes seems to involve some measures of altruism and idealism, or a readiness to sacrifice some personal advantages in the hope of achieving a more just social order'. However: 'It is a liberalism which does not extend far into the area of domestic economic arrangements. Here, the middle classes generally act on the basis of self-interest as much as the working classes' (p. 210).

3.3.4.1. 'The Nature of Belief Systems in Mass Publics' (Converse, 1964). Converse's approach to liberalism-conservatism is essentially unidimensional (p. 214): 'One judgemental dimension or "yardstick" that has been highly serviceable for simplifying and organizing events in most Western politics for the past century has been the liberal-conservative continuum on which parties, political leaders, legislation, court decisions and a number of other primary objects of politics could be more — or less — adequately located'.

The author does not expect, however, that such an abstract continuum will actually be used by the general public, or will be recognized as underlying a number of issue-positions [36].

This seems to be confirmed by some research evidence. In the electorate, only low correlations among 4 domestic and 3 internationalism-items are found while in the elite (congressional candidates) these correlations are rather high. Moreover, in the electorate there is only a weak relation between issue-position and party-preference. It is concluded that: 'It cannot therefore be claimed that the mass public shares ideological patterns of belief with relevant elites at a specific level any more than it shares the abstract conceptual frames of reference' (p. 231).

In addition, the stability of beliefs over a 2-year period is extremely low, thus indicating the non-existence of idiosyncratic patterns of belief. Beliefs are most stable for opinions regarding highly visible objects like political parties and ethnic groups. It is concluded that: '. . . large portions of the electorate do not have meaningful beliefs even on issues that have formed the basis for intense political controversy among elites for substantial periods of time' (p. 245) (cf. Lane, 1962).

Finally, the upper classes (and also the better educated and informed) presumably show far more ideological constraint than the lower classes; the former hold views on *most* issues [37].

A few comments are in order.

In the *first* place, it should be noted that the empirical basis of Converse's study is extremely narrow when compared to the broad generalizations. Responses to single-items (though of a rather general and enduring nature, see Luttbeg, 1968, below) are apt to be relatively unreliable, and therefore neither high intercorrelations nor high stability in time may be expected (see Lentz, 1938: 542–544).

Second, for the public at large the correlations between domestic items and between foreign items are still rather substantial (and of course, statistically highly significant). They are both .23 on the average. So at least *within* the domains of domestic welfare and foreign policies it would seem that, however weak it may be, some underlying dimension does exist. This is ignored by Converse.

Third, the difference in constraint between the elite and the mass may be exaggerated by the differences in wording between the questions. The difference in item format is roughly that the mass public is requested to respond yes or no to such statements as: 'The government in Washington ought to see to it that everybody who wants to work can find a job' whereas the elite is asked: 'Do you think the federal government ought to sponsor programs such as large public works in order to maintain full employment, or do you think that problems of economic readjustment ought to be left more to private industry or state and local government?' (p. 257, note 21). In other words, the elite is offered alternative response categories, put forward in moderate terms; the mass is confronted with simplistic statements of the agree-disagree type.

Although one may agree with Converse's hesitation in presenting simplistic statements to elitist groups, one might ask oneself why the elite format was not *also* used for the mass. I tend to agree with one of Converse's critics (see Luttbeg, 1968: 406) that 'the difference between the items . . . would tend to support the hypothesis', even for some other reason than Luttbeg's [38]: 2 *alternative response-categories* are presented to the elite, whereas the mass has to decide for itself whether it will agree or disagree. In conclusion, Converse's evidence, and hence his 'theory', should not be regarded as conclusive.

3.3.4.2. Critics of the 'lack of constraint' theory. Axelrod (1967) reanalyzes Campbell et al.'s (1960) data and finds that, indeed, a clear left-right dimension is lacking but this is also valid to a large extent for the informed and the concerned, the educated, the rich and the 'participants' rather than just for the uneducated, the uninformed, the poor.

The most meaningful cluster, however, is one that may be labeled 'populism'. It includes items favoring government aid to education, job guarantees and Medicare, and also items in favor of tax-reduction, firing suspected communists and isolationism (p. 57). In this cluster *liberal* welfare positions are combined with *conservative* non-economic positions. This dimension is most meaningful for *non*-voters.

This study is especially important for 2 reasons: (a) it shows that some meaningful structure of beliefs may be found when data are analyzed in an *exploratory* way rather than in a *preconceived 'traditional'* manner i.e. from the liberalism-conservatism perspective; (b) it shows that some configurations are not only typical of the masses, (often meaning, by implication, the inarticulate, uneducated, uninformed), but *also* of some *semi*-elites, like college-graduates, and that some structure may even manifest itself most strongly in groups such as non-voters.

A recent study by Nie (1974) might perhaps solve the dispute between the 'elitists' and the 'populists' (see Brown, 1970: 60) [39].

His study is mainly based on secondary analyses of election studies by the Survey Research Center, University of Michigan (SRC).

For 7 consecutive years similar items (whose actual similarity will be discussed later) in the fields of domestic welfare, foreign policy and racial integration in schools were intercorrelated. The correlations increased dramatically over this period. The average correlation for all issues increased from .14 to .38, for domestic welfare issues it increased from .24 to .49. The major increase occurred between 1960 and 1964: an overall liberalism-conservatism dimension somehow emerged in that period. Since 1964, the level of constraint of issue-positions along this continuum equals or even exceeds the level of constraint found for congressional candidates in 1958 [40].

Results are interpreted in terms of the *increased salience of politics* in the 1960's. However, around 1970 'campaign interest' was no longer a valid indicator of the salience of politics. Between 1968 and 1970 there is a sharp increase in consistency for the 'disenchanted' (as measured by a political cynicism-scale) indicating that in these people politics have become 'negatively salient'.

In conclusion, '. . . the pattern of attitudes found among Americans in the 1950's was a transient phenomenon and not an inevitable characteristic of mass politics . . . the structure of mass attitudes may be affected by politics in the real world. The average citizen may not be as apolitical as has been thought' (p. 580).

There is, however, a nasty methodological issue that should be raised: there is a suspicious change in the question-wording, parallel to the observed emergence of 'ideology'. *Until* 1960, respondents were asked whether they had an opinion on a statement (i.e. whether they agreed or disagreed on a 5-point scale). *Since* 1964, the question-format was such that *2 points of view* were presented and the respondents were asked which position they agreed with the most (see the discussion on Converse's study above). Nie is of course aware of this problem, and discusses it at length (pp. 550–551). Though admitting that the evidence in favor of the 'validity' of the change is not conclusive, he mistakenly judges the agree-disagree format of the pre-1964 period as similar to the more recent NORC and SRC formats, where *2 polar* positions along a 7-point scale are presented.

Nie's is a fascinating trend-study, but as Converse's study it is limited in scope as far as the definition and conceptualization of liberalism-conservatism are concerned. There are only 4 specific issue-items in the social welfare area, while the other 4 areas (black welfare, school integration, size of government and Cold War) are covered by only one item. Apart from the general differences in format noted above, some items in these areas change their content over the years. For example in the foreign area on Cold War, there are items on the Vietnam War (which was not so cold). Moreover, again like in Converse's study, there is some evidence for a 2-dimensional structure (i.e. 2 weakly related economic vs. non-economic dimensions), which is ignored.

3.3.5. Factor-analytic studies at the item level

Numerous attempts have been undertaken to assess progressive-conservative dimensions through factor-analysis of more or less intuitively grasped items.

The earliest approach in America is probably that of Hayes (1939 a, b), which is also one of the first studies based on a non-student sample. A large number of opinions on political and economic issues were inter-correlated on the basis of a sample of 8419 voters from 37 states. The author notes '. . . the coexistence of logically quite contradictory attitudes in the minds of so many voters . . .' (1939a: 375).

In a second paper an attempt was made to assess general factors by way of a factor-analysis of the same data (1939b: 393). The first main factor was called 'liberalism', mostly including items of the conventional social welfare type. The second factor was a curious one: 'Intranationally, it was liberal. Internationally it was not. However, the isolationist attitudes would fit in perfectly with the name suggested above, a general attitude of "national socialism"' (p.395). A similar "national-socialist" syndrome was observed by Hartmann (1936: 350) and later by Axelrod (1967), as discussed above.

The work of Hayes has remained rather unique for the U.S. In Europe, however, many studies of this type were carried out around 1950 at the University of London (see Eysenck, 1944, 1947, 1951, 1954; Sanai, 1950, 1951; Sanai and Pickard, 1949).

3.3.5.1. Eysenck's and other English studies.

By reanalyzing earlier studies by e.g. Thurstone and Ferguson, Eysenck (1944) finds a more 'meaningful' and invariant structure when the factors are left unrotated. In all these studies, the first factor may now be labeled 'radicalism-conservatism': radical attitudes are those in favor of e.g. communism, divorce, birth-control, evolution; conservative, those in favor of e.g. patriotism, religion, capital punishment, law (p. 214). The second factor is more difficult to interpret but is called 'practical vs. theoretical' (p. 214).

A similar structure is found in a preliminary research project. In a subsequent study (1947) 2 main factors explaining 18 and 8 percent of the variance are found. They are interpreted in terms of *radicalism-conservatism* and *tough-tendermindedness*. The first factor is validated by testing on the 'known groups' of liberals, conservatives and socialists. The second factor again causes more problems and obviously needs further validations. This is reported in later studies (1951, 1954) [41].

The 1951-study confirms the hypothesis that communists are 'tough-minded radicals' and that, with party allegiance controlled, working class respondents are *more conservative* than the middle class, even towards an issue like: 'Ultimately, private property should be abolished and complete socialism introduced' (p. 205) [42].

According to the author, one cannot 'maintain the superficially plausible hypothesis that there are two kinds of conservatism involved, one dealing with economic matters, the other with ideational causes, in such a way that working-class people are economically radical and ideationally conservative, while middle class people are economically conservative and ideationally radical'; obviously the working-class is not the 'true breeding ground of radicalism' (p. 205) [43].

The 1954-publication contains validating evidence for the tender- vs. tough-mindedness factor [44]. There is a positive relationship between tough-mindedness and extroversion (p. 178), aggression and dominance (pp. 198–236); thus the dimension can be seen as a projection of personality tendencies in the field of attitudes.

This early work of Eysenck has been severely criticized (see Christie, 1956 a, b; Rokeach and Hanley, 1956 a, b). Eysenck did formulate a reply (1956 a, b), but it was not very convincing.

I will not go into the details of it here, but will add some critical notes on Eysenck's work:

1. It is not clear why only *2 out of 40* items refer to socio-economic opinions. Both items discriminate best between conservatives and socialists, and may even have had a strong influence on the resulting factor-structure (see Eysenck, 1971: 211). Nowhere is a principle underlying item-selection presented, and the result is a hotchpotch of items (see for example items such as: There should be far more controversial and political discussion over the radio, and There will be another war in 25 years).

2. Samples used do not allow for generalization. They are severely limited as to age group and social class and, as far as the communists are concerned, to membership of the party.

3. Factor-analysis without rotation to some form of simple structure is often a doubtful procedure. One could of course agree with Eysenck's theoretical stand on this matter: '. . . different methods of factor-analysis are appropriate to different types of problems, and in every case one should seek evidence that the method of analysis chosen is in actual fact the most appropriate one to use' (1947: 64), but one wishes

that he had applied this procedure to his own data (see also Kerlinger, 1967: 116).

4. Procedures of measurement are not at all clear. In the first place, not all items loading highly on one or both factors are in fact used in measurement, and nowhere are the reasons made explicit! (compare Tables 1 and 5, 1947: 76–81). Taking a loading of .35 as the minimum, the radicalism-scale is constructed *ignoring* 7 items which load sufficiently high. On the tough-mindedness scale, 2 such items are excluded, but 9 are included which have loadings that are *too low*. Only 5 have sufficiently high loadings. There are 14 items in both scales: 5 common items are scored identically and 6 in opposite ways. Furthermore, items are 'keyed': only agreements or disagreements indicating *radicalism or tender-mindedness* are counted. For the tender-mindedness scale, there are 9 *disagreements* and 5 *agreements* which are counted as tender; the distribution is equal for the radicalism-scale. This is of course, all quite arbitrary and may have all kinds of 'odd' consequences; the critics cited above show an abundance of them. Even if no errors had been made (some critics find this highly improbable) the measurements would still be extremely doubtful.

In a recent paper, Eysenck (1971) again considers this area of research. The study was based on a national, cross-sectional sample taken from the British population including 28 questions on 'social attitudes'; again only 2 refer to politico-economic issues (on government interference and on the immorality of capitalism). A central objective of the study was to investigate whether different attitudinal structures would emerge for the various social classes. Another question was whether the working class, which has often been found to be economically left-wing, also shows conservative and authoritarian tendencies to a greater extent than the middle class [45]. The conclusion is reached that '. . . working class people, in summary, are nationalistic, even jingoistic, xenophobic, anti-semitic, racialist, inhumane, narrowly moralistic in sexual matters and unconcerned with ethical or religious issues' (p. 205).

In the middle class the factor-structure was 'tighter' (more variance explained) but essentially similar to that found in the working class. The 2 main second-order factors were now labeled 'humanitarianism vs. authoritarianism' and 'religionism vs. permissiveness' (both labels were introduced earlier by Ferguson, 1939) [46].

The most obvious difference in this work as compared to the earlier study (see Eysenck, 1954) is that there seems to have been a '*rotation of axes*' of about 45° (now, second order factor-analysis is used). Eysenck's explanation of this: '. . . in the original analysis the conservative-radical factor was *centered* [my emphasis; CPM] on questions relating to economic radicalism and conservatism, e.g. "abolish private property" and "nationalisation is inefficient" ' (1971: 210), is completely incorrect since there were only 2 economic items in *both* studies. Although new evidence in favor of another structure has been gathered, Eysenck keeps to his original interpretation in terms of radicalism-conservatism and tender-toughmindedness.

In conclusion, it may be suggested here that:

(a) Rotation of the factors in Eysenck's original study (1947, 1954) would have yielded a structure similar to that found earlier by Ferguson (1939) and again later by Eysenck (1971).

(b) Item-selection (which, according to Eysenck, appears so invaluable to the final structure that will be found; 1971: 211) *lacks a sufficient theoretical rationale* as to lead to much confidence in the nature of the factors that were found [47].

(c) Eysenck's work at best suggest that the structure of the *non-economic domain of social attitudes and opinions* (including those on religious, sexual, racial, family, military, punitive, and 'moral' matters) is 2-dimensional rather than unidimensional.

I will now briefly comment on some other studies similar to those of Eysenck. Sanai and Pickardt (1949) find a clear 2-factor structure with most items (of 'general' politico-economic nature) loading on the first unrotated factor.

Sanai (1950) carried out a factor-analysis over 16 items (very similar to Eysenck's; only 3 items on capitalism and nationalization were included) and again found one general unrotated factor.

In a second study (Sanai, 1951), 30 items — again similar to those of Eysenck and Sanai 1950), including 5 items on socialism and capitalism — were factor-analyzed in a similar way. Once again a general factor is found. (All these studies were based on student samples.)

There are some rather interesting discussions as to the name that should be given to the general factors found: '. . . it does not seem very satisfactory to use the term radicalism. In its political aspect, it may be called a factor of 'left vs. right' or socialism versus laissez-faire (or conservatism). In its religious aspect it may be called a factor of rationalism, agnosticism or atheism vs. orthodox religious dogma. In its social aspect it may be called progressivism or modernism vs. conservatism . . .' '. . . The writer thinks that the term progressive vs. conservative is a better term for this factor, but of course the term should be used without giving it an ethical connotation and meaning by it simply advocacy of change and openness to new ideas' (1950: 176). This latter reasoning as to the meaning of 'progressiveness vs. conservatism' is not uncommon, but is of course unacceptable. Liberalism as a label for the general factor is also considered unsuited because liberalism is a political philosphy which has undergone evolution (see Sanai, 1951: 257–259, for a reasoning similar to e.g. that of Campbell et al., 1960, McClosky, 1958, Free and Cantril, 1967, discussed above. In England, modern social liberalism was advocated by Green, 1911, and especially Hobhouse) [48].

3.3.5.2. Kerlinger's 'criterial referents'. According to Kerlinger (1967) there are 2 basic factors underlying positions on social attitudes. (His work is mainly, though not completely, based on student- and teacher-samples.) 'Social attitude referents — e.g. private property, religion, civil rights — are differentially criterial (relevant) for different sets of individuals. Their structure is dualistic: two basic orthogonal dimensions span the attitude domain due to a press toward dichotomizing referents into criterial and non-criterial and to the culture that offers two main ideologies (liberalism and conservatism)' (1967: 110).

In an early study (1958) on educational attitudes 2 orthogonal factors were found after rotation and called 'progressiveness' and 'traditionalism'. This is the first evidence of a basic duality of the attitude-structure (see 1958: 130).

In a second study (Kerlinger and Kaya, 1959), those results were replicated and elaborated upon. Methodologically, it is important to quote the following: ' . . . Some attempt should be made, in brief, to identify the factors behind the attitudes being measured before constructing and administering attitude scales. Otherwise, psychological and educational measurement falls victim to the 'mindless empiricism' of the philosophers. Procedures like Thurstone's, Likert's and Guttman's, while effective in identifying 'good' items and, in the Guttman case, in attaining unidimensionality, are severely limited. The Thurstone and Likert methods are limited in that, in and of themselves, they give little or no clue to the factors behind the attitudes being measured. . . . Moreover, they are perhaps often multidimensional, and thus conceal the true nature of the variables presumably being measured. The Guttman-procedure is limited in that we emerge from it with very short scales of extremely homogeneous items which probably rarely tap much of the richness of any complex attitude structure' (1959: 28) (see also Kerlinger, 1967: 116) [49].

The structure of the broader domain of 'social attitudes' is assessed in a third study (1968). Here, there is a more or less clear procedure of item-selection (1968: 1) [50]. A 4-factor rotated solution was judged best (various numbers of factors were rotated, in search of a 'best solution')

[51]. However, after the 10-factor oblique solution, 2 relatively orthogonal factors, one *'liberalism'* and one *'conservatism'*, emerged, as predicted. With the 26 best items, similar results were obtained in replication (i.e. using new data): a best 4-factor orthogonal solution and 2 second-order factors: one liberal and one conservative.

In the 4-factor othogonal solution, the *first* factor is called 'liberalism' or 'socialism' (the well-known economic welfare-items) [52]. The *second* factor ('government aid to education') overlaps heavily with the first one, both in loadings and item-content. The *third* factor is labeled 'religionism' or 'religionism-conventionalism', but 4 of its items do not refer to this general term. The *fourth* factor is termed 'economic conservatism', with 3 of its 6 items referring to business. Two other items (property rights and internationalism) have a double loading on both third and fourth factors. This structure is not very clear indeed, so the second-order solution is preferred.

The labeling of the 2 second-order factors seems somewhat simplistic, however. The first is clearly the 'welfare-government interference' factor, with some emphasis on education. The second factor may be interpreted as a mixture of *non-economic* and *economic* conservatism items (the latter type not referring to *specific* welfare measures but to more *general phrases* on business, property rights and enjoyment of wealth) [53]. In discussing the literature, we have already seen on numerous occasions that respondents tend to react to general, more abstract items in a different way than to specific items (see e.g. McClosky, 1964; Free and Cantril, 1967). Kerlinger's liberalism and conservatism factors may thus be reinterpreted in the sense suggested above.

As already outlined above, Kerlinger (1967) interprets his findings in terms of the *criteriality* of attitudinal *referents*. In most Western societies, 2 'supersets' of attitudinal referents are postulated: the liberal and the conservative one [54]. It is reasoned that for most individuals, reality is too complex for attitudes to all those referents to be developed; there is a tendency to regard only one of the 2 supersets as relevant: those referents become *criterial* and the attitudes developed are either pro or con. The other set is *non-criterial*: there tends to be a random, or at least an inconsistent reaction to this. Only few individuals will develop criteriality for *both* supersets of referents, and thus develop a bipolar unidimensional attitude structure. Those are the more interested and involved, the better-educated or the ideologically 'extreme' persons [55].

The theory can evidently be more fully substantiated when the referents of attitudes themselves are studied. Research of this type has been reported in a recent paper (see Kerlinger, 1972) and the results are indeed more convincing. A 'referent' is a name, a recurrent, a category (Brown,

1958 in Kerlinger, 1972: 614). In other words, a referent is a set of 'things' toward which an attitude may be directed.

Conservative and liberal referents were selected from the literature. Twenty-five liberal and 25 conservative referents were again presented to samples of graduate students, teachers and businessmen. Again, 2 second-order factors were found.

The first-order oblique factors were labeled: 1. *'religiosity'*, with such referents as religion, church, faith in God (but also 'moral standards in education' and 'patriotism'); 2. *'educational traditionalism'*, e.g. school discipline; 3. *'economic conservatism'*, e.g. free enterprise, private property, capitalism, (but also national sovereignty and scientific knowledge) (!); 4. *'civil rights'*, e.g. Negroes, civil rights; 5. *'child-centered education'*, e.g. a pupil's personality, children's needs and 6. *'social liberalism'*, e.g. social security, poverty program, socialized medicine (but also the United Nations). Factors 1, 2 and 3 form the conservative second-order factor; 4 to 6 the liberalism factor.

This approach may open up new lines of research especially when it is systematically linked to approaches on a 'statement'-level as well as to those on a 'value'-level. (Referents may provide a link between research on attitudes and values; see Kerlinger, 1972: 628.)

A few final comments:

1. In Kerlinger's work (unlike Eysenck's) there is an increasing awareness of the necessity to base the selection of items on 'theoretical' considerations (see Kerlinger, 1972). Still, the items are not derived systematically from some 'conceptual model' of liberalism and conservatism; their selection remains rather intuitive and idiosyncratic (i.e. Kerlinger's bias towards including 'educational' items).

2. The samples used are always 'ad hoc', obtained in unspecified ways. It remains to be seen whether similar results would have been obtained with cross-sectional national or local samples. These 'unsophisticated' people may have less 'criterial referents', making their attitudinal structure (much) weaker (see e.g. Kerlinger, 1967: 119, note 6).

3. The analytical technique used does not always yield easily interpretable results: many first-order factors appear difficult to label (i.e. to interpret) and many items prove to have multiple loadings. Kerlinger seems to reject a 'preconceptualization' of the attitudinal domain through the construction of unidimensional scales (e.g. Guttman-scales). Nevertheless, in the light of his own results and e.g. those of Comrey and Newmeyer (1965), this seems much to be preferred.

4. The introduction of the concept of the 'criterial referent' of attitudes is a significant contribution, and is also relevant to the present study: the level of abstraction as regards 'referents' is higher than that of

'statement-items'. Since Kerlinger's theory is most convincingly confirmed in case the referents themselves are used as stimuli, it may be suggested here that Kerlinger's theory (generalized to include European ideologies such as socialism) may be quite useful at this 'abstract-ideological' level, rather than at the more specific issue-level.

3.3.5.3. Other recent studies. The work of both Eysenck and Kerlinger has evolved over the decades. Eysenck begins with an analytical ad hoc sample, intuitively selected items and factor-analysis without rotating axes. More than 20 years later he ends up with a similar collection of statements, but with second-order factor-analysis of the data based on a cross-sectional sample. Results are similar to those obtained more than 30 years earlier by Ferguson (1939), but are somewhat curiously reinterpreted to correspond with his earlier results in terms of radicalism-conservatism and tender-toughmindedness factors. The groups of items contain conspicuously few politico-economic items.

Kerlinger begins by considering educational attitudes and from that finds evidence in favor of 2 relatively independent 'progressive' and 'traditionalist' factors. He is then able to generalize this finding and apply it to the field of 'social attitudes' (including political and politico-economic ones) where, using second-order factor-analysis and on the basis of ad hoc student- and non-student-samples and an initially rather ad hoc set of statement-items, 2 relatively independent liberalism and conservatism factors are found. A theory of criterial referents of attitudes is developed to explain the findings and subsequently the theory is tested, using the referents themselves as stimuli. The theory is confirmed using referents which have been selected from a study of the literature on (the ideologies of) liberalism and conservatism, with data based on similar ad hoc samples.

This review suggests that the item-selection, item-format, samples and analytical procedures used may all influence the results obtained. This is further shown by 2 studies (see Comrey and Newmeyer, 1965 and Wilson, ed., 1973) in which similar procedures are followed . . . but with differing results.

Comrey and Newmeyer (1965) used factor-analysis to 'preconceptualize' a broad attitudinal domain. Twenty-five sets of 'homogeneous items' thus obtained were factor-analyzed and rotated obliquely. The 9 'oblique second-order factors' (e.g. welfare, punitive attitudes, nationalism, religiosity and racial tolerance) were again factor-analyzed. Only one third-order factor (called radicalism-conservatism) appeared. Results are interpreted in the light of varying procedures for the rotation of factors. In the U.S. it has been customary to *rotate* factors towards simple structure, a procedure which according to the authors, 'tends to organize the attitude domain around several distinct variables (such as religionism, nationalism, humanitarianism and so on) with no Radicalism-Conservatism factor' (p. 368). They conclude: 'These same factors factor-analyzed without rotation will show Radicalism-Conservatism as the first general factor, but will not reveal appropriately the correlated primary factor-level components of Radicalism-Conservatism. The present analysis, which uses oblique rotation to [obtain; CPM] the correlated primary factors, and then second-order analysis is the appropriate means for demonstrating the existence of both the general factor and its correlated primary components'.

It is doubtful, however, that the controversy on the dimensionality of liberalism-conservatism will be solved if the *only* thing that one applies is the appropriate analytic technique. Kerlinger, for example, used *similar* ad hoc samples, applied *similar* techniques, obtained *similar* first-order factors, but not one general second-order factor (perhaps due to rotation of factors).

Wilson and his colleagues (see Wilson, ed., 1973) provide further evidence that the problem is more complicated. They begin with a new conceptualization of conservatism in terms of 'the ideal conservative' as outlined above (see par. 3.2.4.). Their work constitutes a mixture of quasi-model construction, its rather loose operationalization in terms of 'brief labels or catch phrases' (1973: 50; similar to Kerlinger's referent-items), an initial measurement reflecting a unidimensional conceptualization, and a subsequent assessment of the dimensionality of the 'scale' through first- and second-order oblique factor-analysis. Their work can be considered as a partial integration of Eysenck's and Kerlinger's approaches. Results, however are more similar to Eysenck's than to Kerlinger's, probably due to a definition of conservatism only in non-economic terms (p.7).

The operationalization of the 'ideal conservative' seems dubious: the catch-phrases are not systematically derived from the model and there are curious ones like 'Learning Latin'.

The items are factor-analyzed on the basis of an 'ad hoc' sample. The first unrotated factor explains 18.7% of the variance; factors 2 to 4 respectively, 6.5, 5.4 and 4.6%. So there is a general factor, but since 18 out of 50 items load less than .35 on it, it is certainly too weak to conclude, as Wilson does, that the scale is predominantly unidimensional (p. 59). Multidimensionality is in fact clearly shown in subsequent second-order analysis. Here, the first-order factor-structure shows the by now familiar picture of dubious interpretation and double-loading items. Three of the 5 promax-factors correlate moderately (around .35): these factors are labeled 'militarism-punitiveness', 'anti-hedonism' and 'racialism'. The fourth factor, 'religious fundamentalism', is weakly related to the other 3; and the fifth one, 'anti-art', is unrelated to the other 4.

Five additional promax-factors are extracted and, subsequently, 2 second-order promax-factors appear which are .60 related to each other: they are termed *'conservative-religious'* and *'anti-intellectual-racialist'* (loadings of the first-order factors on these second-order ones are not presented). Though the results point to 2 types of conservatives (a 'tender' and a 'tough' type, so to speak; see p. 84) they are again taken as confirming the 'general factor finding'.

In comparing their results with previous findings (those of Eysenck and Ferguson), Wilson notes a similarity between the first and second unrotated factors and those obtained by Eysenck (1947, 1954) and, after rotation, by Ferguson (1939). In this context, some curious remarks are made, misinterpreting Eysenck's design and results (see p. 86).

Let us conclude for the moment that the work of Wilson et al. is possibly of value for its criticism of the conventional 'statement'-item type because of the latter's susceptibility to acquiescence (see in particular pp. 42–47).

While Kerlinger and Wilson both use referents and ad hoc samples, Kerlinger finds a clearly 2-dimensional structure whereas Wilson finds that responses to liberal and conservative items become, as they 'should', negatively correlated, rather than mostly uncorrelated, as is the case for the 'old' item format (see p. 64).

These conflicting results may be due to sampling variability and cross-cultural differences, but perhaps mainly to the fact that Kerlinger uses far more referents in the politico-economic and the political sphere (compare Wilson, 1973: 52, Table 1, and Kerlinger, 1972: 622, Table 3). To develop more explicit rationales for item-selection seems of overwhelming importance.

3.4 SOME NOTES ON DUTCH RESEARCH

3.4.1. Introduction

The major Dutch study on progressiveness-conservatism (mainly in the politico-economic realm) is that by Hoogerwerf (1964), based on a local sample from a medium-sized town.

Lange et al. (1968) and Lange (1971) have later elaborated to some extent on Hoogerwerf's work.

Other general studies are those of Verzijden and Van de Brug (1969, based on secondary analysis) and Kroes' (1971). Recently, Roe (1975) completed an interesting study on the empirical dimensionality of the 'theoretical' left-right antithesis among psychology students. Another rather general approach is contained in a preliminary report on the Dutch National Election Survey of 1972–1973.

Some more limited approaches, mostly based on secondary analysis of data in the Steinmetz Archives, will also be mentioned [56].

In addition, some studies on what may be called the 'political party system' will be discussed (see e.g. Stapel, 1968, 1971; Daalder and Rusk, 1972). Finally, some typical Dutch studies on traditionalism among farmers will be mentioned.

3.4.2. Hoogerwerf's 'socio-political conservatism'

Hoogerwerf (1964) is among the few who clearly recognize the necessity of a *criterion* as a basis for the conceptualization of progressiveness vs. conservatism. After an extensive examination of the literature on conservatism (both empirical and philosophical) the value of *equality* is chosen as such a criterion for a working definition of political conservatism: 'Political conservatism is an opinion characterized by the aim of leaving the existing inequality in society as regards the distribution of a certain value, according to a certain distribution-criterion, unchanged' (p. 28) (my translation; CPM) [57].

Progressiveness and reactionism are defined accordingly, as *opinions* with the aim of respectively decreasing or increasing existing inequalities. From this, a socio-political conservatism(SPC)-index is constructed (without scaling-evidence) which comprises items on equality of income and property, on aid to developing countries and 'democratization' (an increase in the 'say' of workers and employees in industrial and other organizations).

Three limitations of Hoogerwerf's conceptualization can be pointed out. In the first place, the value of *equality* has not been derived from an analysis of conservatism as an ideology to the extent that a conceptual model has been constructed (although many quasi-models of conservatism have been studied; pp. 40–48). The author frankly admits the relativity of his criterion: it could even have been replaced by the criterion of *freedom* (!) (p. 29). Thus, for practical reasons so it seems, only one of at least 2 possible criteria has been chosen. (Note other inconsistencies in describing what is 'progressive', etc., pp. 49–50.)

Another limitation is that conservatism is defined in terms of *opinions* and *aims*, and not as constituting an *ideology* itself.

This seems unwarranted in view of the historical developments in Western Europe, and in the light of almost all conservative 'philosophies' from Burke (1790) on. (This will be discussed in the next chapter.) Although Hoogerwerf is of course aware of this tradition, he chooses to regard all this as non-essential, thereby reducing the notion of conservatism in fact to rigid 'standpattism' (see Rossiter, 1962). Only one aspect of conservative ideology (in terms of aims) is taken as the defining one for political conservatism — see e.g. Hoogerwerf's comment on McClosky (1958) (p. 39), on Kirk (1954) (pp. 40–41) and others.

Thirdly, and as a possible consequence of the second 'reduction', *aims* are separated from *means*. Hereby, Hoogerwerf's approach is further isolated from almost all other conceptualizations and operationalizations of politico-economic conservatism, in which *the role of government(-interference)* is always taken as a *defining*, essential element [58]. Again, the author shows uncertainty as to the choice of his criterion (see e.g. p.51). In a discussion on the extent of 'progressiveness' regarding social policy among Dutch religious groups and political parties, he often suggests that the extent to which one is in favor of government interference to solve the 'social problem' is an indication of 'progressiveness' (pp. 117–141) [59].

In conclusion, Hoogerwerf's conceptualization of socio-political conservatism seems too narrow. The author is the prisoner of his own criterion and so broader and possibly more profitable perspectives have remained outside the scope of his study.

A final point of criticism concerns the fact that the 4 SPC-items have not been tested for scalability. In secondary analysis (see Lange et al., 1968) it has been shown that the SPC-index does not constitute a unidimensional scale (in particular, the item on 'aid to developing countries' is unrelated to the others). However, Hoogerwerf's (1968) 'theoretical unidimensionality' is not an acceptable alternative (see Galtung, 1967: 78–79; Stinchcombe, 1973, a,b,) [60].

Lange et al.'s (1968) approach to constructing a new scale measuring progressiveness-conservatism is also unacceptable, because there a definition of progressiveness is lacking: 15 items were selected from Hoogerwerf's questionnaire, including items on class relationships, social planning and on e.g. 'change' in some social institutions. It was found that a cluster of 7 items formed a unidimensional and more reliable measuring-instrument. Results, however, were similar to Hoogerwerf's.

3.4.3. *Other general approaches*

Verzijden and Van de Brug (1969) made a secondary analysis of a study based on a national cross-sectional sample [61] to assess dimensions of political conservatism. Hoogerwerf's criterion (see above) was used for item-selection but it is not always clearly reflected in the items. Three major scales were found (one on *'provo's*, one on *'civil liberties'* and one on *'social welfare laws'*) [62], which were relatively independent of each other.

A more general approach is found in the study by Lange (1971), based on a local sample of religious groups [63]. Again on the basis of Hoogerwerf's criterion, 41 items were selected from previous studies [64] and submitted to Mokken-scale procedures (see Mokken, 1970) [65].

According to Lange, the criterion of equality can be applied to areas outside the politico-economic field: e.g. to the fields of sexuality, internationalism, religion, etc. However, quite a few of Lange's items do not seem to clearly reflect this criterion [66].

The Mokken-scaling procedures yield 2 scales:

1. *socio-political progressiveness*, including items from Hoogerwerf (1964) and Verzijden and Van de Brug (1969) on e.g. social welfare laws and equality of income and property; and

2. *sexual progressiveness*, including items on pre- and extramarital sexual permissiveness, abortion, divorce, homosexuality, etc.

Both scales are moderately correlated (.30) and *negatively* related to an authoritarianism-scale, sexual progressiveness the most strongly so.

Another, and (as far as conceptualization is concerned) a very general approach to progressiveness-conservatism (though in terms of 'radicalism') is that of Kroes (1971) [67]. Contrary to Hoogerwerf, Kroes defines radicalism in terms of *norms, goals* and the *means* by which to reach those goals (see e.g. Kroes, 1971 a: 246). A number of 'theoretical' dimensions or aspects of radicalism are formulated (pp. 266-267); this quasi-model is operationalized and assessed empirically by way of cluster-analysis on the basis of a sample of students and their parents.

There are, then, 2 problems: first, only 65% of the items appear in the same clusters for both samples, and second, the *'empirical'* clusters do not correspond to the *'theoretical'* dimensions. (Unfortunately, the author does not try to tackle these problems, e.g. through some procedure of reconceptualization.)

It is interesting to note that Kroes makes a distinction between 'central' vs. 'peripheral' radical elements and that he develops a *'radical credo'* in terms of opinions regarding 'man and society': radicals tend to be optimistic as regards human nature and tend to attribute the causes of agression and violence to the 'social system'. They disagree that man will never be able to create an ideal society (see Kroes, 1971 a: 127-128; see also Portes, 1971 b). 'Democratization' is mentioned as perhaps the most direct embodiment of the ideal: the integration of aims and means (p. 129). (Compare results of the present study, to be presented in Chapter 6.) Finally, there are 2 fairly recent studies which should be mentioned. In a preliminary report on the Dutch National Election Study 1972–1973 (Werkgroep Nationaal Verkiezingsonderzoek, 1973), the authors develop 2 scales on progressiveness and conservatism: one is based on 5 items, selected according to the criteria of *freedom and equality* (freedom to demonstrate and for young people; equality in terms of opportunity to acquire the proper education and occupation, and on workers having a say in matters); the other is based on 4 items on *change* in the Dutch political system (the items load highly on a factor after principal component-analysis and promax-rotation). No rationale for the operationalizations is given, however [68].

The other study is Roe's (1975) assessment of the dimensionality of political attitudes among students [69]. On the basis of suggestions made by Lipschits (1969), Roe takes the left-right antithesis as a theoretical starting-point. He distinguishes 8 ideologies: 3 on the left (socialism, democracy and New Left) and 5 on the right (liberalism — the Dutch version — , conservatism, confessionalism — also more or less typically Dutch: the relationship between religion and politics — , fascism and national socialism). These ideologies are briefly introduced (no conceptual models are developed) and subsequently extensively operationalized: there is a total of 210 items involved in their measurement. The ideologies are defined in terms of principles but in addition, Roe develops a battery of almost 60 items on *means* which can be used to reach certain goals indicated by the principles. This is much more than has ever been done by psychologists in their attempts to assess the left-right dimensionality.

However, the design of the study might be criticized in that the author terms too many 'points of view' full-fledged ideologies. Liberalism, conservatism and socialism are ideologies, and to a certain extent so are fascism and national socialism. However, democracy, confessionalism and New Left are not. Moreover, where does communism fit in?

In addition, the analyses are not carried out properly. The author should first have tried to develop measurements for his 'ideologies', e.g. through factor-analysis in order to find out to what extent the ideologies 'exist' empirically in his group of students (first-year undergraduate students in psychology at the University of Amsterdam). Instead, a cluster-analysis is carried out and the over-all correlations between the 4 or 5 clusters per ideology are not even reported; nor are names given to the clusters, i.e. as aspects of the ideology. A similar analysis is carried out over the 'means'-items: no clear picture emerges. The same is true for the over-all analysis: there is no clear factorial analysis over the principles — and means — sub-scores. Therefore, the author's conclusions as to the multidimensionality of the left-right antithesis are highly doubtful: there is, in fact, more evidence for unidimensionality. The effect of political information on this structure is at best marginal. (For more detailed criticism, see Middendorp, 1976 e.)

In conclusion, when there is a broad and interesting definition and conceptualization, the Dutch studies on progressiveness-conservatism are mostly based on specific local (Lange, 1971) or student samples (Kroes, 1971; Roe, 1975). When national samples are used, conceptualization is either insufficient (The National Election Study 1972–1973) or specific and limited in scope.

In the present study an attempt will be made to fill the gap created by the lack of studies based on broad conceptualizations as well as national samples, as already outlined in Chapter 2.

3.4.4. Specific approaches

There are a number of other Dutch studies which are more limited in scope in that only certain *specific* dimensions of progressiveness-conservatism are assessed [70]. Weima (1965), for example, formulates a number of characteristics of religious conservatism without much theoretical rationale. Both this small quasi-model and its operationalization seem doubtful, e.g. rigidity in adherence to traditional ideas as a model-element and e.g. sexual intercourse before marriage is always wrong as an operationalization. There are a number of other studies which are all based on a secondary analysis of data in the Steinmetz Archives. Koomen and Winnubst (1968) [71] constructed a 10-item Mokken (1970) — scale on religious orthodoxy but included an item on church attendance. Using cluster-analysis, Middendorp et al. (1970) [72] constructed a conservatism-scale in the area of marriage and family life. Conceptualization was based on a definition in terms of 'adherence to conventional norms'.

Brinkman and Koster-Sweers (1972) constructed 5 scales in the field of 'sexuality' (on tolerance, premarital permissiveness, masturbation, romantic love and 'naturalness') [73]. The 5 scales were factor-analyzed. After rotation, 2 orthogonal factors appear ('tolerance-permissiveness' vs. 'romantic love-naturalness') with the masturbation-scale loading on both.

3.4.5. Studies on the Dutch party system

Stapel (1968) finds the following rank-order of the political parties from left to right: Communists, Pacifist Socialists, Socialists, Democrats, Radicals, Farmers' Party, Liberals, Christian Democrats (in terms of party-labels: CPN, PSP, PvdA, D'66, PPR, BP, VVD, ARP, CHU, KVP) [74].

For 'progressive' vs. 'conservative', Stapel (1971: 208) finds roughly the following rank-order: Democrats, Socialists, Radicals, Liberals, Pacifist Socialists, Anti-Revolutionaries, Roman Catholics, Communists, Democratic Socialists, Christian Historians, Farmers' Party [75].

Another attempt to structure the complex Dutch party system has been reported by Lipschits (1969), and was made on the basis of the party-programs. Curiously enough, the left-right antithesis is conceptualized in terms of 4 dimensions: Christian vs. non-Christian, capitalistic vs. socialistic (free enterprise vs. government interference), totalitarian vs. democratic and . . . conservative vs. progressive. When the political parties are ordered from left to right along 3 of the 4 dimensions and no identical rank-orders are found, it is concluded that the (one) left-right antithesis does not 'exist'. However, it is clear that the dimensions are strongly related to each other as is shown by Lehning (1970) and can be seen very easily: *It does make sense to think in terms of an over-all left-right continuum as far as the party-programs are concerned.* The rank-order of the major parties obtained in this way is different from that found by Stapel (1968) [76].

Other approaches to the party structure are those that work with preferences, or that are made on the basis of voting-behavior, and which subsequently apply analytical techniques to detect dimensions along which the parties can be ordered. Using a local sample, preference-rank-orders for the various parties and factor-analysis, Koomen and Willems (1969) find a 2-dimensional structure. One dimension could be labeled 'progressive-conservative'; this only roughly corresponds to the left-right dimensions found by Stapel (1968) and Lipschits (1969). Liberals are now clearly most conservative: much more so than Christian Democratic parties. There is another dimension (labeled 'Christian' vs. 'non-Christian') [77] which resembles but is not identical to Stapel's (1971) rank-ordering of the parties from . . . progressive to conservative [78].

Van Tijn-Koekebakker et al. (1970) base their multidimensional scaling analysis (Kruskal, 1964 a, b) upon roll-call data from the House of Commons (i.e. the Second Chamber of Parliament). They find a heavily-clustered 2-dimensional structure which is difficult to interpret.

One dimension clearly distinguishes communist and socialist parties from the others, which, however, are split up along the second dimension. Finally, Daalder and Rusk (1972) apply Kruskal's (1964 a, b) and Coombs' (1964) procedures of multidimensional scaling to data based on distance-scores towards other parties of M.P.'s in the House of Commons. With both the Kruskal procedure and the Coombs' procedure, a left-right dimension emerges which is similar (although with slight variations) to those mentioned earlier. In the Kruskal-method, the left-wing parties are heavily clustered and there is a second dimension which again somewhat resembles Stapel's (1971) rank-ordering of the parties in terms of progressive vs. conservative and the second dimension found by Koomen and Willems (1969) [79]. The second dimension found in applying Coombs' method is less interpretable: it seems to distinguish 'system' parties from 'anti-system' parties (1972: 180). When the anti-system parties are eliminated from the data, a somewhat clearer left-right vs. 'progressive-conservative' dimensionality appears (p. 182), though it is still not very convincing.

In conclusion, it seems that a clear rank-ordering, or positioning of the Dutch political parties along progressive-conservative or left-right dimensions does not become apparent due to a lack of 'objective' measures for these dimensions. Subjective rank-orderings are bound to be very unstable and non-valid due to the fact that most people are unable to conceptualize the progressive-conservative or left-right dimension (cf. Stapel, 1968, 1971). Therefore, their party preferences can hardly be based on such considerations; hence, they do not yield a clear structure. Lipschits' (1969) approach comes closest to an 'objective' standard but suffers from insufficient conceptualization, 'obscure' content-analytical procedures and gross rank-ordering.

In the present study an attempt will be made to develop objective measurements for progressive-conservative dimensions on which the parties can then be positioned, both on the basis of voters' positions and those of M.P.'s.

3.4.6. Studies on farming: the 'modern dynamic culture pattern'

Although the Netherlands is no longer a predominantly agricultural country, there is a research tradition which has a special interest in farming and the farmer's orientation towards 'modern dynamic culture' (as opposed to traditional culture) [80]. Of central concern is the farmer's attitude (and related behavior) towards innovation and modernization, both in his work orientation and also in more general matters. The 'modern dynamic culture pattern' is conceptualized in terms of an 'ideal type', but mainly defined as an 'attitude towards change' (see e.g. Hofstee, 1962). It is implicitly understood that a positive attitude to 'change' means, among other things, optimism, openness and a willingness to invest and to take risks. Due to this insufficient conceptualization and to unsophisticated procedures of measurement and analysis, there is no agreement as to the dimensionality of the 'modern-dynamic' vs. 'traditional' antithesis [81].

3.5. DISCUSSION AND CONCLUSIONS

Due to serious limitations in definitions and conceptualizations, the over-all picture is rather confused. Rather than summarize, let us concentrate on the *promising starts* that have already been made, and which, in the present study, will be integrated in one design which includes the definition of conservatism as an ideology by means of the construction of an ideal type model of this construct, and its conceptualization by means of what has been called Type-1 analysis.

1. Definitions
We have seen that attempts at definition in many studies have been weak and insufficient. Researchers frequently (a) do not define the progressive-conservative antithesis at all, (b) give very ad hoc, simplistic definitions, for instance in terms of 'government interference' or 'attitude to change', or (c) complain about their problems in this respect and do not solve them sufficiently.

The first is typical of most factor-analytic studies, From Thurstone (1934) and Carlson (1934), Ferguson (1939) and Hayes (1939) through to e.g. Eysenck (1947, 1971), Kerlinger (1968), and Comrey and Newmeyer (1965). Only recently more attention has been paid to the problem of definition in this branch of research (see e.g. Kerlinger, 1972; Wilson, 1973; Roe, 1975). Other early studies which attempt to construct liberalism-conservatism tests either do not give a definition or only a very simplistic one (see e.g. Vetter, 1930; Lentz, 1935; Hartmann, 1938). This 'tradition' is carried on later to a large extent in political research, where the definition of liberalism-conservatism is often taken 'for granted'. Various dimensions are often distinguished, after which one 'jumps' to the operational level (see e.g. Lipset, 1963; Lenski, 1961; Kelly and Chambliss, 1966; Converse, 1964; Nie, 1974). Campbell et al. (1960) again end up with notions such as on 'government interference' and 'attitude to change'. Problems of definition, anticipating conceptualization, are reported by Pollack (1943) and Kerr (1952) and later again by e.g. Middleton and Putney (1963) and Wiley (1967). The most promising approaches have been reported by Levinson (1950) and McClosky (1958) and later by Free and Cantril (1967). McClosky's (1958) study no doubt comes nearest to what is meant by the construction of an ideal type model of conservatism, at least within a research context [82]. In 2 types of study in related fields (*fascism* in the 1930's and 1940's, *liberal democracy* in the 1960's), some other promising starts in conceptual model-construction have been made (see e.g. Stagner, 1936; McClosky, 1964).

Of the Dutch studies, Hoogerwerf's (1964) is important in that it makes explicit the need for a *criterion* with which to select items. In fact, as has been indicated in Chapter 2, the 2 approaches should be combined: a conceptual model should be constructed more systematically than has been done by e.g. McClosky and from such a model, criteria (if more than one) should be derived more systematically than has been done by Hoogerwerf, in order to define progressive-conservative attitudes at a lower level of abstraction. The lack of studies in which the progressive-conservative antithesis has been defined and subsequently conceptualized in a sufficiently broad, explicit and systematic manner (i.e. as an *ideological* controversy and by way of an *ideal type* conceptual model) has hampered research immensely and seems to be a major factor in contributing to the present confusion and plethora of contradictory findings.

Early definitions and operationalizations (with the limitations outlined above) have tended to be *broad*, covering almost every field of social life. Later as a result of the Great Depression, there has been a tendency to define the antithesis mainly (or solely) in politico-economic terms. Subsequently, there was a tendency on the part of political scientists to split off 'social' and 'religious' aspects from the 'political' ones, whereas psychologists and sociologists continued to define the antithesis in a somewhat broader manner. In defining the progressive-conservative antithesis, not only does it seem important to be able to derive *criteria* from such a definition (i.e. an ideal type model) for operationalizations at lower levels of abstraction, but it also seems important to define the *various fields* in which it can be applied and may be relevant.

That this is important, especially in view of the evidence on the relevance of the economic vs. non-economic distinction is shown by the work of Eysenck (see e.g. 1947, 1971) and Wilson, ed. (1973) and as early as 1939 by the studies of Ferguson (see also e.g. the criticism on McClosky's definition). In short, the necessity of constructing, somehow, a model of i.e. conservatism in defining this construct, rather than attempting to conceptualize 'vague notions' as to what constitutes the progressive-conservative antithesis, has become obvious after our survey of the literature.

2. Conceptualizations

(a) The relevance of distinguishing the various levels of *abstraction* of items (operationalizing a construct) has been shown in early studies such as those of Allport (1929) and Hartmann (1936), and in recent work by Prothro and Grigg (1960), McClosky (1964) and in particular by Free and Cantril (1967).

In the *abstract* people may tend to be in favor of general notions like e.g. 'the family', 'private property', 'social harmony'. With something more concrete, however (one might guess: in terms potentially closer to actual behavior), they might not react so favorably. This has been suggested by Kerlinger (1972: 624–626) and also by many other studies referred to above, in which it has been shown that people's reaction to general, abstract notions or statements may well be contrary to their reaction to specifics [83]. To put it in another way: *specific* orientations may not be 'backed up' by an appropriate (abstract) *ideology*. Therefore, a model of an ideology should be empirically assessed at both an abstract and at more specific levels, as will be attempted in the present study.

(b) Kerlinger has suggested that bipolar items should not be used in order to avoid 'artificial bipolarity' of the liberal-conservative antithesis. When, however, conservatism 'itself' (i.e. a body of statements constituting conservative ideology) is multidimensional (i.e. its various components would evoke a differential response in most people, as is suggested by many studies in terms of economic vs. noneconomic conservatism), then the use of bipolar items would *not* yield unidimensionality. It has been suggested in Chapter 2 that if more than one criterion can be derived from a model of a construct, then people might react differentially to these criteria in their responses to the stimuli in the operationalized model.

(c) It has been suggested as early as 1938 (Lentz) that *specificity* is a characteristic of *items*; and that evidence as to the generality or specificity of 'traits' like conservatism should consequently *not* be assessed on the basis of single items. Nevertheless, in recent research some political scientists have done so, and consequently found evidence refuting the 'existence' (at least in cross-sectional samples) of one dimension of liberalism-conservatism (see e.g. Converse, 1964). Others, however, also using intercorrelations of items, have later found evidence contrary to this (see e.g. Nie, 1974).

That scales rather than single items should be used to assess the dimensionality of a progressive-conservative antithesis has been implicitly recognized by those authors whose work involved conceptualizing and intercorrelating such scales (see e.g. Kerr, 1952; Campbell et al., 1960; Anderson et al., 1965; Kelly and Chambliss, 1966), and by those researchers who used second-order factor-analysis (see e.g. Comrey and Newmeyer, 1965; Kerlinger, 1968, 1972; Wilson, ed., 1973).

(d) It has been suggested by Kerlinger (1967, 1972) and by Wilson, ed. (1973) that referent- (in Kerlinger's terms) rather than statement-items should be used. This may be a promising new approach, but basically it may be considered similar to working with attitude-scales as units of analysis. Such scales are often described 'in terms of their object', e.g. a scale on 'nationalism', 'social welfare laws', 'civil liberties', etc. It remains to be seen, then, whether an assessment of attitudes through presentation of the general labels as the stimuli, rather than deriving such attitudes from 'scaling' statement-items, is not inferior to the latter in terms of reliability and perhaps validity (referents are more *abstract* than statements; see (a) above).

(e) It has been shown that the researchers who have considered the definition and conceptualization of the progressive-conservative antithesis most seriously have often found it inappropriate to apply analytical techniques to assess its possible empirical *multi-dimensionality* (see e.g. Levinson, 1950; McClosky, 1958). This same attitude is manifested in some early test-constructions; upon subsequent analyses, these have often appeared to be multidimensional (see e.g. Vetter, 1930, 1947; Lorr, 1951; Hunter, 1951; Rubin Rabson, 1954).

The liberal-conservative antithesis is sometimes defined in unidimensional terms but then the 'non-existence' of this antithesis is too readily concluded if results (in scaling and intercorrelating scales) are not as expected (see e.g. Campbell et al., 1960). The opposite can also happen: several dimensions are 'conceptualized' from the literature and when they subsequently prove to intercorrelate, the antithesis is taken to be a 'real' empirical one (see e.g. Ferdinand, 1964; see also Lentz, 1938). If the scales used in such approaches are unidimensional, this type of procedure allows for dimensionality-assessment (see Kerr, 1952; Kelley and Chambliss, 1966; O'Kane, 1970). It would be even better if factor-analysis were applied, but such approaches seem more typical of the earliest studies on the generality of attitudes, rather than of recent studies (see Ferguson, 1939; Lorr,

1951; see also, however, Brinkman and Koster-Sweers, 1972; Roe, 1975). Given the often confused nature of oblique primary factors (see e.g. Kerlinger, 1968; Comrey and Newmeyer, 1965; Wilson, ed., 1973) it would also seem that the preconceptualization of sub-dimensions is superior to second-order factor-analysis (although in such a case the data speak less 'for themselves').

(f) The research evidence presented above suggests that apart from variations in definitions, operationalizations and analytical techniques, variations in the *samples* used have been one of the main reasons for the present state of contradictory findings.

There has been a tendency for psychologists to use samples of students and 'related' groups and for sociologists to use special groups, but it has been the political scientists who have drawn attention to the systematic variation of results in various types of samples, especially between national cross-sectional samples vs. samples from (political) elites. Of course, research on public opinion has also contributed to an increasing use of national cross-sectional samples. The development of sampling techniques has been crucial here.

The effects of sampling on the interrelatedness of variables have been noted by various authors. Early evidence as to the effects of using cross-sectional rather than special or student samples has been shown in the work of Hayes (1939) and Smith (1948). Prothro and Grigg (1960) observed that the '*educated*' were more consistent than others in their responses to 'abstract principles' vs. 'specific applications' of liberal democracy. This is also noted (for specific issues) in 'leaders' (congressmen) vs. 'followers' by McClosky et al. (1960), and by McClosky (1964). Converse (1964) shows that, unlike the general public, to such elites the liberal-conservative antithesis is a reality. He proposes a distinction between (a) a unidimensional liberal-conservative antithesis for the elite and (b) the irrelevance of this antithesis to the population at large (cf. also Anderson et al., 1965; Wiley, 1967).

Although there is some (weak) evidence to the contrary (see e.g. Axelrod, 1967; Luttbeg, 1968; Brown, 1970), it may be that progressiveness-conservatism is an 'elitist' conceptualization which is not immediately relevant to the population at large. However, this should not imply that a dichotomy of 'elites' vs. 'masses' exists in the sense that elites show unidimensionality, whereas for the masses no structure at all can be seen (see e.g. Luttbeg, 1968). Neither would a unidimensional structure necessarily exist for *both* the elite and the general population, as is suggested by Nie (1974).

In the present study an attempt will be made to assess the dimensionality of the progressive-conservative 'antithesis' in both the general public (i.e. the Dutch population) and a strategic elite, on various levels of abstraction of this domain of ideological controversy.

In conclusion, it has been seen that various elements of Type-1 analysis as outlined in Chapter 2 have already partly been realized, or at least noted, in previous studies. So far they have not been integrated into one research-design, however, and it is exactly this for which an attempt will now be made in the present study. We will start in the next chapter with the development of the ideal type model of the construct of conservative ideology.

NOTES ON CHAPTER 3

1. The terminology in the present chapter will predominantly be that used by the authors whose work is discussed. Thus, 'progressiveness' may be indicated by either 'liberalism' (in American studies) or by 'radicalism' (in American and English studies). (Note that Dutch studies will be discussed separately in par. 3.4.). For a very brief review of the research-literature, see Ray (1973).
2. See Chapter 2: note 25. The present study is a partial replication of earlier studies which did not aim at a conceptualization of the progressive-conservative antithesis. Therefore, those studies were first analyzed secondarily from this theoretical perspective (see Chapter 5).
3. The trend outlined here is of course only partial, as is shown by the work of e.g. Ferguson (1939, 1940, 1942, 1944 a, b); Lentz (1935, 1938); Hunter (1942); Pollack (1943), and Hayes (1939 a, b).
4. Other factors that might have contributed to the relative lack of interest in ideological dimensions in the 1950's and early 1960's have already been outlined in the introductory chapter.
5. Similar phenomena are reported in many other studies, e.g. those of Raskin and Cook (1938: 205); Menefee (1936); Edwards (1941, 1944); Gundlach (1937) and Katz and Cantril (1940).
6. Centers does not define radicalism-conservatism either (1949: 39-40); his 'battery' of politico-economic attitudes is clearly based solely on common sense. In recent studies somewhat more attention has been paid to the definition of liberalism and conservatism; see e.g. the study by Wilson, ed. (1973), working in the Eysenck-tradition.
7. When here and below I speak of 'attempts at conceptual model construction', it should be noted that such attempts have not been successful: a model in the sense of the present study has not been developed. (See the notion of 'quasi-model', Chapter 2: 2.2.1., which will sometimes be used when referring to such 'attempts at model construction'.)
8. This will be discussed further in the next chapter (par. 4.3.6.2.). In America, the relationship between fascism and certain forms of European conservatism (especially in Germany, as has been convincingly shown by Von Klemperer, 1968, and indicated by Mannheim, 1953, esp. p. 161, note 2; p. 162, note 2), has not been clearly recognized.

9. Results were, however, consistent with those of Stagner (1936) and Raskin and Cook (1938: 205), who validated the Stagner-scale by testing it on 'known groups'.

10. In this context, a significant remark may be noted: 'This way of thinking assumes that the individual has "freedom" economically to the extent that there are no government restrictions on him; it overlooks the fact that economic freedom for most people today is limited to the greatest degree by economic forces originating in business monopoly' (p. 156). Note, however, that Levinson's approach to politico-economic conservatism is broader than usual, i.e. not limited to the socio-economic field.

11. The work of the English conservatives — Burke (1790), Hearnshaw (1933), White (1950), Hogg (1947) — and the American New Conservatives — Kirk (1954), Rossiter (1962), Wilson (1951) and Viereck (1962), among others — has been studied in formulating these elements. Compare Hoogerwerf's comments (1964: 57-58) in terms of the fact that McClosky did not restrict himself to *defining* characteristics of conservatism only, but also included *related* aspects. This may be true, but it could only have been decided upon by comparison with a conceptual model of conservatism. This has not been presented by Hoogerwerf, but his comments correctly point to the fact that the 7-point list does not constitute such a model (see below).

12. There is an inconsistency regarding the relationship between liberalism and conservatism in McClosky's paper. It is first noted that liberalism and conservatism may be 'natural' or polar positions (p. 28); but it is then concluded (without evidence) that liberalism-conservatism may not be variables, 'paired in such a way that a high score on one necessarily signifies a low score on the other' (p. 44). Evidence for this latter point of view is later presented by Kerlinger (1968, 1972), and will be discussed below.

13. Dimensions of liberalism-conservatism are conceptualized somewhat differently by different authors. Campbell et al. (1960) distinguished domestic welfare, foreign policy and attitude toward change (i.e., the items included in the McClosky classical conservatism scale, which will be discussed below); Converse (1964) distinguishes between domestic welfare (including e.g. aid to education) and foreign policy (i.e. internationalism); McClosky et al. (1960) make distinctions within the domestic welfare section between public ownership of resources, government regulation of economy, equalitarianism, human welfare and tax policy; Key (1968: 171) adds a section on civil liberties, as does Nie (1974: 561); Hero Jr. (1969), includes one on civil rights (race relations).

14. It is curious that the authors tend to misinterpret both scales.

15. It may be noted that here, 'ideological' is used to refer to a coherent philosophy to rationalize specific programs. Such a philosophy should be expressed in general, abstract terms. Other researchers use the word 'ideology' in different ways. Campbell et al. (1960: 203-204) make a distinction between 'ideology' and 'primitive self-interest': '. . . it is important to distinguish between behavior impelled by self-interest in a primitive and short-sighted sense, and the operation of self-interest within a structure of attitudes that might reasonably be labeled an "ideology". We have no quarrel with the view that ideological position is largely determined by self-interest. But we do maintain that it matters whether self-interest proceeds in a simple and naked sense or has indeed become embedded in some broader ideo-

logical structure . . . One important implication . . . is that the person is sensitized to the existence of "roundabout" routes that, despite a superficial detour, will better secure ultimate gratification' and, on the basis of their findings, they criticize Lipset's (1963) distinction between 'economic' and 'non-economic' liberalism: '. . . even the connotations of the term "economic liberalism" may be unrealistically broad. If these attitudes have internal coherence, they are expressions of self-interest, not "liberal ideologies" ' (note 6).

Mitchell (1966) and Selznick and Steinberg (1969) make a similar distinction between 'ideology' and 'ideas based on (primitive) self-interest' (see also McClosky et al., 1960: 423). The concept of 'ideology' will be discussed in the next chapter.

16. Some other studies of lesser importance are e.g. those by Messick (1956), Nettler and Huffmann (1957), and Wright and Hicks (1966). Quinney (1964: 375); Wiley (1967: 144) and Schindeler and Hoffman (1968: 437) made studies on religious and political attitudes. The last 3 studies are all unsatisfactory in that they fail to give an adequate definition of religious conservatism. Note, however, the interesting discussion by Schindeler and Hoffman in interpreting their findings (p. 441):

'At the level of general principles, one can readily see a relationship between theological conservatism and political conservatism. "Deference to authority", "tradition", "order", "community", "suspicion of reason", "resistance to change", "acceptance of inquality", "the belief that man by his nature is imperfect and may be made perfect only by redemption and grace" and other phrases that have been used to describe political conservatism apply equally well to theological conservatism . . .'

17. There seems to be a clear overlap between the concepts of liberalism-conservatism and liberal-democratic principles, for example in civil rights and civil liberties and the principle of minority rights (see note 18).

18. It is curious that neither Prothro and Grigg nor McClosky note the *anti-democratic implications of conservatism*. These implications are obvious: conservatism is generally conceptualized in terms such as opposition to free speech (i.e. civil liberties); opposition to social and ethnic equality (i.e. civil rights) and especially opposition to economic equality (i.e. domestic welfare, government aid to the needy, etc.). Almost the only aspect of political conservatism which is *not* opposed (according to McClosky's definition) to liberal-democratic principles is *nationalism* (see also e.g. Lipset, 1959: 500).

There seems to be a discrepancy between the ease with which McClosky describes the basic principles of liberal democracy, and the way in which Free and Cantril (1967) see the lack of a 'liberal ideology' which would sustain 'liberal policy' in the modern sense of government interference and social welfare measures. The solution may be that the 'egalitarian' aspects of liberal democracy have not been fully worked out, as McClosky (1964: 368) notes. This particularly applies to *economic equality*. Lichtman (1970) speaks of the 'façade of equality' in liberal-democratic theory, which is 'the ideology of capitalism'. *It is exactly this economic aspect of equality which is lacking in liberal democracy.* Of course, in Europe and elsewhere, there is such an ideological framework: socialism (see e.g. Middendorp, 1974: 168).

19. Studies in which not much attention has been paid to problems of definition but in which the relevance of a distinction between 2 levels of abstraction of

statements is also shown are those by Selznick and Steinberg (1969) and Mann (1970). Earlier studies in which similar phenomena have been observed (see e.g. Hartmann, 1936; Stagner, 1936; Edwards, 1941, 1944) will be discussed below (par. 3.3.3.1.).

20. Lentz's study may be interpreted as an early argument for assessing the *sub-dimensions* of a broad progressive-conservative domain at the *attitude-level* rather than at the single-item level (see Chapter 2).

21. Some of these groups and items are quite surprising. There are groups on 'the subway fare', 'social limitations in mating', 'attitude towards incest', 'the prohibition question', 'gambling', 'the qualifications of Mr. Hoover', 'the Fascist government', 'our Latin-American policy' and 'the Nordic race'. The list of items covers almost all relevant fields: e.g. socio-economic policy and economic inequality, internationalism, civil liberties, social matters such as divorce, abortion, birth-control and (premarital) sexual relations, attitudes toward attempts at social progress, respect for traditions, the church and religion, trade-unions and race relations.

22. For an additional criticism on the use of positive and negative items, see the discussion on Kerlinger's work below.

23. It is noted that the best items are those dealing with the functioning of government, ownership of utilities, control on business, limitations on income and unions; items that are all socio-economic in the 'classical' sense (see Levinson, 1950: 166).

24. McClosky's scale has been criticized precisely for the content and form of its items, and the relationship of the items to the 'creed', i.e. to conservatism as a social and political philosophy; see e.g. Kendall (1958). Frisch (1958) also criticizes the 7 tenets of conservatism as an essentially 'doctrinized' version of the conservative political mood and considers that this has been brought about by 'armchair neo-conservative interpreters' (p. 1111); see also McClosky's rejoinder (1958a).

25. It has been noted that the origin of the dispute on the nature and relevance of the New Conservatism to the American scene lay in the New Conservative's tendency to go back to the roots of the conservative tradition: they were inspired by typical European (classical) conservatives such as Burke (1790) (see e.g. Freund, 1955; Schlesinger, 1953; Horowitz, 1956; Chapman, 1960).

26. Wiley's (1967) study is interesting in that he distinguishes between the laity and priests and nuns, i.e. the Catholic 'general public' vs. a 'strategic elite'. A much higher intercorrelation between religious and political conservatism is found in the latter. Religious liberalism is most strongly associated with political tolerance. Schindeler and Hoffman have found another high correlation (.43) for Baptist ministers (1968: 439).

27. Compare the later discussion on abstract vs. specific items; par. 3.3.3. Ferdinand seems to 'intuitively grasp' that most people will be inclined to endorse general platitudes or slogans. One wonders, however, whether most people would endorse general phrases on a 'negative attitude to the dominant social institutions' or a 'willingness to utilize political institutions in perfecting the social and economic conditions of man'. Free and Cantril's (1967) findings on this latter aspect seem to be contrary to this. It would have been more interesting if Ferdinand had in fact tested his intuitive notion. There is a lack of data on people's reactions to general *liberal* phrases as compared to *conservative* ones (like Free and Cantril's) and on

their reactions to *platitudes* about (economic) equality as compared to *specifics* (see e.g. McClosky, 1964).

28. The operationalization of the 3 dimensions seems doubtful. Humanitarianism, for example, includes a 'punitive' item on criminals, and items on civil rights, labor unions and women's rights. Aconventionalism includes 2 PEC-scale items (nos. 71 and 78, Form 78), one item on church attendance and one on premarital sex.

29. The alternative terms status-integration, status-congruence, etc., are well known. They all refer to different ranks people may occupy according to status criteria such as education, occupation, race, etc.

30. Operationalization again seems rather doubtful. The 'civil rights' scale incorporates items on attitudes towards Negroes and racial discrimination in general; attitude towards 'civil liberties' deals mostly with communists. Internationalism deals, for the most part, with items on trade with communist countries.

31. Each scale consists of 20 items; again of doubtful validity: the non-economic liberalism-conservatism scale is heavily loaded with items on disarmament, foreign aid, internationalism in general and awareness of possible communist threat, but also includes items on aid to education, the general role of the federal government, government actions to reduce inequalities of power and opportunity and America becoming a socialist state. The latter items all seem to belong to the economic rather than the non-economic dimension, though they are phrased in somewhat more general terms than the items included in the economic scale.

32. There is, indeed, sometimes a tendency to regard only those positions which are *contrary* to (economic) self-interest as *ideological*. Thus Campbell et al. suggest that one should expect low status Republicans and high-status Democrats to have strong ideological views. This does not prove to be so. The social welfare scale shows low status Republicans to be almost as radical as Democrats of similar status (pp. 206–207). High status Democrats are also only slightly more liberal than high status Republicans; yet the difference is greater than at lower class levels, class being measured on the basis of educational level only (see McClosky et al., 1960: 422, for the positions of Republican and Democratic leaders vs. those of their followers).

33. Other relevant findings from this study will be dealt with in the context of our own research (Chapters 6 and 7).

34. In interpreting the finding that, on average, 27% of the elite and 47% of the electorate are in favor of economic equality McClosky is certainly too pessimistic in noting that 'support for economic equality is only slightly greater among the electorate'; see p. 367. Note that McClosky's items are not as 'concrete' as Free and Cantril's, 1967: 11–15. The author refers to the by now almost familiar inconsistency in the response of the American public to, in Free and Cantril's terms, 'ideological' vs. 'operational' items (Free and Cantril, 1967: 32): 'The pattern, furthermore, is extremely spotty, with some policies strongly favored, and others as strongly rejected. Thus approval is widespread for *public policies* [my emphasis; CPM] (such as social security) that are designed to overcome gross inequalities, but is equally strong for certain features of economic life that promote inequality, such as private enterprise, economic competitions and unlimited pursuit of profit' (p.367). Neither is evidence for this generalization presented nor is the reference to

earlier work relevant (i.e. to McClosky et al., 1960: 413; see p. 367, note 18), but in the light of Free and Cantril's study, the observation seems fairly plausible (similar inconsistencies have been noted by McClosky, 1964: 373).

35. Smith gives a good description of the functional nature of economic conservatism amongst the better educated and informed section of the public: 'They . . . are status-striving and see their purposes best served by "rugged individualism" and "free enterprise" with the rules set by the business men . . .' (A higher education) '. . . is important in setting the pattern of their thinking along traditional American lines. One of the functions of the public schools — which are staffed predominantly by middle-class teachers — is to drill 'common values' into American youth and it is well known that these values are largely dictated by vested voices of the established order' (p. 77; see also Mann, 1970: 436).

36. Campbell et al. (1960, Chapter 10) found that only 3.5% of the voters could be regarded as such 'ideologues', and about 15% as 'ideologue' or 'near-ideologue' (see Converse, 1965: 218).

37. A few notes are in order here. First, Converse's notion of 'issue politics' and 'groups' as central objects of belief is clearly related to Kerlinger's (1967) notion of *'criterial referents of attitudes'*. But Kerlinger distinguishes 2 fairly comprehensive groups of referents rather than small groups of specific referents, centering around (visible) groups or issues (see Kerlinger, 1967: 119, note 6 and the discussion below). Second, Converse's observation that 'the elites of leftist parties enjoy a natural numerical superiority, yet they are cursed with a clientèle that is less dependable or solidary in its support' (Converse, 1964: 248) has consequences which Converse aptly describes as follows. ' . . . for leftist parties, the transmission of gross, simple, group-oriented cues is a functional imperative. For rightist parties, there is much to lose and nothing to gain in such publicity, for the basic clientèle can be counted on for fair support without blatant cues, and the tactical needs are to avoid the alienation of potentially large-scale "haphazard" support from the lower-status clientèle' (p. 249). For further observations on this matter, see e.g. Lipset (1963) and Campbell et al. (1960: 348), and particularly Bittner (1963) and Sartori (1969). See e.g. Merelman (1969), Bowles and Richardson (1969) and Mann (1970) on the differential (i.e. positive) relationship between the development of 'ideology' and social class (see Chapter 6).

38. Luttbeg (1968: 407) notes that 'The stimuli [for the mass public; CPM] encourage independence in responses, which, in turn, is judged low constraint'.

39. Luttbeg (1968) and Brown (1970) are 2 other critics of the 'lack of constraint' theory. The evidence presented by them is not particularly convincing, however. In both studies elites are identified by the 'reputation'-method. Luttbeg's conceptualization of liberalism-conservatism is very weak: specific local issues, assessed in a local sample, are factor-analyzed, and leaders prove to show slightly more 'constraint' on more 'enduring' issues (p. 408). Luttbeg's observation that: ' . . . belief systems cannot be classified merely as either unidimensional or nonconstrained and fragmented. Rather, it is possible to have multidimensional belief systems . . . ' (p. 409), is a valid and interesting one. Brown (1970) considers the issue of whether belief-systems are relatively stable. Forty-eight state-

ments (from Lane, 1962), covering political, economic and social affairs and the general values of *freedom* and *equality* were used (pp. 62–63). In small samples of articulates as well as non-articulates stability was shown. In the discussion, the author maintains that ' . . . the elitists . . . impose a *specific* kind of logic as though it were one of the *general* characteristics of consistency . . .' (p. 67), whereas the 'populists' contend that whether or not they can be articulate about this, virtually all people have political belief systems (see e.g. Lane, 1962; Rogow and Lasswell, 1963; see also Bluhm, 1974: 10–12).

40. One should remember that e.g. Converse's (1964) data are based on 1958–1960 surveys. Nie shows that the increase in 'constraint' among and between domestic and foreign issues also extends to some social issues (pp. 563–564) as well as to some issues on civil liberties which, as many see it, are an integral part of a true liberal ideology (pp. 561–562).

41. Members of the Liberal Party occupied a position between that of the socialists and conservatives on almost all radical-conservative issues. ' . . . Socialists were found to be more "liberal" in their attitudes than professed liberals' (p. 72). Contrary to what Eysenck claims (p. 73) the primary attitudes have not been derived from a correlation-matrix based on attitude-scales.

42. Table III, p. 203, shows, however, that the differences for conservatives and communists are negligible. On the only other socio-economic item, this relationship is only found for liberals; both facts are not mentioned by Eysenck. Only recently (Eysenck and Coulter, 1972), data on the personality of communists and fascists were fully reported.

43. It should be noted that such conclusions are unwarranted to the extent that they smack of prejudice against the working class. The relationship between social class and political party preference, and between both these variables and radicalism, has been completely *ignored* by controlling for political party choice. With reference to Rosenberg's work (1968: 94–98), political party choice acts here as a 'distorter' variable: controlling for such a variable *reverses* the over-all relationship, because, as in this case, many more working class people vote Labour and Labour voters are more radical than conservatives; a fact that Eysenck knows, of course, but chooses to ignore. Moreover, there are only 2 items on socio-economic matters in the radicalism-scale (see note 42); the other item referred to in note 42 is: '*The nationalisation of the great industries is likely to lead to inefficiency, bureaucracy and stagnation*'. Both items are presented in *general* terms, and it is by now well known that working class people's reaction to such items will often not be a 'radical' one. (See Eysenck's (1951) description of the working class, pp. 204–205, and note that items relating to class interests in the socio-economic sense, as meant by Centers . . . have been completely disregarded! Obvious inconsistencies are also disregarded, e.g. the working class is *more* in favor of unrestricted freedom of discussion, and is in *fuller* agreement that human beings are all born with the same potentials; opinions which could hardly be considered conservative.)

44. This concept has originally been developed by James (1908) but does not seem very convincing. A rationalistic and dogmatic(!) approach would be tender-minded, whereas an irreligious and sceptical (as opposed to dogmatic) one would be tough! (1954: 130–132).

45. Compare earlier views on these matters (see Eysenck, 1947: 54; 1951: 205).
46. The loadings of the single *items* on second-order factors are plotted in Fig. 1 (p. 209). The procedure is unclear: one would have expected to see the loadings of the first 10 factors which were rotated obliquely for second-order analysis.
47. Many items are similar to or identical with F-scale items, e.g. item 5, p. 202: 'Nowadays, more and more people are prying into matters which do not concern them'; see also items 7, 9, 13. There seems to be an overrepresentation of items on *race, sex* and *criminals*. (In addition, note that in the 1971 study, age and sex are included as variables in the factor-analysis.)
48. Sanai finally proposed the terms 'alterationism' vs. 'preservationism'. Note that this is then considered 'alterationist': e.g. agreement with opinions such as (abbreviated) capitalism is immoral, abortion should be made legal, there is an irreconcilable conflict between the capitalist element and the workers.
49. Some of Kerlinger's further remarks seem to imply that factor-analysis of a number of Guttman-scales to assess people's more complex attitudes is not permitted. If this interpretation is correct, I disagree with his position (as will become evident in Chapter 6). The present study has been set up exactly along the lines suggested by McNemar more than 30 years ago (see McNemar, 1946: 355-356).
50. See Kerlinger (1967: 118-119; 1970: 379-383), Robinson et al. (1968: 98-101), Shaw and Wright (1967: 322-324). I would like to thank Professor Kerlinger for having made available the paper upon which the comments below are based.
51. A preliminary comment on this factor-structure is in order: it is far from clear and not really convincing. Factor A is labeled 'economic and social liberalism', but includes an item on internationalism. Factor B, 'economic and social conservatism', includes items on internationalism, racism and some on 'radical professors', and 'scientists taking part in politics'. Factor C, 'government aid to education', includes items on unemployment insurance, the U.N., and Medicare. Factor D, 'religionism-conventionalism' also includes the item on radical professors.
52. There must be some error in presentation. The item 'Large fortunes should be taxed fairly heavily over and above income taxes' appears twice, with *different* loadings. There is an emphasis on 'government aid to education' items; one item refers to 'throwing out old ideas and customs'.
53. There is one '*abstract*' item in the list of (economic) liberalism-factors, and one non-economic item, However, some items seem to be a mixture of 'abstract' and 'concrete' elements for example: 'Unemployment insurance (specific) is an inalienable right (abstract) of the working man'.
54. Kerlinger's reasoning here is only directed towards the situation in the U.S.A. In Europe, there is an additional ideological set of referents in the form of Marxism or socialism. In some countries like France and Italy, there is, moreover, communism and fascism to be considered. This matter will be discussed in more detail in Chapters 4, 6 and 8.
55. As Converse sees it (1964: pp. 234-238, 245-246), criterial referents may be considered as broad sets of social groupings and issues on which people structure their beliefs. But Converse observes much more specific, unrelated sets of beliefs pertaining to differing social groups and issues rather than a dual ideological structure. Referring to the work of Campbell et al. (1960)

and Converse (1964), it has been suggested that the dual structure observed by Kerlinger is related to his relatively sophisticated samples of (mostly) students (Kerlinger, 1967: 119, note 6). Kerlinger's experience is, however, that 'the man in the street does have attitudes', though he does leave the possibility open that the unsophisticated may have relatively few 'criterial referents' and that not everybody has a 'complete' set of either liberal or conservative referents. For a possible explanation of factorial duality in terms of 'acquiescence', see Ray (1972).

56. Many studies in the Steinmetz Archives have been used (mostly after secondary analysis) in designing the questionnaire for the present study (see Chapter 5).

57. Equality is in itself a 'value', but not an 'immanent' one such as e.g. income, power, property, etc.

58. By including one 'generally phrased' item on 'state interference', the author succeeds in putting forward misleading suggestions (see Hoogerwerf, 1964: 256) as will be shown in our own research (Chapter 6),

59. See e.g. Berting (1968) for a conceptualization of politico-economic progressiveness in terms of goals and means (i.e. government policy).

60. Hoogerwerf's data are available from the Steinmetz Archives ('Protestantisme en Progressiviteit'; no. P0004).

61. The study is entitled 'Politiek in Nederland' (Steinmetz Archives no. P0026).

62. Provo was a movement in Amsterdam in the late 1960's, which organized itself around 'provocating' actions by groups of young people against the police in 1966. Later, it developed into a movement which propagated an 'alternative' life style. It was followed by the so-called 'Kabouter' movement and its history has still to be written.

63. Data are in the Steinmetz Archives (no. P0133).

64. Many of these studies are also available from the Steinmetz Archives: 'Het Jaar 2000' (no. P0047); 'Protestantisme en Progressiviteit' (P0004); 'Huwelijk en Gezin in Nederland' (P0008); 'Nederland en Politiek' (P0026); (items are sometimes reversed or slightly modified).

65. See Chapter 5 for a critical comment on such a *direct* application of Mokken's procedure to a heterogeneous set of items.

66. For example, items on how to attain 'peace' (see Lange, 1971: 187) items on 'change' (p. 188) and 'religion' (p. 190). For other items (e.g. homosexuality, abortion, sex) it seems more obvious to acknowledge the underlying criterion of 'freedom'. However, non-economically, as will become clear in Chapter 6, freedom and equality (in the 'egalitarian', 'of equal value' sense) can be taken as being identical.

67. Data are available through the Steinmetz Archives: 'Conflict en Radicalisme', no. P0099.

68. The data are in the Steinmetz Archives, study no. P0131.

69. The data are in the Steinmetz Archives, study no. P0192.

70. Hoogerwerf's (1964) empirical research was limited to the socio-political sphere, but philosophically as well as historically and 'analytically' it made use of a broader framework.

71. The study is based on data from 'Godsdienst in Nederland', Steinmetz Archives no. P0027.

72. The study is based on data from 'Huwelijk en Gezin in Nederland'; Steinmetz Archives no. P0008.

73. The study is based on data from 'Sex in Nederland', Steinmetz Archives no. P0067.

74. More details on the (major) political parties will be given in Chapter 6. For a more 'proper' rank-ordering of some parties see Jacobs and Jacobs-Wessels (1968: 48), a study based on a student-sample.

75. This rank-ordering is not 'absolute', and has been based on responses to questions such as: 'Which parties do you find really progressive?; Which ones are really conservative and which ones are in between?' Not all respondents gave every party a score; so no party is even mentioned by a clear majority (see Stapel, 1971: 208).

76. The over-all rank-ordering of the parties along the 2 major dimensions (*capitalism-socialism* and *progressive-conservative* (Christian-non Christian does not seem to be a continuum at all and all parties claim to be democratic) by summation is: CPN (3), PSP (4), PPR (6), PvdA (7), D66 (11), KVP (13), ARP (13), VVD (16), CHU (18), BP (21). It can be seen (see Lipschits, 1969: 137) that the KVP is slightly more in favor of government interference than the Democrats, but that the Liberals are the most 'capitalistic'. The VVD is also more conservative than the ARP, and only less conservative than the KVP and CHU. The ranks are generally only 2 points or less apart on both dimensions. Only the KVP is more conservative than capitalistic by 3 points while the reverse is true for the Farmers' Party (BP).

77. There seems to be no proper translation of the Dutch *confessioneel* which roughly means: 'organized on a religious basis, and approaching society through a religious point of view'.

78. Confusion in terminology is evident here: Stapel's rank-ordering according to 'left-right' corresponds roughly to Koomen and Willems' progressive-conservative approach as well as to Lipschits' mixed 'capitalist-socialist, progressive-conservative' (but generally 'left-right') rank-ordering.

79. However, small left-wing (CPN) and right-wing (BP, SGP, GPV; the latter 2 have a strong religious background) parties are, together with the liberal VVD, between Christian Democratic and left-wing parties on this dimension. It is difficult to accept that these rightist parties are more 'progressive' than the Christian Democrats.

80. See e.g. Hofstee (1962, 1966), Van den Ban (1963), Bergsma (1963), Benvenuti (1961), Constandse (1964), Op 't land (1966) and Nooy (1964, 1969).

81. The items assembled for dimensionality assessment are often extremely heterogeneous and refer to (reported) behavior, opinions, expectations, norms, etc. In a situation where a development is postulated in which there is a tendency for certain groups to gradually accept new forms of behavior, opinions, etc., Mokken-scaling appears to be the most suitable technique (see Mokken, 1970).

82. Apart from this, there are, of course, other worthwhile attempts at model-construction, as will be seen in the next chapter, e.g. Lenski (1966); Rossiter (1962); Huntington (1957); Kendall and Carey (1964); Von Klemperer (1968) and others.

83. In a recent personal communication from Kerlinger, it is suggested that there are 'attitude' and 'value' referents, differentiated by their degree of 'abstractness'. Attitude-referents are for example: 'real estate' and 'trade unions', and value-referents: 'capitalism', 'equality', 'freedom'.

Empirically, however, as Kerlinger reports, the 2 types of referents could not be distinguished. It had earlier (1972: 628) been found that referents may provide a bridge between research into attitudes and values. This may be interpreted in such a way that higher-order constructs appear over and above attitudes; these may refer to values (see Chapters 4 and 6 and e.g. Rokeach, 1968, 1973).

CHAPTER 4

The Definition of the Construct of Conservative Ideology: The Construction of the Ideal Type Model

4.1. INTRODUCTION

It has been argued in Chapters 2 and 3 above that what is needed in order to properly define and subsequently conceptualize conservative ideology is an ideal type model of this (theoretical) construct. This model will be presented in the present chapter. It has been developed on the basis of a systematic analysis of the literature on 'conservatism': outlines as to what constitutes conservatism to either self-styled conservatives, liberal critics of conservatism or independent scholars. There are roughly 2 stages in this process of model construction. The first stage is 'inductive'; characteristics of conservatism are listed in an inventory (see Chapter 2: par. 2.2.1.). In the second stage, these elements are combined and mutually related in a 'deductive' way: there is a set of basic elements from which others can be derived in a more or less logical manner. Finally, a 'treestructure' emerges, although this structure need not be *completely* consistent.

This process of model construction which has, of course, been rather complicated, will not be presented. Instead, the model will be introduced by a brief sketch of the history of European political thought from the Enlightenment until the present. This is done in order to put conservatism in a historical perspective, a perspective which is too often lacking in reports on empirical studies. Hopefully this historical introduction will sufficiently clarify the process of model construction, for which it forms the background.

The approach to the history of political ideas will be 'ideological'; schools of thought (e.g. liberalism, socialism, conservatism) will be considered as expressions of the interests of certain social groups and categories (i.e. social classes). The development of ideas will be related to the interests of (new) social classes. Ideologies will partly be defined in terms of underlying values by which their various elements are related to each other (see next paragraph). These values will then be used as criteria for the operationalization of conservative ideology at the attitude level (see Chapter 5). In addition to the general outline (mainly based on the development of ideologies in England, France and Germany), there will be some notes on (a) the unique development in the Netherlands, and (b) the differences between American and European liberalism and conservatism.

After its presentation, the model of conservative ideology will finally be discussed in terms of the 2 values that seem to underlie most of its elements: *freedom* and *equality*.

4.2. ON IDEOLOGY

The history of the concept of ideology has been well documented [1]. The notion of 'ideology' arose during the period of the French Enlightenment, or, to be more precise, during its decay in Napoleonic times. Destutt de Tracy (1801) introduced the term as meaning a 'science des idées'. The thinkers of the period (les Philosophes, les Encyclopédistes: Diderot, Voltaire, d'Alembert, Condillac, Condorcet, etc.) were convinced that many people had distorted or incorrect ideas about 'reality' (i.e. society). Destutt de Tracy and his school realized that a new science was necessary in order to study how this had come about. This science, or 'idéologie' was to become part of 'zoologie'.

These French philosophers were not the first to consider such matters. In England, Francis Bacon (in Novum Organum) had already introduced his 'theory of idols' (see e.g. Remmling, 1967: 118ff.), a systematic outline of the various mechanisms 'clouding' the human mind and preventing it from a rational insight.

The Philosophes, like Bacon, were still optimistic about the power of *human reason* to overcome the forces which prevented it from full development. The most radical and materialist Enlightenment thinkers like Helvetius and Holbach still believed in the value of education. However, Bacon's notions were radicalized by those thinkers in the sense that the forces which prevented many people from the full development of rationality — and hence, insight into (social) reality — were now clearly located in the *traditional social order*: the forces of *religion* (priestly fraud) and *vested interests* (the nobility).

It seems that the 'neutral' sense of the word ideology (i.e. as a science) suffered from Napoleon's reaction to the ideologues. His reaction had been positive at first, but he soon realized the danger of a school of thought which was atheistic, egalitarian, rationalistic and extremely critical of the established social order. He subsequently referred to the ideas of the ideologues as 'idéologies', i.e. *unrealistic, impractical* ideas (see e.g. Naess, 1956: 150–153, and especially Barth, 1945: 21–27) [2].

Marx's radicalization of the word gives it one of its modern meanings. In Marxian terms, the word ideology refers to all those doctrines and other ideas prevalent in capitalist society. According to Marx, any social order is dominated by the ideas of the ruling class which is able to impose them on the other classes. Those ideas legitimize the social order, and hence the position of the dominant class. Thus to Marx all thinking and all ideas in a capitalist society are 'ideological': expressions of the class-society and the vested interests of the bourgeoisie [3]. Marx's notion of ideology was *'total'*, but there was still the perspective of an inevitable development towards the 'classless society' in which, by definition, 'non-ideological' ideas would prevail [4].

This is no longer apparent in the 'sociology of knowledge'. Here, all ideas are somehow related to the social situation in which they emerge. There is no clear picture of 'objectivity' or 'truth' left: by definition, ideas are limited by the social reality of a certain epoch. Marxism itself could now be considered as such an expression: a set of ideas related to the era in which it arose, and to the social position of the proletariat therein [5].

For our purposes, a further survey of the history of the notion of 'ideology' is unnecessary [6]. From this brief sketch (and the literature on which it has been based), and taking into account more systematic studies of ideology [7], let us rather outline a number of relevant characteristics of (an) ideology.

(a) *An ideology refers to a doctrine, or at least to a number of related ideas or a belief system.* In empirical research, this seems to be central defining characteristic (see e.g. Campbell et al., 1960, Converse, 1964). Still, in the early discussions, this notion is at best implicit. The reason may be that before and during the French Enlightenment, there were no 'bodies' of thought in the modern sense to which the Philosophes could refer. They could only refer to religion and traditional ways of thinking as 'irrational'. By ideology, Marx meant all 'cultural manifestations' in capitalist society, but he did not always explicitly refer to ideologies such as classical liberalism or conservatism. (He discussed classical economics and the utopian socialists, however; see e.g. Bendix, 1964: 309). Mannheim (1930: 183-184) has referred to ideologies and utopias in the sense of 'systems of ideas', of *ideal type* nature. Elsewhere (1953: 115) he also refers to conservatism (i.e. 'conscious traditionalism') as an ideology. Most authors writing on ideologies (more so than authors on 'ideology', see e.g. Geiger, 1953) agree that such phenomena consist of related ideas or patterns of ideas (see e.g. Minar, 1961: 312-362; Shils, 1968: 66; Mullins, 1972: 507; see also Naess, 1956: 161-163) [8]. It may be noted, however, that the notion of 'systems of ideas' is a problematic one for Naess (1956: 183, 190) who considers the relatedness of various ideological elements a matter of social research (pp. 174-176) [9].

(b) *The 'elements' of an ideology incorporate value-judgements about man and society and the relationship of one to the other.* There is hardly any disagreement amongst scholars about this. Shils (1968: 63) notes: 'Ideology is one variant form of those comprehensive patterns of cognitive and moral beliefs about man, society' (see also Minar, 1961: 321; Loewenstein, 1953: 691; Williams, 1961: 374). Naess (1956: 181-182) makes the additional, important distinction between *explicit* and *implicit* value-sentences.

(c) *Ideologies are 'shared' ideas, which are adhered to as a doctrine by certain groups.* It is generally acknowledged that ideologies are systems of ideas (or: doctrines) which are adhered to by certain groups, not by individuals only [10]. Naess (1956: 162) gives several examples of definitions of ideology which he is in agreement with, and which imply this point (p. 183), which is also stressed by Minar (1961: 325).

(d) *Ideologies reflect the social position of certain groups or categories of people, and are either oriented towards legitimizing this position* (and thereby legitimizing the social order, society as a whole) *or towards legitimizing a position which is aspired towards* (and in pursuing this objective, thereby aiming at social change). This point is, of course, essentially Marxian and was later adopted by Mannheim (1930) in the context of the sociology of knowledge. It was clearly anticipated by the French Enlightenment (see above). In all these instances, groups or categories are taken to mean social classes or estates, like nobility, bourgeoisie, proletariat. This notion of 'ideology' seems, then, to be more typically European than American [11]. This aspect is not mentioned by Shils (1968), for example.

In a European context it is often noted, and almost generally accepted, that *liberalism* (i.e. classical economic liberalism) is the 'political expression' of the rising bourgeoisie while *socialism* and *communism* are the political expression of the proletariat (see e.g. Laski, 1936; Mannheim, 1930). Conservatism may be considered the ideology of the aristocracy (see e.g. Freund, 1955: 11; Huntington, 1957: 454; Spitz, 1964: 138; Mills, 1963: 210–211). Huntington rejects the aristocratic definition of conservatism but not in a convincing manner. Spitz and Mills note that there are also *other* classes which may become carriers of conservatism [12]. This can be seen in relation to Marx's notion of the ideology of the upper classes dominating society as a whole, i.e. being accepted by other strata as well (see below). For the moment, let us assume that ideas and ideologies emerge as a function of the 'socio-cultural constellation' during a certain epoch and are related to the positions which certain groups (i.e. social classes) find themselves in. Such ideologies 'reflect' the social position of such groups i.e. they are an expression of the *interests*, often of an economic nature, of such classes (see e.g. Mannheim 1953: 128). As indicated above, an ideology may either 'legitimize' or *reject* the existing order. In the latter case, it will advocate another social order, arranged according to its own principles; this would imply a different social position for that particular class (and, consequently, for other classes as well).

(Note that the *actual carriers* of an ideology — groups of people manifesting to some extent the opinions and orientations of the ideology, and perhaps acting accordingly, i.e. organizing themselves on this basis — need not be identical to, or belong to, the social group whose interests are in fact reflected in the ideology. The extent to which a social group adheres to ideological notions which are 'in its interest' is a matter of social research, and may vary in time and place [13]. The example of this which is pertinent to the present study is the following. When it arose in Western Europe in the first half of the 19th century, conservatism, as 'conscious traditionalism' (Mannheim, 1953: 95, 98) was mainly upheld by aristocrats and priests and was (partly) a conscious defense of their social position, a privileged one which was threatened by the bourgeoisie. However, it was probably also adhered too, at least in sentiment, by other classes who did not belong to the rising commercial bourgeoisie, e.g. the 'petit bourgeoisie', farmers, perhaps even workers such as farmworkers, craftsmen, etc. (see Mannheim, 1953: 87–88; see also Spitz, 1964: 138; Mills, 1963: 210–211). Later, as has already been mentioned above, Marx made it quite explicit that the ideology of the upper classes tends to dominate *all* social classes, including the proletariat (see e.g. Lichtmann, 1970: 175). It is frequently pointed out in modern studies that the established classes have many ways of making lower classes accept the ideology which legitimizes the existing social order, i.e. through the primary school system, mass media, etc. (see e.g. Lipset, 1963: 280–282 and 1968: 161). It need hardly be mentioned that socialism has not been 'carried' first, let alone developed, by the working class, for example.)

(e) *An ideology refers to a few central, underlying values.* This characteristic may partly be concluded from points (a) and (b) above: when ideas, expressing value-judgements, are somehow related to each other (i.e. form a 'system'), they should have something in common, i.e. they should all refer to some *common, general value or values.* But a direct reference to such a view of central values as a characteristic of ideologies is also often made in the literature (see e.g. Shils, 1968: 66; Loewenstein, 1953: 691; Minar, 1961: 321; see also Naess, 1956: 164–165; compare Lichtmann, 1970: 177, and Mannheim, 1930: 207, for references to 'liberalism' as centred around the value of 'freedom' and socialism as centered around 'equality' and 'equality and freedom'; see e.g. Mühlenfeld, 1952: 15, 88–90, 331–332, for a conceptualization of conservatism as *opposed* to *both* freedom and equality; to be discussed below).

4.2.1. Discussion

The problem with an abstract construct like ideology is, as Mullins (1972: 498) notes, the establishment of its *boundaries.* It has been argued in Chapter 2 that with a complex construct like conservatism, ideal type models should be constructed in order to define them.

The above outline does not constitute an ideal type of the construct of ideology. Rather, it is a rationale for including certain elements in the definition of ideology which seem pertinent to the present study [14]. The following aspects of ideology (at least often mentioned as such) are *not* considered here as constituting defining elements:

(a) *The extent to which ideology or an ideology refers to incorrectness, untruth,* etc.; in other words: the extent to which ideological thinking refers to an incorrect perception of reality (see e.g. Naess, 1956: 165–166, 190; Geiger, 1953). This notion is intimately related to the history of the concept, but has later been modified by Marx and Mannheim as ideas related to the interests of certain groups (i.e. social classes). *Essentially, ideologies incorporate value-judgements that are themselves neither true nor false.* The notion of truth is only partly retained in that some elements of an ideology may contain implicit value-judgements (see Naess, 1956) and thereby refer to characteristics of reality (i.e. man, society) which may be obvious distortions, or at best one-sided points of view (e.g. society is a harmonius whole). In most cases, however, such ideological statements are unverifiable (e.g. human nature is intrinsically bad; traditions are indispensable to mankind; see Mann, 1970: 436–437; McClosky, 1958: 39).

(b) *The several 'functions' of ideology* (as regards the motivation of the individual, the organization of political movements and political action generally, the manipulation of the masses, etc.) are also outside the present definition of the concept (see e.g. Naess 1956: 164; Loewenstein, 1953: 691; Mullins, 1972: 498; Minar, 1961: 322–324; Putnam, 1971: 655; see also Barnes, 1966; Sartori, 1969).

(c) The extent to which an ideology is *consciously held* (see e.g. Putnam, 1971: 655; Barnes, 1966: 514).

(d) *The type of belief system that would constitute an ideology* — often in combination with specific behavioral consequences — especially: ideology as a rigid and inflexible system which is dogmatically or fanatically adhered to by the individual (see e.g. Putnam, 1971: 655). Obviously, this point is a combination of points a-c above, and may be of special relevance to the so-called *'end of ideology'* debate (see e.g. Bell, 1960; Lipset, 1963; Waxman, 1969).

Briefly, points such as those mentioned above are matters of empirical research. As defined earlier, ideologies may be *investigated* or analyzed for the truth or incorrectness of their elements, their functions for the individual and organizations, the extent to which they are consciously held, etc. In particular, some of these investigations might serve to *validate* ideological positions or ideological continua once they have been identified. For example, if one has constructed a left-right ideological continuum, one would predict that those who *consciously* consider themselves as left-wing occupy more left-wing positions on the continuum than those who consider themselves right-wing; those who have a preference for left-wing political parties should take more leftist positions than those with a right-wing political party preference.

In conclusion, an ideology is defined here as *a system of general ideas on man and society, centered around one or a few central values, which has manifested itself historically as a doctrine adhered to by some groups and categories, and which expresses the interests of some important social category, i.e. a social class.* The major political ideologies [15] in Western Europe during the last 2 centuries are considered to be *conservatism, liberalism* and *socialism.*

In the next paragraph an attempt to give a rough outline of the emergence and subsequent development of these ideologies will be made [16].

4.3. HISTORICAL BACKGROUND: A ROUGH OUTLINE

Since modern (European) conservatism first developed as a reaction against the rationalism of the (French) Enlightenment and the French Revolution (which was more or less based on Enlightenment ideas; see e.g. Mannheim, 1953: 77ff and Remmling, 1967: 132–133; Burke, 1790 — often regarded as the founder of modern conservatism — explicitly refers to this revolution), a historical outline might well begin with a brief description of the ideas of the Enlightenment [17].

4.3.1. The Enlightenment

A fine summary of Enlightenment thought is given by Zeitlin (1968: 9–10): 'Knowledge of reality, whether natural or social, depends on the unity of reason and observation in the scientific method. The Enlightenment thinkers were as interested in society and history as they were in nature, and these were treated as an indivisible unity. By studying nature — including the nature of man — one could learn not only about what *is*, but about what is *possible*; likewise, by studying society and history one could learn not only about the workings of the existing factual order, but about its inherent possibilities . . .' '. . . These premises, as will be seen, were either accepted, modified, or rejected in the subsequent development of *sociological* thought'.

The beginnings of the Enlightenment are generally linked with the work of Locke. Although Locke laid down the foundations of what was later called 'liberal democracy', it has convincingly been shown that his theory can be regarded as the first ideological expression of capitalism (see Lichtmann, 1970: 170) which, with the Industrial Revolution, first arose in England. By defining the state in economic terms (i.e. as the protector of property) the value of *'freedom'* could only come to mean 'freedom *from* state interference' *in property rights*, whereas the value of *'equality'* was formalized as 'equality before the law', and could never be substantiated in an economic and democratic sense. There is a 'façade of equality' and of generally egalitarian phrases which can be seen in liberal democracy as early as Locke. 'Having begun with the value of equality, then, we proceed through the institution of property to a distinctly unequal system of class domination' (Lichtmann, 1970: 181).

Although according to some (see e.g. Laski, 1936; Remmling, 1967: 134) the Enlightenment in France was essentially a bourgeois movement it can still be argued that the Philosophes radicalized Locke's ideas. This may be related to the different social positions of the bourgeoisie: in France it had no rights against church and nobility, whereas in England, a parliamentary system had already been introduced in 1688.

In France, the democratic implications of Locke's work were (gradually) taken more seriously by the bourgeoisie-philosophers and were *substantiated* in order to draw support from the lower classes. 'Notwithstanding their position in the bourgeoisie, the Philosophes found their best friends in the working class' . . . 'The question of the masses received the Philosophes undivided attention: should simple man, mostly lacking in even basic education, be permitted to play a role in political life?' . . . 'The shift toward radicalism, toward belief in the possibilities of universal Enlightenment, became a general characteristic of the philosophers in the second half of the eighteenth century . . .' (see Remmling, 1967: 135) [18].

At a more philosophical level, Locke's ideas were also elaborated on and radicalized during the French Enlightenment, especially by Condillac (see Zeitlin, 1968: 9; Remmling, 1967: 131) who used Locke's empiricism in his attack on the metaphysics of the 17th century. Helvetius and Holbach extended this even further into *materialism*, and then made use of this to attack religion and the clergy (see Remmling, 1967: 139–144).

Certainly, Locke's conception of the mind as a 'tabula rasa' at birth is the first 'environmentalist' expression and could well be taken up by the Philosophes as implying that 'society shapes the human mind and that, therefore, if society would be altered in a positive way, a better mankind would result' (see e.g. Phillips, 1959: 756).

Condillac significantly modified Locke's theory by attributing a *creative* and *active* role to the mind. 'Condillac now argues that once the power of thought and reasoning is awakened in man, he is no longer passive and no longer merely adapts himself to the existing order' (see Zeitlin, 1968: 9). The Philosophes were impressed by the results of natural science, especially by the discoveries of Newton. 'Order is immanent in the universe . . . and is discovered not by abstract principles but by observation and compilation of data' (see Zeitlin, 1968: 5–7).

It is clear, then, that a firm empirical stand was characteristic of the

Philosophes. They added to this a strong belief in the power of reason and the value of the scientific approach in the study of society, which might, as in the physical world, lead to the discovery of 'natural laws' . . . 'these thinkers waged constant war against the irrational, and *criticism* became their major weapon. They fought what they considered to be superstition, bigotry or intolerance; they attacked the prerogatives of the feudal classes and their restraint upon the industrial and commercial classes; and finally, they tried to secularize ethics . . .' (Zeitlin, 1968: 3–4).

There is no need to go any further into the exact relationship between the Philosophes, the Jacobins and the French Revolution. There is little doubt that many of their ideas had an influence on and were accepted by the revolutionaries, whose slogan was the famous '*freedom, equality* and *brotherhood*'.

In conclusion, it can be stated that the French Enlightenment considered traditional society in a negative and critical way; most traditions and traditional institutions were dismissed as irrational and contrary to the nature of man. Since their belief was in human reason, they were necessarily individualistic and their views on any 'rational' society were necessarily somewhat atomistic, although 'natural laws' and, consequently, 'natural rights' could be discovered through the scientific approach.

4.3.2. The romantic conservative reaction

Edmund Burke (1790) was the first exponent of the *reaction* to these Enlightenment ideas, which quickly grew into a movement which was later called 'conservatism' [19]. His immediate and passionate reaction to the French Revolution already contains the major arguments of the anti-revolutionary 'romantic' movement.

A few citations will set the tone of this reaction [20].

(A) *On the Enlightenment conception of 'natural rights':*
'Whatever each man can separately do, without trespassing upon others, he has a right to do for himself; and he has a right to a fair portion of all which society, with all its combinations of skill and force, can do in his favour. But as to the share of power, authority and direction which each individual ought to have in the management of the state, that I must deny to be amongst the direct original rights of man in civil society. It is a thing to be settled by convention' (p. 87).

'In this sense, the restraints on men as well as their liberties are to be reckoned among their rights. But as the liberties and restrictions vary with times and circumstances, and admit of infinite modification, they can not be settled upon any abstract rule and nothing is so foolish as to discuss them upon that principle' (p. 89).

'The pretended rights of these theorists are all extremes; and in proportion as they are metaphysically true, they are morally and politically false. The rights of man are in a sort of middle, incapable of definition but not impossible to be discerned' (p. 92).

(B) *On the democratic and egalitarian ideals of the Enlightenment:*
'The characteristic essence of property, formed out of the combined principles of its acquisition and conservation, is to be unequal' (p. 75).

'The rich indeed require an additional security from the dangers to which they are exposed when a popular power is prevalent' (p. 260).

'. . . that the votes of the masses were rendered equal, and that the votes within each mass were proportioned to property. In any other light I see nothing but danger from the inequality of the masses' (p. 261).

'A perfect democracy is, therefore, the most shameless thing in the world' (p. 139).

(C) *On the value of conventions and traditional ways of life, even the value of prejudice:*
'When men are encouraged to go into a certain mode of life by the existing laws and protected in that mode as in a lawful occupation, when they have accomodated all their ideas, all their habits to it . . . I am sure it is unjust in legislature, by an arbitrary act, to offer a sudden violence to their minds and their feelings, forcibly to degrade them from their state and their condition and to stigmatize with shame and infamy that character and these customs which before had been made the measure of their happiness and honour' (p. 230).

'You derive benefits from many dispositions and many passions of the human mind, which are of as doubtful a color in the moral eye as superstition itself . . . But is superstition the greatest of all possible vices? . . . Superstition is the religion of feeble minds; and they must be tolerated in an intermixture of it; in trifling or some enthusiastic shape or other, else you will deprive weak minds of a resource found necessary to the strongest' (p. 234).

(D) *On the distrust of the individual and human reason* (according to Barth, 1958: 15, Burke did not have an organic conception of society):
'But in a question of reformation, I always consider corporate bodies,

whether sole or consisting of many, to be much more susceptible of a public direction by the power of the state, in the use of their property and in the regulation of modes and habits of life in their members, than private citizens ever can be, or perhaps ought to be . . .' (p. 239).

(E) *On social change* (obviously, Burkean conservatism was not opposed to change; rather, it had to be brought about with great prudence, and gradually [21]):
'At once to preserve and to reform is quite another thing. When the useful parts of an old establishment are kept, and what is superadded is to be fitted to what is retained . . .' (p. 247).
'Such a mode of reforming possibly might take up many years! Without question it might, and it ought. It is one of the excellencies of a method in which time is amongst the assistants, that its operation is slow, and in some cases almost imperceptible' (p. 248).
'By a slow but well-sustained progress, the effect of each step is watched; the good or ill success of the first gives light to us in the second and so, from light to light, we are conducted with safety through the whole series. We see that the parts of the system do not clash' (p. 249) [22].

In France, or in exile, De Bonald, De Maistre and others attacked the revolution in a more reactionary manner, and from a decidedly more religious point of view: they wanted a restoration of the 'Ancien Régime'. In fact, their traditionalism, their image of traditional society, was modeled on the medieval order [23].
In pointing to the disrupting effects of the French Revolution, the romantic-conservative reaction generally accused Enlightenment thought of naive optimism in the goodness and rationality of man. Moreover, society was not seen as organized according to abstract, mechanical laws; in its traditions and customs, it was considered as intimately related to man and invaluable to the development of the human personality. It was generally seen as a complex and organic whole, which was difficult to 'grasp', if at all, by human reason.
Zeitlin (1968: 54-55) summarizes various propositions of the conservative reaction:
1. Society is an organic unity with internal laws of development and deep roots in the past, not simply a mechanical aggregate of individual elements.
2. Man has no existence outside a social group or context and he becomes human only by participating in society.
3. The individual is an abstraction and not the basic element of a

society. Society is composed of relationships and institutions. The existence and maintenance of small groups is essential.

4. Customs, beliefs and institutions are organically intertwined so that changing and remaking one part will undermine the complex relationships maintaining the stability of society as a whole.
5. Man has constant and unalterable needs, which every society and each of its institutions serve to fulfill. If these agencies are disturbed or disrupted, suffering and disorder will result.
6. The non-rational aspects of human existence have a positive value and are essential.
7. Status and hierarchy are essential to society. 'Equality' will destroy the natural and time-honored agencies by which values are passed from one generation to another [24].

This early romantic conservative reaction perhaps found its fullest development in Germany [25]. Mannheim (1953: 80ff) accounts for this by noting certain characteristics of German society at that time, i.e. the lack of both a middle class (bourgeoisie) and a parliamentary tradition. Taking Germany in the beginning of the 19th century as an example, Mannheim gives perhaps the best account of the 'basic intentions' underlying conservative thought: Conservatism is *conscious traditionalism* (1953: 95, 98): the attempt to rationalize the world, parallel to the development of the new capitalist economic system emerging with the rising bourgeoisie, had 'suppressed all those vital relationships and attitudes, and their corresponding modes of thought' (p. 87), which were now raised to a new level of consciousness by those strata which were unaffected by modern developments, (e.g. the peasants) and also by those strata whose position was threatened, notably the 'petit-bourgeoisie' and the nobility.

The sociological background to this modern conservatism is the rise of the class society: static society becomes dynamic, different classes arise, with more or less homogeneous ideas and reactions to events of a political nature (pp. 100–101).

There are only few basic intentions underlying conservative thought.

(a) *Concreteness:* attention paid towards particular detail. 'Progressive reformism tends to tackle the system as a whole, while conservative reformism tackles particular details' (p. 103) [26]. Progressiveness sees the actual in terms of the *norm*; conservatism tries to see the actual in terms of *real factors*: it tries to see the norm in terms of the actual (p. 109).

There is, then, a related difference in the *experience of time*. The conservative experiences the present in terms of the past; the progressive sees the present in the light of the future, the possible, the norm. The conservative tries to interpret the present as an 'intuitively reached whole'. He tends to see '. . . the past as being one with the present, hence his concept of history tends to be *spatial* rather than temporal'. Land is the *real* foundation on which the state rests and develops, and only land can really make history. The transient individual is replaced by the more durable factor, land, as the foundation of events. The conservative, then, tends to trace history back to 'organic' entities, of which the family is the prototype [27].

(b) *The qualitative idea of liberty*, as opposed to the revolutionary liberal idea of liberty, of which equality is the 'logical corollary' (p. 105). 'Revolutionary liberalism understood by liberty in the economic sphere the release of the individual from his medieval connection with state and guild. In the political sphere, they understood by it the right of the individual to do as he wishes and thinks fit, and especially his right to the fullest exercise of the inalienable rights of man. Only when it encroaches on the liberty of fellow citizens does man's freedom know any bounds . . .' [28].

The qualitative idea of liberty, however, starts from the premise of the inequality of man. Here, freedom means the right to develop according to the law and principle of each unique personality. Mannheim has convincingly shown how this conception of freedom, close as it may come to subjective anarchism, is transformed by transferring it from the individual to the 'true bearers': the organic communities, the 'estates'.

Finally, this 'liberty' became a matter which concerned private life only, whereas social relations were subordinated to the principles of order and discipline. What was needed to prevent a clash between both these spheres was the assumption of a pre-established harmony in society. Here again, through the concept of liberty, a tendency towards nationalism becomes evident: 'Only the state, developing freely according to its own laws of growth, is ever really free. The individual is bound and can only achieve usefulness within those wider units' (p. 108).

Mannheim then sets out to analyze the theoretical core of conservative thought by a systematic comparison with the contents and methodology of 'natural law' thought.

The contents of the latter are defined as the doctrines of the 'state of nature' and 'social contract'; 'popular sovereignty' and the 'inalienable rights of man' (life, liberty, property, the right to resist tyranny). Methodologically, it is characterized by 'rationalism' and the 'deductive method' [29], the claim of the 'universal validity' of every individual, 'universal applicability' of all laws to all historical and social units; an 'atomistic and mechanistic' view of social units such as society and 'static thinking' (a belief in the autonomy of reason) (p. 117).

By now, it will be clear why conservatism opposed this way of thinking: reason was opposed by concepts such as history, life, the nation; reality was viewed as essentially irrational; human individuality became problematic; the universal applicability of social laws was questioned by postulating the organic nature of social units; the autonomous concept of reason was replaced by a dynamic conception of reason [30].

In conclusion, in this early version of conservative thought there is relatively little emphasis on the principle of 'inequality', the necessity of 'orders and classes', the need for a leading aristocracy and for limited government. Of course, the principle of equality was rejected, as was the notion of popular sovereignty, but as we have seen, those principles were not very prominent in Enlightenment thought, either (see Mannheim, 1953: 106; Lichtmann, 1970). As indicated above, there is evidence that those principles were taken most seriously during the French Enlightenment and by the French revolutionaries (Remmling, 1967: 135). After the revolution, it was perhaps too self-evident that such principles could not be applied for much attention to be given to them in anti-revolutionary thought (see also Napoleon's reaction to the egalitarian ideals of the ideologues; Barth, 1945: 25–26). *Moreover, in actual politics, there was no 'opposing' egalitarian ideology at the beginning of the 19th century. When such an ideology arose (i.e. Marxism), the anti-egalitarian ideas in conservatism were reemphasized and elaborated on* (see e.g. Mühlenfeld, 1952: 183)]31].

4.3.3. The heirs of the Enlightenment: classical liberalism and Marxism [32]

As had happened earlier in England, the bourgeoisie came to power in France after the Napoleonic wars. So with the exception of Germany, the dominant ideology became one of 'classical liberalism', which was based on classical economic theory. Its central thesis was opposition to state intervention in economics, in order to optimalize economic freedom and competition by free enterprise (see e.g. Free and Cantril, 1967: 1–4). This ideology of early capitalism was based on the economic ideas of the Manchester School, but, as indicated earlier, it also reflected Locke's theories (and later those of J. S. Mill). It had, of course, its 'idealistic' components such as individualism, self-reliance, the full development of personality. However, its social philosophy was essentially one of 'social Darwinism'. Classical liberalism was an heir of the Enlightenment not only in its relation to Lockean ideas, which had a great influence in America, but also in its belief in progress and in its optimism regarding human nature and social development. But although it followed Locke's theory, this movement lacked the latter's 'egalitarian façade' (see Lichtmann, 1970): its emphasis was on individual *liberty*, freedom *from* state (especially economic) interference, and the protection of the rights of property. The democratic and substantially egalitarian ideals of some of the French Enlightenment and the French Revolution were completely lost: equality was formalized as 'equality before the law' and democracy (i.e. extending the suffrage to lower, non-property owning classes) was feared for its possible threat to property-rights and free economic competition (see above).

It is clear, then, that as far as most anti-egalitarian aspects were concerned, classical liberalism and conservatism were not opposed to each other: both emphasized the value of private property and neither were in favor of full democracy or extension of the suffrage [33].

Thus the first heir of the Enlightenment was classical liberalism, which emphasized the value of liberty but stopped at its egalitarian implications (see e.g. Mannheim, 1930: 182; see also Lichtmann, 1970: 177). It required the emergence of a new social class, the proletariat, to re-emphasize those implications.

Such well known phenomena as the effects of the industrialization-process on traditional society, the emergence of the fully fledged class society (in particular the urban proletariat) and the rise of Marxism as the ideology which 'reflected' the social position of that proletariat hardly need to be mentioned. Neither is it necessary to consider Marxism in detail. The characteristics of Marxism and its development into the various forms of communism and social-democratic ideas that are of importance to the present study are already well known.

Marx's notion of ideology has already been mentioned. Essential to this notion is the existence of the class society. For heuristic purposes, 2 classes were distinguished: the owners of the means of production (the capitalist bourgeoisie) and the proletariat (selling its labor on the market). In brief, Marx predicted a dialectic and revolutionary development (albeit natural and inevitable) towards a classless society, but he was ambivalent as to how this process would come about [34], and most vague when it came to defining the nature and characteristics of such a classless society. In the present context, what is important are the strongly *egalitarian* aspects of Marxism which were later developed by social-democrats [35].

The originally weak egalitarian ideals of the (French) Enlightenment were incorporated into Marxism, but this time in a radical and revolutionary way. Capitalist society was utterly rejected, precisely for its lack of democracy and egalitarian attitudes, for its exploitation of the working class and its gross inequality of wealth[36].

4.3.4. Liberalism and conservatism and their reaction to Marxism

In the same way that it affected sociology and social theory (see Zeitlin, 1968), Marxism also seems to have had a profound influence on the ideologies of liberalism and conservatism that dominated the first half of the 19th century. But it was not *only* Marxism that gave rise to the modifications in liberal and conservative ideology.

At the beginning of the century, the industrialization process, guided by the liberal bourgeoisie, had disrupting effects on the traditional mode of life (this was one reason why conservatives were opposed to the materialism of the industrials, and to liberalism as the ideology legitimizing this process), but new structures were not really evident until mid-century. The new harsh social class structure with its gross inequality of opportunity did affect the old ideologies to the extent that they split up to form new variations on traditional themes. Since this was also soon to be the case with Marxism, the *ideological spectrum* in the second half of the 19th century became much more complex than it had been at the beginning of the century, when it was composed of a mixture of liberal-conservative thought.

In the first half of the 19th century, the structure of ideologies was 2-dimensional: some liberals were influenced by conservative ideas on e.g. the community, the nation, the value of traditions, the necessity of hierarchy (especially in Germany; see Mannheim, 1953: 81), whereas some conservatives sooner or later accepted industrialization and the new (bourgeois) elite. Here the first distinction between *reactionary*, *static* and *developmental* conservatism appears (see e.g. Kendall and Carey, 1964: 409–410). *Reactionaries* wished to return to pre-industrialized traditional society. As noted above, especially in France there was a nostalgia, resulting from the traumatic effects of the revolution, for the *Ancien Régime* or even for the Middle Ages. This was also inspired by the strong influence of roman catholicism (see Mannheim, 1953: 146). On the other hand, *developmental* conservatives tended to accept industrialization as a 'natural, inevitable' development, and sometimes only attempted to soften its disrupting effects (especially in England, where industrialization had started early, and political developments had been gradual during the 18th and 19th centuries so that it was not difficult for the landed aristocracy to accept the rise of the class structure in a pragmatic way, as the latter's power had hardly been threatened at all by the emergent bourgeoisie) [37].

For some conservatives, the social situation in the mid-19th century, together with Marx's criticism of classical economic theory, was an inspiration to reconsider their *original* criticism of the liberal principles underlying capitalism. Conservatives had always been in favor of the view that people should be *accommodated* by society, i.e. one should be able to live quietly and happily, immersed in the traditions and customs of one's own position in life (this notion is of course typical of a static, traditional society). This ideal was threatened by the industrial revolution's disrupting effects on 'quiet country life'. Initially one could, as a conservative, still hope that new organic communities (i.e. in the cities, in the factories) would soon come into being, but after a few decades, this hope was proven unfounded, and some conservatives reconsidered their old notion of a 'strong state upholding moral values', in the sense that the government now had a task to do in reaccommodating the unsettled masses. As a natural consequence of their 'organic' and 'harmonistic' view of society, this task was of course a limited one: *unlimited economic individualism was rejected, but the capitalist system of production was not: a rejection of this would be contrary to their attitude toward private property and their fundamental acceptance of the class society as an expression of 'natural inequality'* (see also Rossiter, 1962: 35). Their first and major appeal, then, was to the moral standards and conscience of the entrepreneurs themselves, and to the working class to (at least temporarily) accept its natural and inevitable lot. Their approach was essentially paternalistic, although it left room for social legislation if no other solution appeared to prevent further upheaval or revolution [38].

In addition to this, conservatism developed its legitimation of social inequality somewhat further. It became bitterly opposed to Marxist ideas on social development (dialectical, revolutionary), and on private property (means of production should be in the hands of the people, i.e. the democratic government), and to the idea that man could only fully develop his faculties in a *completely new and different type of society* (i.e. the classless society). On these and other points, conservatism was able to attack Marxism more consistently than liberalism, with its partly revolutionary, democratic and more or less egalitarian tradition in the French Enlightenment, and its 'egalitarian façade' in the English Enlightenment [39]. Conservatism now maintained more strongly than before that orders and classes were indispensable as was a leading elite which should live in luxury so that it was able to attend to the moral and cultural values so essential to man and to society. It reemphasized the rights of property, the intimate relationship of property to personality (the fruits of one's labor) and therefore the inevitability of an unequal distribution of wealth. It became strongly opposed to the *democratic* implications of Marxism i.e. to social-democrats demanding extension of the suffrage, and also reemphasized its distrust in the whims of the masses, the wisdom of the common man, and majority rule.

During the second half of the century, it became evident to scme liberals that the system of free enterprise and unlimited competition was having social effects that classical liberalism in its naive optimism had not foreseen, and which were contrary to liberal and Enlighten-ment ideals on the free development of human personality. It was realized that the economic system left little room for most people (i.e. the working class) to develop their potential. Hence some liberals (again, especially in England where the situation of the working class was harsher than elsewhere) gradually came to accept the idea that the state should interfere in the economy through social legislation. Some even went further and became in favor of extension of the suffrage to the lower classes. On the continent, however, most liberals remained 'classical' and were opposed to social legislation and other forms of government regulation of unbridled capitalism, as well as to the exten-sion of suffrage. Those 2 issues made a deep split in the liberal move-ment during the second half of the 19th century (see e.g. Smith, 1968: 279).

It is not surprising that in their principled opposition to Marxism and as part of the leading elite, a large number of classical liberals now tended to accept many ideas put forward by the conservative opposi-tion to Marxism. Conversely, conservatives who accepted capitalism thereby tended to accept classical liberal principles more than was done earlier during the 19th century (see e.g. Rossiter, 1962: 55; Chamberlin, 1963: 249; Freund, 1955: 16; Livingstone, 1956: 643, note 6; Phillips, 1956: 38; 1959: 754, note 2). The main ideological controversy during the second half of the 19th century, then, was that between *classical liberalism* and *conservatism* on the one hand [40], *Marxism* in its various forms (which later included the social-demo-cratic movement) on the other.

But, as indicated above, there were branches of liberal and conserva-tive thought that, although they accepted the established society for the most part, wished to modify it and thus took a stand between both ex-tremes on certain issues [41] whereas the ideological situation was further complicated by the well known split in the Marxist movement between revolutionary communists and social-democrats and later by the attitude of various socialist or social-democratic movements to proposed social reform by liberals and conservatives.

The general outline of Marxism's development is well known. The *communist* movement did not believe that the owners of the means of production would ever agree to do away with their property by peaceful means, e.g. through legislation brought about in a democratic way once the proletariat had the right to vote. As mentioned before, Marx had observed that in a class society the ideology of the bourgeoisie (i.e. the dominant class) tends to dominate: the proletariat would also be susceptible to it and hence would not easily develop a revolutionary (class) consciousness on its own (see notes 34 and 35). The more or less logical consequence of this point of view was developed by Lenin: the necessity of a *leading elite*, which would guide the masses at the proper time. Hence, an undemocratic and almost aristocratic element crept into the communist version of socialism, emphasizing purity of doctrine. There emerged a somewhat disciplinarian and punitive quality, which was intolerant of deviant opinions, which set severe limits to freedom of expression and which was opposed to democratic procedures in the Western (parliamentary) sense [42].

The *social-democrats* were generally optimistic about attaining their revolutionary aims by peaceful means, i.e. through legislation in a parliamentary democracy, based on universal suffrage. Roughly speaking, however, they have been proven mistaken. In England, where socialism never had these revolutionary aims [43], a long period of gradual extension of the suffrage passed before universal suffrage was unenthusiastically introduced by Disraeli's government (see e.g. McKenzie and Silver, 1968). But the conservatives believed that the English working class, used as it was to gradual reform, and tied as it was to the traditional ways of life, would tend to trust their 'natural' (conservative) leaders and would not vote so largely Labour that this would constitute a threat to the (traditional) establishment. They were *not* mistaken: until today, one third of the English working class votes conservative; sufficient to keep this party in power for most of the time [44].

It was the same on the European continent. Universal suffrage was introduced during the First World War, which contributed to an increase in nationalistic feelings and removed the emphasis from the 'class struggle': instead of uniting, European workers were fighting each other. During the period after the war, which is always a time when people want tranquility and harmony and prefer to enjoy themselves rather than be involved in a class struggle, general elections did not yield the vast socialist majorities that the social-democrats had expected. Many workers and lower-middle class people voted for royalist, nationalist, liberal, conservative or religion-based parties. This has remained the case in most European countries, even during the depression of the 1930's.

In conclusion, the *'ideological domain'* in Western Europe during the second half of the 19th and the first part of the 20th century consists of a *basic triangle of liberal, conservative and 'socialist'* (Marxist, not communist however; see below) *ideologies*. These 3 ideological 'foci' can be considered as ideal types. Under the influence of Marxism and structural developments in the class society, there have been both *converging* and *polarizing* tendencies: the ideal types of classical liberalism and (romantic) conservatism have been modified to varying extents by all kinds of parties and movements. In addition, Marxism itself developed into various forms. Such modifications have led to constellations which have differed from country to country.

Convergence means that there have been tendencies for parties to adopt elements from other ideologies (i.e. they 'move into the triangle', or at least alongside one of the axes). *Polarization* means that unidimensionality may emerge when there is a predominant tendency for 2 of the 3 ideologies to converge in their opposition to the third ideology. *It has been suggested above that such polarization has taken place between liberalism and conservatism on the one hand and Marxism on the other, with some liberal, conservative and socialist groups in between.*

There is, however, a special type of polarization which occurs when some group reinterprets an ideal type in such a way that it 'leaves the arena' of political debate, i.e. moves outside the basic ideological triangle. Such tendencies have been most apparent in the early part of the 20th century when Marxism developed into *Leninism* and *Stalinism*, and conservatism into *national socialism* and *fascism* (see below, par. 4.3.6.2.). The ideological situation was further complicated by the rich variation in the *nomenclature* given to movements and parties occupying differential positions within the ideological triangle [45].

Finally, it seems that *convergence* has been more typical of the situation in England; *polarization* (and rigidly keeping to ideal type positions) has been more typical of the continent of Europe. Due to classical liberalism developing into its more 'social' variety in England, conservatism gradually incorporated a large number of classical liberal views. There has traditionally been little difference between Whigs and Tories (see note 20 above), so that this process did not in any case cause much trouble. But compared to similar movements on the continent, British conservatism has been relatively pragmatic and developmental and British socialism rather moderate and reformist (in the Fabian tradition), though there has also been militant trade union influence.

On the other hand, as mentioned above, liberalism on the continent has tended to keep to classical economic principles (see e.g. Smith 1968: 279–280); conservatism has sometimes become reactionary (i.e. in France, where it was strongly influenced by Roman Catholicism) or has developed into national socialism and fascism (i.e. in Germany and Italy; see Von Klemperer, 1968) and Marxism has undergone a serious split into communism (e.g. France, Italy, Germany before the Second World War) and reformist social-democratic movements.

If one bears all this in mind, the development in the Netherlands seems rather unique and deserves some special attention.

4.3.5. A note on the Netherlands: the emancipatory religious movements [46]

(a) From the 17th century onwards (trade and shipping in the 'Golden Age'), the bourgeoisie ('burghers') has occupied a dominant position in the Netherlands. Radical Enlightenment ideas did not therefore have much influence during the 18th century.

(b) The Netherlands were one of the last European countries to become industrialized, hence 19th century liberalism, though based on classical economics, was open to the influence of conservative thought in Germany (e.g. Thorbecke's early acceptance of the 'organic' nature of society). In the first half of the 19th century, conservatism was embedded in the liberal tradition.

(c) Under French influence, Dutch liberalism was strongly in favor of a separation between church and state. As a consequence, the liberal government did not want to support private, religion-based schools.

(d) During the second half of the 19th century, the 'schoolstrijd' (school struggle) which had started already around 1830 dominated the political scene for several decades: it was one of the main factors which led to the formation of the political party system. First, the Calvinists organized themselves into the Anti-Revolutionary Party. Then, liberal, roman catholic and social-democratic party organizations were formed. One of the major school-struggle issues was: should the government give full financial support to private, religion-based schools over which it had no control?

(e) The religious parties (and the social-democrats) were 'emancipatory movements'. The protestants were mainly concerned with the educational issue, and so were the roman catholics, but in a more general way: they had long felt discriminated against in a country which was first dominated by protestantism after the war with Spain (1568–1648), and then later by liberalism.

(f) Although protestants were overrepresented in the lower-middle class (e.g. farmers, shopkeepers; there were many 'liberal' protestants amongst the bourgeoisie) and there was a greater proportion of roman catholics in the working class, the religious parties were not based on class: religion, influenced and helped on by the school struggle, was a sufficient basis for their existence.

(g) Marxism did not have a strong influence in the Netherlands at the end of the 19th century, but was a cause of much debate. There was an early split in the party into social-democrats and communists. Its influence was weakened by the poorly industrialized state of the country at that time (hence there was only a small urban proletariat) and the preoccupation with religion, stimulated by the school-issue, of many of its potential adherents.

(h) The conservative reaction to Marxism was hardly noticeable as an independent movement. Conservative ideas became an integral part of the religious emancipatory movements during the second half of the 19th century, but because these movements were emancipatory and drew support from various classes, they were often divided on issues such as legislation on social welfare and extension of the suffrage (see e.g. Hoogerwerf, 1964: 116, 140–141, and 222–223), as were the liberals. Generally, the religious movements became more in favor of gradual extension of the suffrage and social legislation than the liberals, who became split into many factions. The dominant 'Liberale Unie' remained mostly inspired by classical-liberal and conservative principles.

In conclusion, conservatism did not manifest itself as strongly in the Netherlands as in other European countries because its 'social basis' was either too weak (nobility) or was engaged in emancipatory religious movements (i.e. the lower-middle class). Liberalism, which had been upheld by a leading bourgeoisie since the 17th century, became dominant in the 19th century. Because of this, and because the country was poorly industrialized, it was a traditional form of liberalism, receptive to German conservative ideas, which embraced most of Dutch conservatism in the early 19th century. Dutch liberalism has predominantly remained 'conservative' and 'classical'. Gradually, conservative ideas became incorporated in the religious emancipatory movements, but for that reason this conservatism was moderate, or rather the aforementioned movements were internally divided on the most important progressive issues [47]. This was aided by the fact that Marxism has not been a threat to the existing social order during the second half of the 19th century due to the lack of a large urban proletariat, caused by the slow start of the industrialization process.

4.3.6. Discussion

The emergence of ideological constellations in Western Europe in the 19th and early 20th century has been outlined on the basis of a postulated triangular model of ideological controversy between ideal types of liberalism, conservatism and socialism. It has been shown that empirically, when political parties or movements are considered, constellations with more or less mixed versions of the ideal types have emerged, varying in time and from country to country.

Liberalism and Marxism have been considered as 'expressions of the emerging class structure'; each of these philosophies is closely related to the interests of newly emerging social classes during the process of industrialization. As such, their ideological nature seems rather clear.

The ideological nature of conservatism appears to be more complicated. Originally, in the first half of the 19th century, it was the expression of the interests of the nobility in its defense against the emergent bourgeoisie. This is shown for example by the fact that it became most fully developed (and had most influence) in countries where the nobility held a strong position (e.g. Germany, England). However, as indicated above, conservatism has not been *completely* opposed to (classical) liberal ideas. Rather, it opposed the ideology of its predecessor, the French Enlightenment, and also the ideas of the French Revolution. Although from a different approach, conservatism largely accepted the liberal notions on private property and (at best) limited democracy. For example, a statement like Burke's 'All men have equal rights, but not to equal things. He that has but five shillings in the partnership has as good a right to it as he that has five hundred pounds has to his larger proportion' is acceptable both to conservatives and to classical liberals (see Burke, 1790: 331–332; cited from Horowitz, 1956: 3). So there was already an overlap of some important and substantial ideas in the 2 competing ideologies which reflected the interests of 2 groups concerned (nobility and bourgeoisie).

Second, conservatism was more than just an attempt at a defense of the interests of a threatened elite: *as 'conscious traditionalism', it expressed the traditional ways of life that many people were still leading in the class society. So it probably also had an appeal to other classes, who were outside the frames of reference provided by the 2 'progressive' ideologies: farmers, shopkeepers, craftsmen, people living in the country generally.* One could even postulate that conservative ideas also had an appeal to people who were really affected by the class-society (whose traditional way of life was shaken by its emergence) but who were still 'sensitive' to traditional notions: the *proletariat. Socialism* is the expression of *economic* interests of the proletariat, but *conservatism* may well have appealed to this group because of the *non-economic* sentiments it embodied.

Third, conservative ideas have often been put forward in the context of religious social philosophy, which often pretends to be unrelated to the interest of specific groups or social classes.

Finally, and related to the first point mentioned above, *there is a developmental aspect in conservatism which made it gradually accept capitalism (and also most of the premises of classical liberalism) as a natural development.* On the other hand, once an emergent class is successful (as e.g. the bourgeoisie in Western Europe) in that it becomes a supplementary 'leading elite', it is natural that *it may start to use elements of thought that were previously used by its former opponents. Here, the positional or situational aspects of conservatism become clear (see e.g. Huntington, 1957): certain elements of conservative thought can indeed be used to defend any social system* (I am referring here to elements such as distrust of human rationality and the 'goodness' of human nature; hence the emphasis on stable, civilizing institutions, customs, traditions and the necessity of gradual and prudent social reform, etc.).

Conservatism first was developed mainly as a defense of traditional society. It was subsequently developed further as a defense of capitalism. This tendency was finally strengthened in its opposition to Marxism. So although it can be maintained that *some* conservative ideas can be used by almost any elite that wishes to legitimize its social position, in Western Europe the first elite to do so was the nobility, which tried to legitimize its particular position in the (traditional) social order. Gradually, a *new* elite emerged alongside the old one; to legitimize the position of this new elite, conservatism incorporated some of its ideas, whereas the new elite adopted some conservative notions. Therefore, it is not surprising that conservatism has often been regarded *not* as constituting a definite 'school of thought', but as an attitude towards life' [48]. It is also not surprising that many conservatives have been reluctant to outline their principles: conservatism may have an appeal to *non*-elites, but a clear delineation of principles might be too obvious an indication of its ideological nature, i.e. its legitimation of the position of an elite (see Converse, 1964: 249; see also Chapter 3, note 37).

It is obvious from the above discussion that conservatism, liberalism and Marxism or socialism are 19th-century ideologies, related to the emergence of the class society. What is the meaning of these ideologies today? A preliminary answer is that they are relevant to the extent that present day society can *still* be considered a class society. It is well known that this notion was challenged after the Second World War. Society was seen as 'pluralist'; most people's position along the relevant dimensions was a variable one, so no single position could be the basis for the formation of an ideology [49]. On this basis, the 'end of ideology' could at least be partially explained (see e.g. Bell, 1960; Lipset, 1963). In recent years, this notion has been challenged, however, and ideological controversy has again become salient. Social class is still a reality, and consequently we may expect that the nature of ideological controversy can still be conceptualized in terms of the 'classical' 19th-century ideologies.

We can also predict that in countries *without* a traditional society, and *without* a nobility or aristocracy to give the conservative reaction to revolutionary thought, attempts to destroy the traditional order, and 'modern developments' (i.e. the Industrial Revolution and the transformation of the old order), a phenomenon like European conservatism could not emerge at all. In such countries, the meaning of conservatism must be quite different. The obvious example is the U.S.A.

4.3.6.1. A note on the United States. The United States has generally been considered as an essentially liberal society (see e.g. Hartz, 1955). Much of its constitution has been based on the ideas of Locke, and to some extent on typical classical liberal principles such as individualism, competition, free enterprise, self-reliance and as little government interference as possible. The *Declaration of Independence* embodies the egalitarian ideals (or phrases) of the Enlightenment in the Lockeian sense: the natural rights of life, liberty and the pursuit of happiness [50]. In the *Constitution* other typically 'conservative' ideas have been laid down, like the principle of 'checks and balances' to prevent majority rule, the emphasis on !ocal government and limited federal power, and the protection of property. It has been shown above that such principles could well have been developed from Locke, but in addition, Burke also had a strong influence (see e.g. Hartz; see also the Federalists' reaction to the French Revolution, Huntington, 1957: 465). There was no aristocracy whose interests would be threatened by the emergent class of the bourgeoisie; no traditional ways of life were so shaken that traditionalism could become a conscious movement. American society was in itself the embodiment of the *new* way of life (see also Bluhm, 1974: 65). There were no classes that could be the carriers of a creed that was opposed to, or criticized the liberal principles legitimizing the new developments. Moreover, in America, liberalism had been infiltrated by conservative ideas from the start, even more openly than in Europe where it originally opposed the romantic conservative reaction [51]. This conservatism was quite different from what might now be termed 'American conservatism'.

After outlining the principles of European Conservatism, (pp. 64–66), Rossiter (1962: 198–219) has systematically documented the differences between European 'Conservatism' and American 'conservatism'. It seems essential that the American right 'embraced and still cherishes the principle of economic liberalism' (p. 211) [52]. '. . . first, American conservatism is clearly more *optimistic* about the nature of man, the uses of reason, the possibilities of progress, and the prospects for democracy. Second, it is clearly more *materialistic*. The orientation of its political theory is to economics rather than ethics or even politics, and its feeling for religion, history and higher law is cheapened by the assumption that these mighty forces reserve their special blessings for American economy. It is happily at home in the modern world and worries hardly at all about the ways of life and thought that industrialism has weakened or wiped out. Finally, American conservatism is clearly more *individualistic*. In rejecting the primacy of society, in underrating the capacity of government to do good, in passing lightly over groups and institutions that serve as buffers between man and political authority, it has pushed the precious concept of the free individual to an extreme position that no genuine (European) Conservative can occupy with peace of mind. The notion of society as a mass of struggling individuals who must root or die — all on their own — has no place in the Conservative tradition. While the contemporary Right is turning away slowly from the exaggerated optimism, materialism, and individualism of the full season of laissez-faire conservatism, it has 'miles to go before it sleeps in the plain bed of Conservatism' (see Rossiter, 1962: 201).

American conservatism appears to accept only a few European conservative principles, like those of the superiority of *liberty to equality*, the *fallibility and potential tyranny of majority rule* and the prime importance of *private property* in the maintenance of *liberty, order and progress* (p. 198) [53]. We have seen above that those ideas are in agreement with those of Locke and J. S. Mill (see e.g. Lichtman, 1970). All other European conservative ideas are reinterpreted, only partially accepted, or rejected like those on the nature of man, natural inequality, the rights of man as something to be earned rather than given, the need for a ruling aristocracy, the uncertainty of progress and the primacy of the community.

Not only has American liberalism not been challenged by aristocratic romantic conservative notions, the 'mentality of a victorious middle class' (after Shklar, 1966: 89) has also hardly been challenged from below, i.e. by proletarian Marxism or socialism. Although there are, of course, social classes in the United States, it has never been a class society in the European sense. Hence a completely different and more homogeneous ideological structure has emerged, dominated by the classical liberal principles outlined above, which have been and largely still are accepted by a vast majority, which includes what might well be considered the working class [54]. The question of 'Why is there no socialism in the U.S.?' (see Sombart, 1906) need not be considered further here. Generally speaking, it is not too difficult to recognize factors that might have contributed to this phenomenon: the frontier mentality, the enormous opportunities for expansion, the immigration (immigrants starting at the bottom of the ladder but not forming a class, perhaps partly due to ethnic and racial differences), etc. All this forms the background to a lack of ideological thinking in the U.S.: the basic 'ideology' is too widely accepted. In such a case, one can hardly speak of 'ideology'; there is no ensuing fundamental ideological debate which could integrate opinions and beliefs along ideological lines (see e.g. Hartz: 1955: 141; 229; 231–232). American political parties, then, have tended to be non-ideological; political thinking has been pragmatic and oriented towards problem-solving within the framework of the generally accepted 'ideology' (see e.g. Grimes, 1956 and again Free and Cantril, 1967). During the 19th century, the only issue which aroused widespread ideological debate was that of slavery and the controversy between the industrialized North and the agrarian South. This caused the southerners to turn to Burke in order to defend their position (see e.g. Huntington, 1957: 466–467; Rossiter, 1962: Chapter 4). In a sense, this was the first liberal-conservative antithesis in the United States; however, it soon died down after the Civil War, although in the South conservative attitudes remained rather strong.

It was not until the depression of the 1930's and Roosevelt's New Deal that there was serious ideological debate in a modern sense, centred around issues regarding the New Deal policy and the interference by the federal government in the system of free enterprise (see e.g. Grimes, 1956: 677; Ladd, 1969: 38–40). This new antithesis between liberalism and conservatism was certainly classbound: 'Liberalism was the ideological statement of the interests of a 'have-not' class of industrial workers and their allies who found the good society not in some agrarian past but in a future of more humanized industrialism and who invoked government to get there. And conservatism was the ideological defense of those of an elitist inclination opposed to the use of government on behalf of a broader extension of values' (see Ladd, 1969: 40). Here, liberals were those who, like the modern English liberals, returned to the *humanitarian ideals* of liberalism and accepted (but in a less principled way than e.g. Green did in England) that there was a task for the (federal) government in e.g. unemployment relief, housing, and medicare. Conservatives were, in fact, *conservative liberals* who kept to the 'property rights' version of liberalism, which is opposed to government interference and government welfare policy resulting in increased taxation (see e.g. McGovern and Collier, 1957).

Thus, in the United States in the 1930's, a liberal-conservative antithesis emerged which centered around socio-economic issues (as discussed in Chapter 3) but both for liberals and (especially) conservatives, *the liberal tradition was retained as the predominant ideological framework* [55]. As has been noted by Hartz (1955) and later shown by Free and Cantril (1967): liberal reform has not been backed up by an *ideology* as, for example, socialism in Europe. Thus, although up to the present day most Americans, and certainly those who identify with the working class, are in favor of *liberal programs* by the federal government, their 'abstract' ideology from the classical liberal perspective is still largely *conservative*.

That American conservatism, embedded in the classical liberal tradition, has been different from European conservatism does not imply that European conservative ideas did not have any appeal at all in the U.S., however. *Ideas* will not constitute *ideologies* when there are no 'carriers' in the social structure, but that does not mean that in specific groups or individuals such ideas might not be taken up. In fact, *European conservative ideas appealed to many American philosophers after the Second World War.* This war aroused a reaction among some American scholars (but on a much smaller scale) similar to that in Europe after the French Revolution. After the Second World War (during a period where there was an upsurge of romanticism, traditionalism and increasing demands for new harmony, order and security), some Americans became disgusted with the liberal society around them, with its 'vulgar materialism', 'ethical relativism' (see Viereck, 1962), general superficiality and lack of culture as seen in the mass media (see also Chapman, 1960; Huntington, 1957).

There emerged an American 'New Conservatism' which turned to Burke, Metternich and other European conservatives and which tried to establish a truly American tradition of conservatism . . . which, however, only existed in the agrarian South before the Civil War [56]. This movement, which conservative liberals such as Barry Goldwater sometimes mistakenly associated themselves with (Rossiter, 1962: 219–220), aroused enormous debate which still seems to be going on (see e.g. DuBois Cook, 1973) [57]. As a movement, then, the New Conservatism may be considered 'out of step' with American reality: its nostalgia for the past (which did not exist in America in the way that they saw it) certainly had *reactionary* implications: it wanted a less *free* and less *egalitarian* society and was in favor of order, hierarchy and authority, with traditions and customs as agents of social control. Its return to Burke was for the most part not inappropriate, since Burke's influence on the American constitution and the Federalists had been substantial. However, it tended to interpret Burke from the standpoint of European traditional society, not from the American liberal one.

The New Conservatives have stimulated a renewed interest in conservatism by their systematic analyses of conservative principles. So far, however, only one empirical study has been inspired by their work (McClosky, 1958) [58].

4.3.6.2. Some final comments. Conservatism has been defined as an ideology from the Western European perspective: in terms of a system of ideas on man and society, expressing the interests of a certain social group. In the case of conservatism, these characteristics are somewhat more complicated than with classical liberalism and Marxism [59]. Conservatism embodies ideas related to the interests of differing social classes: it incorporates *economic* elements which may be considered the expression of the ideas related to the interests of (economic) elites like the aristocracy (and later the bourgeoisie), but it also incorporates *non-economic* elements: expressions of what might be called the 'psychological interests' of other classes like the petit bourgeoisie and the farmers. Even new classes, still susceptible to traditional ways of life — like the proletariat — may be influenced by it. (Compare Wolfe's (1923) distinction between 'interested' and 'disinterested' conservatism; see Spitz, 1964: 138; Mills, 1963: 210–211.)

In a sense, classical liberalism could be considered '*progressive*' in its opposition to traditional authoritarian society and its legitimation of a new social order based upon individual freedom from the state. Seen in the light of the French Enlightenment, however, it should be considered *regressive* or *reactionary*, due to its disregard of the egalitarian ideals incorporated in that body of thought. (Accordingly, in the American context, *classical liberal* positions are labeled *conservative* — see e.g. Free and Cantril, 1967; see also Livingstone, 1956: 643, note 6; Bluhm, 1974: 122–124.)

Marxism incorporated these egalitarian ideals in a much more radical fashion than did the French Enlightenment. Hence, Marxism is opposed to both classical liberalism and conservatism. Some developments have been sketched within this basic triangular pattern which suggest that at the level of political parties and groups, there is a tendency for a major ideological antithesis to exist between *conservatism*, which has incorporated *classical liberal* ideas on capitalism on the one hand (or vice-versa: classical liberalism which has incorporated conservative ideas), and *Marxism* or *socialism* on the other.

It may well be, however, that such a unidimensional antithesis is too simple to describe the structure of ideological controversy in the general public. The problem here may be that socialism opposes liberalism and conservatism mainly on *economic* grounds. Marxism has predicted a social development on the basis of an economic development. Although the concept of *alienation* was central to the young Marx, and socialism became a strongly *democratic* force and re-emphasized solidarity, fraternity and moral values (with egalitarian implications), Marxism, like liberalism, seems rather poorly developed in formulating ideas which oppose the conservative ideals on e.g. the value of traditions and customs, authority, the family, the nation, etc. In other words, socialism, even more than liberalism, has failed to develop 'libertarian' ideas in opposition to 'traditional' conservative ones; there has not been a 'libertarian Marxism' (see Guérin, 1971) [60].

So it is possible that socialism appeals to the same groups (i.e. the lower classes) that are also susceptible to conservative ideas outside the area of their perceived economic interests. This may be due to limited horizons, lack of education, authoritarian family life and work experiences, or generally traditional ways of life. (In the empirical part of the study, this matter will be investigated at length.)

Finally, developments in the 20th century have considerably complicated the already complex ideological scene at the end of the 19th century. Developments of 2 of the 3 major ideologies (conservatism and Marxism) in the beginning of the 20th century and especially between the 2 world wars can be considered as movements *away* from the basic triangle of ideological controversy in Western Europe, as has already been suggested above (par. 4.3.4.). Seen from the original Marxist position, communism (i.e. Leninism and Stalinism) swings away from the liberal and conservative positions rather than converging towards them. From the conservative standpoint, fascism and national socialism may be considered as similar centrifugal developments. It can easily be seen that fascism and national socialism 'radicalized' a number of important conservative principles. Here we may recall the fascist ideas on the 'leader' vs. the common people, which is a radicalized version of conservative elitist ideas (i.e. in terms of aristocracy); fascist extreme irrationalism with an emphasis on 'action' ('der Tat') and the value of myths, which is an extreme version of conservative ideas on the weakness of human reason and the value of traditions, customs and even prejudices; and the fascist ideas on 'Blut und Boden' and conventionality in family matters, which are extreme versions of conservative ideas on the value of organic units like the nation and the family and its generally 'spatial' orientation. (See e.g. Mannheim, 1953: 103–109 and also Stagner, 1936a and Edwards, 1941, 1944, who have been mentioned in Chapter 3.) (See Von Klemperer, 1968, for a convincing description of the development of German conservatism into fascism) [61].

This obvious potential of ideologies to develop into radicalized versions, which could have disastrous consequences, led to a general distrust of ideologies after the Second World War. The Cold War strengthened this tendency, especially regarding communism. As mentioned above, it was suggested that the whole issue of ideology was time-worn; the old 19th-century ideologies of liberalism, conservatism and socialism were found to be outdated. In modern society a consensus, where once there had been disagreement, on the major issues of political debate seemed to have been reached. The way in which communism had evolved in the U.S.S.R. seemed to legitimize the capitalist system of free enterprise. On the other hand, the depression of the 1930's legitimized a certain amount of government regulation of the economy. The system of parliamentary democracy on the basis of universal suffrage had now been accepted by both liberals and conservatives, and the value of traditions and authority relations was generally accepted after the disrupting experience of the Second World War [62]. The 'end of ideology' was therefore proclaimed. However, events in the late 1960's and early 1970's have proven this movement to be wornout. In the terminology of the present study, such extreme *convergence of 'traditional' ideological positions* may perhaps have temporarily come about during the 1950's; it clearly does not exist any longer today. Similarly, ideological controversy may have withered away during the 1950's in the general public, but seems to have been clearly reestablished during the 1960's.

This study will attempt to assess the nature of this controversy. We begin by presenting, on the basis of the above sketch of the historical background, the ideal type of conservative ideology, which will subsequently be discussed and analyzed.

4.4. CONSERVATISM AS AN IDEOLOGY: AN IDEAL TYPE CONCEPTUAL MODEL [63]

4.4.1. Introduction

Some quasi-models of conservative ideology, i.e. some outlines of conservative statements, have been helpful in constructing the model to be presented below.

Some such models have already been presented above, i.e. those of McClosky (1958) and Zeitlin (1968). Some attention has also been paid to the similar approaches by Levinson (1950), Mannheim (1953) and of course Burke (1790). Quasi-models are unsatisfactory insofar as they are unsystematic and incomplete. Still, such approaches like those of Kendall and Carey (1964), Kirk (1964), Wilson (1960), Rossiter (1962), Huntington (1957), Von Klemperer (1968) and Lenski (1966) have been useful, in addition to the content-analytical approach to many other studies.

The model is hierarchical in that it 'unfolds', so to speak, from basic premises, and that gradually, more and more elements can be derived from previous ones. The model is comprised of a number of sections, outlined in Table 4.1.

The list of statements below constitutes a *model* insofar (a) it *represents* the ideal type of conservative ideology to be operationalized in subsequent research; (b) the statements are mutually related in a logical or deductive way (in that sense, the model has system-characteristics). The mutual relationships between the model-elements are given by way of a reference to earlier elements from which later elements have been derived (see above and note 1 of the model).

Table 4.1. *The sections constituting the model of conservative ideology*

	No. of elements
Section 1: basic assumptions: the nature of man	6
Section 2: basic assumptions: the nature of society	11
Section 3: the relation between man and society: (a) general	16
Section 4: the relation between man and society: (b) on the implementation of change	14
Section 5: the relation between man and society: (c) a specification for a fundamental social institution: the family	9
Section 6: the relation between man and society: (d) on authority and democracy	21
Section 7: the relation between man and society: (e) on private property and social classes	15
Section 8: the functions of government: (a) general	9
Section 9: the functions of government: (b) the socio-economic field	20
Total	121

4.4.2. The model

Section 1. Basic assumptions: the nature of man

1.1.   Human reason is weakly developed; people are fundamentally irrational, motivated by intuition and emotion.

1.2.   Human nature is complex and intricate.

1.3.   Man is basically inclined to evil more than to goodness; is egoistic rather than altruistic; is aggressive and destructive.

1.4.   Human nature is unchangeable; it cannot be improved.

1.5.   People are unequal in all respects (i.e. their qualities and abilities). They are only equal in the possession of a unique, valuable personality.

1.6.   Man is basically a weak and 'dependent' creature.

Section 2. Basic assumptions: the nature of society

2.1.   Society is an organic, growing whole: all parts are intimately related to and dependent upon each other.

2.1.1.   There is a natural development taking place in society; an organic process of growth.

2.1.2.   Only society (i.e. the nation) is really free: it develops freely and naturally.

2.2.   Society is built up of organic wholes like the family and the community (later: the industrial organizations). They form its basic and most valuable elements.

2.2.1.   Each of such elements has an identity of its own. They should be as autonomous as possible within the larger whole in order to be able to develop freely and naturally, and fully realize their potential.

2.3.   Society is a harmonious whole; all elements are basically in harmony with each other.

2.4.   In its institutions, and in the norms, habits, traditions and values which these embody, society incorporates the heritage and the wisdom of the past.

2.4.1. In its institutions, society incorporates transcendental moral values, absolute moral standards.

2.5.   Society is a complex whole.

2.5.1. It requires wisdom to be able to understand and interpret society.

2.5.2. What is happening in society (the course of its development) can only partly be grasped by intuition and experience.

Section 3. The relation between man and society
(a): general

3.1.   Man is logically and morally secondary to society (i.e. the nation, the community and the family) (1.6., 2.2., 2.4.)*

3.2.   Man can be 'civilized' (i.e. become 'human' by restraining basically evil impulses) by living through ('internalizing') the values, norms and customs incorporated in social institutions. (1.3., 1.6., 2.4.)

3.2.1. Man is dependent upon society for becoming 'human'.

3.2.1.1. The values, norms, customs and traditions of society, even if they are in fact prejudices, are indispensable.

3.2.1.2. There should be 'law and order' in society to enable people to live through (internalize) its values, norms and traditions (civilization should be protected).

3.2.2. Civilization is a precious good though only a thin veneer, covering man's basically immoral, complex, and irrational impulses. (1.1., 1.3., 1.4.)

3.3.   The traditions, institutions and customs that have existed for a long time are especially suited to human nature (1.2., 2.4., 3.2.)

3.3.1. By living through social institutions and internalizing the values, norms and customs incorporated by them, man will be free in a substantial and optimal way (i.e. he will be able to fully develop his potential).

---

* Numbers in parentheses refer to earlier statements from which the statement has been (partly) derived. A reference to broader categories implies a reference to narrower ones derived from it.

3.4.   In the interest of society as a whole, the task of interpreting (and attending to) its development should be entrusted to the ablest, wisest and most experienced members (1.1. 1.5., 2.4., 2.5.)

3.5.   Man is unable to fundamentally improve society (1.1., 2.5.)

3.5.1.   It is due to the frailty and basic immorality of human nature rather than to the way in which society is organized, that society will never be 'ideal' and that there will always be evil (1.3., 2.4.)

3.6.   A society cannot be judged according to general, abstract principles (1.1., 2.5.)

3.6.1.   A society cannot be judged 'from outside', i.e. without an intimate knowledge and experience of it (2.5.)

3.7.   People's rights and duties are settled by social conventions (2.4., 3.1., 3.2., 3.3., 3.6.)

3.7.1.   People don't have 'abstract', general, or 'inalienable' rights

3.7.2.   To be considered a member of a society or community, and enjoy their proper rights, people should fulfil their duties (i.e. live according to accepted social standards).

Section 4. The relation between man and society (b): on the implementation of change

4.1.   Human nature cannot be improved by altering society (1.4., 3.2.2.)

4.2.   It is futile and dangerous to try to change society according to general, abstract principles (1.1., 2., 3.5., 3.6.)

4.2″.   It is futile and dangerous to try to create an 'Utopia' by changing society according to some general scheme or 'blueprint' of an ideal society (1.1., 2., 3.5., 3.6.)*

4.3.   The natural development of society should be interrupted as little as possible by human endeavors (1.1., 2.1., 3.5.)

4.3.1.   One should only deliberately change society when there is an obvious need to do so (e.g. to preserve fundamental institutions, restore harmony and the past heritage and to adapt to changing standards).

4.3.2.   Deliberate change should always be moderate and prudent (so as not to disturb the 'precious fabric' of society) (1.1., 1.6., 2.1., 2.4., 2.5., 3.2., 3.3., 3.5.)

4.3.2.1. Radical change would be likely to create chaos.

4.3.2.2. Trying to implement radical change would result in but a

---

* The statement 4.2″. is included as an alternative to 4.2. Both phrases are often used for this rather fundamental conservative principle, and are essentially similar.

caricature of what was intended

4.3.2.3. After a radical change, results would be worse than the original situation

4.3.3. Deliberate change should be in harmony with existing traditions and customs and the absolute moral values that are incorporated by them (2.4., 3.2., 3.3.)

4.3.4. Deliberate change should be in harmony with the natural development of society (2.1.1.)

4.3.5. Deliberate change should aim at the preservation of the past heritage (2.4.)

4.3.6. Deliberate change should aim at restoration of the past heritage if this has been lost (2.4., 3.3., 4.3.2.)

4.3.7. In the implementation of change, one should be guided by the lessons of history (1.1., 2.4.)

4.4. Decisions regarding deliberate change should be taken by the ablest, wisest and most experienced (3.4.)

Section 5. *The relation between man and society (c): a specification for a fundamental social institution: the family**

5.1. In the family, the heritage should be passed on from one generation to the next (2.4., 3.1., 3.2.)

5.1.1. It is the duty of parents to pass on this heritage

5.1.2. It is the duty of children to accept and internalize this heritage

5.1.3. Parents have authority over their children†

5.2. The family-relations between parents and children are a 'model' for relations of authority in the community and in society at large

5.3. The relation between parents and children is harmonious (2.3.)

5.3.1. There is harmony between the duty of the parents to exercise authority and the need of the children to have this authority exercised over them (3.2., 5.1.)

5.4. 'Blood relationships' are of special value; they imply the right to inheritance of property (5.1.)‡

5.5. In addition to the natural inequality of people (through

---

* The community forms the 'organic unit' between the family and the nation. Many statements of special relevance to the family are also, possibly in a somewhat modified form, applicable to the community.

† For the elaboration on the concept of 'authority', see the next paragraph.

‡ For the elaboration on the concept of 'property', see section 7.

inheritance), further inequality among people is created through differential 'civilizing' of children by their parents (1.5., 3.2., 5.1.)

Section 6. The relation between man and society
(d): on authority and democracy

6.1.   Authority is needed (1.6., 3.2., 3.4., 4.4.)
6.1.1.   The authority of absolute moral values, incorporated in social institutions and embodied in traditions, norms, habits and customs, is needed (3.2.)
6.1.2.   The authority of able, wise, experienced people is needed (4.4.)
6.1.2.1. Society has need of a 'natural aristocracy' entrusted with authority
6.2.   Authority should be legitimate (i.e. be accepted as legal)
6.2.1.   Authority should be in harmony with existing traditions and customs (4.3.3.)
6.2.2.   Authority should be in harmony with the natural development of society (4.3.4.)
6.2.3.   Authority should be exercised (as much as possible) in harmony with what 'lives' among the people
6.2.3.1. There should be certain institutions which transmit the wishes of the people to the elite who are in positions of authority
6.2.3.2. The elite has the responsibility to translate and interpret those wishes into some concrete policy (if necessary)
6.2.3.3. The procedures through which the elite is responsive to the wishes of the people may vary in time and place
6.3.   People should abide by the rules laid down by authority (1.1., 1.3., 1.6., 3.1., 3.2., 3.3., 4.4., 5.2.)
6.3.1.   When authority is no longer considered legitimate (i.e. by a majority of the people) it may be necessary to enforce (traditional) authority in order to prevent radical change (4.3.)
6.3.2.   The 'ultimate' legitimacy of authority is its upholding of the absolute moral values incorporated in the social institutions and traditions (2.4., 3.2.)
6.4.   Government may develop naturally into some form of 'democracy' (2.1., 6.2.3.)*
6.4.1.   It is impossible and dangerous to try to bring about democratic forms of government deliberately in any country at any time (4.2., 6.2.3.3.)

* For an elaboration on the theme of 'government': see par. 8–9 below.

6.4.2.   The principle of 'popular sovereignty' has to be rejected (1.3., 2.2., 2.4., 3.4., 3.7.1., 4.4., 6.1., 6.3.)

6.4.2.1. The principle of popular sovereignty implies 'majority rule' and the majority is not always right (3.4., 6.3.2.)

6.4.2.1.1 The people are often subject to the 'whims of the times', i.e. fads, fashions and foibles (1.1., 1.2., 1.6.)

6.4.2.1.2 People often have only a thin veneer of civilization (3.2.2.)

6.4.3.   Forms of 'direct democracy' on a more limited scale have to be rejected (4.4., 6.1., 6.4.2.)

Section 7. The relation between man and society
(e): private property, social classes

7.1.   Everyone has a right to the fruits of his labor

7.1.1.   Everyone has a right to his own property

7.2.   The fruits of one's labor should be related to the value of that labor for society

7.2.1.   Through their work people have unequal value to society (1.5., 4.4.)

7.2.2.   Differential contributions to society as a whole should be rewarded accordingly because 'incentives' are needed to stimulate people to become 'civilized' (1.3., 3.2.)

7.2.2.1. Incentives are needed to stimulate people to develop their abilities fully

7.2.2.2. Incentives are needed to stimulate people to accept responsibility

7.2.2.3. Incentives are needed to stimulate people to exercise authority (4.4.)

7.2.3.   Private property is naturally distributed unequally

7.3.   Property is intimately related to personality and the private sphere (i.e. the family) (5.4., 7.1.1., 7.2.)

7.3.1.   Everyone should be free to do as he wishes with regard to his own property

7.3.1.1. Private property is essential for freedom

7.4.   Social classes are natural and inevitable phenomena (7.1., 7.2.)

7.4.1.   Social classes benefit society as a whole (7.2.)

7.4.2.   Social classes can and should live in harmony with each other (2.1., 2.2., 2.3.)

Section 8. The functions of government (a): general*

8.1.   Government should be 'reticent' (2)
8.1.1.   Government should be moderate and prudent (4.2., 4.3.)
8.2.   Government should primarily preserve the moral standards embodied by social institutions, traditions and customs (6.3.2.)
8.2.1.   The main function of government is to keep 'law and order' (3.2.1.2.)
8.3.   Government should attend to harmonious developments in society (2.3.)
8.4.   Government should respect the relative autonomy of the organic parts that constitute society, e.g. communities, families (2.2.1.)
8.4.1.   Government should only interfere when people are clearly no longer 'accommodated' by the 'organic wholes' in which they live (4.3.1.)
8.5.   Government should be exercised by a civilized, aristocratic elite (able, wise, experienced people) (6.1.2.)
8.5.1.   Government should be legitimate (responsive to the wishes of the people, in harmony with traditions etc.) but should not ultimately be exercised by the people (popular sovereignty must be rejected) (6.4.2.)

Section 9. The functions of government (b): the socio-economic sphere

9.1.   Industrial organizations have developed naturally in society (2.1.1.)
9.1.1.   Industrial organizations constitute an 'organic part' of society (2.1., 2.2.)
9.1.2.   Industrial organizations should be as autonomous as possible (2.2.1.)
9.1.3.   Industrial organizations are in themselves harmonious wholes (2.2.)
9.1.4.   The economic system that has developed in society is best suited to human nature (3.3.)
9.2.   Government should interfere as little as possible in natural economic developments (8.1.)
9.2.1.   Government should only interfere when there is a clear necessity to do so (8.4.1.)

---

* Under this heading, a summary is given of earlier more general statements, which now all focus on the functions of government. Those functions are implicit in many earlier statements.

9.2.2. In case of a possible necessary interference, government should first encourage the involved parties to arrive at a solution (which should always be possible) (9.1.3.)

9.2.2.1. It should first be made clear to the most powerful party involved that it has a moral obligation to find ways to accommodate the other party (or parties) (8.4.1.)

9.2.3. Much government interference would lead to a stifling bureaucracy rather than to a solving of problems (4.3., 8.1.)

9.3. Government should respect the rights of property (7.3.)

9.3.1. Government should refrain from attempts at 'leveling' (7.4.)

9.3.2. Economic relationships in society are natural and inevitable (7.4., 9.1.)

9.3.3. Private enterprise should be left to develop freely in the general interest (3.3., 9.1.)

9.3.4. Impingment on the rights of property would soon lead to other impingments by the government on basic freedoms (7.3.1.1.)

9.4. Government should not take away responsibilities from people by taking too much care of them (7.2.2.)

9.4.1. The 'welfare state' should be as limited as possible in scope

9.4.2. Government should only interfere when people are unable to take care of themselves because they are not given sufficient opportunities to do so (9.2.1.)

9.4.2.1. People should be free to take the initiative and to live their own lives within the economic system

9.4.2.2. Much government interference would lead to a slackened way of life by taking away too much of this basic freedom

.5. DISCUSSION

'he model that has been presented constitutes a loosely interconnected, ierarchical body of ideas on man, society and social institutions, and ᴀeir mutual relationships. It is constructed from basic assumptions or ᴘemises on man and society (Sections 1 and 2), which clearly reflect ᴀe conservative reaction to Enlightenment thought: they constitute the ᴋact opposite of Enlightenment ideas. The Enlightenment held man ᴐ be basically rational and good; therefore he should be *free and qual*. To the extent that man is *not* rational and good, this is *because* ᴇ is not treated as, or allowed to be, free and equal in traditional ᴐciety.

The complement to this dim view of human nature is conservatism's glorification of traditional society and social institutions as reflected in section 2. Whereas the Enlightenment was extremely critical of traditional society (with its many irrational institutions and traditions and its arbitrary authority relations) and glorified the individual, freed from his bonds, conservatism maintains that society is an organic and harmonious whole which incorporates the wisdom of the past and absolute moral standards which are indispensable to man and to civilization and which should be left free to develop naturally.

Unlike the 'simplistic' Enlightenment notions on human nature and society, conservatism postulates their complexity in that their true nature may never be completely understood. These basic conservative premises may well be taken as notions marking and legitimizing the rise of the social sciences to study these complex phenomena (see e.g. Nisbet, 1952).

An attempt has been made to show how the whole fabric of conservative thought may be derived from these few basic assumptions on man and society. The relationship between man and society in general terms (section 3) is partly implicit in the basic assumptions. If, for example, one assumes that human reason is poorly developed and that society incorporates wisdom, man would do better to leave society alone rather than meddle in its affairs. Since man alone is but a lonely beast, he is in need of the civilizing influence of social institutions and hence is secondary to the community. Here, by the way, more specific issues such as 'nationalism' and 'militarism' may be justified in terms of a conservative ideology (see also note 61, and above, on the relationship between fascism and conservatism).

Similarly, a cry for 'law and order' and concomitant punitive attitudes may find their justification in such notions as the civilizing effect of social institutions on individuals. A similar attitude is reflected in item 3.7.2.: as soon as one does not live according to the norms and laws of society, *one has no rights*: this may legitimize a punitive or aggressive attitude towards e.g. criminals, foreigners, and in general minority groups with a different life-style (note item 3.2.1.1. on the value of prejudice). Some paradoxical patterns of ideas come to the fore, for example the idea that one can only be 'really' or 'substantially' free by . . . conforming to traditions and customs (item 3.3.1. see Mannheim, 1953: 115ff. and pp. 217ff).

Item 3.5.1. reflects the difficulty conservatism has in glorifying an imperfect society: however, evils are attributed to man's wickedness. In this context, it is also clear why people have no 'abstract', 'general' rights: if they had, it would be immediately clear that society is incapable of realizing such rights: (revolutionary) reform would be a natural consequence. A final paradox is that, however much society and its institutions are glorified, man remains fundamentally unchanged by this: his basically evil impulses forever lurk behind the façade of civilization, which is but a thin veneer. Of course, conservatism cannot accept any other principle since in that case, progress and a better society would be envisaged, as well as the (Enlightenment) notion that if we start changing society for the better, a better mankind could result.

In section 4, various implications of such notions are worked out with regard to social change. If only for semantic reasons, ideas on social change have occupied a central place in definitions of conservatism, both in a research and a philosophical context (see e.g. Huntington, 1957). They have often been isolated from their proper context, however. From Burke on, there has been debate as to whether conservatism is opposed to *any* change, to *fundamental* change, or only to *rational, planned* change of the social order. The problem here is perhaps that conserva*tives* may well be against (proposed, conscious) change on specific issues, whereas conserva*tism* as an ideology need not, therefore, be opposed to *any* change of that kind.

The major problem may be that conservative ideas on change are *positional* to the extent that they largely depend on the situation. (See Mannheim, 1953: 95 who distinguishes 'traditionalism' from 'conservatism' in this respect.) *This means at the same time that conservative ideas on change cannot constitute an essential part of the ideology: conservatism has no definite point of view as regards change in the abstract.* Its only definite point of view regarding change generally is that it should be brought about (a) only when strictly necessary and (b) gradually and with great prudence. (Note that both points are extremely positional: *when* is something 'strictly necessary'? *how* 'gradual'?.)

The important thing here is that the conservative view on change immediately points to criteria, dimensions along which the effects of certain types of change can be measured. This is in keeping with the notion that, by definition, not every change is progressive. Hence, paradoxically, conservatism may be in favor of *retrogressive* change, if this is necessary to restore part of the heritage that has been lost (e.g. under the influence of progressive forces; see item 4.3.6., and note 61). But under certain circumstances, conservatism may also be in favor of *progressive* change, or even initiate such change (see e.g. item 4.3.1. and note 38).

Of course, conservatism is against change that is based on abstract ideas or blueprints of a better society, since this would imply *radical* or even *revolutionary* change, a disturbance of the civilizing fabric of society which would only lead to barbarism and disaster (see items

4.2., 4.2″. and 4.3.2.). This fundamental conservative notion, which is opposed to radical change, can be immediately derived from the conservative position on the relationship between man and society (especially items 3.2. and 3.3.): in case of radical change, people would lose their foothold on life and civilization would crumble. Such ideas no doubt resulted from the conservative perception of the effects of the French Revolution.

The conservative position on *gradual* change is quite different. First we have to distinguish between *deliberate* (man-made, intended) and *natural* change. As soon as change can be considered a natural development, conservatism will not oppose it (item 4.3.). The problem here is one of perception: when is a development natural and when is it man-made? The most important example seems to be that of *industrialization*. Originally, this development could be conceived of as man-made, disrupting traditional society (at least large parts of it). Hence it was opposed by conservatism. Gradually, however, it became clear that the process of industrialization was irreversible. In such a case, conservatism tends to accept these developments as natural. The conservative position is somewhat more complicated when certain proposals on change are clearly intentional, aiming to change the traditional order, but not by revolutionary means. When the proposed change is in the progressive direction, as will mostly be the case, such proposals could be accepted under certain circumstances; in a case when a more or less obvious *need* for such change can be discerned, conservatives may even take *the initiative* — for example, when such change seems inevitable or when such change being inevitable, has important 'tactical' advantages (e.g. Bismarck's social legislation and Disraeli's extension of the suffrage).

However, in times of progressive change, the conservative is often much more enthusiastic about *retrogression*: to restore as much of the past (the lost heritage) as possible. In fact, conservative notions of change always tend to center around ideas like: change should aim to preserve or: change should essentially aim to restore; even progressive change is looked upon this way: when engaged in such change, the ultimate conservative goal is to preserve the essentials of the old order (item 4.3.5.). Finally, conservatism may turn to *revolutionary, reactionary* change when progressive change becomes too radical. When, to conservative eyes, it seems that there is a threat of revolution (and consequently chaos, nihilism, anarchy etc.), conservatism provides the legitimation for an enforcement of traditional authority by, for example, a *coup d'état* (see item 6.3.1.) [64].

In summary: from the 2 sets of basic premises on man and society, here follows another basic section on the fundamental relationship between man and society, which culminates in a section on social change, the elements of which have often erroneously been taken as constituting the essential elements of conservatism. *In this sense, the very word 'conservatism' is a misleading, formalized indication of the ideas of some philosophers wishing to preserve a specific social order: at first the traditional European social order, and later, a mixture of this traditional order and modern capitalism.*

In the model, the bridge which spans the more fundamental premises and formal notions of conservative ideology and the more substantial ones is the section on the family (section 5). In conservative thought, the family is the prototype for broader social relationships. It constitutes the very core of the process of civilization: parents having a natural authority over the (at least initially) helpless and dependent children. There are mutual needs, rights and duties in the unit. Parents exercise authority over their children and exert discipline in order to civilize them. Notwithstanding this situation of inequality and lack of freedom, there is harmony and mutual respect. Moreover, a link between the family and society is made through the institution of the inheritance of property and the effects of the socialization process.

Substantial elements in conservative ideology on authority-relations and the idea of democracy (section 6) can be traced back to fundamental premises on the inequality of men (item 1.5.), the complexity of society (2.5.) and the consequent desirability of the ablest being in power (3.4.) and having the authority to implement change, if at all necessary (4.4.). There is only a seeming paradox in the fact that on the one hand, it is postulated that 'man is irrational, wicked, weak and dependent', and on the other hand, in the conclusion, that 'society is in need of a natural aristocracy' (item 6.1.2.) to exercise authority and to exemplify the moral values. The family, with its natural inequality, caused by inheritance and socializing processes (5.5.), together with additional socializing agencies like schools and universities, is the breeding ground for an elite which is most able to internalize the values and norms embodied in social institutions. The ultimate authority rests with moral values, but those should be embodied by a leading elite (see items 6.1.1., 6.1.2.1. and 6.3.2.).

In par. 6.2., the moderating and limiting conditions set to the exercise of authority are listed, and in 6.3. and in 6.4. its demanding and restricting elements are set out. There seems no doubt that conservatism was the major anti-democratic force in Western Europe during the 19th century. Unlike classical liberalism, it had an ideology legitimizing an authoritarian government by a ruling elite, which was only moderated by vague notions of 'responsiveness to the people', of being 'legitimate', and of the responsibility to 'accommodate'; all this to protect moral values and valuable ancient institutions from the 'whims of the masses'. Classical liberal antidemocratic ideas were more nakedly and frankly expressed in terms of the protection of property rights but as we have seen above, even early European conservatism also had firm ideas on this and (with the rise of the class society) on the class structure as well.

Section 7 considers these notions. From simple premises such as (item 7.1.), that one has a right to the fruits of one's own labor and that (item 7.2.3.), through one's labor, differing contributions to society — however that may be measured — should be rewarded accordingly, it is concluded that property is intimately related to personality and so necessarily *unequally* divided; this is said to be essential for freedom (item 7.3.1.1.).

Item 7.2.2. and its sub-items constitute a small theory which maintains that social classes as the expression of the unequal distribution of property are not only natural or inevitable, but even desirable for the common good.

Given such *substantial* notions as those on the value of the traditional social order, authority, democracy, private property and social classes, it is clear that conservatism had to develop a set of ideas on the *functions of government*. Initially, in the early 19th century, government (i.e. the influence of the state upon society, as it is often put) was limited. Therefore, it could be proposed that the major task of government (and conservatism, as opposed to liberalism, was quite in favor of this task) was the upholding of moral values (see item 8.2.). This was often seen as a 'strong state' in a moral sense, but not in the sense that government should *direct* society. On the contrary: government should be a guardian of law and order, ensuring that harmonious developments took place, and leaving as much as possible to the smaller organic social units (see items 8.2.1., 8.3., 8.4.). A natural consequence of the conservative view on man and society is that government should *not* be noticeable; that it should be moderate and prudent and that the power to govern should only be entrusted to the most capable and civilized (in other words, to an aristocratic elite) who are *responsive* but not *responsible* to the people (items 8.1., 8.5.). Upon the rise of the class society during the 19th century, it became increasingly important to (re)define the role of government in socio-economic terms; in other words: to also apply notions on the limited role of government to the socio-economic field. Section 9 considers such notions.

In one sense, conservatism was less well prepared than classical liberalism to oppose increasing demands for government participation in solving the so-called 'social problem': (European) conservatism includes notions such as e.g. the state taking care that people are 'accommodated' by society (i.e. in their traditional social roles and positions). The dilemma of conservatism is that one should let natural developments take place as much as possible but when such developments get 'out of hand', the government has a task of redirecting, restoring, reharmonizing social developments and social relationships. This *could* include moderate government interference in redressing the effects of unbridled laissez-faire capitalism (see item 8.4.1.).

However, in its principled opposition to Marxism, conservatism has generally tended to accept classical liberal ideas on limited government interference in the socio-economic field, as becomes clear in section 9. The system of private enterprise has developed 'naturally' (item 9.1.) and consequently industrial organization form organic, harmonious wholes (item 9.1.3.). Further, government should respect the rights of property (item 9.3.) and certainly not make attempts at leveling (item 9.3.1.). From ideas on private property stem those on the threat to other freedoms' when the rights of property are impinged upon (item 9.3.4.).

Another paradox in conservative thought is that although men are held to be weak and dependent, government should *not* 'take away' man's responsibility by taking too much care of him (item 9.4.). Rather, 'society' should provide the incentives for man to live his own life. This notion starts with the premise that man should be sheltered by the traditions, customs and moral values available to him. But it may easily end up with the idea that the individual should be 'free from government care' in the economic sphere, since society is supposed to offer a sufficient number of such opportunities. Conservatism tends to accept capitalism to the extent that it accepts the rise of industrial organizations (and hence notions such as 'individualism', 'competition' and the necessity of incentives to stimulate individual effort). Conservatism is only in favor of government interference in moderating the effects of unbridled capitalism in certain circumstances, i.e. when people are clearly no longer 'accommodated' and are obviously powerless to do something about this themselves (see items 9.2.1. and 9.4.2.). Generally speaking, government interference should be as limited as possible since most problems should be solved by society itself, which offers the necessary and most suitable stimuli and incentives.

4.6. CONSERVATISM AS AN IDEOLOGY: AN ANALYSIS IN TERMS OF UNDERLYING BASIC VALUES

Let us now consider the following question: does conservatism constitute an *ideology* in the sense as defined above (par 4.2.). In the light of our historical review and the way in which the model has been presented, it appears that condition (a) has been fulfilled: conservatism is a doctrine: it constitutes a number of related ideas.

Condition (b) seems to be partially fulfilled: the model-elements refer to ideas on man and society and their mutual relationship, but not all these ideas appear to refer directly to *value-judgements*. A value-judgement implies an *evaluation* of e.g. goals, means, a state of affairs, or norms of behavior. In this sense, some model-elements do not constitute *explicit* value-sentences but at best *implicit* ones (see Naess, 1956: 181–182). Some elements, however, especially those on 'human nature' in section 1 do not seem to imply a value-judgement at all. They are merely statements of 'fact', for example 'people are fundamentally irrational', notions on the complexity of human nature, or its immutability, the statement on human inequality. On the other hand, value-judgements can be seen clearly in notions on the goodness or badness, or the weakness and dependence of human nature.

It is much easier to derive value-implications from the model-statements on *society*: apart from item 2.5., all elements imply a positive evaluation of society, social institutions, norms, etc.; at least their acceptance as they are. Gradually then, value-judgements become increasingly more 'explicit'.

Accepting for the moment that conservatism is an ideology in the other respects (as outlined above: par. 4.2., points c and d), we may now turn to the final question which is most important for our purposes: is conservatism an ideology in the sense that one or more (but only a few) central values underlie this body of thought?

After the outline above it is not too difficult to see now that there are such values, i.e. the values of *freedom* and *equality* [65].

In statements on the relation between man and society in general, and in the ideas on social change, the underlying value of *freedom* seems dominant: the individual is requested to conform to existing traditions and customs and not to try to change social institutions and social relationships. Both the values of *freedom* and *equality* are integrated in the sections on the family and on authority and democracy; here, *some* have the authority to impose laws and norms on others, but *all* are bound to these laws and norms.

In the section on private property and social classes, the meaning of the values of freedom and equality gets a special twist; the inegalitarian aspect implying lack of freedom for *all* is no longer there: now there is much more freedom (i.e. in the sense of the ability to develop one's potential, to choose from among alternative life styles and behavioral possibilities) for *some* — i.e. the well-to-do — than for *others* — i.e. the poor.

It is also clear that in defining the role of the government in this sphere, conservatism is only in favor of freedom so that *inegalitarian* relationships may remain intact. *It is only in this limited economic sense that conservatism is more in favor of freedom than equality (see e.g. Rossiter, 1962); in the non-economic sense, conservatism is opposed to freedom since it needs to maintain absolute norms.*

So, conservatism generally opposes the value of equality: (a) *economically* in terms of opposition to equality of income, status, power; and (b) *non-economically* in terms of a *non*-acceptance of various types of behavior as 'of equal value' as long as the freedom of others is not impinged upon. However, conservatism *only* opposes freedom in the *non-economic* sense, since there freedom would have . . . egalitarian consequences, as described above. It is paradoxical that in this sphere, conservatism is at the same time in *favor* of equality in the sense of conformism to absolute moral standards, which it sees embodied in traditions and in civilization in general.

Thus, there seems to be a theoretical 2 × 2 design underlying conservative ideology (see Table 4.2.).

Table 4.2. *The structure of conservative ideology in terms of fields and values*

		FIELDS	
		Economic	*Non-economic*
VALUES	*Freetown*	Conservative	Progressive
	Equality	Progressive	Progressive-Conservative*

*Progressive in the sense of: various behavior is of equal value;
  conservative in the sense of: all should conform to absolute moral standards (i.e. be equal in this respect).

Economically, conservatism is in favor of freedom, with inegalitarian consequences, whereas non-economically it is in favor of equality in the sense that everybody should abide to absolute moral standards (which has the implication of non-freedom). (Compare Rokeach, 1968, 1973, who disregards, like so many others, the distinction between the economic and non-economic fields.)

In conclusion, in terms of the underlying values, there does not seem to be much unity in conservative thought. For this unity to come to the fore, we have to return to the ideological nature of conservatism in the sense of its legitimization of the established social order. In this sense, conservatism has especially tended to legitimize the position of the aristocracy (or the upper classes) in that social order. At first (i.e. in the first half of the 19th century) conservatism defended the traditional order against the disrupting effects of the industrialization process, carried by the new liberal bourgeoisie and supported by the ideology of liberalism. The value most central to this ideology was *freedom*, but already Mannheim (1953: 106) noted that 'The counter-revolutionary opposition . . . [i.e. conservatism; CPM] . . . had a sound enough instinct not to attack the idea of freedom as such; instead, they concentrated on the idea of equality which stands behind it'. The conservative idea of freedom (as it was originally developed in the first half of the 19th century) did not apply to the individual, however: 'Only the state, developing freely according to its own laws of growth is ever really free' (Mannheim, 1953: 108), which in fact means that the individual should *conform* to the state's development, and so be *unfree*. Conservatism opposes *freedom* which has *egalitarian* consequences in a moral sense, but it does *not* oppose freedom which has *in*egalitarian consequences in a '*non*-moral' (i.e. economic) sense. Therefore, it is not surprising that when a new elite emerged (i.e. the liberal bourgeoisie) as the expression of an irreversible process of industrialization, it was not too difficult for conservative thought to incorporate the value of freedom in this sense. Thus, in terms of fields and values, an *interaction* effect emerged: conservatism is in favor of *economic freedom* (like classical liberalism, defending the position of a new elite) but opposed to *non-economic freedom* (i.e. sticking to absolute moral values of behavior, incorporated in the traditional social order, and carried by the old elite, the aristocracy). Consequently, it is against *economic equality* (in the sense of a leveling of incomes and property) but in favor of *non-economic equality* (i.e. all abiding to the same absolute norms of behavior).

So, we can define 'progressiveness' as an orientation in favor or *equality* in an economic sense and *freedom* in a non-economic sense, but we should be aware of the fact that this implies *opposition* to economic freedom to the extent that this has inegalitarian consequences, and an egalitarian orientation in non-economic matters in the sense of 'various forms of behavior being of equal value' [66].

4.7. IMPLICATIONS FOR EMPIRICAL RESEARCH

The ideal type model of conservative ideology has been developed and basic values underlying this model have been found, although the application of these values to the economic field is not identical to that in the non-economic field. This model, representing the theoretical construct of conservative ideology, and its underlying values will now be used in the empirical part of this study.

First, the model itself will be put into an operational form (i.e. direct operationalization). The dimensionality of this domain of (bipolar) statements will be assessed in (a) the population at large, (b) some subgroups and (c) the strategic elite of M.P.'s. Among other things, we will see whether the possible dimensionality of this domain of statements will somehow reflect the underlying values which have been discerned. Since the unity of conservative thought mainly seems to stem from the defense of elitist positions in society, one may wonder whether the progressive-conservative antithesis is an elitist construction, so that it may only emerge as a unidimensional antithesis in the strategic elite.

Second, the values of freedom and equality will serve as *criteria* for the selection of items which form part of attitude scales reflecting these values in some respect, i.e. in some field. This is the indirect operationalization of the model at a more specific and concrete level. Attitude scales will be considered as the units of analysis of the progressive-conservative domain at this level. In order to optimalize the results of the construction of scales, a number of studies (Dutch national surveys of the mid-1960's) have been secondarily analyzed from this freedom-equality perspective; items have been selected which somehow reflect these values and their scalability has been tested by way of factor-analysis and Mokken-scaling (1970). Thus, a basis for the *further* definition of sets of items to be submitted to similar procedures in order to obtain attitude scales for the present study has been obtained. The results of the scaling procedures are reported in Chapter 5.

The dimensionality of this attitudinal domain will be investigated in the general population. Both domains (i.e. the abstract and the specific) will then be integrated so that the dimensionality of the complete *ideological* domain can be assessed. This will be the central part of Chapter 6.

NOTES ON CHAPTER 4

1. On the history of the concept of 'ideology', see e.g. Barth (1945), Naess (1956: 148–161); Bendix (1964: 294–318); Geiger (1953); Lenk (1961), Lichtheim (1967: 3–46) and Remmling (1967: Ch. 10–14).

2. According to Naess (1956: 152), the word can also be used in a derogatory manner, as by e.g. De Bonald (exponent of the conservative reaction to the French Revolution). So, Napoleon's use of this word was in line with the already popular way in which it was employed by those outside Destutt de Tracy's circle.

3. Marxian ideas are modified (on the subject of the upper class manipulating the ideas of the lower classes) but essentially accepted by sociologists such as Pareto and Mosca (see e.g. Zeitlin, 1968, Ch. 12, 13).

4. Since Marx's own theories are not considered 'ideological', there is still the notion of an ability to 'rise above' ideological forms of thought to a non-ideological, 'true' understanding of reality (see e.g. Bendix, 1964: 309-310).

5. I will not go into any detail on Mannheim's thoughts about the sociology of knowledge. As is well known, Mannheim distinguished 'particularen' from 'totalen' ideologies (see Mannheim, 1930: 8) and *'ideologies'* from *'utopias'*. Roughly speaking, liberalism, conservatism and socialism are all regarded as 'ideologies' — which are bound to the historical epoch in which they arose — as well as *'utopias'* — which incorporate elements aiming at transcending this (historical) reality — ; see Mannheim (1930: 183-184).

6. Related to the notion of 'ideology' is the notion of rationality, or trust in the power of human *reason*: for the past 2 centuries this has steadily been declining. Remmling (1967) shows, for example, that this process begins with Locke and Kant. During the French Enlightenment, there was a renewed belief in rationalism (see e.g. Zeitlin, 1968: 9) but it was realized at the same time that there were powerful forces in society which opposed rational insight. Subsequently, in the work of Hegel, Dilthey, Marx, Nietzsche, Freud, Mannheim and others, there is a consistent 'road to suspicion' regarding human reason.

7. For systematic, 'analytical' approaches to 'ideology' see e.g. Minar (1961), Naess (1956), Shils (1968) and Mullins (1972).

8. It should be noted that the 'organization' of the ideas constituting an ideology is not completely 'logical', nor completely 'idiosyncratic'. A distinction should be made, however, between the ways in which the various ideas can be interrelated. Some more specific ideas may be partly derived 'deductively' from general premises, but the *actual* interrelation of these ideas in various categories and groups of people is still a matter of empirical research (see Chapter 6).

9. I agree with Naess' view that the degree of interrelation of ideas in an ideology (i.e. the extent to which the ideology constitutes a 'system' of beliefs) is a matter of empirical research (see note 8). However, it is difficult to conceive of measuring a 'system' other than by correlations (p. 176).

10. There are, in addition, some who also consider that individualistic constellations of beliefs with a certain 'stability' form an ideology; see e.g. Lane (1962), Brown (1970), Converse (1964), Naess (1956: 161-162).

11. The often noted 'lack of ideological thinking' in the American electorate may be related to the lack of a class-structure in the European sense (e.g. the lack of an old aristocracy) and the dominance of one class (i.e. the 'middle class') and its ideology; see Hartz (1955: 141, 231-232) and further discussion below.

12. It is sometimes denied that liberalism and conservatism constitute 'ideologies' related to 'class interest'. On liberalism, see Smith (1968: 276, 279);

on conservatism, Mühlenfeld (1952: 19, 177, 351–355).

13. Of course, such a discrepancy between the group (i.e. social class) whose interests are 'expressed' by an ideology and the actual *support* for the ideology in such (a) group(s), or even the 'reality' or 'existence' of the ideology in such a class (the degree to which the various ideological elements form a system), may be called, in Marxist terms, a state of relative 'false consciousness'. Here the concept of ideology becomes 'heuristic' in nature, in that it provides guidelines for research. Note that there may be groups or categories other than 'social classes' which manifest an ideology, but that the major ideological controversies seem to be 'class-based'.

14. See the Weberian notion that ideal types may be constructed by an *eclective selection* of elements for special research purposes; a point of view which is rejected in the case of 'conservatism' but may be accepted in the case of 'ideology' (see Chapter 2, note 12).

15. Those ideologies are in the main, though not exclusively, political (see Mannheim, 1953: 77).

16. See the introduction to this Chapter.

17. Huntington (1957: 463ff) distinguishes 4 major manifestations of conservatism in Western political history. He locates the first of these before that which emerged as a reaction to the French Revolution: '. . . the response in the 16th and 17th centuries to the challenge of centralized national authority to medieval political institutions and the challenge of the Reformation to established church relationships'. The others are the responses to Marxism, industrialization, and the opposition to slavery in the American south. The first conservative reaction is outside the scope of the present study: it is not considered as the beginning of *modern* conservatism. The exclusively 'positional' approach to conservatism by Huntington is rejected here: the *substantial* elements in Western European conservatism will be emphasized.

18. Laski (1936; in Shklar, 1966: 79–89) is more sceptical about this. See his notes on Voltaire (pp. 83–84). He observes that Diderot was in favor of property rights (p. 84). 'He [Diderot] felt sentimentally for the poor, but he had no criticism to make of the general contours of liberal and economic doctrine'. However, . . . 'Progressive taxation, a more equitable distribution of wealth, less luxury, a greater tenderness for the poor, a wider attention to education, it is difficult to see in Diderot's program very much more than this' (p. 85). Remmling's point of view seems to be the more correct one, if only because of this statement. See also Gay's (1964: 119) statement on the relation between 'Philosophes' and 'Jacobins' (in Remmling, 1967: 132).

19. The word 'conservative' was first used by Chateaubriand in 1818 (i.e. in his journal *Le Conservateur*) and subsequently adopted by many other groups and movements opposed to the ideas of the French Revolution e.g. the Tory's in England in the 1830's (see Freund, 1955; Chapman, 1960: 29).

20. There was not much difference in England between the Whigs and the Tories at that time (see Mannheim, 1953: 81). Hence, even Burke could be considered by many as a Whig. Note the later discussion on the *similarity* between conservative thought and the earliest expressions of the English Enlightenment (liberalism) in e.g. Locke. There are many examples of early liberals (e.g. those in favor of free trade) who *also* accepted conservative

ideas in response to the revolution (see e.g. Huntington, 1957: 465–466).

21. The notion that conservatism is *not* opposed to change *as such* has been repeated again and again by later scholars, e.g. Freund (1965: 10–11); Chapman (1960: 31); Phillips (1956: 30); Barth (1958: 3–11). Others have made distinctions between 'static' and 'developmental' conservatism (see Kendall and Carey, 1964) or 'standpattism' vs. conservatism (see Rossiter, 1962: 12–13).

22. For a discussion in Dutch on Burke and other 'right-wing' theorists, see Sizoo (1971).

23. For most conservatives, religion was important as a set of 'moral values' embodied in the traditions and institution in society (see also Burke, 1790: 134). This element does not seem to have been generally accepted by conservatives, however, and does not seem to be essential to conservatism. The relationship between religion (roman catholicism, protestantism) and conservatism does seem rather complicated. It will not be discussed in the present study. See e.g. Rossiter (1962: 232–234) on the conservative nature of roman catholicism. Perhaps it may be put in this way: most *conservatives* attach great value to religion, but a religious point of view need not necessarily have (although it mostly has) conservative implications.

24. This is one of the many quasi-models of conservatism which have been helpful in constructing the ideal type conceptual model used in the present study. Other quasi-models will be mentioned below.

25. It should be noted that Germany as a nation did not exist at that time.

26. According to Mannheim, this, 'concreteness' finds a special application in the concept of 'property', which was now regarded as having close connections with the person, far more so than in bourgeois thought. Note however, that such an intimate relationship already existed in Locke's and in J. S. Mill's work (see Lichtman, 1970: 181–183 and 191).

27. Note here the clearly *nationalistic* implications of a spatial, organic approach to history. On conservative attitudes to the family and to nationalism, see also Rossiter (1962: 10, 31, 37–38) and Horowitz (1956: 15).

28. Note Burke's citation above. The liberal idea of liberty implies 'equality' because 'without the assumption of political equality for all men it is meaningless. Actually however, revolutionary liberalism never thought of equality as anything more than a postulate. It certainly never took it as a matter of empirical fact, and indeed never demanded equality in practice for all men, except in the course of economic and political struggles' (see Mannheim, 1953: 105–106). It is not clear here whether Mannheim is referring to the Philosophes and the French Revolution.

29. Note, however, the difference between this view on 'natural right' and Zeitlin's approach to the Philosophes (see above).

30. Seen in regard to the sociology of knowledge, it is not surprising to find Mannheim rather enthusiastic about this 'contribution' made by conservative thought. He considers this notion as 'One of the most important logical weapons against the natural law style of thought' and as 'something new . . . new insights which played a momentous role in later evolution' (p. 118).

31. Other elements were also further developed, e.g. the role of moral values and the duty of the state to uphold them, as against (the liberal principle by now largely accepted) the limited role of the state in economics, and other points

to be made clear below. See, however, Horowitz (1956: 2): 'And last in theory but first in actuality was Burke's social elitism, a stress on the inherent worth of socio-economic stratification and the attendant duties and rights of class to class and man to man'.

32. In the remainder of this chapter, in some cases the terms Marxism and socialism will be considered as more or less equivalent: Marxism is seen as the basis from which an extensive socialist movement developed. It is realized, of course (and will be discussed below), that this movement split up into revolutionary communism and Leninism on the one hand, a reformist social-democratic movement on the other; these originally had quite similar aims, but proposed different means of reaching those goals.

33. Conservatism was opposed to classical liberalism for its libertarianism, its indifference towards traditions and customs, its 'vulgar materialism', its individualism and optimism (regarding human nature and social progress), its rationalism and, of course, its threat to the nobility and its disruption of the traditional social order. Generally, it opposed its 'abstractness' in defining social relations (see e.g. Mannheim, 1930: 215ff).

34. On the one hand, Marx predicted a 'natural' development of a dialectic nature. On the other hand, he was well aware of the fact that the proletariat had been subjected to indoctrination by the dominant ideology of the bourgeoisie, and might therefore not develop a sufficient amount of 'class consciousness' to bring about the 'natural' development. This was later modified by Lenin, who postulated the necessity of a leading elite 'to bring about the inevitable through hard work'.

35. Here, the later split in Marxism is referred to: the social-democrats trusted in being able to bring about socialism through a majority in parliament, once there was universal suffrage; and the communists rejected this notion because they believed that capitalists would never give up their privileged position without the use of force.

36. Marxism, like liberalism, was an expression of the modern class society. Both ideologies reflected the interests of a newly emerging social class. Both ideologies had a firm materialistic basis, but also 'idealistic' components. In Marxism, the notion of economic equality was connected to a concern for '*freedom*' (i.e. liberation) and full development of the personality (see e.g. Spitz, 1964: 130). The difference between classical liberalism and Marxism is that the latter demanded *equal* freedom (*equal chances*) for all to develop their full potential. (Of course, it should again be noted that this is quite different in later varieties of Marxism like Leninist communism, which has elitist characteristics and also sets many limits to individual freedom of expression.) Both Marxism and liberalism were antagonistic towards, or indifferent to the traditional social order.

37. Germany however, was (a) not a nation which (b) had experienced a revolution or (c) an early industrialization with (d) the introduction of parliamentary life. Here, conservatism was thus least influenced by liberal ideas or 'liberal situations' and could develop into its purest form (see Mannheim, 1953).

38. Bismarck and Disraeli are notorious examples of conservatives who used *progressive* means for *tactical* reasons of this type, e.g. Bismarck's social welfare legislation to get support from the working class for his military plans; Disraeli's extension of the suffrage to the lower classes (see below).

39. In the present study, the view is taken that originally the egalitarian ideals in liberalism were weak and insubstantial, except in pre-revolutionary France. Others, however, stress the original liberal ideals in terms of freedom and equality (see e.g. Hallowell, 1943: 73–74; see also Barth, 1958: 4; Grimes, 1956: 634–636).

40. It should be remembered that the class society in Marxian sense was a 'heuristic abstraction'; almost an ideal type in the Weberian sense of a selection of elements which were considered essential to the development of social theory (see Chapter 2, note 12). Large sections of society were still *traditional* and as such most susceptible to *conservative* notions, e.g. people living in small villages in the country, farmers, small shopkeepers and craftsmen, as well as those in aristocratic circles. (See comments below on 'conservatism as an ideology'.)

41. A complication is that 'modern' liberals and 'modern' conservatives do not take *similar* positions on the main continuum of ideological controversy. Modern (English) liberals went further towards *social legislation* and *government regulation* than most modern conservatives. The latter were almost completely against extension of the suffrage whereas many modern liberals were in favor of it.

42. This aspect is stressed in modern research literature on the organization of left-wing movements; see Chapter 3: e.g. Converse (1964); Bittner (1963).

43. This is probably related to the gradualness of social development in England, its long parliamentary tradition (the Glorious Revolution of 1688), the pragmatic, developmental nature of conservatism and the early 'social' nature of its liberalism, both representing (partial) alternatives to socialism.

44. See the many English studies on working class conservatism, e.g. McKenzie and Silver (1968), Runciman (1966), Parkin (1967), Nordlinger (1967) and a recent article by Pinto-Duschinsky (1973). See also Lipset (1963, 1968), where working class conservatism and authoritarianism is presented as being essential to parliamentary democracy (see Chapter 7).

45. Of course, when parties and movements occupy positions between ideal type ones, or within the ideological triangle, they seek names to identify these positions. Those names often do not refer to their position relative to the *ideal type corners* of the triangle. Party names may refer to one major issue central to the party program, such as republican, royalist, democratic. Often, specific views (especially conservative ones) have been put forward from a religious viewpoint, both roman catholic and protestant. Thus, there are many christian (-democratic) parties. (On the conservative nature of those parties, see e.g. Fogarty, 1957; and MacDonald, 1957: 75.) Sometimes, however, such parties (e.g. the Dutch Anti-Revolutionaries) have not used a 'christian' label. There are also party names which refer to the groups whose interests the parties represent, like farmers' parties, middle-class parties, labor parties. Such nomenclature obscures underlying ideological positions along the three axes of the ideological triangle.

46. A certain amount of literature on Dutch society is available in English: see e.g. Bone, 1962, Goudsblom, 1967 (and the references and bibliographical note) and a recent bibliography in Sociologia Neerlandica (see Ellemers et al., 1974).

47. The protestant movement later split up into Anti-Revolutionaries and Christian-Historians. The latter were more 'liberal' in their attitude towards

religion (Dutch Reformed based) and overrepresented among the upper class. (The nobility was rather well represented.) They were less in favor of extension of the suffrage and social welfare legislation than the Calvinist, lower-middle class based Anti-Revolutionaries.

48. That conservatism does not constitute a definite body of thought, that it has few principles or no principles at all, that it is hard to define, etc., has been outlined by many scholars, e.g. Rossiter (1962: 20), Freund (1955: 10–11), Chapman (1960: 31), Spitz (1964: 133–134), Phillips (1959: 755), Barth (1958: 7), Mühlenfeld (1952: 179–180). On the other hand, many have found it relatively easy to outline the (few) principles of conservatism, e.g. Kirk (1954), Huntington (1957: 456, 469), McClosky (1958), Zeitlin (1968: 54). Few argue for the 'ideal type' approach; see, however, e.g. Neuman (1968: v, xvii; in: Von Klemperer), and also Lenski (1966: 22–23 and 441–443) and Kendall and Carey (1964: 421) on Burkean principles (see Chapter 1, notes 11, 12).

49. With regard to social class, such points of view emphasized the multidimensionality of the class phenomenon and gave special attention to phenomena such as status-inconsistency. Others emphasized the effects of social mobility rather than social class (see Chapter 7).

50. Spitz (1964: 130) notes that in the Declaration of Independence, Locke's 'property' has been replaced by 'pursuit of happiness' and that the 'Constitution does not incorporate the notion that property is a natural right. It does stipulate, however, that the deprivation of property must 'accord with due processes of law'.

51. See e.g. Huntington (1957: 465) for early mixtures of liberal and conservative ideas in the reaction to the French Revolution in Europe.

52. It is noted that, on the contrary, the European Conservative 'refuses to go all the way with economic individualism' but 'at the same time that he expresses doubts about unqualified laissez-faire, the Conservative expresses horror over unqualified socialism' (see Rossiter, 1962: 40–41).

53. Rossiter also mentions 'the essential role of religious feeling in man and organized religion in society'.

54. Compare Free and Cantril (1967: 37, discussed in Chapter 3) pointing to discrepancies between the appeal of *slogans* of a classical liberal (i.e. conservative) nature, and *specific opinions* on liberal policy.

55. Both 'liberalisms' had been combined in the work of Locke, but now became opposed in the class society in times of crisis. See e.g. Huntington (1957: 468).

56. Some well known American New Conservatives are Viereck (1962), Kirk (1954), Wilson (1941, 1951, 1960), Meyer (1964, 1969), McGovern and Collier (1957), Butler (1955), Kendall (1960), Kendall and Carey (1964). See e.g. Rossiter (1962: 223–226) for an exhaustive list. The agrarian southern conservatives they often refer to are e.g. Adams, Calhoun, Randolph, Fitzhugh, and Babbitt.

57. The New Conservatism is critically discussed (seen in relation to the American liberal tradition) by e.g. Huntington (1957: 470–472), Rossiter (1962: 219–232), Lewis (1953), MacDonald (1957), Brown (1955), Chapman (1960), Freund (1955), Horowitz (1956) and Schlesinger, Jr. (1953).

58. Huntington (1957: 470–471, note 38) has correctly noted that conservativism has been ignored by political scientists; that there are no decent histories of

political thought which deal with conservatism. Phillips (1959: 755) notes that there has never been a systematic study of conservative principles. There are various reasons why this might be so, which will not be discussed here, but the New Conservatives have been invaluable in helping to fill this gap.

59. Some maintain that conservatism itself is not an ideology but that it *opposes* ideological ways of thought (or: modern, materialistic ideologies) like liberalism and socialism, which only lead to lack of freedom and inequality (see Mühlenfeld, 1952: 88, 177, 351).

60. Since Marx considered all ideas in the class society as ideological, there was certainly an implicit tendency to reject such typical conservative ideas on family, discipline, sex, patriotism and conventions. When Marxism was first 'realized' (i.e. in Russia), there was a relatively short period during which a libertarian policy was followed. However, a more traditional policy was quickly returned to (see e.g. Flugel, 1945: 298).

61. The apparent confusion as to the relationship between fascism and national socialism and conservatism seems to be related to the fact that in the former ideologies, these radicalized conservative ideas were *used* in a way which is quite opposite to conservative aims, i.e. to arouse and activate people in order to overthrow an old order and create a new one. In this sense, fascism and national socialism appear truly *reactionary*. We will see below, however, that this reactionary potential is inherent in conservative thought and constitutes an essential aspect of it, as well as of conservative policy.

62. Some even attribute the 'loss of civilization' to the materialist ideologies of liberalism and socialism, which sprang from 18th century rationalism. Conservatism is then seen as necessary to oppose such ideologies to bring back civilization; see e.g. Mühlenfeld (1952: 15-19; 31-42).

63. Other authors on conservatism which have inspired the present approach are Barth (1958), Baxa (1924, 1931), Kissinger (1954), Lewis (1953), Livingstone (1956), MacDonald (1959), McGovern and Collier (1957), Mühlenfeld (1952), Phillips (1956, 1959, 1963), Wolfe (1923), Wolin (1953, 1954). Some others are mentioned in the bibliography.

64. Recent examples of such *coup d'états* are those of the Greek colonels in 1967 and the Chilean junta in 1973.

65. Approaches to the progressive-conservative antithesis in terms of the values of freedom and equality are not uncommon. See e.g. Brown (1955: 2-7), Barth (1958: 21, 26), Hallowell (1943: 73-74), Huntington (1957: 472, note 34), Horowitz (1956: 2), Kendall and Carey (1964: 420), Lewis (1953: 636), Lichtmann (1970), Mannheim (1953: 105; 1930: 182), Mühlenfeld (1952: 43-69, 90), Rossiter (1962: 24, 35, 293) and Smith (1968: 276). They have never been properly derived from a model of conservative ideology, however.

66. Progressiveness is also an elitist phenomenon, which implies an inconsistency, e.g. in being in favor of *freedom* from traditional norms and customs, but *not* being in favor of freedom from government interference for the individual businessman. A certain consistency in the progressive point of view may be found however, in the notion of '*equality of freedom*', which means that one should only limit those freedoms which would render the *general distribution* of freedom less equal (see e.g. Rawls, 1972).

PART TWO

The Empirical Assessment of Progressive-conservative Dimensions and an Attempt at Theory Construction

CHAPTER 5

Operationalizations of Conservative Ideology: The Abstract and Attitudinal Progressive-conservative Domains

5.1. INTRODUCTION

The ideal type model that is needed as the basis for the operationalization of the construct of conservative ideology has been developed in Chapter 4. *Fundamental values* underlying the various model-elements (ideological statements or sentences – see Naess, 1956: 181ff) have been derived from it. They will serve as criteria to identify *attitudes* which can be considered as indicators of progressiveness and conservatism in various fields. Attitudes are considered as middle-range constructs which lie between abstract values and broad ideological dimensions on the one hand, and specific opinions, assessed by single items on the other. In order to assess whether an attitude underlies a set of items (i.e. opinions, beliefs), some procedure of scale-construction is required (see Chapter 2).

The first step will be to indicate the way in which the model of conservative ideology has been operationalized *directly* i.e. how model-elements have been selected and 'translated' into an operational form. It will then be shown how, on the basis of the 2 criteria of *freedom* and *equality*, sets of opinion-items have been constructed to be submitted to scale-analysis. Here, extensive use has been made of a number of Dutch surveys carried out during the 1960's. Items were selected from those surveys on the basis of the above-mentioned criteria, and submitted to various scale-analyses. Through this procedure, a basis for the final establishment of the domain of attitudes of progressiveness and conservatism in various fields was acquired.

5.2. DIRECT OPERATIONALIZATION: THE ABSTRACT LEVEL [1]

The operationalized model is presented in Table 5.1. Of the 9 sections of statements, 6 have been (partly) operationalized. Progressive counterparts have been added to the conservative poles, which were derived directly from the model (for the rationale of this, see Chapter 2).

Section 2: '*Basic assumptions on the nature of society*' has not been operationalized, due to the abstractness of the elements contained in this section. It was felt that for the general public, no meaningful responses to such items could be expected.

Table 5.1. *Direct operationalization of the model of conservative ideology*

No. Model-no.(a)	Quest. no.(b)	Items on: BASIC ASSUMPTIONS: THE NATURE OF MAN (SECTION 1).
1. 1.1	469	(c)C: Most people are guided by irrational inclinations and impulses
		(d)P: Most people are guided by reason
2. 1.3.	463	P: Man is naturally inclined to help his fellowmen when necessary, even when this is not in his own interest
		C: Man is by nature egoistic
3. 1.3.	464	P: Man is naturally inclined to do what is right
		C: Man is naturally less inclined to do what is right than to do what is evil
4. 1.3.(e) (7.2.3.)	462	C: Most people are only prepared to exert themselves when this results in a higher salary
		P: Most people are prepared to exert themselves when necessary
5. 1.4. (4.1.)	465	P: A better society will lead to a better mankind
		C: Man cannot be changed for the better by changing society
6. 1.4.	466	P: Personality is almost exclusively determined by social environment and education
		C: Personality is mainly determined by inherited abilities
7. 1.5.	468	P: The existing social differences between people are mainly caused by the unequal opportunities they get to develop themselves
		C: The existing social differences between people are mainly caused by differences in inherited abilities
8. 1.6.	467	C: At heart, man is a weak and dependent being
		P: Man is an independent and self-reliant, rational being

Table 5.1. (*continued*)

No. Model-no.(a)	Quest no.(b)	Items on: THE RELATION BETWEEN MAN AND SOCIETY: (1) GENERAL (SECTION 3).
9. 3.2.1.1.	445	C: The customs and traditions of society are of indispensable value to mankind
		P: The customs and traditions of society often restrict people's freedom
10. 3.2.1.2.	446	C: The maintenance of law and order is essential to the sound development of society
		P: It is essential to the sound development of society that all kinds of groups disturb law and order now and again, to demand reform
11. 3.3.	512	C: When a social institution has been in existence over a long period of time, it is probably of value to mankind
		P: When a social institution has existed for a long time, it probably contains ideas that are for the greater part out of date
12. 3.3.1.	511	C: By living according to the customs and traditions of society, man is best able to fully develop himself
		P: Man is best able to fully develop himself when he does not adjust to the customs and traditions of society
13. 3.5. (4.2., 4.2.")	514	C: The organization of society is far too complex to be improved upon by man and his ideas
		P: Society can be improved through ideas
14. 3.5.1.	513	C: The origin of most social abuse like war and poverty mainly lies in human nature
		P: The origin of most social abuse like war and poverty mainly lies in the organization of society
15. 3.6. 3.6.1.	449	C: Each society is too complex a whole for people to have an opinion about it
		P: The structure of each society can be judged by generally accepted norms and principles
		Items on: THE RELATION BETWEEN MAN AND SOCIETY: (2) THE IMPLEMENTATION OF CHANGE (Section 4).
16. 4.3.	454	P: One should be critical of society's development and change its direction when necessary
		C: One had better let society develop naturally than attempt to change its direction
17. 4.3.1.	450	C: Social change should only be introduced when this has proven to be necessary
		P: Society should be changed as much as possible in order to realize certain ideals

Table 5.1. (*continued*)

No. Model-no.(a)	Quest. no.(b)	Items on: THE RELATION BETWEEN MAN AND SOCIETY: (2) THE IMPLEMENTATION OF CHANGE (Section 4).
18. 4.3.2.	447	P: When implementing social change it is not really necessary to set to work gradually and carefully C: When implementing social change, it is imperative to set to work gradually and carefully
19. 4.3.2.1.	448	P: Implementing change in various fields can enhance the smooth development of society C: Society is so complex that bringing about change in various fields would soon cause chaos
20. 4.3.2.3.	453	P: A better society can only be realized through a radical change of the present social structure C: A better society is best realized by introducing gradual reform within present-day society
21. 4.3.6.	452	C: Social change should above all aim at restoring the past heritage, some of which has got lost in modern times P: Social change should above all aim at eradicating antiquated ideas that are still in existence today
22. 4.3.7.	451	C: When implementing social change, one should above all be guided by the lessons of history P: When implementing social change, one should exclusively be guided by the goals set
		Items on: THE RELATION BETWEEN MAN AND SOCIETY: (4) AUTHORITY AND DEMOCRACY (Section 6).
23. 6.1.1. 6.1.2. 6.3.	475	P: The freedom of many people is limited by existing authority C: The existing authority is best suited to the welfare of all
24. 6.1.2. 6.1.2.1.	509	C: It is necessary that a small group of able men exercise authority in order to realize a sound society P: In a sound society, everybody must be able to have a say in matters that directly or indirectly concern him
25. 6.4.1.	474	C: Some countries have not yet developed fully enough to realize democratic principles P: Democratic principles can be directly realized in any country

Table 5.1 (*continued*)

No. Model-no.(a)	Quest. no.(b)	Items on: THE RELATION BETWEEN MAN AND SOCIETY: (4) AUTHORITY AND DEMOCRACY (Section 6).
26. 6.4.2.	510	C: Complete democracy is impossible because people have such varying abilities P: The fact that people have varying abilities does not mean that complete democracy would not be possible
27. 6.4.2.	473	P: Complete democracy can be satisfactorily realized in present-day complex society C: In present-day complex society, complete democracy cannot be realized
		Items on: THE RELATION BETWEEN MAN AND SOCIETY: (5) PRIVATE PROPERTY, SOCIAL CLASSES (Section 7).
28. 7.4.1.	470	P: The existence of social classes is unjust C: The existence of social classes is necessary for the welfare of all
29. 7.4.2.	471	P: The most important social antithesis is still that between the social classes C: In present-day society, social classes no longer form an important social antithesis
30. 7.4.2.	472	C: All social groups can live together in harmony without having to change social relations P: If all social groups were to live in harmony together, the existing social relations would have to be drastically altered
		Items on: THE FUNCTIONS OF GOVERNMENT: (2) THE SOCIO-ECONOMIC SPHERE (Section 9)
31. 9.2.3.	457	C: A great deal of government interference can only lead to bureaucracy and economic stagnation P: A great deal of government interference leads to planning and therefore to a more efficient economy
32. 9.3.2.	460	C: From an economic point of view, the existing social relations are inevitable P: The existing social relations are created by an economic policy, which can be changed
33. 9.3.3.	458	C: Private enterprise is essential to economic growth P: Economic growth can only be realized when the government restricts private enterprise

Table 5.1. (*continued*)

No. Model-no.(a)	Quest. no.(b)	Items on: THE FUNCTIONS OF GOVERNMENT: (2) THE SOCIO–ECONOMIC SPHERE (Section 9)
34. 9.3.3.	459	P: In a society based on private enterprise, insufficient attention is usually paid to the necessary public services
		C: In a society based on private enterprise, the welfare of all is best guaranteed
35. 9.3.3.	456	C: Human needs are generally best satisfied in a capitalist society
		P: In a capitalist society, all sorts of artificial needs are frequently thrust on people
36. 9.3.4.	455	C: If freedom of enterprise is restricted, other freedoms will also disappear
		P: Restricting freedom of enterprise does not endanger the loss of other freedoms
37. 9.4.2.2.	461	C: Government care from the cradle to the grave leads to a slackened way of life
		P: Government care provides many with the feeling of security necessary to develop their potential

Notes:
(a) See the model presented in Chapter 4, par. 4.4.2.
(b) This refers to the Dutch questionnaire; see Appendix 1 for the general outline of this questionnaire
(c) C=conservative pole
(d) P=progressive pole
(e) When a statement refers to more than one model-element, alternatives have sometimes been indicated

Section 5: '*The relation between man and society: a specification for a fundamental social institution: the family*' was also thought to be relatively abstract. Moreover, a number of these model-elements could be dealt with at the attitude level. So, this section has not been operationalized either.

Section 8: '*The general functions of government*' constitute a body of ideas more or less explicitly contained in many other elements, so this section was also not operationalized.

Section 1: '*The nature of man*' has been almost fully covered, the only exception being the statement on the 'complexity of human nature'. About 50% of section 3: '*The relation between man and society: general*' has been covered. In section 4: '*The implementation of change*', about 75% of the model-statements were operationalized. There is much less coverage for sections 6, 7 and 9.

The operationalization of the model has been based on several principles. *First*, a selection has to be made for (obvious) practical reasons.
Second, most sections had to be covered, at least to some extent. *Third*,
those elements had to be selected which could be operationalized in a
form that would not be too far removed from the model-statement, and
that would still be easily understood by the majority of the general
public.

At the time of the actual questionnaire construction, only a first draft
of the model was available. This original version has been revised and
considerably expanded. Therefore, the operationalized model used in the
present study should be regarded as a preliminary approach.

A few points need to be discussed briefly. First there is the question
whether the 2 poles form a 'real' antithesis, i.e. are *logically* opposed to
each other. Strictly speaking, this may not be so in some cases, but the
polar positions seem generally to sufficiently express opposite points of
view. Second, the order of presentation of the items has essentially been
random, though not completely so, as this might have caused too much
confusion: the items have been grouped more or less according to the
model-sections. Third, the order of presentation of the polar positions
has also been random. It can be seen, however, that of the 37 bipolari-
ties, 23 start at the conservative pole.

5.3. INDIRECT OPERATIONALIZATION: THE ATTITUDE LEVEL

5.3.1. Stage 1: item selection by means of secondary analysis

5.3.1.1. Introduction. Needless to say, there are practical limitations to
survey research, both as regards costs and interviewer-respondent relations, which set limits to the length of the questionnaire. When one still
wants a comprehensive approach to a subject, it is most helpful to use
items of so-called '*known scalability*'.

Evidence for the scalability of items can be gathered by *secondary
analysis* or on the basis of evidence from primary research. In setting up
the present study, 5 Dutch surveys were secondarily analyzed in order to
gather evidence on items constituting part of an attitude-scale within the
progressive-conservative domain. In addition, items from 2 other studies
were incorporated on the basis of their proven scalability in primary
analysis. The studies used are presented in Table 5.2. They have all been
made available through the Steinmetz Archives [2].

5.3.1.2. Procedures followed and results. Since the 2 values of *'freedom'*
and *'equality'* were the criteria for item-selection, every selected item
from the 7 studies indicated in Table 5.2. in some way allows respondents
to express their views on these basic values. Response-categories were
dichotomized near the median and in each of the 5 studies that were
secondarily analyzed the items were intercorrelated (tetrachoric coefficients) and factor-analyzed (principal components; the maximum
number of factors extracted was roughly one-third of the number of
items). Rotations were carried out with varying number of factors, both
promax and varimax: all solutions from 2 to the maximum number of
factors were rotated in both ways [3]. Items loading highly on a factor in
any solution were defined as a variable or scale if they were *interpretable*
as such, i.e. if the factor could be *labeled* in terms of some attitude [4].

Table 5.2. *Studies submitted to secondary analysis to select items of 'known
scalability' for the construction of progressive-conservative attitude-
scales*

Steinmetz Archives study-number	Title + subject (translated)	Original investigator(s)	Year of study	Sample size	Universe sampled
1. P0004	Protestantism and progres-siveness	A. Hoogerwerf, Soc. Wet. Inst., Afd. Politico-logie, Vrije Uni-versiteit, Amsterdam	1962	912	Pop. of Delft, aged 21 and over(a)
2. P0014	Aid to developing countries	Netherlands Org. for Intern. Relations, (NOVIB); NV v/h Ned. Sticht. v. Statistiek, Den Haag	1962	2198	Pop. aged 18–70
3. P0008	Marriage and the family	De Geillustreerde Pers BV, A'dam; NOVUM BV, Haarlem; Interact BV, Dongen	1965	1704 (b)	Pop. aged 17–70
4. P0026	Politics in the Netherlands	idem	1966	1790 (b)	Pop. aged 17 and over
5. P0027	Religion in the Netherlands	idem	1966	1142 (bc)	Pop. aged 17 and over

Table 5.2. (*continued*)

Steinmetz Archives study-number	Title + subject (translated)	Original investigator(s)	Year of study	Sample size	Universe sampled
6. P0075	Homo-sexuality(d)	Sticht. Bevorder-ing Soc. Onderz. Minderheden, A'dam; S. Meilof-Oonk; Interact BV, Dongen	1966	1671	Pop. aged 21 and over
7. P0067	Sex in the Netherlands(d)	De Geillustreerde Pers BV, A'dam; NOVUM BV, Haarlem; Interact BV, Dongen	1968	1285	Pop. aged 21–65
8. P0042	The year 2000(e)	Polemologisch Inst. Rijksuniv. Groningen; Inter-act, BV, Dongen	1967	774	Pop. aged 15–40(a)

Notes:
(a) 'Universe' is not the entire population (Delft is considered a typical, medium-sized city)
(b) Weighed by means of card duplication
(c) Only people who consider themselves as church-members
(d) Study not secondarily analyzed; items incorporated on the basis of primary research evidence
(e) No items used in attitude scales *within* the progressive-conservative domain (see below)

In addition, scaling procedures according to Mokken's search-method were carried out (see Mokken, 1970) on the same sets of items in order to test the sets for stronger unidimensionality [5].

A relatively large number of scales, which sometimes overlap, has become available in this way (see Table 5.3.) [6]. From these, sets of scaling items were selected for inclusion in the new questionnaire.

It can be seen in Table 5.3. that a wide range of fields is covered by the many attitude scales, i.e. the fields of politics, marriage and the family, sexuality and religion. So, at this level, our approach is not exclusively *political*, although many attitudes in the non-political fields do have a political relevance. These are considered to be the major fields in which social attitudes can manifest themselves.

Table 5.3. *Labels for attitude-scales in the progressive-conservative domain, obtained through secondary analysis* (a)

Title and subject(b)	Scale label	Number of items	Scale-type(c)
1. Protestantism and progressiveness(e)	1. att. to equality of income, property status, power	5	FM
	2. att. to social change(d)	3	FM
	3. politico-religious conservatism	5	FM
2. Aid to developing countries	4. att. to procedures to be followed and amount of aid to be given	3	F
	5. att. towards the government's task	3	F
3. Marriage and the family	6. family traditionalism	5	F
	7. tolerance regarding daughter's choice of husband	3	F
	8. extramarital sexual permissiveness	3	F
	9. premarital sexual permissiveness	3	F
	10. general sexual libertarianism	4	M
	11. conventionality regarding family life	4	F
	12. authoritarian parent-child relationship	3	F
4. Politics in the Netherlands (e)	13. political freedom of expression (civil liberties)	6	F
	14. idem	3	M
	15. attitude to social welfare laws	6	F
	16. idem	5	M
	17. nationalism, royalism	3	F
5. Religion in the Netherlands (e)	18. orthodoxy (doctrine elements)	12	FM
	19. conformism	5	F
	20. tolerance	3	FM
	21. tough-mindedness	3	F
	22. att. to 'pillarization' (segmentation)	6	FM
	23. general conservatism	18	M
	24. idem(f)	22	M
6. Homosexuality(g)	25. extreme intolerance/aggression towards homosexuals	2	M
7. Sex in the Netherlands (eg)	26. premarital sexual permissiveness	12	M

Notes:

(a) See Appendix 3 for individual items incorporated into the new study. Many other scales were constructed, but finally, no items from these were used. There were also many small Mokken-scales of less than 3 items; with the exception of a scale on 'aggressiveness towards homosexuals' these are not mentioned, either

(b) See Table 5.2. for further details on the studies

(c) F: scale based on factor loadings higher than .40
M: scale is a Mokken-type (1970) scale

(d) Incorporated for special reasons (see next chapter)

(e) From this study, a number of single items have also been used

(f) Almost all items in the scales mentioned load highly on this general 'Religious conservatism' factor which in fact has not been used. This indicates, however, that the intercorrelations between the resulting scales will be relatively high

(g) The study has not been submitted to secondary analysis

5.3.2. Stage 2: Defining sets of items to be tested for scalability

In Appendix 3 it is indicated how, to a large extent on the basis of (scaling) items which have become available by means of secondary analysis, 'sets' of *potentially* scaling items (i.e. scaling in *this* study) have been defined. Some sets have been defined 'directly', i.e. on the basis of the (homogeneous) content of the items, which clearly refer to a concept (i.e. an attitude). Others have been defined on the basis of a factor-analysis over more extensive sub-domains of items (see par. 5.3.3.).

Of course, the new items that have been constructed — and added to the scalable items that have become available by means of secondary analysis — have all been inspired by (a) the 2 criteria of *freedom* and *equality* (they should somehow reflect one of these values), (b) the items already available, and (c) the construct of conservative ideology.

The various sets can now be described as follows (the reader is referred to Appendix 3 for details):

(a) Items most clearly indicating the value of *equality* in the politico-economic field are in sets 1 and 2. The *goals* of egalitarian socio-economic policy are seen in set 1; in set 2, the *role of the government* in realizing those goals is referred to.

From an examination of the model of conservatism, it can be observed that the role of *government* had been clearly defined, and it has been seen in Chapters 3 and 4 that it is mainly in these terms that many researchers and scholars define the progressive-conservative antithesis [7]. The role of the government is further reflected in fairly general terms in set 3, which comprises items on *social welfare laws*. Social welfare laws are one way of realizing a more egalitarian income-distribution, and also greater equality as regards social security.

(b) Items in set 4 refer to 'equality of opportunity'. An attempt to collect a group of items on the *perception* of equality is made, with special reference to working class children's opportunities.

(c) The items in sets 5–7 refer to *specific government policies* for bringing about more egalitarian socio-economic relations through *education, income policy and tax policy*. Set 8 contains items of a directly socialistic nature: *direct* government interference. Here, it is clearly implicit that the aims of such a policy would be egalitarian. Items in set 9 refer to a type of welfare policy which costs money, but which is directed towards a specific group or purpose; there is a *non-economic* dimension to it [8].

(d) Finally, 2 items on *trade-union policy* are included (set 10), since this policy is relevant to the attainment of egalitarian goals. (There is nothing on trade unions in the model, since this concentrates on man, society and the state and does not include details on how government should respond to pressure groups.)

Comments. The sets of items discussed above reflect the domain of specific politico-economic issues as incorporated in the various (politico-economic) liberalism-conservatism scales discussed in Chapter 3. There is no reference to e.g. capitalism, big business, or socialism, as in e.g. the PEC-scale (in Adorno et al., 1950), and in Eysenck's (1954) and Sanai's (1950) scales since such notions belong to, and have actually been covered in, the abstract domain (see Table 5.1.). Issues like 'Negro housing' or 'black welfare' are not covered, either, as they are not relevant to the Dutch setting (see e.g. Nie, 1974; Converse, 1964). Other issues concerning government interference are also dealt with in a different manner (compared to many American studies) because of differences in social setting. The politico-economic domain is now *preconceptualized*, anticipating the actual construction of attitudes within this field. This is considered the proper level of abstraction for assessing the dimensionality of broad domains (see Chapter 2: par. 2.2.2.).

(e) Set 11 refers to democracy or rather *democratization*, in the sense of 'equality of power'. There is a strong emphasis on freedom in this set, in addition to obvious egalitarian implications. The items do *not* refer to liberal-democratic principles, like those used by Prothro and Grigg (1960) and McClosky (1964). Other issues which are frequently conceptualized as belonging to liberal democracy such as 'free speech', 'civil rights' and 'political tolerance' are dealt with elsewhere (see below).

(f) *Political freedom of expression* (set 12) is a set of items, approximating to what is meant in most American studies by 'civil liberties'. There is no reference here to e.g. 'communistic and atheistic teachers in our schools'; differences in setting are further expressed by the inclusion of items on 'conscientious objectors' and 'the right to strike'; these are not often found in American studies. *Political tolerance* is indicated by the small set 15 on the rights of communists and fascists.

(g) *Internationalism* is divided into 2 sets (sets 13 and 14): one on aid to developing countries and the other on internationalism proper, a set which includes items similar to those on the 'American way of life', but which, of course, does not include items such as 'fighting communism abroad' or 'leaving the U.N.'. There are references to European integration and to the royal family.

(i) Further political or semi-political issues on 'tolerance' and 'freedom of expression' are covered by *'law and criminals'* and *'mass-media tolerance'* in sets 16A and 17.

Comments. The above sets (i.e., sets 11–17, with the exception of 'rest-set' 16) refer fairly directly to the value of *freedom* in a *non-economic* sense. Aid to developing countries is a special case as it refers to increasing the freedom of others abroad. It shows how the values of freedom and equality are in fact intimately related. Internationalism, for example, refers to freedom in a specific egalitarian sense: consider other ways of life as being equal in worth and value; tolerate deviant expressions. Criminals are a particular case here. Another minority group is dealt with in set 23: homosexuals.

(j) The value of *freedom* seems to underlie the sets of items on *moral* and *family* issues even more clearly; these sets include *parent-child* and *male-female role issues* (sets 18–22).

Comments. Admittedly, conceptualization is somewhat arbitrary here: certain items in the family traditionalism set also refer to moral libertarianism, and to male-female roles, for example. (Both sets are distinguished statistically: those items *not* referring to moral issues related to family-life proved to form a separate scale; see below.) If, for example, the construct of *feminism* or *women's lib* had been defined, items from the family traditionalism and conventional male-female role sets could have been combined.

Here, the political aspects have become less central and entangled with non-political ones. The moral libertarianism items are still all political, as are some of the family traditionalism set (e.g. those on abortion, divorce, euthanasia). In the sets on parent-child relationships (sets 20–21) there is only one item which is politically relevant — 'young people of 18 should be able to marry without their parents' consent'. Conventional male-female roles, as conceptualized here, does not contain politically relevant issues. There is only one item on attitude to homosexuals (set 23) which is politically relevant: the government's legalizing of the Society for Homosexuals was an issue at the time of the survey [9]. Generally, it seems that the distinction between political and non-political is rather irrelevant to the attitude structure of the individual: there is a complex of attitudes covering both sub-fields. (This is one reason why the present study has not been set up exclusively from the limited point of view of political science. It has been noted earlier (see Mannheim, 1953) that the progressive-conservative antithesis is perhaps for the most part, but not exclusively, political in nature.)

(k) Two final sets of items on *sexual permissiveness* (sets 24 and 25) seem completely non-political. The distinction between pre- and extra-marital permissiveness seems relevant — see, e.g., Reiss (1967, 1971) and Middendorp, et al., (1970, 1974b).

(l) Five sets of items have been distinguished in the *religious* field (sets 26–30). Two of these contain issues which have possible political relevance. *Politico-religious conservatism* refers to items which, from a religious point of view, express scepticism about or the undesirability of social reform. The set of items on *'pillarization'* (also indicated by *'segmentation'* or the Dutch *'verzuiling'*) is typically Dutch. (The role of religion and its strong political relevance in the Netherlands has been briefly outlined in Chapter 4.) Not only political parties have been organized along religious lines in the Netherlands, the impact of religion on society has been much greater since the 'school-struggle': all kinds of organizations have been formed on a religious or neutral basis; some of these are mentioned in set 30: e.g. the *school system, trade unions* and *broadcasting companies*. Matters of *orthodoxy, conformism to church rules* and *religious tolerance* will no doubt have a political *impact* (i.e. on voting behavior), but are not in themselves directly political.

(m) Finally, 3 items on *attitude to social change* have been included for special reasons: in social research, the attitude in favor of or against social change has often been considered adequate in defining conservatism vs. progressiveness (see e.g. Campbell et al., 1960; Lipschits, 1969; see Chapter 3). The view held in the present study is that attitude to change is not essential or decisive in conservatism, as has been repeatedly pointed out by philosophers on the subject. This is reflected in the construct of conservative ideology as defined in the present study and has been discussed in Chapter 4. Some empirical evidence might now be gathered to support this view.

In summary, the domain of progressive-conservative attitudes has been preconceptualized by the definition of sets of items forming potential attitude scales. The preconceptualization of sets of items constituting an attitude scale seems preferable to *second-order* factor-analysis (see e.g. Kerlinger, 1968; Comrey and Newmeyer, 1965). This procedure is in accordance with the programmatic suggestions of Lentz (1938), McNemar (1946) and Eysenck (1947) but has not been realized previously. Thus, according to the 2 criteria of freedom and quality — central values underlying conservative ideology — 30 sets comprising a total of 147 items (including 6 items in a 'miscellaneous' set), have been defined.

5.3.3. Stage 3: attitude scale construction [10]

5.3.3.1. Introduction. As has been mentioned above, some sets of items have been defined directly (these seemed to refer clearly to a specific attitude), others have been defined indirectly, i.e. after factor-analysis over broad sub-domains (here, factor analysis has been used heuristically: with the aim to conceptualize variables which could be defined in terms of a meaningful construct) [11].

Attitude scales have only been constructed for the sample from the population at large (see Appendix 2 for details of this sample as well as the 'sample' from the strategic elite of M.P.'s). In subsequent analysis, it has been assumed that identical scales would exist for the M.P.'s [12].

A brief description of Mokken's search method, which was applied to either directly or indirectly defined sets of items, will now be given (see Mokken, 1970: 182–194).

Basically, in applying this technique, a scale is constructed from a set of items by (a), selection of the 2 items with the highest H-value and (b), adding to these the item from the set with the next highest H-values when it is related to the items which are already in the scale. H is essentially Loevinger's coefficient, but Mokken adds both an *item-scale* H-coefficient and also a *total* H-coefficient for all items in the scale at every stage of its construction. It is clear that the toal H-value drops gradually [13]. The lowest acceptable H-value is set, somewhat arbitrarily, at .30. The method is stochastic in contrast to the deterministic Guttman-procedure (giving Rep-values). Setting Rep = .90 as a scaling criterion for a total set is (a) more arbitrary than H = .30 and (b) unreliable, since Rep may be artificially raised by some distribution of the item-dichotomies. There is, nevertheless, a relation between H and Rep, which will be illustrated later on. Mokken considers that a scale with an H-value of $.30 \leqslant H \leqslant .40$ is 'weak'; when: $40 \leqslant H \leqslant .50$, the scale is *'medium'*; when $.50 \leqslant H$, the scale is *strong*.

(It is clear that the search-method may pose a dilemma: one may have to make a choice between a *long* but *weak* scale and a *short* but *strong* one. Very *homogeneous* sets of items may yield *long-strong* scales. *Heterogeneous* sets, potentially indicating a broad, generalized attitude (or general view of life, like authoritarianism and anomia) may yield one long-weak scale and/or one or more short-strong scales, or even only a few short-weak scales or no acceptable scale(s) at all.)

A well-known limitation of Guttman-type scaling procedures is the fact that response-categories have to be *dichotomized*. It appears to be common practice to count only positive responses (in terms of one polar position of the variable intended to be measured) as high and *all others* (non-response, middle categories and negative response) as low. In the present study, this was considered too rigid and also unwarranted from certain theoretical and methodological points of view.

Methodologically, it was found unacceptable that people who were unable to formulate opinions on many items in a scale, or people to whom the scale-items were mostly not relevant, would be identified with the negative-response group. They ought, in fact, to be near the middle of the scale. The *theoretical* argument is that items have been selected for their (potential) ability to differentiate positions of respondents along progressive-conservative continua in terms of the criteria of freedom and equality. However, there is no rigid distinction between progressive, conservative or even reactionary positions as far as their responses to single items are concerned. The consideration of *continua* at the *attitude* level, rather than *specific positions* on the *item* level is not in line with an approach in which there are rigid distinctions on the item-level between progresive-conservative positions.

The rigidity of traditional Guttman-scaling has been reduced by Mokken's stochastic search method. It may be rendered even more flexible by using *alternative cutting points* in dichotomizing response categories of items in the sets to be submitted to scaling procedures.

The procedures followed in the present study are that: (a) a maximum of 3 different '*constellations*' of cutting points has been used per *set* of potentially scalable items; (b) sometimes less than 3 were used for *statistical* reasons [14]; (c) sometimes one constellation was used for purely *theoretical* reasons [15]; (d) the 'best solution' was chosen as constituting the scale (see above, on dilemmas).

The 3 constellations per set were determined as follows:
1. the traditional way, i.e. only positive responses high
2. half of the *cumulative percentage* of middle categories plus non-response were high; the others (i.e. the middle categories plus non-response of the other items) were low [16].
3. the opposite of 2.

This procedure has been found most valuable: various constellations yielded quite different results so that a choice as to the best solution could always be made.

5.3.3.2. Results. Results are presented in Appendix 3 and are summarized in Tables 5.4. and 5.5.

It can be seen in Table 5.5. that the average Mokken-type scale consists of almost 4 items and tends to be *strong*, although close to *medium* (average H = .51; but without the religious scales it is .48). This average is quite acceptable. About half of the scales are (very) small, however: 5 consist of only 2 items. Most of the small scales are *strong* ones; only 2 are weak. In 2 cases (sets 4 and 25, see Table 5.4.) no Mokken-scale could be constructed [17].

The weakest scale is the 2-item scale on 'Tolerance regarding controversial TV-programs', which may have been caused by the fact that the 2 items are worded in opposite directions (Appendix 3, set 17). The same applies to the weak 3-item scale on 'Tolerance towards criminals'. The medium 2-item scale on 'Tolerance regarding daughter's choice of husband' contains items referring to behavior in certain situations. Here, there is reference to both *race-* and *class-antagonism*; these may in fact be quite different from one another. This scale is conceptualized rather weakly. The other 2-item scales are strong, or even very strong: 'Government interference for equality of income, etc.', 'Political tolerance' and 'Militant trade-union policy'. Almost all 3-item scales are medium or strong, but most of the 4- and 5-item scales are medium or weak: *as soon as the scales become longer, they also tend to become weaker*. The only strong 4-item scale is 'Tolerance towards homosexuals', an attitude to a clearly defined group, which is also highly 'visible' (compare Converse, 1964).

Table 5.4. *Attitude-scales in the progressive-conservative domain*(a)

Set-no.	Scale label	No. of items	Scale characteristics(b)
1.	Attitude to equality of income, property, status	4	H=.49, Rep=.94 I=.48 medium
2.	Government interference in bringing about equality of income, property	2	H=.79, strong
3.	Attitude to social welfare laws	4	H=.47, Rep=93 I=.46 medium
4.	Equality of opportunity (for working class children)(c)	3	
5.	Government aid to education	4	H=.35, Rep=.93 I=.31 weak
6.	Government income policy	3	H=.46, medium
7a.	Tax policy (1): higher incomes	3	H=.59, strong
7b.	Tax policy (2): lower incomes	3	H=.43, medium
8.	Government direct economic interference	3	H=.41, medium

Table 5.4. (*continued*)

Set-no.	Scale label	No. of items	Scale characteristics(b)	
9.	Government (non-directly economic) welfare policy	3	H=.40,	medium
10.	Militant trade-union policy	2	H=.54,	strong
11.	Democratic attitudes	6	H=.44, Rep=.92 I=.49	medium
12.	Freedom of political expression	6	H=.41, Rep=.90 I=.36	medium
13.	Aid to developing countries	3	H=.54,	strong
14.	Internationalism	5	H=.42, Rep=.93 I=.45	medium
15.	Political tolerance	2	H=.94,	strong
16A.	Tolerance towards criminals	3	H=.37,	weak
17.	Tolerance regarding controversial TV-programs	2	H=.33,	weak
18.	Moral libertarianism	4	H=.36, Rep=.91 I=.35	weak
19.	Family traditionalism	8	H=.39, Rep=.92 I=.34	weak
20.	Tolerance regarding daughter's choice of husband	2	H=.40,	medium
21.	Authoritarian parent-child relationship	5	H=.41, Rep=.93 I=.36	medium
22.	Conventional male-female roles	4	H=.38, Rep=.93 I=.33	weak
23.	Tolerance regarding homosexuals	4	H=.72, Rep=.98 I=.70	strong
24.	Premarital sexual permissiveness	6	H=.53, Rep=.92 I=.43	strong
25.	Extramarital sexual permissiveness(d)	2		
26.	Religious orthodoxy	8	H=.68, Rep=.94 I=.62	strong
27.	Politico-religious conservatism	4	H=.38, Rep=.93 I=.39	weak
28.	Conformism to church rules	3	H=.64,	strong
29.	Religious tolerance	3	H=.78,	strong
30.	Attitude to 'pillarization'	7	H=.58, Rep=.94 I=.59	strong
31.	Attitude towards change(e)	3	H=.55,	strong

Notes: (See Appendix 3 for individual items)
(a) In Appendix 3 it has been indicated which items (from 'sets' submitted to scaling-procedures) belong to the scales mentioned. It has also been indicated how the 'missing data' and 'middle categories' have been dealt with
(b) According to Mokken (1970). Rep and I are not computable for scales of less than 4 items; I is Green's index of consistency, of Type S_2 (see Mokken, 1970: 58)
(c) Scale based on correlation (a cluster)
(d) Scale based on correlation (product-moment; r=.32)
(e) This scale has been included for exploratory reasons (see text)

There is, however, a relatively large number of 'long-strong' scales, 2 of which are in the field of religion, where one might expect a more consistent attitude-structure. Another fine long-strong scale is that on 'Premarital sexual permissiveness'. Here, the item-*format* is for the most part 'Guttman-type'. The subject itself is most specific, highly 'visible' and suitable for a 'stepwise' approach: various types of behavior and degrees of 'feeling' towards the partner can easily be distinguished (set 24). In the case of the long-weak scale on 'Family traditionalism', shorter and stronger scales could of course have been used, but here priority was given to the variety in content: it was felt that items on divorce, abortion, the working wife, birth-control, etc., belonged to this subdomain, and therefore that they should be included. Finally, a number of satisfactory long-medium scales have been constructed (e.g. 'Political freedom of expression', 'Democratic attitudes', 'Internationalism', and 'Authoritarian parent-child relationship'), and there are also a number of fine 4-item medium scales (e.g. 'Attitude to social welfare laws', and 'Equality of income, etc.').

Table 5.5. *A survey of characteristics of the progressive-conservative attitude-scales* (Mokken-type)

	No. of items				
	Small scales (N=14)		Medium-size scales (N=7)	Large scales (N=8)	Total no. of scales (N=29)
Strength(a)	2	3	4	5 ≥ 6	
Weak	1	1	4	– 1	7
Medium	1	4	2	2 2	11
Strong	3	4	1	– 3	11
Total No. of scales	5	9	7	2 6	29

Note:
(a) According to Mokken (1970)

Table 5.6. *The effect of including items of 'known scalability' on the results of the scaling-procedures*

	Items of 'known scalability'			New items	Total	Total Non-religious
	Religious	Non-religious	Total			
No. of items in sets	25	40	65	76	141	116
% Non-scalable(a)	0	10	6	21	14	17

Note:
(a) According to Mokken (1970)

As indicated above, there have been various attempts to optimize the number of scaling items per set. This has proved quite successful (see Table 5.6.). Out of a total of 141 items, only 20 could not be incorporated in a scale (i.e. 14%). The total number of items in 31 scales is 121. Of these, 116 form part of a Mokken-scale; 3 are in a cluster on 'Equality of opportunity for working class children' and 2 are in a cluster on 'Extramarital sexual permissiveness' (see Table 5.4.). Excluding the religious attitudes, the total number of non-scaling items remains the same and then constitutes about 17% of the 116 items in the 25 sets. The *non-religious* domain of progressive-conservative attitudes is covered by 26 scales containing a total of 96 items.

As might have been expected (and as aimed at), scaling-results are better for those items included on previous evidence of scalability (i.e. mostly on the basis of secondary analysis). A total of 65 items from other studies have been included (25 in the 5 religious sets). This amounts to 46% of the total number of items. Sixty-one of these (94%) could be included in a scale. Thus, 6% proved unscalable, as against 21% of the 76 'new' items. In the religious sub-domain, all items were from an earlier study and all of them could be rescaled. Thus outside this sub-domain, 10% of the items of known scalability in fact proved to be unscalable.

5.3.4. Discussion and summary

We have seen that for various reasons, the operationalization of the ideal type model of conservative ideology is far from perfect. An investigation will be made to see if this operationalization (by means of the 37 bipolar statements presented in Table 5.1.) has nevertheless been successful. As has been outlined in Chapter 2, a successfully operationalized construct will yield useful yardsticks for subsequent analysis, i.e. its dimensionality should be interpretable and 'clarifying'. The same is true of the attitude scales which have been derived from the model through its underlying values of freedom and equality.

It has been outlined how, from more than 25 progressive-conservative attitude scales obtained through secondary analysis of studies in various fields, items could be incorporated into the new study. It has been seen that items of so-called 'known scalability' rescaled better than originally formulated items.

Most scales in the progressive-conservative attitudinal domain are of the Mokken type. Mokken's (1970) search-method has been applied to preconceptualized sets of items, either defined directly on theoretical grounds, or by preliminary *heuristic* procedures of factor-analysis, used as a 'retrieval-device' to find clusters of items which might be interpretable as a variable.

The application of this method has further been optimalized by the use of various constellations of dichotomies within the sets of items. This explains the success of the scaling-procedures: the 31 scales that have been constructed comprise a total number of 121 items. Only 20 items proved unscalable. Almost half of the items in the various scales were derived from earlier studies; of these, only 4 proved unscalable.

In most cases, it is not too difficult to set up ad hoc rationales as to why certain items did not scale in terms of Mokken's lower-boundary of H = .30 (they often do so in factor- or cluster-analysis, and have often formed a scale in another constellation of dichotomies) [18].

In many cases non-scaling items have a reversed wording. No items have been excluded from a scale in order to increase its strength. The H-value has been the only criterion used. Even weak scales were considered sufficiently unidimensional for our purposes [19].

In Table 5.4. it can be seen that there is a certain correlation of both Rep and I with H, but it can also be seen that Rep may be e.g. .93 for *weak* scales (scales no. 5 and 27) and .92 for a *strong* scale like no. 25. Rep is never below .90, its traditional criterion, but H-values may vary considerably for similar Rep-values. Further technical details will not be given here (see Mokken, 1970: 48ff).

Some final comments must be made on the tax items set (no. 7). Campbell et al. (1960: 205ff) have complained that people in favor of increased government spending are nevertheless in favor of tax reduction rather than higher taxation (which would seem logical). In challenging their interpretation of this finding, it has been argued that it may well be considered ideological if people were in favor of a more equal distribution of 'life chances' through both tax policy and other government activities. *To disentangle people's attitudes on taxation, however, one should distinguish the groups to be taxed* (see Chapter 3).

It might be hypothesized that lower income groups are in favor of tax reduction *for themselves*, but a tax *increase* for middle- and upper-income groups (or only in favor of the latter). (See e.g. Hamilton, 1972: 99.) The upper class might consistently be in favor of tax reduction, or a less 'progressive' taxation, which might even imply, given the same tax level, a tax reduction for the upper-income group and an *increase* in the lower-income groups (or at least a greater reduction for upper- than for lower-income groups) [20].

The present study shows that the attitude to taxation is indeed not a simple one. Seven questions have been asked on various kinds of taxation; these formed a structure (again, a best solution) of 2 (related) dimensions, to the extent that 2 4-item scales, with one common item (taxation of middle-incomes!) could be constructed. One scale measures an attitude towards a tax increase (vs. decrease or maintenance of status quo) which is relevant in particular to middle- and upper-income groups (i.e. including items on taxations such as surtax and death-duties). The other scale measures an attitude towards a tax decrease (vs. increase or maintenance of status quo) which is particularly relevant to middle- and lower-income groups (i.e. including items on indirect taxes).

There seems to be a widespread tendency in the population at large to be either in favor of or opposed to a tax policy aiming at greater equality of the income distribution. However, 2 attitudes can be distinguished: one focuses on increasing or decreasing taxation on *upper*-income groups, the other focuses on decreasing or increasing taxation on *lower*-income groups [21]. Both attitudes refer to leveling; the difference between them is that the former type of leveling (i.e. increasing taxation on upper-income groups) implies the possibility for more government spending for social welfare, whereas the other type of leveling implies less such government spending. Therefore, we may consider the former attitude to be the more left-wing (see the analysis in the next chapter).

In summary, we have operationalized the theoretical construct of conservative ideology in 2 ways: (a) by way of a set of 37 bipolar items which are directly related to the ideal type model-elements (Table 5.1.), and (b) by way of a set of 31 attitude scales, mostly of the Mokken-type, comprising a total of 121 items. Five scales belong to the religious field, and are only relevant for people considering themselves to belong to a church or religious community; these will not be involved in the general analysis, to be presented in the next chapter, regarding the dimensionality of the attitudinal domain. Thus, the *general* attitudinal domain consists of 26 scales comprising 96 items.

The empirical assessment of the 2 operationalizations of the progressive-conservative antitheses (one has been considered 'abstract', the other 'concrete' or 'specific') will be carried out (a) in the Dutch population at large, (b) in some 'strategic subgroups', and (c) in the strategic elite of M.P.'s. (Note that the attitude scales have only been constructed for the population at large; the elite has been assigned scores on these 'mass' attitudes.)

No hypotheses as to the structures to found in the mass, the semi-elites and the elite have been formulated, but some suggestions have been made in the previous discussions:

1. to the extent that the progressive-conservative antithesis is an elite phenomenon, we can only expect a unidimensional antithesis in the

elite. In this case, the general question is: what is the meaning of the antithesis at the mass level? More specifically: will the antithesis be somehow reflected in the mass, or will there be no meaningful structure of ideological controversy at the mass level at all?

2. if we find a *multi*dimensional structure in the general population, we expect this structure to be interpretable;

3. we expect that a multidimensional structure will somehow *reflect* the underlying values which have been identified for conservative ideology, and which have been used in selecting and constructing the sets of items which have been submitted to scaling procedures to obtain progressive-conservative attitudes;

4. given the evidence in the literature that people tend to react differently, even inconsistently, to abstract vs. concrete items (e.g. abstract principles vs. concrete applications), we expect certain differences between the structure(s) of both operationalizations.

NOTES ON CHAPTER 5

1. The questionnaire has been tested in a small pilot study on 50 respondents in Amsterdam, stratified as to age, sex and social class (which was estimated on the basis of neighborhood characteristics). This resulted in a large number of modifications of original formulations of items, as well as in elimination and addition of (new) items.

2. All studies in Table 5.2. are available from the Steinmetz Archives, (Steinmetzarchief), Social Science Information and Documentation Center, Royal Netherlands Academy of Arts and Sciences, Amsterdam (see also Chapter 3: 3.4.). Actually, the secondary analyses were carried out in 1969 when the predecessor of the Steinmetz Archives, the Steinmetz Stichting (Steinmetz Institute), was still in existence. I would like to thank Dr. Harm 't Hart and Mr. Ho Yam Yok for their assistance in making these studies available.

3. All secondary analyses were carried out by Peter Haringhuizen at the Mathematical Center (Mathematisch Centrum), Amsterdam.

4. Of course, a check was made to see if such items were in fact highly correlating. As is well known, the latter need not always be the case. Factor analysis was thus used in a 'heuristic' manner, i.e. to detect *meaningful clusters* of items.

5. It could be expected that for practical reasons not all items identified as constituting a scale by factor-analysis could be incorporated into the new questionnaire. Further selection would have to take place, for which it was thought advantageous to have *statistical* criteria. However, Mokken-scaling was not applied in an optimum manner here; all items were 'rigidly' dichotomized as much as possible near the median. Consequently, results have almost never been a decisive criterion for item selection.

6. For reasons of space, the scales are not presented in full. In Appendix 3, however, the sets of items used (i.e. submitted to scale analysis) have been

indicated. Which items could be incorporated into a new scale has also been indicated. From the scale labels in Table 5.3. and the names of the item sets in Appendix 3, it is not too difficult to see which items belong to which scale in Table 5.3.

7. See Chapter 3 par. 3.4.2. for arguments against Hoogerwerf's (1964) definition of progressiveness solely in terms of goals.

8. This set is not particularly homogeneous. The items on housing and sex instruction seem doubtful.

9. This is one of the few 'issue-of-the-day' items that have been included. In most instances, this has been avoided. Other 'issues of the day' are: 'Is the occupation of buildings allowed (e.g. schools, universities) in order to enforce justified demands?'; 'Should a mayor be elected?' (rather than appointed by the government, as is the case at present); 'The students' right to a say in the management of the university' and other 'democratic' issues; 'Should pornography be free like in Denmark?' and some issues on economic policy, like 'The raising of the minimum income' and 'The control of mergers'.

10. All analyses were carried out at the Mathematisch Centrum, Amsterdam, by Hans van Vliet.

11. The procedures that have been followed here are similar to those followed in secondary analyses: sub-domains were factor-analyzed, applying varimax rotations (no promax rotations this time because the solutions were always found to be highly similar) to a varying number of factors (i.e. from 2 to n — n being roughly one-third of the number of items involved). A large number of overlapping sets of items have been defined. Here, in Appendix 3 and Table 5.4., only those that yielded the best results are presented.

12. This has been done for the sake of comparability and to simplify the analysis somewhat. Later we will see that it is unlikely that in the case that a scale exists for the population at large, it will *not* exist for a group like M.P.'s, though occasionally items might prove unscalable for the latter group.

13 It is clear that the search-method is much more flexible than the rigid testing of the scalability of a fixed set of items. The order in which items are included in the scale indicates, for example, their centrality vs. their peripheral nature. Processes of *innovation* may be assessed at one point in time; a *continuum* of behavior-types involving certain sections of the population or group may exist (see the discussion on Dutch farming-studies: Chapter 3).

14. Less than 3 alternative constellations were possible if a number of items in a set could only be dichotomized in one way for reasons of discrimination. It was generally felt that at least 10% of the cases would have to fall into one response category. This principle has been erroneously violated in 3 instances (see Appendix 3).

15. Sets scaled for theoretical reasons on the basis of the traditional cutting points only are: Appendix 3, set 15 ('Political tolerance') and set 26 ('Religious orthodoxy'). In set 1, items 3 and 4, the response 'decrease' has been considered as the only progressive one. In some cases, a choice as to the best solution was (partly) made on such theoretical grounds, i.e. sets 3, 11 and 13 (see text on dilemma's).

16. (2) means that if in a set of items the sum of the percentage 'middle score plus non-response' equals x%, then scores are counted 'high' for those items which yield a sum-score which comes nearest to $x/2$. The third constellation

is then the logical opposite of this one. In using these 2 alternative constellations in addition to the traditional one, we sometimes not only obtain better scales, with the consistent 'middle-of-the road' scores and/or the consistent non-response nearer to the scale-middle, we also avoid 'spurious' scales which can come about by such consistent non-response. We obtain all this by recognizing the essential trichotomy of response to (survey) questions (see Galtung, 1967: 94).

17. In case of 'equality of opportunity' in the sense of 'awareness of the situation of working-class children', a Mokken-scale could be constructed, but this has been rejected for reasons of 'inconsistent' item-content.

18. There are, of course, 2^n 'constellations' of dichotomies per set (n = number of items in the set) and at times even more if one or more items have more than 2 acceptable cutting points.

19. Still, as mentioned previously, in most cases the *stronger* scale was preferred to the *weaker*, even if the items in the former were dichotomized in the classical manner, so that 'consistent non-response' would score extremely low.

20. Compare Barry Goldwater's view that '. . . progressive taxation is repugnant to my notions of justice' (see Spitz, 1964: 132).

21. The relationship between the scales will be assessed in the next chapter. The 'middle-income' item has been left out of both scales. The pattern is consistent to the extent that this item was *weakest in both scales*, i.e. when constructing the scales according to Mokken's search-method this item was added as the last one to the other 3.

CHAPTER 6

Type-1 Analysis: Dimensions of Ideological Controversy in the Progressive-conservative Domain

6.1. INTRODUCTION

The Type-1 analytical scheme was developed in Chapter 2, par. 2.2.2.3. We have now assembled the necessary tools to carry out this analysis. The theoretical construct of conservative ideology has been operationalized in 2 ways, i.e. by way of a direct translation of the elements of the construct and by way of attitude scales which could be derived from it.

The attitude scales have been constructed on the basis of the national cross-sectional sample which was drawn from the general Dutch population. Elite data were obtained from M.P.'s in the Second Chamber of Parliament (see Appendix 2). The elite was assigned scores on the mass attitude-scales.

We will start with an investigation of the dimensionality of the abstract domain in the population at large. In anticipation of the empirical assessment in the elite, the structure of this domain will be investigated in some strategic subgroups (this is in fact an extension of the basic Type-1 design).

The second round of Type-1 analysis will start with the empirical assessment of the structure of the progressive-conservative attitude scales in the general population. The next stage of the analysis to be presented below will again be an extension of the Type-1 design: the abstract dimensions that have been found in the general population will be brought into the attitudinal domain in an attempt at mutual validation of the abstract and attitudinal mass-dimensions. This integration will yield the fundamental dimensions of *ideological* controversy, encompassing both abstract, philosophical notions and their specific applications at the attitude level. We will then proceed by testing this ideological domain in some strategic subgroups before we assess its dimensionality in the strategic elite.

The technique that will be applied in Jöreskog's (1966) factor-analysis; various numbers of factors will again be rotated orthogonally (according to the varimax criterium) in search of the best theoretical solution [1].

6.2. DIMENSIONS AT THE ABSTRACT (PHILOSOPHICAL) LEVEL

6.2.1. The general population

Results are presented in Tables 6.1. and 6.1a. In Table 6.1., both un-rotated and rotated 4-factor-solutions are presented. Table 6.1a. shows the alternative rotated 2-, 3- and 5-factor solutions. *The rotated 4-factor solution is taken as best-interpretable* (the 4 factors explain 23.2% of the total variance). The rationale behind this choice is the following:

(a) There is one major factor and 3 minor ones in the unrotated solution. (The Eigenvalues of the matrix S^* are 6.7, 3.5, 2.7 and 2.5; the fifth factor has an Eigenvalue of 1.84, the sixth, 1.76; so there is a slight indication of a 'natural break' after the fourth factor.) Although items from 5 of the 6 areas covered by the operationalized model load highly on the first factor it was decided *not* to accept this un-rotated solution as the best one. The variance explained, relative to the other factors, seems too low: too few items (less than half) are loading highly on it and it seems that for one, the second factor cannot be disregarded. Moreover, examination of the correlation matrix proves that not all variables which load highly on the first factor intercorrelate sufficiently. The structure seems rather weak and too complicated to be explained by one factor. Therefore, an attempt to interpret the structure by rotation of factors was made [2].

(b) At first 2 factors were rotated, explaining 16.3% of the variance. The solution in Table 6.1a. shows that here the major *un*rotated factor is somewhat modified, and that the second *un*rotated factor has become stronger in this particular rotation. Variables loading doubly on the first and second unrotated factors have turned to the second one only, but the first unrotated factor is 'enriched' by 2 items on 'government interference'.

(c) The 3-factor rotated solutions is very similar to the 2-factor one; only 2 items on the 'nature of man' appear separately on the third factor.

(d) The 4-factor solution is quite different in that a new factor breaks off from the major one: 4 items on *government interference* load highly on it, 3 of which previously loaded highly on the main factor. The 5-

factor solution is less interesting, since the first 4 factors remain intact, but a fifth one is added, which introduces a double loading and takes away one variable from the second factor. It is not easily interpretable, either.

The major reason for regarding the 4-factor solution as the best was that in this solution, the 4-variable factor on government interference appeared. (This break-off proved to be stable in subsequent 5- and 6-factor solutions, and seems well justified on the basis of the correlation matrix.)

The interpretation of the 4-factor solution may now be as follows (see Table 6.1.):

1. The *first* major factor may be called *'general conservatism'* or *'classical conservatism'* (see the discussion in Chapter 4). On this first and major factor, items from all sections load sufficiently high. *General notions on the relationship between man and society* (section 3) is almost fully covered, i.e. the value of (traditional) society to mankind and to human nature. Traditions and customs are indispensable, long-established institutions are invaluable and law and order are essential. Consequently one should live according to traditions and not try to improve society (society's faults are due to the imperfections in human nature). In the next section on *social change* it is stated on the conservative side that one should only change 'when necessary'. There are some items pointing to the inherent *reactionary* tendencies of this body of thought: i.e. change should aim at restoring the past; in introducing change, one should be guided by history; in addition, (these items are at least partly reactionary by implication) a small group of able men should exercise authority, and complete democracy is impossible. Finally, there are items on harmony in society, accepting social inequality (as item 32 implies) and the economic system of capitalism (item 35), which is interesting in the light of the third factor.

2. The *second* factor may be called *'socialism'* with an emphasis on the inequality of opportunity, the necessity of radical change, the fact that the existing relations of authority are not legitimate, that social classes and the system of private enterprise (which tends to neglect necessary public utilities) are unjust.

3. The *third* factor may be called *'classical liberalism'*; its emphasis is on the necessity of private enterprise and non-acceptance of government interference (which would lead to stifling bureaucracy, would endanger fundamental freedoms by setting limits to private enterprise or would easily make people slack and lacking in incentive by granting too much social security).

4. The *fourth* factor is a minor one, with just 3 variables on the *nature of man* which load highly. This factor may be interpreted as not being at all 'ideological'. It seems to indicate 'trust in people', and refers to a belief in man's basic goodness or evilness.

Table 6.1.   *The dimensionality of the abstract domain in the general population; the 4-factor unrotated and rotated solutions*(a)

Item labels			Unrotated				Rotated		
			1	2	3	4	cons	soc	lib(b)
1. 1.1	469	Most people are irrational							
2. 1.3	463	Man is naturally inclined to help				.51			.52
3. 1.3	464	Man is naturally good				.53			.58
4. 1.3	462	Man only strives for a higher salary						.36	
5. 1.4	465	Better mankind through better society		.36					.36
6. 1.4	466	Personality determined by social environment							
7. 1.5	468	Differences due to inequality of opportunity		.37				.47	
8. 1.6	467	Man is a weak and dependent being							
9. 3.21.1	445	Traditions and customs necessary to mankind	.50				.39		
10. 3.21.2	446	Law and order essential to society	.53				.40		
11. 3.3	512	Long-established institutions invaluable to mankind	.42				.41		
12. 3.31	511	Full development by living according to traditions	.47				.37		
13. 3.5	514	Society too complex to be improved	.38		.–36		.54		
14. 3.51	513	Origin of social abuses in human nature	.43				.39		
15. 3.6	449	Any society is too complex to be assessed by outsiders							
16. 4.3	454	Critical of the natural development of soc.		.36					
17. 4.31	450	Social change only when necessary	.43				.51		
18. 4.32	447	Social change not gradually-carefully						.37	
19. 4.32.1	448	Change can help towards smooth development							
20. 4.32.3	453	Better society only through radical change			.37			.48	
21. 4.36	452	Change should aim at restoring the past	.47				.53		
22. 4.37	451	Implementation of change: guided by history	.37				.43		

Table 6.1. (*continued*)

Item labels			Unrotated				Rotated		
			1	2	3	4	cons	soc	lib(b)
23. 6.11	475	Authority limits freedom	.35	.42			.53		
24. 6.12	509	Authority in the form of a small group of able men	.49				.47		
25. 6.41	474	Some countries not ready for democracy							
26. 6.42	510	Full democracy impossible due to varying capacities	.39				.45		
27. 6.42	473	Full democracy can be realized in a complex society							
28. 7.41	470	Existence of social classes unjust	.45	.39				.54	
29. 7.42	471	Social classes most important antithesis		.35				.40	
30. 7.42	472	All groups can live together in harmony	.55				.44		
31. 9.24	457	Government interference leads to bureaucracy							.49
32. 9.32	460	Social relations inevitable economically	.48				.46		
33. 9.33	458	Private enterprise essential for economical growth			.39				.55
34. 9.33	459	Private enterprise: no attention given to public utilities						.40	
35. 9.33	456	Capitalist society best fulfils human needs	.47				.37		
36. 9.34	455	Restricted freedom of enterprise: other freedoms lost	.41						.43
37. 9.43	461	Too much care on the part of the government will lead to a slackened way of life							.41
		Variance explained					23.2%		

Notes:
(a) Only loadings $\geq$ .35 are given. Sample size: N=1937. All scores have been recoded to run from progressive to conservative. The second number indicates the corresponding model-element. The third number indicates the question-number in the questionnaire. Questions are indicated by a label referring to their left-hand pole (see the model in Chapter 4: par. 4.4.2. amd Table 5.1.)
(b) cons=conservatism factor; soc=socialism; lib=liberalism
Note on sections (see Chapter 4):
Items 1– 8: basic assumptions: the nature of man
         9–15: the relation between man and society: general
     16–22: idem: the implementation of change
     23–27: idem: authority and democracy
     28–30: idem: private property, social classes
     31–37: the functions of government: the socio-economic sphere

6.2.1.1. Discussion. In the Dutch population, there is no evidence of the existence of one progressive-conservative antithesis on an abstract level. But there is also no evidence of no structure at all existing. Rather, 3 relatively independent dimensions can be observed. It seems possible to interpret these dimensions in terms of the basic triangle of the Western European ideologies: conservatism, socialism and (classical) liberalism (see Chapter 4).

Table 6.1a. *The dimensionality of the abstract domain in the general population; the 2-, 3-, and 5-factor rotated solutions* (a)

Item labels	2 fact's	3 factors	5 factors	
1. Most people are irrational				
2. Man is naturally inclined to help		.53	.55	
3. Man is naturally good		.55	.60	
4. Man only strives for higher salary				
5. Better mankind through better society	.39	.36	.39	
6. Personality determined by social environment				
7. Differences due to inequality of opportunity	.45	.46	.49	
8. Man is a weak and dependent being				
9. Traditions and customs necessary to mankind	.48	.42	.40	
10. Law and order essential to society	.51	.46	.42	-.36
11. Long-established institutions invaluable to mankind	.43	.40	.42	
12. Full development by living according to traditions	.45	.38	.38	
13. Society too complex to be improved	.41	.42	.53	
14. Origin of social abuses in human nature	.41	.41	.39	
15. Any society is too complex to be assessed by outsiders				
16. Critical of the natural development of society	.39	.39		
17. Social change only when necessary	.42	.40	.51	
18. Social change not gradually-carefully		.35		
19. Change can help towards smooth development				
20. Better society only through radical change	.35	.36		-.44
21. Change should aim at restoring the past	.48	.46	.53	
22. Implementation of change: guided by history	.39	.39	.43	
23. Authority limits freedom	.51	.54	.51	
24. Authority in the form of a small group of able men	.48	.47	.47	
25. Some countries not ready for democracy				-.37
26. Full democracy impossible due to varying capacities	.40	.41	.45	
27. Full democracy can be realized in a complex society				

Table 6.1a. (*continued*)

Item labels	2 fact's	3 factors	5 factors		
28. Existence of social classes unjust	.52	.55	.54		
29. Social classes most important antithesis	.42	.44	.45		
30. All groups can live together in harmony	.53	.48	.44		
31. Government interference leads to bureaucracy				.55	
32. Social rel. inevitable economically	.48	.48	.46		
33. Private enterprise essential for economical growth	.40	.43		.58	
34. Private enterprise: no attention given to public utilities		.36	.42		
35. Capitalist society best fulfils human needs	.45	.41	.36		
36. Restricted freedom of enterprise: other freedoms lost	.45	.47		.41	
37. Too much care on the part of the government will lead to a slackened way of life	.35	.40		.49	
Variance explained	16.3%	19.9%	25.3%		

Note:
(a) For notes see Table 6.1. See also Table 6.1. for references to model-elements and question-numbers

The structure seems triangular or even 'pyramidal' rather than uni-dimensional. As will become clear from the measurements of the 3 dimensions, liberalism and socialism are virtually *independent* of each other (rather than being opposed, as might have been expected) and conservatism has a moderately positive relation to liberalism and only a weakly negative relation to socialism.

There seems to be a certain parallel between the way in which ideological controversy has 'unfolded' historically in Western Europe (as sketched in Chapter 4) and the way in which the factor structure 'unfolds' from the data. We begin with one weak, general factor which incorporates *some* liberal and *some* anti-socialist elements. This may be interpreted as corresponding to early 19th century conservatism.

The 2- and 3-factor rotated solutions reflect the *independent* socialism-factor which, from a historical point of view, should have been *opposed* to the combined conservative-liberal factor, since this latter factor reflects the opposition to Marxism: it indicates *post-Marxist* conservatism, which incorporated classical liberal ideas.

Finally, the 4-factor rotated solution shows the emergence of a relatively independent classical liberalism factor, which may find its historical parallel in late 19th century ideological constellations in Europe (at least in some countries, like the Netherlands) where conservatism became somewhat independent of classical liberal ideas whereas, together with classical liberalism, it remained opposed to Marxism and socialism generally.

In short, the empirical structures that emerge from the data seem to satisfactorily reflect the historical development of conservatism which, stimulated by its response to Marxism gradually accepts liberal ideas but then becomes somewhat independent of such ideas [3].

The main phenomenon that needs explanation is why socialism, as an empirical factor, emerges as *independent of* rather than *opposed to* both conservatism and liberalism. This means that many people accept both socialist and liberal ideas, and combine socialist and conservative ideas as well.

The fact that in the population as a whole, the 3 classical Western European ideological positions appear as relatively independent dimensions rather than as one bipolar ideological antithesis can be explained by a generalization of Kerlinger's (1967, 1972) theory of the 'criteriality of attitudinal referents' (see Chapter 3, par. 3.3.5.2.) as follows: *Whatever their format (from single 'referents' to complex bipolar statements), abstract stimuli evoke responses in the general public in terms of the prevailing ideological 'superstructure' of a country which has evolved in the course of its history.* In *America*, liberalism and conservatism are the prevailing, historically evolved ideological positions, with liberalism close to (moderate) socialist positions (from a European point of view) and conservatism close to classical liberal positions (see Chapter 4). In Western Europe, however, there are at least 3 classical ideological positions which are still relevant today: conservatism, classical liberalism and socialism: hence we find a *'trinity'* rather than a duality of ideological controversy. Although the ideal type model of conservative ideology embraces both liberal and anti-socialist elements, even in its present (limited) operationalized form, these ideological opponents to conservatism are singled out as separate factors due to the *differential criteriality* of such ideological positions to most people, even if such positions and their opposites are presented together in bipolar format.

There are 2 methodological complications. One reflects the above rationale: the construction of the anti-conservative and anti-liberal 'poles' was often found to be a little 'uneasy' or artificial. The cases in which it was *not* found artificial are among the items which load on the socialism-factor. Thus, there is some intuitive evidence on the 'naturalness' of the 3 ideological 'foci'. However, in Table 6.1. it can be observed that the construction of bipolar items has possibly not ruled out *response-set* effects: all conservative items have the conservative item-pole presented first, all socialism items the socialist pole, and all liberalism items the liberal pole. Although the placing of the poles to the left or right has been arbitrary, the fact that no formal random procedure has been applied could have resulted in the most 'natural' referents being put first without the researcher being aware of it. Anyway, evidence on the *validity* of the 3 dimensions is badly needed in the light of this methodological issue.

Another matter is the relationship of the 3 ideological dimensions to the 2 basic values that have been derived from the model. *It seems that the 3-factor structure can be interpreted in terms of these 2 values. The conservatism factor seems to incorporate the tendencies against freedom as well as those against equality* (or at least tendencies against an increasing 'realization' of these values). The items on the value of traditions, customs, old institutions, etc. all imply conformism (i.e. lack of *freedom*); the items on authority and democracy imply both lack of freedom and inequality, and the items on 'harmony', socio-economic relations and capitalism imply inequality.

The socialism-factor seems to imply an orientation in favor of increasing both freedom and *equality* (i.e. the items on authority, social classes, public utilities).

Thus in terms of *basic values*, there appears to be a *consistent opposition* between conservatism and socialism. However, the items appear on separate factors as relatively independent of each other. This is another way in which this seemingly inconsistent pattern may be interpreted: *many people may not have integrated their views on basic values, as these have in fact been integrated in the ideological controversy between conservatism and socialism.* Many people may be in favor of freedom but not equality, for example. Thus, they tend to respond negatively to what they see as egalitarian in socialism and positively to what they perceive as *in*egalitarian in conservatism. But they are not in favor of freedom; therefore they tend to respond negatively to socialism and positively to conservatism. Consequently, both dimensions become relatively independent. This (hypothesized) phenomenon may also be described by yet another generalization of Kerlinger's (1967) theory, i.e. in terms of *'differential criteriality of values'* [4].

In the *liberalism-dimension*, a field is referred to in which the values of freedom and equality stand in special relationship to each other: that of socio-economic freedom of enterprise vs. government interference. Here, and this may be difficult for many people to grasp, freedom of enterprise (especially big business) should be limited by government interference in order to guarantee (more) equality in the socio-economic sense (see e.g. Levinson's remarks, 1950: 156; and Rawls, 1972; see the discussion in Chapter 3 on e.g. McClosky, 1964; Free and Cantril, 1967). In terms of adherence to values, this unique relationship of the 2 values underlying the classical liberalism dimension might (partly) explain its relative independence: *in socialism and conservatism (as assessed above) the values of freedom and equality are in harmony with each other; in liberalism they are opposed to each other in the sense that freedom (for some) should be limited in order to bring about greater equality (for many).*

In conclusion, it seems that the factorial structure may be interpreted to some degree in terms of peoples' views on underlying values and their somewhat differential application to certain fields.

There are, then, 3 alternative interpretations of this structure — one in terms of *response set*; another in terms of *criterial referents*, a third in terms of *underlying value-positions*. It seems unlikely that response set plays an essential role, though it may have had some effect. The latter 2 interpretations do not exclude each other: they can be integrated in the notion of *the criteriality of values.*

All interpretations would predict that in more sophisticated subgroups of the population, and especially in (strategic) elites, there would be a strong tendency towards unidimensionality: elites are *less* sensitive to response-set, have *more* criterial referents (see Kerlinger, 1967) and may be expected to adhere more *consistently* to the underlying values which have been integrated into ideologies as they have appeared in the course of history, and which have mainly been *upheld* by political elites.

Before turning to evidence in favor of this position, which exposes some interesting incongruencies between ideological postures of (semi-) elites vs. those of the 'masses', let us first briefly return to the data in Table 6.1. and consider some of its implications.

(a) The 'theory' suggested by the operationalized model is largely confirmed: more than 75% of the items (29 out of 37) load highly on one of 4 factors, 3 of which have been interpreted above in what might be described as a meaningful way. The fourth is a minor factor on 'human nature'.

Although optimistic ideas on human nature have been a part of progressive thought from the Enlightenment until Marxism there has been a movement *away* from such optimism during the late 19th and 20th centuries. As is well known, both liberalism and socialism have gradually incorporated more pessimistic ideas on human rationality and goodness. The experience of fascism and the Second World War have probably raised further doubts in this area [5]. There is no evidence that a more or less consistent pattern of ideas on 'human nature' exists today, and certainly there is not much evidence of 'human nature conservatism' (see Anderson et al., 1965: 191-192). Ideas on 'human nature' are rather isolated within the broader ideological structure.

Some ideas on human nature (and this happens in a consistent manner) are, however, still integrated with ideological positions. Conservatism includes an item on 'the ability to improve society on the basis of men's ideas' (which is rejected) and one on 'the origin of abuse in society lies in human nature' (this is accepted). A statement like 'complete democracy is impossible because people have such varying abilities' is also accepted, and therefore the idea of human inequality and the implications of this in the power-structure. Conservatism still implies a belief in the limited power of rational ideas and in human 'badness', but items which try to *directly* tap such attitudes are unrelated to it (see Table 6.1., items 1–3). Socialism accepts that 'inequality of opportunity' is most important in creating differences in social status (i.e. socially relevant differences) but a straightforward environmentalist position is no longer upheld, nor is the ethical implication of such a position (see Table 6.1., items 5 and 6). Finally, liberalism incorporates a consistent item on 'the necessity of incentives of a materialistic nature' (see Table 6.1., item 4).

(b) A systematic discussion of the non-loading items will not be gone into. If one turns from Table 6.1. to Table 5.1., it can be seen that the 8 items all have some weakness in wording or are somewhat irrelevent (see Table 5.1., items 1, 6, 8, 15, 16, 19, 25, 27). In secondary analysis or in replication these items might be left out, or their wording changed. It does not seem necessary to alter the theoretical model to any great degree because of this.

(c) Our results are at variance with the influential notion of the *lack of ideological structure in the general public* (see e.g. Converse, 1964; Campbell et al., 1960). Admittedly, the structure is weak, but it is there. It has not been formed according to theoretical expectations (then it would have been *uni*dimensional), but it is *multi*dimensional (see Luttbeg, 1968: 409) and although the matter of why positions that should 'theoretically' be opposed to each other in fact tend to appear as relatively independent dimensions, still needs further investigation, the structure could be interpreted in terms of historical developments of ideological constellations in Western Europe; some additional rationales for its interpretation could also be developed. Though less than 25% of the variance is explained, it should also be remembered that compared to other attempts to assess ideological structure, *the items are all of an extremely abstract and rather complicated nature for use with unsophisticated samples.*

It is not easy to evaluate our results in the light of previous research. Most American research based on cross-sectional samples and indicating a lack of ideological structure was carried out in the 1950's and was based on single items of the 'issue' type, which had not been systematically selected from a definition of a construct by means of a model. In addition, the studies were generally very limited in scope.

McClosky's (1958) study is the obvious exception. He does find an ideological structure of items at an *abstract* level, but the procedures through which he arrives at his single scale are unclear (cluster-analysis 'by hand'; personal communication) and, as shown above, the definition of conservatism by means of his quasi-model is not really satisfactory. In addition to this, bearing in mind the author's intention *not* to cover issues on government functions, free enterprise and welfare measures, and seeing the inclusion of notions on democracy, private property and social classes in his quasi-model, one wonders how this has been operationalized. Comparing McClosky's items 3 and 9 (Chapter 3: par. 3.3.1.2.) and 2 items in our conservatism-factor (nos. 11 and 30), a similarity can be seen between this factor and McClosky's scale. The lack of our other 2 (actually 3) dimensions in McClosky's study can perhaps be explained by his operationalization of the quasi-model in combination with the limited analytical techniques available at that time.

My criticism of other studies, e.g. the recent work by Eysenck (1971) and others, need not be mentioned again here.

Two rationales may finally be suggested to explain the abstract dimensions, found in the Dutch population in 1970, as compared to the lack of ideological structure found in the U.S. in the 1950's and early 1960's.

One is *cross-cultural*: it has often been observed that, in comparison to people in Europe, the American public does not 'think' ideologically. Some evidence has been presented that there has been less ideological controversy in the U.S. due to a fairly general acceptance of the business society and liberal ideology. Historically, there has never been a 'romantic' conservative reaction and there has also never been a strong socialist influence (see the discussion, Chapter 4, par. 4.3.6.1.), certainly not at the philosophical level. American political debate has remained pragmatic, centering around issues or 'problems' (see Hartz, 1955; Converse, 1964; Free and Cantril, 1967) [6].

The other explanation is *longitudinal*. Although there seems to be some methodological weakness in his study, Nie (1974) presents evidence of an emerging liberal-conservative antithesis in the U.S. in the mid-1960's, which has been present ever since. Contrary to suggestions made by e.g. Converse (1964), Nie's evidence shows that it was *not* the general improvement in educational level during the 1960's which caused the emergence of ideological controversy. Hence it would *not* be the *intellectual* ability to 'grasp' an abstract ideological dimension which would lead to more consistent views on issues along such a dimension. Rather, Nie's study suggests that the *increasing salience of politics* in the 1960's, reflected in growing political interest, has been the major cause of the increase in attitude-consistency, and hence of the emergence of ideology in the American public.

Before turning to an investigation of the dimensionality of the abstract domain of bipolar items in the elite of M.P.'s, we will first test the 2 'theories' suggested by Converse (1964) and Nie (1974) and also, albeit in a somewhat different terminology, by Kerlinger (1967).

One theory (Converse's) maintains that the abstract dimension of liberalism-conservatism (in the terminology of American authors) is too difficult for the general public to grasp. It suggests that a relatively high level of education is therefore necessary. The theory predicts that *in the highly educated, at least a tendency towards a unidimensional structure will be visible.*

The other theory (Nie's) denies this, and maintains that it is rather the salience of politics, which in most instances can be measured by a scale for *political interest*, which causes the emergence of (again) a unidimensional structure, or at least a tendency in that direction.

However, both theories start from the premise that there is either no ideological structure at all (i.e. in the uneducated and/or the politically apathetic) or a unidimensional structure (i.e. in educated, politically interested groups). Since we have found, in fact, a weak multidimensional structure in the general population, the above theories could also lead to the prediction that in the 2 'semi-elite' groups mentioned above, *this same structure will emerge more clearly* (i.e. the same factors will emerge, but with higher loadings). In case *both* tendencies appear, we can expect a structure which might not be very easily interpretable.

6.2.2. Semi-elites: the highly educated and the politically interested

In the present study, 4 educational levels have been distinguished and political interest has, in this instance, been indicated by political party membership. The overall effects of education and political interest on the structure of the abstract domain can be seen in Table 6.2.

Table 6.2. *Overall effects of educational level and political interest on the structure of ideological controversy at the abstract level*

	Eigenvalues of matrix S* (Jöreskog)				Variance explained (%)		
	1st factor	2nd	3rd	4th	2 factors	3	4
Educational level (a)							
1. Attended university (N=114)	33.7	7.3	6.1	4.8	32.0	36.4	40.0
2. Grammar school (N=331)	12.4	3.9	3.2	2.9	21.9	25.4	28.7
3. Secondary modern school (N=550)	6.2	3.8	3.1	2.6	14.8	18.7	21.9
4. Primary school (N=932)	5.9	4.2	2.8	2.2	15.9	19.7	22.3
Political party membership							
1. (Former) members (N=286)	11.7	4.1	3.2	2.7	20.9	24.5	27.4
2. Non-members (N=1641)	6.3	3.6	2.8	2.4	15.7	19.5	22.7

Note:
(a) Highest type attended. For both variables, see Appendix 6. Total N=1927; see Appendix 2

Table 6.2. shows that *both* tendencies predicted above do indeed manifest themselves, and most strongly so for educational level: (a) there is a tendency towards unidimensionality in the semi-elites; and (b) there is more variance explained in these groups. For the highly educated, for example, the first Eigenvalue of matrix S* is 5 times as strong as compared to the population at large, and the 4 factors explain almost twice as much variance! These effects are much weaker for the party members, whereby Nie's theory is *not* confirmed (this is, of course, not a final test of his theory).

As mentioned above, we may now expect an actual structure in the semi-elites which is not very easily interpretable.

The data are presented in Table 6.3. [7].

The 4-factor solution indicates 2 *conservatism*-factors for the members of a political party: the one original factor appears to have split (with 2 double loadings, i.e. factors 1 and 3 in Table 6.3.). The first factor incorporates almost all *classical liberal* items. The second factor is a somewhat enriched *socialism* factor (appearing already in the 2-factor solution) and the fourth one is on human nature. The 2 conservatism factors are difficult to interpret. The second conservatism factor already appears in the 3-factor solution, with 8 items loading highly, 4 of which have a double loading with the first conservatism-factor. Only in the 5-factor solution do the classical liberalism items tend to load on a separate factor.

Obviously, the structure of the ideological domain is so 'tight' that it becomes more 'difficult' for the separate 'national' dimensions to

Table 6.3. *The dimensionality of the abstract domain in 2 semi-elites: the highly educated and the politically interested; 4-factor rotated solutions* (a)

Item labels	Those who attended university (N=114) (b)			(Former) party members (N=286)		
1. Most people are irrational						
2. Man is naturally inclined to help			.62			.44
3. Man is naturally good			.73			.48
4. Man only strives for higher salary						
5. Better mank. thr. better society		.37	.42	.54		
6. Pers. determ. by soc. environment						
7. Differences due to inequality of opp.	.36	.34		.56		
8. Man is a weak and dependent being			.48			
9. Trad. and customs necessary to mank.	.64			.41		
10. Law and order essential to soc.	.80			.47		
11. Long-establ. inst. invaluable to mankind					.46	
12. Full dev. by living acc. to tradit.	.69			.44		
13. Soc. too complex to be improved		.41			.51	
14. Origin of soc. abuses in hum. nat.	.36	.46		.40	.44	
15. Any soc. is too complex to be assessed by outsiders		.45				
16. Crit. of nat. developm. of society		.51				
17. Soc. change only when necess.	.36	.46				.51
18. Soc. change not gradual/careful	.48			.37		
19. Change can help tow. smooth devel.		.68		.37		
20. Better soc. only thr. radical change	.60			.38	.47	
21. Change sh. aim at restoring the past		.42				.40
22. Implementation of change: guided by history		.38				.39
23. Auth. limits freedom	.72				.47	
24. Auth. in the form of a small group of able men	.55			.43		
25. Some countr. not ready for democr.	.52			.48		
26. Full dem. imposs. due to var. capac.		.39		.43	.38	
27. Full dem. can be real. in a compl. soc.						
28. Existence of soc. classes unjust	.70				.46	
29. Soc. classes most imp. antithesis	.49	.37		.49		
30. All groups can live together in harmony	.74	.38				.46
31. Govern. interf. leads to bureaucracy		.43		.46		
32. Soc. rel. inevitable economically	.43	.47				.36
33. Priv. enterpr. essent. for econ. gr.	.49	.49		.64		
34. Priv. enterp.: no att. given to publ. util.	.56				.39	
35. Capit. soc. best fulfils hum. needs	.62			.42		
36. Rests. freed. of enterpr.: other freed. lost	.44	.52		.56		
37. Too much care on the part of the governm. will lead to a slackened way of life		.63		.53		

Notes:
(a) See notes on Table 6.1. See also Table 6.1. for references to model-elements and questionnaire-positions of items
(b) N is a bit small for factor-analysis

appear. The *unrotated* first factor has 21 items which load highly (over .35), and which cover the conservatism, socialism and liberalism dimensions. Only the items on human nature and some items on procedures and aims of change are excluded.

Judging from these results, one could expect that it would be even more difficult for 'national' dimensions to appear (if at all) for people who have attended university. This is indeed so. For this group, 28 of 37 items load highly on the first unrotated factor. Apart from 5 items on human nature, only 2 items on the implementation of change, one on the complexity of society and one on the possibility of full democracy in a complex society do not load highly. (Note that 3 of these 4 items do not load highly on any factor in the 4-factor rotated solution in the general population either.) The 'human nature' dimension is present in the second rotated as well as in the unrotated solution. In the 3-factor rotated solution, there is already a tendency for a separate liberalism-factor to appear. This factor, though somewhat 'enriched', is still present in the 4-factor solution. The separate 'conservatism' factor that can be seen there may be interpreted as a dimension indicating an attitude in favor of or against the *implementation of social change*. (Note that the only 2 items from the section on the implementation of change which do not load highly refer to *procedures to be followed* in implementing change (radicalism, gradualness) rather than to an attitude *in favor of or against* change — in some sense or direction! With the exception of 2 items on social classes and conflicting groups in society, which have a rather low loading, the other 3 items which load on the factor all refer to change.) Neither in the 4- nor in the 5-factor solution does a separate *socialism* factor appear.

6.2.2.1. Conclusions. There is a much stronger tendency in the highly educated group than in the party-members for a unidimensional structure to appear. With the exception of items on human nature, there is a clear tendency in these semi-elites for the abstract ideological progressive-conservative antithesis to constitute a 'real entity'. This would mean that *the 'reality' of the progressive-conservative antithesis can be understood once people are sufficiently involved politically and/or have an educational background which enables them to organize their ideas in a consistent manner along this highly abstract continuum, either because more referents are 'criterial' to them, or because they are able to integrate their views in terms of both (rather than only one) values that seem to underlie the progressive-conservative antithesis.*

Still, this tendency is only *partial* which is proven by the fact that rotation of 2 to 5 factors still yields meaningful solutions.

Leaving aside the 'human nature' factor, which is particularly clear in the case of the highly educated, a *socialism* factor is clearly apparent in *party members*, and a separate *liberalism* factor in the *highly educated*. In addition, there is a combined liberalism-conservatism and another conservatism factor in party members in the 4-factor solution and a separate liberalism-dimension appears in the 5-factor solution in this group.

For the highly educated group there first appears an integrated liberalism-conservatism-socialism factor and, later, a factor which could be interpreted in *positional* terms: *attitude to change* (in the 4-factor solution). Of course, there are many double loadings here. Rotation of factors seemed hardly justified in the light of the strong unidimensional unrotated solution.

In summary, 2 phenomena are important for our present purposes. *First*, there is indeed a tendency towards unidimensionality which increases our trust in the *reality* of a progressive-conservative antithesis. *Second*, upon 'unfolding' the structure through rotation of 2 to 5 factors, and comparing this to the mass structure, similar though not identical dimensions emerge and in addition, some unique dimensions [8].

It may now be safely predicted that in a *real strategic elite* such as members of parliament, in whom extremely high levels of political involvement and education are combined, a strong unidimensional structure will emerge and no meaningful subdimensions will appear.

6.2.3. The elite: members of parliament

Results are presented in Table 6.4. and clearly confirm expectations. The factor-structure is plainly unidimensional, with only a few items on human nature which do not load highly (as might have been expected) and also 2 other items, which have already been proven 'wrong' in the over-all 'best solution' (see Table 6.1.).

The first Eigenvalue of matrix S* is much higher than that of the highly educated group (84.2 compared to 33.7), and 4 factors now explain more than half the variance (as compared to 40% for the highly educated). The 4-factor rotated solution can be seen as almost meaningless. When 2 factors are rotated, a separate human nature factor becomes more apparent. In the 3-factor rotated solution, a third factor already appears with almost nothing but double loadings on the first factor. This remains the case in the 4-factor rotated solution.

Table 6.4. *The dimensionality of the abstract domain in members of parliament; 4-factor unrotated and rotated solutions* (a)

Item labels	Unrotated				Rotated			
1. Most people are irrational				.60	.58			
2. Man is naturally inclined to help	.38	.63	.39		.79			
3. Man is naturally good		.72			.71	.38		
4. Man only strives for higher salary	.61				.50			
5. Better mankind thr. better soc.	.59				.48	.38		
6. Person. determ. by soc. environm.	.48						.45	
7. Differences due to inequality of opportunity	.77				.43	.67		
8. Man is a weak and dependent being			.35	.40	.55			.36
9. Trad. and customs nec. to mank.	.74				.61	.49		
10. Law and order essent. for soc.	.80				.56	.62		
11. Long-establ. inst. invaluable to mank.	.59				.47			
12. Full devel. by living acc. to trad.	.67				.66			
13. Soc. too complex to be improved	.66				.50			
14. Origin of soc. abuses in human nature	.67				.45	.46		
15. Soc. too complex to be assessed by outsiders		.42			.38			
16. Critical of natur. devel. of soc.		.55			.37	.39		
17. Soc. change only when necessary	.63			.44	.36			.70
18. Soc. change not gradual/careful	.72				.50	.35		
19. Change can help tow. smooth dev.	.64				.41	.46		
20. Better soc. only thr. radical ch.	.63				.63			
21. Change aim at restoring the past	.57				.44	.35		
22. Implem. of change: guided by hist.	.53				.38			
23. Auth. limits freedom	.83				.58	.56		
24. Auth. in form of small gr. of able men	.73				.50	.48		
25. Some countr. not ready for democr.	.54							
26. Full dem. imposs. due to varying capac.								
27. Full dem. real. in complex soc.	.52							
28. Existence of soc. classes unjust	.80				.47	.65		
29. Soc. classes most imp. antithesis	.77				.63	.48		
30. All groups can live together in harmony	.85				.79			
31. Governm. interf. leads to bureaucr.	.76				.74			
32. Soc. rel. inevitable economically	.70				.67			
33. Priv. enterpr. ess. for econ. growth	.82				.80			
34. Priv. enterpr.: no att. given to public util.	.82				.67			.43
35. Capital. soc. best fulfils human needs	.80				.60			.65
36. Rest. freed. of enterpr.: other freed. lost	.84				.72			
37. Too much care on the part of the governm. will lead to a slackened way of life	.84				.80			
Variance explained					53.5%			

Note: (See notes on Table 6.1. and Table 6.1a.)

(a) N=81 (See Appendix 2); N is a bit small for factor-analysis

5.2.4. Conclusions

The progressive-conservative antithesis at an abstract (philosophical) level constitutes a real entity, but for the political elite only. Here, from the perspective of the construct of 'conservatism', a clear antithesis appears between progressive and conservative points of view, including the classical liberal implications of conservatism.

In the first test of the operationalized construct of conservative ideology (in a sample taken from the general population), quite a different picture emerges: here, there are *relatively independent conservative, liberal* and *socialist* dimensions. This means that *the pattern of ideological controversy is much more complicated at the mass level than at the level of political elites.*

At the *mass level*, conservatism need not imply liberalism or anti-socialism and socialism does not necessarily imply anti-liberalism or anti-conservatism. Such ideological positions may vary relatively independently of one another. Returning from this to the *elite level*, we find a clear tendency for all such implications to indeed hold good: there is a clustering of (in terms of mass dimensions) conservative, liberal and anti-socialist positions on one side; socialist, anti-conservative and anti-liberal positions on the other. We will now try to obtain some evidence on the validity of the mass and elite dimensions.

5.3. THE VALIDITY OF THE ABSTRACT DIMENSIONS IN THE GENERAL POPULATION AND IN THE ELITE

5.3.1. Measurements and interrelations: 'false consciousness' [8a]

Since factor-analysis is mainly considered as a heuristic device, measurements have not been based on factor-scores, but on a summation of the raw scores of highly loading items [9]. The items that have been used in constructing the measuring instruments are presented in Appendix 4 [10]. The intercorrelations of the 3 dimensions for the general population, semi-elites and the elite of M.P.'s, are presented in Table 6.5. [11]. Table 6.5. simplifies but at the same time clarifies the various structures of the abstract domain that have been found.

In the population as a whole ('the mass'), conservatism is moderately *positively* related to liberalism and moderately *negatively* related to socialism. The negative relation of the latter 2 variables is only very weak; this constitutes the major *ideological inconsistency* (i.e. false consciousness) at the present level of abstraction.

Table 6.5. *Intercorrelations of the abstract mass dimensions in (a) the genera*
population, (b) some semi-elites and their corresponding non-
elitist groups, (c) the strategic elite of M.P.'s (a)

		Elite (b)		Mass (b)	
		lib	soc	lib	soc (c)
	cons	.82	—.86	.31	—.28
	lib		—.78		—.12
		Semi-elites		Non-elites	
		very high	high (yes)	low (no)	very low
		lib soc	lib soc	lib soc	lib soc
Educational *level*	cons lib	.56 —.77 —.56 (N=114)	.42 —.54 —.46 (N=331)	.27 —.26 —.04 (N=550)	.28 —.11 .08 (N=932)
Social class(d)	cons lib	.36 —.46 —.33 (N=279)	.34 —.42 —.25 (N=379)	.31 —.26 —.04 (N=829)	.30 —.07 .08 (N=440)
Membership of *a political* *party*(e)	cons lib		.47 —.39 —.29 (N=286)	.28 —.25 —.07 (N=1641)	
Political *interest*(f)	cons lib	.45 —.50 —.35 (N=509)			.21 —.13 .05 (N=645)

Notes:
(a) Correlations are product-moment
(b) See Appendix 2
(c) cons=conservative dimension; lib=(classical) liberalism; soc=socialism.
These dimensions have been recoded to 10-point scales with the following
characteristics: conservatism: M=4.14, s=1.61 (scale range from 0-9);
liberalism: M=5.27, s=2.10; socialism: M=4.96, s=1.78. It can already be
seen here that there is a tendency towards liberalism, but also towards
socialism in the general public (see Free and Cantril, 1967: 32)
(d) For the variable of social class: see Appendix 6
(e) See Table 6.2
(f) For the measurement and categorization of political interest: see also
Appendix 6

The enormous increases in consistency in (a) the highly educated, (b)
the upper classes, (c) members of political parties, and (d) the politically
interested, are clearly shown. *Educational level* and *political interest*, in
that order, have the strongest effects; *social class* and *party membership*
have weaker effects (income and occupation seem to moderate the effect
of education in the social class index).

It is even more interesting to see what happens when we go 'down' the
scale from the semi-elite level to the non-elites of (a) the uneducated, (b)

he working class, (c) non-party members, and (d) the politically dis-
nterested. *The relationships that disintegrate most are those between
ocialism vs. liberalism and conservatism, and in particular between
iberalism and socialism.* All semi-elites, especially the highly educated,
ire rather *consistent* in showing a rather strong negative relationship
between liberalism and socialism, but at the lower-middle levels of
ducation and social class, in non-members and the politically apathetic,
his relationship has already vanished.

The relationship between conservatism and socialism also weakens
onsiderably but is maintained at the 'lower-middle' levels of education
ind social class, and in non-members of political parties.

The relationship between conservatism and liberalism weakens a great
deal (except for social class), but maintains itself rather well. (This is in
ine with the historical analysis of the development of both ideologies,
presented in Chapter 4). Obviously, it is the relationship between
iberalism and *socialism* which is most susceptible to the influence of
actors such as educational level and political interest and involvement.
or a substantial majority of the population, there is *no* relationship
between liberalism and socialism, whereas for the well-educated, the
ipper classes and the politically interested there is a substantial
elationship.

The implications of this phenomenon can be described in more detail.
n case one recodes, in a rather arbitrary manner, socialist positions to 3
evels and liberal positions to 4 levels, it can be seen that in those who are
strongly liberal, 34% are also strongly socialist. Among those who are
strongly anti-liberal, only 45% are also socialist, whereas in this category
23% are still also anti-socialist. For those who are strongly liberal, only
32% are anti-socialist. The (relatively) uneducated, the lower classes and
he politically apathetic show even more inconsistency. Although they
were found more than 5 years later, in another country, and by quite
different measurements, the general results are very similar to those of
Free and Cantril (1967: 32). As these authors note, it can be concluded
hat about one quarter of the population shows *false consciousness* in
that it takes inconsistent positions along such (abstract) ideological
continua as liberalism (in Free and Cantril's terms: *ideological* liberalism) and socialism (Free and Cantril term this: *operational* liberalism).
Our data are not yet fully comparable to those of Free and Cantril, however, since the socialism-dimension does not include such *specific* notions
on government policy as their 'operational liberalism', but more comparable data will be presented below.

It is important to note that already at this stage *most false consciousness appears in the lower strata of the population.* At the same time, it

should be noted that since political apathy is related to social class and educational level, it remains to be seen whether this has an independent effect on false consciousness, although such an independent effect does seem plausible.

6.3.2. Validity [12]

Four tests will be carried out on the validity of the various dimensions found in the population at large and in the strategic elite. The 3 mass dimensions will be related to (a), identifying oneself as progressive vs. conservative; (b), identifying oneself as left-wing vs. right-wing and (c), political party preference. Finally, (d) for the elite dimension, the various positions of M.P.'s belonging to the major political parties will be investigated. Results are presented in Table 6.6. They clearly confirm the validity of the dimensions. Self-identification as progressive vs. conservative is most strongly related to *conservatism*, most weakly (but consistently) to *liberalism*. Self-styled left-wing vs. right-wing, on the contrary, is most strongly related to *socialism*, again most weakly to *liberalism*, but also rather strongly to *conservatism*.

Both self-identified types are only moderately related to each other (Tau = .21): many *right-wingers* consider themselves *progressive* — in fact more than 50% do so. On the other hand, only a few left-wingers — less than 10% — consider themselves conservative. Right-wing is much more 'popular' than conservative; progressive however, is

Table 6.6. *The validity of the 3 abstract mass dimensions and the abstract elite dimension; tests on 'known groups'*(a)

Self-description as (b)		Mass-dimension			Elite-dimension
		Conserva-tism	Liberalism	Socialism	Progressive-Conservative (c)
conservative	(N= 434)	4.87	5.73	4.59	(f)
neutral(d)	(N= 462)	4.43	5.19	4.82	
progressive	(N=1011)	3.67	5.15	5.19	
Tau-beta(e)		—.29	—.05	.11	
right-wing	(N= 775)	4.64	5.65	4.28	
neutral	(N= 722)	4.20	5.26	5.08	
left-wing	(N= 450)	3.18	4.66	5.93	
Tau-beta		—.26	—.14	.30	

Table 6.6. (*continued*)

Political partisanship(g)	Mass-dimension			Elite-dimension
	Conserva-tism	Liberalism	Socialism	Progressive-Conservative (c)
voters(h)				M.P.'s(i)
liberal (VVD) (N= 218)	4.66	6.48	4.00	5.78
christian-democratic CHU (protestant) (N= 106)	4.87	5.33	4.29	5.00
ARP (prot-Calvinist) (N= 104)	4.56	5.47	3.86	5.17
KVP (roman catholic) (N= 280)	4.70	5.23	4.70	4.14
progressive(j) PPR (radicals) (N= 29)	3.45	5.90	6.00	(k)
D'66 (democrats) (N= 128)	3.47	5.51	5.36	2.50
PvdA (labor) (N= 248)	3.95	4.72	5.42	1.61
extreme left PSP (pacifist soc.) (N= 44)	2.23	3.45	7.20	(k)
CPN (communists) (N= 36)	2.94	4.53	7.19	(k)
new party DS'70 (right-wing splinter party of PvdA-Labor Party)(l)				3.60

Notes:
(a) Except for the Tau-beta's, figures indicate mean scores on the 10-point scales (see Appendix 4)
(b) See Appendix 6 for details
(c) High=conservative
(d) This includes the non-response
(e) See Kendall (1948)
(f) Self-descriptions of M.P.'s are not available
(g) See Appendix 6 for details on the parties and the party labels
(h) Vote-intention if there were parliamentary elections now (see Appendix 6)
(i) See Appendix 2 for details and N's
(j) These parties form a coalition under that name since 1972
(k) Too few M.P.'s; communists did not participate at all
(l) This party has been founded in the year of the survey (1970); in 1971, when the M.P.'s were approached, it had 8 seats in the Second Chamber of Parliament

most popular. For many people, progressive does not imply socialism or anti-liberalism, but self-styled left-wing orientation is strongly related — relatively speaking — to both socialism and anti-conservatism. Self-styled left-wing is more strongly negative in its relation to liberalism than self-styled progressive is.

All dimensions seem to be valid indicators of progressiveness vs. conservatism, but relationships are sufficiently weak to allow for a considerable amount of false consciousness in this sense of inconsistency: many people consider themselves progressive, but according to 'objective' standards, they are not. The alternative is also true: many people who are 'progressive' do not consider themselves as such. According to Barnes' (1966) definition such people could not be considered as being 'ideologues' [13].

The relationship between *political partisanship* and the abstract-ideological dimensions seems sufficient for trust in the validity of the dimensions to be strengthened. At the same time, new and revealing information is obtained on the opinions of various groups of voters [14].

Christian-democratic voters are the most *conservative*, but liberal voters are a close second. Labor Party voters come next; they are somewhat more conservative than other progressive voters. The most anti-conservative are communists and pacifist-socialists.

Liberals are most *liberal*, but it is interesting to note that non-labor progressive voters (PPR and D'66) tend to be even more liberal (in their opposition to government interference) than most christian-democratic voters. (As is well known, this has sometimes been a source of tension within the present progressive coalition: the Labor Party is clearly more in favor of the government playing an active role. In this respect, the progressiveness of democrats and radicals seem very limited indeed.) Again, as could be expected, pacifist-socialists and communists are most anti-liberal.

Finally, liberal voters are least *socialist*, followed by (on average) the christian-democratic voters. The progressives are more socialist, and the most socialist are the pacifist-socialists and communists. There are, however, some interesting deviations from the general pattern within these various 'blocks'. Anti-Revolutionaries, for example, are *least* socialist and radicals are even *more* socialist than labor voters [15]. This might partly be explained by the content of the socialism dimension, which contains items on *'radical change'* and *'authority relations'*: Anti-Revolutionaries seem disproportionately in favor of existing authority; radicals may be disproportionately in favor of 'radical change'.)

Along the elitist progressive-conservative dimension, liberal M.P.'s score most *conservative*, followed by the christian-democrats, of which

he roman catholics clearly score as less conservative than the 2 protes-
ant parties. Democrats and especially labor M.P.'s are the most progres-
.ive. Democratic socialists score as slightly more progressive than roman
:atholics but are more conservative than the democrats: they obviously
:onstitute a conservative splinter-group of the Labor Party.

In conclusion, these results are in general agreement with those of
Lipschits (1969) made on the basis of party-programs — if the latter's
data are correctly (re)analyzed, as is discussed above, par. 3.4.5. — and
with evidence on how the positions of the parties along progressive-
:onservative or left-right continua are often seen or assessed.

5.3.3. Discussion and summary

Very briefly, we have found the following:

a) The theoretical progressive-conservative antithesis, operationalized
   at an abstract, philosophical level by means of bipolar statements,
   falls apart in the general Dutch population in 3 relatively independent dimensions. These dimensions could be interpreted in terms of
   the 3 major foci of ideological controversy as they have manifested
   themselves in Western Europe since the beginning of the 19th
   century: conservatism, classical liberalism and socialism.

b) There seem to be 2 major rationales for this finding. Both are in
   terms of a generalization of Kerlinger's (1967) theory of the criteriality of referents of attitude. The first generalization considers that in
   Western Europe, contrary to the United States, these are the 3 ideologies mentioned above, rather than only liberalism and conservatism in the American sense. Hence we might expect a 3-dimensional
   structure of ideological controversy. The other generalization of
   Kerlinger's theory is in terms of the basic values of freedom and
   equality underlying the progressive-conservative controversy. In the
   abstract, conservatism is opposed to increasing freedom and
   equality, as compared to socialism, which is in favor of that.
   Liberalism is a special case, since it applies to the socio-economic
   field, where freedom (of enterprise) is opposed to equality (through
   government interference). That all 3 dimensions are relatively
   independent could be explained in terms of the differential
   criteriality of the *values* of freedom and equality in their application
   to various fields.

c) The weak though clearly visible structure of dimensions of ideological controversy in the general population, even at this abstract
   philosophical level, is contrary to evidence from American studies,
   carried out in the 1950's and early 1960's (e.g. Converse, 1964) where

no structure at all in the general public was found. This difference could be explained in terms of cross-cultural differences between Western Europe (i.e. the Netherlands) and the United States, but also, perhaps, by the increasing salience of politics all over the world which has taken place during the 1960's and which has probably caused the (re)emergence of ideological controversy along (vague, but visible) dimensions, even at an abstract level. Evidence for such an emergence of ideological controversy (in terms of a uni-dimensional liberal-conservative dimension in the American public) has been presented by Nie (1974).

(d) Contrary to Nie, educational level proved to be a factor which has a much stronger effect on the structure of the abstract domain than political interest. Both effects were similar, however, in that in the highly educated and the politically interested, there was (1) a tendency towards a unidimensional structure, (2) more variance explained than in the general population, and (3) the structure of ideological controversy was *similar but not identical* to the one in the general population, and generally rather confused.

(e) In the elite of M.P.'s, a clearly unidimensional progressive-conservative antithesis was found, thus confirming the reality of this construct as an elitist phenomenon. Obviously, for the highly politically involved and highly educated elite, the whole domain of elements constituting the abstract progressive-conservative antithesis is 'criterial' (in Kerlinger's terms) and/or the 2 values of freedom and equality are (also) criterial and can be brought into harmony with each other, in the socio-economic realm as well as in the non-economic sense. In the elite, even more variance is explained than in the highly educated and the first Eigenvalue of the matrix S* is more than twice as strong. (These results are in line with Converse's theory of 'increasing constraint' of belief systems in (semi-)elitist groups, as compared to the general public, but this theory is too simplistic in that it only makes a distinction between an amorphous 'structure' (interpreted in terms of 'issue publics') at the mass level, as compared to the unidimensional ideological controversy at the elite level.)

(f) By interrelating the 3 mass dimensions of conservatism, liberalism and socialism for the general public, the various semi-elites (and their corresponding non-elites) and the elite, the variations in ideological structure between these groups at the present abstract level have become even clearer. These findings have been described in terms of false consciousness.

As against the very consistent elite, the mass shows only moderately high correlations between conservatism and liberalism and (negatively) between conservatism and socialism. The relationship between socialism and liberalism which, theoretically, should be highly negative — which it is indeed in the elite: —.78) is only —.12 in the general population: this is the major inconsistency at this abstract level which can be described as a manifestation of false consciousness of large sections of the mass public. (This finding is in line with Free and Cantril's, 1967). Many people in the mass public do not see the anti-socialist implications of a classical liberal posture or vice versa, and substantial minorities do not see the anti-socialist implications of conservatism either.

Such inconsistencies are not distributed at random in the population at large, however. It can clearly be seen in Table 6.5. that the highly educated, the upper classes and the politically interested are much more consistent in both respects than the poorly educated, the lower classes and the politically uninvolved. In fact, the differences are rather dramatic. There is much more false consciousness in the lower echelons of society than in the upper parts of it. Still, although it is weaker, these lower echelons do show a clearly visible and well-interpretable ideological structure which is similar to the one in the general public.

It should be noted that the relationship between conservatism and liberalism (.82 in the elite and .31 in the general public) is most capable of maintaining itself in the poorly educated, the lower classes and the politically uninvolved. These 2 ideologies are seen as most strongly related by all social strata. The strongest negative relationships in (semi-) elites are found between conservatism and socialism.

(g) Evidence in favor of the validity of the mass and elite dimensions has been presented by several tests on 'known groups'. This has rendered it quite unlikely that the dimensions (especially the mass dimensions) were only artefacts which had come about by way of a response-set mechanism. An interpretation of the dimensions in terms of the differential criteriality of elements in the political culture of a nation, or of the differential criteriality of basic cultural values, seeems more likely.

It is still possible, however, that the very weakness of the mass structure has (partly) been caused by our *elitist* approach from the progressive-conservative perspective. It could be postulated that the mass has a quite different frame of reference in its perception of the political culture, and consequently uses a different language in expressing its views, as compared to the elite (see e.g. Lipsitz, 1970). In this case, elitist notions yield only a very weak response in the mass, and particularly in its lower echelons, not because the mass does not have any strong ideological postures at an abstract level, but because we are still insufficiently aware of them, and hence have not developed the constructs which would be most suited for a fruitful approach.

For the second stage in Type–1 analysis, we will now go *back* to the general population and *down* to the attitude level, and an attempt will be made to assess the dimensions of ideological controversy there, using the same technique (i.e. Jöreskog factor-analysis) and the same procedure (i.e. rotation of 2, 3 etc. factors according to the varimax criterion in search of a best solution).

First, we will make a *general* approach, leaving aside the 5 religious attitudes, but including 2 attitudes on social change in order to obtain evidence on the fact that notions on 'social change as such' do not really belong to the progressive-conservative domain.

The second stage will entail an *integration* of the abstract dimensions of liberalism, conservatism and socialism and the attitudinal domain in search of an (additional) validation of both types of dimensions, and the establishment of truly *ideological* ones. (A short F-scale will also be added.)

The analysis in the general population will be finished by an excursion into the *religious* field, drawing into the design the 5 religious attitude-scales and truncating the sample by selecting those that consider themselves to belong to a certain church. This excursion will yield an interesting and more complicated ideological structure which can be seen as an extension of earlier findings of Ferguson (1959) and Eysenck (1954, 1971).

The general ideological structure will then be tested for semi-elitist groups and for the elite of M.P.'s in a way which is similar to the one applied above at the abstract level.

6.4. DIMENSIONS AT THE ATTITUDE LEVEL

6.4.1. The general population

The results for the 26 attitude scales plus 1 item and 1 small scale on 'attitude towards change', are presented in Table 6.7.: the unrotated 2-factor solution and the rotated 2- and 3-factor solutions.

It immediately clear that evidence for unidimensionality is only slight, given the Eigenvalues of 9.93, 4.67, 2.31, 1.75 and 1.65, respectively, of matrix S*. One factor is not the best interpretation of the correlation matrix: 9 scales load highly on the second factor. The third factor is already meaningless (there are no loadings $\geqslant .35$.)

Table 6.7. *The dimensionality of the attitudinal domain in the general population: the 3-factor unrotated solution and the 2- and 3-factor rotated solutions* (a)

Attitude scale names	Unrotated		Rotated 2 factors Litr	Leri	Rotated 3 factors Litr	Leri	Auth (b)
1. Attitude to equality of income, property, status	.45	.47		.63		.60	
2. Government interference in bringing about equality of income, property	.37	.45		.57		.53	
3. Attitude to social welfare laws				.36		.36	
4. Equality of opportunity (for working class children)							.42
5. Government aid to education	.47	.36		.55		.56	
6. Government income policy		.60		.68		.70	
7. Tax policy (higher incomes)	.39	.37		.51		.47	
8. Tax policy (lower incomes)		.38		.38		.42	
9. Government direct economic interf.	.38	.44		.56		.56	
10. Government non-directly economic welfare policy	.50		.38	.34	.38	.34	
11. Militant trade-union policy		.38		.42		.45	
12. Democratic attitudes	.68		.52	.46	.42	.43	.35
13. Freedom of political expression	.65		.61		.50		.38
14. Aid to developing countries	.35		.33				.45
15. Internationalism	.63		.69		.43		.59
16. Political tolerance			.36				.31
17. Tolerance towards criminals							.30
18. Tolerance reg. controv. TV-programs	.41		.41		.50		
19. Moral libertarianism	.60		.68		.62		
20. Family traditionalism	−.60		−.64		−.65		
21. Tolerance reg. daughter's choice of husband							
22. Authoritarian parent-child relationship	−.59	.37	−.69		−.49		−.50
23. Conventional male-female roles			−.42				−.40
24. Tolerance regarding homosexuals	.54		.60		.50		.34
25. Premarit. sexual permissiveness	.51		.54		.61		
26. Extramarit. sexual permiss.	.41		.48		.53		
27. Attitude towards change(c)	.43						.40
28. Government implementation of change(c)	.41			.35			
Variance explained			28.2%		31.7%		

Notes:

(a) Only loadings ⩾ .35 are given, except for some between .30 and .35 which clarified the meaning of a factor. For the meaning of the scales and their characteristics: see Appendix 3 and Chapter 5, Table 5.4.

(b) See text for the meaning of these names

(c) See Appendix 3, set 31

The 2 rotated solutions are much more interesting. We will first discuss the 2-factor solution. Here, 2 clearly distinguished factors emerge, with only 2 double loadings. The 2 factors explain 28.2% of the variance.

The *first factor* includes all non-economic political attitude scales, with a low loading of .33 only for 'Aid to developing countries' and a rather low loading for 'Political tolerance' (.36). All scales on 'social' attitudes regarding marriage, family life and sexuality load highly, with the exception of 'Tolerance towards criminals' and 'Tolerance regarding daughter's choice of husband'.

In European terminology, the factor could be labeled *non-economic progressiveness vs. conservatism*, but I would rather suggest the name *libertarianism vs. traditionalism (LITR)*. The factor seems to point to a dimension reflecting the value of *liberty*, applied to non-economic aspects of social life. All scales appear to indicate a *libertarian* attitude which aims at the optimalization of individual liberty and freedom of expression in the broadest sense of the word (e.g. 'Freedom of political expression', 'Moral libertarianism', 'Tolerance regarding homosexuals' and 'Sexual permissiveness'). However, some scales also incorporate *egalitarian* aspects, like 'Democratic attitudes', 'Internationalism', '(Anti-)authoritarian parent-child relationship' and 'Conventional male-female roles'. Thus the factor may be interpreted as predominantly non-economic and libertarian, but also including egalitarian aspects. (As indicated earlier, one may interpret this as confirming the rationale that the values of *liberty* and *equality* are in harmony with one another *non-economically*, when equality refers to 'of equal value', rather than to uniformity, especially as regards certain forms of behavior and the rights of certain minority groups. From this viewpoint, both values may even be taken as 'identical'; see Table 4.2. in Chapter 4.)

Non-economically, the value of freedom implies equality of freedom. A positive attitude towards 'Freedom of political expression', for example, implies a positive attitude to *various forms* of expression. Internationalism, on the other hand, implies that one tends to consider one's own nation or country as being 'equal' (i.e. of equal value) to most other nations, but also that e.g. the individual should be free, if he so chooses, *not* to live according to 'national standards'. 'Moral libertarianism' implies a positive attitude towards individual liberty in the moral sense, but naturally also an egalitarian attitude to various types of behavior relevant in this area. Most clearly, perhaps, libertarianism implies equal rights for certain *groups* in expressing themselves freely in a wide sense, like political 'outcasts' (communists, fascists), directors of TV-programs, children, women and homosexuals.

The opposite of libertarianism may be called '*traditionalism*' because many non-libertarian attitudes seem to refer to traditional, customary or common situations and opinions which were predominant in the past. 'Freedom of political expression' has always been very limited in most countries; 'Aid to developing countries' is a recent phenomenon, 'Nationalism' has been common, 'Political tolerance' mostly limited. Some other examples of topics that also come into this category are: 'Family traditionalism', 'Authoritarian parent-child relationship' and 'Conventional male-female roles'. These have all been customary in most Western European countries, and such standards are still kept today by many people.

The factor under consideration refers to a meta-attitudinal dimension which aims, at one pole, at a liberation from such traditional ways of life. Hence, the term libertarianism-traditionalism seems suitable.

A few additional remarks are in order. In the first place the fact that both the scales on 'Democratic attitudes' and (with lower loadings) 'Government non-directly economic welfare policy' have a double loading can be explained in terms of the hypothesized value-reference of the first factor. A discussion of this phenomenon will be postponed until after the second factor has been discussed.

Second, why do the scales on 'Tolerance towards criminals' and 'Tolerance regarding daughter's choice of husband' not load on the first factor? The scale on criminals may tap a *punitive* rather than an (anti-) libertarian or egalitarian attitude. The tendency to advocate 'change' or 'cure', rather than punishment of criminals may not really reflect libertarianism. The same applies to the item on the reintroduction of the death penalty. The 2 items on tolerance regarding daughter's choice of husband are somewhat atypical in that reference is made to (1), a specific personal situation and (2), the variables of race and social class. It may be that items of the first kind elicit responses that are different to other items, and also that items on race and social class have a special aspect which renders them unfit for a broader libertarianism dimension.

We may now turn to the second factor. This is clearly *economic* in nature, and refers in particular to the role of government in creating more *economic equality* in society. Almost all relevant scales load highly on this second factor; the 'Social welfare laws' scale however, has a rather low loading compared to the other scales. In American terminology, this meta-attitudinal dimension clearly refers to *economic liberalism-conservatism*, but in European terminology it seems better to refer to it as socialism or *left-right (LERI): to the left there are socialist opinions and attitudes which, through government policies and trade-union strategies, aim at equality of income, etc.; to the right there are those who are opposed to such aims and means.*

One may wonder, however, why the scale on the 'Equality of opportunity for working class children' does not fit into this factor. The reason for this may be that the scale-items all imply an *awareness of a situation*: the awareness of the intelligence or laziness of working class children and an awareness of opportunity in society today. The items were meant to *indirectly* tap the attitude towards equality of opportunity (since, if this had been done *directly*, it was expected that an insufficient number of people would state that they were opposed to equality of opportunity) but since the scale does not load on this factor, it may be wondered whether this attempt has been successful (see note 18 below for further comments).

The 2 factors seem clearly distinct: on the one hand a libertarianism-traditionalism dimension in the *non-economic* field; on the other hand an egalitarian left-right dimension, with a strong emphasis on government policies and a specific aim of achieving egalitarian *economic* goals. The 2 dimensions clearly seem to reflect *differential value orientations*, i.e. value-orientations differentiated according to the fields of application in which they have a (partially) different relationship to each other.

Non-economically, both values which define the domain of progressive vs. conservative attitudes, i.e. freedom and equality, seem to coincide: they appear on the same dimension. Here the *libertarian* aspects (i.e. the value of freedom) dominate, however. In other words, in a non-economic sense, the egalitarian implications are somewhat less obvious than the libertarian ones: it is liberty that is requested for certain types of behavior and certain groups.

Economically however, the value of *equality* dominates, with 'liberating', but also with anti-liberal (anti-liberty) connotations: economically a greater amount of equality can only be attained through a government policy which would set limits to the freedom of those individuals whose economic freedom would create (further) economic inequality (see Rawls, 1972). Economically more than non-economically, it is clear that in order to achieve an *egalitarian* ideal, *freedom* should be limited to the extent that is necessary to realize such goals. (Compare the interpretation of the abstract liberalism dimension; above, par. 6.2.1.1.) Of course, non-economically there cannot be absolute or unlimited liberty either, if one is to achieve equality: the rather generally accepted limits set to individual liberty are those which define the liberty of others. Otherwise, a state of 'equal freedom' could not be reached. In a different way, and in a sense more directly, the same seems true for the economic field. The *overlap* between both dimensions (for the 2 scales with double loadings: see Table 6.7.) now seems especially interesting.

On the one hand, the scale on '*Government non-directly economic welfare policy*' reflects an attitude towards government spending, and consequently, by implication, towards tax policy, social welfare laws, etc. On the other hand, the focus of such policies is on *non-economic* libertarian ideals, e.g. grants for artists and support for working wives. There is no reference to the broader socioeconomic class differentiation.) From this, the reason why the scale loads (poorly) on both major meta-attitudinal dimensions can be explained.

That the scale on '*Democratic attitudes*' loads *highly* on both major dimensions can be explained as follows. On the one hand, a democratic attitude (as indicated by the scale items on e.g. increasing the influence and power of workers, students and pupils, and that of citizens on local and regional policy) clearly refers to *non-economic* libertarian (and egalitarian) ideals. Hence its loading on the first factor. On the other hand, its specific reference to inequality of power and influence in society may well be perceived as related to *economic* inequality and hence to the left-right dimension: the striving for economic equality has strongly liberalizing implications for those groups whose opportunities are limited by their low social position, i.e. low income, educational level and occupational status.

Obviously, the egalitarian ideals incorporated in the left-right dimension particularly refer to class distinctions and it may be hypothesized that the variable of social class is related to it ideologically: it would be in the economic interest of the lower class to support leftist attitudes, as defined by the left-right factor, in order to promote such left-wing policies. The libertarian ideals incorporated in the LITR-dimension do not refer to the social position of specific groups in this economic sense. They refer to various types of behavior and to groups that may be 'liberated' in various ways, e.g. women and homosexuals. The 2-factor structure shows that there must be important groups in society which are libertarian in the latter, general, non-economic sense, but right-wing in the specific socioeconomic sense, and that there must be groups which are traditional but also socioeconomically left-wing.

It may be hypothesized that here, social class is an important differentiating variable (see e.g. Lipset, 1963; Kelly and Chambliss, 1966; Lenski, 1961). If this were indeed true (and evidence will be presented below), the left-right dimension could possibly be considered the most clearly ideological in the sense that it reflects the economic interests of the lower classes on its left-wing side. The LITR-dimension would perhaps be less obviously ideological, but it might be argued that libertarianism is in the psychological interest of the upper classes, who require as much freedom as possible to 'express' themselves (the liberating role of education, for example, has often been noted). As the lower classes have less opportunity for expression (and a lower educational level), they may have to keep to the existing, 'given' ways of life which have meaning to them (i.e. make their lives meaningful) and which may provide the necessary psychological security which they are unable to obtain in other ways. (See Chapter 7 for a test of this rationale.)

The above reasoning might be expressed in terms of values and their differential criteriality to certain social classes (see Kerlinger, 1967; and the discussion above: par. 6.2.1.1.). It can be reasoned that the value of *freedom* is mainly criterial to the upper classes, and has perhaps been taken by them from the non-economic field and applied to the economic one. The value of *equality* may be criterial to the lower classes; it might have been taken from the *economic* field and applied to other forms of behavior in the sense of: a general tendency to require people to abide by certain standards (which are, by definition almost, the given traditional ones).

Hence, the relationship between social class and libertarianism-traditionalism would be *negative* and that between social class and left-right would be *positive*. The extent to which the dimensions may be considered ideological in this special sense, and the extent to which false consciousness would exist under the same terms, depends, then, on the differing strengths of these relationships.

If social class were indeed negatively related to left-wing positions along the LERI-dimension, this factor still need *not* be interpreted as an expression of *primitive self-interest* of the various social classes (see Campbell et al., 1960: 203–209). In the *first* place, there is a high consistency in the setting of egalitarian *goals*, and in the adherence to certain *means* in order to reach such goals in the LERI-dimension. *Secondly*, some of these means do not seem 'direct' or 'obvious', for instance 'Government aid to education' and 'Direct economic interference by the government'. *Third*, and perhaps most important: there is a *link* between the predominantly socioeconomic and the more general libertarian and egalitarian views in the form of the 'Democratic attitudes' scale and, to a somewhat lesser extent, the 'Government non-directly economic welfare policy' scale. The 'Democratic attitudes' scale (with the highest loading on the first unrotated factor) reflects the *common underlying value orientation* of both factors and thus appears *insensitive* to those variables in the social structure which, in terms of these values, elicit inconsistent responses leading to the appearance of 2 relatively independent meta-attitudinal dimensions. (More evidence on the ideological nature of the LERI-dimension rather than an interpretation in terms of primitive self-interest will be given and discussed below; see e.g. the consistent loadings of the 2 tax policy scales.)

Some final remarks may be added on the 2 social change variables. *'Attitude to change'* is only very weakly positive in its relation to both libertarianism and left-wing orientation. 'Government interference to bring about change' is only weakly related to LERI. Both variables are of course strongly related (.51), but when the 2 factors have been extracted the residual correlation is still relatively high (.32).

It seems likely that a conceptualization of progressiveness vs. conservatism in terms of an attitude to change stems from the section in the model of conservatism on the implementation of change (see Chapter 4); but even there, it is obvious (1), that conservatism need not imply 'standpattism' (see Rossiter, 1962), i.e. complete opposition to any change, and (2), that conservatism mainly implies opposition to certain *types* of change rather than opposition to change as such.

Therefore, the progressive-conservative antithesis could theoretically and ideologically be conceptualized in terms of certain *values*. Those values (freedom and equality) underlie the attitude scales that have been assembled here. It can now be seen that `empirically`, the attitude to change is only very weakly related to progressive-conservative dimensions. (The fact that 'Government interference in order to bring about change' is weakly related to left-wing orientation may be due to a 'halo-effect': many scales in the left-right dimension refer to government interference and it may be that to some extent groups which tend to score left-wing realize that socioeconomic egalitarian goals can only be reached through government policy. From this perspective they may tend to react positively to general statements on government interference in order to bring about change, though not very strongly so.) In any case, as has been predicted, the attitude to change 'as such' seems peripheral to the major dimensions which underlie progressive-conservative attitudes.

Let us now examine the 3-factor rotated solution. It appears that the 2-factor structure is remarkably stable. The left-right factor remains completely unaltered in the 3-factor solution, whereas the libertarianism-traditionalism factor is only modified in that some scales with too low loadings now appear on the third factor: 'Equality of opportunity for working class children', 'Aid to developing countries' and, though low: 'Tolerance towards criminals'. The third factor shows the highest loadings for 'Nationalism' and 'Authoritarian parent-child relationship' (both with a double loading on the libertarianism-traditionalism dimension) and for 'Aid to developing countries' and 'Conventional male-female roles' (the latter scale originally loaded rather highly on the libertarianism-traditionalism factor). 'Freedom of political expression' (.38), 'Democratic attitudes' (.35), 'Political tolerance' (.31) and 'Tolerance regarding homosexuals' (.34) all have low loadings.

This factor may tentatively be interpreted as constituting a dimension of authoritarianism (AUTH). In the classical F-scale there is a separate theoretical subdimension of 'conventionality' and there are items implying children's submission to their parents (Adorno et al., 1950: 255–257, Forms 45 and 40 of the F-scale, items nos. 1, 27 and 13) as well as nationalism (items nos. 13 and 23) and a punitive attitude regarding homosexuals and sexual criminals (items nos. 25 and 39). The relatively high loading of the 'Equality of opportunity' scale is consistent with earlier conceptualizations of fascism by Stagner (1936 a, b) and Stagner and Katzoff (1942) which imply a 'middle-class consciousness' aspect (i.e. a superior attitude towards the working class and a 'lack of sympathy for the underdog').

All other (low) loadings also seem consistent with the interpretation of the factor in terms of authoritarianism. To be opposed to aid to developing countries, for example, implies both nationalism and a lack of concern for the underdog.

The interpretation of this third factor as an *authoritarian subdimension of the major libertarianism-traditionalism* dimension, as well as the interpretation of the 2 major dimensions, will be tested below.

6.5. IDEOLOGICAL DIMENSIONS: INTEGRATION OF ABSTRACT DIMENSIONS AND THE ATTITUDINAL DOMAIN

6.5.1. The general population

The 2 sets of dimensions that have been assessed so far in the general population (the abstract philosophical and the attitudinal ones), immediately suggest their integration into one design. Both dimensionalities could at least partly be interpreted in terms of the same postulated underlying values. Moreover, the names that could be assigned to the various dimensions also strongly suggest an at least pairwise similarity, i.e. between the conservatism and the libertarianism-traditionalism dimension and between the socialism and the left-right dimension. In both domains, the distinction between the economic and non-economic fields in applying the underlying values seemed to be a relevant one.

On the other hand, there also seem to be some interesting differences between the 2 sets of dimensions. At the abstract level, for example, there appears to be a clear distinction between the socialism and the liberalism dimension (constituting one of the major indications of the existence of what has been called a type of false consciousness in large parts of the population) whereas at the attitude level, there is a clear integration of goals and means in the left-right dimension (i.e. obtaining socioeconomic equality to a greater extent by means of a large number of government policies). As indicated above, the 2 major dimensions at both levels seem to be related to each other, but each domain has a unique subdimension: *liberalism* at the abstract level and *authoritarianism* — so it is postulated — at the attitude level. (Note the interpretation of the liberalism dimension above — par. 6.2.1.1. — in terms of a conflict between the application of the values of freedom and equality in the socioeconomic field, in particular government interference versus free enterprise.)

In the integrated approach to both domains that will be carried out, it is predicted that *socialism* will be the philosophy behind the meta-attitudinal *left-right* dimension and that *conservatism* will be the philosophy behind the *libertarianism-traditionalism* dimension. These dimensions will then be considered as *ideological* dimensions [16].

If these predictions will be borne out, then liberalism will obviously *not* be the philosophy behind a right-wing, anti-egalitarian and anti-government interference dimension, and we must consider the possibility that liberalism, which is rather widely adhered to in the general population, is not integrated with many of its specific applications at all.

The integration of both domains will also offer an opportunity to test the nature of the third dimension at the attitude level, which has been defined as one of authoritarianism. This will be done by including a short version of the classical F-scale (for measurements, see Appendix 6).

The results in Table 6.8. clearly show that all predictions are borne out: ideological dimensions, in which abstract notions and their specific applications are integrated, have been empirically assessed. In the 2-factor solution, conservatism and socialism consistently load on the libertarianism-traditionalism and left-right dimensions respectively, although the short F-scale loads even slightly higher on the first factor. *Liberalism only loads very low on the left-right dimension, by which another, more extensive form of false consciousness has been established: the lack of integration between abstract tendencies against government interference and attitudes towards specific government policies in favor of a more egalitarian distribution of income, property, opportunity, etc. There are, in fact, large majorities in favor of such specific policies (see Appendix 3) whereas mostly there also appear relative majorities generally against government interference (see Appendix 4).*

In the 3-factor solution, the stability of the left-right dimension is again shown. The third dimension of authoritarianism is indeed validated by the high loading of .64 of the short F-scale. The only minor incon-

Table 6.8. *The dimensionality of the ideological domain in the general population; a first approach; 2- and 3-factor rotated solutions*(a)

Attitude scale names	2 factors		3 factors		
			Litr	Leri	Auth
1. Attitude to equality of income, property, status		.64		.65	
2. Government interference in bringing about equality of income, property		.58		.58	
3. Attitude to social welfare laws		.36		.36	
4. Equality of opportunity (for working class children)					−.46
5. Government aid to education		.55		.55	
6. Government income policy		.68		.68	
7. Tax policy (higher incomes)		.51		.52	
8. Tax policy (lower incomes)		.38		.39	
9. Government direct economic interference		.56		.56	
10. Government non-directly economic welfare policy	.36	.36	.38	.35	
11. Militant trade-union policy		.45		.45	
12. Democratic attitudes	.51	.47	.44	.45	
13. Freedom of political expression	.60		.51		−.35
14. Aid to developing countries	.36				−·46
15. Internationalism	.71		.43		−.59
16. Political tolerance	.37				
17. Tolerance towards criminals					−.32
18. Tolerance reg. controversial TV-programs	.40		.48		
19. Moral libertarianism	.67		.62		
20. Family traditionalism	−.61		−.66		
21. Tolerance reg. daughter's choice of husband					
22. Authoritarian parent-child relationship	−.70		−.48		.52
23. Conventional male-female roles	−.46				.45
24. Tolerance regarding homosexuals	.59		.50		−.34
25. Premarit. sexual permissiveness	.51		.61		
26. Extramarit. sexual permissiveness	.45		.53		
Abstract dimensions					
27. Conservatism	−.50	−.35	−.33	−.34	.40
28. Socialism		.49		.49	
29. Liberalism		−.31		−.31	
30. Authoritarianism (shortened F-scale)	−.59				.64
Variance explained	29.1%		32.8%		

Note:

(a) See note a, Table 6.7. The dimensions of conservatism, liberalism, socialism and authoritarianism have been measured by means of 10-point scales (see Appendix 4 and for authoritarianism: Appendix 6)

sistency is the somewhat higher loading of conservatism on the AUTH-dimension (.40) as compared to its loading on the LITR dimension (.33), whereas its negative loading on the LERI-dimension is —.34 [17].

As we have seen in Chapter 3, the F-scale cannot very well be considered as a measure of fascist ideology. We have maintained in Chapter 4 that fascism can be seen to a large extent as a radicalized version of conservative ideas, which has thus moved outside the basic triangle of ideological controversy in Western Europe and does not constitute an element within the progressive-conservative domain. Now we have seen that *empirically*, in the general population, there appears a dimension at the *attitude* level which is a subdimension of the LITR dimension that could indicate what might be called a 'fascist potential'. The implication may be that there are sentiments and ideas of this type at the mass level which are not reflected at the abstract philosophical level, at least not within the basic triangle of ideological controversy.

The other, complementary, phenomenon is the rather isolated position of liberalism in the ideological domain: this posture is not reflected in the general population at the attitude level. So, philosophical debate in terms of classical liberal notions may be philosophical in the worst sense: there is no 'practical' basis for this debate in the attitudes of most people. As mentioned above, this phenomenon is considered as a major form of false consciousness.

In summary, we have found that the major abstract dimensions and the major attitudinal ones have pairwise validated each other in the ideological domain. In addition, the assessment of this domain in the general population has indicated the theoretical limitation of the definition of the abstract domain (i.e. not including fascist ideas, of which authoritarianism might be seen as the attitudinal components) and the isolated nature of classical liberalism, ideas which do not seem to be reflected at the attitude level.

6.5.1.1. Exploration and modification: towards a 'best' solution

Although the 2- and 3-factor solutions presented in Table 6.8. were quite satisfactory, some investigations of the position within the structure of some specific single items was found useful: those on 'Tax policy for middle incomes' (an item originally belonging to *both* tax scales; see Appendix 3 and Chapter 5, par. 5.3.3.), 'State interference' generally (compare Hoogerwerf, 1964: 256), 'Government policy to bring about equality of opportunity' and 'Government spending' (as a logical consequence of many forms of government policy). Moreover, the scale on 'Equality of opportunity for working class children' was reduced to a single item, leaving out the 2 items on the awareness of the attitudes of working class children [18]. The resulting 2- and 3-factor rotated solutions are presented on the left-hand side of Table 6.9. They explain 27.0 and 30.7% of the variance respectively, which is somewhat less than the solution in Table 6.8.

The 2-factor solution is very similar to the former one; the 2 items on 'Government interference for equality of opportunity' and 'Government spending' load, consistently, on the left-right dimension. The items on '*Tax policy* for middle incomes' and '*State interference*' do not show up on any factor, nor does the item on 'Everybody deserves what he earns'.

In the 3-factor solution, the authoritarianism dimension proves somewhat unstable: it is weakened to a noticeable degree. Moreover, the item on 'Tax policy for middle incomes' shows up on it. No immediate interpretation of this phenomenon is available.

It can be seen that, as in previous research, the item on 'There is too much state interference' is unrelated to any of the major dimensions (see Hoogerwerf, 1964: 256). However, one should not, as Hoogerwerf did, interpret this phenomenon as an indication of the fact that many people are in favor of 'progressive' (i.e. leftist) goals but 'do not perceive the state as the big leveler' or that this would indicate 'trust in the natural development in society towards more economic equality'. This is indicated by the high loadings on the LERI-dimension of all the government interference scales (e.g. the scale on government interference to bring about greater equality of income and property). The item on 'State-interference' may be considered a very general and suggestive one, but its being unrelated to the left-right or to any other dimension emphasizes the sensitivity of many people towards items which express *an attitude that is generally anti-government (especially 'state') meddling in private affairs, independent of their positions on ideological dimensions.* The very fact that the liberalism dimension shows up as relatively independent from the socialism dimension and only loads weakly on the left-right dimension may be due to this same phenomenon: a general attitude against state interference, independent of specific goals to be attained through government policy. This tendency is possibly related to a strong antagonism towards 'bureaucracy', 'civil servants' etc., which stems from basically liberal sentiments [19].

A '*best solution*', also presented in Table 6.9., was finally reached by eliminating a few items and the scale on 'Tolerance regarding daughter's choice of husband', which never loaded on any factor. The item on 'Everybody deserves what he earns' was excluded because it could be seen that the more explicit item on 'Government actions to bring about equality of opportunity' loaded more highly on the left-right factor. The 2 newly introduced items on 'Tax policy for middle incomes' and 'State interference' were also left out.

In the 'best 3-factor solution', the authoritarianism dimension again shows up very clearly. Compared to the earlier solutions, the left-right factor is strengthened and further validated by the inclusion of the 2 single items on 'Government policy'. The item on 'Government spending' only has a low loading [20]. The high-loading item on 'Equality of opportunity through government interference' seems an important addition to the left-right factor [21].

Table 6.9. *The dimensionality of the ideological domain in the general population: exploration and best solution; 2- and 3-factor rotated solutions*

Attitude scale names	Exploration 2 factors		3 factors			Best solution 2 factors Litr	Leri	3 factors Litr	Leri	Auth
1. Attitude to equality of income, property, status		.65		.66			.63		.65	
2. Government interference to bring about equality of income, property		.59		.61			.59		.60	
3. Attitude to social welfare laws		.37		.36			.36		.36	
4. Everybody deserves what he earns (single item)(a)										
5. Government aid to education		.57		.55			.56		.55	
6. Government income policy		.68		.68			.68		.68	
7. Tax policy (higher incomes)		.51		.53					.52	
8. Tax policy (lower incomes)		.39		.37			.38		.37	
9. Government direct economic interf.		.56		.56			.56		.56	
10. Government non-directly economic welfare policy	.34	.38		.36		.36	.37	.38	.36	
11. Militant trade-union policy		.44		.44			.45		.44	
12. Democratic attitudes	.48	.49	.50	.47		.50	.47	.43	.47	
13. Freedom of political expression	.58		.59			.60		.49		.35
14. Aid to developing countries	.36				.40	.36				.47
15. Internationalism	.70		.61		.39	.70		.42		.59
16. Political tolerance	.36		.33			.36				
17. Tolerance towards criminals										.33
18. Tolerance regarding controversial TV-programs	.40		.46			.40		.47		
19. Moral libertarianism	.66		.68			.67		.62		.32
20. Family traditionalism	-.60	-.67				-.61		-.66		
21. Tolerance reg. daughter's choice of husband										
22. Authoritarian parent-child rel.	-.70		-.63		-.32	-.70		-.47		-.54
23. Conventional male-female roles	.46		.37		-.30	-.45				-.45
24. Tolerance regarding homosexuals	.58		.58			.59		.49		.34
25. Premarital sexual permissiveness	.50		.59			.51		.60		
26. Extramarital sexual permissiveness	.45		.52			.46		.52		
Abstract dimensions										
27. Conservatism	-.47	-.39	-.43	-.38		-.49	-.36	-.33	-.36	-.38
28. Socialism		.50		.50			.49		.49	
29. Liberalism		-.32		-.33			-.31		-.32	
30. Authoritarianism (shortened F-scale)	-.60		-.44		-.52	-.59				-.64

Table 6.9. *(continued)*

Attitude scale names	Exploration 2 factors	Exploration 2 factors	Best solution 2 fact. Litr Leri	Best solution 3 factors Litr Leri Auth
Exploratory Items				
31. Tax policy (middle income groups)(b)		.40		
32. The state interferes too much(c)				
33. Government policy to create equality of opportunity(d)	.54	.57	.53	.54
34. Government spending(e)	.36	.35	.36	.35
Variance explained	27.0%	30.7%	29.9%	33.4%

Notes: (see note Table 6.7.)

(a) Item-text: In present-day society everybody earns what he deserves
   (5-point scale, from strongly agree to strongly disagree)
(b) See Appendix 3, set 7
(c) Text of item: responses from strongly agree to strongly disagree (5-points)
(d) Item-text: Are you in favor of or against the government taking *radical* measures so that everybody will really get an equal opportunity to be successful in society? Response-categories: strongly in favor, in favor, neither for nor against, against, strongly against
(e) Item-text: Do you think that the government should have more or less money at its disposal to make all sorts of public provisions possible? Response-categories: a great deal more, a bit more, leave it as it is, a bit less, a great deal less

6.5.1.2. An excursion: people considering themselves to belong to a certain church

The *religious attitude scales* which have been defined in the present study as belonging to the progressive-conservative domain (see Chapter 5, par. 5.3.2. and Table 5.4.; see also Appendix 3, sets 26–30) have only been considered relevant to people who are willing to indicate that institutionalized religion (i.e. one of the established churches) appeals to them in the sense that they consider themselves to belong to such a church (see Appendix 6). Now that we have identified a best solution for the ideological domain in the general population, an investigation will be made as to how the religious attitudes fit into this structure among people who fulfil the above criterion (N = 1196, i.e. 62% of the sample).

Results are presented in Table 6.10. The unrotated solution is the least interesting; it is highly similar to the one for the overall attitudinal domain (see Table 6.7.). In the 2-factor rotated solution, it can be seen that, without altering the overall best solution to any significant extent, all religious attitude scales load highly and consistently on the libertarianism-traditionalism dimension. *Thus, in the way the LITR dimension has been interpreted, it can be seen that the religious attitude scales refer to a non-economic application of the value of freedom.* 'Orthodoxy' refers to an adherence to many elements of belief and dogma that are common to both roman catholicism and protestantism. 'Conformism to church rules' implies an element of 'limited freedom' by definition.

'Politico-religious conservatism' can be regarded as the philosophical element in religious conservatism; it includes rather abstract notions on the relation between man, God and society, all implying a conservative attitude in a sense of passivity, submission to the will of God, and scepticism. This implies a tendency to leave things as they are, both in terms of freedom and equality (see e.g. item 3, Appendix 3, set 27). Finally, the attitude to 'pillarization' or 'segmentation' refers to the spheres of life that are arranged according to the principles of a certain religion, which also by definition implies a certain amount of limited freedom. (Of course, religious tolerance is the only scale which, as it suggests, implies a certain amount of freedom — see the opposite loading in Table 6.10).

Table 6.10. *The dimensionality of the ideological domain (the best solution extended with 5 religious attitude scales) in people who consider themselves to belong to a certain church; 2-factor unrotated and 2- and 3-factor rotated solutions (N = 1196)*

	Unrotated		Rotated				
Attitude scale names	2 factors		2 factors		3 factors		
1. Att. to equality of income, property, status	.39	.49		.62		.63	
2. Govern. interf. in bringing about equality of income, property		.45		.53		.54	
3. Att. to social welfare laws				.33		.33	
4. Governm. aid to education	.45	.41		.57		.57	
5. Governm. income policy		.60		.65		.65	
6. Tax policy (higher incomes)		.35		.42		.43	
7. Tax policy (lower incomes)		.35		.37		.37	
8. Governm. economic interference		.41		.48		.48	
9. Governm. non-dir. econ. welfare policy	.46		.35	.33	.31	.33	
10. Militant trade-union policy		.40		.42		.42	
11. Democratic attitudes	.64		.49	.44	.32	.44	.39
12. Freedom of political expression	.61		.57		.37		.46
13. Aid to develop. countries							.49
14. Internationalism	.59		.62		.30		.62
15. Political tolerance	.31		.32				.30
16. Tolerance towards criminals							.30
17. Tol. reg. controv. TV-programs	.43		.43		.48		
18. Moral libertarianism	.60		.64		.55		.34
19. Family traditionalism	-.62		-.63		-.60		
20. Authorit. parent-child rel.	-.55	.31	-.63		-.35		-.59
21. Covent. male-female roles	-.30		-.39				-.43
22. Toler. reg. homosexuals	.53		.56		.38		.44
23. Premar. sex. permissiveness	.49		.49		.56		
24. Extramar. sex. permissiveness	.44		.46		.48		

Table 6.10. (*continued*)

Attitude scale names	Unrotated 2 factors		Rotated 2 factors		3 factors		
Items added later							
25. Governm. policy: equality of opportunity (a)	.30	.42		.51		.52	
26. Government spending (b)	.39			.37		.37	
Abstract dimensions							
27. Conservatism	−.54		−.44	−.33	−.30	−.33	−.33
28. Socialism	.40	.30		.45		.45	
29. Liberalism							
30. Authoritarianism (short F-scale)	−.36	.35	−.48				−.62
Religious attitude scales(c)							
31. Religious orthodoxy	−.48		−.48		−.64		
32. Conformism to church rules	−.49		−.50		−.50		
33. Politico-religious conserv.	−.47		−.55		−.45		−.31
34. Attitude to 'pillarization'(d)	.48		.49		.60		
35. Religious tolerance	.48		.49		.60		
Variance explained			25.8%		30.3%		

Notes: (see note a Table 6.7. and 6.8.)
(a) Single item; see Table 6.9., noted (d)
(b) Ibid, Table 6.9. note (e)
(c) See Appendix 3, sets 26–30
(d) Might also be labeled: attitude to segmentation

The 3-factor solution is most interesting. The most noticeable phenomenon is the strengthening of the third dimension of authoritarianism. As compared to the overall best solution, scales such as those on 'Democratic attitudes', 'Freedom of political expression', 'Authoritarian parent-child relationship' and 'Tolerance regarding homosexuals' now have a (much) higher loading on authoritarianism than on LITR! The structure of the ideological domain has become more clearly 3-dimensional. *It seems that the religious attitudes split the original LITR dimension into 2 sets of components: (a) a set of moralistic, non-political attitudes, including scales on sexual attitudes and the 5 religious conservatism scales, and (b) a set of political-authoritarian attitudes, including 'Aid to developing countries', 'Freedom of political expression' and 'Internationalism'.* The distinction is not complete, however, since the 'political authoritarianism' factor still includes scales on 'Authoritarian parent-child relationship', 'Conventional male-female roles' and 'Tolerance regarding homosexuals'.

There seems to be an interesting similarity between these findings and those of Ferguson (1939) and Eysenck (1971) which have been discussed in Chapter 3. These authors almost completely leave out politico-economic items, but include religious ones. They then find factors labeled 'religionism' and 'humanitarianism'. These factors appear to be highly similar to the 'religious-moralistic-sex' factor and the 'political authoritarianism' factor found in the present study. Obviously, the politico-economic left-right factor, which was also found in the present study, could not appear in the earlier studies . . . because there were not enough items included which could load on such a factor.

These results show the importance of proper conceptualization and careful, 'complete' operationalization. Politico-economic attitudes should occupy a prominent place in the domain of progressive-conservative attitudes: they show up as a stable, separate factor. When religious attitudes are not included, factor-analysis shows one major additional factor (libertarianism-traditionalism) and a minor one, which breaks off from this factor: authoritarianism. When religious items are subsequently included (and the sample truncated accordingly), the basic pattern becomes more full-fledged 3-factor. Two of these factors have already been found in a fairly early study among students in the U.S. in 1939 (Ferguson), and e.g. in a quite recent study by Eysenck (1971) made on the basis of an English national cross-sectional sample. This 3-factor structure is more complicated than the original 2-factor solution, which could be interpreted in terms of the underlying values of freedom and equality.

One final question may now be raised: is it possible to interpret the 3-factor structure for the ideological domain, including religious attitudes, in terms of the values of freedom, equality and *brotherhood*, the famous slogan of the French Revolution? It does not seem easy to apply the brotherhood-principle either to the 'religious moralistic' factor or to the 'political authoritarianism' factor, however (see Kuypers, 1967). Perhaps the political authoritarianism factor comes closest to an interpretation in terms of brotherhood (i.e. anti-authoritarianism implies humanitarianism; compare also the scales on 'Internationalism' and 'Aid to developing countries'). On the other hand, the religious moralistic factor shows that those who conform most closely to what might be called 'the dogmas of the churches' are conservative in most family matters and generally in social and sexual matters, which implies *non*-permissiveness and *intolerance*. So, both non-economic dimensions have, on their conservative side, anti-brotherhood implications as well as implications which set limits to individual freedom.

In the present report, this distinction between the 2 non-economic factors is not dealt with any further. The religious subscales are not included in the basic design. However, the religious excursion has been clarifying and fairly rewarding. A starting point has been found for further (secondary) analysis on the role of religious ideology and attitudes within the progressive-conservative domain.

6.5.1.3. Discussion

The implications of our findings presented in this and the previous paragraph seem to be far-reaching.

In paragraph 6.4. we have seen that the social and political attitudes within the progressive-conservative domain show a basically 2-dimensional structure in the population at large and that in the 3-factor solution the third factor could be interpreted in terms of one of the best known constructs that have ever been developed in this area: *authoritarianism* which, placed in its proper context, proved to be a subdimension of the meta-attitudinal dimension of libertarianism-traditionalism. The other meta-attitudinal dimension has been called left-right in a politico-economic sense.

Like the abstract philosophical dimensions, the major meta-attitudinal ones could be interpreted in terms of the 2 postulated values underlying the attitudinal domain: freedom and equality. However, a clearer distinction between the economic and non-economic realms had to be made in the attitudinal domain. In the socioeconomic field, the value of *equality* seems to be the dominant one, although liberalizing and liberating implications for most people can clearly be seen; in the non-economic realm the value of *freedom* seems to dominate, although here the egalitarian aspect is manifested in the sense of various types of behavior being regarded as 'of equal value'.

More clearly than at the abstract level, the structure of conservative ideology in terms of fields and values, which has been derived from the model of the construct of conservatism, has been confirmed at the attitude level, but in terms of 2 relatively independent dimensions (see Table 4.2.). Economically, the progressive is in favor of *equality* — the conservative is opposed to it — and the conservative is in favor of *freedom from governmental interference*, i.e. against government policies to reach egalitarian goals and against the goals themselves. Non-economically, the progressive is in favor of *freedom*, which has egalitarian consequences whereas the conservative is opposed to freedom, which has the 'egalitarian' consequence that everybody should abide to the same norms ('absolute standards' for behavior).

The fact that both progressive-conservative dimensions (LITR and LERI) are relatively independent of each other may now, even more clearly than in the case of socialism and conservatism, be interpreted in terms of the differential criteriality of the values of freedom and equality, as applied to the economic and non-economic realms of social life (see Kerlinger, 1967). It has been suggested in paragraph 6.4. that the variable of *social class* plays an essential role in determining the conditions under which either the value of freedom in the non-economic

sense or the value of equality in the economic sense become criterial to
people. This will be investigated below.

Given the fact that the major meta-attitudinal dimensions could be interpreted in terms of the same underlying values which have been derived
from the definition of the construct of conservatism and which could be
used to interpret the abstract dimensions we have found earlier, we hypothesized that there would be an intimate relationship between the dimensions at both levels. One important piece of evidence in favor of the
ideological nature of the meta-attitudinal dimensions could be obtained
by relating them to the abstract, philosophical dimensions (which have
been found on the basis of a *direct* operationalization of conservative
ideology). Thus the next step in our analysis has been the integration of
the abstract dimensions and the attitudinal domain. We hypothesized
that socialism would load on the left-right dimension and that conservatism would load on the libertarianism-traditionalism dimension. In order
to validate the third dimension of authoritarianism, we also predicted
that a short version of the classical F-scale would load highest on this
dimension.

*All our predictions were borne out; we obtained 2 fundamental dimen-
sions of ideological controversy in the general population — labeled left-
right (LERI) and libertarianism-traditionalism (LITR) — and 1 subdimension of LITR: authoritarianism (AUTH).* (The specific nature of
this latter dimension will be examined below.)

Not only at the abstract level is there a well-interpretable, multidimensional structure of ideological controversy in the general population, but
the 2 major dimensions at that level are also well integrated with many of
their 'specific applications' at the attitude (and item) level. For the third
dimension (liberalism) this is not so and in addition, the meta-attitudinal
AUTH dimension is not reflected in e.g. an abstract fascism dimension,
since fascism is an ideology which has been considered outside the triangle of major ideological controversy in Western Europe, consisting of
the ideologies of liberalism, conservatism and socialism. The lack of integration between liberalism and the left-right dimension can again be
interpreted in terms of false consciousness in the sense of Free and
Cantril (1967).

On the one hand, these results are at variance with earlier findings; on
the other hand, they imply an important extension of earlier evidence on
the nature of ideological controversy in general populations.

*Unlike suggestions by Campbell et al. (1960) and Converse (1964),
there is no complete lack of ideological structure in the mass population,
at least not in the Netherlands in 1970* (see the discussion in par. 6.2.1.1.
on the possibility that cross-cultural differences between the United

States and the Netherlands, and/or the phenomenon of the 'emergence of ideology in the 1960's' explain the different findings in those studies; see also the discussion below). Neither does Nie's (1974) suggestion seem correct that during the 1960's there has emerged *one* overall liberal- (progressive-) conservative antithesis in the general population (i.e. in the United States). We have shown that possibly during the 1960's there emerged a structure of ideological controversy in the Dutch population which is basically *2-dimensional* and which can be interpreted in terms of the somewhat differential application of the 2 basic values of freedom and equality to the socio- (politico-) economic vs. the non-economic realms. This result is in line with early suggestions made by Smith (1948) which were later adopted by Lenski (1961), Lipset (1963) and O'Kane (1970) and which are reflected in results presented by e.g. Ferdinand (1964) and Kelly and Chambliss (1966). But of course our results are much more final than the rather scattered evidence of limited scope presented in these studies. By our comprehensive approach we have been able to show a number of phenomena in addition to the simple notion of a 2-dimensional structure of the liberal- (progressive-) conservative antithesis:

(a) there is a clear tendency that abstract notions, such as those involved in the socialism and conservatism dimensions, are consistently related to their specific applications in the LERI and LITR meta-attitudinal dimensions. But of course this integration is only a partial one; the average correlation is about .30, which leaves enough room for inconsistency which could, in terms of Free and Cantril (1967) and Mann (1970), be interpreted as a manifestation of false consciousness in large sections of the population. We have seen above that such false consciousness in terms of a lack of relationship between liberalism and socialism is greatest in the lower echelons of society (i.e. the uneducated and politically apathetic: the lower classes). However, the relationship between the 2 pairs of dimensions at both levels of abstraction has confirmed their ideological nature. (The lack of a *complete* consistency is in line with suggestions made by Prothro and Grigg (1960) and McClosky (1964) as far as liberal democracy is concerned.)

(b) there is additional evidence — see (a) above — that the left-right dimension should *not* be interpreted in terms of 'primitive self-interest', although a left-wing orientation of the lower classes (and a right-wing orientation of the upper classes) would indeed be in their interest. The extent to which this is the case will be investigated below.

(c) alongside the 2 major dimensions, there appeared an additional one at both the abstract and the attitude levels: *liberalism* and *authoritarianism*, respectively. The structure of ideological controversy in the general population is not *simply* 2-dimensional. Thus, the lack of integration between abstract and specific notions could be *specified*: liberalism should logically be opposed not only to socialism but especially to the left-right dimension which includes so many attitudes on government interference — the very notion to which liberalism, being in favor of free enterprise, is generally opposed. However, liberalism is almost completely independent of LERI, whereas socialism, as we have seen, is moderately related to the attitudes comprising this dimension. Thus the *major* indication of the existence of false consciousness in substantial parts of the general population is given by the almost complete lack of a relationship between liberalism and LERI. We will see below whether this is again especially so in the lower classes. (The uniqueness of the authoritarianism dimension at the attitude level — validated by its relationship to a short F-scale — could be explained in terms of our theoretical approach.)

(d) by extending the domain of attitudes into the religious realm (and by truncating the sample accordingly) we have shown that a more fully-fledged 3-factor structure emerges of which 2 factors are highly similar to those found by Ferguson (1939), Eysenck (1971) and also Wilson, ed. (1973). These 2 factors can now be interpreted in *religious-moralistic* terms (cf. Ferguson's and Eysenck's 'religionism'; Wilson's 'conservative-religious' factor) and in *(political-) authoritarian* terms (compare Ferguson's and Eysenck's 'humanitarianism' — the opposite of authoritarianism — and Wilson's 'anti-intellectual-racialist' factor). Our more comprehensive and systematic approach has shown serious bias in item selection in these studies, however, due to which there could not appear a socio-economic left-right factor, the third factor in our 3-factor solution.

Both the general domain and the one for religious people, including religious elements, show a meaningful structure, but they should be clearly distinguished! Religious attitudes are no longer relevant to an ever-increasing number of people, so they should not be involved in an analysis in the population at large. We have seen that when they are left out the basic 2-dimensional structure can be seen, and that when they are included the structure becomes somewhat more complicated and 3-dimensional. So, as at the theoretical level (see Chapter 4, note 23), religion seems to be a complicating factor at the empirical attitude level as well. Here lies an important opportunity for further research by means of secondary analysis.

A final question that could be asked is: Are our results, to the extent that they are at variance with results from earlier studies, typical for the Dutch population in 1970, after the 'radical' 1960's with the increased 'salience of politics', or are they the result of the present approach to the progressive-conservative antithesis, which may be described as e.g. being based on a more proper construct-definition, a more systematic and comprehensive attitude-selection and more proper procedures of conceptualization in general?

To suggest a possible answer to this question, let us return to the evidence presented in some of these earlier studies, which pointed to the non-existence of dimensions of ideological controversy in the general population (cf. par. 6.2.1.1.c). Campbell et al. (1960: 195ff; see also Key Jr., 1961) base their pessimistic conclusions on items such as the non-scaling tax-item and the one on 'business', which has already been criticized above (par. 3.3.2.3.). In our data, we see that differentiating tax-items for their relevance to upper vs. lower income groups yields the predicted structure: both scales (i.e. *lowering* taxes for lower incomes, *increasing* taxes for upper incomes) load consistently on the LERI dimension: this dimension reflects an ideology which is in favor of (or against) a more egalitarian income-distribution rather than 'primitive self-interest' (see above).

Another finding presented above is consistent with the lack of scalability of the 'business' item reported by Campbell et al. (and similar 'inconsistencies' as reported by e.g. McClosky, 1964): the loading for classical-liberalism is only very low on the LERI dimension. This phenomenon may now be interpreted in terms of (a), *differential* responses to *abstract* vs. *specific* notions; (b), the predominance of classical liberal positions (for America, see Free and Cantril, 1967) and (c), 'anti-state' sentiments and 'fear of bureaucracy' (see par. 6.5.1.1.).

Other evidence which the authors of *The American Voter* presented as indicating a lack of ideological structure in the masses are the lack of a relationship between the 'Domestic welfare' scale, the 'Internationalism' scale and McClosky's somewhat shortened 'Classical conservatism' scale (now interpreted as: 'Posture towards change'; see Campbell et al., 1960).

First, the authors erroneously define liberalism-conservatism in terms of *'attitude to change'* (see Campbell et al., 1960: 197, and above, Chapter 3). Therefore, the lack of a relationship between *'attitude to change'* and the other 2 scales could be taken as evidence of a lack of an integrated ideological structure. (In the present study, progressiveness vs. conservatism has been defined and conceptualized in terms of underlying *values*, from which it could be *predicted* that 'Attitude to change' would *not* be substantially related to ideological continua. This prediction has been confirmed.)

Second, the lack of a relationship between 'Domestic welfare' and 'Internationalism' has also been confirmed in the present study: *but it could be shown that 'Internationalism' loads on a different dimension of ideological controversy to scales that assess 'Domestic welfare' attitudes, like 'Government aid to education' and 'Social welfare laws'*. In other words, when the classical American distinction between 'domestic issues' and 'international issues' is given a more comprehensive, philosophical and attitudinal framework, the 2 basic dimensions of ideological controversy appear and rationales for this 2-dimensional structure (rather than a unidimensional one or no structure at all) can be developed, as has been attempted above. The actual though limited evidence presented by Campbell et al. is not very different to the evidence presented here. In fact, there are remarkable similarities. But the present interpretations are radically different. It has been shown that by redefinition and reconceptualization, and by placing scales which are similar to previously developed ones in their proper and more comprehensive context, it is possible to arrive at such radically different interpretations of the ideological structure at the mass level. To some extent, the same holds true for the evidence presented by Converse (1964) and Key, Jr. (1961), which is at the single-item (issue) level: the issues should be embedded in a scale, tapping the more reliable and more relevant *attitude*; subsequently, broader ideological dimensions may be identified by dimensionality-research based on such attitude-scales. Thus, there is some evidence that the notion of the low level of ideological constraint in the masses during the 1950's was not so much a phenomenon of the era, as due to misconceptualization, misinterpretation of evidence and limited research designs. This suggests that Nie's (1974) findings may not be as much a reflection of the *emergence* of ideology in the 1960's as an artefact (at least partly) of changes in question-wording in 1964, which would in itself be an important methodological phenomenon. But of course, this is still in the realm of speculation rather than being an empirical fact.

All this does not imply that the ideological structure at the mass level is as strong as at the (semi-) elite level (it is in fact much weaker); nor that in the poorly educated and in the disinterested, apathetic working class ideological structure might not wither away until it becomes virtually non-existent. A minimum level of education and political information seems necessary. It has already been shown at the abstract level that although the general structure remains largely intact, the mutual relationships between conservatism, liberalism and socialism become very low indeed (or disappear completely) in the poorly educated, the working class and the politically disinterested, whereas for semi-elites the structure becomes so tight that mass-dimensions can only partly manifest themselves (see above, Tables 6.3. and 6.5.).

We will now see whether these same phenomena appear in the ideological domain. The analysis will be somewhat more extensive than at the abstract level and the following predictions can be made: (a) there will be a tendency towards a unidimensional structure in semi-elitist groups, (b) more variance will be explained in semi-elites by the same number of factors, (c) in non-elites — e.g. the politically apathetic, the lower classes — the structure will be similar to the one in the population at large, but weaker, (d) the structure in semi-elites will be partly similar to that in the mass, and partly unique.

6.5.2. *Some semi-elites and their corresponding non-elitist groups*

The overall effects of semi-elitism (and the corresponding non-elitism) are presented in Table 6.11.: the first 3 Eigenvalues of matrix S* and the explained variance by the first 2 and 3 factors. Of the 5 variables that have been used to define these groups (educational level, social class, income level, political party membership and political interest), *educational level* has again the strongest effect on unidimensionality and explained variance; the first Eigenvalue in the highly educated (those who attended university) is 3 times that in the population at large, and the explained variance of the first 3 factors is about 40% higher. However, this effect can have come about at least partly by the manner in which the 5 variables have been categorized: only 6% of the population have ever attended a university, whereas the upper class comprises, in this instance, about 14% of the sample and about 15% are or have been a member of a political party. Even about 25% are considered as highly politically interested. Income is clearly an exceptional case: those who earned a reported income in 1970 of Dfl. 24,000 or more comprise about 10% of the population, but the effect of semi-elitism here is weak and irregular; there is a similar effect in the more than 20% who earn between Dfl. 12,000 and Dfl. 18,000.

In any case, the educational effect towards unidimensionality is so strong that in the highly educated there are only 4 scales which do not load over .40 on the first unrotated factor. Still, rotation with 2 and 3 factors yields a structure which is highly comparable to the one in the general population; there is only slightly more overlap between the factors [22] (see Table 6.12.). Scales like those on 'Democratic attitudes' and 'Freedom of political expression' now have higher loadings on the authoritarianism factor in the 3-factor solution.

The most interesting phenomenon that should be noted in the highly educated group, however, is the fact that *all abstract dimensions load very high on the left-right factor.* In the 2-factor solution, these loadings are .78 for socialism, —.70 for conservatism and —.62 for liberalism; in the 3-factor solution they are somewhat lower. Conservatism and socialism (*not* liberalism) load low on LITR in the 2-factor solution and somewhat higher — but still lower than on LERI — on AUTH in the 3-factor solution.

The short F-scale loads moderately high on both LERI and LITR and then switches consistently to AUTH in the 3-factor solution.

Table 6.11. *Over-all effects of semi-elitism and non-elitism on the structure of ideological controversy*(a)

	N	Eigenvalues factors			Variance explained	
		1st factor	2nd	3rd	2 factors	3
Educational level						
1. attended university	114	33.5	9.3	4.0	42.5	46.4
2. grammar school	331	15.6	6.8	3.3	33.4	37.7
3. secondary modern school	550	10.2	5.1	2.5	27.0	30.5
4. primary school	932	9.6	3.7	2.2	24.8	27.8
Social class						
1. upper class	279	16.0	6.3	3.5	33.6	38.5
2. upper-middle class	379	13.5	5.7	3.1	31.3	35.5
3. lower-middle class	829	11.9	4.6	2.4	29.2	32.5
4. working class	440	8.7	3.9	2.4	22.8	26.1
Income level						
1. over Dfl. 24.000	191	14.7	7.2	3.2	32.5	36.4
2. 18–24.000	175	11.9	6.6	3.1	28.9	32.8
3. 12–18.000	421	13.9	6.1	3.2	32.3	36.7
4. less than 12.000 (per year)	789	10.7	4.4	2.4	27.2	30.4
Political party membership						
1. (former) members	286	16.4	6.8	2.8	36.1	39.3
2. non-members	1641	10.5	5.3	2.4	28.7	32.2
Political interest						
1. high	509	15.5	6.2	2.8	34.1	37.6
2. low	645	7.3	4.8	2.3	22.5	25.7
Over all	1927	11.1	5.5	2.5	29.9	33.4

Note:
(a) See Appendix 6 for the measurement of variables; compare Table 6.2.

Table 6.12. *The dimensionality of the ideological domain in the highly vs. poorly educated; 2- and 3-factor rotated solutions*

Attitude scale names(a)	Attended university (N=114) 2 fact. Leri	Litr	3 factors Leri	Litr	Auth	Primary school level (N=932)(b) 2 fact. Leri	Litr	3 factors Leri	Litr	Auth
1. Attitude to equality of income, property, status	.76		.70			.50		.51		
2. Govern. interference in bringing about equality of income, property	.80		.77			.45		.47		
3. Attitude to social welfare laws	.45		.48		.37	.31		.30		
4. Government aid to education	.48	.38	.52	.39		.62		.61		
5. Government income policy	.73		.74			.68		.68		
6. Tax policy (higher incomes)	.68		.68			.41		.43		
7. Tax policy (lower incomes)			.36			.39		.38		
8. Government direct econ. interfer.	.68		.72			.54		.53		
9. Government non-directly economic welfare policy	.38	.43	.37	.36		.37	.34	.35	.37	
10. Militant trade-union policy	.49		.51			.36		.35		
11. Democratic attitudes	.51	.55	.44	.35	.50	.51	.48	.48	.47	
12. Freedom of political expression	.37	.56		.37	.49		.57		.51	
13. Aid to developing countries	.57		.49		.40					.32
14. Internationalism	.45	.64	.35	.38	.61		.61		.43	.46
15. Political tolerance					.48		.34			
16. Tolerance towards criminals	.47	.38	.35		.55					
17. Tolerance regarding controversial TV-programs		.44		.44			.41		.48	
18. Moral libertarianism		.70		.69			.57		.59	
19. Family traditionalism		-.70		-.72			-.56		-.61	
20. Authoritarian parent-child rel.		-.63		-.38	-.58		-.59		-.44	-.41
21. Conventional male-female roles		-.40			-.41		-.37			-.42
22. Tolerance regarding homosexuals		.66		.45	.54		.51		.45	
23. Premarital sexual permissiveness		.80		.75			.42		.55	
24. Extramarital sexual permissiveness		.49		.55			.45		.51	
25. Government policy: equality of opportunity(c)	.56		.51			.54		.54		
26. Government spending(c)	.57		.54			.41		.40		
Abstract dimensions										
27. Conservatism	-.70	-.38	-.62		-.49		-.45		-.34	-.31
28. Socialism	.78	.41	.72		.44	.31		.31		
29. Liberalism	-.62		-.59							
30. Authoritarianism (short F-scale)(d)	-.42	-.43			-.63		-.45			-.55

Notes: (note that LERI is now presented as the first, major factor)
(a) See note a, Table 6.7
(b) See Appendix 6
(c) See notes d and e, Table 6.9
(d) See note a, Table 6.8

The fact that all 3 abstract dimensions now load on one factor should not surprise us too much, given their high intercorrelation which has been presented in Table 6.5. But we have now seen that this rather consistent clustering of abstract philosophical positions is related to or integrated with the *left-right* dimension rather than with libertarianism-traditionalism, which implies that *the left-right dimension is the most 'ideological' in this sense in the highly educated.* Moreover, the left-right dimension is 'enriched' with many non-economic attitude scales as well in this group, such as 'Aid to developing countries', 'Internationalism' and 'Tolerance towards criminals'.

If we compare these results with those in the uneducated group, 2 things are immediately clear: (a) like at the abstract level (see note 7), *there is a dimensionality of ideological controversy in the uneducated which is somewhat less tight, but highly similar to the one in the general population* (compare Table 6.9.), so, even in that part of the 'mass' which consists of the about 50% which have followed no further education than primary school ('the true mass'), there are meaningful dimensions of ideological controversy; (b) *the relationship between the abstract dimensions and LERI, which was so strong in the highly educated, has virtually disappeared.* In the population at large we have seen that socialism loads highly on LERI, conservatism weakly negative and liberalism not at all; in the poorly educated we see that only socialism loads *very weakly* on LERI. This contrasts with the relatively high loading for conservatism on LITR in the 2-factor solution and the high loading for the short F-scale on AUTH in the 3-factor solution. This seems to warrant the conclusion that *whereas LERI gets a full 'philosophical backing' in the highly educated, it is at the same time the only dimension which completely lacks such a philosophical basis in the poorly educated.* Thus, educational level seems to be a major factor determining the capacity to integrate abstract philosophical notions and their specific applications in one ideological dimension [23].

As has been shown in Table 6.11., the dimensionality of the ideological domain has also been tested on various social class levels. The actual structures obtained in the upper class vs. the working class are highly similar to those in the highly educated vs. the poorly educated. The structures are less 'extreme' in that in the 2-factor solution in the upper class, all abstract dimension load on LERI but somewhat lower than was the case in the highly educated. The same is true in the 3-factor solution, where socialism now also loads relatively high on AUTH (-.51 as against .54 on LERI), whereas conservatism loads .37 on AUTH and, as in the highly educated, hardly at all on LITR. In the working class, socialism loads somewhat higher — still very low: .35 — on LERI in the

2-factor solution and .38 in the 3-factor solution (both values were .31 in the poorly educated). Thus it is less clear in the working class than in the poorly educated that especially LERI lacks a 'philosophical' foundation.

It seems that income is a variable 'disturbing' the picture in the educational groups within the various class levels (which have been constructed on the basis of educational level, occupation and income; see Appendix 6B). We have already seen that income has an irregular effect on Eigenvalues and explained variance (see Table 6.11.), and this is confirmed in the actual solutions found in the high vs. low income groups. The 2-factor solution in the high income group is similar to the one found in the upper classes, though the loadings for the abstract dimension on LERI are again weaker with conservatism now loading as high on LITR as on LERI (.48) and liberalism only loading –.40 on LERI. The 3-factor solution is *unique*: however, there appears no AUTH dimension (conservatism and the short F-scale remain loaded .45 and .52 on LITR), but the LERI dimension splits into 2 factors with socialism loading highly on a factor including the first 2 scales (implying 'goals'), the 'Tax policy: higher incomes' scale, the one on 'Democratic attitudes' and the one on 'Aid to developing countries'. Most of the other LERI variables are on the other factor, which is similar to the fourth factor which has been found in the general population (see note 17).

The dimensionality in the low income group is highly similar to the one found in the general population with relatively high loadings for conservatism and socialism on LITR and LERI, respectively, in the 2-factor solution (.55 and .42) and still a relatively high loading of socialism on LERI in the 3-factor solution (.43) where conservatism now loads highest on AUTH (.44) together with the short F-scale (.59) as in the general population. Liberalism, however, does not load on LERI anymore. So, although *socialism* is still (very) weakly related to LERI in *some* non-elites such as the working class and the low income group, the *anti-liberal* implications of left-wing ideology are clearly seen in *all* semi-elites and are *not* seen at all in the non-elites.

In summary, we have found that (a) educational level has the strongest effect on the unidimensionality of the ideological progressive-conservative antithesis, thus confirming, like at the abstract level, the partial 'reality' of this antithesis in semi-elitist groups. This tendency is much weaker, however, in the semi-elite of the upper class, where it is probably disturbed by the atypical income-effect, which is very weak indeed; (b) in the highly educated, rotation of 2 and 3 factors still yields a meaningful structure which is, unlike at the abstract level, tighter but *similar* to the structure in the general population. This is also true in the upper class, but in the high income group there appears a unique third factor similar

o the 4th factor in the general population, and no authoritarianism
factor; (c) apart from a certain enrichment of the LERI factor with a
number of non-economic attitude scales in the highly educated, the
major finding is that in this group all abstract dimensions load very high
on the LERI factor and much weaker (i.e. conservatism and socialism)
on LITR and AUTH (in the 2 and 3 factor solutions, respectively). On
the other hand, it is this same LERI factor which completely lacks such a
philosophical basis in the poorly educated, as compared to LITR in the
2-factor solution in that group and AUTH in the 3-factor solution. These
effects are similar, but weaker — probably again due to the atypical
income-effect — in the upper class vs. the working class.

Finally, we have seen in Table 6.11., that educational level also has
much stronger effects on the dimensionality of the ideological domain
than the other form of semi-elitism which has been indicated by political
party membership and political interest (compare Table 6.2. where the
similar effects have been given for the abstract domain).

Rotation of 2 and 3 factors again yields a pattern which is similar to
the one in the highly educated, but less 'extreme': Table 6.13. gives this
pattern in (former) members of a political party. Again, in contrast to
what was the case at the abstract level, dimensions appear which are similar to those in the general population. All abstract dimensions load
rather high on the LERI dimension, but not as high as in the highly educated group, whereas conservatism loads high on LITR in the 2-factor
solution, together with the short F-scale.

In the 3-factor solution it can be seen even more clearly that the major
ideological antithesis (i.e. the one backed up with or embedded in
philosophical notions) in party members is the left-right dimension. (For
non-members, results are similar to those of the general population).

We will now see whether the combination of a high educational level
and extremely high political interest in the elite of M.P.'s will yield the
expected unidimensional progressive-conservative antithesis in the
ideoligical domain, with no meaningful factors appearing after
rotations.

6.5.3. The elite: members of parliament

A rationale behind the prediction that in the elite of M.P.'s the ideological progressive-conservative antithesis will show a unidimensional
structure can now be presented in terms of the criteriality of the 2 values
of freedom and equality which, as we have seen, seem to underlie the
ideological controversy that we are dealing with here. The major dimen-

sions of ideological controversy at the mass level have been interpreted in terms of these 2 values and their somewhat differential application to the economic vs. non-economic realms. It has been suggested that in the general population there may be structural mechanisms at work, like those related to social class, which render the upper classes especially sensitive to the value of freedom and the lower classes to the value of

Table 6.13. *The dimensionality of the ideological domain in (former) members of a political party: 2- and 3-factor rotated solutions*(a)

Attitude scale names	2 factors		3 factors		
	Leri	Litr	Leri	Litr	Aut
1. Attitude to equality of income, property, status	.67		.69		
2. Governm. interference to bring about equality of income, property	.66		.70		
3. Attitude to social welfare laws	.44		.42		
4. Government aid to education	.59		.56		
5. Government income policy	.73		.71		
6. Tax policy (higher incomes)	.65		.66		
7. Tax policy (lower incomes)	.41		.39		
8. Governm. direct econ. interfer.	.63		.61		
9. Government (non-directly economic) welfare policy	.49	.30	.45	.38	
10. Militant trade-union policy	.61		.59		
11. Democratic attitudes	.52	.50	.48	.47	
12. Freedom of political expression	.38	.60	.34	.49	.39
13. Aid to developing countries		.37			.44
14. Internationalism		.68			.66
15. Political tolerance		.31			.36
16. Tolerance towards criminals		.32			
17. Tolerance regarding controversial TV-programs		.49		.53	
18. Moral libertarianism		.67		.53	.43
19. Family traditionalism		.65	-.64		
20. Authoritarian parent-child relationship		.69		-.38	-.59
21. Conventional male-female roles		.43			-.45
22. Tolerance regarding homosexuals		.64		.42	.49
23. Premarital sexual permissiveness		.52		.65	
24. Extramarital sexual permissiveness		.58		.56	
25. Government policy: equality of opportunity	.62		.63		
26. Government spending	.46		.44		
Abstract dimensions					
27. Conservatism	.45	-.50	-.44	-.36	-.37
28. Socialism	.54		.54		
29. Liberalism	-.46		-.43		
30. Authoritarianism (short F-scale)		-.61			-.72

Note:
(a) See notes Table 6.12. For the measurement of political party membership: see Appendix 6

quality (see the discussion in par. 6.4.). Hence we find a basic 2-dimensional structure in the general population. In semi-elites, this differential criteriality diminishes (as we have seen above) and in elites it becomes virtually irrelevant.

In addition to this, it has been suggested in our discussion on the results of the empirical assessment of the operationalization at the abstract level that the progressive-conservative antithesis is an *elitist* construction. If this is true, we will also expect a unidimensional anti-thesis in such an elite.

The results as presented in Table 6.14. confirm these predictions. First, there is clearly 1 major factor in the unrotated solution, with almost all scales loading (very) highly. The degree of unidimensionality is quite similar to that for the abstract-ideological domain (see Table 6.4.; the first Eigenvalue of matrix S* is here 86.8 as compared to 84.2 in the abstract domain). There are only 3 non- or low-loading scales: 'Tax policy: lower incomes' (i.e. tax-reduction), 'Government (non-directly economic) welfare policy' and 'Conventional male-female roles'. Almost all other variables load over .60 [24]. The 2 major abstract ideological dimensions load highest. The second factor reflects double loadings for some 'sex' scales only.

It can be seen that rotation of this highly unidimensional structure does not yield meaningful results: only the 4 'sex' scales load on the second rotated factor without a double (and mostly higher) loading on the first factor. The same is true of the 'non-economic welfare' scale. There is, then, a slight tendency for some sort of 'sex-factor' to split off, but there is so much overlap with the first factor that the structure is meaningless. All ideological scales remain highly loaded on the first factor. In the 3-factor rotation, most variables have double or even triple loadings.

6.5.4. Conclusion

It has been shown above that, like at the abstract level, the progressive-conservative antithesis constitutes a 'real entity' only for a political elite. We have found that in this political elite of M.P.'s, the 3 abstract philosophical dimensions of liberalism, conservatism and socialism are all integrated with almost all attitudes in the progressive-conservative domain, which have been derived from the construct of conservatism by means of the 2 underlying values of freedom and equality.

Table 6.14. *The dimensionality of the ideological domain in members of parliament: 2-factor unrotated solution and 2- and 3-factor rotated solutions* (a)

Attitude scale names	Unrotated prog cons		Rotated 2 factors		Rotated 3 factors		
1. Attitude to equality of income, property, status	−.75	.38	−.68		−.77		
2. Governm. interference to bring about equality of income, property	−.70		−.76		−.76		
3. Attitude to social welfare laws	−.69		−.58	−.39	−.45		−.43
4. Government aid to education	−.84		−.69	−.48	−.62	−.43	−.38
5. Government income policy	−.80		−.76		−.56		−.60
6. Tax policy (higher incomes)	−.85		−.85		−.75		−.45
7. Tax policy (lower incomes)							
8. Governm. direct econ. interfer.	−.83		−.62	−.56	−.43	−.47	−.57
9. Government non-directly economic welfare policy	−.31			−.41		−.44	
10. Militant trade-union policy	−.71		−.65		−.40		−.66
11. Democratic attitudes	−.81		−.71	−.40	−.67	−.36	
12. Political freedom of expression	−.78		−.62	−.47	−.53	−.42	−.40
13. Aid to developing countries	−.74		−.74		−.76		
14. Internationalism	−.74		−.56	−.50	−.50	−.46	
15. Political tolerance	−.80		−.77		−.58		−.58
16. Tolerance towards criminals	−.69		−.51	−.46	−.58	−.48	
17. Tolerance regarding controversial TV-programs	−.65		−.37	−.61		−.53	−.47
18. Moral libertarianism	−.71	−.46		−.78		−.74	
19. Family traditionalism	.73	.51		.83		.80	
20. Authoritarian parent-child relationship	.75		.56	.51	.45	.45	.42
21. Conventional male-female roles	.36	.35					.48
22. Tolerance regarding homosexuals	−.71	−.38	−.38	−.71	−.41	−.71	
23. Premarital sexual permissiveness	−.70	−.51		−.81		−.77	
24. Extramarital sexual permissiveness	−.52	−.43		−.65		−.60	
25. Government policy: equality of opportunity	−.70		−.56	−.43	−.58	−.43	
26. Government spending	−.83		−.80		−.72		−.40
Abstract dimensions							
27. Conservatism	.89		.81	.40	.66		.53
28. Socialism	−.89		−.83	−.36	−.63		−.63
29. Liberalism	.83		.81		.71		.44
30. Authoritarianism (short F-scale)	.65		.59		.50		.36
Variance explained			58.2%		61.7%		

Note:
(a) See notes Table 6.12. and Appendix 2 for the strategic elite sample

Obviously, if our reasoning is correct, the elite is able (a) to integrate its positions on both values — although their application to the economic and non-economic realms seems to be somewhat different (this again confirms our reasoning as to the intimate relationship of the 2 values, non-economically but also in an economic sense — see the discussion in par. 6.4.) — and (b) to integrate its attitudes with abstract philosophical stands into one over-all ideological dimension. The general population does not have these capacities. Hence, we have found there a 3-dimensional structure at the abstract level — liberalism, conservatism and socialism as relatively independent dimensions — and a basically 2-dimensional structure at the attitudinal and ideological levels, left-right and libertarianism-traditionalism, with an interesting subdimension of authoritarianism.

These are the results of our Type-1 analysis (see the scheme in Chapter 2, Table 2.1.) which are rather gratifying in that (a) the *'reality'* of the construct of the progressive-conservative antithesis has been confirmed twice in the strategic elite (at an abstract level and in the overall ideological sense) and (b) the *'fruitfulness'* of the construct has been proven twice in the general population where the conceptualization of the construct of conservative ideology has yielded meaningful and well-interpretable *dimensions* of ideological controversy at the 2 levels of abstraction. Moreover, the dimensions at both levels proved to be related to each other and to partially validate each other; thus the ideological dimensions could be constructed. The empirical assessment of the construct of conservatism at both levels of abstraction in semi-elites and non-elitist groups has also yielded interesting results in that (a) some possible mechanisms leading to unidimensionality in the elite have been identified (i.e. educational level and political interest) and (b) the consistency between abstract dimensions and between these and the left-right dimension rather than the libertarianism-traditionalism dimension has been shown in semi-elites, whereas in non-elites there appeared only a very weak integration of the abstract philosophy of socialism with the left-right dimension and no integration at all of an anti-liberal orientation with socialism and left-right ideology.

As a final extension of Type-1 analysis, we will now make an attempt to assess the validity of the ideological dimension. First, however, we will describe their measurement and their interrelations, as well as their relations to the abstract dimensions of liberalism, conservatism and socialism (compare par. 6.3.1. above).

6.6. THE VALIDITY OF THE IDEOLOGICAL DIMENSIONS IN THE GENERAL POPULA-
TION AND IN THE ELITE

6.6.1. Measurements and interrelations: 'false consciousness'

The 3 ideological dimensions which have manifested themselves in the
general population have been measured by means of a 'double weighed
summation' of the scores on their highly loading attitude scales, items
and abstract dimension. (See Appendix 5 for the details of the measurement; the scale scores have been recoded to 10-point scales.) [25].

The intercorrelations of these dimensions as well as their correlations
with the 3 abstract dimensions are presented in Table 6.15. for (a) the
elite of M.P.'s, (b) the general population (i.e. the mass) and (c) some
semi-elites vs. their corresponding non-elites on the variables of (1)

Table 6.15. *Intercorrelations of the ideological mass dimensions and the
abstract mass dimensions in (a) the general population, (b) some
semi-elites and their corresponding non-elitist groups, and (c) the
strategic elite of M.P.'s(a)*

	Elite(b)					Mass(b)				
	Soc	Lib	LITR	LERI	AUTH	Soc	Lib	LITR	LERI	AUTH (c)
Cons.	−.76	.70	.73	.78	.65	−21	22	.39	.28	.27
Soc.		−.68	−.68	−.79	−.63		−08	−.21	−.41	−.14
Lib.			.63	.71	.60			.04	.16	.03
LITR				.72	.77				.28	.66
LERI					.64					.11

	Semi-elites						Non-elites				
Educational Level(d)	Att. university			Grammar school			Sec. Mod. school			Primary school		
	LITR	LERI	AUTH	LITR	LERI	AUTH	LITR	LERI	AUTH	LITR	LERI	AUTH
Cons.	51	57	53	43	34	34	42	27	31	35	24	19
Soc.	−48	−64	−51	−38	−50	−32	−20	−43	−14	−21	−32	−13
Lib.	39	47	34	19	28	21	09	15	09	07	04	02
LITR		47	72		31	72		26	63		35	57
LERI			50			21			11			13
Social Class(d)	Upper class			Upper-middle			Lower-middle			Working class		
Cons.	42	41	34	42	35	31	40	28	28	32	21	21
Soc.	−34	−48	−33	−27	−41	−21	−27	−42	−20	−12	−31	−06
Lib.	13	30	13	10	19	12	06	12	07	07	04	02
LITR		35	70		32	67		38	65		35	57
LERI			30			19			22			13

Table 6.15. (*continued*)

Political party membership(d)	(Former) members			Non-members		
Cons.	*44*	*39*	26	*38*	26	27
Soc.	-24	*-48*	-13	-21	*-40*	-15
Lib.	20	32	08	01	13	02
LITR		*34*	66		27	67
LERI			14			11

Political interest(d)	Very inter.			Interested			Uninterested			Very uninter.		
Cons.	*49*	*41*	37	*40*	23	26	*35*	22	26	*27*	19	14
Soc.	-36	*-51*	-27	-19	*-44*	-11	-16	*-38*	-12	-15	*-31*	-08
Lib.	21	32	16	06	13	03	-06	11	-05	-03	09	-02
LITR		*36*	71		*21*	64		23	64		23	59
LERI			21			06			06			03

Notes:
(a) Coefficients are Tau beta's; compare the Tau's with the product-moment coefficients in Table 6.5. for elite and mass
(b) See Appendix 2
(c) The abstract dimensions of conservatism, socialism and liberalism are indicated by Cons, Soc. and Lib, respectively; see Appendix 4 and Table 6.5. For LITR, LERI and AUTH, see Appendix 5
(d) See Appendix 6 for measurements

educational level, (2) social class, (3) membership in a political party and (4) political interest.

The data in Table 6.15. constitute a major elaboration of the data that have been presented in Table 6.5. Table 6.15., like Table 6.5., simplifies but also clarifies the structure of the ideological domain and its relation to the abstract domain. (Note that the coefficients in Table 6.5. are product-moment correlations and that the coefficients in Table 6.15. are Tau beta's.) It can be seen that in the population as a whole, LERI and LITR are moderately related (Tau = .28), as are conservatism and socialism (see Table 6.5.). LERI is only slightly related to AUTH; there are indeed many '*left-wing authoritarians*' (see Shils, 1954; Barker, 1958), but it should be remembered that left-right ideology has a predominantly *economic* meaning here. In other words, LERI is relatively independent from the non-economic LITR dimension, but even *more* independent from the (also non-economic) AUTH dimension, at least in the general population. Although the concepts of LITR and AUTH overlap a great deal, to distinguish between the two does seem to make sense, given their differential relationship to LERI and also, for example, to conservatism and socialism. The distinction between liberalism and conservatism also seems of some value, given their differential relationships to all ideological dimensions (note the rather isolated position of liberalism at the 'mass' level: it is only moderately related to conservatism — see Table 6.5. — and right-wing ideology). Socialism and AUTH are also weakly related: there is a relatively large number of *'authoritarian socialists'*.

From the point of view of the 'theoretical' unidimensional progressive-conservative antithesis, the empirical reality of which is again so clearly manifested in the political elite, the relatively low correlations for the general population may again be described in terms of false consciousness. The very dimensionality of the progressive-conservative domain which exists at the mass level seems to simultaneously show 2 things. First, there is obviously a *structuring of ideological positions*, so that there is some measure of 'ideological consciousness' in the population as a whole. Second, however, since this structuring occurs along several subdimensions rather than only along one, as is the case for the political elite, the weak relationships between the various dimensions point to serious inconsistencies in ideological stands.

One of the clearest examples is the weak relationship between liberalism and LERI (.16), which becomes .71 for the political elite. Contrary to the population as a whole, the *elite is able to integrate both abstract and specific notions on government interference*! Generally speaking, the liberalism-dimension, which is rather, or completely independent from all other dimensions at the mass level, is very strongly related to LITR, LERI and AUTH in the elite. The *integration* between abstract and ideological dimensions has generally become much stronger in the elite, as have the mutual relationships among the ideological dimensions. This again suggests that the lack of such relationships points to a state of false consciousness in large parts of the general public. There may be a link between Kerlinger's theory of the 'criteriality of referents' and false consciousness. False consciousness would then be created by the complexity of the 'superstructure' of ideological referents. This would cause many people to select only one of the 2 underlying values as 'critical'.

The 'mechanisms' through which an integration between both orientations might come about are also shown in Table 6.15. It can be seen that the structure in the highly educated most closely approaches that for the elite, especially regarding the relationship of conservatism and socialism to AUTH (the relationships between the abstract dimensions are discussed in paragraph 6.3.1.). The above mentioned relationships as well as that between liberalism and LERI and the one between LERI and AUTH are most sensitive to this educational factor.

The relationships of LITR to the other (abstract) ideological dimensions seem least sensitive to educational level. The relationship between the 2 major ideological dimensions (LITR and LERI) even shows a deviant pattern of slight curvilinearity: it drops from .35 to .26 for the secondary modern school, then rises again slightly to .31 for the grammar school and then again to .47 for the university level. (This is in sharp contrast to the huge rise in the correlation between the 'abstract' counterparts of these dimensions: conservatism and socialism; this is an even sharper rise than that seen for the relationship between liberalism and socialism; see Table 6.5.).

Social class has an effect on the strengths of the relationships between the (abstract-) ideological dimensions which is similar to that of educational level, but obviously income and occupation weaken the education effect. So the relationship between liberalism and conservatism does not increase very much going from working class to upper class (see Table 6.5.), whereas liberalism remains rather independent of LITR and AUTH. Its relationship to LERI increases to .30, however, while LERI and LITR remain related at .35. (Social class acts as a suppressor of the relationship between these variables; the average correlation *within* social class levels increases from .28 overall to .35; see Chapter 7.)

It can again be seen that such phenomena as the lack of relationships between liberalism and socialism (see Table 6.5.) and, as can be seen in Table 6.15., the lack of relationship (though less so) between liberalism and socialism on the one hand, and left-right ideology on the other, are typical for the uneducated and the working class. It is here that we find most false consciousness in this sense. Similar to what has been found in the U.S. (see Free and Cantril, 1967) and as has been noted by Mann (1970), these groups seem largely unable to translate their specific, concrete left-wing opinions into a consistent abstract philosophy.

According to Mann (1970: 436ff), it is the primary school system which is mainly responsible for this situation: 'The essential point is that "the realities of the political process" (to use Litt's phrase) and the populist deviant tradition of the lower class are ignored in the classroom. As the child gets older, he becomes increasingly cynical in his political and social attitudes (Hess and Easton, 1960; Hess, 1963; Greenstein, 1965), but he has difficulty in putting them into abstract terms. What has been ignored in childhood is unlikely to be grasped in adulthood, given working class difficulties with abstract concepts (cf. Bernstein, 1961; findings replicated by Hess and Shipman, 1965). Hence we see agencies of political radicalism, like the trade unions and the British Labour Party, struggling against their opponents' ability to mobilize the national and feudal symbols to which the population has been taught to respond loyally in schools and in much of the mass media (McKenzie and Silver, 1968: 245)'.

We have seen that since the relationships between socialism and left-right and AUTH are so weak in the working class, there must be many

working class people who are left-wing and socialistic but still authoritarian. Hence, these people may be sensitive to right-wing appeals to the
national and feudal notions referred to by Mann above.

Mann concludes that it is the absence of a consistent deviant ideology
which makes the lower classes ' "accept" their lot' (1970: 437) [26].

Finally, as can also be seen in Table 6.15., political interest and political party membership have similar effects on the relationships between
the (abstract) ideological dimensions as educational level and social class
have. However, since political apathy is not unrelated to educational
level and social class, the independent effect of this phenomenon on the
relations between the various dimensions still has to be established. We
will first gather some evidence on the validity of the ideological
dimensions.

6.6.2. Validity

The validity of the ideological mass-dimensions and the one dimension in
the political elite has been assessed in a similar way to the one used in
assessing the validity of the abstract dimensions (see par. 6.3.2. and
Table 6.6.), i.e. LITR, LERI and AUTH have been related to the 'known
groups' of (a) those who describe themselves as progressive or conservative, (b) those who describe themselves as left-wing or right-wing and (c)
those willing to indicate their vote intention 'if there were elections
now' — i.e. political partisanship. The progressive-conservative
dimension for M.P.'s has, of course, been related to their respective
party membership (d).

Results are presented in Table 6.16. and summarized in Table 6.16a.,
where some additional data on the validating 'instruments' are also
presented. They help to inspire confidence in the validity of all ideological dimensions.

Self-identification as progressive vs. conservative is most strongly
related to LITR and AUTH; and less strongly, but positively, to LERI.
Self-identification as left-wing vs. right-wing is about as strongly related
to LITR as to LERI, and in a somewhat weaker manner to AUTH.

Along the LITR dimension, the relationships for political partisanship
are almost identical to those along the conservatism dimension (see Table
6.6.): the christian-democrats are most traditional, followed by labor
and liberals. *Liberals and labor have changed positions here, however:
the position of liberal voters on the abstract dimension is relatively
conservative as compared to their traditionalism.* (The opposite is true
for labor voters.)

Along the LERI dimension, the picture is identical to that for socialism, with liberals again clearly most right-wing, followed by the christian-democrats (with roman catholics most left-wing), radicals, democrats and labor, in that order.

An interesting picture emerges on the AUTH dimension. Here, christian-democrats, together with labor voters are the most authoritarian, followed by liberals, radicals and democrats. Pacifist socialists score as the least authoritarian. As on the LITR dimension, but even more strongly here, *labor voters have changed their position relative to liberals, to the extent that they now form a part of the most authoritarian groups!*

Along all dimensions, pacifist socialists again prove to be the most progressive, followed by communists (note the relative *anti*-authoritarianism of communists: they are only slightly more authoritarian than

Table 6.16. *The validity of the 3 ideological mass dimensions and the ideological elite dimension; tests on 'known groups'*(a)

	Mass-dimensions			Elite-dimension
Self-description as	*LITR*	*LERI*	*AUTH* (b)	*Prog-cons*(c)
conservative	5.22	3.84	5.89	
neutral	4.99	3.81	5.89	
progressive	3.67	2.95	4.52	
right-wing	5.02	3.98	5.57	
neutral	4.52	3.44	5.47	
left-wing	2.96	2.21	4.02	
Political partisanship voters				M.P.'s
liberal (VVD)	4.09	4.79	5.07	4.00
christian-democratic CHU (protestant)	5.46	4.01	5.75	3.40
ARP (prot.-Calvinist)	5.53	4.12	5.71	4.50
KVP (roman catholic)	5.44	3.57	5.94	2.86
progressive PPR (radicals)	3.28	2.79	3.97	—
D'66 (democrats)	3.15	2.61	4.18	.83
PvdA (labor)	4.34	2.50	5.75	.21
extreme left PSP (pacifist socialist)	1.55	1.11	2.07	—
CPN (communists)	2.78	1.44	4.25	
new party DS'70 (right-wing splinter-party of PvdA — Labor Party				2.00

Table 6.16a. *Intercorrelations between validating variables and ideological dimensions in the general population*(d)

	Self. Lr	PPP(1)	PPP(2)	LITR	LERI	AUTH
Self-ident. prog-cons.	.21	.15	.20	.33	.18	.28
Self-ident. left-right		.44	.33	.33	.31	.21
Political party pref(1)			.31	.18	.42	.07
Political party pref(2)				.44	.18	.30

Notes:

(a) See Table 6.6. for additional information on N's; neutrals; political parties, etc.

(b) 10-point scales have been used (see Appendix 5). Figures are mean scores. Over-all means are: LITR: 5.35; LERI: 3.37 (tendency to the left); AUTH: 5.17 (tendency to authoritarianism)

(c) Total score has been constructed by summation of the scores on LITR and LERI, assessed like for the population as a whole, and recoded to 10-points

(d) Correlations are again Tau-beta (Kendall, 1948). All correlations are based on the recoded 4-level variables; see Appendix 5

Political party preferences have been rank-ordered according to the position of the parties on 2 ideological dimensions: (1) LERI (2) LITR. According to the LERI criterion, the rank-ordering is: (from left to right) PSP-CPN, PvdA, PPR-D'66, KVP, AR-CHU, VVD (see Appendix 6 for the key to the party-labels). According to the LITR criterion, the rank-ordering is, from libertarian to traditional: PSP-CPN, PPR-D'66, VVD, PvdA, KVP, AR-CHU. The latter ranking is based on the positions of voters and party members; not on those of members of parliament. Other parties have not been included (n = 1211)

radicals and democrats, but much less authoritarian than labor voters and liberals).

On the over-all dimension for M.P.'s the relative shift for liberals from extreme conservatism in abstract terms to moderate conservatism in ideological terms can be seen. This may be interpreted in terms of the following: liberals are strongly in favor of the existing social order, but somewhat lenient when it comes to the application of general (conservative) principles in private life. It is no wonder, then, that Anti-Revolutionaries prove most conservative. KVP M.P.'s again tend to be relatively progressive, but there is still a wide margin between them and the extreme progressiveness of both democrats and especially labor M.P.'s. Democratic socialists are again in between christian-democrats and progressives.

Although the overall dimension is quite clear in the M.P.'s with liberals and christian-democrats on one side, democrats and labor on the other, it is also clear that voters may not be ordered along the various dimensions in the same way. Here, this is more evident than in the case of the abstract dimensions in Table 6.6.

In order to acquire a measure of association between political partisanship and ideological dimensions, the parties have been rank-ordered in 2 ways: (1), according to the position of voters on the LERI dimension and (2), idem along the LITR dimension (see note on Table 6.16a.). It can be seen that, if 'properly' rank-ordered, political partisanship is more strongly associated with ideological positions than self-identification is [27]. Self-identification as left- vs. right-wing is most strongly related to 'left-right' political partisanship but also more strongly related to 'libertarian-traditional political partisanship' than self-identification as progressive or conservative is (.33 vs. .20); it is more strongly related to AUTH than *actual* LERI position is (.21 vs. .11; see Table 6.15.). Self-identification as left-wing or right-wing is the best predictor for political partisanship and ideological as well as abstract ideological positions. But again, as has been noted above, there is room for additional false consciousness: the self-identified positions of many people are not consistent with their positions on 'objective' measurements of ideology (see also note 13).

Thus there are at least 2 types of false consciousness: (1) inconsistent (abstract) ideological positions, i.e. from the consistent elite and theoretical progressive-conservative perspective, and (2) self-descriptions in ideological terms vs. positions on 'objective' measures of ideological stands. We have seen this in validating the abstract dimensions (par. 6.3.2.) and we see it now again in validating the ideological dimensions.

In the present chapter there is one thing that remains to be done: a full assessment of the 'ideological' nature of the abstract as well as the ideological dimensions by relating these dimensions to social class (see note 16).

It has been suggested above that the basically 2-factor structure in the general population points to the fact that there must be important groups in society which are both libertarian and right-wing or vice versa, and that social class may be an important differentiating variable because the underlying values of freedom and equality may be differentially criterial to upper vs. lower classes (see par. 6.4.). It has also been suggested that the left-right dimension could perhaps be considered the more ideological one since left-wing positions are so much in the (economic) interests of the lower classes, right-wing positions being in the interest of the upper classes. (Libertarian positions can be seen as in the 'psychological interest' of the upper classes; traditionalism could be in the psychological interest of the lower classes — i.e. providing the necessary psychological security; see below.)

Anticipating a further investigation, a third type of false consciousness has been suggested in terms of the relative strength or weakness of the relationship between social class and ideological positions 'in the interest' of the various social classes. Having validated the abstract and the ideological dimensions and having presented evidence on their 'ideological' nature — as opposed to their being 'just' expressions of 'primitive self interest' (see Campbell et al., 1960) — we can now turn to this final question of the relationship of both types of dimensions to social class.

6.7. (ABSTRACT) IDEOLOGICAL DIMENSIONS AND SOCIAL CLASS: A FINAL ASSESSMENT OF THE IDEOLOGICAL NATURE OF THE MASS — DIMENSIONS

It has been argued in Chapter 4 that a 'body of ideas' constitutes an ideology if the ideas (a), constitute a 'doctrine', or are at least related to each other in some meaningful way, and perhaps form a 'system'; (b), they incorporate value-judgements about man and society; (c), they are followed by certain groups (i.e. are not completely idiosyncratic); (d), they are related to each other by virtue of their reference to common underlying values; and (e), they reflect the social position of certain groups or categories (i.e. the interests of social classes).

This definition, in which the concept has been stripped of many other connotations, has been helpful in sketching the historical background of modern Western European ideologies, especially their development during the 19th century. In 'analyzing' the model of conservatism for example, the underlying values of freedom and equality could be detected. In this sense, the notion of ideology has been of heuristic value.

Still, this notion becomes relatively simplistic as soon as one starts empirically assessing ideological structures among certain groups and categories of people, for instance, political elites vs. the population as a whole. Additional complications may arise as soon as one realizes that a conceptual model may be operationalized at various levels of *abstraction*. The definition of ideology which has been used does not specify *how many* values (should) underlie a set of model-statements defining an ideology, the *nature* of their mutual relationship and the *way* in which they should be applied in certain fields.

In empirically assessing a model of an ideology, various structures may emerge, due to the fact, for example, that as Kerlinger (1967, 1972) led us to suggest, the underlying values may be differentially criterial to various groups. In yet other groups (i.e. 'strategic elites'), all values may be criterial: hence such groups are able to comprehend their mutual relationships in various fields. The ideology, so to speak, becomes a 'reality' (i.e. a real, unidimensional antithesis) whereas in the population as a whole, several dimensions may prove to exist. This is in fact what has been shown in the present study.

That the progressive-conservative antithesis constitutes an ideological controversy from the point of view that certain groups tend to adhere to either position, has been confirmed: this antithesis is characteristic of political elites like members of parliament [28]. They are the carriers of such an ideological antithesis, and it has been seen that the M.P.'s of various political parties can be meaningfully ordered along this continuum. At the mass level, with its various ideological continua, the positions of voters along the various dimensions could also be meaningfully distinguished. What remains is the relationship of ideological positions to the structural, social positions of individuals.

It has been suggested that the actual 'carriers' of an ideology need not be identical to those groups whose interests the ideology aims to reflect. It has been maintained that modern ideological controversy arose as an expression of the industrialization process and the rise of the class society. Two classes, the bourgeoisie and the working class, became opposed to each other for predominantly economic reasons. There were other classes however (in a non-Marxian sense), which were threatened by the process of industrialization (i.e. nobility — very small in the Netherlands; see Chapter 4 — , farmers, and a petit bourgeoisie of shopkeepers, craftsmen etc.) or which remained relatively unaffected by it. Such groups often reacted to this process by keeping to the security of a traditional way of life, for *economic* or for *psychological* reasons.

Modern society is of course much more complicated than it appears from this rough sketch of the 19th century class-structure, but there are still many similarities. Thus, certain predictions can be made about the position of various classes along the several ideological dimensions.

Historically, one would predict that, since the upper class contains almost no nobility but represents today's bourgeoisie [29], it will generally be in favor of liberalism, and be anti-socialist and right-wing. The lower-middle class will tend to be most conservative and traditional, and the working class most in favor of socialism, anti-liberal and left-wing.

From the *value-criteriality* perspective, one could, in addition, postulate that the value of freedom will be most criterial to the upper classes (see par. 6.4.). Hence, the upper classes would be least conservative and most libertarian. It can also be predicted that the value of equality will be most criterial to the lower classes for economic reasons. This value may be generalized to non-economic fields, where it would result in egalitarian tendencies which would require 'similar' behavior according to given traditions, norms, etc. This would imply that, in addition to their economic left-wing positions, the lower classes would also be most conservative, traditional and authoritarian (for this rationale, see again the discussion above in par. 6.4.).

The extent to which the various (abstract) ideological dimensions are in fact 'ideological' in this sense, is shown in Table 6.17.

Table 6.17. *The relationship of the (abstract) ideological dimension to social class*

	Conservatism	Socialism	Liberalism	Libertar.-Trad.	Left-right	Authoritarianism
1. Upper class (N = 279)	4.03	4.77	5.61	3.49	4.14	4.04
2. Upper-middle (N = 379)	4.08	4.71	5.65	3.98	3.71	4.58
3. Lower-middle (N = 829)	4.07	5.00	5.11	4.43	3.18	5.33
4. Working class (N = 440)	4.36	5.23	5.02	5.06	2.92	6.11
Tau's	−.04	−.08	.11	−.22	.19	−.30
Over-all means	4.13	4.96	5.27	4.35	3.37	5.17

Note:
Means are based on 10-point scales.
Correlations (Tau-beta's) are based on the 4-level recoded variables (see Appendix 4 and 5). For the measurement of social class, see Appendix 6.

It is clear from Table 6.17 that the abstract dimensions are only *weakly* related to social class, although in the predicted direction. The positions of various classes along these dimensions are often similar: note that only the working class distinguishes itself from the other 3 classes on conservatism. On the socialism- and liberalism-dimensions, upper and upper-middle classes take almost identical positions. The same is true for both lower classes on the liberalism-dimension. On the abstract dimensions, the working class obviously does not hold very 'deviant', progressive positions on socialism and liberalism, whereas it appears slightly more conservative than other classes (see Mann, 1970). It seems that the abstract dimensions are not very 'ideological' in the sense of their relatedness to social class. On the ideological dimensions, it appears that the working class does hold more left-wing positions. At the same time, it is far more traditionalist and authoritarian than the upper(-middle) classes. Here there are clear distinctions between all social class levels. In particular the relationship between authoritariarianism and social class is relatively strong.

The dimensions of LITR, AUTH and LERI are ideological in that they are differentially adhered to by various social classes. These relationships imply an empirical confirmation of the proposition that ideologies incorporate elements expressing the interests of social classes, although the exact nature of these interests as far as AUTH and LITR are concerned has yet to be defined (for LERI, they are clearly economic).

However, the relationship between social class and the ideological dimensions are still rather weak. Thus, although the dimensions are supposed to reflect the 'interests' of social classes, such differential interests are not understood by all.

Many working class people are obviously fairly right-wing; many upper-class people are relatively left-wing; a situation which points to a substantial amount of false consciousness in this sense. The relatively weak relationship between left-right ideology and social class (.19) seems especially interesting because of the more or less obvious economic relevance of left-wing opinions to the working class and of a right-wing ideological stand to the upper class. This poses a challenge to the researcher: *which factors are responsible for the weakness of this relationship and which factors may therefore increase it*? This will be the major issue in the next chapter. (Additional rationales for choosing this relationship as a starting-point in Type–2 analysis — see Chapter 2 — will be outlined there.)

Finally, the negative relationships of social class to traditionalism and authoritarianism should be considered. The latter is the strongest of the two, which suggests that, given the overlap between the 2 dimensions, *the authoritarianism components of LITR are most sensitive to social class differences.* This is another matter which has to be discussed shortly: the fact that a variable like social class is related to a broad, general construct like libertarianism-traditionalism does not imply that it is related to the same extent to every subdimension within this broader construct, although all these subdimensions are sufficiently related to each other to warrant the construction of the broader dimension (see Stinchcombe, 1973 a, b).

Social class and the various strengths of its relationship to the various

LITR subscales might perhaps also explain the phenomenon of 'working class conservatism'. Of course, many suggestions have been put forward (e.g. Lipset, 1963; Parkin, 1967; Nordlinger, 1967; Lipsitz, 1965; Miller and Riesman, 1961), but the relationship between such explanations and the 'ideological' nature of the LITR dimension is not so clear: which *interests* of the working class, for example, are at stake for its need to be (relatively) traditional and authoritarian, in combination with its relatively left-wing views?

6.7.1. A note on 'working class conservatism'

Before making speculations, as has so often been done before on this well-known phenomenon, some more detailed data will be examined. In Table 6.18., the overall relationship between social class and LITR and AUTH, respectively, is broken down into its various components (so-called 'component-analysis'; see Rosenberg, 1968). The 'marginals' give the relationships between (a) social class and AUTH components and (b) AUTH and LITR and social class components.

The relationship between social class and LITR (working class traditionalism) is indeed mainly caused by the relatively strong relationships between social class and the AUTH components of LITR. The average Tau for the non-AUTH LITR components is only .08, whereas for the AUTH LITR components it is about .19. Hence, there is working class *authoritarianism*, rather than *traditionalism*. (Conservatism is, of course, a much too general term, given the working class' left-wing views).

Attitudes regarding certain aspects of *family life* play a prominent role in this: the lower classes are especially differentiated from other classes by their ideas on parent-child relationships and by their definition of male-female roles. Their attitudes towards family traditionalism generally and extramarital sexual permissiveness are consistent with this. The same seems to be true of their intolerant attitude towards homosexuals.

Outside their attitudes regarding family life, working class notions on authoritarianism seem mainly to consist of *nationalism* (including notions such as 'patriotism', keeping up typically Dutch ways of life, respect for national symbols etc.; see Appendix 6 for the scale-items; this is consistent with their negative attitude to 'Aid to developing countries') and personality factors as included in the shortened version of the *classical F-scale* (including tendencies such as those towards stereotypy and paranoia, cynicism about people generally, conformism, punitive atti-

Table 6.18. *The relationship between social class components and the component subscales of the ideological dimensions of LITR and AUTH*

	Social class components			
	Educ. level	*Occup. level*(a)	*Income level*(b)	*Social class*(c)
Non-AUTH components				
Conservatism	–10	–04	02	–05
Freedom of political expression	16	07	04	09
Democratic attitudes	13	03	02	04
Political tolerance	18	09	12	11
Gov. (non-dir. econ.) welfare pol.	08	04	–04	03
Tolerance reg. controversial TV-programs	07	01	–04	02
Moral libertarianism	23	13	11	13
Family traditionalism	–21	–12	–14	–15
Premar. sex. permissiveness	10	–03	–03	–02
Extramar. sex. permissiveness	16	05	06	12
AUTH-components				
Aid to develop. countries	20	14	10	15
Nationalism	–32	–25	–18	–22
Auth. parent-child relationship	–32	–22	–17	–24
Convent. male-female roles	–22	–22	–17	–21
Tolerance towards homosexuals	24	15	11	15
Tolerance towards criminals(d)	13	12	04	10
Classical F-scale(d)	–31	–23	–16	–22
LITR(e)	–33	–20	–17	–22
AUTH(e)	–40	–28	–24	–30

Notes:
(a) Housewives and students not included (N = 1089; see Appendix 6B).
(b) Non-response not included (N = 1576; see Appendix 6B).
(c) The social class index is not a simple summation of the scores on the 3 class-indicators (see Appendix 6B).
(d) Scales have not been included in the LITR-measurement.
(e) For the measurements of these dimensions, see Appendix 5.

tudes and submission to a strong leader; see Appendix 6B). The rather weak relationship between 'Tolerance towards criminals' and social class is consistent with this authoritarian tendency.

So, it has been shown that working class authoritarianism does *not* imply (or hardly) that the working class (and the lower-middle class) are, for example, more opposed to civil liberties, less democratic (in the concrete sense of equality of power), less tolerant about controversial TV programs or more opposed to premarital sexual relations, than the upper classes (cf. Middendorp, 1974: 173; see also Hamilton, 1972: Ch. 11).

How, then, should working class authoritarianism be interpreted if it does not include these tendencies? In the first place, it can be seen in Table 6.18. that *educational level* is the social class indicator which is most strongly related to AUTH-components, as well as to other LITR-components. So, although it has not yet been established whether occupation and income do have an independent effect on AUTH [30], working class authoritarianism seems mainly to have been caused by the generally low educational level of that class. Educational level is by far most strongly related to authoritarianism as measured by the AUTH dimension (—.40), and to its specific components of nationalism, authoritarian parent-child relationship, and the classical F-scale (all about —.32).

This suggests that authoritarianism is largely brought about by what might perhaps be termed 'limited horizons' or 'a limited view of life'. In the context of the present study, and certainly at this stage of the present analysis, one can only speculate as to why education seems to have such a relatively strong positive effect on internationalism and egalitarian opinions about the parent-child relationship [31]. The fact that there is a strong tendency in primary schools to instill a feeling of nationalism in pupils has often been noted (see e.g. Mann, 1970: 436 and the references given there; see also Converse, 1964: 237). Obviously, further education is needed to 'free' the individual from such indoctrination. If only in this sense, education seems to be 'liberating'.

The same may be true of the parent-child relationship. If people develop themselves further through education, they may possibly develop a positive attitude towards individual freedom and tolerance, which they may then extend to the parent-child relationship. They may also become increasingly aware of alternative life-styles and the relativity of specific cultural traditions; hence, they may tend to be less conventional as regards male-female roles, more tolerant towards, for example, homosexuals, more libertarian in a moral sense, etc. Of course, exposure to such expressions of other cultures and life-styles as experienced through mass-media, books, films, theatre and travel, may also play an important role here.

In general, the effects of educational level on non-AUTH aspects of the LITR dimension are much weaker; they are strongest for 'Moral libertarianism' and 'Family-traditionalism'. An explanation could be that education has stronger effects in fields of (potential) immediate concern to people, like the family and the nation.

Finally, the effects of education on AUTH-components could also perhaps be interpreted in terms of a mechanism which might be called 'lack of social security', 'lack of sense of control of one's social environment' or 'lacking the ability to find one's bearings in a complex world';

n short: *anomia* [32]. Where there is such an anomic situation, in seeking 'psychological security' people may develop 'authoritarian' personality tendencies as outlined above (see also par. 6.4.). In addition, they may tend to abide by the rules of the existing social system, and adhere to traditional norms and habits. It seems plausible that in such a situation one begins to accept the system as it stands (i.e. tends to be nationalistic) and organizes one's *immediate* social environment along 'secure' lines (e.g. one requires obedience of children, defines sex-roles in a rigid and conventional way, keeps to traditional ways of family life generally). Subsequently, one may reject 'deviant' minority groups like homosexuals, criminals, etc., or even develop a punitive attitude towards them, because they are experienced as 'threatening' this 'precious fabric'. Other attitudes referring to situations which are of less immediate concern to the individual's personal life (i.e. democratic attitudes) or views phrased in very general terms (i.e. lacking in appeal to the specific personal situation), would not — because of this sense of anomia — show such a strong relationship to educational level [33]. In the next chapter, this theory on working class traditionalism will be tested.

In summary, we have found that:

(a) the abstract dimensions of conservatism, liberalism and socialism are *not* ideological in that they are virtually unrelated to social class;

(b) the ideological dimensions are *weakly* ideological in that their relationship to social class is rather weak. This means that in the Netherlands there is no strong class antagonism along these fundamental ideological dimensions — especially the left-right dimension — which has been put forward by some political sociologists as a prerequisite for liberal (parliamentary) democracy. Therefore, the relationship between social class and LERI — as the dimension most clearly related to the economic interests of the various classes — will be taken up in the next chapter as the central relationship in Type-2 analysis;

(c) the notion of 'working class conservatism' is erroneous. The working class is more left-wing than other classes and the traditionalism of this class — in terms of the LITR dimension — could first be specified as 'authoritarianism' and secondly, working class authoritarianism proved to consist mainly of nationalism, an authoritarian orientation regarding parent-child relationships, conventionality in male-female role definitions and authoritarian personality tendencies in terms of the classical F-scale. In addition, the working class is more intolerant regarding homosexuals and more opposed to aid to developing countries (see e.g. Hamilton, 1972: 127). Hence, the working class is *not* authoritarian in the sense of being opposed to freedom of political expression or anti-democratic in specific attitudes; the relationships between such and other attitudes and social class are very weak indeed;

(d) to the extent, then, that working class conservatism exists, it is mainly caused by the factor of educational level. The effect of a relative lack of education on the emergence of certain authoritarian attitudes regarding nationalism and the family has been interpreted in terms of 'limited horizons' and an attempt to fight anomic tendencies by means of the creation of a secure psychological environment in fields that are of immediate concern to the individual's daily life. In the next chapter an attempt will be made to gather evidence in favor of this rationale.

6.8. SUMMARY

In this chapter we have empirically assessed the operationalizations of conservative ideology according to the Type–1 analytical scheme which was outlined in Chapter 2. The basis for this procedure was laid in Chapter 4 where we defined the construct of conservative ideology by means of an ideal type model of 121 statements.

This model was operationalized in Chapter 5 in 2 ways: (a) by means of a direct translation into 37 bipolar statements, and (b) by way of about 30 attitude scales derived from the model by means of its 2 underlying values of freedom and equality, which served as selection-criteria.

We started the analysis at the *abstract* level (the bipolar statements) and in the *general Dutch population*. Here we found that the progressive-conservative domain falls apart into 3 relatively independent dimensions which could be interpreted in terms of the 3 major ideologies which have dominated Western European political thought since the first half of the 19th century: liberalism, conservatism and socialism. Hereby, 3 things were proven: (a) contrary to much research evidence gathered in the U.S. around 1960, there is, even at an abstract philosophical level, a meaningful structure of ideological controversy in the general Dutch population in 1970; (b) this structure is rather weak: 4 factors (one factor does not refer to an ideological dimension) explain 23.2% of the variance; (c) this structure is much more complex than the simplistic notion of *one* progressive-conservative antithesis would suggest.

Two major rationales have been developed to explain why this unidimensional structure does not emerge in the general population. Both are generalizations of Kerlinger's (1967) theory of the criteriality of attitudinal referents. One rationale generalizes Kerlinger's theory to the Western European scene, where liberalism and conservatism have somewhat different meanings as compared to the U.S. and where, in addition, there is the ideology of socialism. The other rationale generalizes the theory to the criteriality of values instead of referents, and postulates a differential criteriality of the values of freedom and equality to broad sections of the general population. Differences between our findings and those in the U.S. referred to above, pointing to a complete lack of ideological structure in the American public, were explained in the first instance in 2 ways. One is cross-cultural: the American public has been notorious for its lack of ideological thinking, probably due to the dominant business ideology of the middle classes (see Hartz, 1955). Neither has there been an aristocracy that could be the carrier of typical European notions of conservatism, nor has there been a strong socialist ideology; the ideological scene has been much more homogeneous in the liberal tradition. The other explanation is longitudinal: Nie (1974) noted the increasing salience of politics in the 1960's with an increase in political interest which — at least until recently — led to the emergence of, so Nie maintains, *one* liberal-conservative antithesis at the mass level. This notion, and Converse's one that education would play an important role in people's ability to grasp abstract continua like the liberal-conservative one, was tested by an extension of the basic Type-1 analytical design, which formed the second phase of the analysis; the structure of ideological controversy at the abstract level was tested in 2 so-called semielites, anticipating its assessment in the elite the highly educated and the politically interested (i.e. party members).

Three things have become clear from these analyses: (1) in both semielites, but especially in the small highly-educated group, there is a tendency for a unidimensional structure to emerge, (2) (much) more variance is explained by the same number of variables, and (3) rotations of factors yield partly unique, partly similar factors, as compared to the general public. Especially in the highly educated, there is such a strong tendency towards unidimensionality — whereby the reality of the progressive-conservative antithesis is at least suggested for this and similar groups — that the mass dimensions find it almost too difficult to manifest themselves.

The expectation that was formulated after these analyses, that in the elite of M.P.'s the progressive-conservative antithesis would exist as a unidimensional structure, was indeed confirmed. Thus, after the first part of Type-1 analysis, we have found that at the abstract level in the mass population the progressive-conservative 'antithesis' falls apart into 3 dimensions, while at the elite level there is 1 unidimensional antithesis.

At semi-elite levels, there are constellations which are between these various structures. Thereby we have proven 2 things: (1) the progressive-conservative antithesis, as operationalized at the abstract level by means of the bipolar items, constitutes a 'real entity' in the elite of M.P.'s, and (2) it yields well-interpretable dimensions of ideological controversy at the level of the general population. These results could be obtained although the direct operationalization of the model of the construct of conservative ideology was far from perfect.

After the assessment of the structure of ideological controversy at the abstract philosophical level in the general population, some semi-elites and the elite of M.P.'s, the fourth phase in the analysis — and another extension of Type–1 analysis — was the measurement and validation of the dimensions in these same groups, based on the mass-dimensions. These measurements and interrelations have yielded results which point to the existence of substantial amounts of false consciousness in the mass, in particular in the non-elite mass groups such as the relatively un-educated, the working class and the politically uninterested. In the general population, the relationship between the dimensions is not very strong, and especially the relationship between liberalism and socialism (which theoretically should be highly negative, which it is in the elite) is only $-.12$. In most non-elites, this relationship vanishes com-pletely — or even becomes positive — while the relationship between conservatism and socialism also weakens considerably. Generally, the structure of ideological controversy at this abstract level becomes much weaker in these non-elitist mass groups. Finally, the validity tests for the various mass-dimensions as well as for the one elite-dimension yielded satisfying results.

The next stage in Type–1 analysis was to go down to the *attitude level* (excluding for the moment the 5 religious attitudes) and back to the *general population*, in order to test the structure of 'ideological' con-troversy at the meta-attitudinal level.

Here we found a basic 2-factor structure which could well be inter-preted in terms of the underlying values of freedom and equality, although the application of these values to the economic vs. non-economic realm should now be made more explicit. At the abstract level, both values could be seen as underlying the conservatism and socialism dimensions more or less in the same manner, and the separate liberalism dimension could be 'explained' by pointing to the differential application of these values to the economic realm of government interference vs. the freedom of enterprise. At the attitude level, one dimension (the left-right dimension) seemed clearly to reflect the value of socio-economic equality as a goal, but including a positive orientation regarding a large number of government policies aiming to reach this goal; here the liberating implications, though clearly visible, seem to be secondary. The other dimension, the libertarianism-traditionalism one, seems to be dominated by the value of freedom applied in a non-economic sense with the secondary egalitarian implication of 'various behaviors of various groups' being of 'equal value' and hence to be tolerated and accepted. Thus, this basically 2-dimensional structure of ideological controversy at the meta-attitudinal level in the general population — as opposed to the theoretical unidimensional antithesis — could again be interpreted in terms of the differential criteriality of the values of freedom and equality to large sections of the population, but now it became clearer which structural variable would effect this differential criteriality: *social class*; it has been suggested that the upper classes would have the value of freedom as the major criterial one and that the lower classes would adopt the value of equality as such.

Finally, when 3 factors were rotated orthogonally, there appeared an interesting third factor alongside the 2 major ones, which was tentatively interpreted in terms of authoritarianism. (This structure is now much more tight than at the abstract level: 3 dimensions explain 31.7% of the variance.)

The next stage was again an extension of the basic Type-1 analytical design: an integration of the abstract dimensions of liberalism, conservatism and socialism, plus a shortened version of the classical F-scale, into the attitudinal domain in order to validate (at least partially) the dimensions that had appeared at the meta-attitudinal level and to see whether the abstract philosophical dimensions would be related to their specific and more concrete applications at the attitude level.

The results of this procedure were quite interesting. In the general population, the abstract dimension of socialism proved to be the philosophy behind the left-right dimension, thus partially confirming the ideological nature of this dimension. The same proved to be the case for the abstract dimension of conservatism and the meta-attitudinal dimension of libertarianism-traditionalism. Finally, the third dimension of authoritarianism was validated by the short F-scale. (The explained variance has increased to 32.8%.) The most intriguing finding was the lack of a relationship in the general population between the abstract dimension of liberalism and the left-right dimension; although liberalism explicitly refers to government interferences vs. free enterprise and although many left-right attitude scales refer to specific government policies, the attitude towards liberalism is virtually unrelated to the left-right orientation.

After some exploration, the establishment of a 'best solution', (in which the explained variance increased to 33.4% for the 3 factors) and an interesting excursion into the religious realm (where it was found that instead of a basic 2-dimensional structure, the structure becomes more fully fledged 3-dimensional, with alongside the left-right dimension, a religious-moralistic and a politico-authoritarian dimension which are highly similar to dimensions found earlier by Ferguson [1939], Eysenck [1971] and Wilson, ed. [1973]), the next stage in the analysis was the establishment of the structure of the ideological domain (abstract dimensions and attitudes in the 'best solution' in the general population) in some semi-elites and their corresponding non-elitist groups along the variables of educational level, social class, income, political party membership and political interest. In semi-elites along these variables, and in particular in the highly educated, 2 tendencies appeared which are similar to those at the abstract level: (1) a tendency towards a unidimensional structure, and (2) more explained variance. The actual solutions were quite similar to the ones for the general population: contrary to the abstract domain, there appeared no unique factors. Only for income levels did there appear a deviant pattern which cannot be explained.

The most notable phenomenon at this stage of the analysis was the confirmation of the left-right dimension as the major ideological one: in semi-elites all abstract dimensions loaded very high on this dimension rather than on the LITR or AUTH dimensions. (Earlier it had been suggested that the ideological nature of the left-right dimension would be most clear due to the fact that the economic interests of various social classes would be most clearly related to this dimension, whereas the other dimensions would reflect the 'psychological' interests of the various classes; see below.)

It has been clear throughout this chapter that the Type–1 analytical scheme that was presented in Chapter 2 (i.e. the 2 × 2 scheme according to which the operationalizations of a complex construct such as conservatism should be assessed at 2 levels of abstraction in both the general population and a strategic elite) has not been carried out rigidly. At the abstract level, the analysis in semi-elites was introduced — anticipating the analysis in the elite — and at the attitudinal level it was soon found useful to return partially to the abstract level in order to obtain evidence in favor of the validity of the abstract and meta-attitudinal dimensions and to reach the 'real' ideological level of analysis. This ideological domain was again submitted to subgroup analysis in semi-elites and their corresponding non-elites, and so the final stage of Type–1 analysis does not consist of an analysis of the structure of the attitudinal domain in the strategic elite, but rather of an analysis of the structure of the complete ideological domain in that group. Of course, the prediction that was made was that the structure of ideological controversy in that group would be clearly unidimensional; a prediction that was clearly confirmed.

Thus, in terms of our modified Type-1 analysis, we have found the following results (see Table 6.19.).

Table 6.19. *The results of Type-1 analysis (see Table 2.1.)*

UNIVERSE SAMPLED	OPERATIONALIZATIONS OF CONSERVATISM	
	The abstract philosophical level	The ideological level
The general population	3 dimensions: conservatism socialism liberalism	3 dimensions: LITR LERI AUTH (subdimension)
The strategic elite	1 dimension: progressive-conservative	1 dimension: progressive-conservative

These results have been considered satisfactory in that (a) the reality of the progressive-conservative antithesis as an elitist phenomenon has been established twice, and (b) at the mass level there appeared meaningful dimensions of ideological controversy, even though the perspective from which these various domains were defined was an elitist one.

Our findings as to the nature of ideological controversy in the general population are at variance with findings in the U.S. in the late 1950's and early 1960's. Some rationales for these differences could be developed, but it could also be shown that it might well be the limited definitions and conceptualizations used in previous studies which led to erroneous interpretations of the evidence.

The last extension of Type-1 analysis was the establishment of evidence in favor of the validity of the ideological mass-dimensions and the one dimension for the elite. Therefore, the dimensions were measured and mutually related in (a) the elite of M.P.'s, (b) the mass, and (c) some semi-elites and their corresponding non-elites. In addition to this, the ideological dimensions were related to the abstract dimensions in all these groups. In terms of false consciousness, results again point unequivocally to the existence not only of substantial amounts of false consciousness in the general population (e.g. the weak relationship between liberalism and left-right ideology), but also to the fact that such false consciousness is again most prominent in non-elites such as the uneducated, the working class and the politically apathetic. It should be remembered, however, that although there is from the consistent elite perspective a substantial amount of various types of false consciousness in such non-elitist groups, even in these groups is there a meaningful structure of ideological controversy which is weaker but similar to the one in the general population, although one major difference is the fact that in particular the left-right dimension as a meta-attitudinal one is not 'backed up' with a socialist and anti-liberal philosophy, whereas in the semi-elites the left-right dimension is the one on which all abstract dimensions load very highly. The evidence in favor of the validity of the ideological dimensions which was gathered in a way similar to the one used in the case of the abstract dimensions, has been quite satisfactory.

The final stage in the analysis in the present chapter was the establishment of the relationship between the (abstract) ideological dimensions and social class in order to assess whether the dimensions are truly ideological — given our definition of ideology, among other things, in terms of the interests of various social classes. It was then found that the abstract dimensions are virtually unrelated to social class, hence are not ideological in that sense. The ideological dimensions are weakly related to social class in that there is a negative relationship between social class and LITR and AUTH and a positive relationship between social class and LERI, i.e. the working class is more left-wing but also more traditional and authoritarian than the upper class. The weakness of the relationship between social class and LERI has been especially intriguing because obvious economic interests seem to be at stake. This relationship will be the central one in the Type-2 analysis to be presented in the next chapter.

The negative relationship between social class and LITR and AUTH has led to a preliminary analysis of the well-known phenomenon of working class traditionalism, which has actually proven to be working class authoritarianism and to consist mainly of negative relationships between social class and nationalism, authoritarian parent-child relationship, conventional male-female role definitions, aggression against homosexuals, opposition to aid to developing countries and anti-authoritarian personality characteristics in terms of some classical F-scale items. It was found that educational level is the major factor behind this type of working class authoritarianism. A rationale for these relationships has been given, and this will also be tested in the next chapter.

1. A detailed description of the advantages of Jöreskog's factor-analysis over other methods will not be given here. Very briefly it can be seen as an approximation to maximum likelihood factor analysis. However, it is a new model with an extra assumption about communalities, which makes the estimation of the parameters simpler and solves the identification-problem. The assumption is that the unique variances of the variables is proportional to $1-R^2$ (R is the multiple correlation-coefficient of the i-th variable with all other variables). Jöreskog has shown that this is a reasonable approximation to the general model if the number of variables is large and if the factors are well-identified. We will see in the present study that these conditions are generally satisfied.

2. In assessing multidimensionality through factor-analysis, factors should always be rotated to simple structure (unless there is one 'overwhelming' factor), though not necessarily via an orthogonal solution (e.g. according to the varimax-procedure). It has been the author's experience that oblique and orthogonal solutions are mostly quite similar (a fact that seems inherent in factor-analysis) and for that reason, that oblique rotations are only useful in second-order factor analysis. This technique does have disadvantages from the point of view of conceptualization (see e.g. the discussion on the results of Kerlinger, 1968; Chapter 3). In spite of this, as a control for the 4-factor (best) solution, using Jöreskog's method and varimax-rotation, a simple 'principal components' analysis with both varimax- and promax (oblique) rotations has nevertheless been carried out. For all practical purposes all solutions had identical results. The same applied to a separate factor-analysis after elimination of duplicated cases (N = 1718).

3. I have been reluctant to incorporate the classical-liberal 'operationaliza-tions' in the conservatism-model for this very reason. The statements in section g of the theoretical construct better reflect the somewhat more *moderate* conservative position (e.g. statements 9.2.1.; 9.4.1.). It can be seen that even in the 4-factor rotated solution, some liberal elements which do not directly refer to 'government interference' or 'free enterprise' are maintained in the conservatism factor.

4. See the discussion on this generalization below.

5. The influence (after its popularization) of psychoanalysis may also be mentioned. Generally speaking, modern psychology has not tended to find evidence in favor of basic human rationality or goodness. It has emphasized man's tendency to satisfy drives and needs, with strong irrational and amoral implications (expectations of negative vs. positive sanctions and rewards; enhancement of power and self-esteem, etc.). Still, most people tend to respond positively to items which deal with human nature.

6. This may be one reason, by the way, why ideological controversy is so often empirically assessed in American research in terms of the individual's position on *specific issues*. There are only a few studies which attempt to assess liberal democratic principles in general terms (see e.g. Prothro and Grigg, 1960). We should also recall the uniqueness and subsequent misinterpretations of McClosky's (1958) study (see Chapter 3: par. 3.3.1.2.).

7. Results for the uneducated (primary school only) and non-members of a political party are not presented, as they are highly similar to the over-all

results, only somewhat less 'tight'. All unpublished results (including 2-, 3 and 5-factor solutions) are available upon request. This applies to all find ings referred to throughout this and the next chapter, which have not bee presented in full.

8. Results are not only at variance with Nie's (1974) suggestions about th effects of educational level upon ideological constraint, but also wit Eysenck's (1971) finding that social class only has a positive relationship t the *tightness* of the factorial structure (i.e. the variance explained), but tha the type of structure is identical for upper vs. lower classes. It may be note that the effects of *political interest* have been found highly similar to thos of party membership, and that *social class* has an effect similar to that o educational level.

8a. The term 'false consciousness' is used in a *descriptive* way only. As yet, w have no conclusive evidence on the 'falsity' of the 'consciousness' involved.

9. As might have been expected, the Mokken-procedures applied to these item have been rather unsuccessful. These ideological dimensions are obviousl 'too broad' (or: too vague) to attain the strong unidimensionality that i required, even for a weak Mokken-scale. Only liberalism showed a weak scale, which has not been used. (See Mokken, 1970.)

10. Item 35 has not been used in measuring conservatism. In measuring social ism, item 18 has been left out (it is similar to item 20, which has a highe loading). In measuring liberalism, item 4 has been excluded (see Table 6.1.) No weighing for variations in loading has been found necessary. Total sum scores have been recoded to 10 points scales (see Appendix 4). High score indicate conservative, socialist and liberal positions.

11. Although we have seen that not quite the same dimensions appear for ever semi-elite in Table 6.5., it seems justified to compute scores on the mas dimensions for these groups and their corresponding non-elite groups. Fo the elite, the mass dimensions may be distinguished as 'aspects' of the over all progressive-conservative dimension.

12. Validation procedures presented here and below are essentially on the basi of 'known groups', although the positions of political parties along ideologi cal continua are only partly known. In this sense, the validation is 'predic tive' (see the research-evidence on the position of Dutch political partie along progressive-conservative and left-right dimensions in Chapter 3 3.4.5.). By the way in which they have been constructed, the dimension have a high degree of *content* validity, although judging by the label attached to them (i.e. conservatism, socialism), their content does no pretend to represent all or even most elements of these ideologies. Construct validity seems essential, but can only be gathered gradually, in the course o subsequent analyses.

13. False consciousness exists only *to the extent that one accepts the validity o the indicators for the various ideological dimensions.* But this validity i assessed on the same basis as the degree of false consciousness. Though con ceptual model-construction guarantees a high degree of content-validity what is clearly needed is *additional* evidence of the validity of the dimen sions. What is lacking in the present study (due to its progressive-conserva tive perspective) is evidence on the relationship of self-identification a liberal and socialist to the various dimensions; a typical matter for replica tion. What is also lacking is an assessment of a respondent's adherence t

values like *freedom* and *equality*. In that way, our reasoning as to a respondent's attitude on such values *underlying* positions on abstract-ideological dimensions, could have been substantiated. Evidence of this kind on the validity of the dimensions has been gathered in a number of subsequent studies; see e.g. Middendorp, 1977b.

4. Predictions could have been made in the light of what has been made known from previous research on the parties' varying stands regarding progressive-conservatism issues, from perception of the parties' positions along (imaginary) left-right or progressive-conservative dimensions, on the basis of M.P.'s awareness of distances between parties and from voting behavior in parliament (see again Chapter 3: 3.4.5.). Evidence has recently (Fall, 1974) been gathered by the Dutch Institute for Public Opinion and Marketing Research (NIPO), following suggestions put to them by Van Cuilenburg of the Free University of Amsterdam (Dept. of Mass Communication; Social Science Institute), where it is again quite clear that both along the left-right and the progressive-conservative dimensions, the christian-democratic parties and the liberal VVD are *seen* in the population at large as the most right-wing and conservative; the progressive parties (especially the radicals and labor) and the communists are seen as the most left-wing and progressive. On 7-point scales, there are 2 clear clusters with margins of about 2 to 3 points (data available on request).

15. Radicals take a rather inconsistent position; they are both more *liberal* and more *socialist* than labor voters. It seems that both radicals and democrats are strongly in favor of socialist *goals*, but not in favor of using the traditional socialist *means*, i.e. government interference.

16. Whether these dimensions are ideological in a more general sense, i.e. are consistently related to social class, will be investigated below.

17. The left-right dimension is less stable in the 4- and 5-factor rotated solutions. In these solutions, there is a tendency for a certain split between goals-scales (nos. 1 and 2) and socialism on the one hand, and government policy scales (and the one on 'Democratic attitudes') on the other. This tendency is not consistent, however, since the scale on tax policy for higher incomes remains loaded on the 'goals' dimension. Moreover, liberalism, albeit very low again, also remains loaded on that dimension.

18. This was done because it was hypothesized that (a), many people might be unwilling to admit prejudices against working class children and (b), the relationship between social class and educational achievement may be too complicated for many people to have an opinion about it, which could be interpreted in terms of an attitude to equality of opportunity.

19. In the 5-factor rotated solution, the item 'The state interferes too much' appears together with the liberalism scale and some other variables on a separate factor. The item is moderately related to liberalism (.22).

20. Many people may consider the present level of government spending acceptable, but find that the government should spend available resources *in a different way*. This is suggested by the fact that 44% of all respondents are of the opinion that *military spending* should be sharply cut; an additional 18% are in favor of a little less military expenditure and 31% have no opinion or find that the present level is satisfactory. Only 7% want an increase, mostly a small increase. This is also consistent with the fact that the 'Tax-reduction for lower-incomes' scale (including indirect taxes) loads on

the LERI-dimension: *only taxes on higher incomes should be increased* (compare Campbell et al., 1960: 203ff; note also the somewhat atypical position of the item on taxes on *middle*-income groups).

21. Strictly speaking, there is not one best solution; both the 2-factor and the 3-factor solutions in Table 6.9. are acceptable as 'best solutions'. Both dimensionalities were again found in a similar factor-analysis using single records only (N = 1718) and in principal component analysis after rotations according to the varimax and promax criteria. (Thus, *principal component* analysis and *promax* rotation yielded results which, for all practical purposes, were identical to those obtained with *Jöreskog factor*-analysis and *varimax*-rotation.) The structure of the ideological domain was also tested by applying MINISSA-multidimensional scaling, using Tau-beta's as measures for the similarity. This technique yields a clear 2-dimensional structure, also in terms of libertarianism-traditionalism and left-right, but is unable to detect the third authoritarianism dimension. (The program was made available by H. Verheyden, Psychological Laboratory, University of Amsterdam, and the analysis was carried out by Ms. Lucienne Storm, Technisch Centrum, Faculty of the Social Sciences, University of Amsterdam.)

22. This result is in line with Eysenck's (1971) for social class (see below), and contrary to results at the abstract level where unique dimensions appeared in semi-elites like the highly educated and the members of a political party (see Table 6.3.). Note that the tendency towards unidimensionality is somewhat stronger at the abstract level (where the first Eigenvalue increased from and overall 6.7 to 33.7 in the highly educated) than in the ideological domain (where the increase was from 11.1 to 33.5), and that the explained variance also increased more at the abstract level (from 23.2% to 40.0% in the 4-factor solution) than in the ideological domain (from 33.4 to 46.4 in the 3-factor solution). In the ideological domain, more variance is generally explained, both in the general population and in the highly educated (the difference is about 10%, i.e. 4 factors in the abstract domain explain 23.2%, whereas 3 factors in the ideological domain explain 33.4% in the general population).

23. Note that in the highly educated, the scale on 'Tax policy; lower incomes' (i.e. a tax *reduction* for these groups as the left-wing stand) loads only very low on LERI; obviously, this attitude is not so relevant to people with a higher educational level and hence, mostly, a high income. Note, however, the low loadings of 'Attitude to social welfare laws' for the poorly educated group, for which this aspect of left-right ideology would seem relevant enough!

24. The scales on 'Tax policy on lower incomes' and 'Conventional male-female roles' do not differentiate very well for M.P.'s. The non-loading of the tax policy item may be due to the irrelevance of this item to high income groups. However, it never loaded very highly either in general or for e.g. the upper class. The same is true of the 'Government non-economic welfare policy' scale: both scales are relatively weak. 'Conventional male-female roles' generally only comes out clearly on an authoritarian factor.

25. Again, no factor-scores have been computed. As mentioned before, factor-analysis has mainly been regarded throughout the present study as a *heuristic* device. However, since there were so many discrepancies in the various loadings, these together with a correction for scale-length have been

used as a weighing-factor. Double loadings have been disregarded, i.e. high loadings on a factor ($\geqslant .35$) have been included in the measurement of a dimension, whether or not the same subscale loaded on another dimension as well. Hence, the correlation between the various dimensions is 'inflated' (especially between libertarianism-traditionalism and authoritarianism, of course), but correctly reflects the lack of (complete) independence between the dimensions, and their 'conceptual overlap'. (The correlations between abstract and ideological dimensions are also sometimes inflated.)

26. Mann does not hold the view that the extent of present-day false consciousness is a sufficient explanation of the 'pragmatic role acceptance' of the working class, or that 'manipulative socialization' would be such an explanation. He is in favor of a *mixed* approach, in which both the manipulative practices of the ruling class (in 'closing the political universe' by incorporating working class political and industrial movements during the 19th and 20th centuries into the existing structures) and elements of genuine and voluntary compromise may play a role: ' . . . one obstacle to the development of a more precise mixed theory in the past has been the failure of most sociologists to take the Marxist tradition in social theory seriously. In particular they have dismissed the crucial concept of "false consciousness" as being non-scientific' (1970: 437).

27. This estimate is biased, however: political party preference could only be assessed for a subsample (n = 1211).

28. This does not mean that M.P.'s either agree or disagree with all conservative principles. However, the high correlations between the various conservative positions do justify their location somewhere along one progressive-conservative dimension, both at an abstract, at a meta-attitudinal and at an ideological level.

29. Of course, the upper class does not only contain (big) businessmen, but also professionals, higher civil servants, managerial staff, etc.

30. The establishment of one of these (possible) independent effects (that of income) will be investigated in the next chapter.

31. Further analysis, which is outside the scope of the present study and a typical matter for secondary analysis, might involve the investigation of a relationship through component analysis down to the item-level, i.e. one could investigate the relationship between education and *specific items* in AUTH-components. Perhaps some opinions are extremely sensitive to education, and others far less so.

32. The anomia-scale developed in the present study (see Appendix 6) is as strongly related to education as the shortened F-scale (—.32).

33. If it could be shown that social class components such as occupation and income do have independent effects on AUTH-components, it would not be too difficult to develop rationales interpreting these effects in terms of 'anomia' as well.

CHAPTER 7

Towards Theory Construction

.1. INTRODUCTION

In the previous chapter we identified 2 major dimensions of ideological controversy in the general Dutch population: the left-right dimension and the libertarianism-traditionalism one. In the present chapter an attempt will be made to put these dimensions, and especially the left-right one, into an empirical perspective. The type of analysis that will be used has been called 'Type-2' and was outlined in Chapter 2.

As was outlined there, Type-2 analysis aims at the construction of 'theory' or 'theories' — although this aim may not be attained to any significant extent — by means of an inductive approach to the data and by the inclusion of deductive moments on this basis, i.e. in testing causal models which have been developed around the central relationship of this analysis.

What is needed in Type-2 analysis, then, is (a) one or more thoroughly conceptualized constructs, i.e. dimensions which measure the initial dependent variable(s); (b) a large number of other variables of various kinds, their mutual relationships and their relationships to the initial dependent variables; and (c) an initial relationship around which Type-2 analysis will 'unfold'.

It is clear that the variables described under (a) are already available: the ideological dimensions of left-right and libertarianism-traditionalism and in addition, the subdimension of authoritarian ideology.

We will now briefly describe the process of the construction of the many other variables to be used in Type-2 analysis. Subsequently the rationale for the choice of the initial relationship will be given.

7.2. THE CONSTRUCTION OF VARIABLES TO BE USED IN TYPE-2 ANALYSIS

These variables are described in Appendix 6. Where variables have been constructed on the basis of some scaling procedure, the sets of items which have been submitted to such procedures are also presented in Appendix 6. The definition of these sets has essentially been similar to the procedure followed in the case of the progressive-conservative attitude scales (see Chapter 5: 5.3.2. and Appendix 3). Some of these variables have been built upon scales which were obtained by means of secondary analysis of previous studies, in a way which is also similar to the one followed in the case of the attitude scales in the progressive-conservative domain (see Chapter 5: 5.3.1.). An indication of the scales that have been obtained in that way is given in Table 7.1. It is indicated in the sets of items in Appendix 6 which items have been taken over on this basis from previous surveys (note the correspondence between the scale labels in Table 7.1. and the names for the sets of items in Appendix 6). It is also indicated in Appendix 6 which items form the actual scale or index that has been used in Type-2 analysis.

Table 7.1. *Labels for scales to be drawn into Type-2 analysis which have been obtained through secondary analysis*

Name of study(a)	Scale label(b)	No. of items	Scale-type
1. Protestantism and Progressiveness	1. satisfaction with living conditions, society	3	F(c)
	2. general optimism-pessimism	2	F
2. The Year 2000	3. dogmatism (intolerance, time-perspective, anomia)	10	F
	4. anomia	3	F
	5. dogmatism (submissiveness to ideals and leaders)	5	F
	6. optimism-pessimism regarding living conditions in the year 2000	9	F
	7. idem	3	M(d)
3. Politics in the Netherlands	8. political alienation (from the party system)	3	F
	9. political interest	3	C(e)
4. Homosexuality	10. religious involvement	4	F
	11. F-scale item, from a shortened version of the scale		

Notes:
(a) For more details on the studies: see Table 5.2. and note 2 of Chapter 5
(b) Details on the scales are available upon request. For individual items: see Appendix 6
(c) F = scale based on factor-loadings
(d) M = Mokken (1970)-type scale
(e) C = scale based on a cluster

There are 5 types of variables in Appendix 6:
1. *personality variables*, i.e. characteristics of people that are assumed to be relatively stable, like authoritarianism (the classical F-scale in a shortened version, which was used in Chapter 6 to validate the AUTH-dimension), dogmatism and optimism vs. pessimism;
2. *background variables*, i.e. (relatively) stable characteristics of people which are easily observable and/or easily notable by questioning, like age, sex, residence, occupation;
3. *personal history variables*, i.e. variables referring to the parental family of respondents or to the situation in their youth, like social class of parents and degree of urbanization of residence in youth;
4. *situational variables*, i.e. variables which pertain to less stable characteristics of people or situations in which they find themselves, like satisfaction with living conditions, political interest and political information;
5. *consequential or validating variables*, i.e. variables that may be considered as dependent in relation to the ideological dimensions, such as self-description in terms of left-wing or right-wing, progressive or conservative, and political party preference (these variables have already been used as validating ones in Chapter 6).

Most of the personal history and background variables have been assessed on the basis of single items (exceptions are, for example, 'relation to parents in youth' and 'social class'). Most personality and situational variables have been assessed on the basis of some procedure of scale analysis. Personality variables, like dogmatism, authoritarianism and anomia are well-known (and complex) constructs. For practical reasons, their measurements had to be limited (i.e. no 'conceptual model-construction' has been carried out).

As is evident from Table 7.1., secondary analysis was of no great help here; few items of known scalability could be incorporated. The majority of the items finally included in the sets of items on authoritarianism, dogmatism and anomia were selected from the literature; this selection entailed a systematic scrutiny of the 'classical' scales [1]. Items selected to indicate optimism-pessimism could be partly taken from results of secondary analyses (see Table 7.1.). Items for measurement of 'general satisfaction', 'self-evaluation/anxiety' and the tendency to respond in 'socially desirable' ways were taken from the literature and partly resulted (in case of self-evaluation/anxiety) from attempts at the empirical assessment of other constructs, i.e. dogmatism [2].

Many items on 'situational' variables, indicating 'political interest' and 'satisfaction with living conditions' could also be taken from results of secondary analyses. Others, on 'social integration', 'political information' and 'awareness of a possible communist threat' are original to the present study. Items on 'alienation from the political party system' could also be taken from previous research.

The various scales and indices that have become available this way and the single items that have been used in the analysis are summarized in Table 7.2. There it can be seen that almost 40 variables have been constructed to be used in Type–2 analysis. (The 4 validating variables are already well-known; vote-intention will again be used in the final stage of Type–2 analysis.)

Table 7.2.   *A survey of scales and other variables outside the progressive-conservative domain, incorporated into Type-2 analysis*

Scale label	No. of items	Scale-characteristics
A. *PERSONALITY VARIABLES*		
(1) Authoritarianism	7	Factor-loadings ≥ .40
(2) Militant dogmatism	6	Factor-loadings ≥ .45
(3) Submissive dogmatism (a)	6	Factor-loadings ≥ .40
(4) Anomia	5	Mokken-scale; H = .43; Rep = .90; I = .43
(5) Political alienation (b)	3	Factor-loadings ≥ .60
(6) Misanthropy	3	Factor-loadings ≥ .60
(7) Optimism-pessimism, in the year 2000 (a)	4	Mokken scale; H = .43; Rep = .96; I = .49
(8) General optimism-pessimism	2	Mokken scale; H = .43
(9) General satisfaction-neuroticism	4	Mokken scale; H = .45; Rep = .94; I = .46
(10) Self-evaluation/anxiety	5	Factor-loadings ≥ .60
(11) Social desirability	5	Cluster; Tau (b) coefficients; p < .001
B. *BACKGROUND VARIABLES*		
(1) Educational level (c)	1	
(2) Occupational level (c)	1	
(3) Social class (interviewer rating) (d)	1	
(4) Income level	1	
(5) Social class (objective)	3	Index (see Appendix 6B)
(6) Social mobility (intergenerational)	4	Index (idem)
(7) Status-inconsistency	2	Index (idem)
(8) Social class (subjective)	1	
(9) Social mobility (subjective) (see C4)	2	Index (idem)
(10) Age	1	
(11) Sex	1	
(12) Degree of urbanization of residence		Index (idem)
(13) Province (a)	1	
(14) Religion	1	
(15) Church-attendance	1	

Table 7.2. (*continued*)

Scale label	No. of items	Scale-characteristics
C. *PERSONAL HISTORY VARIABLES*		
(1) Socio-emotional relationship with parents	6	Cluster based on Chi-2's: $p < .0001$
(2) Normative-instrumental relationship with parents	5	Cluster based on Chi-2's: $p < .0001$
(3) Social class of parents (objective)	2	Index; see Appendix 6C
(4) Social class of parents (subjective) (see B9)	1	
(5) Degree of urbanization of residence in youth	1	
(6) A religious upbringing	1	
(7) Party-preference of father	1	
D. *SITUATIONAL VARIABLES*		
(1) Social integration	3	Cluster of Chi-2's; $p < .05$
(2) Satisfaction with living-conditions	4	Cluster; Tau-b; $p < .10^{-10}$
(3) Religious involvement	3	Mokken-scale; $H = .45$
(4) Political interest	4	Mokken-scale; $H = .58$; $Rep = .94$; $I = .63$
(5) Political information	2	Cluster: Chi-2: $p < .10^{-10}$
(6) Awareness of a possible communist threat	2	Mokken-scale; $H = .90$
(7) Political alienation (see A5)	3	Factor-loadings $\geqslant .60$
E. *CONSEQUENTIAL AND VALIDATING VARIABLES*		
(1) Identifying oneself as progressive vs. conservative	1	
(2) Idem: left- vs. right-wing	1	
(3) Political party membership	1	
(4) Vote-intention 'if parliamentary elections were to be held now'	1	

Notes: (See Appendix 6 for individual terms and questions and for more detailed information.)
(a) Not used in subsequent analyses
(b) Later considered a 'situational variable'
(c) Data on 'head of family' or 'father' are used for index-construction only (e.g. social mobility)
(d) Used for index-construction only (i.e. social class; see Appendix 6)

The results, as far as the characteristics of the various scales is concerned, are quite different from the ones *within* the progressive-conservative domain, i.e. the progressive-conservative attitude scales (compare Table 5.4. and Appendix 3). Satisfactory Mokken-scales could not always be constructed; often the scales are based on factor-loadings or clusters.

Let us now briefly describe the various scales and the procedures that have been used in constructing them.

1. It has already been mentioned that the domains of authoritarianism, dogmatism and anomia have been 'purified'. A *shortened F-scale* could be constructed on the basis of factor-loadings (no satisfactory Mokken-scale resulted) after elimination of items on criminals; an *anomia-scale* of the Mokken-type could be constructed, and simultaneously it could be shown that notions which are often taken as implicit in the concept of anomia (like *'political alienation'* from the party system and *'misanthropy'* — a negative evaluation of human beings in general) are relatively independent of 'general' anomic tendencies such as 'normlessness' and an 'uncertain view of the future' [3]. *Dogmatism* constitutes an interesting case: in the first place, the *self-evaluation* items taken from the classical scale (see Rokeach, 1960) proved to be loading on a separate factor. In addition, however, the (proper) dogmatism-items showed 2 factor-analytic patterns: in orthogonal rotation with 4 factors, 2 *'militant'* dogmatism items joined the *basic* 4 items on one factor; in rotation with 3 factors, these were replaced by 2 *'submissive'* items (see Appendix 6A: set 2): both pairs of items were related to the basic 4, but were *unrelated* to each other [4]. This clearly shows the value of rotation with various numbers of factors, a procedure which has consistently been applied here as in the progressive-conservative domain [5].
2. The optimism-pessimism set (Appendix 6, set 4) has been divided into 2 medium Mokken-scale: optimism-pessimism in *specific* terms (with a clear time-referent: the year 2000) is almost unrelated to *general* optimism-pessimism.
3. Items for sets A 9 and A 11 and the anxiety-items in set A 10 have partly been taken from well-known scales, i.e. the Amsterdam Biographical Questionnaire (ABV) (see Wilde, 1964), and the Crowne-Marlowe (1964) scale on social desirability. In the social desirability scale, only the *desirable* responses have been distinguished from all others (i.e. non-response was considered as evading the undesirable response).
4. After careful examination, the 2 scales on 'relationship with parents' emerged from the data. One intuitively feels that this distinction makes sense (see items in Appendix 6C: 1, 2).
5. 'Social integration' is the weakest scale of all.
6. 'Satisfaction with living conditions' is a more or less purely 'economic' cluster, referring to income, social status and housing.

In summary, a total number of 29 items from previous research have been used; 25 proved to be scalable, (i.e. 86%; see Table 7.1.). In Appendix 6 it can be seen that, in comparison with the scaling ones, many non-scaling items again prove to be reversals, as is the case for the authoritarianism, dogmatism and anomia reversals which have been formulated in the present study [6].

Finally, the basic data that form the starting point for Type–2 analysis have been obtained (1) by relating available independent and intervening variables to the 2 major ideological dimensions of LERI and LITR and the subdimension of AUTH; and (2) by relating all these variables to each other. The results are presented in Appendices 7 and 8, respectively. They will not be commented upon at this stage (see the comments in Appendix 8 and the notes to the tables).

7.3. THE INITIAL RELATIONSHIP: SOCIAL CLASS AND LEFT-RIGHT IDEOLOGY

Several rationales can be given for the choice of the relationship between *social class* and *left-right ideology* as the initial one in Type–2 analysis. In the first place, the role of social class in the emergence of ideological controversy in Western Europe was emphasized in Chapter 4. Secondly, the LERI dimension — predominantly though not exclusively in a politico-economic sense — are obviously related to the major structural variable reflecting inequality in several respects: social class.

We have seen in Chapter 6, however, the social class is only weakly related to left-right ideology in the predicted direction: Tau=.19. It has already been noted that this is an intriguing phenomenon, given the obvious economic interests that are at stake (see e.g. Bertrand et al., 1974). One wonders which factors are *suppressing* this relationship or under which conditions it is strengthened or weakened. An attempt will be made to answer these questions in the analysis to be presented below. (Compare the outline of Type–2 analysis in Chapter 2.)

From still another point of view, an investigation of the possible factors weakening the relationship between social class and left-right ideology seems important. Given the fact that leftist ideology is quite strongly related to voting behavior in favor of leftist parties [7], political scientists and political sociologists have often admitted that *the very existence of a democratic political system is dependent upon a fairly weak relationship between these variables* (see e.g. Lipset, 1963: 31, 279–282). The reason is that the lower classes (working class and lower-middle class) have a *substantial numerical majority in society*. If *economic* factors *only* (or predominantly) would determine voting behavior, the parties of the left (e.g. socialists, social-democrats, communists) would have a 'natural' majority in parliament in all Western societies. Then, however, there would be no 'real' democracy in the present western sense, with at least 2 parties struggling to gain a majority (or simply as many votes as possible) with about equal chances of winning (or forming part of a coalition government if there were 3 or more parties involved).

Thus, Lipset (1963: 40) maintains that 'It is obvious that the distribution of wealth is the most important source of interest-conflict in complex societies'. 'A stable democracy requires a situation in which all the major political parties include supporters from many segments of the population. A system in which the support of different parties corresponds too closely to basic social divisions [i.e. social class; CPM] cannot continue on a democratic basis, for it reflects a state of conflicts intense and clearcut as to rule out compromise' (p. 31).

Thus, from the point of view of an economic self-interest, Lipset almost advocates a state of 'false consciousness' to make democracy in the common, western, parliamentary sense, possible '. . . phenomena such as the Tory worker or the middle-class socialist are not merely deviants from class patterns, but basic requirements for the maintenance of the political system' (i.e. liberal parliamentary democracy) (p. 31) . . . 'Marx accounted for such support (which he called "false consciousness") by postulating (1) that the lower classes enter the body politic accepting the legitimacy of the existing stratification arrangements. and (2) that the basic institutions of a society — religion, education, the mass media — propagate ideas and values which support the existing order and are necessarily accepted by all strata to some extent' (see Lipset, 1963: 280).

Thus the central prerequisite for a democratic system seems to be that class differences are *not* recognized by voters as the principal basis of political division, although in fact they are (see Lipset, 1963: 40). 'To the extent, therefore, that the conservative parties can make elections revolve around non-economic issues [i.e. foreign policy, morality, the personality of the candidates; CPM.] they can reduce the pressure for reform and increase their chances of electoral victory. Their greater access to the press and other mass media helps them to define the issues of the election, particularly in periods of prosperity when economic needs are not salient' (p. 282).

In conclusion, there is indeed a weak relationship between both social class and left-right ideology, as well as between social class and left-right voting behavior (this will be discussed below). Since such a weak relationship is often posited as constituting a major prerequisite for the very existence of a democratic system in the western parliamentary sense, it seems worthwhile to investigate which factors are responsible for this situation.

Thus there are the following reasons to take the relationship between social class and left-right ideology as a starting point for Type-2 analysis in the present study: (a) the role of social class in the emergence of ideological controversy in Western Europe in the 19th and 20th centuries, (b) the clearly ideological nature of the left-right antithesis, referring to the economic interests of various classes and having a strongly egalitarian basis — on its left-wing side (remember also the much more 'ideological' nature of the left-right dimension in semi-elites; see Chapter 6: 6.5.2.), and (c) the weakness of the relationship, which has been seen by many as a prerequisite for the very existence of parliamentary democracy.

7.4. TYPE-2 ANALYSIS: SYSTEMATIC EXPLORATION

Our analysis (see again Chapter 2: 2.3. for the general outline), which may be considered one of 'systematic exploration', will start with an attempt to *clarify* the initial relationship itself: what does a Tau = .19 mean in terms of e.g. a 4 by 4 table and how does it come about in terms of the relationships of its various components? (Compare the analysis of the phenomenon of working class conservatism in Chapter 6: 6.7.1.) Given the nature of the variable of social class, which was constructed out of the indicators of educational level, occupation and income — see Appendix 6B — component analysis will lead us to an investigation of the effect of at least one type of *status-inconsistency* on left-right ideology.

We will proceed by bringing those variables into the design which have a special relationship to social class, such as subjective social class and social class of parents. This will lead us to an investigation of the possible effects of phenomena such as *social mobility* and '*class consciousness*' (of particular importance in the present context) on left-right ideology (this will be called 'within analysis').

Subsequently we will bring other variables into the design in an attempt to construct *causal models* around the initial relationship. This will lead us to an assessment of the *determinants* of left-right ideology, as far as they can be established on the basis of the present design (this will be called 'between analysis').

The final 2 stages of the first round of the systematic exploration process are of particular importance in the present study, given the intriguing weakness of the initial relationship.

First, we will try to *specify* this relationship, i.e. determine the conditions under which it can be strengthened or weakened; second, we will try to locate variables which *suppress* this relationship, i.e. variables which 'by their very existence' weaken the relationship between social class and left-right ideology and might therefore, from the perspective of the above outline of at least one prerequisite of parliamentary democracy, be considered as stabilizing factors.

At that stage, we will see whether we will extend the analysis any further.

7.4.1. Clarification

7.4.1.1. Social class and left-right ideology: the 4 by 4 table. Table 7.3. shows in somewhat more detail what a correlation of Tau = .19 means.

Table 7.3. *Social class and left-right ideology; the 4 by 4 table*

Social class (b)	Left-right ideology(a)				M(d) 100%
	Left +	Left	Right	Right +	
Working class	17.7 (78) (c)	50.2 (221)	27.1 (119)	5.0 (22)	1.19 (440)
Lower-middle	17.0 (141)	42.5 (353)	29.5 (245)	10.9 (90)	1.34 (829)
Upper-middle	12.7 (48)	33.0 (125)	36.0 (136)	18.4 (70)	1.60 (379)
Upper class	11.1 (31)	23.7 (66)	40.5 (113)	24.8 (69)	1.79 (279)
Tau = .19	(298)	(765)	(613)	(251)	N = 1927

Notes:
(a) See Appendix 5 for measurement and recoding to 4 levels
(b) See Appendix 6B for measurements and the index-construction. Categorization into 4 levels has been carried out according to the principle of the 'big lower-middle class' (see point 5 c)
(c) N's per cell are in brackets. Other figures are row percentages
(d) M = mean scores per class level

It can be seen that a relatively weak relationship in terms of 'explained variance' (a Tau of .19 corresponds roughly to a product-moment correlation of .20 to .25, which explains about 5% of the variance) can still be very meaningful. In the upper class for example there are, relatively speaking, about 5 times as many extremely right-wing people as in the working class and the total percentage of right-wing people in the upper class is about 65%, as against less than half this percentage in the working class. On the left-wing side, the opposite pattern appears. Even between both middle classes there are clear differences: almost 60% in the upper-middle class are right-wing, as against about 40% in the lower-middle class.

Still, various types of false consciousness can clearly be seen: *more than one third of the lower classes (this amounts to about 25% of the total population) has a right-wing ideological stand, about half of these people are in the moderately right-wing lower-middle class.* The same is true in the upper classes: about 40% are left-wing, but this amounts to only about 14% of the population. About half of these are in the moderately left-wing upper-middle class. (All these percentages are of course arbitrary to the extent that the categorizations are arbitrary, i.e. the cutting points.)

7.4.1.2. Component analysis. Component analysis further clarifies the nature of the relationship between social class and left-right ideology. The results are presented in Table 7.4.

Table 7.4. *The relationship between social class components and the component subscales of left-right ideology*

	Social class components			
	Educ. level	*Occup. level*	*Income level*	*Social class*(a)
The components of left-right ideology(b)				
Att. to equality of income, property, status	.06(c)	.15	.15	.13
Government interference to bring about equality	.03	.06	.12	.11
Att. to social welfare laws	.04	.05	.05	.07
Government aid to education	.01	.05	.03	.03
Government income policy	.15	.18	.20	.22
Tax policy, higher incomes	.03	.04	.07	.12
Tax policy, lower incomes	.13	.20	.17	.14
Governm. direct econ. interference	.06	.14	.08	.10
Governm. (non-directly econ.) welf.	−.08	−.04	.04	−.03
Militant trade-union policy	.16	.18	.18	.19
Democratic attitudes	−.13	−.03	−.02	−.04
Item on: government policy; equality of opportunity(d)	.02	.09	.09	.09
Item on: government spending(d)	−.02	.02	.01	.04
Socialism	.03	.10	.12	.08
Left-right ideology(e)	.08	.17	.16	.19

Notes:
(a) The 3 social class components have all been recoded to 4 levels (see Appendix 6B). For occupation, students and housewives have been left out (N′ = 1089); for income, the non-response has been eliminated (N′ ″ = 1576). See also Appendix 6B for the class-index
(b) See Appendix 3 for the full scale names and details on their characteristics. Scoring is from left-wing to right-wing
(c) Coefficients are Tau-beta's
(d) For item-text, see Table 6.9., notes d and e
(e) For the measurement of this dimension, see Appendix 5

In Table 7.4. the following can be seen:

(a) the relationship between social class *components* and left-right ideology is weakest for educational level; this confirms the predominantly socio-economic nature of this dimension. Thus, there is hardly any tendency for the highly educated to be right-wing. We will see below whether educational level, which has, of course, a positive relationship to both occupational level and income (see Appendix 8B) has an independent effect on left-right ideology at all, and whether there is perhaps an interaction effect with income (i.e. an effect of status-inconsistency).

(b) There is a great deal of variation in the strength of the relationships between social class and LERI-components. The strongest relationship (.22) is between social class and government income policy. The 3 items in this scale refer fairly directly to the economic interests of the lower classes: control of prices after a wage-increase, a large increase in minimum incomes and workers sharing in profits. It comes as no surprise, then, that income is the social class component which is most strongly related to this subscale. As in the case of the relationship between social class components and authoritarianism components — Table 6.18. — the overall relationships are stronger than the 'average' relationship between components: evidently, subscales tend to furnish an independent contribution to the overall result (see, however, Table 7.4., note (a)). Only the subscale that has been mentioned above is more strongly related to social class than LERI ideology as a whole. Trade-union policy shows another relatively strong relationship to social class: in its 2 items, the interests of employees and workers are again directly referred to [8]. All other subscales are (much) more weakly related to social class than LERI-ideology. Tax policy scales are next in strength; they also refer fairly directly to economic interests, as do the scales on equality of income, property and status and the scale on government interference to effect these latter aims. All other scales are only related at the level of .10 or weaker, and 2 subscales (which also load highly on the LITR dimension) are even related in a weakly positive manner to social class — 'Government non-directly economic welfare policy' and 'Democratic attitudes' — note the direction of the scoring in Table 7.4.

In summary, the picture that emerges from the 'marginals' in Table 7.4. is a fairly consistent one: the social class components that are the most *strongly* related to LERI are those that are most *directly* economic in nature, and social class as a whole is most *strongly* related to the LERI-components that incorporate elements which are most *directly* and concretely related to the economic interests of various social classes.

(c) Only few deviations from both overall pictures appear in the 42 coefficients into which the overall relationship between social class and LERI has been broken up.

Educational level is moderately positive (note again the direction of the scoring in Table 7.4.) in its relation to 'Democratic attitudes' and weakly positively related to the other 'deviant' left-right component: 'Government non-directly economic welfare policy'. It is also moderately negative in its relation to 'Government income policy' and 'Militant trade-union policy'. Its relationships to the other components are very weak indeed.

For occupation and income there are few deviations from the overall social class pattern. The only exception seems to be their weak relationship to 'Tax policy, higher incomes'.

It may finally be noted that educational level is virtually unrelated to socialism, while income is most strongly related: at the level of .12.

Thus, component analysis has shown 2 things: (1) that from the perspective of the marginals, the relationship between social class and left-right components and vice versa varies a great deal and that this variation could be interpreted in terms of the nature of both the dimensions and their components, and (2) that there is a great deal of variation in the strengths of the relationships between the various components, which varies from .20 to —.13. Although social class as a whole is positively related to right-wing ideology, one of its components (educational level) is *positively* related to the *left-wing* orientation of 'Democratic attitudes'. One should be very careful in generalizing an overall relationship between 2 complex variables to every single relationship between their components. (In fact, this has already been shown in our reduction of the notion of 'working class traditionalism' in Chapter 6: 6.7.1.)

We will now see whether educational level and income have any independent effects at all on left-right ideology and/or whether there is an interaction effect between these 2 variables: an effect of *status-inconsistency*.

7.4.1.3. Status-inconsistency [9]. The results are presented in Table 7.5.

Table 7.5. mainly shows 2 things. First, the educational effect on LERI virtually disappears and even turns positive at various income-levels. So at first sight it seems that educational level does not have an independent effect on LERI. However, its potentially negative effect on LERI in the lowest income group after the secondary modern school does not result in a negative correlation only because there are so few

Table 7.5.   *The effects of status-inconsistency between education and income on left-right ideology*(a)

Educational level(b)	Income level(b)					
	<12.00	12-18.000	18-24.000	>24.000	Tau-beta	D(c)
Primary school	1.24(d) (517)	1.13 (173)	1.51 (41)	1.88 (32)	05 (763)	.68
Sec. modern school	1.31 (196)	1.24(d) (142)	1.74 (72)	1.82 (57)	16 (467)	.51
Grammar school	1.06 (63)	1.38 (88)	1.62(d) (42)	1.77 (60)	22 (253)	.71
University	.69 (13)	1.24 (17)	1.40 (20)	2.00(d) (42)	38 (92)	1.31
Tau-beta	-.02 (789)	.07 (420)	-.01 (175)	-.04 (191)	N = 1575	

Notes:

(a) Entries are mean scores on the 4-level LERI-scale (see Appendix 5); N's per cell in brackets.
   The marginals are Tau-beta's

(b) For measurement: see Appendix 6B

(c) Difference scores between highest and lowest income level

(d) Status-consistent positions (10)

cases with a *low* income combined with a *high* educational level. The few people who have attended university (or: are attending university) but who report a low income level are probably mostly students (not living with their parents), who are clearly more left-wing than other groups with low incomes.

For upper income groups, weak curvilinear relationships appear. The weak positive overall trend is only found in 'lower-middle' income levels. The effects of income on various levels of education are more interesting: educational level strongly determines the income-effects on LERI ideology. There seem to be both an income and an interaction-effect. However, here again we should look more closely at the N's per cell. For those who have only attended primary school, there is in fact a rather strong *positive* effect of income on right-wing ideology which is not reflected in Tau because there are so few people with a high income in this category. (Again, as in the low income group, there is also weak curvilinearity caused by the 'second-lowest' level.) At the secondary modern school level, differences in mean scores between low and high income groups are slightly smaller and weak curvilinearity remains. Still, Tau can rise to .16 since the distribution is less skewed. At the grammar school level, the N's per cell are even more equal and curvilinearity disappears due to the sharp increase in left-wing opinions of those with low incomes; hence, a Tau of .22. Finally, Tau can rise sharply for those at the university-level due to further 'polarization' at both extremes.

At first sight, 2 effects seem predominant: (1), the education-effect is *interpreted* by income (in many cases, education may lead to relatively high income through occupation) [11] and (2), the income-effect itself is *specified* by education. However looking more closely at the data, the picture then becomes more complicated.

There are at least 2 types of status-inconsistency: (a) higher income than educational level (top row in Table 7.5., and all cases to the *right* of the diagonal from top-left to bottom-right) and (b) higher educational level than income (left-hand column in Table 7.5. and all cases to the *left* of the diagonal from top-left to bottom-right). Both types are clearly complementary, centering around 'consistent' positions, but *the effects of status-inconsistency seem to depend upon whether one considers the data from an educational or an income point of view*. From the educational point of view, there seems to be a clear trend (with only minor exceptions) that higher income leads to right-wing, lower income to left-wing positions. From the income point of view, the effect of educational level is much less clear.

The overall index of status-inconsistency (see Appendix 6B) is weakly related to LERI ideology (.13), which means a tendency towards right-wing positions if income is *higher* and towards left-wing positions if income is *lower* than educational level. On the basis of Table 7.5., one may wonder whether constructing such an index is not more confusing than enlightening; it mainly reflects an income-effect which exists at various levels of education, and even increases at higher educational levels, in particular university level [12].

In fact, status-inconsistency has opposite effects at low vs. high educational levels: at *low* levels, increasing *inconsistency* (increasing income) leads to stronger right-wing opinions; at *high* levels, increasing *consistency* (also: increasing income) leads to stronger right-wing opinions. Hence, the overall effect of status-inconsistency is misleading although the income-effect on right-wing positions at various levels of education may (partly) be interpreted in terms of differential effects of status-inconsistency, as indicated in note 12 above.

In conclusion, we have seen that educational level does not have an independent effect on left-right ideology at all (it may have such an independent effect — although probably weakly — on certain components of LERI, but this is a matter for further analysis) and that various types of status-inconsistency have *opposite* effects due to a dominant effect of *income*. Thus, in this instance, the construct of status-inconsistency is a rather dubious one.

7.4.2. *Within-analysis: social mobility and class consciousness*

Within-analysis centres around variables which are 'related to', or somehow 'belong to the family' of the independent variable in the initial relationship in Type–2 analysis, i.e. the social class variable. It seeks to assess whether it is social class 'as such' which is related to LERI ideology, or whether other variables belonging to the social class 'family' are responsible for the (apparent) social class effect. This leads to analysis of the concepts of *social mobility* and *class consciousness* since (a), social class of parents (both objectively and subjectively; see Appendix 6C) [13] and (b), subjective social class, belong to the family of social class variables.

7.4.2.1. *Social mobility*.

There are numerous studies in which an attempt has been made to assess the effects of (intergenerational) social mobility on political attitudes, liberalism-conservatism, political party preference, etc. [14]. For our purposes, the most important thing to note is that there seem to be 2 'schools': one finds evidence that the upwardly mobile are more *conservative*, the other that these people are more *liberal* than their class of destination [15].

Then, O'Kane (1970) makes a distinction between economic and non-economic liberalism and finds that although mobility potential is *positively* related to non-economic liberalism for a very special group, it is *unrelated* to economic liberalism. 'Perhaps, as the Marxian interpretation of social classes as economic entities would suggest, the individual's identity is far more dependent on economic positioning and socialization than other factors. Consequently, economic orientations provide a foundation for one's political-ideological framework and mobility probably plays a minor role in reshaping these economic attitudes' (1970: 504).

Most studies on social mobility appear to be rather limited in scope, both as regards the measurement of mobility and in the assessment of its effects. No study seems to exist, for example, in which the differential effects of social mobility are assessed on various levels of parents' social class (class of departure) and present social position (class of destination). This situation is in fact similar to that found in studies on status-inconsistency (see above, note 9).

The differential effects of social mobility on LERI ideology are presented in Table 7.6. (Social class and social class of parents are of course strongly related to each other (Tau = .61; see Appendix 8H.) The first thing that is shown in Table 7.6., especially Table 7.6a., is that both the effect of parents' social class (i.e. the *socialization*-effect) and the effect of social class itself (i.e. the class *identification* effect) are weakened or virtually disappear at the various levels of the controlling variable. So both independent effects are weak and seem to be strongest for the middle classes (Table 7.6a.), and especially for the lower-middle class (Table 7.6b.), a phenomenon which is no doubt related to varying skewness of the distributions [16].

Table 7.6. *The effects of social mobility on left-right ideology*(a)

Table 7.6a.

Soc. class parents(b)	Social class				Tau	
	Working class	Lower-middle	Upper-middle	Upper class		
Working class	*1.19* (421) →	1.22 (383)	1.46 (52)	—	.04	(856)
		↓				
Lower-middle	1.32 (19) ←	*1.38* (346) →	1.55 (138)	1.55 (29)	.08	(532)
		↑	↓			
Upper-middle	—	1.63 (93) ←	*1.67* (153) →1.87(d)(109)		.09	(355)
			↓			
Upper class	—	2.00 (7)	1.69(d)(36) ←*1.79*	(141)	.03	(184)
Tau (beta)	.04 (440)	.13 (829)	.07 (379)	.01 (279)	N = 1927	

Table 7.6b.

Soc. class parents(c)	Social class				Tau	
	Working class	Lower-middle	Upper-middle	Upper class		
Working class	*1.22* (315)→1.17(d) (178)		1.42 (12)	1.22 (9)	.02	(514)
	↑	↓				
Lower-middle	1.06(d)(102)←*1.25*	(394) →	1.51 (106)	2.18 (11)	.16	(613)
		↑	↓			
Upper-middle	1.31 (16)	1.60 (214) ←	*1.65* (155) →	1.69 (74)	.06	(459)
			↑	↓		
Upper class	1.57 (7)	1.60 (43)	1.65 (106) ←	*1.83* (185)	.10	(341)
Tau (beta)	.05 (440)	.16 (829)	.06 (379)	.06 (279)	N = 1927	

Notes:

(a) LERI recoded to 4 levels as in Appendix 5; in Table: mean scores; N's in brackets; non-mobile cases cursive. As has been explained in Appendix 3C, the social class of parents has been assessed *indirectly* by subtracting 'objective social mobility' (assessed on the basis of differences between educational level and occupation of the respondent and his father) from present social class position, and recoding the difference-scores to a 10-point scale. Regarding the reported *occupational level* of the father, one wishes that there had been a social class of parents index with about equal percentages in the working class and in the lower-middle class. However, the 10-point scale which resulted from the above procedure did not allow for such cutting-points, so there was either a *smaller* working class, or a *larger* working class than the lower-middle class. The latter categorization seems to be preferable.

(b) Social class of parents recoded to 4 levels, reflecting social mobility; i.e. the second recoding as described in Appendix 3C; a 'large working class'

(c) Social class of parents recoded to a similar distribution to that of present social class, i.e. a relatively large lower-middle class and a smaller working class

(d) Showing an irregular pattern (see text)

The effects of social mobility from the point of view of the class of *departure* (parents' social class) will be examined first. They are quite clear: the upwardly mobile tend to be more right-wing, the downwardly mobile more left-wing than their class of departure (with only a few exceptions). This points to effects of *class identification*.

However, from the point of view of the class of *destination*, the opposite effects appear. Now, the upwardly mobile tend to be more left-wing and the downwardly mobile more right-wing. The effects are rather weak; still they point to a *socialization*-effect, in the class of departure on LERI ideology. So, due to both the effects of socialization and class identification, the mobile tend to take positions on LERI that are between those of the non-mobile in their class of departure vs. their class of destination but (a) the effects tend to be weak and highly sensitive to class definitions (i.e. cutting points), (b) there are some exceptions to this pattern, and (c) sometimes, socialization seems to be the dominant factor and sometimes class identification seems to be [17].

In conclusion, the virtually zero relationship between the index of social mobility (see Appendix 6B) and LERI ideology (see Appendix 7) could be specified and meaningfully interpreted: social mobility has no overall relationship to LERI because there are 2 opposing forces at work, socialization and class identification, locating the position of the socially mobile in between that of the socially non-mobile. Hence, the value of an index of social mobility, like the index for status-inconsistency, is indeed open to question [18].

The same applies to the value of an index for 'subjective' social mobility [19]. For subjective mobility, however, there appeared an interesting specification of the 'objective' effects: in the *upwardly* mobile, the *socialization* effect is clearly dominant; in the *downwardly* mobile the *class identification* effect. The upwardly mobile tend to stick to the left-right positions that are dominant in their class of departure, while the downwardly mobile tend to accept the left-right positions which are dominant in their class of destination. So, from the perspective of the class of departure, only downward mobility has an effect on left-right ideology, whereas from the point of view of the class of destination, the upwardly mobile are much more left-wing.

These phenomena may be interpreted as follows: in case of subjective 'success' (upward mobility) there is a feeling of solidarity shown towards one's class of departure, probably because having been brought up in a lower class one 'knows what it means', so to speak. This is in line with a suggestion made by O'Kane (1970: 504) referred to above. In case of subjective 'failure' (downward mobility), one probably blames the 'social order' for the downward mobility. One feels dependent on government measures and tends to be in favor of a generally egalitarian policy in the hopes of restoring a level of welfare that one has perhaps been accustomed to. However, only about 10% of the population reported downward mobility, as against about 20% reporting upward mobility.

7.4.2.2. Class consciousness. The concept of class consciousness is of course rather complicated and 'smacks of Marxism' even more than the concept of social class itself does (see Kelly and Chambliss, 1966: 302). Still, there are low levels of class consciousness (e.g. the ability and willingness to identify oneself with a social class, at the lowest level) which may very possibly be operationalized, and the effects of which may be investigated. In the present study, 2 simple variables which have already been introduced (subjective social class and subjective social class of parents), will be used in combination with similar objective measures to construct 6 indices of class consciousness. The general hypothesis that will be tested is that the higher the level of class consciousness, the stronger the relationship between social class and left-right ideology.

Before turning to this analysis the question of whether objective social class has an independent effect on LERI when controlled for subjective social class, will be investigated. It could be that subjective social class *interprets* to some extent the relationship between objective social class and LERI. (The alternative hypothesis — that social class *explains* the relationship between subjective social class and LERI — seems less likely, but may also be tested in the usual way; both variables are strongly related to each other: Tau = .52.) The data are presented in Table 7.7.

First it can be seen in Table 7.7. that the subjective social class effect on LERI, though weakened (overall, Tau: .23), remains rather strong

Table 7.7. *The (independent) effects of objective and subjective social class on left-right ideology*(a)

| Objective social class | Subjective social class | | | |
	Working class	Lower-middle	Upper-middle + Upper class	Tau
Working class	*1.06* (237)	1.25 (138)	1.38 (26)	.14 (401)
Lower-middle	1.10 (167)	*1.32* (400)	1.43 (180)	.11 (747)
Upper-middle	.91 (22)	1.62 (105)	*1.72* (178)	.13 (305)
Upper class	.78 (9)	1.50 (24)	*1.90* (195)	.20 (228)
Tau	.02 (435)	.10 (667)	.19 (579)	N = 1681

Note:
(a) See note (a) Table 7.6. Cursive figures indicate 'consistent' cases for which objective and subjective class are identical

The partial correlation for the effects of social class on LERI controlled for subjective social class, is .10; when the order is reversed, the effect of subjective social class is .16. The effects of social class on LERI, controlled for both subjective social class and social class of parents (cutting points as in Table 7.6a.) is negligible (.03), while the effect of subjective social class on LERI, controlled for both objective social class and social class of parents, is still .16. The relationship between social class of parents and LERI, controlled for both objective and subjective social class, is still .10 (compare the test of Model 1, Fig. 7.2. below) and consistent. If one 'belongs' to the working class but 'identifies' with higher classes, one has a correspondingly more right-wing ideology [20]. The opposite is also true, and even more apparent. There are very few upper-middle and upper-class people who identify with the working class, but the few that do have an extremely strong left-wing ideology [21]. This ideology is also more left-wing than that of 'consistent' workers. (Still, social class does not seem to have an effect on subjective workers, but this is obviously due to the skewness of the distribution and weak curvilinearity.) For those identifying with the lower-middle or upper classes, objective social class does have an effect which is, again, consistent with its general effect.

In conclusion, subjective social class does not interpret the relationship between social class and LERI; rather it specifies it. In the working class the reverse tends to be true (though Tau is virtually zero, due to the extreme skewness of the distribution), in the lower-middle class it is somewhat weakened due to slight curvilinearity and it is maintained in the upper classes. On the other hand, social class does not explain away the effect of subjective social class [22].

Let us now return to our general hypotheses that (a) class consciousness increases the strength of the relationship between (objective) social class and left-right ideology, and (b) the higher the level of class consciousness, the stronger this relationship will be.

It is clear that subjective social class, i.e. the ability and willingness to assign oneself to a social class at all, is the lowest level of class consciousness (and consequently, the unwillingness and/or inability to do so constitute the *highest* level of a *lack* of class consciousness).

It could be considered somewhat more difficult to assign one's parents to a social class. The third level could be the ability and willingness to assign both oneself (i.e. one's family) and one's parents to a social class.

Another level of class consciousness would be reached if one were able and willing to assign oneself to the 'correct' social class (we have seen above — Table 7.7. — that people's objective vs. subjective social class positions may differ from each other and we may assume that those people are more class conscious that place themselves in their 'true' social class [23]).

Again we may consider it somewhat more difficult to place one's parents in the correct social class (if not living with one's family) [24] and the highest level of class consciousness that we are able to assess in the present study may be considered the ability to place both one's own family and one's parents' into the correct social class.

Hence, we have established 6 levels of class consciousness and non-class consciousness, and we predict that the relationship between social class and left-right ideology will be strongest in the most highly class conscious group and weakest in the group which completely lacks the ability and willingness to assign itself to a social class. From low to high class consciousness there should be a more or less gradual increase in the strength of the relationship between social class and left-right ideology, while in the non-class conscious groups, this relationship should remain rather low. Results are presented in Table 7.8., which shows that our predictions are largely confirmed, although there is also some irregularity.

Table 7.8. *The relationship between social class and left-right ideology on various levels of class consciousness*(a)

	Lowest level					Highest level
	Self-ass. soc. class	Parents ass. soc. class	Self + parents	Self-ass. correct soc. class	Par. ass. correct soc. class	Self + parents correct
	1	2	3	4	5	6
Yes (Consc.)	.21 (1680)	.18 (1127)	.21 (1060)	.28 (1009)	.29 (547)	.35 (368)
No	-.03 (246)	.19 (799)	.15 (866)	.07 (917)	.14 (1397)	.14 (1558)

Note:
(a) Correlations are Tau-beta's; N's are in brackets.

For the most non-class conscious group, the relationship between social class and left-right ideology vanishes completely (—.03), while in the most class conscious group it almost doubles to .35. However, in groups 1–3 the relationship does not increase at all; this only happens in the 3 most conscious groups.

There is no explanation available for the fact that there is no difference between the strengths of the relationship at the second level of consciousness (groups no. 2) which presumably also disturbs the relationship at the third level.

In conclusion, we have seen that class consciousness is indeed an important specifying variable of the relationship between social class and left-right ideology. If more people would become class conscious, class antagonism along the left-right dimension would increase, which could lead to a stronger left-wing vote in the lower classes and a stronger right-wing vote in the upper classes, and to a more or less permanent left-wing majority. Those that are highly class conscious are probably the more extremely left-wing and right-wing 'ideologues'.

Before we turn to an investigation of other specifying variables, an attempt will first be made to construct causal models around the relationship between social class and left-right ideology, in what has been called 'between-analysis'.

7.4.3. An attempt to construct causal models

7.4.3.1. Introduction. Causal models can be 'derived' from the basic data that are available and which have been presented in Appendices 7 and 8. This means that in these 2 appendices one might look for those variables which are positively (or negatively) and substantially related to both social class and left-right ideology [25]. These variables could, depending on their nature, be either interpreting or explaining variables (see Hyman, 1955).

7.4.3.2. Model 1. It is perhaps somewhat surprising to see that the number of variables, available in the present design, which could either interpret or explain the relationship between social class and left-right ideology, is very limited indeed: there are only 2 such variables:
1. Political party choice of father (PPCF) and
2. Satisfaction with living conditions (SLC) [26].

PPCF is related .20 to social class and .25 to left-right ideology; SLC is related .15 to social class and .18 to left-right ideology (coefficients are Tau-beta's). Since PPCF seems to be more intimately related to social class of parents (SCP) rather than to social class (Tau = .21), it was decided to bring SCP into the (possibly) causal model, which is presented in Fig. 7.1.

Fig. 7.1. *Model 1*

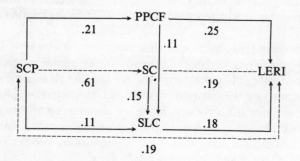

Note:
Coefficients are Tau-beta's. The dotted lines indicate the 'social mobility model' tested above in within-analysis — see Table 7.6.

The model is rather self-evident:

(a) the effect of SCP on LERI may be interpreted by PPCF and/or SLC. We have already seen that social class only partially interprets the SCP effect (see Table 7.6.) but together with the other 2 variables it could completely interpret the SCP effect;

(b) SCP might explain away most of the relationship of PPCF and SLC with LERI (we have already seen that it partly explains away the relationship between social class and LERI); and

(c) SLC could either interpret the relationship of PPCF and/or social class to LERI or both the relationship between SLC and LERI could be explained away by either or both of these variables.

The model has first been tested by means of elaboration and subsequently by means of partial correlations. No evidence in favor of any of the postulated interpretations or explanations has been found, with the exception of the fact that SLC interprets the SCP effect on LERI. So, apart from the already known fact that social class and social class of parents form a 'syndrome' in that both factors explain or interpret most of each other's affects on LERI, no other explaining or interpreting factors have been found so far. Instead, we have found 2 other 'determinants' of LERI: *PPCF* and *SLC*. The next step will be an investigation of the question whether the relationships of these factors with LERI can be interpreted or explained away by other variables.

7.4.3.3. Model 2. There are again only very few variables in the design which are related to either PPCF and/or SLC and LERI in a similar way so as to be building blocks for a possible causal model, they are:

1. Having had a religious upbringing (RU);
2. Considering oneself to belong to a certain church (i.e. religion: REL); and
3. Sex (for measurements: see Appendix 6)

The relationships between these 3 variables and the other 3 are sometimes rather complicated and difficult to express in terms of correlations, due to the nominal character of RU, REL and sex, in addition to PPCF. However, when RU and REL are rank-ordered as follows: no religion, roman catholic, Dutch reformed and Calvinist, and PPCF as in note 26, some meaningful correlations appear.

Let us introduce the causal model to be tested by a small excursion into the religious realm: an investigation as to process of dechristianization that is going on in the Netherlands: many people who report to have had a religious upbringing no longer consider themselves as being a member of a church (see Table 7.9.).

Table 7.9. *A religious upbringing vs. considering oneself as belonging to a* church

| | Considering oneself as: | | | | | |
Brought up as:	Non-believer	Roman catholic	Dutch reformed	Calvinist	Total	100%
Non-believer (no church)	89.9 (338)	2.9 (11)	6.1 (23)	1.1 (4)	21.7	(376)
Roman catholic	18.5 (136)	80.7 (592)	0.7 (5)	0.1 (1)	42.4	(734)
Dutch reformed	40.2 (176)	1.1 (5)	55.5 (234)	3.2 (14)	25.3	(438)
Calvinist	19.5 (36)	1.1 (2)	9.2 (17)	70.2 (130)	10.7	(185)
Total	39.6 (686)	35.2 (610)	16.6 (288)	8.6 (149)	100%	(1733)

Note:
Other churches have been left out of consideration. See Appendix 6B for the Dutch names of the 2 protestant churches.

Table 7.9. shows that of those who have been brought up in a non-religious way, 90% consider themselves as not belonging to a church; of those who have been brought up as a roman catholic 80% still consider themselves to be roman catholic; of those who have been brought up as a Calvinist, 70% still consider themselves to be Calvinist, but of those who have been brought up Dutch reformed, only 55% still consider themselves to belong to this church.

Half of those not considering themselves to belong to a certain church have been brought up in a certain religion, and half of these have been brought up in the Dutch reformed faith. Almost 20% of those who have been brought up either roman catholic or Calvinist do not consider themselves to belong to a church anymore. For the Dutch reformed group, this percentage is 40! The dechristianization process is finally indicated by the fact that slightly more than 20% of the population have not been brought up in a religion, but that almost 40% do not consider themselves to belong to a church anymore.

Let us now return to the possible causal model to be constructed. RU and REL are related .41 to each other; they are virtually unrelated to sex; RU is strongly related to PPCF (Chi-2 is 485.6 when both variables are dichotomized 'religious-non-religious'); they are hardly at all related to SLC and related .16 and .18, respectively, to LERI (correlations are Tau-beta's). Sex is related .12 to SLC and .11 to LERI.

The model that may be tested on the basis of this evidence is presented in Fig. 7.2.

Fig. 7.2. *Model 2*

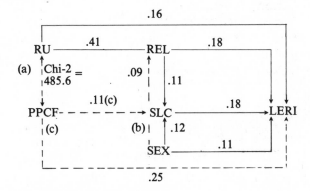

Notes: (Correlations are Tau-beta's)
(a) This relationship is a syndrome rather than a causal one: more than 80% of those reporting a religious upbringing also report that their father voted for a christian-democratic party. For both RU and PPCF dichotomized 'religious-non-religious', the Pearson coefficient is .64.
(b) This relationship is not strictly 'causal', but women may be more 'sensitive' to a religious upbringing and hence remain more religious (this is the case, but not for Calvinists).
(c) Relationships already tested in Model 1.

The model is again rather self-evident:
(a) REL could interpret the RU effect, or RU could explain the REL effect away.
(b) SLC could either interpret the REL and/or SEX effect, or it could be explained away by one or both of these variables; and
(c) REL could (partly) interpret the SEX effect.
In testing this model, first again by means of elaboration and subsequently by means of partial correlations, the only thing that could be shown was that the RU effect is interpreted by REL: in those who no longer consider themselves to belong to a certain church, their religious upbringing does not have an effect on their left-right ideological stand. The sex effect is only slightly weakened when controlling for SLC. All other relationships remain unaffected [27].

Instead of finding another causal model, we have again identified 2 other determinants of left-right ideological positions: *religion* and *sex*: these variables do not interpret or explain away the effects of the other determinants, i.e. PPCF and SLC. The final step in causal model construction attempts will be an investigation of variables which are possibly interpreting the religion effect on left-right ideology.

7.4.3.4. Model 3. There are only 2 variables available which could possibly interpret the religion effect:
1. General optimism-pessimism (GOP);
2. Awareness of a possible communist threat (APCT) (see again Appendix 6).
The final, rather simple model, is presented in Fig. 7.3.

Fig. 7.3. *Model 3*

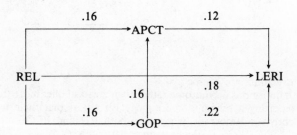

Note:
Coefficients are Tau-beta's.

The model is tested again by means of elaboration and partial correlations, by which it is shown that (a) the religion effect could not be interpreted by APCT or GOP or both, (b) the GOP effect is not interpreted by APCT or explained away by REL, (c) The APCT effect largely disappears when controlling for REL and GOP. (In elaboration, a number of irregular patterns appeared, which could not be explained or interpreted.) So, the net result of our testing of this final model has been the identification of another determinant of left-right ideology: *general optimism-pessimism* (GOP).

7.4.4. Conclusions: determinants of left-right ideology.

We have seen above that the relationship between social class and left-right ideology is not a simple one. First, it has been shown that educational level does not have an independent effect on LERI and that *income* seems to be the social class component with the strongest independent effect [28]. Second, it has been shown that the social class effect is partly explained away by 'social class of parents' (partial correlation becomes .07) and by 'subjective social class' (partial correlation becomes .13). Since these variables together take away the complete social class effect (partial correlation, second order, becomes .03), we have to conclude that the relationship between social class and left-right ideology is brought about by a combination of *'socialization'* and *'class identification'* mechanisms. Since income remains to have an independent effect on left-right ideology when controlled for these factors (second order partial = .11), and since 'parents' social class' and 'subjective social class' remain to have independent effects on left-right ideology when controlled for each other plus income (second order partials are .08 and .13, respectively), the social class effect has in fact been broken up into these 3 factors. In addition, however, it can be seen that the multiple correlation between these 3 factors and left-right ideology is much stronger than the relationship between social class and left-right, which will be discussed below.

In the previous analysis we have found 8 determinants of left-right ideology [29].
1. social class parents' (SCP)
2. subjective social class (SC-subj.)
3. income (INC)
4. satisfaction with living conditions (SLC)
5. political party choice of father (PPCF) [30]
6. considering oneself as belonging to a certain church (REL) [31]
7. sex
8. general optimism-pessimism (GOP)

An attempt has been made (a) to assess the independent effects of these determinants on left-right ideology, and (b) to assess the predictability of this variable by means of multiple correlation. The results are presented in Table 7.10., which also includes the social class variable. (Note the direction of the relationships between the determinants and left-right ideology, and see therefore notes 30 and 31. All scores go from 'low' to 'high' in terms of the variable name. Women are somewhat more right-wing than men.)

It can be seen in column 3 that the 4 'social class' variables (variables 1–4) when not controlled for each other have effects on left-right ideology that are about as strong as the effects of 2 other variables: GOP and PPCF (all partials are about .20); it can also be seen that these variables have stronger effects than SLC, REL and especially SEX. (The effects of the 'non-social class' variables are controlled for each other and for social class.)

However, when the effects of the social class 'determinants' (variables 2–4) are controlled for each other, as well as for 3 other variables, their independent effects drop to a level around .10 (as is shown in columns 4 and 5), and the effect of non-class variables (especially GOP and PPCF), even when controlled for the social class determinants, proves stronger (it remains at levels of around .20).

Obviously, the 3 social class determinants form a syndrome. Neither of these factors has a strong effect independent of the others and, as can be seen in the first row of the bottom part of Table 7.10., their multiple correlation with left-right ideology is not very much higher than the 'direct' relationships of SC (subjective) and INC (.32 vs. .27 and .25, respectively).

Going down from the top row of the bottom part of Table 7.10., it can be seen that the multiple correlations for non-social class variables are

Table 7.10. *Determinants of left-right ideology: direct relationships, partial correlations and multiple correlations* [32]

Variable label	Direct relat.(a)		4th-order partials(b)		5th-order partials(c)		5th-order partials(d) (N = 1364)	5th-order partials(e) (N = 881)
	1		2		3		4	5
		N =		N =		N =		
1. SC(obj)	.19	1926	.21	1816	.19	1162	—	—
2. SCP	.18	1926	.23	1816	.19	1162	.10	.07
3. SC (subj)	.27	1680	.23	1586	.17	1018	.10	.07
4. INC	.25	1576	.21	1498	.18	970	.09	.12
5. SLC	.16	1926	.14	1816	.12	1162	.14	—
6. PPCF	.25	1220	—	—	.20	1162	—	.22
7. REL	.15	1816	.16	1816	.16	1162	.18	.17
8. SEX	.08	1926	.09	1816	.07	1162	—	—
9. GOP	.21	1926	.21	1816	.21	1162	.22	.21

Multiple correlations	R =	N =
1. SCP, SC (subj), INC	.32	1436
2. SLC, REL, SEX, GOP	.36	1816
3. SLC, REL, SEX, GOP, PPCF	.43	1162
4. SC (obj), SLC, REL, SEX, GOP	.41	1816
5. SC (obj), SLC, REL, SEX, GOP, PPCF	.46	1162
6. SCP, SC (subj), INC, SLC, REL, SEX, GOP	.45	1436
7. SCP, SC (subj), INC, SLC, REL, SEX, GOP, PPCF	.48	1018

Notes: For variable labels and measurements see text and appendices. One case was lost during processing. N's lower than 1926 indicate missing data or categories left out of consideration — i.e. in the case of REL and PPCF.

(a) For variables drawn into model construction, the direct relationship means the independent effects established there i.e. highest order partial correlations pertaining to the variables in the model. For income and subjective social class, the uncontrolled product-moment coefficients are given; these are, of course, higher than their independent effects. However, no variable belonging to the family of social class variables has been controlled for other similar variables (see text above for these partials).

(b) Variables 1–4 controlled for variables 5–8 and variables 5–8 controlled for each other plus social class.

(c) Like b, but including variable 6.

(d) Variables 2, 3, 4, 5, 7, 9 controlled for each other.

(e) Variables 2, 3, 4, 6, 7, 9 controlled for each other.

somewhat higher (about .40) than for the social class variables and that when the 2 sets of variables are combined, the multiple correlation approaches .50, thus explaining between 20 and 25% of the variance. (This percentage is a little inflated, though, since the highest coefficients are obtained when the variable of the political party choice of father is included, which particularly truncates the sample due to missing data (32.6%) and parties left out of consideration (4%). It is obvious that since PPCF is an important determinant of left-right ideology, an attempt should be made to improve the measurement of this variable in future research. The same applies to GOP and to a somewhat lesser degree to SLC, SC (subjective) and INC.)

In addition to the social class determinants, left-right ideology seems to be determined by a *socialization* variable (PPCF), a *personality* variable (GOP), a *situational* variable (i.e. how one's economic situation is experienced: SLC) and what might be called a special *'ideological'* variable (REL). So there is quite a variety in the types of variables which prove to be determinants of left-right ideology, but (a) none of these has a strong independent effect; and (b) together they explain still less than 25% of the variance. This may be partly due to weak measurements, as indicated above, but it may be taken for granted (and this is no unusual conclusion in social research) that there are other determinants of left-right ideology which have still to be identified. A replication of the present study with improved measurements, as well as additional (potential) determinants is to be recommended. In secondary analysis, it might be interesting to carry out a contrasting groups analysis to further clarify the mutual effects of the determinants of left-right ideology that were identified (see e.g. Morgan and Sonquist, 1963).

In conclusion, although left-right is clearly an ideological dimension which is related to a number of 'social class' determinants, left-wing vs. right-wing ideological positions also depend on how 'satisfied' one is in one's class position and on a number of factors that are not (directly) related to class position. Perhaps we should search for additional 'cultural mechanisms' affecting people's positions along the left-right dimension in future research. The conditions *specifying* the relationship between social class and left-right ideology, to be assessed in the next section, could also provide hunches for future study.

7.4.5. *Attempts at specification*

From the very beginning of the analyses presented in this chapter, a major aim has been to identify those conditions under which the relationship between social class and left-right ideology could be strengthened or weakened. One set of conditions has already been identified: the higher the degree of *class consciousness*, the stronger the relationship between social class and left-right ideology indeed becomes (see section 7.4.2.2.).

In the present section, we will systematically explore the domain of available variables for their possibly specifying effects. (Such a rather unscholarly exploration is inevitable since the basic data that we have at our disposal — presented in Appendices 7 and 8 — do not give us any clue as to the possibly specifying nature of the variable. A theory on the basis of which predictions could be made is also lacking.) In the present study, a selection has been made of those variables which have more or less clearly and unambiguously specifying effects.

7.4.5.1. Specifying variables: a description of their effects. The following variables specify the relationship between social class and LERI [33]:

(a) The urban-rural continuum
(b) Political partisanship of father (PPCF)
(c) Religion and religious variables
(d) Age
(e) Authoritarianism (shortened classical F-scale)
(f) General optimism-pessimism (GOP)
(g) Alienation from the political party system (APPS)
(h) Abstract-ideological dimensions [34].
(i) Self-identification as left- vs. right-wing (SLR) [35]

(ad a)   There are 2 specifying variables here: degree of urbanization of residence in youth (URY) and degree of urbanization of present residence (URP) (for measurements see Appendices 6 and 7). Both variables are unrelated to LERI, but are moderately related to social class (Tau's are .18 and .12, resp.).
The relationship between social class and LERI proves to be somewhat weakened in the country (.15) but strengthened in the 3 large cities (.25) with small towns in between. URY has a stronger specifying effect, which may help to explain the former specification: for those who have been raised in the country, the relationship between social class and LERI drops to .10; for those who have been raised in a large city, it increases to .28 (small towns lie in between, at .23).

(ad b)   In people from a 'liberal background' (see section 7.4.3.2. above), the relationship between social class and LERI is somewhat increased: .24. It is maintained in those from a christian-democratic background but is weakened to .09 and .05 in people from a progressive and extremely left-wing background.

ad c)   Some specification occurs for REL as well as for RU (see section 7.4.3.3. above). In non-religious people for example, the relation between social class and LERI is somewhat increased (.21) and in roman catholics and Dutch-reformed it is somewhat weakened (.14, .16, respectively). Surprising enough, in Calvinists it is again increased to .27. (A similar pattern appears for RU.) This is the more surprising since church-attendance and religious involvement prove to have a moderating effect on the relationship between social class and LERI: for those who go to church at least once a fortnight or once a week, the relationship weakens to .13 and .15, respectively, whilst for those who are highly involved it only reaches .15. On the other hand, Calvinists are among the most frequent church-attenders and are also the most highly involved as far as religion is concerned (see Appendix 8). The other phenomenon in need of explanation is why in the group of people attending church less than once a month (but who still regard themselves as belonging to a certain church) and/or people who are not greatly involved in religious matters, the relationship increases to .32 and .28, respectively.

(ad d)   Age proves to be a strongly specifying variable: in young people (17–24) the relationship between social class and LERI drops to .07; in old people (55–70), it increases to .31. (In between, it remains at more or less the original level.) On the other hand, the originally-zero relationship between age and LERI increases to .11 for the upper-middle class and to .24 for the upper class. The phenomenon to be queried is why the older upper-middle and upper class, unlike the older lower class people, become so strongly right-wing.

(ad e)   The shortened classical F-scale (see Appendix 6A) specifies the relationship between social class and LERI in a somewhat irregular manner. The relationship for the 4 levels from low to high authoritarianism increases from .15 and .20 to .26 and .20. The opposite specification is more interesting: the original zero-relationship between authoritarianism and LERI ideology becomes weakly negative in the working class, weakly positive in the middle classes and increases to .16 in the upper class: only in the upper class does authoritarianism have a positive relationship with right-wing ideology.

(ad f)   General optimism-pessimism (GOP; see section 7.4.3.4.) has another strongly specifying effect: for pessimists, the relation increases to .27. On the other hand, the relationship between GOP and LERI (.22) decreases to .10 in the working class, but increases in the upper-middle and upper classes to .32 and .27 resp.

(ad g) Alienation from the political party system (APPS; for measurement, see Appendix 6D) only specifies the relationship between social class and LERI ideology to some extent: it becomes .11 for the non-alienated and .24 for the strongly alienated. The originally weak negative relationship between APPS and LERI (—.10) increases somewhat in the lower classes (—.13, —.14), but disappears in the upper class (.05).

(ad h) It has been shown in Chapter 6 that the relationship between abstract ideological dimensions and LERI is specified by social class: the upper classes show a much stronger interrelated pattern of ideological positions (see Table 6.15.). It could have been predicted, then, that the relationship between social class and LERI would not remain unaffected by abstract ideological dimensions. Indeed, the relationship between social class and LERI for the conservative, liberal and anti-socialist positions is increased to .36, .35 and .28, respectively; for 'progressives', liberals and socialists, it weakens (or disappears completely) to .13, —.03 and .05. On moderate positions along the abstract ideological dimensions, it remains roughly at its original level.

(ad i) A similar pattern is shown by self-identification as left-wing vs. right-wing (SLR; see Appendix 6E), a variable which is unrelated to social class: for those who consider themselves right-wing, the relationship increases to .28; for those who consider themselves left-wing the relationship is weakened to .14.

7.4.5.2. *Attempts at interpretation* [36].

The relationship between the various specifying variables, and their respective relationships to social class and left-wing ideology are given in Appendices 7 and 8; they will not be repeated here. After some regrouping, it becomes clear that these variables form 3 clusters: (1) the 2 urban-rural continuum variables (URP and URY), PPCF and the religious variables; (2) age and the 2 personality variables: the short F-scale and GOP; and (3) and 3 abstract ideological dimensions and self-description as either left- or right-wing (SLR).

Specifying variables that are related to each other could possibly 'interpret' each other's effect, but since the specifying effects themselves are sometimes already difficult to 'explain', our attempts at interpretation will be limited: we will see whether

(a) The effect of present residence is explained by the effect of the degree of urbanization of the residence where one has been brought up (i.e.

whether URY explains the URP effect).

(b) The socialization effect of PPCF is interpreted by the socialism dimension.

(c) The religion effect is interpreted by the self-identification as left-wing vs. right-wing SLR).

(d) The SLR effect is explained by the abstract ideological continua of socialism, conservatism and liberalism.

(e) The age effect is interpreted by the 2 personality variables of authoritarianism and GOP.

(ad a)   Here, further specifications emerge when the relationship between social class and left-right ideology is simultaneously controlled for URP and URY: for those living in the country, the original URY effect is strengthened, but for those who have been raised in big cities, the specifying effect of URP is reversed.

(ad b)   *Socialism* seems indeed to interpret the PPCF effect: it is the socializing effect of PPCF along the socialism dimension which leads to its specifying effect (see below).

(ad c)   SLC does not interpret the religion effect.

(ad d)   *Liberalism* explains the SLC effect: the fact that the relationship between social class and LERI is strengthened in those who consider themselves as right-wing seems to be caused by the liberalism of those people (see again below for a further discussion on the specifying effects of the abstract dimensions).

(ad e)   The age effect is interpreted by the general pessimism of older people: it is in pessimists that the relationship between social class and LERI increases, due to the extreme right-wing tendency in upper class pessimists. Authoritarianism does not interpret the age effect.

In conclusion, let us briefly consider 3 phenomena that have appeared.

First, the specifying effects of the abstract dimensions of socialism and liberalism can be seen in the light of our previous analysis on the existence of certain forms of false consciousness in the general population, but especially in the poorly educated and the lower classes (see Chapter 6, Table 6.15.). We have seen there that liberalism is virtually unrelated to left-right ideology in the lower classes, but .30 in the upper class, and also that socialism is more weakly related to LERI in the working class (—.31) than in the upper class (—.48). This means that in the lower classes we find relatively many 'anti-socialist left-wing' and 'liberal left-wing' positions and hence, in anti-socialist and liberal groups, there are relatively many left-wing lower class people, which increases the relationship between social class and left-right ideology in these groups.

Second, the fact that the relationship between social class and left-right ideology is so relatively strong in Calvinists may be related to the particular Calvinist views on the government and its public duties. Generally, Calvinists may tend to see the government's task in terms of 'accommodation', i.e. taking care of people to the extent that is necessary to make them feel comfortable in their social 'station'. In its principled version, this may lead to moderately left-wing positions to be adopted by lower class Calvinists but also to extremely right-wing positions to be adopted by upper class Calvinists (cf. Hoogerwerf, 1964: Chs. 3 and 9).

Third, we have seen that pessimism (GOP) has a stronger effect on right-wing positions in older people than in younger ones. The relationship between social class and left-right ideology is much stronger in older pessimists (Tau = .37) than in young ones (Tau = .21), while the difference disappears in the optimistic groups. The question is why the older pessimistic working class still remains relatively left-wing. There is no definite answer to this question at this stage (the matter needs further investigation) but we may suggest that an interpretation in a slightly Marxian way is appropriate: the economic situation of most older working class people is such that they lack a perspective of a 'better future' to be reached by personal initiative; hence, although their pessimism would lead them to adopt right-wing positions, they remain in favor of (certain) government policies with an egalitarian aim, which could improve their living conditions.

We have now reached the final stage in the first round of Type–2 analysis: the assessment of variables that *suppress* the relationship between social class and left-right ideology.

7.4.6. Suppressor variables

When, as in our case, the initial weakness of a relationship is one reason to start a process of systematic exploration around it, special attention should be paid to the detection of variables that suppress such a relationship. In our case, we have postponed an investigation of such variables to the last stage of the analysis [37].

As has been indicated in Chapter 2, those variables suppress or cloud a certain relationship which are related in *opposite* ways to both variables involved (if the variables themselves are positively related, which, in our case, they are). In fact, we have already identified 2 important supressor variables: libertarianism-traditionalism (LITR) and authoritarianism (AUTH) as the subdimension of LITR, consisting of components that are particularly sensitive to social class and educational level (see Table

6.18.). We have seen in Table 6.15. that LITR is *positively* related to LERI (.28; when both variables are recoded to 4 levels, Tau increases to .30) [38] and that AUTH is also *positively* related to LERI, although weaker (Tau = .11 but increases to .13 after recoding the variables to 4 levels). We have seen in Table 6.18. that LITR and AUTH are both *negatively* related to social class (Tau's are —.22 and —.30, respectively).

The conclusion seems inevitable: *the second fundamental dimension of ideological controversy (LITR) and its subdimension of AUTH act as variables which suppress the relationship between the first major dimension (LERI) and the crucial structural variable of social class.* It is the traditionalism and authoritarianism of the lower classes (or rather, as we have seen in our previous analysis on working class authoritarianism, the fact that in the lower classes, due to a poor level of education, many show some symptoms of authoritarianism in the areas of nationalism and family life) which prevents them from a stronger left-wing position; conversely, it is the libertarianism and anti-authoritarianism of the upper classes which moderates their right-wing stand [39].

But this is not all. Two other suppressing variables have been found: 'Self-identification as progressive vs. conservative' (SPC) and 'Political interest' (POLINT) which are related —.14 and .15, respectively, to social class and .18 and —.14, respectively, to LERI. Thus, it is the fact that the upper classes see themselves as progressive which prevents their right-wing tendency to become very strong; the same applies to their political interest. For the lower classes, it is their lack of political interest and the fact that they tend to describe themselves as conservative (compared to the upper classes) which prevents them from a more extreme left-wing position. (For the measurement of SPC and POLINT: see Appendix 6.)

The extent to which these 4 variables suppress the relationship between social class and left-right ideology (Tau = .19 over-all) is shown in Table 7.11.

Table 7.11. *The effects of the suppressor variables on the relationship between social class and left-right ideology* (a)

| Suppressors | Relationship between social class and left-right ideology | | | | | | |
	very low	low	medium	high	very high	average Tau-beta	partial correl.
LITR	.21	.34		.30	.29	.29	.37
AUTH	.15	.37		.28	.19	.25	.32
SPC		.19	.24	.33		.25	.27
POLINT	.16	.22		.26	.24	.22	.26

Note:
(a) entries are Tau-beta's except for the right-hand column.

LITR is the strongest suppressor: on its 4 levels, the average Tau increases from .19 to .29 (when measured as a 10-point scale the average Tau increases to .31). AUTH and SPC are weaker suppressors, and POLINT is the weakest. A clear picture is shown by the partial correlations. When the relationship between social class and LERI is controlled for LITR, SPC and POLINT, the partial correlation rises to .38 which indicates that alongside the major suppressor-variable (LITR), the other 2 have almost nothing to contribute (AUTH is excluded because of its overlap with LITR — note that the suppressing effect of LITR is slightly exaggerated due to its overlap in measurement with LERI.)

It is clear that the relationship of suppressor-variables to each of the variables whose relationship is suppressed may itself be suppressed by each of the other variables. So, the relationship of LITR to social class is suppressed by LERI (partial correlation is .40) and the relationship of LITR to LERI is suppressed by social class (see Chapter 6: Table 6.15.) [40]. The same applies to AUTH and SPC and also to POLINT.

Relationships are not always so simple, however: potentially suppressing variables, like potentially interpreting or explaining variables, may in fact prove to be specifying. It has been shown in Chapter 6 for example, that the relationship between AUTH and LERI is not only suppressed by social class (it rises to an average Tau of .22) but that it is also *specified*: in the working class it remains at the level of .13, in the upper class it rises to .30. Thus in the upper class AUTH has a much stronger effect on right-wing orientations than in the working class (with the middle classes somewhat irregularly in between) [41]. (The same is true for self-identification as progressive vs. conservative: .16 in the working class; .31 in the upper class; and in the middle classes .23.)

Table 7.12. *The effects of social class and political interest on left-right ideology* (a)

Social class	Political interest				
	very low	low	high	very high	TAU
Working class	.43 (205)	1.16 (89)	.96 (79)	.81 (75)	− .27 (440)
Lower-middle	.53 (287)	1.46 (135)	1.32 (183)	1.06 (224)	− .18 (829)
Upper-middle	.88 (83)	1.66 (80)	1.59 (98)	1.37 (118)	− .17 (379)
Upper class	.81 (70)	1.88 (49)	1.82 (68)	1.70 (92)	− .05 (279)
TAU	.16 (645)	.22 (344)	.26 (429)	.24 (509)	(1927)

Note:
(a) Mean scores on the 4-point left-right dimension; N's in brackets. For categorizations: see Appendix 5.

A most interesting specification-effect of social class can be observed in the relationship of the weakest clouding variable — political interest — to left-right ideology. It has been shown above (see Table 7.11.) that political interest, as a variable suppressing the relationship between social class and LERI, is also weakly specifying. The relationship between POLINT and LERI, however, is *strongly* specified rather than increased at various levels of social class. In workers, POLINT has a relatively strong effect on LERI: —.27. So when workers become interested in politics, they tend at the same time to become much more left-wing, as can be seen in Table 7.12. In the middle classes, the original Tau (—.14) is only slightly increased, but in the upper class, it almost vanishes to —.05.

The strong effect of political interest upon left-wing ideology in the working class has only a small overall effect however, since so few working class people are politically interested — only 17% are very interested, 35% are interested; in the upper class, these figures are 33% and 57%, respectively.

Whereas AUTH and SPC mainly act as suppressor variables 'through the upper class', political interest has its strongest effect in the working class. If workers became less apathetic politically, there would be a strong tendency for them to become more left-wing ideologically and this would increase the relationship between social class and LERI [42].

7.4.7. Conclusions

The first round of Type-2 analysis — around the initial relationship between social class and left-right ideology — has been completed by the identification of a number of variables which suppress this relationship. According to some, one could say that these variables are important to the political system of parliamentary democracy because they prevent the relationship between social class and left-right ideology from becoming too strong so as to endanger this system. (A little scepticism about this rationale is in order, however: in some Scandinavian countries there have been solid left-wing majorities for decades *within* a parliamentary system.) We have started the process of systematic exploration by a clarification of the initial relationship by means of an assessment of the relationships between the various components of the variables involved. There is a great deal of variation in the strengths of these various relationships and we could disentangle the social class effect on LERI to some extent by establishing that *educational level* does not have an independent effect on LERI and that the social class effect is mainly brought about by *income*. A further disentanglement of the relationship of social class to LERI ideology has been brought about by 'within-analysis'; the social class effect proved to be brought about mainly by parents' social class (a socialization factor) and subjective social class (the class one feels to belong to; a class identification factor).

Subsequently, we have found, after the rather unsuccessful attempts to construct causal models, that there are a number of variables outside the realm of social class which are relatively important determinants of left-right ideology, i.e. a political socialization factor such as 'political party choice of father', a personality variable such as 'general optimism-pessimism' and a factor such as religion. These variables even tend to be better predictors of left-right ideology than social class variables.

Our attempts to find variables that specify the relationship between social class and left-right ideology have been moderately successful. We have found, for example, that, as predicted, the relationship increases rather sharply in categories manifesting high levels of class consciousness (it doubles in the highest class conscious groups and vanishes completely in the non-class conscious groups). After more systematic exploration, we later found that the relationship increases e.g. in people living or having been brought up in big cities, in people from a liberal (i.e. VVD) background, in Calvinists, in older people, in pessimistic people and in anti-socialists, liberals and conservatives according to the abstract dimensions which have been conceptualized in Chapter 6. No variables could be found that could either explain or interpret the class consciousness effect, but some other specifying effects could be explained or interpreted by means of variables in the design, e.g. the PPCF effect is interpreted by the socialism dimension, the age effect is interpreted by the optimism-pessimism dimension and the SLR effect is explained by the liberalism dimension.

Finally, we have been rather successful in identifying some variables which suppress the relationship between social class and left-right ideology in a substantial manner: its strength approaches .40 when controlling (by means of partial correlation) for the major suppressing variable, which happens to be the other fundamental dimension of ideological controversy which was identified in the present study in the previous chapter: libertarianism-traditionalism.

In summary, we now know a great deal more about (a) the relationship between social class and left-right ideology, and (b) the determinants of left-right ideology. In the present study we will not go back and make an attempt, for example, to assess the effect of class consciousness on the multiple correlation of parents' social class, subjective social class and income and LERI; to what extent this relationship can be specified in other ways or to which extent it is suppressed. We will also not go back into a more extensive assessment of determinants of LERI ideology by including suppressing variables and those that have been used as validating variables. If we did all this, we might well end up with a number of rather high correlations, indicating the conditions under which social class variables act as substantial predictors of left-right ideology, as well as the extent to which left-right ideological stands might be predicted at all. However, we leave this as a matter of secondary analysis.

Rather, we will carry on the analysis and make an attempt to investigate the relationship between *social class and libertarianism-traditionalism*, in line with our previous analysis into the phenomenon of working class traditionalism in Chapter 6: 6.7.1. The rationale behind this procedure is twofold: (1) LITR is the second major dimension of ideological controversy in the general population identified in the present study, (2) LITR is the major suppressor variable of the relationship between social class and left-right ideology. If we would know more about the relationship of LITR to social class (i.e. by means of a shortened repetition of the Type–2 analysis carried out around the relationship between social class and LERI), we would know more about one of the major 'mechanisms' keeping the relationship between social class and LERI rather low.

7.5. TYPE-2 ANALYSIS EXTENDED: (1) SYSTEMATIC EXPLORATION AROUND THE RELATIONSHIP BETWEEN SOCIAL CLASS AND LIBERTARIANISM—TRADITIONALISM

7.5.1. Introduction

Now that we know that the relationships between social class and the major dimensions of ideological controversy in the progressive-conservative domain in the general population (left-right and libertarianism-traditionalism) are so weak mainly because the 2 ideological dimensions *suppress* each other's 'effects', and after our systematic exploration around the relationship between left-right ideology and social class, one is intrigued by the results of a systematic exploration along similar lines around the relationship between social class and libertarianism-traditionalism.

The analysis presented below will yield results that will often be discussed in the light of a comparison with the results of the previous analysis presented in section 7.4. It will be more limited in scope in that (a) the effects of *class consciousness*, which seem so intimately related to the economic interests of the various social classes, will not be assessed (it has been suggested in Chapter 6: 6.4. that LITR is probably related to the psychological interests of people in various social class positions), and (b) it will not be attempted to assess *determinants*, *specifying* variables or *suppressors*. We limit ourselves to (1) *component-analysis* on the basis of our previous analysis into 'working class authoritarianism', (2) *within-analysis* and (3) *between-analysis*. We will see, for example, whether such phenomena as status-inconsistency, social mobility and class identification have effects on LITR which are somehow comparable to those they (don't) have on LERI. Between-analysis will finally yield a number of factors *interpreting* working class authoritarianism, which confirm, to some extent, the rationales that have been developed in section 6.7.1. on this phenomenon.

7.5.2. Component analysis

The data have already been presented in Table 6.18. and they have been discussed in the context of our preliminary investigation into the phenomenon of working class conservatism. A reconsideration of these data is particularly interesting in the light of the similar component analysis of the relationship between social class and left-right ideology (see Table 7.4.). In particular a comparison of the relationships among the social class components and LERI, LITR and AUTH yields an interesting picture (see Table 7.13.).

Table 7.13.   *The relationships between the social class components and the ideological dimensions*

Social class components	Ideological dimensions		
	LERI	*LITR*	*AUTH*
Educational level	.08	−.33	−.40
Occupational level	.17	−.20	−.28
Income level	.16	−.17	−.24
SOCIAL CLASS	.19	−.22	−.30

Note: see Tables 6.18. and 7.4. for measurements and coefficients. (Tau-beta's over 4 × 4 tables)

We see in Table 7.13. that although occupation and income are related at about the same level to LERI and LITR, the somewhat weaker relationship between social class and LERI as compared to the relationship between social class and LITR is caused by the fact that educational level is virtually unrelated to LERI (we have seen in section 7.4.1.3. that there is no independent education effect at all when controlled for income), but rather strongly to LITR; most strongly, of course, to its AUTH components. Not only is social class *positively* related to one dimension of ideological controversy (LERI) and *negatively* to the other (LITR), there is the additional complication that the component of educational level is unrelated to LERI and *strongly* related to LITR. This is one major difference between the 2 dimensions: their differential sensitivity to education. If we accept the weak positive relationship between LERI and LITR, the highly educated must experience some cross pressure: as soon as they *also* have a high income, their libertarianism would incline them towards a left-wing stand, but their income towards a right-wing stand.

We will see below which mechanisms lead to the traditionalism and especially the authoritarianism of the poorly educated. First we will see whether income, the weakest 'predictor' of LITR, remains to have an independent effect when controlled for educational level (i.e. we will investigate the possible effects of status-inconsistency; compare Table 7.5.).

7.5.2.1. Status-inconsistency. The results are presented in Table 7.14.[43]

Table 7.14. *The effects of status-inconsistency between education and income on libertarianism-traditionalism*(a)

Educational level	Income level								
	<12.000		12-18.000		18-24.000		>24.000		Tau-beta
Primary school	1.82(b)	(517)	1.55	(173)	1.63	(41)	1.53	(32)	-12 (763)
Sec. modern school	1.39	(196)	1.19(b)	(142)	1.28	(72)	1.19	(57)	-07 (467)
Grammar school	.89	(63)	1.06	(88)	1.00(b)	(42)	1.12	(60)	08 (253)
University	.08	(13)	.53	(17)	1.00	(20)	1.05(b)	(42)	37 (92)
Tau-beta	-.32	(789)	-.25	(420)	-.24	(125)	-.16	(191)	N = 1575

Notes:
(a) See Table 7.5.
(b) Status consistent positions

It can be seen that unlike LERI, where the education effect largely disappeared on the various income levels, here the education effect is somewhat specified in that it gets weaker (but does not disappear) in the higher income groups. On the other hand, the income effect on LITR *reverses* itself for low vs. high educational levels (and almost disappears in between): at low educational levels, it remains negative (though weaker), at the university level it becomes rather strongly positive. *Obviously, income does not have an independent effect on LITR. It seems to be dominated by the effects of status-inconsistency:* at both high and low educational levels, increasing discrepancies between educational level and income level lead to increasing libertarianism.

Thus, contrary to its effects on LERI, status-inconsistency seems — at first sight — to be a meaningful construct here: there is one main education effect and in interaction effect. However, this is only true from the *educational* perspective. From the *income* perspective, increasing *inconsistency* at low levels and increasing *consistency* at high levels both lead to libertarianism: the education effect clearly dominates the status-inconsistency effect, especially at low income levels.

Here we have found other differences between the 2 major dimensions of ideological controversy in their relationship to social class components. For LERI we found that (a) there is no independent education effect, (b) there is an independent income effect, particularly at the higher educational levels, and (c) status-inconsistency is no meaningful construct at all. For LITR we find that (a) there is an independent and rather strong education effect, (b) there is no independent income effect, and (c) status-inconsistency is a meaningful construct from the education perspective (where inconsistency leads to libertarianism, particularly in the highly educated group) but not so from the income perspective, where it is overruled by the education effect.

In conclusion, the positive relationship between social class and LERI is mainly brought about by income while the negative relationship between social class and LITR is mainly brought about by education which shows an interaction effect with income that can be interpreted in terms of status-inconsistency. This last finding suggests that the actual 'social class situation' (i.e. the actual position of people along the educational dimension and its relation to income) is an important determinant of libertarian vs. traditional stands. This will now be investigated by means of within-analysis.

7.5.3. Within-analysis: social mobility and class identification

7.5.3.1. Social mobility. Both objectively and subjectively, present social class continues to have a similar effect at various levels of parents' social class. The effects of the latter variable are clearly interpreted by present social class position. In terms of social mobility, there is a consistent trend that upward social mobility is positively related to libertarianism and downward mobility to traditionalism. There are (weak) tendencies — both in the objective and subjective groups — that the downwardly mobile are more traditionalist than their class of destination, whereas the upwardly mobile tend to be more libertarian. (There are only

2 exceptions to this rule: objective downward mobility from lower-middle to working class and subjective downward mobility from upper classes to lower-middle class.)

It is clear that the effects of present social class position (as we have seen above: educational level) dominate the possibly socializing influences which one has undergone in the parental family. This is again quite different as compared to LERI ideology; there we saw (see Table 7.6.) that social class of parents and social class formed a syndrome: both variables took away most of each others effects on LERI, while the effects of the parents' social class (i.e. socialization) seemed to dominate. Objectively, there were both socialization and class identification effects; subjectively, the socialization effect dominated in the upwardly mobile, the class identification effect in the downwardly mobile.

Regarding LITR the effects are less complicated and the construct of social mobility seems (only) necessary to possibly explain the (weak) tendency, both objectively and subjectively, that the mobile 'over-conform' as compared to their class of destination.

7.5.3.2. Class identification. The effects of social class on LITR at various levels of subjective social class are somewhat specified, but are largely maintained: the average Tau drops to .12 (from the original —.22) in those who identify with the working class but is maintained at —.18 in those who identify with the upper classes (the partial correlation drops from an original —.25 to —.20).

The effects of subjective social class within objective class levels are less clear: workers who identify with lower-middle and upper classes are slightly more traditional (Tau turns positive: .10), but very weak negative relationships appear in the other class levels: the partial correlation drops from an original —.16 to —.02. Thus, subjective social class does not interpret the objective social class effect on LITR; this latter effect remains mostly intact.

Regarding left-right ideology, we have again seen a quite different picture (see Table 7.7.). There, the effect of class identification was somewhat stronger than that of social class. There was even a tendency, in those that identified with the working class, of a negative relationship between social class and LERI. Here again both variables seemed to form a syndrome, each taking away (large) parts of the other's effects on LERI, with subjective social class clearly dominant. We have even seen that the social class effect on LERI was completely explained away and interpreted by parents' social class and subjective social class, respectively, i.e. the combined effects of 'class' socialization and class identification.

Regarding LITR we see the predominant effect of social class itself, i.e. educational level. We have seen before (section 6.7.1.) that the notion of working class traditionalism should be reduced to the authoritarianism of the poorly educated and that even this notion is more limited in scope than has sometimes been suggested (it amounts to nationalism and authoritarianism in the area of family life). We have now seen that the effect of educational level cannot be explained away or interpreted by other 'social class' variables. In the final stage of this extension of Type-2 analysis we will make an attempt to locate 'mechanisms' bringing about this effect.

7.5.4. An attempt to construct causal models

There are 8 variables available (see Appendices 7 and 8) which are substantially related in opposite ways to social class and LITR and which could thus explain or interpret the relationship between these variables:

(a) The 2 *'urbanization'* variables: level of urbanization of residence in youth (URY) and present level of urbanization of the residence (URP) (see Appendix 6B and 6C).

(b) The 3 *personality* factors of *authoritarianism* (F, as measured by the shortened classical scale; see Appendix 6A), *dogmatism* (D, idem) and *anomia* (A, idem).

(c) *Political information* (POLINF; see Appendix 6D) and *political interest* (POLINT; idem).

(d) *Social integration* (SOCINT; see Appendix 6D).

(ad a) It is not immediately clear how a causal model could be constructed using these variables. Both URY and URP are most strongly related to educational level (.23 and .16, resp.), and most weakly to income (.13 and .07, resp.). It may be that the country offers less stimuli and opportunities for higher education, so being brought up in the country predisposes one to a lower educational (later: occupational) level.

Country traditionalism may also play a role here: children may be socialized into assuming traditional roles, rather than stimulated to accept other roles, which would require a higher educational level (e.g. higher than the parents' level). If this reasoning is correct, the 'theory' could be that the relationship between social class — in particular educational level — and LITR is partly explained by URY. This 'theory' is not confirmed. However, the relationship between URY and LITR is weakened and specified for social class and even more strongly for educational level. The original relationship (Tau = .23) is maintained in the working class and lower-middle class, but is weakened in the upper-middle class (.16) and vanishes in the upper class (.04). (Here, it can be observed how 'misleading' a partial correlation can be: the original product-moment correlation of .26 only drops to .21.) The relationship also disappears at the 2 highest educational levels; it is only maintained for those with primary school education and weakened (.15) for those with a secondary-modern school background. Obviously, higher social class (in particular: education) renders one independent of the effects of socialization (in the country vs. large cities) on one's libertarian or traditional attitudes.

A 'complementary' rationale could be that the upper classes (or people from an upper class background) tend to live in the larger cities since these offer more opportunities for higher educational and occupational levels to be reached. The social class effect could then partly be interpreted by URP. This is only slightly confirmed: the correlation between social class and LITR only drops somewhat for people living in the 3 large cities (Tau = .15). So, whereas there is more 'polarization' between the classes on left-right ideology in large cities, there is at the same time more agreement along the libertarianism-traditionalism dimension (the opposite is true in the country).

The relationships between the 2 urbanization variables, social class and LITR seem to be rather complex; they do not allow us to construct and test a causal model. We have seen an indication of the 'liberating' effects of education (the highly educated are independent from the socializing effects of URY) and that, whereas class antagonism along the left-right dimension is strongest in big cities, antagonism along libertarianism-traditionalism is strongest in the country. These phenomena are probably brought about by (a) the left-wing urban proletariat and (b) the traditional ways of life of many people in the country, in combination with a tendency in the urban (upper-) middle class to leave the bigger cities and live in the country [44].

(ad b) These variables seem to offer better opportunities for causal model construction. Let us therefore return to section 6.7.1. and Table 6.18. and our attempt there to explain the authoritarian tendencies in the poorly educated in terms of *anomia*, and the development of authoritarian personality traits (i.e. the classical F-scale, not to be confused in this context with the AUTH subdimension of LITR — which includes the F-scale). The fact that the poorly educated tend to be so *nationalistic* in various ways (including, for example, intolerance towards deviant political minorities such as communists and fascists) and authoritarian and traditional in *family matters* (including, for example, intolerance regarding homosexuals and being opposed to moral libertarianism) has been interpreted there in terms of 'limited horizons' and a 'limited view of life' which may lead to a 'lack of a sense of control of one's social environment', i.e. anomia. Authoritarianism as a personality trait (see the items in the F-scale in Appendix 6A) can then be interpreted as an attempt, at the personality level, to obtain a sense of *'psychological security'* (compare our original interpretation of the relationship between social class and the LITR dimension in terms of the 'psychological interests' of classes in section 6.4.; note also the discussion on the 'differential criteriality' of the value of freedom to upper vs. lower classes there and later in section 6.7.). If we inspect the F-scale items, we see that many of them are attempts to 'structure the world' (nos. 1, 3, 5 and 6) by searching for scapegoats (no. 4) or express scepticism (no. 2) or anxiety (no. 7).

We have now assembled the necessary data to test this theory: the anomia scale is positively related to LITR (.24) and even stronger to AUTH (.43) and negatively related to social class (-.25) and even stronger to educational level (—.32) (all coefficients are Tau-beta's). So, anomia could interpret the relationship between social class (educational level) and LITR (AUTH).

The F-scale is also positively related to LITR (.36) and to AUTH (.66, but this relationship is inflated because the F-scale is a component of AUTH) as well as negatively related to social class (—.24) and in particular educational level (—.31). In addition, the F-scale is positively related to anomia (.44) so it could interpret the relationship between anomia and LITR and AUTH, respectively.

Finally, we have constructed a short dogmatism scale. Dogmatism is a construct which was developed by Rokeach (1960) as a measure of *general* authoritarianism, as opposed to the supposedly 'right-wing' orientation of the F-scale. If we inspect the various items in the scale (the militant version has been used, including items 1–6 in Appendix 6A), we see that many, like in the F-scale, reflect tendencies to 'structure the world' and hence might be taken as another attempt by the anomic uneducated to obtain 'psychological security'. Dogmatism and authoritarianism are positively related (.46) and so are dogmatism and anomia (also .46). Dogmatism is also negatively related to social class and educational level (—.24 and —.29, resp.) and to LITR and AUTH (.32 and .46, resp.); these are all correlations which are highly similar to the corresponding ones for the F-scale. We may predict that dogmatism constitutes an alternative variable interpreting the relationship between anomia and LITR resp. AUTH.

So, we have 3 mechanisms possibly interpreting the relationship between social class (educational level) and LITR (AUTH). Anomia is seen as a consequence of a lack of education. To suppress these anomic tendencies, personality syndromes such as authoritarianism and dogmatism are developed. These mechanisms lead to a further search for 'psychological security' and perhaps a sense of 'meaning' in the social world by an acceptance of the social system in which one lives (i.e. the nation) and opposition to potentially threatening outsiders, and by a rigid structuring of one's immediate social environment (i.e. the family) around secure traditional lines leading to intolerance towards those that might threaten those traditions (e.g. homosexuals). The model that we may now attempt to test is represented in Fig. 7.4.

Fig. 7.4. *Model 4*

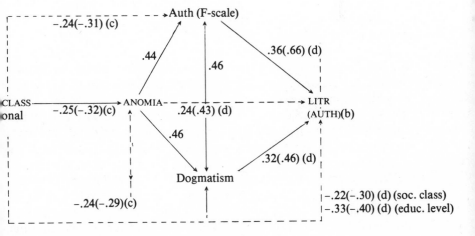

Notes: (dotted lines represent uninterpreted effects; coefficients are Tau-beta's)
(a) the most important social class component
(b) aspects of LITR which are most sensitive to social class
(c) coefficients in brackets refer to educational level
(d) coefficients in brackets refer to AUTH

The model has (again) been tested by means of elaboration and partial correlations. Below, the results of both types of tests will be given. Anomia, authoritarianism and dogmatism will be indicated by the letters A, F and D, respectively. The results can be described as follows:

1. The social class effect on LITR is weakened when controlled for A, D and F separately, but especially when controlled for all of the factors at once, and when controlled for F and D only (partials are —.15 and —.14, resp.).

2. When the educational effect is controlled for A, D and F, the relationship with LITR is only partly interpreted. The partial correlation drops from —.37 to —.26; the same holds when it is just controlled for D and F [45]. Room remains for other interpreting factors.

3. The effects of social class on dogmatism and authoritarianism is only partly interpreted by anomia: the original relationships of .29 and .28 both drop to .16.

4. The effect of educational level on dogmatism and authoritarianism is not completely interpreted by anomia either: correlations drop from —.33 and —.36 to —.17 and —.21, resp. Room remains for other factors interpreting the relationship between educational-level and dogmatism and authoritarianism.

5. The anomia effect on LITR almost disappears when controlled for F and D (average Tau's become .06 and .08, resp.; the partial correlations are .11 and .14, resp.). For both F and D controlled, the partial correlation almost disappears completely to .05.

6. The anomia effect on LITR is not only interpreted by F and D, but also partly *explained* away by social class, especially educational level. When controlling for educational level, the original Tau = .24 drops to an average of .12; the original product-moment correlation of .31 drops to a partial of .19. The anomia effect on LITR is completely explained away and interpreted by educational level, F and D (partial = .00).

7. F and D effects are weakened when controlled for one another, but remain substantial (average Tau: .24 and .17, resp.; partial correlations: .29 and .19, resp.). Both effects are also specified for one another, which suggests a syndrome: at low levels of D, the F effect is maintained at .40 and .28; at high levels it is weakened to .12 and .15. When the order is reversed, the D effect is maintained, though much more weakly, at low levels of F (.21 and .22), but is further weakened at higher levels to .13 and .11. Thus the D effect is partly interpreted by F, but essentially, in case either of the factors is low, the other 'takes over' with a relatively independent effect. In a case when either of them is high, this is probably due to some kind of a ceiling effect.

In conclusion, model 4 is partly confirmed (note that it has only been tested with LITR as a dependent variable due to the fact that the F-scale is part of AUTH). The clearest result has been the interpretation of the anomia effect by authoritarianism and dogmatism; our rationale that the effects of anomia on LITR are interpreted by personality mechanisms has been confirmed. (Anomia does not explain away the F and D effects.) However, the relationships between social class and educational level with F, D and LITR are only partially interpreted by A and A, D and F together, respectively. There is room for other interpreting factors regarding these relationships.

In our design, there are 2 other variables which might have something to contribute here: political information and political interest (POLINF and POLINT, resp.).

(ad c) The rationale is that political information and/or political interest could interpret the relationships between social class (educational level) and anomia, and perhaps authoritarianism and dogmatism. Although the measurements of both variables are very limited, one might hypothesize that a poor educational level might lead to a low level of political information and/or political interest, which might lead to anomia and so on. (POLINF is related .25 to social class, .37 to educational level and .30 to anomia; these figures are .15, .23 and .22, respectively, for POLINT; both variables are related —.28 and —.26 to LITR, respectively; these correlations are again Tau-beta's.)

At first an investigation to see whether POLINT and POLINF explain or interpret each other's effect on anomia was made. The original correlation between POLINT and anomia is largely — but not completely — interpreted by POLINF (partial = .12), whereas the original relation of POLINF to anomia is largely maintained when controlling for political interest (partial is —.27). So, again there is some indication of the existence of a 'syndrome' which may well have been caused by the limited measurement of POLINF [46]. In any case, POLINT seems to have only a weak independent effect on anomia and POLINF a relatively strong independent effect. The next step has been to investigate whether, as predicted, these variables interpret to some extent the relationship between social class — especially educational level — and anomia. However, this interpretation is only partial. For social class, the partial correlation is —.21 when controlled for POLINF. For educational level, the coefficient becomes —.27. (POLINT has no additional interpreting effect at all.)

When controlled for POLINF, D and F, the relationship between social class and LITR drops to a partial correlation of —.10 (controlling

F and D only, the partial became —.15) and the relationship between educational level and LITR drops to —.20. Not only does there remain an independent effect of social class and educational level on LITR, but POLINF also continues to have such an independent effect: the original relation with LITR only drops to —.23 when controlled for F and D.

The relationship between social class — educational level — and F and D is only slightly more satisfactorily interpreted when controlling for *both* anomia and POLINF: POLINF does not substantially add to the anomia interpretation, which may again be related to its weak measurement.

(Social integration, the final interpreting variable, has no interpreting power at all, which may also be due to its very weak measurement; see Appendix 6D).

In conclusion, we have established the following:

(a) POLINF has a moderate additional interpreting effect as far as the relationships between social class (educational level) and A, F, D and LITR are concerned; it continues to have an independent effect on LITR.

(b) The anomia-authoritarianism-dogmatism syndrome together with POLINF interprets the relationship between social class (educational level) and LITR in a substantial way; the remaining partial correlations are about half of the original product moments. This means, for example, that the uninterpreted effect of social class on LITR is only .10 (partial correlation) and that the effect of educational level on LITR is .20; that social class remains related .14 to both F and D and that the independent relationship of POLINF to F and D are below .10 (the latter effects are largely interpreted by anomia).

(c) The relationships between A, D and F are, of course, not explained away by social class, educational level and POLINF; the interrelationships remain substantial and F proves to have the strongest effect on LITR (partial is .28 as compared to D: .11).

(d) There are, of course, other determinants of LITR (see Appendix 7), but it was considered outside the scope of the present analysis — as has been mentioned before — to make an attempt to assess all determinants of LITR at this stage.

(e) Our theory as to the mechanisms, causing a negative relationship between educational level and the authoritarian components of traditionalism has been partly confirmed, but there remains room for additional interpreting mechanisms, although the weakness of the measurement of some variables may also play a role here.

(f) There are many more variables in the present design that could potentially interpret or explain the relationship between social class and LITR than there were variables that could explain or interpret the relationship between social class and LERI. However, we have seen that mainly the 3 well-known personality variables of anomia, authoritarianism and dogmatism could in fact be brought into a causal model. These variables are among the most well-known and used constructs in social psychology and political sociology: researchers have been rather concerned about these phenomena which happen to characterize the poorly educated and the working class. These phenomena are generally negatively evaluated in the well educated and the upper classes, but seldomly has their nature been made explicit as *mechanisms* leading to the traditionalism of the poorly educated which weakens the relationship between social class and left-right ideology.

7.6. TYPE-2 ANALYSIS EXTENDED: (2) THEIR RELATIONSHIP BETWEEN SOCIAL CLASS, LEFT-RIGHT IDEOLOGY AND VOTING BEHAVIOR

7.6.1. Introduction

In this final stage of the extended Type-2 analysis we will return to our choice of the initial relationship around which to develop the process of systematic exploration (see section 7.3.). The choice of this relationship — the one between social class and left-right ideology — was based on several considerations, but one of these was its very weakness, which has been seen by some political sociologists as a prerequisite for liberal (parliamentary) democracy. Implicit in this rationale has been the idea that left-right ideology is the major determinant of voting behavior along this dimension (for which there was some evidence since it had already been shown in Table 6.16a. that the relationship between left-right ideological positions and voting — with the parties ordered along this dimension on the basis of the ideological stands of their voters — was Tau = .42).

The implicit model behind this rationale was that social class leads to LERI ideological positions which in turn lead to voting along this dimension. This model will now be tested. First, we will inspect the relationship between social class and voting along the left-right dimension (see Table 7.15.).

Table 7.15.　*The relationship between social class and voting behavior*

	Social class (a)					
Voting for: (b)	*Working class*	*Lower-middle*	*Upper-middle*	*Upper class*	*M=*	*Total N(100%)*
1 PSP-CPN (extr. left)	14.8(12)	49.9(40)	22.2(18)	13.6(11)	1.35	(81)
2 PvdA (labor)	39.0(97)	49.0(122)	9.2(23)	2.8(7)	.76	(249)
3 D'66-PPR (democrats, radicals)	17.0(28)	47.3(78)	23.0(38)	12.7(21)	1.32	(165)
4 KVP (roman cath.)	29.1(82)	43.6(123)	19.9(56)	7.4(21)	1.06	(282)
5 AR-CHU (protestant)	23.0(49)	52.6(112)	18.3(39)	6.1(13)	1.08	(213)
6 VVD (class. liberal)	3.2(7)	25.8(57)	40.3(89)	30.8(68)	1.99	(231)
	22.7(275)	43.9(532)	21.7(263)	11.6(141)	N = 1221	

Notes: (entries are percentages except for the right-hand column which gives mean scores on the 4-point social class dimension; N's are in brackets)
(a)　See Appendix 6B
(b)　See Appendix 6E (see Table 6.16. for the rank-ordering of the parties along the left-right dimension)

7.6.2. Social class and vote-intention

Social class is slightly better related to vote intention 'if there were elections now' (for those capable and willing to tell; note the total N = 1221) than to left-right ideology: Tau = .24. It can be seen in Table 7.15., however, that the correlation is 'suppressed' by an irregular pattern on the left-hand side of the party spectrum: the extreme left-wing and the moderate left-wing draw only about 65% of their votes from the lower classes (about 50% from the lower-middle class), whereas the Labor Party (PvdA) draws almost 90% from the lower classes (almost 40% from the working class as against the extreme and moderate left-wing about 15%). The lower class basis of the christian-democrats is even somewhat 'better' than that of the extreme and moderate left-wing (between 70–75%); the liberal VVD draws more than 70% of its vote from the upper classes.

A partial explanation of this phenomenon could be that there are 2 opposed tendencies among the upper classes. Some take the left-wing ideology 'seriously' but then tend to be more extreme (one could also say: consistent) than the Labor Party elite and certainly the lower class labor voters. (We have seen in Chapter 6 that the upper class has more consistent ideological positions both 'within' and 'between' mass ideological dimensions.) This may have been one reason why in 1962 the Pacifistic Socialist Party split off from the PvdA — see Van der Land, 1962. Other upper class groups may not be willing to accept the liberals' rather extreme right-wing ideology, nor feel attracted by the more moderate positions of the christian-democrats (e.g. because they do not belong to a church) but are also not 'socialistic' in an abstract ideological way . . . in the sense that they tend to be 'liberal' in their philosophy of limited government interference in the system of free enterprise. (In Chapter 6 it has been shown that D'66 and PPR voters are even more liberal in this respect than the christian-democrats, although not so liberal as the liberals — see Table 6.6.) These people are faced with a dilemma: they tend (as is also shown in Tables 6.6. and 6.16.) to be philosophically anti-conservative and socialistic, but to reject 'traditional' (they often call it 'dogmatic') socialist means to attain socialist goals: government interference. In addition, they tend to be libertarian and anti-authoritarian, and almost as left-wing as the labor voters.

The solution of this hypothesized dilemma has often been, so it seems, the foundation of new parties (i.e. D'66 and PPR). Until now, these solutions have not been very successful: D'66 almost ceased to exist in 1974, and the PPR has remained small up to the present day. Given their somewhat atypical class basis — and lacking another basis such as religion — this is not really surprising [47].

If we compare the 'class basis' of the various parties in Table 7.15. with their ideological positions in Tables 6.6. and 6.16., it becomes clear that the ideological stands of the voters for the 2 protestant parties, as well as the ideological positions of the M.P.'s of these parties, are much more right-wing and conservative than their class basis would suggest. Since the class basis of the 2 protestant parties is much closer to that of the Labor Party as compared to that of the liberals, and since the ideological position of voters and M.P.'s for these parties is much closer to that of the liberals than that of the Labor Party, the conclusion is inevitable that the 2 protestant parties *draw away much of the lower class vote into the right-wing camp* (this is also the case for the roman catholic party, but to a lesser extent).

Thus, although the parties can be ordered in a meaningful way along the left-right dimension — as has been shown in Table 6.16. — there is no 'consistent' class basis for the vote, due to a moderate or even extreme left-wing tendency in parts of the upper (-middle) classes (see note 47), whereas the Labor Party, which is ideologically in between these positions, lacks such a substantial vote of the upper (-middle) classes. Some 'mechanisms' which might bring this tendency about have been outlined above. In addition, one might postulate a tendency in the lower classes to vote for the traditional, established left-wing party rather than for new, anti-establishment parties like D'66 and PSP, which also lack a working class image or a program which would appeal to the lower classes.

7.6.3. Social class, left-right ideology and vote-intention

Turning now to a direct test of the model that left-right ideology inter-prets the relationship between social class and left-right voting, it can be seen that such an interpretation only appears in those who have a left-wing ideology (there Tau's become .04 and .09, respectively) but that in those with a right-wing ideology there remains an independent social class effect (Tau is .27 in the moderately right-wing and .45 in the extremely right-wing).

At first sight this seems to be an interesting specification: in those who have a left-wing ideology, social class does not affect voting anymore, whereas in those who have a right-wing ideology, the social class effect is maintained or even increased (i.e. for the extremely right-wing). This means that the impact of a right-wing ideology on voting is less than the impact of a left-wing ideology. However, the high correlation in the extreme right-wing is mainly caused by the fact that many lower-middle class people vote christian-democratic rather than liberal (there are very few extreme right-wingers in the other parties) whereas most extreme right-wingers in upper-middle and upper class vote liberal.

In those who are moderately left-wing, the relationship with social class is weakened because of serious curvilinearity: liberal voters and the extremely left-wing and progressive (D'66, PPR) voters tend to belong to the middle classes, others (i.e. labor and christian-democratic voters) to the lower classes. In the extreme left-wing there is also some curvilinear-ity: roman catholic (KVP), progressive and extremely left-wing voters tend to come from the lower-middle class and labor voters from the working class (there are almost no liberal and protestant voters). In con-clusion, the left-wing vote in the right-wing 'ideologues' is limited to christian-democratic votes in the lower-middle class; the lack of a rela-tionship between social class and the vote in left-wing ideologues is caused by the differential class basis of the 'new' moderate and extreme left-wing parties, as compared to labor and even to the christian-demo-crats. Although both the relationship between social class and left-right ideology (see Table 7.3.) and the relationship between left-right ideology and the vote (see Table 6.16.) lack any curvilinearity, the appeal of some new left-wing parties to certain parts of the upper (-middle) classes com-plicates the over-all picture.

In a situation of 'polarization' where (classical) liberals and socialists take rather extreme positions on the left-right ideological spectrum (see Tables 6.6. and 6.16. for the positions of voters along mass dimensions; the positions of M.P.'s along these dimensions are even more extreme — see Middendorp, 1976 b), the moderately left-wing non-religious parts of the upper (-middle) classes find themselves in a difficult situation as far as their vote intention is concerned. Ongoing processes like the dechristianization process (see Table 7.9.), and the processes of 'deconfessionalization', 'depillarization' or 'desegmentation' increase the number of such people 'in need of new parties'. Attempts to create such new parties sometimes involve split-offs from the major parties, such as PPR (split-off from KVP) and DS'70 (split-off from the Labor Party in 1970 — see again Tables 6.6. and 6.16.). The dilemma of many people in the (upper-) middle classes, rejecting individualistic liberalism and 'collectivist' socialism and — being non-religious — the christian-democrats, complicates the relationship between social class and the vote, at least since the mid-sixties.

We will finally investigate whether social class affects the relationship between left-right ideology and the vote. We have seen in Chapter 6 that the upper classes show a much higher level of consistency between ideological mass dimensions, and hence lower levels of false consciousness (see Tables 6.5. and 6.15.). On this basis we may predict that the relationship between left-right ideology and the vote will be stronger in the upper class than in the working class.

This prediction is confirmed. The original relationship (Tau = .42) is maintained in the middle classes, but in the working class it drops to .24 and in the upper classes it is raised to .51. We have found an additional type of false consciousness — *a lack of consistency between ideological position and voting behavior* — which is again most prominent in the working class as compared to the upper class. The relationship between LERI and voting in workers is particularly weakened by (a) the relatively right-wing position of KVP workers, and (b) the relatively left-wing position of D'66 and PPR workers. There is no curvilinearity in the upper class. Here we find some confirmation of the notion that, although the left-wing parties have a 'natural majority', since their ideology is based on the interests of the lower classes, this majority is much less dependable in their voting behavior than the upper class (see e.g. Converse, 1964: 248).

7.6.4. Possible developments in the 1970's

We have seen that in the Netherlands, the christian-democratic parties are the major agents that 'draw away the lower class vote into the right-wing camp'. We have also seen that, as a result of the ongoing processes of dechristianization and deconfessionalization, these parties have suffered serious losses during the past decade. At this stage, a coalition with the liberals does not yield a 'workable' majority in parliament anymore.

We have seen in addition that the establishment of new political parties, somewhere left of the political center, for which there was a need in certain groups that are not attracted to either liberals, labor or christian-democrats, has so far been rather unsuccessful. New parties such as D'66 and DS'70 have almost ceased to exist during the past couple of years; others (PSP, PPR) have remained rather small [48].

The 'politization' process of the past decade has yielded a certain polarization between liberals and labor (under the influence of the New Left movement in the second half of the 1960's and the partial collapse of the christian-democrats). There is some indication that this process has caused the emergence of ideological controversy in the mass public — as we have shown in Chapter 6 — together with an increase in political interest and information — through the mass media — in the general population (see Middendorp, 1975 e). The emergence of ideological controversy probably has a polarizing effect on the ideological positions of various parties, although the pattern at the mass level is more complicated than a simple left-right or progressive-conservative antithesis, which is found in the elite of M.P.'s. *The multidimensional structure of ideological controversy in the general population may confuse many people who do not see their ideological stands clearly reflected in the major political parties.* This could yield a converging tendency towards a unidimensional antithesis in the mass public and consequently, a further polarization between liberals and labor and a further collapse of the christian-democrats. It is such a polarization which could, together with an increasing political interest and political awareness in the lower classes (see Table 7.12.) eventually lead to a more or less stable left-wing majority of the Labor Party, together with other parties of the left and perhaps with some new party 'left of center'.

The opposite development is also possible, however, and perhaps more likely. Since the establishment of the Den Uyl government in 1973, based on the 3 progressive parties and 2 of the 3 christian-democratic parties (ARP and KVP) there has been a tendency towards *depolarization.* Before the elections of 1972, the progressives refused to cooperate in one government with the christian democrats unless these parties made it clear *before* the elections that they preferred a coalition with labor and the other progressives, which the christian-democrats refused to do. The results of the election were such, however, that the only possible government with a majority in parliament had to be based on a coalition between progressives and christian-democrats. So, after the longest cabinet formation in the history of the country, a complicated 'formula' was found to nevertheless form this coalition. The Den Uyl government, then, is one of complicated compromises on many major policy issues.

Moreover, after the many big strikes and general labor unrest of the years 1971–1972, there has been the oil crisis and the increasing awareness of the energy problem in general in 1973, and since then there has been the most serious economic crisis since the 1930's, with a huge unemployment rate and the necessity to set serious limits to government spending in general. The real income of most people will probably not increase during the next few years and many are talking about setting limits to the general level of social welfare that has been realized so far.

It seems that the conditions to realize a left-wing policy have never been so bad since the early 1960's. It is not unlikely that there will emerge '*individualistic*' tendencies in the general population now that the socio-economic position of many is uncertain as far as income and employment are concerned. Perhaps there will even be a stagnation of the dechristianization process and a stability in the attractiveness to the voters of the christian-democratic parties, united in the Christian-Democratic 'Appeal' (CDA). This could mean that in the next elections there could again be a christian-democratic and liberal majority and probably, a corresponding coalition in government.

As long as there is no progressive majority nor a liberal-christian-democratic majority, but only a progressive-christian-democratic one, the political situation in the Netherlands will probably remain rather unstable, given the fact, as we have seen in Chapter 6 (see Tables 6.6. and 6.16.) that the positions of christian-democratic M.P.'s along the progressive-conservative dimensions at both levels of abstraction are much closer to those of the liberal M.P.'s than to those of labor M.P.'s (see also Middendorp, 1976 b). (Here we assume, of course, that the M.P. positions, on the average, adequately reflect the 'party' positions.)

In summary, our analysis of the relationship between social class, left-right ideology and voting behavior has led us to an attempt to sketch some possible developments in Dutch politics in the 1970's. One is towards a *progressive majority*, under the influence of ongoing processes such as the polarization between liberals and labor, the withering away of the christian-democratic 'middle', the increasing 'polarization' and 'salience of politics' at the mass level, increasing the political interest of many people which will lead to a strengthening of left-wing ideology in the lower classes and the convergence of the mass dimensions of ideological controversy to one progressive-conservative dimension in the general population.

The other, perhaps more likely development is one that will lead us back to a liberal-christian-democratic majority under the influence of the depolarizing effects of the present government's compromises in major areas of policy and the depolarization due to the overwhelming economic problems of the mid-1970's, which could even lead to a fading away of the structure of ideological controversy that has been found to exist at the mass level in 1970 and to an increasing individualism and a corresponding appeal of the liberal party. The growth of this party, together with a stagnation in the losses of the christian-democrats, perhaps due to the CDA, could yield this majority [49].

7.6.5. The construction of theory

Type-2 analysis has aimed at the construction of 'theory' or 'theories' as mentioned above, but we have intentionally left aside the matter of what is meant by 'theory'. It seems that, roughly speaking, there are at least 2 notions of 'theory'; (1) a systematic body of *knowledge* about the way a number of variables are interrelated, and (2) a number of interrelated *hypotheses* about the relationships between a number of variables [50]

When we maintained that Type-2 analysis 'aims at the construction of theory', this means that this type of analysis should yield (a) a systematic body of knowledge about the interrelations of variables, which (b) *suggest* a number of hypotheses as to how *other* variables will 'behave' within this domain. (Other variables may be either completely 'new' variables or 'old' variables which are defined and/or conceptualized in another (better) way in a new research design.) The extent to which hypotheses can be formulated — and the extent to which these hypotheses are interrelated so as to constitute a theory — depends on the body of knowledge that has become available and on the theoretical skills and inventiveness of the researcher. However, this is essentially a matter of replication and, perhaps, secondary analysis (see Middendorp, 1976c and 1977a).

Here, an attempt will be made to integrate the 'body of knowledge' that has become available on the basis of the analyses in the present chapter (of course, in relation to the results which were obtained in Chapter 6). One of the major objectives of social research, in particular of political sociology seems to be the identification of the interrelation between '*structural*' and '*cultural*' variables (and/or behavioral variables). Structural variables refer to the individual's social position within the broader social structure, i.e. in relation to the social positions of others. Cultural variables refer to the individual's ideas, opinions, feelings, motivations, etc., as far as they are shared by others who find themselves in similar social positions [51].

The present study focussed on one of the major *'cultural'* variables: the ideological progressive-conservative antithesis, and subsequently an attempt was made to relate this to one of the major *'structural'* variables: social class. Both constructs are in widespread use and belong to the 'folklore' of social scientific terminology. *However, one of our main findings seems to be that these constructs obscure rather than clarify our insight into social reality. Both seem to be inspired by an elitist approach to society, whereby it is assumed that 'things' that always tend to go together in the elite also tend to do so in the general population.*

This has, in particular, become very clear regarding the progressive-conservative antithesis which was exposed as an elitist phenomenon in Chapter 6. At both levels of abstraction on which this 'antithesis' was conceptualized, it fell apart into 3 relatively independent dimensions in the mass population.

In the present chapter we have not only seen that social class — which is basically a Marxist construct — is inversely related to the major dimensions of ideological controversy within the progressive-conservative domain, but that the *positive* relationship between social class and left-right ideology is mainly, if not only, brought about by the *income* component, and that the *negative* relationship between social class and libertarianism-traditionalism is brought about by the *education* component of social class. *Thus, the 2 major social class components suppress each other's relationship to the 2 major ideological dimensions.* However, the *degree* of suppression is unequal: because educational level is much more strongly related to libertarianism than income is related to right-wing ideology, a lack of education more strongly suppresses a left-wing tendency in the lower income groups than a high income 'liberates' the traditionalism in the uneducated (probably through lessening somewhat the anomic tendencies in that group; see above, Table 7.14.). (See Fig. 7.5.)

Fig. 7.5. *The relationships between income and education (as social class components) and left-right ideology and libertarianism-traditionalism as the major ideological dimensions*

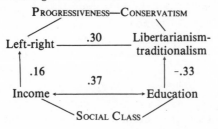

Note: Coefficients are Tau-beta

We cannot maintain that the elitist perspective of the progressive-conservative antithesis was unfruitful in applying it to the mass public: its conceptualization there has yielded well-interpretable dimensions of ideological controversy. We also will not maintain that the construct of social class is in every case unfruitful; the various components are highly related indeed. But we do maintain that relating these constructs 'as such' to each other does not make sense and obscures our insight into the actual mechanisms at work.

In our attempt to find the building stones for (further) theory construction around the relationship between social class and left-right ideology, the weakness of which has struck us, we found the income determinant of LERI and, subsequently, we found a number of variables and conditions that 'repress' this relationship between income and left-right ideology [52]. *Obviously, the 'naked' fact of having a low income is insufficient as a mechanism to bring about a strong tendency towards a left-wing ideology: there are factors at work in the social system which prevent this.* One major factor has been indicated above: those who have a low income also tend to be poorly educated, those who are poorly educated tend to be traditional (in fact, authoritarian in a limited sense, as we have seen above), and those who are traditional tend towards a right-wing ideological stand. Actually, we now know a little more about this mechanism: the traditionalism of the poorly educated is partly interpreted by the anomic tendency in this group, and also by its lack of political information; this leads to personality syndromes such as authoritarianism and dogmatism (F and D scales), which in turn lead to traditionalism.

Another suppressor is the lack of political interest in both the low income group and the poorly educated [53]. It is not yet quite clear why political interest increases a left-wing tendency (or why a lack of interest goes together with a right-wing tendency) but the fact is that this is particularly so in the working class, where only a few people are politically interested.

Given these suppressing mechanisms at work, we have been unable to identify determinants of left-right ideology which, including income, explain more than 20–25% of the variance. In addition, we have identified a number of variables which *specify* the relationship between social class (in fact: income, we may assume) and LERI. *From this point of view, we may place the income effect in a network of conditions that have to be fulfilled in order to strengthen it, to prevent that it becomes weaker, or to prevent that it becomes repressed by independent mechanisms.* We will first discuss the alternative *determinants*: this means that if people in the lower income groups do *not* show the 'values' on these variables that imply a left-wing tendency, then there will be a right-wing tendency; hence, the relationship between income and left-wing ideology will be repressed.

First we have seen 2 '*socialization conditions*' that have to be fulfilled: having been raised in a lower class family and in a family in which at least the father had a left-wing party preference. This means that if the individual has been brought up in some (upper-) middle class family, or in case the party preference of his father was christian-democratic or liberal, his tendency towards a left-wing ideology diminishes, *although* he has a low income. *Second*, there are 2 conditions that seem to be more directly related to the *actual income situation* of the individual, which have nevertheless to be fulfilled to prevent that the income effect on LERI will become weakened: the class one identifies with and the extent to which one is in fact satisfied with one's living conditions. This means that to the extent that low income groups actually *feel* to belong to the (upper-) middle class(es) or to the extent that they feel satisfied with their living conditions, they will tend towards a right-wing ideology, or rather their tendency towards a left-wing ideology will be weakened. *Third*, there are a number of variables *unrelated* to social class (the above 4 variables are all, of course, related to social class) which define some *conditions* which prevent the income effect from becoming very strong: (a) general pessimism regarding future social developments, (b) considering oneself to belong to a certain church, in particular the Calvinist church, but also the Dutch Reformed and Roman Catholic church, in that order, and (c) being a woman [54].

Above, we have defined 7 conditions, 4 of which do *not* tend to appear in low income groups (they do appear, of course, though less so than in other income groups) and 3 of which are independent of income, which *repress* the 'naked' relationship between income and left-right ideology. Some of these variables are also *specifiers* of the relationship between social class and left-right ideology, to which we will turn now.

First, in the country, the antagonism between the various classes along the left-right dimension is diminished, probably under the influence of country traditionalism and the lack of an 'isolated' urban proletariat, implying more intimate relationships between various social class levels. *Second*, we have seen the increasing strength of the relationship between social class and left-right ideology in older people as compared to younger people: it seems to be the general pessimism of older people in the upper classes that brings about right-wing tendencies, whereas older working class people remain rather left-wing. In other words, young upper class people are still relatively optimistic and therefore tend to be relatively left-wing as compared to the older generations in their class.

Third, we have seen that in Calvinists the original relationship between social class and left-right ideology is increased; in the other religious groups it is decreased. *Fourth*, we have seen that generally 'conservative' positions on the abstract dimensions of conservatism, liberalism and socialism (this interprets the specifying effect of political party choice of the father) increase the relationship between social class and left-right ideology due to the fact that the relationship between these abstract philosophical dimensions and left-right ideology is much weaker in the lower classes than in the upper classes.

The abstract dimensions form a separate case: they point to the importance of *philosophical* stands for *ideological* ones; i.e. as soon as one has a 'progressive' philosophy, the effects of social class are diminished, or in other words, *overruled*.

Last but not least, there is the variable of *class consciousness*. To the extent that the low income groups are not *aware* of their social class position, the effect of income is almost completely nullified. This is the complement of the effect of *class identification: one has to be aware of one's class position (and that of the family one has been brought up in) in order for the income effect on left-wing ideology to become substantial.*

In summary, we have outlined above the mechanisms which repress the relationship between income and left-wing ideology: this might be called the *'repression theory'*; we have identified real suppressor variables, specifying variables and alternative determinants of left-wing ideology. (What is lacking in this theory is a *systematic* outline of the determinants of traditionalism which might *indirectly* suppress left-wing tendencies. This has been left a matter for secondary analysis.)

Perhaps we may draw 2 broad conclusions from the results of our analysis so far:

(a) The relationships between, on the one hand, income and left-right ideology, and on the other, education and libertarianism-traditionalism (i.e. its authoritarian components) are not only different in *strength*, they also appear to be different in *kind*. The *income* effect could not be interpreted at all; instead we have found a relatively large number of variables, related or unrelated to income, which appear to have independent effects or specify the effects of income on left-right ideology [55]. On the other hand, the *education* effect could be (partly) interpreted by the anomia, authoritarianism-dogmatism syndrome, and in addition, political information. As indicated above, the present analysis is a little asymmetrical in that no attempt has been made to construct causal models around the libertarianism-traditionalism dimension independent of the social class or educational variables. It is clear in Appendix 7 that there are many (potential) determinants of traditionalism and authoritarianism, some of which are also determinants of right-wing ideology, such as pessimism, sex, religion and political party choice of father. Others are unique to LITR, such as — apart from the ones already involved in the analyses — social desirability, age, church attendance and religious involvement and the perception of a possible communist threat.

Regarding 'social class related variables', however, there seems to be a difference between the income effect on LERI and the education effect on LITR. As we have outlined above, the income effect seems to be embedded in a number of *'subjective'* variables, i.e. variables related to the individual's 'experiences' and to his 'awareness' of his social class position. From the lower class perspective, the individual has to be 'socialized into' a left-wing ideology (i.e. the effects of variables such as political party choice of father and parents' social class), and he has to be *aware* of his social class position and *dissatisfied* with his living conditions; only then does the (suppressed) relationship of 'all these variables' to left-right ideology become substantial. Another 'awareness' variable is the suppressor 'political interest', which has its strongest effect in the working class. *Of course it has often been maintained that the lower classes should become more 'aware' of their social position before they could adopt a consistent left-wing ideology. Here, we have assembled some evidence in favor of that position.*

When we compare this to the education effect on LITR, the difference is clear: there, the *'objective'* effect of education is dominant with additional marginal effects of the 'actual' social class position of the individual, in terms of status positions and mobility instead of how this position is 'experienced'. Rather, the lack of education seems to lead to anomic experiences which are not 'linked' to social class and which evoke mechanisms suppressing the relationship between social class and left-right ideology.

(b) Not only have we seen that 'progressiveness-conservatism' and 'social class' are elitist and Marxist constructs, respectively, which should be used very carefully and which have no 'meaning' — in relation to each other — in the general population, *we have also seen that both in the progressive-conservative domain and in the domain of social class, social research has tended to focus, during the last couple of decades, on phenomena that are marginal or peripheral to these domains.*

We have seen that *authoritarianism*, one of these constructs, constitutes a *subdimension* of the libertarianism-traditionalism dimension and entails those elements from this dimension which are in particular sensitive to educational level. In research, there has been confusion on whether authoritarianism constitutes an *ideologica* dimension — derived, as it originally was, from fascist ideology — or a *personality* syndrome. We have now seen that the original F-scale notions (if we accept these as personality-tendencies) are in fact integrated with the ideological notions based on attitude scale scores, and also that the F-scale notions act as a mechanism interpreting the anomia effect on traditionalism. Thus we have put 'authoritarianism' in an empirical context which shows its essential — but modest — role both within the progressive-conservative domain and in the relationship between one dimension in this domain and the social class component of educational level.

Finally, there are many studies in which it was attempted to assess the effects of *status inconsistency* and *social mobility*, which could 'refine' the gross social class effect, which some researchers even found too Marxist or of which they believed that it would not be related to ideological postures at all (see e.g. Kelly and Chambliss, 1966 and Levinson, 1950). We have found that the construct of social class (when we operationalize it on the basis of components such as income and education) is not always a fruitful one, i.e. when its various components manifest different relationships to other important variables in a research design, as has been the case here (see e.g. Stinchcombe, 1973 a, b), but we have *also* seen that in such cases, constructs such as status inconsistency and social mobility may have only marginal effects. Regarding the relationship between social class and the fundamental dimensions of ideological controversy within the progressive-conservative domain, it has proven more fruitful to assess the *independent* effects of social class *components*.

NOTES ON CHAPTER 7

1. Although many items in the dogmatism and anomia-sets (Appendix 6) are similar to items used in The year-2000 study, statistical evidence of their scalability has not been used, due to (a) the limited sample of The year-2000 study and (b) the atypical response-categories used in that study. The work of Adorno et al. (1950), Rokeach (1960) and Srole (1956) has been studied as well as some Dutch studies in which F, D and A-items were used, e.g. Weima (1963) and Nooy (1969).
2. The field of concepts such as authoritarianism, dogmatism, anomia and e.g. self-evaluation, misanthropy and tolerance towards criminals is not notable for its clear conceptualization: the constructs overlap each other. The statistical analysis in the present study resulted in the disentanglement of some of these overlapping concepts.

3. The total anomia-alienation domain has first been factor-analyzed. The item 'You hardly know who you can trust now-adays' would logically belong to the 'misanthropy' subset: here a difference in 'direction' wording may again have brought the item into another scale (see Appendix 6A, set 3). Note that one reversed item from the dogmatism set is included in the misanthropy scale. For certain aspects of 'anomia', reflected as fully as possible in the selected items, see e.g. Srole (1956) and especially Seeman (1959).

4. The various factorial solutions for the authoritarianism, dogmatism and anomia-alienation domain are available upon request. The total domain is in need of thorough redefinition and reconceptualization (see also note 5). It seems that this 'complete' domain has not even been studied yet. An attempt will be made to do this in a subsequent secondary analysis (see Middendorp, 1977e). Compare e.g. Fruchter (1958), Kerlinger and Rokeach (1966), Roberts and Rokeach (1956), Rhodes (1961), Rose (1966), Roghmann (1966), Rokeach and Fruchter (1956), Struening and Richardson (1965), Warr et al. (1969) and Warshay et al. (1964).

5. In the present study militant dogmatism was used since it was felt that *dogmatism* had connotations that were more typically 'militant' than 'submissive'. But this decision has been 'intuitive', and not based upon model-construction. Dogmatism as a construct appears to have the *'submission to leaders and ideals'* aspect and also the *'aggression, hate, violence'* aspect. That both tendencies are empirically unrelated to other 'dogmatic' aspects, for instance what might be termed 'narrow-mindedness' (set 2, items 1–4), indicates the multidimensionality of the construct.

6. Since F-, D- and A-reversals did not load on the same factor but tended to form a separate one, Kerlinger's (1967) theory of the criteriality of attitudinal referents could possibly be extended to these domains in that there might be e.g. *'authoritarian'* and *'non-authoritarian'* referents, with a 'differential criteriality'. In the layout of the questionnaire, especially in the section on authoritarianism etc., some reversed items have been inserted here and there in order to 'alert' the respondent and to lessen any tendency simply to agree out of fatigue, boredom or irritation (see Chapter 6, note 4).

   On acquiescence, see e.g. Bass (1955, 1956); Block (1965); Chapman and Bock (1958); Chapman and Campbell (1957, 1959); Christie et al. (1958); Cloud and Vaughan (1970); Cough and Keniston (1960); Cronbach (1946, 1950); Elliot (1961); Frederikson and Messick (1959); Gage and Chatterjee (1960); Helmstadter (1957); Jackson and Messick (1957, 1958); Messick and Frederiksen (1958); Messick and Jackson (1957); O'Neill (1967); Peabody (1961, 1964) and Samelson (1964).

7. This relationship is .42, as is shown in Table 6.16a. It will be further examined below.

8. Note that in Dutch only one word is used: 'werknemers', which more or less means: 'not self-employed, and non-professional'. There are of course 'werknemers' with huge salaries and 'werknemers' who are unskilled workers with a minimum income . . . Of course, trade unions generally represent the interests of workers and (lower) employees.

9. The concept of 'status-inconsistency' (or status-incongruency, status-integration, status-crystallization, etc.) has been introduced by Lenski (1954) and since then been widely discussed and studied. Its effects on political attitudes and on voting behavior have been investigated in numerous studies.

Results appear quite confusing, due to the fact that among other things a variety of statuses are combined in various ways into indexes of status-inconsistency. To my knowledge, however, there is no study in which a simple assessment has been made of the effects of one status on levels of one or more other statuses, so that the effects of one or more *types* of status-inconsistency could be investigated, as has been done in the present study. A discussion of the literature will not be made: the reader is referred to e.g. Blalock (1966), Broom and Jones (1970), Eitzen (1970, 1972, 1973), Hyman (1962), Kelly and Chambliss (1966), Kenkel (1956), Lenski (1967, 1969), Rush (1967), Segal (1968, 1969), Segal et al. (1970) and Smith (1969).

10. Of course, since the income brackets are arbitrary it is also arbitrary to consider these cases, especially the 2 middle ones, as consistent. However, these cases represent the best available approach to the consistent positions.

11. Note that the partial correlation between education and left-right ideology is .00 when controlling for income. So there is no independent educational effect (the income effect remains at .23 when controlling for education).

12. Thus, it may tentatively be concluded that students are particularly sensitive to rises in income: at the university level the most extreme left-wing and right-wing positions are found. Hence, social conflicts along the left-right dimension may first become apparent at this level. There is some evidence that this is indeed the case. A partial explanation could be the typical status-inconsistency experienced by students: they fulfil a crucial condition set for acquiring a higher income (i.e. a high educational level), but in most cases their income is still rather low. The opposite effect of status-inconsistency at low educational levels may be due to the fact that these people realize that 'it is the social order which allows me to have a high income, *although* I do not have the "required" educational level'. They tend to be 'self-made men' and accept the social order which allows people to become such. Hence, they will stress right-wing (classical) liberal points of view such as: individual competition, personal initiative, rewards for 'hard work', etc.

13. Objective social class of parents has been used with various cutting points to arrive at 4 levels; see Appendix 6C.

14. The literature will not be reviewed or discussed here. See e.g. Abrahamson (1972), Hazelrigg and Lopreato (1972), Hetzler (1954), Hodge and Treiman (1966), Jackman (1972 a, b, c), Lipset and Bendix (1959), Lopreato (1967), Lopreato and Chafetz (1970, 1972), Lopreato and Hazelrigg (1970), O'Kane (1970), Segal and Knoke (1968), Silberstein and Seeman (1959), Thompson (1971), Wilensky (1966), Wilensky and Edwards (1959). See also Lipset (1963) and Lenski (1954).

15. It has sometimes been suggested that there is a cross-cultural difference here: in America, upward mobility would lead to conservatism; in Europe, it would lead to liberalism — in the American sense — (compared to the class of destination). For a discussion of this, see e.g. Lopreato (1967). This position is later challenged by Thompson (1971).

16. The effect of parents' social class — with cutting-points as in Table 7.6.A — on left-right ideology controlled for social class is even somewhat stronger than the effect of social class controlled for parents' social class (partial correlations are .11 vs. .07). With the alternative cutting-points, the partials remain somewhat higher: .13 and .09, respectively.

17. The effects of extreme mobility cannot be adequately assessed since there are

so few cases that manifest mobility over more than one class-level. For the extreme upwardly mobile, the same pattern appears, however. Some irregular patterns are shown in Table 7.6A and 7.6B. They occur among the upper classes in Table 7.6A, and among the lower classes in Table 7.6B, hence no attempt at explaining these patterns will be made.

18. Social mobility may only have a strong effect on those people who have reached more or less 'final' classes of destination, i.e. people over 35 years of age, for example. For these people, the socialization-effect of parents' social class, controlled for present social class position remains at zero except for the lower-middle class. However, the effect of social class controlled for social class of parents increases from an average Tau of .06 to one of .14. So it may tentatively be concluded that for people over 35 years of age who have reached a more or less final social class position, the effect of this position relative to that of the 'class of departure' increases in strength.

19. Subjective social class and subjective social class of parents are more strongly related to LERI than the corresponding objective measures: Tau's are .23 and .26, respectively. This already indicates a possible effect of 'class-consciousness'. Both variables are again strongly related: .65. 12.8% could not or would not identify themselves with a social class (see Appendix 1 and 6B). This figure increases to over 20% for parents' social class. (For children living with their parents, it was assumed that subjectively, they consider themselves and their parents as belonging to the same class; hence the question of the social class of parents was 'not applicable' to them.) Non-response plus not applicable (41.5%) were left out of the present analysis (see Appendix 6 for exact response categories). Since only 2.4% considered themselves as belonging to the upper class, and 2.4% also considered that their parents belonged in that category, upper and upper-middle class were combined.

20. This phenomenon is well-known; see e.g. Centers (1949), McKenzie and Silver (1968), Nordlinger (1967) and other English studies on 'working class conservatism' (see below and par. 6.7.1. above).

21. These few cases may be students or young people with a grammar school education, living with their upper (-middle) class parents (n=9+22=31); see e.g. Kenniston (1968), who shows that 'young radicals' are often from an upper-middle class background.

22. Here, it is again clear that through elaboration rather than only through partial correlation one may obtain a far more detailed and clarifying picture. Nevertheless, it is also clear from the partials that the effects of social class are mainly brought about through socialization (i.e. social class of parents) and class identification (subjective social class) and that of these 2 variables, class-identification is the stronger factor (see the note on Table 7.7. and below).

23. Correct social class of parents is objective social class as in Table 7.6A. See also the discussion on the various cutting-points in Appendix 6B.

24. Correct social class is objective social class. Of course, the boundaries are somewhat arbitrary; for the rationale of this see Appendix 6B.

25. Variables related in *opposite* ways to 2 (positively related) variables are suppressor or clouding variables, to be identified later. Here, substantially related does not mean statistically significant. Given the size of the sample, even very weak relationships would be significant at levels like .01 or .001. In

the present study, a rough boundary of Tau = .10 is used, which is roughly significant at least at the level of 10^{-5}. (As is well-known, there is no direct relationship between the value of Tau, the size of the sample and the level of significance: the latter depends on the value of the statistic S; see Kendall, 1948.)

26. For the measurement of PPCF see Appendix 6C and Appendix 8C. Parties are categorized from left to right: 0=PSP—CPN; 1=PvdA—PPR—D66; 2=ARP—KVP—CHU; 3=VVD; others are left out. This measurement has been preferred over the measurement as to the perception of left-wing vs. right-wing or progressive vs. conservative ideological positions of parents. For SLC, see Appendix 6D; this variable has been recoded to 4 levels as indicated in Appendix 7.

27. The relationship between RU and LERI also disappears for those reporting PPCF=non-christian-democratic. In other cases the relationship is maintained.

28. In addition, there is an independent occupation effect (excluding housewives and students, however), but the multiple correlation for income and occupation is only .27, which is only slightly better than the single income effect (.25). (Note that this product-moment for the relation between income and left-right ideology is much stronger than the Tau-beta of .16, which has been noted in Table 7.4.)

29. There are other (possible) determinants of left-right ideology which are left out of consideration for the moment, i.e. *validating* variables like self-description as left-wing or right-wing and political preference, and variables that will be dealt with below as 'suppressors of the relationship between social class and left-right': political interest and libertarianism-traditionalism, the other major dimension of ideological controversy. Note that SCP has been included as a determinant in the 'social class realm' although we have seen in Model 1 that its effect on LERI is mainly interpreted by SLC.

30. See the rank-ordering of the parties — or party combinations — in note 26. Of course, people with a liberal VVD 'background' are the most right-wing; there is no curvilinearity.

31. See the text above for the rank-ordering of the religions. From non-religious via roman catholic and Dutch reformed to Calvinist, people become increasingly right-wing; there is no curvilinearity.

32. The analysis is limited here by the fact that 5th-order partial correlations were the highest possible order in the available computer program.

33. Suppressor variables also proved to be specifying in some cases. This will be discussed in the next section. It can be seen from the list below that some LERI *determinants* also prove to specify the relationship between LERI and social class.

34. See Chapter 6 for specification of the relationships between these variables and LERI at various social class levels. See Appendix 4 for their measurement.

35. This variable has been used as a validating one in Chapter 6. The other validating variable, political party preference, will be reintroduced later in a separate analysis.

36. It should be made clear that in this section 'interpretation' and 'explanation' will be used in a sense different to that used in previous sections: how to

'interpret' or explain *specifying* effects. In terms of analysis of variance, specification is an interaction effect.

37. Again, it should be noted that Type–2 analysis does not follow a fixed or logical order. We could even have started with the determination of the suppressing variables, which would not have been illogical since 2 major suppressors had already been identified in the previous chapter. We have chosen, however, for an approach to the initial relationship from the *social class* perspective in order to assess the effects of such well-known constructs as status-inconsistency, social mobility and class consciousness before turning to causal models, specifying and suppressing variables.

38. This relationship is, of course, inflated due to the 2 common subscales in LITR and LERI (see Appendix 5).

39. In addition, we have gathered evidence that religious conservatism (i.e. measured on the basis of the 5 religious subscales; see Chapter 6: 6.5.1.2.) and thus probably also the religious-moralistic factor which was identified when these 5 subscales were added to the attitudinal domain, act as suppressor variables to the relationship between social class and left-right ideology. It is an interesting matter for further research (i.e. in secondary analysis) to assess the suppressing effect of 'religion', religious attitudes and religious ideology in this respect.

40. In Table 6.15. it has been shown that in every social class level the relationship between LERI and LITR increases to about .35.

41. This, by the way, does not interpret the relationship shown in the previous section between age and LERI in the upper classes. This relationship tends to be specified for AUTH: it increases at high levels and decreases at low levels.

42. It is not suggested that political interest in itself might cause left-wing ideological positions, but political interest could increase class consciousness for example, which could interpret the relationship with LERI.

43. As before, the clearest indicators for assessing status-inconsistency seem to be educational level and income. For education vs. occupation (housewives and students excluded), other effects appear: the education-effect becomes weakened and there is no reversal of the occupation-effect on high vs. low levels of education. For occupation vs. income, the occupation-effect is somewhat weakened and the income-effect is again reversed for high vs. low levels of occupation. This is another indication that the (possible) effects of status-inconsistency are not invariant across statuses.

44. The effect of present residence along the urban-rural continuum (URP) is largely explained away by URY: the original Tau = .17 weakens to .01 and .06 for those raised in large cities or towns and only stays at .12 for those brought up in the country. However, the reverse is also true: the original relationship between URY and LITR (.23) is more than maintained for those living in the country, but weakens to .11, .11 and .09, respectively, for increasing levels of urbanization of present residence (URP). Thus, the 2 variables seem to form a 'syndrome': the place where one was raised is only important to one's present libertarianism when *living* in the country. On the other hand, present residence only has an effect when one has been *raised* in the country.

45. That education is the primary component of social class and that a lack of it leads to anomia, dogmatism and authoritarianism is confirmed when this effect is controlled for occupation and income: although it drops signifi-

cantly (12–14 points), the correlations remain at levels around .20. Occupation and income effects either vanish completely or drop to levels around .10. Occupation tends to have a weak independent effect on LITR (the partial correlation becomes —.14 (original = —.34) when controlled for education — housewives and students excluded) and thus most probably on AUTH. A low occupation may also lead to anomia as a result of 'authoritarian' supervisory structures, limited work-schemes etc.

46. It is clear from Appendix 6D that the measurement of POLINF is very superficial; it does not refer to anything like 'insight into the political system', or 'insight in the political process'. Still, its correlations with e.g. educational level and anomia are rather high. So, the superficial measure may still be a good indicator of broader and 'deeper' constructs. Note, for example, the relationship between POLINF and self-evaluation/anxiety (—.13).

47. Three of the 4 parties on the left with a deviant class basis as compared to the Labor Party are new parties which were founded in the 1960's, i.e. the PSP (pacifist socialists), D'66 (democrats) and PPR (radicals). The 4th party, CPN (communists), does not have a deviant class basis (it also draws about 90% of its votes from the working and lower-middle class). This is an old party which broke away from the social-democrats (i.e. the SDAP-Social Democratic Workers Party) as early as 1913. PPR drew away from the roman catholic KVP in 1968 and has, since 1970, taken a more extreme left-wing position on many issues.

48. The rise and fall of these parties will not be discussed here. Only the PPR is a new party which plays a significant role at the moment and shows some stability (see note 47). Another party which has risen during the 1960's and fallen down again during the early 1970's is the Farmers Party (Boeren Partij). Recently there has been established a roman catholic 'orthodox' party (Roman Catholic Party of the Netherlands — Rooms-Katholieke Partij Nederland) with 1 M.P. Such splinter parties, like the 2 protestant orthodox parties SGP and GPV, have been left out of consideration here. (See Appendix 6C for more details.)

49. The present study was replicated in 1975. These data could give us the necessary clues as to the actual direction of the developments during the 1970's (see also Middendorp, 1977 c, e; both forthcoming).

50. Other forms of 'theory' are e.g. in the realm of the definition and conceptualization of constructs; see Chapter 2.

51. These descriptions of 'structural' and 'cultural' should not be taken as definitions.

52. The term 'repress' is introduced as a general term to include some mechanisms that do not weaken a relationship by means of formal suppression.

53. It can be seen in Appendix 8 that political interest is more strongly related to income and education than to social class, probably due to the way the social class index was constructed.

54. We have seen that the sex effect is very weak indeed (see Table 7.10.).

55. We assume that the findings for social class will be similar for income; this could be tested in secondary analysis.

CHAPTER 8

Summary and Epilogue

In this study we have, in the first place, made an attempt to define and conceptualize the progressive-conservative 'antithesis'.

We have noted the confused state of affairs regarding the nature of this antithesis: the meaning of the terms 'progressive' and 'conservative' in relation to such terms as 'radical' and 'liberal' which, in English and American studies, respectively, are used as alternatives for 'progressive'; the relationship of the progressive-conservative antithesis to other antitheses such as left-wing vs. right-wing, or authoritarian vs. egalitarian; the various meanings of the terms in philosophical and ideological debate and the great diversity of the results of empirical research.

We have seen 2 levels of discourse on the progressive-conservative antithesis: the abstract-philosophical level, i.e. in political debate in Western Europe since the French Revolution, and the attitudinal level in most empirical research. The lack of integration of these 2 levels of discourse has been regarded as the major source of the state of confusion regarding the meaning of the antithesis. Thus, in the present study we have made an attempt to *integrate* both approaches.

First, an attempt was made to *define* the progressive-conservative antithesis by means of the construction of an ideal type conceptual model of conservatism as an ideology. This model, i.e. a systematic outline of a body of thought, consisting of a number of interrelated and hierarchically ordered 'ideological statements' — ideas on man and society and their mutual relationship — was constructed by means of an inductive-deductive process.

First, an inventory was made of the many 'historical' and 'empirical' manifestations of conservative thought: outlines on the nature of conservatism, its emergence in Western Europe after the French Revolution, its varieties in various countries and in various stages of its development during the 19th century in its response to other ideologies, such as liberalism and Marxism; second, an attempt was made to construct a model, as briefly indicated above. The model that has been constructed consists of 121 statements, divided into 9 sections.

The model reflects the development in conservative thought from its original opposition (in theory) to Enlightenment thought and (in practice) to classical economic liberalism, to its gradual acceptance of liberal ideas when the system of free enterprise and capitalism had proven irreversible and when the rise of Marxism proved another, and perhaps even more serious, threat to traditional society and in particular the capitalist system of production.

The first 2 sections form the basis of the model, its 'starting point' of ideas on man and society, which are the exact opposites of those of the Enlightenment: the general irrationality and evilness of human nature and the glorification of traditional society. The next 2 sections are on the relation between man and society: the value of traditions and customs for the development of human personality and the necessity of being careful and prudent in implementing, if at all, social change.

The next sections specify, more or less, these general principles with regard to fundamental social institutions and relationships. We begin with the family, which is regarded as the basis of and a general model for society as a whole (i.e. authority relations and property relations) and subsequently there are sections on authority and democracy and on the value of private property and social classes. Authority should be carried out by a small elite on the basis of absolute moral values; hence democracy should be limited. The conservative ideas on private property already provide a link to classical liberal ideas on this subject: it is seen as intimately related to the individual and essential to freedom. Since it is therefore inevitably divided unequally, the existence of various social classes is seen as beneficial to society as a whole.

Finally, the last 2 sections specify the functions of government in general terms and in the socioeconomic realm. Here, the acceptance of classical economic liberal ideas becomes evident: the main general function of government is to keep law and order and to uphold moral values; generally, however, to 'leave society along' as much as possible. This means that government interference in the socioeconomic sphere, if necessary at all or inevitable to prevent worse social developments, should be very moderate indeed.

In order to obtain a link from this abstract model to empirical research at the attitude level, the model has been 'analyzed' in search of *criteria* which could be used in selecting certain attitudes which would indicate progressive-conservative stands in various fields of social research. A major criticism of previous research has been that generally too little attention is paid to such criteria which would define the progressive-conservative domain at the attitude level. (From the perspective of the terms 'progress' and 'regress', the necessity of such criteria has been obvious from the start: how else could one decide whether 'change' is 'progressive' or 'regressive'?)

We have found that the 2 values of *freedom* and *equality* underlie the model of conservative ideology, but also that the distinction between the *economic* and *non-economic* realms should be made in order to come to grips with the question of the relationship between progressiveness and conservatism on the one hand, and both values on the other: a 2 × 2 design was developed showing that conservatism is only in favor of freedom in the economic sense, i.e. the freedom of the individual businessman, but opposed to freedom, in a non-economic sense, i.e. freedom from traditional ways of life. Conservatism is also opposed to equality (i.e. a greater realization of equality) in the economic sense — equality of income, property, status — but is in favor of equality in the non-economic realm since there it is opposed to individual freedom, which implies an adherence of all to 'absolute' moral values and the concomitant traditional behavior. Thus, progressiveness is economically in favor of equality and non-economically in favor of freedom since it tends to regard various behaviors in that field as of equal value.

In Chapter 2 we developed the methodological rationales for the definition of conservative ideology by means of the construction of the ideal type model, which has been described above, and also a scheme for the conceptualization of such a model, i.e. its operationalization and empirical assessment. This has yielded another 2 × 2 design: we developed rationales for an operationalization of the model at an *abstract philosophical level* and at a *specific attitudinal level* and for its empirical assessment in the *general population* and in a *strategic elite*. These methodological considerations have formed the background (or: the perspective) from which we have critically examined previous research in Chapter 3. The fact that a full Type-1 analytical design, as sketched above, has not been realized so far seems to be the major reason for the present state of confusion as to the results of empirical research on progressiveness and conservatism (of course in combination with the fact that an insufficient amount of attention has been paid to the definition of this antithesis at an abstract philosophical level — in the form of an ideal type model — by means of which criteria for the definition of the attitudinal domain could become available.)

The model has been operationalized at the abstract level by means of 37 bipolar items which, of course, only partly cover the theoretical model. At the attitudinal level it has been operationalized by means of about 30 attitude scales in the fields of politics, family life and sexuality and religion. The political field includes both the economic-government interference area and the non-economic one; the religious scales have been included for a special analysis.

In actual practice, the Type–1 analytical scheme has not been followed rigidly. Several extensions and modifications have been made which seemed obvious given the various results of the analysis, to which we will now turn.

In the *abstract* domain we have shown the existence of 3 relatively independent dimensions of ideological controversy in the *general Dutch population* in 1970: *conservatism* (in a narrower sense), *socialism* and (classical economic) *liberalism*. In addition, there has been a small factor on 'human nature' which is independent of the ideological dimensions. Thus, our 'theory' (which has also been outlined in Chapter 2) that the operationalized model of conservative ideology should yield, upon empirical assessment in some meaningful universe, one or more well-interpretable dimensions of ideological controversy, has been confirmed: 29 out of 37 items load highly on one of the 4 dimensions indicated above.

Conservatism includes items on the value of traditions and customs, law and order, scepticism as to the possibility of improving society, a reluctant attitude to bringing about social change and, if social change should be brought about at all, it should be inspired by history and aim at restoration. Finally, there are items on the necessity of authority in the hands of a small elite, hence of the limitation of democracy, and on the harmony that should exist between various social classes.

Socialism includes items on inequality of opportunity being the cause of social differences, the necessity of radical change, the injustice of the existence of social classes which still form the major social antithesis, and the danger that in a system of private enterprise too little attention is paid to public utilities.

Liberalism is only measured by means of 4 items referring to freedom of enterprise and private initiative as opposed to government interference.

These 3 dimensions are of course insufficiently measured; in particular, socialism and liberalism are ideologies which embrace more ideas on man and society. Therefore, in replication an attempt should be made to cover these ideologies, which have split off from the progressive-conservative antithesis in the general population, more fully. The theoretical model of conservatism could be of some help here, but perhaps this model could also be more fully developed in the above sense.

The model of conservatism, and hence the progressive-conservative domain, has been regarded as the 'core' of ideological controversy in Western Europe since the beginnings of the 19th century, and in particular since the mid-19th century. In Chapter 4 it has been shown that Marxism was developed into social-democratic and socialist movements in most Western European countries during the end of the 19th and the beginning of the 20th century. Leninist and Stalinist communism and fascism have both been regarded as belonging outside the 'basic triangle' of ideological debate in Western Europe, but if a replication of the present study were contemplated in countries like France and Italy, the ideologies of communism and (in Italy) fascism could, of course, not be disregarded.

Several rationales have been developed in order to 'explain' why the 3 dimensions of ideological controversy that we found are relatively independent of each other rather than form a unidimensional progressive-conservative antithesis with, in terms of the 3 mass dimensions, liberalism and conservatism being opposed to socialism. Two have been in terms of a generalization of Kerlinger's (1967) theory of the 'criteriality of attitudinal referents' to (a) Western Europe and (b) the criteriality of the values of freedom and equality which underlie the theoretical model of conservatism and which seem to be reflected in the 2 basic dimensions of conservatism and socialism as measured above: conservatism seems consistently opposed to (increasing) either freedom or equality and socialism seems to be in favor of that.

Regarding these 2 dimensions, the distinction between the economic and non-economic realms does not seem to be essential or dominant, but this seems to be relevant in explaining the existence of the third dimension of liberalism, which is in particular related to the field of socio-economic government interference in the system of free enterprise. Thus, in the abstract domain, the 2 values of freedom and equality are reflected in the resulting dimensionality at the mass level, but (a) the distinction between 'economic' and 'non-economic' does not seem to be very clear-cut — though probably relevant, and (b) there seems to be an alternative mechanism — the other generalization of Kerlinger's theory — which may have disturbed a clearer reflection of the values in the dimensions and their differential application to the 2 fields.

However, another interpretation of the 3-dimensional structure within the population at large has been in terms of 'false consciousness': there are many people who have, from the theoretical unidimensional perspective, inconsistent ideological stands, e.g. they tend to be socialistic but also liberal and/or conservative or vice versa. Such types of false consciousness, in particular the inconsistency between liberalism and socialism, are in line with similar findings elsewhere (see Free and Cantril, 1967).

Some may not be surprised that the well-known 'foci' of ideological debate since the 19th century are reflected in the ideological postures of the general population; still, our findings are contradictory to many other studies in which it has been found that in the general population, in contrast to political elites, no meaningful structure of ideological controversy exists. Some of these studies (see e.g. Converse, 1964, Campbell et al., 1960, Nie, 1974) have been critically reexamined. Apart from limitations in the scope and the general designs of these studies, 2 rationales have been developed to 'explain' why around 1960 the American public did not show a structure of ideological controversy whereas in the Netherlands in 1970, even at an abstract philosophical level, such a structure (though weak — 4 factors explain less than 25% of the variance) is clearly there. One of these is in terms of the non-ideological political culture of the U.S. (dominated by classical liberal notions, the 'middle class' and problem-solving oriented; see Hartz, 1955), the other in terms of the 'increasing salience of politics' (Nie, 1974) during the 1960's which has caused the emergence of ideology in the general public — although the structure is multidimensional rather than, as Nie finds, unidimensional. Finally, at this abstract, 'difficult' level, the generally higher educational level in the general population in 1970 might also have played a role.

In order to test these latter 2 rationales (the first one could only be tested by way of a replication of the present study in the United States), Type-1 analysis was extended by assessments of the dimensionality of the domain in the highly educated and in party members (as a measure of political interest). In these groups, and in particular in the highly educated, 3 phenomena have occurred: (a) a tendency towards unidimensionality, thus suggesting the 'reality' of the progressive-conservative antithesis in these groups, (b) more variance is explained, thus suggesting the increasing 'tightness' of the ideological structure, and (c) the emergence of unique dimensions alongside dimensions which are comparable to those in the general population.

Subsequently, we have found that in the poorly educated, the lower classes and the politically apathetic there exists much more false consciousness than in the well educated, the upper classes and the politically involved. In the former groups the mass dimensions become virtually unrelated, whereas in the latter groups they become rather strongly interrelated, in particular the relationship between socialism and liberalism and conservatism.

These results all suggest that in the political elite of M.P.'s (which has been taken as the strategic elite) the structure will be strongly unidimensional — a prediction which has been confirmed. This proves 2 things: (1) the reality of the progressive-conservative antithesis as an *elitist* phenomenon, and (2) the correctness of our interpretation of the multidimensional mass structure from this elitist perspective in terms of false consciousness. The mass is unable to integrate its ideological stands in elitist terms, or unable to integrate its stands along the 2 basic values of freedom and equality in such terms.

After having established this fact, and the validity of the various dimensions, we have gone *down* to the attitude level and *back* to the general population in order to investigate the dimensionality of the attitudinal domain. Here, we found a basic 2-dimensional structure and a third subdimension. One dimension consists of a number of attitude scales which refer to the value of *equality in the socio-economic field*. including government policies to realize such equality of e.g. income and property, by means of e.g. government aid to education, income policy, tax policy, etc. The other dimension entails attitude scales which all seem to refer to the value of *freedom in the non-economic field*, e.g. political freedom of expression, internationalism, various forms of tolerance, moral libertarianism, pre- and extra-marital sexual permissiveness and opposition to family traditionalism, conventionality in male-female roles and authoritarianism in parent-child relationships. The former dimension has been called *left-right*, the latter *libertarianism-traditionalism*. The third subdimension of the libertarianism-traditionalism dimension has been interpreted as *authoritarianism*: it has high (double) loadings for nationalism, authoritarian parent-child relationships, conventional male-female roles, opposition to aid to developing countries and intolerance regarding homosexuals.

From here on we have introduced a variation of the Type–1 analytical scheme. The integration of the abstract dimensions of conservatism, socialism and liberalism with the attitudinal dimensions seemed too obvious; they could (partly) mutually validate each other. Thus, we constructed the *ideological domain* in which, as predicted, socialism loaded high on the left-right dimension, conservatism loaded high on the libertarianism-traditionalism dimension and a short version of the classical F-scale loaded high on the authoritarianism dimension.

We continued Type–1 analysis by assessing this ideological domain in several semi-elites (and their corresponding non-elites) such as the highly vs. poorly educated, the upper class vs. the working class and the politically interested vs. those who are uninterested. In the semi-elites, similar tendencies appeared as was the case in the abstract domain, i.e. a tendency towards unidimensionality and more explained variance. Again, educational level proved to have the strongest effect. However, in the ideological domain, although no *unique* dimensions occurred, the unique phenomenon that all abstract philosophical dimensions load on the left-right dimension rather than on the libertarianism-traditionalism dimension was observed. This dimension is clearly the most ideological in semi-elites! Perhaps even more interesting has been the fact that it is this same left-right dimension which almost completely lacks a philosophical basis in the poorly educated, the working class and the politically apathetic: socialism loads very weakly on left-right in these groups and liberalism not at all. This is a confirmation and extension of our earlier observation that the most false consciousness is in the lower echelons of society, in particular due to the inability of the poorly educated and the lower classes to put their left-wing tendencies in abstract terms (see Mann, 1970).

Again, we assembled evidence that led us to predict that in the elite of M.P.'s there would be a clear unidimensional progressive-conservative dimension; a prediction which was again confirmed. So at both levels of abstraction, the progressive-conservative antithesis is a reality in the political elite only; it is an elitist phenomenon, although its empirical assessment in the general population again yielded meaningful and well-interpretable dimensions.

We have already seen above that these dimensions can now clearly be interpreted in terms of the 'criteriality' of the values of freedom and equality in their differential application to the economic field (including specific government policies to bring about greater equality) and the non-economic field, where the value of freedom seems dominant but where the meaning of 'freedom' and 'equality' is similar or even identical.

It is interesting to note the 'behavior' of the 'Democratic attitudes' scale within the ideological structure: it loads on both the left-right and the libertarianism-traditionalism dimensions, which can be explained by the fact that in 'democracy' the values of freedom and equality seem to be integrated: democracy forms the kernel of the progressive-conservative antithesis (although this antithesis is clearly much broader) and seems to be insensitive to those factors in the social structure which render people 'differentially sensitive' to both values in the 2 realms.

Finally, it may have come as a surprise that the well-known dimension of authoritarianism showed up as a subdimension of the progressive-conservative domain at the mass level. Authoritarianism, as measured by (variations of) the classical F-scale of Adorno et al. (1950) is one of the best known and most frequently used constructs — mostly seen as a personality variable — in social psychology, and it has also been used quite a lot by political scientists. Here we have seen that this personality variable — originally drawn more or less from fascism as an ideology — has an attitudinal basis which is only a subdimension within a broader and more fundamental ideological structure.

By interrelating all abstract and ideological dimensions to each other in elite and mass as well as in semi-elites and their corresponding non-elites, more extensive evidence was obtained on the differential amounts of false consciousness in e.g. the highly educated vs. the poorly educated, the upper class vs. the working class and the politically apathetic vs. the politically involved.

The major form of false consciousness is already prominent in the general population as a whole: the lack of a relationship between the abstract dimension of liberalism and left-right ideology. Many who are opposed to government interference in the freedom of enterprise in abstract, general terms are still in favor of many specific government policies aiming at a greater amount of equality in the socioeconomic sense (compare again Free and Cantril, 1967, who present highly similar phenomena in the U.S.). In the general population there is a general tendency towards liberalism (opposition to government interference in general terms) as well as to a left-wing ideology (in favor of government policies aiming at equality). We have seen that this particular inconsistency characterizes the poorly educated, the working class and the politically apathetic and almost vanishes in the highly educated, the upper class and the politically aware. The same is true, although to a somewhat lesser extent, for other forms of false consciousness among ideological dimensions or between ideological and philosophical dimensions, e.g. the relationship between left-right ideology and authoritarianism and the relationships of these 2 dimensions and all philosophical ones. The relationship between conservativism and libertarianism-traditionalism remains relatively high in the non-elites, and the relationship between libertarianism-traditionalism and left-right ideology seems rather insensitive to differences in educational level, social class or political interest.

In retrospect, we might perhaps interpret the major form of false consciousness in the general population as follows: most people tend to be in favor of free enterprise because there is a reference to the value of freedom, which is very popular. At the same time, there might be a general fear of 'bureaucracy' or 'state interference' in the private lives of citizens. However, most Western European societies are so-called 'mixed' ones, wherein 'pure' capitalism is moderated by various forms of government regulations and, of course, laws, but such interference is not seen by many as government interference in the system of free enterprise. On the other hand, many specific government policies are also not seen as interfering in this system; according to many, such policies can and perhaps should be realized *within* the framework of a system of production based on freedom of enterprise.

After having assembled evidence on the validity of the ideological dimensions in a way which is similar to the one followed in the case of the abstract dimensions, a final question had to be asked as to the ideological nature of the dimensions and, consequently, their relationship to social class.

In Chapter 4 we briefly discussed the concept of ideology. Subsequently, the outline of the historical background of the development of the major ideologies in Western Europe during the 19th century was in terms of this definition of ideology. One of the elements of this definition is that an ideology reflects the social position of certain groups, in particular the interests of a certain social class. Thus, in the final stages of Type–1 analysis, an investigation was made of the extent to which the philosophical and ideological mass dimensions are in fact related to social class. Here we have found that the philosophical dimensions of conservatism, socialism and liberalism are hardly at all related to social class; these dimensions are not ideological in that sense. However, the so-called ideological dimensions of left-right, libertarianism-traditionalism and authoritarianism are indeed related to social class and in that sense, they are truly 'ideological' but rather weakly. This has especially intrigued us in the case of the left-right dimension. Although this dimension is certainly not one of primitive self-interest (it includes the philosophy of socialism, attitudes regarding both goals and means, the democratic attitudes scales, etc.). it seems obviously related to the economic interests of the various social classes. That its relationship to social class is still so weak has been one of the reasons to take this relationship as the central one in the subsequent analysis.

First, however, we have been intrigued by the *negative* relationship between social class and traditionalism, and in particular authoritarianism, as compared to the positive relationship to left-right ideology. An investigation by means of component analysis (Rosenberg, 1968) was made of the well-known phenomenon of 'working class traditionalism', in particular working class authoritarianism. In this preliminary analysis we have seen that this phenomenon mainly amounts to a negative relationship between educational level and matters related to family life and sexuality and nationalism, i.e. the attitude scales on authoritarian parent-child relationship and nationalism, conventional male-female roles, tolerance regarding homosexuals, aid to developing countries, and family traditionalism. In addition, there is a negative relationship to the short F-scale. This has been interpreted in terms of *anomic* tendencies in the poorly educated which would lead to a tendency to create 'psychological security' in realms which are of immediate relevance to the individual's life. This theory has (partly) been confirmed, and elaborated upon later (see below).

Once we have carried out Type-1 analysis and obtained one or more dimensions (i.e. of fundamental ideological controversy within the progressive-conservative domain), one would like to place these dimensions, or at least one of them, in an empirical context.

One procedure to do this was developed in Chapter 2 and called Type-2 analysis: it starts with the selection of an 'initial relationship' and then proceeds by means of a clarification of that relation through component analysis, 'within-analysis' (i.e. an analysis around variables similar to the independent variable in the original relationship), 'between-analysis' (i.e. the construction of causal models), and the identification of specifying variables and of variables suppressing the original relationship.

As already indicated above, the *relationship between social class and left-right ideology* has been taken as the initial relationship in Type-2 analysis in the present study. The weakness of this relationship has sometimes been put forward as a prerequisite of parliamentary democracy (e.g. Lipset, 1963), but one wonders how such weakness can come about, given the more or less obvious economic interests that are at stake.

By means of *component analysis*, 2 things have been shown: (1) *income* is the social class component with the major independent effect on left-right ideology, in particular on those components of that dimension which have the clearest and most direct relationship to economic interests, i.e. an egalitarian effect on the income distribution, and (2) *education* has no independent effect and the construct of *status inconsistency* is not very meaningful in this context.

By means of *within-analysis* we have also shown a number of things: (a) The socialization variable '*parents' social class*' has an independent effect on left-right ideology which is even somewhat stronger than the social class effect, (b) *class identification* also has an independent effect which is stronger than that of social class, (c) the social class effect is in fact explained away and interpreted by the other 2 variables mentioned above, but income remains to have an independent effect, and (d) *class consciousness* is an important specifying variable of the relationship between social class and left-right ideology: at the highest level of class consciousness, this relationship is almost doubled in strength, whereas at the lowest level, it disappears completely.

The construction of *causal models* by means of between-analysis has not been very successful. These procedures have only resulted in the identification of a number of additional *determinants* of left-right ideology, such as satisfaction with living conditions, political party choice of father, religion, sex and general optimism-pessimism. However, the 3 social class factors mentioned above explain only 10% of the variance, the other variables about 20% of the variance, but together these factors still explain less than 25% of the variance of left-right ideology. Obviously, there are factors that determine left-right ideology which are not included in the present design: their nature is as yet unknown. On the other hand, many determinants are measured in a very limited way in the present design. It is a matter of replication to make an attempt to define and conceptualize these variables more satisfactorily.

In an attempt to *specify* the relationship between social class and left-right ideology, some conditions in addition to class consciousness have been found in which this relationship is indeed increased, e.g. having been brought up and/or living in a big city, being a Calvinist, and being older and generally pessimistic (the latter variable interprets the age effect). Here the abstract philosophical dimensions of conservatism, socialism and liberalism again play a prominent role: due to their weak relationships to social class, we find many relatively left-wing working class people in the anti-socialistic, conservative and liberal groups; hence, in these groups the relationship between social class and left-right is somewhat strengthened. In addition, socialism interprets the specifying effect of political party choice of father. An intriguing finding in this context has been that no determinants at all could be found in the present design of the major specifying variable of *class consciousness*; it seems to be a major task of future research (in replication) to make an attempt (a) to define and conceptualize 'higher order' measures of class consciousness and (b) to identify determinants of this concept (see below).

Finally, some interesting results have been obtained in our search for variables that *suppress* the relationship between social class and left-right ideology. *The major suppressor variable is the other major dimensions of ideological controversy in the mass public: the libertarianism-traditionalism dimension.* (Another suppressor, political interest, has an interesting specifying effect as well: in the working class, political interest has a rather strong positive effect on left-wing ideology, whereas in the upper class, there is no effect at all: once workers become politically interested, they also tend to become left-wing. Since political interest has not been measured very satisfactorily in the present study, this points to the importance of developing concepts that assess the individual's 'perception of the political process' in addition to his perception of and awareness of his own social position — i.e. his class consciousness.)

That libertarianism-traditionalism has been found to be the major suppressor of the relationship between left-right ideology and social class, while it is the other major dimension of ideological controversy as well, has been sufficient reason to extend Type–2 analysis and to make an attempt to clarify and interpret the relationship between social class and libertarianism-traditionalism. This analysis is in line with our previous component analysis on this relationship in order to clarify the phenomenon of working class traditionalism. This phenomenon mainly consists of a negative relationship between educational level and certain authoritarianism-components. In further component analysis we have found that income does not have an independent effect on libertarianism-traditionalism. What we immediately see then is that the relationship between the 2 social class components of income and educational level and the 2 major ideological dimensions is quite different: income is *positively* related to right-wing ideology and not at all to libertarianism-traditionalism, while education is *negatively* related to traditionalism and not at all to left-right ideology. Because the class components and the ideological dimensions are positively related to each other, each class component suppresses the relationship of the other component to one of the major dimensions of ideological controversy. Neither social class nor the progressive-conservative antithesis seem fruitful constructs to be related to each other.

Other differences between the 2 ideological dimensions and their relationship to 'social class' variables are shown in the within-analysis on the relationship between social class and libertarianism-traditionalism: neither social class of parents nor class identification have an independent effect. Instead, there is a marginal effect of social mobility, as there has been a marginal effect of status-inconsistency; it is the *objective* education effect which seems to determine libertarianism whereas *subjective* factors have proven so important in determining left-right ideology. These factors, e.g. subjective social class, political party choice of father, class-consciousness, pessimism, satisfaction with living conditions, religion, all tend to 'repress' the pure, 'objective' income-effect.

Finally, whereas the income effect on left-right ideology could not be interpreted at all, we have found a number of factors which (partly) interpret the education effect on traditionalism (i.e. the authoritarianism components of that dimension). In line with our previously developed rationale, the major mechanism has been the *anomia* of the poorly educated. But in addition we have seen that the anomia effect is almost

completely interpreted by the 2 personality syndromes of authoritarianism (short F-scale) and dogmatism (short D-scale). Thus, there is some
evidence indeed that a poor education sets severe limits to people's ability
to orientate themselves in a complex society. Probably in search of
'psychological security', such people tend to develop authoritarian and
dogmatic personality tendencies which then act as vehicles towards the
acceptance of the traditions (implying authoritarian attitudes) offered by
the social system, or rather: the culture. In this way, a poor education
prevents the relationship between income and left-right ideology from
becoming 'too' strong: left-wing policies and ideals generally aim at the
elimination of traditions and customs that set limits to individual
freedom although basically they aim at a greater equality in an economic
sense. In addition to anomia, a lack of political information also contributes to interpret the relationship between educational level and libertarianism-traditionalism. This all points to the importance of developing, in replication, better defined and conceptualized constructs on the
individual's 'awareness of the social process' (in addition to his awareness of the political process, which has been mentioned above) and his
own social position. In the first place, so it seems, the anomia-authoritarianism-dogmatism syndrome needs further clarification by means of
better definitions and conceptualizations (see Middendorp, 1977d), and
the measurement of political information should also be improved.

In conclusion, we have not only seen that such mechanisms as outlined
above, and in addition the lack of political interest in the lower classes,
suppress the relationship between income and left-right ideology, we
have also seen that the fact that there are so many other determinants of
left-right ideology, often of a 'subjective' nature (i.e. based on the individual's experiences and perceptions of social reality), tends to *repress* this
relationship: all this has tentatively been called the 'repression theory'.

In addition, however, there seems to be a repressing mechanism
inherent in the very structure of ideological controversy in the electorate,
as against the unidimensional antithesis in the political elite. This means
that ideological debate at the elite level (from which level it 'comes down'
to the electorate through the mass media) is '*alienated*' from the actual
controversies which exist at the mass level. This seems to repress the
democratic process (see Middendorp, 1976b). Again this repression is
strongest in the lower classes, in particular the working class; the relationship between left-right ideology and voting is much weaker there as
compared to the upper class.

In general, the relationship between social class, left-right ideology
and voting has proven more complicated than expected. Left-right
ideology does not simply interpret the (weak) relationship between social

class and the vote: some upper (-middle) class people vote moderately or even extremely left-wing whereas some lower (-middle) class people vote christian-democratic. Given their relatively right-wing stands, the christian-democrats, and in particular the 2 protestant parties, draw away part of the lower class vote into the right-wing camp.

On the other hand, some new, relatively left-wing parties such as D'66 and the PPR (democrats and radicals) tend to draw away part of the upper (-middle) class vote into the left-wing camp. (However, these parties tend not to accept the 'traditional' left-wing policy of government interference in the system of free enterprise, i.e. are liberal in this sense, as compared to the 'traditional' left-wing Labor Party).

In a situation in which the Labor Party and the liberals occupy 'polarized' positions along the left-right dimension, we have noted the voting dilemma for the moderate but non-religious middle classes; this could be an impulse for a new party to emerge 'left-of-center' now that the PPR has become more radical and the democrats have almost ceased to exist. Some possible developments in voting behavior in the light of the present economic crisis and the policies of the Den Uyl government have been sketched.

It is of course a matter of replication to assess such developments as well as developments in the structure of ideological controversy in the general population, as compared to the structure among the political elite of M.P.'s. In addition, not only the actual structure could be reassessed from time to time to keep track of developments, the positions of various groups on these dimensions could also change, as well as the relationship between the positions of voters vs. those of M.P.'s (see Middendorp, 1975e and 1976b).

In fact, the present study was replicated in 1975 in order to assess cultural change over the last decade (see Middendorp, 1977 c, e). In this study an attempt was also made to improve the measurements of some variables that have proven to be 'important' in the original design, e.g. class consciousness, political interest and information, anomia and alienation, awareness of the political process, political socialization, etc. (see above). In addition, variables have been included which could further validate the various abstract and ideological dimensions, e.g. self-identification as liberal, conservative, socialist, etc., and the adherence of respondents to the basic values of freedom and equality [1].

In another study, which might be called an 'indirect replication' an attempt was made to assess the structure of the criterial referents of attitudes in the Netherlands. In this study, carried out together with Prof. Fred Kerlinger, the latter's theory, implying that people are differentially sensitive to ideas reflecting the dominant ideological 'foci' of a political culture, was tested. Many attitudinal referents included in the design have been inspired by the abstract dimensions and the attitude-scales which were used in the present study. The results do not unequivocally confirm the theory: Dutch political culture, as assessed in the general population by means of attitudinal referents, seemed to be even more complex than it was proven to be in the present study [2].

NOTES ON CHAPTER 8

1. This study was carried out together with the Sociaal en Cultureel Planbureau (Social and Cultural Planning Office) of the Ministerie van Cultuur, Recreatie en Maatschappelijk Werk (Ministry of Culture, Recreation and Social Work). It is based on a representative sample from the Dutch population aged 16–74 (N = 1977). Fieldwork was carried out by the Netherlands Institute for Public Opinion and Marketing Research (NIPO BV), Amsterdam under the direction of Drs. Ger Schild. The questionnaire was designed in cooperation with Dr. Aat Nauta and Dr. Jos Becker of the Social and Cultural Planning Office.

   Replication of the present study implies that all basic variables are again included in the new design.
2. I would like to thank NIPO BV, and in particular Mr. Jan Stapel and Drs. Ger Schild, for having made this study possible. It is also based on a representative sample from the Dutch population aged 18 and older (N = 815).

Bibliography

ABRAHAMSON, P.
 1972 'Intergenerational Social Mobility and Partisan Choice'. *Am. Pol. Science Rev.*, 66: 1291-1295.
ADORNO, T. W., E. FRENKEL-BRUNSWIK, D. J. LEVINSON, R. N. SANFORD
 1950 *The Authoritarian Personality*. New York, Harper and Row
ALLPORT, G.
 1929 'The Composition of Political Attitudes'. *Am. J. of Sociology*, 35: 220-238
ANDERSON, B., M. ZELDITCH, P. TAKAGI, D. WHITESIDE
 1965 *On Conservative Attitudes; Acta Sociologica*, 8, 3: 189-204
APTER, D.
 1964 *Ideology and Discontent*; New York, The Free Press
AXELROD, R.
 1967 'The Structure of Public Opinion on Policy Issues'; *Publ. Opin. Quart.*, 31 (Spring): 51-60
BACHRACH, P.
 1962 'Elite Consensus and Democracy'; *J. of Politics*, 24 (August): 449-452
 1967 *The Theory of Democratic Elitism*; Boston, Little Brown
BAN, A. W. VAN DEN
 1963 *Boer en landbouwvoorlichting; de kommunikatie van nieuwe landbouwmethoden*; Assen, Van Gorcum en Co.
BARKER, E. N.
 1963 'Authoritarianism of the Political Right, Center and Left'; *J. of Soc. Issues*, 19: 63-74
BARNES, S. H.
 1966 'Ideology and the Organization of Conflict, On the Relationship between Political Thought and Behavior'; *J. of Politics*, 28: 513-530
BARTH, H.
 1945 *Warheit und Ideologie*, Zürich, Manesse Verlag
 1958 *Der konservative Gedanke*, Stuttgart, K. F. Koehler Verlag

BASS, B. M.
 1955 'Authoritarianism or Acquiescence'; *J. of Abnormal and Soc. Psychology*, 51: 616-623
 1956 'Development and Evaluation of a Scale for Measuring Social Acquiescence'; *J. of Abnormal and Soc. Psychology*, 53: 296-299
BAXA, J.
 1924 *Gesellschaft und Staat im Spiegel deutscher Romantik*; Jena, Gustav Fisher
 1931 *Einführung in die romantische Staatswissenschaft*; Jena, Gustav Fisher
BECKER, H.
 1940 'Constructive Typology in the Social Sciences'; *Am. Soc. Rev.*, 5 (Feb): 40-55
BELL, D.
 1960 *The End of Ideology; On the Exhaustion of Political Ideas in the Fifties*; New York, Free Press
BELL, D. (ed.)
 (1955), 1964, *The Radical Right*; New York, Doubleday Anchor Book
BENDIX, R.
 1964 'The Age of Ideology; Persistent and Changing'. In: D. Apter, *Ideology and Discontent*; Glencoe, The Free Press: 294-318
BERG, G. VAN BENTHEM VAN DEN
 1969 *De ideologie van het Westen*; Amsterdam, Van Gennep
BENVENUTI, B.
 1961 *Farming in cultural change*; Assen, Van Gorcum en Co
BERGSMA, R.
 1963 *Op weg naar een nieuw cultuurpatroon*; Assen, Van Gorcum en Co
BERKOWITZ, N. H., G. H. WOLKON
 1964 'A Forced Choice Form of the F-Scale-Free of Acquiescent Response Set'; *Sociometry*, 27: 54-65
BERNSTEIN, B.
 1961 'Social Class and Linguistic Development: A Theory of Social Learning'. In: A. H. Halsley et al. (eds.), *Education, Economy and Society*; Glencoe, The Free Press, 288-314
BERTING, J.
 1968 *In het brede, maatschappelijke midden*; Meppel, Boom en Zn.
BERTRAND, T., L. DE BRUIJN, A. HOOGERWERF, T. NOLDUS, P. SUIJKERBUIJK
 1974 'Political Opinion and Class Identification in the Netherlands'; *Sociologia Neerlandica*, 2, 121-143
BEZEMBINDER, Th. G. G.
 1970 *Van rangorde naar continuum; Een verhandeling over data-structuren in de psychologie*; Deventer, Van Loghum Slaterus
BITTNER, E.
 1963 'Radicalism and the Organization of Radical Movements'; *Am. Soc. Rev.*: 928-940
BLALOCK, H. M.
 1960 *Social Statistics*; New York, McGraw Hill
 1961 'Correlation and Causality; The Multi-variate Case'; *Soc. Forces*, 39: 246-251
 1962 'Four-Variable Causal Models and Partial Correlation'; *Am. J. of Soc.*, 68: 182-194

1962 'Further Observations on Asymmetric Causal Models'; *Am Soc. Rev.*, 27: 542-544

1964 *Causal Inferences in Non-experimental Research*; Chapel Hill, Univ. of North Carolina Press

1965 'Some Implications of Random Measurement Error for Causal Inferences'; *Am. J. of Soc.*, 71: 37-47

1966 'The Identification Problem and Theory Building; The Case of Status Inconsistency'; *Am. Soc. Rev.*, 31: 52-61

1969 'Theory Construction; From Verbal to Mathematical Formulation'; Englewood Cliffs, N.J., Prentice Hall

BLALOCK, H. M., A. BLALOCK

1968 *Methodology in Social Research*; New York, McGraw Hill

BLOCK, J.

1965 *The Challenge of Response Sets*; New York, Appleton Century Crofts

BLUHM, W. T.

1974 *Ideology and Attitudes; Modern Political Culture*; Englewood Cliffs, N.J., Prentice Hall

BOLDT, W. J., STROUD, J. B.

1934 'Changes in the Attitudes of College Students'; *J. of Educ. Psychology*, 25: 611-619

BONE, R. C.

1962 'The Dynamics of Dutch Politics'; *J. of Politics*, 24, 1: 23-49

BONJEAN, C. M., R. J. HILL, S. D. MCLEMORE

1967 *Sociological Measurement*; San Francisco

BORGATTA, E. F., G. W. BOHRNSTEDT (eds.)

1969 *Sociological Methodology*; San Francisco

BOUDON, R.

1965 'A Method of Linear Causal Analysis; Dependence Analysis'; *Am. Soc. Rev.*, 30: 365-374

BOWLES, R. T.

1965 'The Organization of Individual Political Ideologies'; Proceedings of the South-Western Sociological Association; Dallas: 158-163

BOWLES, R. T., J. T. RICHARDSON

1969 'Sources of Consistency in Political Opinion'; *Am. J. of Soc.*, 74, 6: 676-684

BREMNER, R. H.

1953 'The Political Techniques of the Progressives'; *Am J. of Econ. Soc.*, 12: 189-200

BRINKMAN, W., A. L. KOSTER-SWEERS

1972 'Traditionalisme en sexualiteit'; *Mens en Maatschappij*, 47, 1: 141-166

BROOM, L., F. L. JONES

1970 'Status-Consistency and Political Preference; The Australian Case'; *Am. Soc. Rev.*, 35, 6: 989-1002

BROWN, R.

1965 *Social Psychology*; New York, The Free Press

1968 *Words and Things*; Glencoe, The Free Press

BROWN, S. G.

1955 'Democracy, the New Conservatism and the Liberal Tradition in America'; *Ethics*, 66: 1-9

BROWN, S. R.
1970 'Consistency and the Persistence of Ideology; Some Experimental Results'; *Publ. Opinion Quart.*, 34: 60-68
BURKE, E.
1790 'Reflections on the Revolution in France'; *Works II; 1854-1857*
BUTLER, G. G.
(1914), 1957 *The Tory Tradition*; London, Conservative Political Centre
CAMPBELL, A., Ph.E. CONVERSE, W. MILLER, D. STOKES
1960 *The American Voter*; New York, John Wiley & Sons
CARLSON, H. B.
1934 'Attitudes of Undergraduate Students; *J. of Soc. Psychology*, 5: 202-213
CASE, C. H.
1952 'Guttman Scaling applied to Centers' Conservatism-Radicalism Battery'; *Am. J. of Soc.*, 58: 556-563
CAUTE, D.
1966 *De linkse traditie in Europa*; Amsterdam, Meulenhoff
CENTERS, R.
1949 *The Psychology of Social Classes*; Princeton, Princeton University Press
CHAMBERLIN, W. H.
1963 'Conservatism in Evolution; *Modern Age*, 7: 249-254
CHAPMAN, Ph.C.
1960 'The New Conservatism: Cultural Criticism v. Political Philosophy'; *Pol. Sci. Quart.*, 75, 1: 17-34
CHAPMAN, L. J., R. D. BOCK
1958 'Components of Variance due to Acquiescence and Content in the F-Scale Measure of Authoritarianism'; *Psychol. Bull.*, 55: 328-333
CHAPMAN, L. J., D. T. CAMPBELL
1957 'Response Set in the F-Scale; *J. of Abnormal and Soc. Psychology*, 54:
1959 'The Effect of Acquiescence Response Set upon Relationships among the F-Scale, the E-Scale and Intelligence'; *Sociometry*, 22: 153-161
CHRISTIE, R.
1954 'Authoritarianism Re-examined', In: Christie, R., M. Jahoda, *Studies in the Scope and Method of 'The Authoritarian Personality'*; Glencoe, The Free Press: 123-196
1955 'Review of The Psychology of Politics' by H. J. Eysenck; *Am. J. of Psychology*, 68: 702-704
1956a 'Eysenck's Treatment of the Personality of Communists'; *Psychol. Bull.*, 53: 411-430
1956b 'Some Abuses of Psychology'; *Psychol. Bull.*, 53, 6: 439-451
CHRISTIE, R., JAHODA, M.
1954 *Studies in the Scope and Method of 'The Authoritarian Personality'*; Glencoe, The Free Press
CHRISTIE, R., J. HAVEL, B. SEIDENBERG
1958 'Is the F-Scale Irreversible?'; *J. of Abnormal and Soc. Psychology*, 56: 143-159
CLOUD, J., G. M. VAUGHAN
1970 'Using Balanced Scales to Control Acquiescence'; *Sociometry*, 33: 193-202

COBB, R. W.
1973 'The Belief Systems Perspective: An Assessment of a Framework'; *J. of Politics*, 35: 121-153

CAREY, A. L., J. A. NEWMEYER,
1965 'Measurement of Radicalism and Conservatism'; *J. of Soc. Psychology*, 67: 357-369

CONSTANDSE, A. K.
1964 *Boer en toekomstbeeld; Enkele beschouwingen naar aanleiding van een terreinverkenning in de Noord-Oost Polder*; Wageningen

CONVERSE, Ph.E.
1958 'The Shifting Role of Class in Political Attitudes and Behavior'. In: Maccoby, E. E., T. M. Newcomb, E. L. Hartly (eds.), *Readings in Social Psychology*; New York, Holt, Rinehart and Winston: 388-400
1964 'The Nature of Belief Systems in Mass Publics'. In: D. Apter (ed.), *Ideology and Discontent*; New York, The Free Press

COOMBS, C. H.
1964 *A Theory of Data*; New York, John Wiley & Sons

COUGH, A., K. KENISTON
1960 'Yeahsayers and Naysayers, Agreeing Response Set as a Personality Variable'; *J. of Abnormal and Soc. Psychology*, 60: 151-174

COUWENBERG, S. W.
1959 *De strijd tussen progressiviteit en conservatisme*; Den Haag, N.V. Uitgeversmaatschappij Pax

CRONBACH, J.
1946 'Response Set and Test Validity'; *Educ. and Psychol. Measurement*, 6: 474-494
1950 'Further Evidence on Response Set and Test Design'; *Educ. and Psychol. Measurement*, 10: 3-31

CROWNE, D. P., D. MARLOWE
1964 *The Approval Motive*; New York, John Wiley & Sons

DAALDER, H., J. G. RUSK
1972 'Perceptions of Party in the Dutch Parliament', In: S. C. Patterson and G. C. Wahlke, *Comparative Legislative Behavior; Frontiers of Research*; New York, John Wiley & Sons: 143-198

DAALDER, H.
1974 *Politisering en lijdelijkheid in de Nederlandse politiek*; Assen, Van Gorcum en Co

DIRENZO, G. J.
1966 'Concepts, Theory and Explanation in the Behavioral Sciences'; Proceedings of a Symposium held at Fairfield University, April 1964; New York

DUBOIS COOK, S.
1973 'The New Conservatism Versus American Traditions, Ideals; Institutions and Responsibilities'; *Am. Beh. Scientist*, 17, 2: 205-222

DUMONT, R. G., W. J. WILSON
1967 'Aspects of Concept Formation, Explication, and Theory Construction in Sociology'; *Am. Soc. Rev.*, 32: 985-995
1970 'Aspects of Concept Formation, Explication and Theory Construction in Sociology'. In: D. P. Forcese and S. Richer, *Stages in Social Re-*

search; Contemporary Perspectives; Englewood Cliffs, N.J., Prentice Hall: 40-53

EDWARDS, A. L.
1941 'Unlabled Fascist Attitudes'; *J. of Abnormal and Soc. Psychology*, 36: 575-582
1944 'The Signs of Incipient Fascism'; *J. of Abnormal and Soc. Psychology*, 39: 301-316

EITZEN, D. S.
1970 'Status Inconsistency and Wallace Supporters in a Midwestern City'; *Soc. Forces*, 48, 4: 493-499
1972 'Status Inconsistency and the Cross-Pressures Hypothesis'; *Midwest J. of Pol. Science*, 2: 287-296
1973 'Status Consistency and Consistency of Political Beliefs'; *Publ. Opinion Quart.*, 37 (Winter): 541-549

ELLEMERS, J. E., G. J. A. RIESTHUIS, J. H. J. VERMEULEN
1974 'Selected Bibliography of Social Science Publications on Netherland's Society Published in Foreign Languages'; *Sociologia Neerlandica*: 99-113

ELLIOT, L. L.
1961 'Effects of Item-Construction and Respondent Aptitude on Response Acquiescence'; *Educ. and Psychol. Measurement*, 21: 405-415

EPSTEIN, L. D.
1954 'Politics of British Conservatism'; *Am. Pol. Science Rev.*, 48, 1: 27-48

EYSENCK, H. J.
1944 'General Social Attitudes'; *J. of Soc. Psychology*, 19: 207-227
1947 'Primary Social Attitudes, I: The Organization and Measurement of Social Attitudes'; *Intern. J. of Opinion and Attitude Research*, 1: 49-84
1951 'Primary Social Attitudes as Related to Social Class and Political Party'; *British J. Of Soc.*, 2: 198-209
1954 *The Psychology of Politics*; London, Routledge
1956a 'The Psychology of Politics: A Reply'; *Psychol. Bull.*, 53, 2: 177-182
1956b 'The Psychology of Politics and the Personality Similarities between Fascists and Communists'; *Psychol. Bull.*, 53, 6: 431-438
1971 'Social Attitudes and Social Class'; *British J. of Soc. and Clinical Psychology*, 10: 201-212

EYSENCK, H. J., T. T. COULTER
1972 'The Personality and Attitudes of Working Class British Communists and Fascists'; *J. of Soc. Psychology*, 87: 59-73

FEILING, K.
1953 'Principles of Conservatism'; *Pol. Quart.*, 24, 2: 129-138

FERDINAND, T. N.
1964 'Psychological Femininity and Political Liberalism'; *Sociometry*, 27: 75-87

FERGUSON, L. W.
1939 'Primary Social Attitudes'; *J. of Psychology*, 8: 217-223
1940 'The Measurement of Primary Social Attitudes; *J. of Psychology*, 10: 199-205
1942 'The Isolation and Measurement of Nationalism'; *J. Of Soc. Psychology*, 16: 215-228
1944a 'Socio-Psychological Correlates of the Primary Attitudes Scales;

I Religionism, II Humanitarianism'; *J. of Soc. Psychology*, 19: 81-98
1944b 'A Revision of the Primary Social Attitudes Scales; *J. of Psychology*, 17: 229-247

FIELD, J. O., R. E. ANDERSON
1969 'Ideology in the Public's Conceptualization of the 1964 Election'; *Publ. Opinion Quart.*, 33: 389-398

FINIFTER, B.
1973 'Replication and Extension of Social Research through Secondary Analysis; Paper presented at the ESOMAR-WAPOR Conference at Budapest, September'. In: *Secondary Analysis of Sample Surveys: Use and Needs*: 327-372

FISHBEIN, M., (ed.)
1967 *Readings in Attitude Theory and Measurement*; New York, John Wiley & Sons

FLUGEL, J. C.
1945 *Man, Morals and Society*; New York, Intern. Univ. Press

FOGARTY, M. D.
1957 *Christian Democracy in Western Europe 1820-1953*; London

FREDERIKSEN, N., S. MESSICK
1959 'Response Set as a Measure of Personality'; *Educ. and Psychol. Measurement*, 19: 137-155

FREE, L. A., H. CANTRIL
1967 *The Political Beliefs of Americans*; New Brunswick, Rutgers Univ. Pr.

FREUND, L.
1955 'The New American Conservatism and European Conservatism'; *Ethics*, 66: 10-17

FRISCH, M. J.
1958 'On McClosky's "Conservatism and Personality";' *Am. Pol. Science Rev.*, 52: 1108-1111

FROMM, E.
(1942), 1960 *Fear of Freedom*; London, Routledge and Kegan Paul

FRUCHTER, B., M. ROKEACH, E. G. NOVAK,
1958 'A Factorial Study of Dogmatism, Opiniation and Related Scales'; *Psychol. Reports*, 4: 19-22

GAGE, N. L., B. B. CHATTERJEE,
1960 'The Psychological Meaning of Acquiescence Set; Further Evidence'; *J. of Abnormal and Soc. Psychology*, 60: 280-283

GALTUNG, J.
1967 *Theory and Methods of Social Research*; London, Allen and Unwin

GAY, P.
1964 *The Party of Humanity; Essays in the French Enlightenment*; New York, Knopf

GEIGER, TH.
1953 *Ideologie und Wahrheit; Einde soziologische Kritik des Denkens*; Stuttgart, Sammlung "Die Universitat" Bd. 41

GLAZER, N.
1968 'The New Left and its Limits'; *Commentary*, 46, 1: 31-39

GLENN, N. D.
1973 'The Social Science Data Archives; The Problem of Underutilization'; *The Am. Sociologist*, 8: 42-45

GOUDSBLOM, J.
1967   *Dutch Society*; New York, Random House
GOULDNER, A. W.
1946   'Attitudes of Progressive Trade-Union Leaders'; *Am. J. of Soc.*, 52, 5: 389-392
GREEN, B. F.
1954   'Attitude Measurement'. In: G. Lindzey (ed.), *Handbook of Social Psychology*, Vol. I: *Theory and Method*: 335-369
GREEN, T. H.
1911   'Lectures on Principles of Political Obligation'. In: *Works of T. H. Green*, Vol. II; New York, Longman Green
GREENSTEIN, F. I.
1965   *Children and Politics*; New Haven, Yale Univ. Press
GRIMES, A. P.
1956   'The Pragmatic Course of Liberalism'; *Western Pol. Quart.*, 9, 1: 663-646
GROOT, A. D. de
1961   *Methodologie*; Den Haag, Mouton en Co
GUÉRIN, D.
1971   *Voor een libertair Marxisme, Analyses en commentaren*; Amsterdam, Van Gennep
GUNDLACH, R. H.
1937   'Confusion among Undergraduates in Political and Economic Ideas'; *J. of Abnormal and Soc. Psychology*, 32: 357-367
HACKER, A.
1957   'Liberal Democracy and Social Control'; *Am. Pol. Science Rev.*, 51: 1009-1026
HAILSHAM, VISCOUNT
1959   *The Conservative Case*, Penguin Books
HALLOWEL, J.
1943   *The decline of liberalism as an ideology, with particular reference to German politico-legal thought*; London, Kegan Paul
HAMILTON, R. F.
1972   *Class and Politics in the United States*; New York, John Wiley & Sons
HARMAN, H.
1967   *Modern Factor Analysis*; Second Edition, Revised; Chicago, Univ. of Chicago Press
HARRISON, J. M.
1967   'Finley Peter Dunne and the Progressive Movement'; *Journ. Quart.*, 44, 3: 475-481
HARTMANN, G. W.
1936   'The Contradictions between the Feeling-tone of Political Party Names and Public Response to their Platform; *J. of Soc. Psychology*, 7: 336-357
1938   'The Differential Validity of Items in a Liberalism-Conservative Test'; *J. of Soc. Psychology*, 9: 67-78
HARTMANN, H., R. WAKENLUST
1972   'Zur Dimensionalität gesellschaftlich-politischer Attituden bei underschiedlichen Gruppen'; *Z.f. Sozialpsychologie*, 3: 96-115

HARTZ, L.
1955 *The Liberal Tradition in America; An Interpretation of American Political Thought since the Revolution*; New York

HAYES, Jr., S. P.
1939a 'The Interrelations of Political Attitudes; II: Consistency in Voters' Attitudes'; *J. of Soc. Psychology*, 10: 359-378
1939b 'The Interrelations of Political Attitudes; III: General Factors in Political Attitudes'; *J. of Soc. Psychology*, 10: 379-397
1939c 'The Interrelations of Political Attitudes; IV: Political Attitudes and Party Regularity'; *J. of Soc. Psychology*, 10: 503-552

HAZELRIGG, L. E., J. LOPREATO
1972 'Heterogamity, Interclass Mobility and Socio-Political Attitudes in Italy'; *Am. Soc. Rev.*, 37: 264-277

HEARNSHAW, F. J. C.
1933 *Conservatism in England*; London

HELLER, C. S., (ed.)
1969 *Structured Social Inequality; A reader in comparative social stratification*, New York, MacMillan

HELMSTADTER, G. C.
1957 'Procedures for Obtaining Separate Set and Content Components of a Test Score'; *Psychometrika*, 22: 381-393

HEMPEL, C. G.
1952 *Fundamentals of Concept Formation in Empirical Science*; Chicago, Chicago Univ. Press
1965 *Aspects of Scientific Explanation, and Other Essays in the Philosopy of Science*; New York

HENDRICKSON, A., P. D. WHITE
1964 'Promax; A Quick Method for Rotation to Oblique Simple Structure'; *British J. of Statist. Psychology*, XVII: 65-70

HENDRICKS, J., C. BRECKINRIDGE PETERS
1973 'The Ideal Type and Sociological Theory'; *Acta Sociologica*: 31-40

HERO, Jr., A. O.
1969 'Liberalism-Conservatism Revisited; Foreign versus Domestic Federal Policies 1937-1967'; *Publ. Opinion Quart.*, 33: 399-408

HESS, R. D.
1963 'The Socialization of Attitudes toward Political Authority; Some Cross-national Comparisons'; *Intern. Soc. Science Journal*, 15: 542-559

HESS, R. D., D. EASTON
1960 'The Child's Image of the President'; *Publ. Opinion Quart.*, 24: 632-644

HESS, R. D., V. C. SHIPMAN
1965 'Early Experience and the Socialization of Cognitive Modes in Children'; *Child Development*, 36: 869-886

HETZLER, S. A.
1954 'Social Mobility and Radicalism-Conservatism'; *Soc. Forces*, 33: 161ff

HILL, L. E.
1964 'On Laissez-faire Capitalism and Liberalism'; *Am. J. Econ. Soc.*, 23, 4: 393-396

HODGE, R., D. TREIMAN
1966   'Occupational Mobility and Attitudes toward Negroes'; *Am. Soc. Rev.*, 31: 93-102

HOFSTEE, E. W.
1962   'De Groei van de Nederlandse bevolking'. In: *Drift en Koers*; Assen, Ven Gorcum en Co: 13-84
1966   'Over het modern-dynamisch cultuurpatroon'; *Sociologische Gids*, 13, 3: 139-154

HOGG, Q.
1947   *The Case for Conservatism*; Harmondsworth, Penguin

HOOGERWERF, A.
1964   *Protestantisme en Progressiviteit; Een politicologisch onderzoek naar opvattingen van Nederlandse protestanten over verandering en gelijkheid*; Meppel, Boom en Zn
1968   'Over een sekundaire analyse'; *Acta Politica*, 3, 4: 354-355

HOROWITZ, I. L.
1956   'The New Conservatism'; *Science and Society*, 20, 1: 1-26

HUFFMAN, P. E., D. J. LEVINSON
1950   'Authoritarian Personality and Family Ideology; A Scale for the Measurement of Traditional Family Ideology'; *The Am. Psychologist*, 5:307

HUNTER, E. C.
1942   'Changes in General Attitudes of Women Students During Four Years in College'; *J. of Soc. Psychology*, 16: 243-257
1951   'Attitudes of College Freshmen'; *J. of Psychology*, 31: 281-296

HUNTINGTON, S. P.
1957   'Conservatism as an Ideology'; *Am. Pol. Science Rev.*, 51, 1: 454-473

HYMAN, H. H.
1955   *Survey Design and Analysis*; Glencoe, The Free Press
1972   *Secondary Analysis of Sample Surveys; Principles, Procedures and Potentialities*; New York, John Wiley & Sons

HYMAN, H. H., P. B. SHEATSLY
1954   'The Authoritarian Personality; A Methodological Critique'; In: R. Christie, M. Jahoda; *Studies in the Scope and Method of 'The Authoritarian Personality'*; Glencoe, The Free Press: 50-124

HYMAN, M. D.
1962   'Determining the Effects of Status Inconsistency; A Criticism of Lenski's Method and a Description of an Alternative Approach'; *Publ. Opinion Quart.*, 26:

JACKMAN, M. R.
1972a 'Social Mobility and Attitudes toward the Political System'; *Soc. Forces*, 50: 462-472
1972b 'The Political Orientation of the Socially Mobile in Italy, a Reexamination'; *Am. Soc. Rev.*, 37: 213-222
1972c 'Reply to Lopreato and Chafetz'; *Am. Soc. Rev.*, 37: 226-227

JACKMAN, R. W.
1972   'Political Elites, Mass Publics and Support for Democratic Principles'; *J. of Politics*, 34: 753-773

JACKSON, D. N., S. J. MESSICK
1957   'A Note on Ethnocentrism and Acquiescent Response Sets'; *J. of Abnormal and Soc. Psychology*, 54: 137-140

1958 'Content and Style in Personality Assessment; *Psychol. Bull.*, 55: 243-252

JACOBS, A. A. J., W. JACOBS-WESSELS
1968 '"Duidelijkheid" in de Nederlandse Politiek; Een poging tot operationalisering'; *Acta Politica*, 4, 1: 41-54

JAMES, W.
1907 *Pragmatism; A New Name for Some Old Ways of Thinking*; London

JENNINGS, M. K., R. G. NIEMI
1968 'The Transmission of Political Values from Parent to Child'; *Am. Pol. Science Rev.*, 62: 169-185

JÖRESKOG, K. G.
1966 'Some Contributions to Maximum Likelihood Factor Analysis'; *Research Bulletin, RB 66-41*; Princeton, Educational Testing Service

KAISER, H. F.
1958 'The Varimax Criterion for Analytic Rotation in Factor Analysis'; *Psychometrika*, 23: 187-200

KATZ, D., H. CANTRIL
1940 'An Analysis of Attitudes toward Fascism and Communism'; *J. of Abnormal and Soc. Psychology*, 35: 356-366

KELLY, D., W. CHAMBLISS
1966 'Status Consistency and Political Attitudes'; *Am. Soc. Rev.*, 31: 375-381

KENDALL, M. G.
1948 *Rank Correlation Methods*; London, Charles Griffin

KENDALL, W.
1958 'Comment on McClosky's "Conservatism and Personality" '; *Am. Pol. Science Rev.*, 52, 4: 506-520
1963 *The Conservative Affirmation*; Chicago, Regnery

KENDALL, W., G. CAREY
1964 'Towards a Definition of Conservatism'; *J. of Politics*, 26, 2: 406-422

KENKEL, W. F.
1956 'The Relationship between Status-Consistency and Politico-Economic Attitudes, *Am. Soc. Rev.*, 21: 365-368

KENNISTON, K.
1968 *Young Radicals; Notes on Committed Youth*; New York, Harcourt Brace

KERLINGER, F. N.
1958 'Progressivism and Traditionalism; Basic Factors of Educational Attitudes'; *J. of Soc. Psychology*, 48: 111-135
1961 'Factor Invariance in the Measurement of Attitudes toward Education', *Educ. and Psychol. Measurement*, 21: 273-285
1967 'Social Attitudes and their Criterial Referents: A Structural Theory'; *Psychol. Rev.*, 74, 2: 110-122
1968 'The social Attitudes Scale; A Manual'; Unpublished Report
1969 *Foundations of Behavioral Research; Educational and Psychological Inquiry*; New York, Holt, Rinehart and Winston
1970 'A Social Attitudes Scale: Evidence on Reliability and Validity'; *Psychol. Reports*, 26: 379-383
1972a 'The Structure and Content of Social Attitude Referents; A Preliminary Study'; *Educ. and Psychol. Measurement*, 32: 613-630

1972b   'A Q Validation of the Structure of Social Attitudes'; *Educ. and Psychol. Measurement*, 32: 987-995

KERLINGER, F. N., E. KAYA
1959   'The Construction and Factor-Analytic Validation of Scales to Measure Attitudes toward Education'; *Educ. and Psychol. Measurement*, 19: 13-29

KERLINGER, F. N., M. ROKEACH
1966   'The Factorial Nature of the F and D-Scales'; *J. of Personality and Soc. Psychology*, 4, 4: 391-399

KERR, W. A.
1944   'Correlates of Political-Economic Liberalism-Conservatism'; *J. of Soc. Psychology*, 20: 61-76
1952   'Untangling the Liberalism-Conservatism Continuum'; *J. of Soc. Psychology*, 35: 111-125

KEY, V. O., Jr.
1966   *The Responsible Electorate: Rationality in Presidential Voting 1936-1960*; Cambridge, Mass., Belknap Press
1968   *Public Opinion and American Democracy*; New York, Knopf

KIRK, R.
1954   *The Conservative Mind*; London, Faber & Faber

KISSINGER, H. A.
1954   'The Conservative Dilemma, Reflections on the Political Thought of Metternich'; *Am. Pol. Science Rev.*, 48: 1017-1036

KLEMPERER, K. VON,
1968   *Germany's New Conservatism; Its History and Dilemma in the Twentieth Century*; Princeton, Princeton Univ. Press

KOOMEN, W., J. A. M. WINNUBST
1968   'Onder en boven de Moerdijk; De houding van katholieken tegenover protestanten'; *Sociologische Gids*, 15, 5: 299-307

KOOMEN, W., L. F. M. WILLEMS
1969   'Waarneming van het stelsel van Nederlandse politieke partijen'; *Acta Politica*, 4, 4: 460-465

KROES, R.
1971a   'Studentenparticipatie en studentenradikalisme; Eerste verslag van een sociologisch onderzoek'; *Mens en Maatschappij*, 46, 3: 243-270
1971b   *Conflikt en Radikalisme*; Meppel, Boom en Zn (reference to off-set copy)
1974c   'New Left — Nieuw Links; De radikale jaren '60 in Amerika en Nederland'; *Intermediair*, 9, 37:

KRUSKAL, J. B.
1964a   'Multidimensional Scaling by Optimizing Goodness of Fit to a Nonmetric Hypothesis'; *Psychometrika*, 29: 1-27
1964b   'Non-metric Multi-dimensional Scaling, a Numerical Method'; *Psychometrika*, 29: 115-129

KULP, D. H., A.H. DAVIDSON
1934   'The Application of Spearman Two-factor Theory to Social Attitudes'; *J. of Abnormal and Soc. Psychology*, 29: 269-275

KUYPERS, G.
1967   *Het politieke spel in Nederland; Diagnoses, remedies en een suggestie*; Meppel, Boom en Zn

LADD, Jr., E. C.
1969 *Ideology in America*; New York, Cornell Univ. Press

LAND, L. VAN DER,
1962 *Het ontstaan van de Pacifistisch Socialistische Partij*; Amsterdam (diss.)

LANE, R. E.
1959 'Fathers and Sons; Foundations of Political Belief'; *Am. Soc. Rev.*, 24: 503-511
1962 *Political Ideology*; New York, The Free Press
1966 'The Decline of Politics and Ideology in a Knowledgeable Society'; *Am. Soc. Rev.*, 31: 649-662

LANGE, A.
1971 *De autoritaire persoon in zijn godsdienstige wereld*; Assen, Van Gorcum en Co

LANGE, A., W. BRINKMAN, W. KOOMEN
1968 'Protestantisme en Progressiviteit opnieuw bezien; *Acta Politica*, 3, 4: 340-353

LASCH, Ch.
1965 *The New Radicalism in America, 1889-1963*; New York, Knopf

LASKI, H. J.
1936 *The Rise of European Liberalism; An Essay in Interpretation*; London

LEHNING, P.
1970 'Links en rechts in de politiek'; *De Gids*, 133, 2: 146-147

LENK, K.
1964 'Ideologie, Ideologiekritik und Wissenssoziologie;' *Soziologische Texte*, Bd 4; Neuwied

LENSKI, G. E.
1954 'Status crystallization; A Non-vertical Dimension of Social Status'; *Am. Soc. Rev.*, 19: 405-413
1961 *The Religious Factor*; New York, Doubleday Anchor Book
1966 *Power and Privilege*; New York, McGraw-Hill
1967 'Status Inconsistency and the Vote; A Four-Nation Test'; *Am. Soc. Rev.*, 32, 3: 298-301
1969 'Status Consistency and Inconsistency'. In: C. S. Heller, *Structured Social Inequality*; New York: 206-216

LENTZ, T. F.
(1935), 1950 *Conservatism-Radicalism Opinionaire Test Manual*; St. Louis, Character Res. Ass., Dept. of Education, Washington Univ.
1938 'Generality and Specificity of Conservatism-Radicalism'; *J. of Educ. Psychology*, 29: 540-546

LEVINSON, D. J.
1950 'Construction of the Politico-Economic Conservatism Scale'. In: T. W. Adorno et al., *The Authoritarian Personality*; New York, Harper and Row: 153-207

LEVINSON, D. J., P. E. HUFFMAN
1955 'Traditional Family Ideology and its Relation to Personality'; *J. of Personality*, 23: 251-273

LEWIS, G. K.
1953a 'America and the new British Radicalism'; *Western Pol. Quart.*, 6, 1: 1-27

1953b 'The Metaphysics of Conservatism'; *Western Pol. Quart.*, 6: 728-741

LICHTHEIM, G.
1967 *The Concept of Ideology and Other Essays*; New York, Vintage Book

LICHTMAN, R.
1970 'The Façade of Equality in Liberal Democratic Theory'; *Inquiry*, 12: 170-208

LIKERT, R.
1932 'A Technique for the Measurement of Attitudes'; *Arch. of Psychology*, 22: 110-140

LIPSCHITZ, I.
1969 *Links en rechts in de politiek*; Meppel, Boom en Zn

LIPSET, S. M.
1959a 'Democracy and Working Class Authoritarianism'; *Am. Soc. Rev.*, 24: 482-501

(1959b), 1963 *Political Man*; London, Heinemann, Mercury Book
1961 'Working Class Authoritarianism; A Reply to Miller and Riesman'; *British J. of Sociology*, 12: 278-281
1968 *Revolution and Counterrevolution; Change and Persistence in Social Structures*; New York, Basic Books

LIPSITZ, S. M., R. BENDIX
1959 *Social Mobility in Industrial Society*; Berkeley and Los Angeles, Univ. of California Press

LIPSET, L.
1965 'Working Class Authoritarianism; A Re-evaluation'; *Am. Soc. Rev.*, 30: 103-109
1966 'Communication'; *Am. Pol. Science Rev.*, Dec: 1000-1
1970 'On Political Belief: The Grievances of the Poor', in Ph. Green and S. Levinson, *Power and Community; Dissenting Essays in Political Science*; New York, Vintage Book

LIVINGSTONE, J.
1956 'Liberalism-Conservatism and the Role of Reason'; *Western Pol. Quart.*, 9: 641-657

LOEWENSTEIN, K.
1953 'Political Systems, Ideologies and Institutions; The Problem of their Circulation'; *Western Pol. Quart.*, 6, 1: 689-706

LOPREATO, J.
1967 'Upward Social Mobility and Political Orientation'; *Am. Soc. Rev.*, 32: 586-592

LOPREATO, J., J. S. CHAFETZ
1970 'The Political Orientation of Skidders; A Middle-Range Theory'; *Am. Soc. Rev.*, 35, 3: 440-451
1972 'The Political Orientation of the Socially Mobile in Italy; A Comment'; *Am. Soc. Rev.*, 37: 223-225

LOPREATO, J., L. E. HAZELRIGG
1970 'Intragenerational versus Intergenerational Social Mobility in Relation to Socio-Political Attitudes'; *Soc. Forces*, 49, 2: 200-210

LORR, M. A.
1951 'A Factorial Isolation of Two Social Attitudes; *J. of Soc. Psychology*, 34: 139-142

LUTTBEG, N. R.
1968 'The Structure of Beliefs among Leaders and the Public'; *Publ. Opinion Quart.*, 32: 398-409

LYND, S.
1969 'The New Left'; *Annals of the Am. Acad. of Pol. and Soc. Sciences.* 382: 64-72

LIJPHART, A.
1968a *The Politics of Accommodation: Pluralism and Democracy in the Netherlands*; Berkeley, Univ. of California Press
1968b *Verzuiling, pacificatie en kentering in de Nederlandse politiek*; Amsterdam, De Bussy

MACDONALD, H. M.
1957 'The Revival of Conservative Thought; *J. of Politics*, 19, 1: 66-80

MANN, M.
1970 'The Social Cohesion of Liberal Democracy'; *Am. Soc. Rev.*, 35, 3: 423-439

MANNHEIM, K.
(1927), 1953 'Conservative Thought'. In: Kecskemeti, P. (ed.), *Essays on Sociology and Social Psychology*; London, Routledge and Kegan Paul: 74-164
1930 *Ideologie und Utopie*; Bonn

MARX, M. H.
1956 'The General Nature of Theory Construction'. In: M. H. Marx (ed.), *Psychological Theory*; New York, MacMillan

MASLOW, A. H.
1943 'The Authoritarian Character Structure'; *J. of Soc. Psychol.*, 18: 401-411

MATTHEWS, D. R., J. W. PROTHRO
1966 *Negroes and the New Southern Politics*; New York, Harcourt, Brace and World

MCCLOSKY, H.
1958a 'Conservatism and Personality'; *Am. Pol. Science Rev.*, 52, 1: 27-45
1958b 'Rejoinder to Kendall and Frisch'; *Am. Pol. Science Rev.*, 52: 1111-1112
1964 'Consensus and Ideology in American Politics'; *Am. Pol. Science Rev.*, 58, 2: 361-382

MCCLOSKY, H., P. HOFFMAN, R. O'HARA
1960 'Issue Conflict and Consensus among Party Leaders and Followers'; *Am. pol. Science Rev.*, 54: 406-427

MCCOY, D. M.
1956 'The Progressive National Committee of 1936'; *Western Pol. Quart.*, 9: 454-469

MCGOVERN, W. M., D. S. COLLIER
1957 *Radicals and Conservatives*

MCKENZIE, R., A. SILVER
1968 *Angels in Marble, Working Class Conservatives in Urban England*; London, Heinemann

MCNEMAR, Q.
1946 'Opinion Attitude Methodology; *Psychol. Bull.*, 43: 289-374

MENEFEE, S. C.
1936 'The Effect of Stereotyped Words on Political Judgements'; *Am. Soc. Rev.*, 1: 614-621

MERELMAN, R. N.
1969 'The Development of Political Ideology; A Framework for the Analysis of Political Socialization'; *Am. Pol. Science Rev.*, 63, 3: 750-767
1971a 'The Development of Policy Thinking in Adolescence'; *Am. Pol. Science Rev.*, 65: 1033-1048
1971b *Political Socialization and Educational Climates*; New York, Holt, Rinehart and Winston

MERTON, R. K.
(1949), 1957 *Social Theory and Social Structure*; Glencoe, The Free Press; London, Collier-Macmillan

MESSICK, S. J.
1956 'The Perception of Social Attitudes'; *J. of Abnormal and Soc. Psychology*, 52, 1: 57-67

MESSICK, S. J., N. FREDERIKSEN
1958 'Ability, Acquiescence and Authoritarianism'; *Psychol. Reports*, 4: 687-697

MESSICK, S. J., D. N. JACKSON
1957 'Authoritarianism or Acquiescence in Bass' Data'; *J. of Abnormal and Soc. Psychology*, 54: 424-425

MEYER, F. S.
1964 *What is Conservatism?*; New York
1969 *The Conservative Mainstream*; New Rochelle, N.Y., Arlington

MICHELS, R.
1932 'Conservatism'. In: E. L. A. Seligman (ed.), *International Encyclopaedia of the Social Sciences*, Vol. II (4): 230-233; New York, Macmillan

MIDDENDORP, C. P.
1973 'Cultural Change in the Netherlands in the late Sixties and its Relation to T.V.-Exposure'. Paper presented at the ESOMAR-WAPOR Conference at Budapest, September. In: *Secondary Analysis of Sample Surveys; Use and Needs*; 454-498
1974a 'Culturele veranderingen in Nederland, 1965-1970'; *Intermediair*, 10, 11: 1-9
1974b 'Replication through re-conceptualization: progressiveness and conservatism and the relation between social class and premarital sexual permissiveness'; *Sociologische Gids*, 3: 165-182
1975a 'Verdere culturele veranderingen in Nederland? De periode 1970-1974'; *Intermediair*, 11, 19: 1-5
1975b 'Data-archieven in de social wetenschappen, I: Het Steinmetzarchief'; *Intermediair*, 11, 18: 33-37
1975c 'Data-archieven in de sociale wetenschappen, II: Wetenschappelijke functies van een data-archief'; *Intermediair*, 11, 22: 35-39
1975d 'Data-archieven in de sociale wetenschappen, III: Data-archieven in internationaal perspectief'; *Intermediair*, 11, 26: 45-49
1975e 'Politisering en ideologie'; *Beleid en Maatschappij*, 2, 7-8: 183-190
1976a 'Bespreking van: R. A. Roe, Links en rechts in een empirisch perspectief; een onderzoek naar de dimensionaliteit van politieke attituden

onder studenten; Swets en Zeitlinger BV, Amsterdam, 1975'. In: *Sociologische Gids*, 5:319-324

1976b 'Representation in a parliamentary democracy. Positions of M.P.'s and voters on fundamental dimensions of ideological controversy'. Paper presented at the ECPR-workshop at Louvain; April

1976c Over de methode der (partiële) replikatie, Methoden en Data Nieuwsbrief, 1:50-56

1977a Over de methode der (partiële) replikatie (2), Enkele toepassingen, Methoden en Data Nieuwsbrief, 2:111-132

1977b 'The Structure of Criterial Referents of Attitudes in the Netherlands' (forthcoming)

1977c 'The Structure of ideological controversy in the Netherlands; its development and further validation' (forthcoming)

1977d The anomia-authoritarianism-dogmatism syndrome in the Netherlands; its development and some notes on conceptualization (forthcoming)

1977e 'Culturele veranderingen in Nederland, 1958-1975; (forthcoming)

MIDDENDORP, C. P., W. BRINKMAN, W. KOOMEN
1969 'Determinanten van "permissiveness" t.a.v. premarital sexueel gedrag; een sekundaire analyse'; *Mens en Maatschappij*, 1: 15-32
1970 'Determinants of Premarital Sexual Permissiveness; A secondary Analysis'; *J. of Marriage and the Fam.*, August: 369-379

MIDDLETON, R., S. PUTTNEY
1963 'Student Rebellion against Parental Political Beliefs'; *Soc. Forces*, 41: 377-383

MILIBAND, R.
1961 *Parliamentary Socialism*; London, George Allen and Unwin Ltd.

MILLER, S. M., F. RIESMAN
1961 'Working Class Authoritarianism; A Critique of Lipset'; *British J. of Soc.*, 12: 263-273

MILLS, C. W.
(1963), 1969, 'The Conservative Mood'. In: I. L. Horowitz (ed.), *Power, Politics and People, The Collected Essays of C. W. Mills;* London, Oxford Univ. Press: 208-220

MINAR, W.
1961 'Ideology and Political Behavior'; *Midwest J. of Pol. Science*, V: 307-331

MINOQUE, K. R.
1963 *The Liberal Mind*; New York, Vintage Book

MITCHELL, R. E.
1966 Class-linked Conflict between Two Dimensions of Liberalism-Conservatism'; *Soc. Problems*, 13, 4: 418-427

MOKKEN, R. J.
1970 *A Theory and Procedure of Scale Analysis with Applications in Political Research*; Den Haag, Mouton en Co

MORGAN, J., J. SONQUIST
1963 'Problems in the Analysis of Survey Data'; *J. of the Am. Statist. Ass.*, June: 415-434

MÜHLENFELD, H.
1952 *Politik ohne Wunschbilder; Der konservatieve Aufgabe unserer Zeit*; München, Oldenbourg Verlag

MULLINS, W. A.
1972 'On the Concept of Ideology in Political Science'; *Am. Pol. Science Rev.*, 66: 498-511

MURPHY, G., R. LIKERT
1938 *Public Opinion and the Individual*; New York, Harper and Row

NAESS, A., J. A. CHRISTOPHERSEN, K. KVALØ
1956 *Democracy, Ideology and Objectivity; Studies in the Semantics and Cognitive Analysis of Ideological Controversy*; Oslo, Univ. Press; Oxford, Blackwell

NAGEL, E.
1963 'Problems, of Concept and Theory Formation in the Social Sciences'; in: M. Natanson, *Philosophy of the Social Sciences*; New York, Random House: 189-209

NATANSON, M. (ed.)
1963 *Philosophy of the Social Sciences*; New York, Random House

NETTLER, G., J. R. HUFFMAN
1957 'Political Opinion and Personal Security;' *Sociometry*, 20: 51-66

NEUMANN, S.
1968 'Foreword'. In: K. von Klemperer, *Germany's New Conservatism; Its History and Dilemma in the Twentieth Century*; Princeton, N.J., Princeton Univ. Press

NEWCOMB, T. M.
1945 *Personality and Social Change; Attitude Formation in a Student Community*; New York, Dryden Press

NIE, N. H.
1974 'Mass Belief Systems Revisited; Political Change and Attitude Structure'; *J. of Politics*, 36: 540-591

NISBET, R. A.
1952 'Conservatism and Sociology'; *Am. J. of Soc.*, 58: 167-175

NOOIJ, A. T. J.
1964 'Kultuurpatroon als object van onderzoek'; *Sociologische Gids*, 11: 212-219
1969 *De Boerenpartij; Desorientatie en radikalisme onder de boeren*; Meppel, Boom en Zn

NORDLINGER, E. A.
1957 *The Working Class Tories; Authority, Deference and Stable Democracy*; Berkeley

O'KANE, J. M.
1970 'Economic and Non-economic Liberalism, Upward Mobility Potential and Catholic Working Class Youth'; *Soc. Forces*, 49: 499-506

O'NEILL, H. W.
1967 'Response Style Influences in Public Opinion Surveys'; *Publ. Opinion Quart.*, 31: 95-102

OORBURG, J., T. VAN BOVEN, J. DE BRUYN, D. JOLINK
1974 'His Master's Voice: Yes or No? A provisional report on a research project after dominating influences on the contents of mass media in the Netherlands'; Paper given at the research committee on Mass Communication at the VIIIth World Congress of Sociology, Toronto, Can., August

OP 'T LAND, C.
  1966   'Het cultuurpatroon als analytisch instrument bij de studie van veranderingsprocessen'; *Sociologische Gids*, 13, 3: 130-138
ORTON, W. A.
  1945   *The Liberal Tradition*; New Haven, Yale Univ. Press
PACE, R. C.
  1939   'A Situation Text to Measure Social-Political-Economic Attitudes'; *J. of Soc. Psychology*, 10: 331-344
PALMA, G. D., H. MCCLOSKY
  1970   'Personality and Conformity; The Learning of Political Attitudes'; *Am. Pol. Science Rev.*, 64: 1054-1074
PARKIN, F.
  1967   'Working Class Conservatives; A Theory of Political Deviance'; *British J. of Soc.*, 18: 278-290
PARSONS, T.
  1949   *The Structure of Social Action*; Glencoe, The Free Press
  (1951), 1964, *The Social System*; New York, The Free Press
PARTISAN REVIEW
  1965   'Discussion on the "New Radicalism"'
PEABODY, D.
  1961   'Attitude Content and Agreement Response Set in Scales of Authoritarianism, Dogmatism, Anti-Semitism and Economic Conservatism'; *J. of Abnormal and Soc. Psychology*, 63: 1-11
  1964   'Models for Estimating Content and Set Components in Attitude and Personality Scales'; *Educ. and Psychol. Measurement*, 24
PHILLIPS, N. R.
  1956   'The Conservative Implications of Scepticism; *J. of Politics*, 18, 1: 28-38
  1959   'Genetics and Political Conservatism'; *Western Pol. Quart.*, 12: 753-762
  1963   'The Role of Conservatism Today'; *Modern Age*, 7, 3: 242-248
PINTO-DUSCHINSKY, M.
  1973   'Stratification and Policy in the British Conservative Party'; *Am. Beh. Scientist*, 17, 2: 285-292
POLLAK, O.
  1943   'Conservatism in Later Maturity and Old Age; An investigation Based on Studies in the Field of Market and Public Opinion Research'; *Am. Soc. Rev.*, 8: 175-179
PORTES, A.
  1971a 'On the Interpretation of Class Consciousness'; *Am. J. of Soc.*, 2: 228-244
  1971b 'On the Logic of Post-Factum Explanations; The Hypothesis of Lower Class Frustration as the Cause of Leftist Radicalism'; *Soc. Forces*, 50: 26-44
PROTHRO, J. W., C. M. CRIGG
  1960   'Fundamental Principles of Democracy: Bases of Agreement and Disagreement'; *J. of Politics*, 22: 276-294
PUTNAM, R. D.
  1971   'Studying Elite Political Culture; The Case of Ideology'; *Am. Soc. Pol. Rev.*, 65: 651-682

QUINNEY, R.
1964 'Political Conservatism, Alienation and Fatalism: Contingencies of Social Status and Religious Fundamentalism'; *Sociometry*, 27: 374–381

RASKIN, E., S. W. COOK
1938 'A Further Investigation of the Measurement of an Attitude toward Fascism'; *J. of Soc. Psychology*, 9: 201–256

RAWLS, J.
1972 *A Theory of Justice*; Oxford, Oxford Univ. Press

RAWSON, H. E., S. RETTIG
1962 'Controlling the Effects of Clouding Variables in Multivariate Research Designs'; *Educ. and Psychol. Measurement*, 22, 3: 493–500

RAY, J. J.
1972 'Are Conservatism Scales Irreversible?'; *British J. of Soc. and Clinical Psychology*, 2: 346–352
1973 'Conservatism, Authoritarianism and Related Variables; A Review and Empirical Study'. In: G. D. Wilson (ed.), *The Psychology of Conservatism*; London, Academic Press: 17–35

REED, E. F.
1927 'Does the Individual Tend to be Consistently a Progressive or a Conservative?; *Soc. Forces*, 6: 49–52

REISS, I. L.
1967 *The Social Context of Premarital Sexual Permissiveness*; New York, Holt, Rinehart and Winston
1971 *The Family System in America*; New York, Holt, Rinehart and Winston

REMMLING, G. W.
1967 *Road to Suspicion; A Study of Modern Mentality and the Sociology of Knowledge*; New York, Appleton

RHODES, A. L.
1961 'Authoritarianism and Alienation; The F-scale and the Srole Scale as Predictors of Prejudice'; *Soc. Quart.*, 2: 193–202

RILEY, M. W., J. W. RILEY, J. TOBY
1954 *Sociological Studies in Scale Analysis*; New Brunswick, Rutgers Univ. Press

ROBERTS, A. H., M. ROKEACH
1956 'Anomia, Authoritarianism and Prejudice: A Replication'; *Am. Soc. Rev.*, 21: 610ff

ROBINSON, J. P., J. G. RUSK, K. B. HEAD
1968 *Measures of Political Attitudes*; Survey Research Center, Inst. for Social Research, Univ. of Michigan, Ann Arbor

ROBINSON, J. P., PH.R. SHAVER
1969 *Measures of Social Psychological Attitudes*; Survey Research Center; Inst. for Soc. Research, Univ. of Michigan, Ann Arbor

ROE, R. A.
1975 *Links en rechts in een empirisch perspectief; Een onderzoek naar de dimensionaliteit van politieke attituden onder studenten*; Amsterdam, Swets en Zeitlinger

ROGERS, R. E.
1969 *Max Weber's Ideal Type Theory*; New York, Philosophical Library

ROGHMANN, K
1966 *Dogmatismus und Authoritarismus; Kritik der theoretischen Ansatze und Ergebnisse dreier westdeutschen Untersuchungen*; Meisenheim am Glan, Anton Hain

ROGIN, M.
1968 'Progressivism and the California Electorate: *J. of Am. History*, 35, 2: 297-314

ROGOW, A. A., H. D. LASSWELL
1963 *World Politics and Personal Security*; New York, The Free Press

ROKEACH, M.
1960 *The Open and Closed Mind; Investigations into the Nature of Belief Systems and Personality Systems*; New York, Basic Books
1968 *Beliefs, Attitudes and Values; A Theory of Organization and Change*; San Francisco, Jossy Bass
1973 *The Nature of Human Values*; New York, The Free Press

ROKEACH, M. , B. FRUCHTER
1956 'A Factorial Study of Dogmatism and Related Concepts'; *J. of Abnormal and Soc. Psychology*, 53: 306ff

ROKEACH, M., C. HANLEY
1956a 'Eysenck's Tender-Mindedness Dimension, A Critique'; *Psychol. Bull*, 53, 2: 169-176
1956b 'Care and Carelessness in Psychology'; *Psychol. Bull.*, 53, 2: 183-186

RORER, L.
1965 'The Great Response-style Myth'; *Psychol. Bull.*, 62: 129-156

ROSE A.
1966 'Anomia and the Authoritarian Personality'; *Sociology and Soc. Research*, 50: 141-147

ROSENBERG, M.
1968 *The Logic of Survey Analysis*; New York, Basic Books
1973 'The Logical Status of Suppressor Variables'; *Publ. Opinion Quart.*, 37: 359-372

ROSSITER, C.
(1955), 1962 *Conservatism in America; The Thankless Persuasion*; New York, Vintage Book
1968 'Conservatism'. In: D. L. Sills (ed.), *International Encyclopaedia of the Social Sciences*, New York, Collier, Macmillan, The Free Press, Vol. 3: 290-295

RUBIN RABSON, G.
1954 'Several Correlates of a Liberal-Conservative Attitude Scale'; *J. of Soc. Psychology*, 39, 1: 47-55

RUNCIMANN, W. G.
1966 *Relative Deprivation and Social Justice; A Study of Attitudes to Social Inequality in Twentieth Century England*; London, Routledge and Kegan Paul
1970 *Sociology and Its Place*; Cambridge, Cambridge Univ. Press

RUSH, G. B.
1967 'Status Consistency and Right Wing Extremism'; *Am. Soc. Rev.*, 32, 1: 86-92

SAMELSON, F.
   1964 'Agreement Set and Anti-Content Attitudes in the F-Scale; A Re-
         interpretation'; *J. of Abnormal and Soc. Psychology*, 68: 338-342
SANAI, M.
   1950 'A Factorial Study of Social Attitudes'; *J. of Soc. Psychology*, 31:
         167-182
   1951 'An Experimental Study of Social Attitudes'; *J. of Soc. Psychology*,
         34: 235-264
SANAI, M., P. M. PICKARD
   1949 'The Relation between Politico-Economic Radicalism and Certain
         Traits of Personality'; *J. of Soc. Psychology*, 30: 217-227
SARTORI, G.
   1969 'Politics, Ideology and Belief Systems'; *Am. Pol. Science Rev.*, 63,
         2: 390-411
SCHINDELER, F., D. HOFFMAN
   1968 'Theological and Political Conservatism; Variations in Attitudes
         among Clergymen of one Denomination'; *Canadian J. of Pol.
         Science*, 1, 4: 429-441
SCHLESINGER Jr., A.
   1953 'The New Conservatism in America, A Liberal Comment'; *Con-
         fluence*, 2, 4: 61-71
SCHOENBERGER, R. A.
   1968 'Conservatism, Personality and Political Extremism'; *Am. Pol.
         Science Revl.*, 62: 868-877
SCHUTZ, A.
   1963 'Concept and Theory Formation in the Social Sciences'; In: M.
         Natanson (ed.), *Philosophy of the Social Sciences*; New York,
         Random House: 231-249
SEEMAN, M.
   1959 'On the Meaning of Alienation'; *Am. Soc. Rev.*, 24: 783-791
SEGAL, D. R.
   1969 'Status Inconsistency, Cross Pressures and American Political
         Behavior'; *Am. Soc. Rev.*, 34, 3: 352-358
SEGAL, D. R., D. KNOKE
   1968 'Social Mobility, Status Inconsistency and Partisan Realignment in
         the U.S.'; *Soc. Forces*, 47: 154-158
SEGAL, D. R., M. W. SEGAL, D. KNOKE
   1970 'Status Inconsistency and Self-Evaluation'; *Sociometry*, 33, 3:
         347-357
SELLTIZ, C., M. JAHODA, M. DEUTSCH, S. W. COOK
   (1959), 1963 *Research Methods in Social Relations*; 2nd revised edition;
         New York, Holt, Rinehart and Winston
SELZNICK, G. J., S. STEINBERG
   1969 'Social Class, Ideology and Voting Preference'. In: C. S. Heller (ed.),
         Structured Social Inequality; New York, Macmillan: 216-226
SHAW, M. E., J. M. WRIGHT
   1967 *Scales for the Measurement of Attitudes*; New York, McGraw Hill
SHILS, E.
   1954 'Authoritarianism, Right and Left'; In: R. Christie and M. Jahoda,

Studies in the Scope and Method of 'The Authoritarian Personality', Glencoe, The Free Press: 24-49

1968 'The Concept and Function of Ideology'. In: D. L. Sills (ed.), *International Encyclopaedia of the Social Sciences*; New York, Collier, Macmillan, The Free Press

SHKLAR, J. N.
1966 *Political Theory and Ideology*; New York, Macmillan

SILBERSTEIN, F., M. SEEMAN
1959 'Social Mobility and Prejudice'; *Am. J. of Soc.*, 65: 258-264

SIMON, H. A.
(1957), 1967 *Models of Man, Social and Rational; Mathematical Essays on Rational Human Behavior in a Social Setting*; London

SIZOO, J.
1971 *Inzake rechts; Verkenning van een politieke gedachtenwereld*; Meppel, Boom en Zn

SMELSER, N. J., S. M. LIPSET (eds.)
1966 'Social Structure and Mobility in Economic Development'; Papers presented at a Conference held at San Francisco, January 1964

SMITH, D. G.
1968 'Liberalism'. In: D. L. Sills (ed.), *International Encyclopaedia of the Social Sciences*; New York, Collier, Macmillan, The Free Press, Vol. 9: 276-282

SMITH, G. H.
1948a 'Liberalism and Level of Information'; *J. of Educ. Psychology*, 39, 2: 65-81

1948b 'Information, Radicalism and Internationalism'; *Publ. Opinion Quart.*, 12: 125-127

1948c 'A Rejoinder (to Hugh C. Parry)'; *Publ. Opinion Quart.*, 12: 785-786

SMITH, G. H., J. DOBIN
1948 'Information and Politico-Economic Opinions'; *Publ. Opinion Quart.*, 12, 4: 731-733

SMITH, M. B.
1950 'Review of "The Authoritarian Personality"'; *J. of Abnormal and Soc. Psychology*, 45: 775-779

SMITH, TH. S.
1969 'Structural Crystallization, Status Inconsistency and Political Partisanship'; *Am. Soc. Rev.*, 34, 6: 907-921

SOMBART, W.
1906 *Warum gibt es in den Vereinigten Staaten keinen Sozialismus?*; Tübingen, Mohr

SPITZ, D.
1964 *The Liberal Idea of Freedom*; Tucson, Univ. of Arizona Press

STROLE, L.
1956 'Social Integration and Certain Corollaries; An Exploratory Study'; *Am. Soc. Rev.*, 21: 709-716

STAGNER, R.
1936a 'Fascist Attitudes; An Exploratory Study'; *J. of Soc. Psychology*, 7: 309-319

1936b 'Fascist Attitudes; Their Determining Conditions'; *J. of Soc. Psychology*, 7: 438–454

STAGNER, R., E. T. KATZOFF
1942 'Fascist Attitudes; Factor Analysis of Item Correlations'; *J. of Soc. Psychology*, 16: 3–9

STAPEL, J.
1968 'Wie en wat staat tussen links en rechts'; *Acta Politica*, 4, 1: 32–40
1971 'Progressief Nederland'; *Acta Politica*, 6, 2: 205–211

STINCHCOMBE, A. L.
1968 *Constructing Social Theories*; New York, Harcourt, Brace and World
1973a 'Theoretical Domains and Measurement I'; *Acta Sociologica*, 1: 3–12
1973b 'Theoretical Domains and Measurement II; II'; *Acta Sociologica*, 2: 79–92

STOUFFER, S. A.
1955 *Communism, Conformity and Civil Liberties; A cross-section of the Nation speaks its mind*, New York, John Wiley & Sons, Inc., Science Editions Paperbacks

STRUENING, E. L., A. H. RICHARDSON
1965 'A Factor-analytic Exploration of the Alienation, Anomia and Authoritarianism Domain'; *Am. Soc. Rev.*, 30: 768–776

THOMPSON, K. H.
1971 'Upward Social Mobility and Political Orientation; A Re-evaluation of the Evidence'; *Am. Soc. Rev.*, 36, 2: 223–235

THURSTONE, L. L.
1928 'Attitudes can be Measured'; *Am. J. of Soc.*, 33: 529–554
1929 'Theory of Attitude Measurement'; *Psychol. Rev.*, 36: 224–241
1934 'The Vectors of Mind'; *Psychol. Rev.*, 41: 1–32

TORGERSON, W. S.
1951 *A Theoretical and Empirical Investigation of Multidimensional Scaling*; Princeton (Ph.D. thesis)

TRACY, DESTUTT DE
1801 *Eléments d'Idéologie*; Vol. I

TIJN-KOEKEBAKKER, M. VAN, W. BRINKMAN, W. KOOMEN
1970 'Verschillen in stemgedrag tussen Tweede Kamer-fracties tijdens het kabinet Cals'; *Acta Politica*, 5, 2: 173–177

VERZIJDEN, D., H. H. VAN DE BRUG
1969 'Attituden en sociale omgeving en hun samenhang met politieke voorkeur'; Amsterdam, unpublished thesis

VETTER, G. B.
1930a 'The Study of Social and Political Opinion'; *J. of Abnormal and Soc. Psychology*, 25: 26–39
1930b 'The Measurement of Social and Political Attitudes and the Related Personality Factors'; *J. of Abnormal and Soc. Psychology*, 25: 149–189
1947 'What Makes Attitudes and Opinions "Liberal" or "Conservative"?'; *J. of Abnormal and Soc. Psychology*, 42: 125–130

VIERECK, P.
(1949), 1962 *Conservatism Revisited; Revised and Enlarged Edition*; with the Addition of Book II: *The New Conservatism — What Went Wrong*; New York, The Free Press

WARR, P. B., R. E. LEE, K. G. JÖRESKOG
1969 'A Note on the Factorial Nature of F and D-Scales'; *British J. of Psychology*, 60, 1: 119-123
WARSHAY, L., M. GOLDMAN, E. H. BIDDLE
1964 'Anomia and F-Scales as Related to Social Characteristics'; *J. of Soc. Psychology*, 62: 117-123
WATKINS, J. W. N.
1952 *Ideal Types and Historical Explanation*
WAXMAN, CH. (*ed.*)
1969 *The End of Ideology Debate*; New York, Clarion Books
WEBER, M.
1905 'Die protestantische Ethik und der Geist des Kapitalismus'. In: M. Weber, *Gesammelte Aufsätze zur Religionssoziologie, I*; Tübingen, Mohr (1920-21, 1947)
(1922a), 1956 *Wirtschaft und Gesellschaft; Grundriss der verstehenden Soziologie*; Tübingen, Mohr
1922b *Gesammelte Aufsätze zur Wissenschaftslehre*; Tübingen, Mohr
1949 *Methodology in the Social Sciences*; translated and edited by E. A. Shills and H. A. Finch; Glencoe, The Free Press
1968 *Methodologische Schriften*; Frankfurt aM, Fisher (Studienausgabe)
WEIMA, J.
1963 *Autoritaire persoonlijkheid en anti-papisme*; Hilversum, Paul Brand
1965 'Authoritarianism, Religious Conservatism and Sociocentric Attitudes in Roman Catholic Groups'; *Human Relations*, 18: 231-239
WERKGROEP NATIONAAL VERKIEZINGSONDERZOEK
1973 'De Nederlandse kiezer '73'; Alpen a.d. Rijn, Samsom
WHITE, R. J.
1950 *The Conservative Tradition*; London
WILDE, G. J. S.
(1961), 1963 *Neurotische labiliteit gemeten volgens de vragenlijstmethode*; Amsterdam, Van Rossum
WILENSKY, H. L.
1966 'Measures and Effects of Mobility'. In: N. J. Smelser, S. M. Lipset, *Social Structure and Mobility in Economic Development*; Papers presented at a Conference held at San Francisco, Jan. 1964
WILENSKY, H. L., H. EDWARDS
1959 'The Skidder; Ideological Adjustments of Downward Mobile Workers'; *Am. Soc. Rev.*, 24: 215-231
WILLER, D., M. WEBSTER
1970 'Theoretical Concepts and Observables'; *Am. Soc. Rev.*, 35: 748-757
WILEY, N.
1967 'Religious and Political Liberalism among Catholics'; *Sociological Analysis*, 28, 3: 142-148
WILLIAMS, B.
1961 'Democracy and Ideology'; *Political Quart.*, 32: 375-384
WILSON, F. G.
1941 'A Theory of Conservatism'; *Am. Pol. Science Rev.*, 35, 1: 29-49
1951 *The Case for Conservatism; Three Lectures*; Seattle
1960 'The Anatomy of Conservatives'; *Ethics*, 70, 4: 265-281

WILSON, G. D. (ed.)
1973   *The Psychology of Conservatism*; London, Academic Press
WILSON, R. B.
1959   'The Eisenhower Anti-Trust Policy; Progressivism or Conservatism'; *Western Pol. Quart.*, 12: 559ff
WILSON, W. C.
1960   'Extrinsic Religious Values and Prejudice'; *J. of Abnormal and Soc. Psychology*, 60: 286-288
WOLFE, A. B.
1923   *Conservatism, Radicalism and Scientific Method*; New York
WOLIN, S.
1953   'Richard Hooker and English Conservatism'; *Western Pol. Quart.*, 6: 28-47
1954   'Hume and Conservatism'; *Am. Pol. Science Rev.*, 48, 4: 999-1016
WRIGHT, J. H., J. M. HICKS
1966   'Construction and Validation of a Thurstone-Scale of Liberalism-Conservatism'; *J. of Appl. Psychology*, 50, 1: 9-12
ZEITLIN, I. M.
1968   *Ideology and the Development of Sociological Theory*; Englewood Cliffs, N.J., Prentice Hall

Appendices

APPENDIX 1:
INTRODUCTION TO THE DUTCH QUESTIONNAIRES;
A GENERAL OUTLINE

The research instrument consists of 2 parts: the first part is an interview schedule; the second part a questionnaire to be filled out by the respondent with the interviewer present (M.P.'s filled out a selected number of questions from both parts themselves; they were approached by mail). What follows is a rough outline of the design of the research instrument.

The interview starts with the assessment of a number of background variables and proceeds (roughly) with the assessment of political alienation, freedom of political expression, family traditionalism, sexual permissiveness and the attitude to aid to developing countries. Then the attitude to social welfare laws and socioeconomic equality is tapped. Subsequently there are a large number of questions on religious attitudes. The last part of the interview again covers background variables and variables such as political interest and information and voting behavior.

The questionnaire starts with a large number of questions on the general role of the government and on specific government-policies generally aiming to increase — or decrease — (socioeconomic) equality. Subsequently there are 37 bipolar questions which form the operationalized model of conservative ideology at the abstract level. Then there are questions on social desirability, general satisfaction, relationship to parents in youth, optimism vs. pessimism and democratic attitudes. We proceed with items on trade union policy, working class children and a long list of items mainly on (moral) libertarianism, authoritarian parent-child relationship and conventional male-female role definitions. Then there are questions on the perception of a possible communist threat, political tolerance, satisfaction with living conditions, and opinions on international relations. Subsequently class identification and media exposure are tapped. The last part of the questionnaire measures authoritarianism, dogmatism and anomia by means of a selected number of items taken from the 'classical' scales, and also nationalism. Finally, self-identification as progressive vs. conservative and left-wing vs. right-wing is assessed. The questionnaire is available upon request.

The data can be made available by the Steinmetz Archives, Kleine — Gartmanplantsoen 10, Amsterdam. They are stored as SPSS-system file no. P0079. American scholars can also obtain the data from the Inter-University Consortium for Political and Social Research (ICPSR) at the University of Michigan, Ann Arbor.

APPENDIX 2:
DATA COLLECTION: THE NATIONAL CROSS-SECTIONAL SAMPLE AND THE ELITE SAMPLE

1. The design of the national cross-sectional sample

The sample was designed by Jan Ligthart, Makrotest N.V., Amsterdam. Fieldwork was carried out by the staff of this (former) institute.

The design was essentially a multistage one. At first, from a minimum number of 4 households which had to be approached in a municipality, and a total number of 1650 households, the municipalities that were 'self-selecting' were determined. Thus, those municipalities were included for which

$$\frac{h_i}{H} \times 1650 \geqslant 4 \qquad (1)$$

h_i = number of households in the municipality
H = total number of households in the Netherlands.

There were 64 self-selecting municipalities. On the basis of h_i, the number of households which had to be approached within each self-selecting municipality could easily be determined. This number was rounded to the nearest even number (see below). From the other approximately 900 non-self-selecting municipalities, a selection had to be made in such a way that the chance of being included in the sample was proportional to the number of households, i.e. the number of inhabitants. Therefore, the municipalities were placed in alphabetic order and a cumulative list of the number of households was prepared. Thus, if municipalities A, B and C had x, y and z households, the list was

No.	Cumulative number
A (1)	x
B (2)	x + y
C (3)	x + y + z
etc.	

Subsequently, an interval 'a' was determined according to

$$a = \frac{H - \Sigma\, h_i}{1650 - S} \times 4 \qquad (2)$$

$\Sigma\, h_i$ = number of households in the 64 self-selecting municipalities
S = number of households which had to be approached in the self-selecting municipalities, and
$p < a$ was determined at random.
Those municipalities 'j' were selected for which

$$G_{cum\,j} \geqslant p + a\,(j\text{-}1) \text{ and}$$
$$G_{cum\,(j\text{-}1)} < p + a\,(j\text{-}1) \tag{3}$$

$G_{cum\,j}$ = the cumulative number of the jth municipality
$G_{cum\,(j\text{-}1)}$ = the cumulative number of the j-1th municipality

It is clear that according to (3), the chance of a municipality being included is proportional to its number of households: the larger this number, the greater the chance that a 'p + aj' will fall within its range.

Thus, 199 municipalities were selected in which 4 households would be called on.

Within each municipality, *even* numbers of households (2 in a street, 10 house-numbers apart, random selection of floors if necessary) were determined at random by checking the list of registered houses at the local registry office, with the help of some of the employees. Reserve-addresses were taken as well. (In some cases, addresses had to be taken from other public housing registers or from street maps or telephone books, using the same principle, since some municipalities refused to cooperate.)

The maximum number of call-backs was set at two. At each address, it was first determined how many persons between the ages of 17 and 70 were part of that household, defined as any group of people who had meals together regularly, i.e. including boarders. The chance of interviewing each of those persons was set at 50%. The maximum number of persons to be interviewed in one household was set at two. *One interview per generation* was carried out when possible.

The 'internal weighing' which had to be carried out in order to get a proper individual-based sample by means of the household-approach was very limited: 50% of the 'single person' households (i.e. people between 17 and 70 years of age) was eliminated; in case there were more than 2 children of age 17 or older, only 1 was interviewed, but cards were duplicated or triplicated accordingly. Single adults with 2 or more children were also eliminated in 50% of the cases. In total, only 2.5% of the records had to be duplicated and 4.5% of the records had to be eliminated.

2. Fieldwork and results

Fieldwork was carried out mainly in June 1970. A number of problems had to be solved during the fieldwork; for the population at large, the questionnaire proved to be 15 minutes longer than in the test-series (it was only tested on a small sample from the Amsterdam population — where it lasted 75 minutes on the average) and the selection-procedure for respondents *within* a household was not adequately understood by many interviewers. Thus in September, an additional number of interviews were to be held. The final result was quite satisfactory.

2700 households (an estimation on the basis of about 65% of the cases) were approached. One or 2 interviews were realized in each of 1727 households. There were 28% refusals and 8% were not at home on 3 occasions. Since 2 interviews were held in each of 312 households, a total number of 2039 cases was initially available; in addition, there were 97 'slightly inadequate' reserve-cases, i.e. cases from 'over-sampled' households, people over 70 years of age, etc. Since for reasons of 'internal' weighing, 90 records had to be eliminated and 50 duplicated (see above), the final 'unweighed' sample size equals N = 1999. The present design seems a satisfactory one: more than 30% of all municipalities were covered (thus including many smaller ones) due to the small minimum number of households per municipality. Other optimal procedures were the grouping of only 2 households in one street and the system of fixed addresses and 2 call-backs. The 28% refusal rate seems rather high though, and may be related to lack of motivation on the part of the interviewers in the early stages of the field-work, when they were confronted with an interview which was longer than expected — hence, they felt that they were underpaid.

3. Weighing procedures and results

Careful weighing was considered desirable (a) for descriptive reasons and possible trend analysis; (b) in the light of the problems that had to be coped with in fieldwork, and (c) given the relatively large percentage of refusals. It was felt that weighing could be more 'rigorous' than usual by outweighing cases and using the relatively large amount of 'reserve cases' (N = 187) instead of duplication. Thus, an approximate final sample size of N = 1950 was aimed at through (1) outweighing about 300 records, (2) duplicating about 150 cases and (3) using about 100 of the 'reserve' cases. This would result in about 10% duplication. (All weighing was done on the basis of data made available by the Central Bureau of Statistics, the Hague. It was carried out with the help of a desk-calculator made available by the Department of Group Psychology, at present at the Psychological Laboratory, University of Amsterdam.)

Weighing started with the 20-cells age-sex table as a baseline. Two additional criteria were added later (marital status and district), specifying the cases to be outweighed, duplicated or taken from reserve-cases. The chi-2 contribution per cell (comparing the frequency of 'observed' and 'expected' cases) was only used as rough criterion: within the set boundaries, a 'stratified' random sample was in fact aimed at. In the final stage, the additional criterion of 'degree of urbanization' (see Appendix 6: 14) was introduced (in combination with age and sex), keeping the weighing done so far in as much order as possible.

The results of this weighing procedure are presented in Table App. 2:1. It appears that in the 19 tests measured against the available census data, in 11 cases the sample shows no significant deviance. In the other 8 cases, the sample agrees so strongly with the census data that it is highly unlikely that results could have been reached by chance! This reaches the .005 level in 4 cases.

At what costs has this high degree of representativity been reached? The size of the final sample is 1927, with 209 (11%) duplicated cases; 97 reserve-cases could be used, and 318 cases were outweighed (10 cases got lost during processing afterwards; for some early analysis, they were still available, however.) Results therefore seem quite satisfactory.

4. The data obtained from the elite: members of parliament

The most suitable 'strategic elite' was to be found among politicians. The most influential and 'visible' group of politicians which is of any magnitude seems to be the Second Chamber of Parliament (N = 150).

In September 1971, a selected number of questions were sent to all M.P.'s. The questions were limited to items within the progressive-conservative domain (i.e. the questions in Appendix 3). Response was not particularly unsatisfactory:

81 members returned their questionnaires. The distribution by political party is presented in Table App. 2.2.

Since the average response is 54%, the Labor Party (PvdA) is over-, and the Catholic Peoples' Party (KVP) under-represented. DS'70 is also over-represented. The communists did not participate at all. Although the parties are not equally represented in the 'sample', it was felt that the data could be used in Type-1 analysis (see Chapter 6).

Table App. 2.1. *The representativity of the national cross-sectional sample*

	chi-2 value	*d.f.* (a)	*p-value*
1. age	2.50	9	.025(b)
2. sex	.20	1	.50
3. marital status	.79	2	.50
4. district	.44	3	.10
5. degree of urbanization	1.11	2	.50
6. age × sex	6.03	19	.005(b)
7. age × marital status	20.22	29	.25
8. sex × marital status	.87	5	.05(b)
9. age × sex × marital status	35.15	59	.005(b)
10. age × district	12.71	39	.005(b)
11. sex × district	1.19	7	.01(b)
12. age × sex × district	22.82	79	.005(b)
13. marital status × district	3.43	7	.25(c)
14. age × marital status × district	23.61	23	.75
15. sex × marital status × district	10.09	15	.75
16. age × sex × marital status × district	46.32	47	.25
17. age × degree of urbanization	8.17	11	.50(d)
18. sex × degree of urbanization	2.81	5	.50
19. age × sex × degree of urbanization	11.79	23	.05(b)

Notes:
(a) Number of cells minus 1.
(b) Distributions unlikely to have been reached by chance, to the degree indicated, e.g. the 'fit' is too good.
(c) For tables 13–16; age on 3 levels: 21–34, 35–44, 45–64.
(d) For tables 17–19: age on 4 levels: 17–24, 25–39, 40–54, 55–69.

Table App. 2.2. *The 'strategic elite' of Members of Parliament*

PvdA	(Labor Party)	28 (72%)(a)
KVP	(Catholic People's Party)	14 (37%)
VVD	(People's Party for Freedom and Democracy) ('classical' liberals)	9 (56%)
ARP	(Anti-Revolutionary Party; protestant-Calvinist)	6 (46%)
CHU	(Christian-Historical Union) (protestant)	5 (50%)
D66	(Democrats 1966) ('modern' liberals)	6 (56%)
DS70	(Democratic Socialists 1970) (right-wing socialists, split off from the Labor Party in 1970)	5 (63%)
Smaller parties from the (extreme) left and right		8
	Total	81

Note:
(a) Percentage of the total number of M.P.'s for the various parties (Fall, 1971) in the Second Chamber of Parliament.

APPENDIX 3:
ITEMS AND ATTITUDE SCALES IN THE PROGRESSIVE—
CONSERVATIVE DOMAIN
with indications of the scaling items and scale-characteristics.

Introduction
The sets of items submitted to scaling-procedures (either directly or indirectly;
see Chapter 5) are ordered from politico-economic (sets 1-10) through political
non-economic (sets 11-15) and semi-political (sets 16A, 17-19), to almost purely
social and religious sets (sets 20-30).
   Figures in brackets only refer to where the scale is placed in Analysis-Deck
number 1. Items incorporated from previous studies (mostly through secondary
analysis) have been indicated by 2 *letters*, which refer to the following studies
(see Table 5.1 for more details):

PP = Protestantism and progressiveness   RN = Religion in the Netherlands
AD = Aid to developing countries   HS = Homosexuality
MF = Marriage and the family   Y2 = The Year 2000
PN = Politics in the Netherlands   SN = Sex in the Netherlands

In most cases, Table 5.2 will give a clear reference to the scale(s) that were constructed in the secondary analyses of these studies; from these scales, items have
been incorporated into the new study.
   The 3-digit item-numbers refer to the place of the item in the questionnaire.
Scaling items are numbered from 1 to n.
   The figures in brackets which are sometimes placed to the right of the figures
indicating the percentages counted 'high' in Mokken-scale construction, indicate
the percentage in the middle category which is sometimes also counted high. The
rationale behind this procedure is given in Chapter 5. The middle category
always includes the non-response.

1.(25)   Attitude to equality of income, property, status   % high
1.PP 551 Workers must still struggle for an equal social position   84(19)
2.PP 550 Differences in class should be smaller than is the case at
          present   65
3.PP 217 Do you want the differences between higher and lower in-
          comes to increase, decrease or remain as it is? (If increase
          or decrease) Do you want them to become much larger
          (resp. smaller) or just a bit?   64
4.PP 218 There are individuals who own a lot and others who own
          very little. Do you want these differences in the ownership
          of property to become larger, to become smaller or to
          remain as it is? (If larger or smaller) Do you want it to
          become much larger (resp. smaller) or just a bit?   52
Response categories items 1 and 2:
          strongly agree, agree, neither agree nor disagree, disagree,
          strongly disagree
Scale characteristics:
Medium Mokken-scale; 4 items; H = .49; Rep = .94; 1 = .48
High = egalitarian attitude
Distribution of scale scores: 0 = 7%; 1 = 15%; 2 = 20%; 3 = 24%; 4 = 35%
M = 2.65; S = 1.28

2.(27)   *Government interference to bring about equality*   *% high*
1.   414 Are you in favor or against the government taking *radical* measures to reduce the differences in income levels?   78(22)
2.   415 Are you in favor of or against the government taking *radical* measures to reduce the differences in ownership of property?   43
        413 Are you in favor of or against the government taking *radical* measures so that everybody will really get equal opportunities of being successful in society?
Response categories:
        strongly in favor, in favor, neither for nor against, against, strongly against.
Scale-characteristics:
Strong 2-item Mokken-scale; H = .79
High = positive attitude to government interference to bring about equality
Distribution of scale scores: 0 = 21%; 1 = 39%; 2 = 41%
M = 1.20; S = .76

3.(64)   *Attitude to social welfare laws*   *% high*
Tell me whether the social security provisions mentioned are sufficient or insufficient at the moment:
1.PN 212 Old age pensions   59
2.PN 215 Supplementary benefits (for widows, orphans)   46
3.PN 213 Supplementary benefits   30
4.PN 214 Unemployment benefits   19
   PN 216 National health service
Scale-characteristics:
Medium Mokken-scale; 4 items; H = .47; Rep = .93; I = .46
High = social welfare laws are insufficient
Distribution of scale scores: 0 = 27%; 1 = 24%; 2 = 25%; 3 = 16%; 4 = 8%
M = 1.55; S = 1.26

4.(26)   *Equality of opportunity, especially regarding working class children*
1.   552 Working class children still do not often go to secondary schools and universities because they happen to be less intelligent than children from other social backgrounds
2.   553 Working class children still do not often go to secondary schools and universities because they are not encouraged by their parents
3.   554 Working class children still do not often go to secondary schools and universities because they have too few opportunities to develop their intelligence.
4.   555 Working class children still do not often go to secondary schools and universities because they do not want to make as much of an effort as children from other social backgrounds
5.   563 These days everyone in society achieves what he deserves.

Response categories:
>strongly agree, agree, neither agree nor disagree, disagree, strongly disagree

Scale-characteristics:
Cluster-scale of product-moment correlation-coefficients (p < .000001) (items no. 552, 555, 563)
High = perception of unequal chances
Distribution of scale scores: 0 = 1%; 1 = 5%; 2 = 4%; 3 = 9%; 4 = 11%;
5 = 15%; 6 = 14%; 7 = 18%; 8 = 12%; 9 = 13%
M = 5.72; S = 2.28

5.(31)   Government aid to education   *% high*
1.   420 The government should make many more grants available to children of less well-to-do families.   85
2.   426 The government should make education entirely cost-free up till the age of 18.   78
3.   419 The government should make sufficient provisions for all those children who have no suitable place at home for doing their homework.   78
4.   440 The government should introduce compulsory education up to the age of 18.   44
      726 Lately too much money has been spent on efforts to give a better education to people who are not really capable enough.

Response categories:
>strongly agree, agree, neither agree nor disagree, disagree, strongly disagree

Scale-characteristics:
Weak Mokken-scale; 4 items; H = .35; Rep = .93; I = .31
High = in favor of government aid
Distribution of scale scores: 0 = 4%; 1 = 7%; 2 = 19%; 3 = 37%; 4 = 32%
M = 2.85; S = 1.09

6.(66)   Government income policy   *% high*
1.   423 The government should firmly control prices after wage increases   86
2.   424 The government should allow for the minimum income to rise more sharply than other income-levels   72
3.   421 The government should oblige employees to share in the profits to the same degree that shareholders do.   58

Response categories:
>strongly agree, agree, neither agree nor disagree, disagree, strongly disagree

Scale-characteristics:
Medium Mokken-scale; H = .46
High = in favor of government egalitarian income policy
Distribution of scale scores: 0 = 7%; 1 = 17%; 2 = 29%; 3 = 47%
M = 2.15; S = .95

7.		Government tax policy	
7A.(67)		*Government tax policy on higher incomes*	*% high*
1.	429	Taxes on higher incomes	49
2.	437	Surtax	42
3.	430	Death duties	16

7B.(68)		*Government tax policy on lower incomes*	*% high*
1.	436	Indirect taxes on daily necessities	78
2.	433	Taxes on lower incomes	76
3.	434	Indirect taxes on luxuries	38
	435	Taxes on middle-income levels	

Response categories: (The government should)

> sharply increase, moderately increase, leave as they are, moderately reduce, sharply reduce

Scale characteristics:

7A: Tax policy on higher incomes:

Strong Mokken-scale; 3-item scale; H = .59

High = increase taxes

Distribution of scale scores: 0 = 40%; 1 = 25%; 2 = 25%; 3 = 11%

M = 1.07; S = 1.04

7B: Tax policy on lower incomes:

Medium Mokken-scale; 3-item scale; H = .43

High = diminish taxes

Distribution of scale scores: 0 = 10%; 1 = 18%; 2 = 41%; 3 = 31%

M = 1.92; S = .94

8.(35)		*Government direct economic interference*	*% high*
1.	442	The government should control mergers in trade and industry	71
2.	425	The government should itself exploit natural resources like oil and natural gas	61
3.	427	The government should nationalize large industries and firms	27
	439	The government should make land speculation impossible*	

Response categories:

> strongly agree, agree, neither agree nor disagree, disagree, strongly disagree

Scale characteristics:

Medium Mokken-scale; 3 items; H = .41

High = in favor of government interference

Distribution of scale scores: 0 = 16%; 1 = 29%; 2 = 37%; 3 = 19%

M = 1.59; S = .97

* This item has been invalidated due to a printing-error in the questionnaire: 'possible' had been printed instead of 'impossible'

9.(69)   *Government non-direct economic welfare policy*   *% high*

1.*   422   The government should spend far more money on building
            good but cheap houses   96(7)

2.   444   The government should build more cheap day-nurseries
            where working mothers can leave their children for the day   62

3.   441   The government should extend grants to artists   36

      438   The government should make sex instruction obligatory in
            primary schools

Response categories:
            strongly agree, agree, neither agree nor disagree, disagree,
            strongly disagree

Scale characteristics:
Medium Mokken-scale; 3 items; H = .40
High = in favor of government welfare policy
Distribution of scale scores: 0 = 2%; 1 = 28%; 2 = 43%; 3 = 27%
M = 1.94; S = .80

10.(38)   *Militant trade union policy*   *% high*

1.   548   Trade unions should pursue a more vigorous policy if
            they really want to promote the interests of employees and
            laborers   83(30)

2.   549   Trade Unions should advise their members to vote for
            certain political parties which best promote the interests of
            laborers and employees   39

Response categories:
            strongly agree, agree, neither agree nor disagree, disagree,
            strongly disagree

Scale characteristics:
Strong Mokken-scale; 2-items; H = .54
High = militant trade-union policy
Distribution of scale scores: 0 = 14%; 1 = 52%; 2 = 34%
M = 1.20; S = .66

11.(62)   *Democratic attitudes*

1.   547   Do you think that the citizen's say in the government of
            towns and provinces should: 76

2.PP   219   Do you want workers participation in the management of
            firms to increase, to remain as it is or to decrease?   64

3.   545   Do you think that the student's say in the management of
            the university should: 56

4.   546   Do you think that the say of pupils in secondary schools
            and training colleges should: 55

5.   417   Are you in favor of or opposed to the age of franchise
            being lowered to 18?   54

6.   418   idem, and to 17   11

      416   Are you in favor of or opposed to a mayor being directly
            elected by the citizens of a municipality?

* This item has been mistakenly included: it does not discriminate sufficiently

Response categories: items 1, 3, 4
> greatly increase, moderately increase, stay as it is, be moderately lessened, greatly lessened

Response categories: item 2
> much more, a bit more, remain as it is, a bit less, much less

Response categories: items 5, 6 + 416
> strongly in favor of, in favor of, neither for nor against, against, strongly against

Scale characteristics:
Medium Mokken-scale; 6-items; H = .44; Rep = .92; I = .49
High = democratic attitude
Distribution of scale scores: 0 = 8%; 1 = 15%; 2 = 15%; 3 = 13%; 4 = 20%;
> 5 = 22%; 6 = 7%

M = 3.17; S = 1.77

12.(20)   *Political freedom of expression*

Introduction to the set of items:
On each of the cards in front of you, you will find something mentioned about your country. Looking at each of these cards in turn, would you please tell me whether you think everybody should be free to do what has been mentioned, or whether this freedom should be limited in one way or another. Should you be free:

			% high
1.	154	to say whatever you like in public	82(3)
2.PN	153	To write whatever you like in public	77(3)
3.PN	148	To demonstrate for or against something	79(4)
4.PN	149	To criticize openly members of the Royal Family	54
5.PN	151	To be a conscientious objector	49
6.	152	To occupy buildings (e.g. schools, universities) in order to enforce justified demands	34(5)
PN	150	To strike for pay rises	

Response categories:
> Yes, no

Scale characteristics:
Medium Mokken-scale; 6-items; H = .41; Rep = 90; I = 36
High = positive attitude to freedom of expression
Distribution of scale scores: 0 = 4%; 1 = 8%; 2 = 12%; 3 = 19%; 4 = 20%;
> 5 = 19%; 6 = 17%

M = 3.68; S = 1.69

13.(63)   *Aid to developing countries*   % high

1.AD 209 Which of the following statements do you agree with most?
> a. More developed countries like the Netherlands are perfectly able to contribute regular financial aid to developing countries, even if their own prosperity were not to increase for a while   43
>
> b. More developed countries like the Netherlands are only able to contribute regular financial aid to developing countries during a time of prosperity

c. More developed countries like the Netherlands are only able to contribute financial aid to developing countries now and again.

2.   432 The government should: the aid to developing countries   39

3.PN 210 If everybody would give up 1% of his income for aid to developing countries, would you think that too much, too little or just about right? (If too much or too little) Do you think this far too much/little or a bit too much/little?   14

Response categories:

sharply increase, moderately increase, leave the situation as it is, moderately reduce, sharply reduce

Scale characteristics:

Strong Mokken-scale; 3 items; H = .54

High = in favor of (increasing) aid to developing countries

Distribution of scale scores: 0 = 43%; 1 = 26%; 2 = 21%; 3 = 10%

M = .97; S = 1.01

14.(23)   Internationalism   *% high*

1.PN 211 Do you think that a European government that is superior to our own government should be realized in the future, or do you think that the Netherlands should remain as independent as possible   37

2.   678 Instilling patriotism in pupils is an important educational task   35

3.   711 When striving for international cooperation, we should at the same time guard against the loss of the typically Dutch ways of life   27

4.   710 Every Dutchman should show the necessary respect towards our national symbols such as the flag and the national anthem   17

5.   677 Generally speaking, the Netherlands is better than most other countries   15

       679 Sometimes nationalist feelings are preserved by the very existence of the Royal Family; this can hinder international cooperation

       709 The Netherlands should participate as much as possible in the running of international organizations, even if Dutch interests may sometimes suffer

Response categories: item 1

European government, the Netherlands should remain independent

Response categories: items 2, 5 + 679, 709

completely agree, agree in general, neither agree nor disagree, disagree, completely disagree

Scale characteristics:

Medium Mokken-scale; 5-items; H = .42; Rep = .93; I = .45

High = internationalism

Distribution of scale scores: 0 = 40%; 1 = 24%; 2 = 15%; 3 = 11%; 4 = 8%;
                                                          5 = 3%

M = 1.51; S = 1.42

15.(70) *Political tolerance*   *% high*
1.   619   Do you think that communists should have equal rights?   53
2.   620   Do you think that fascists and national socialists should
            have equal rights?   25
Response categories:
       Exactly the same rights, almost the same rights, certain
       rights but not all
Scale characteristics:
Strong Mokken-scale; 2-items; $H = .94$
High = tolerant (same rights)
Distribution of scale scores: $0 = 46\%$; $1 = 30\%$; $2 = 24\%$
$M = .78$; $S = .81$

16.(16) *Miscellaneous*   *% high*
1.   412   Do you think that the government should have at its dis-
            posal more or less money to make all sorts of public pro-
            visions possible?
2.   431   The government should: Military expenditure
3.PP   564   There is too much state interference
4.   565   It is fair to introduce a compulsory social service for girls
            (e.g. as a nurse)
5.   567   The police should take more severe measures when there
            are disturbances of the peace
6.*   568   It might be a good thing to reintroduce the death penalty
            for certain crimes   51
Response categories: item 1
       a lot more, a little bit more, leave as it is, a bit less, a lot
       less
Response categories: item 2
       sharply increase, moderately increase, leave it as it is,
       moderately reduce, sharply reduce
Response categories: items 3, 4, 5, 6
       strongly agree, agree, neither agree nor disagree, disagree,
       strongly disagree

16A.(16) *Tolerance towards criminals*   *% high*
1.   665   Criminals should not be punished in the first instance but
            one should attempt to change their ways   83(11)
2.   712   Sexual criminals should not be punished in the first
            instance, but one should attempt to cure them   68(11)
3.   568   It might be a good thing to reintroduce the death penalty
            for certain crimes   51
Note: 568 has been combined into a separate scale with 2 items from
           the set of authoritarianism-items on tolerance towards
           criminals (see Appendix 6)

* Item has been included in an other scale (see set 16A)

Response categories:
>strongly agree, agree, neither agree nor disagree, disagree, strongly disagree

Scale characteristics:
Weak Mokken-scale; 3-items; H = .37
High = tolerant
Distribution of scale scores: 0 = 7%; 1 = 15%; 2 = 37%; 3 = 41%
M = 2.12; S = .90

17.(15)   Tolerance regarding controversial TV programs   % high
1.   610   It is not right to ban certain TV programs, even if a certain group of people are offended by them   44
2.   569   TV programs which are morally offensive should be banned   35

Response categories:
>strongly agree, agree, neither agree nor disagree, disagree, strongly disagree

Scale characteristics:
Weak Mokken-scale; 2-items; H = .33
High = tolerant
Distribution of scale scores: 0 = 23%; 1 = 36%; 2 = 42%
M = 1.19; S = .78

18.(13)   Moral libertarianism   % high
1.   557   Games of chance, like roulette, should continue to be forbidden in the Netherlands   62(24)
2.   556   Film-censorship should be abolished   45
3.SN   164   In our country the publishing of books and magazines in which sexual acts are described with the intent to excite (pornography) is not permitted. In a country like Denmark this is allowed. What do you think is better, the situation in our country or that in Denmark?   44
4.   558   Smoking marihuana and hashish should be severely punished   21

Response categories: items 1, 2, 4
>strongly agree, agree, neither agree nor disagree, disagree, strongly disagree

Scale characteristics:
Weak Mokken-scale; 4-items; H = .36; Rep = .91; I = .35
High = libertarian
Distribution of scale scores: 0 = 20%; 1 = 26%; 2 = 26%; 3 = 19%; 4 = 9%
M = 1.73; S = 1.24

19.(12)   Family traditionalism   % high
1.   162   And when there are still children at home that would have to be sent to a day-nursery? (for introduction: see item 161 below)   80
2.   561   If a woman so wishes, it should be possible for her to have an abortion   59(15)
3.MF   160   A married couple decides on principle not to have chil-

dren although there are no medical objections. Can you approve of such a point of view or do you think it unacceptable? 42(14)

4.   562   To check the population expansion, birth-control should be strongly advocated 38(22)

5.RN 144   Suppose a physician is able to put a patient out of his misery, at his own request, by giving him an injection. What do you think he should do? 23

6.SN 173   Are there circumstances in which abortion should be allowed? 18

7.MF 163   When husband and wife don't get on well together and they have children, do you think that a divorce is totally unacceptable, or do you have objections but feel that it is understandable in certain cases; or do you feel it is better for husband and wife to get a divorce? 13

8.MF 159   Today, birth-control is a familiar topic. Do you think that purposeful birth-control is always unacceptable, do you object but feel that it is understandable in certain cases, or do you have no serious objections to it? 3*

MF 161   Do you or don't you object to a woman with children who go to school, having a job in addition to her household duties, or is this to be recommended?

560   Divorce should be possible when one of the partners wants it, even if there are children

Response categories: items 2, 4 and 560
  strongly agree, agree, neither agree nor disagree, disagree, strongly disagree
Response categories: item 5
  give it, depends, should not give it
Response categories: item 6
  yes, no
Scale characteristics:
Weak Mokken-scale; 8-items; H = .39; Rep = .92; I = .34
High = traditional
Distribution of scale scores: 0 = 8%; 1 = 19%; 2 = 22%; 3 = 17%; 4 = 15%; 5 = 10%; 6 = 6%; 7 = 2%; 8 = 1%
M = 2.78; S = 1.79

20.(14)   *Tolerance regarding daughter's choice of husband* % high
1.MF 177   Suppose you had a daughter who wanted to marry a man from another social class (another social background). Would you have no objections, would you accept it, albeit reluctantly, or would you oppose it? 63(20)

2.MF 178   And if she wanted to get married to somebody of another race? 42

Scale characteristics:
Medium Mokken-scale; 2-items; H = .40

* Item has been incorrectly dichotomized. It no longer discriminates sufficiently

High = tolerant
Distribution of scale scores: 0 = 28%; 1 = 39%; 2 = 33%

21.(10)   Authoritarian parent-child relationship   *% high*
1.   572 It is mostly for the good of teenagers that they obey their
            parents   84(23)
2.   574 It goes without saying that children show regard and
            respect for their parents   73
3.   573 The most important thing children should learn is total
            obedience to their parents' wishes   65(19)
4.MF   156 Are you for or against children addressing their parents as
            'jij' (= you instead of thou)   31
5.MF   155 Do you think that the parents of, say, a 20-year-old girl,
            should tell her at what time she has to be back home at
            night, or do you think it better that they leave it to the
            daughter's discretion?   17
  MF   157 Do you think that 18-year old boys and girls should be
            allowed to read anything they like or do you think that
            some books might be unfit?
       158 Do you think it is better for parents to be strict with their
            children and tell them exactly which rules they have to
            stick or do you think it is better to leave the children as
            free as possible?
       575 Parents cannot demand things of their children, whatever
            their age, without explaining why
       559 Young people of 18 should be able to get married without
            their parents' consent
Response categories: items 1, 2, 3, 575, 559
            strongly agree, agree, neither agree nor disagree, disagree,
            strongly disagree
Response categories: item 4
            for, not important, against
Response categories: item 5
            leave it to the daughter, a mutual decision, parents should
            decide
Response categories: item 157
            allowed to read everything, some books are unfit
Response categories: item 158
            parents strict, it depends, leave children free
Scale characteristics:
Medium Mokken-scale; 5-items; H = .41; Rep = .93; I = .36
High = authoritarian
Distribution of scale scores: 0 = 6%; 1 = 14%; 2 = 20%; 3 = 31% 4 = 23%;
                              5 = 6%
M = 2.69; S = 1.29

22.(11)   Conventional male-female roles   *% high*
1.   611 A woman is more capable of bringing up small children
            than a man is   76

2. 613 It is not as important for a girl to get a good schooling
    as it is for a boy   29
3. 614 After all, boys can be educated more freely than girls   28
4. 612 In a firm it is unnatural when women hold a position of
    authority over men   22
    576 Husband and wife should decide together, but when it
    comes to the point, a wife should acquiesce to her hus-
    band's decisions
    615 It is quite acceptable for a girl to tell the boy first that
    she is in love with him

Response categories:
     strongly agree, agree, neither agree nor disagree, disagree,
     strongly disagree

Scale characteristics:
Weak Mokken-scale; 4-items; H = .38; Rep = .93; I = .33
High = conventional
Distribution of scale scores: 0 = 17%; 1 = 38%; 2 = 25%; 3 = 13%; 4 = 8%
M = 1.56; S = 1.14

23.(17)   *Tolerance towards homosexuals*   *% high*
1.HS 168 Homosexuals should be eradicated from society   90(7)
2.SN 174 Do you think that homosexuals should be left as free as
    possible to live their own life, or do you feel that this
    should be opposed as much as possible   76(8)
3.HS 167 Homosexuals should be firmly dealt with   65
4.   443 The government should legalize the Dutch Society for
    Homosexuals (COC)   30

Response categories: items 1, 3
     completely agree, agree in general, neither agree nor dis-
     agree, disagree, completely disagree
Response categories: item 4
     strongly agree, agree, neither agree nor disagree, disagree,
     strongly disagree

Scale characteristics:
Strong Mokken-scale; 4-items; H = .72; Rep = .98; I = .70
High = tolerant
Distribution of scale scores: 0 = 6%; 1 = 13%; 2 = 19%; 3 = 35%; 4 = 27%
M = 2.63; S = 1.18

24.(18)   *Premarital sexual permissiveness*   *% high*
1.SN 170 I think that a girl can have full sexual intercourse with a
    boy even if she doesn't care for him   9*
2.SN 169 I think that a girl can have full sexual intercourse with a
    boy if she cares for him   51(6)
3.SN 166 I think that a girl can pet heavily with a boy if she cares
    for him   55
4.MF 171 A girl should remain a virgin until she gets married   60

* Item does hardly discriminate sufficiently

5.SN 165 I think that a girl can pet heavily with a boy if she is in
love with him   64(6)
6.MF 175 Is sexual intercourse between two people who want to get
married totally unacceptable, do you have objections but
understand it in certain circumstances, or do you have no
serious objections?   90(31)
Response categories:
completely agree, agree in general, disagree but not
wholeheartedly, completely disagree
Scale characteristics:
Strong Mokken-scale; 6-items; H = .53; Rep = .92; I = .43
High = permissive
Distribution of scale scores: 0 = 6%; 1 = 12%; 2 = 15%; 3 = 17%; 4 = 20%;
5 = 22%; 6 = 7%

25.(19)   *Extramarital sexual permissiveness*   % high
1.MF 172 One or two love affairs can do no harm to a good marriage
2.MF 176 Suppose a married man has a love affair with another
woman, do you think that this is totally unacceptable or
is it justifiable in certain cases
Response categories:
completely agree, agree in general, disagree but not
wholeheartedly, completely disagree
Scale characteristics:
Correlation-coefficient (product-moment) = .32
High = permissive
Distribution of scale scores: 0 = 28%; 1 = 6%; 2 = 34%; 3 = 5%; 4 = 27%
M = 1.98; S = 1.51

26.(52)   *Religious orthodoxy*
Note: People who do not consider themselves as members of a certain church
have been left out (N = 730) of all religious attitude scales; N' = 1197

		% high
1.RN 232	Do you think that praying has some meaning?	82
2.RN 225	Do you believe in an eternal life?	67
3.RN 231	Do you regard the Bible as the word of God?	64
4.RN 226	Do you believe in heaven?	57
5.RN 230	Did Adam and Eve exist?	47
6.RN 229	Do you believe in the devil?	33
7.RN 228	Do you believe in hell?	31
8.RN 227	Do you believe in purgatory?	14

Response categories: items 1, 5
yes, perhaps, no
Response categories: items 4, 6–8
yes, no, am not sure ('no' and 'not sure' on item 2 have
been extended by implication, to similar responses to these
items)

Response categories: 3
      yes, partly, no
Response categories: 2
      yes, no, am not sure (if yes, ask 226-229, if no, not sure, to 230)
Scale characteristics:
Strong Mokken-scale; 8-items; H = .68; Rep = .94; I = .62
High = orthodox
Distribution of scale scores: 0 = 7%; 1 = 7%; 2 = 9%; 3 = 7%; 4 = 7%;
                        5 = 6%; 6 = 5%; 7 = 11%; 8 = 4%
                        (9 = non-religious: 38%)

		% high
27.(54)	*Politico-religious conservatism*	
1.PP 238	Sin makes a better society impossible	61(14)
2.PP 239	Man should let God decide his destiny	53(5)
3.PP 237	The existing society is according to the will of God	28
4.PP 236	Poverty and injustice should not distress us too much, for everything will be alright in the life hereafter	19

Response categories:
      completely agree, agree in general, neither agree nor disagree, disagree but not wholeheartedly, completely disagree
Scale characteristics:
Weak Mokken-scale; 4-items; H = .38; Rep = .93; I = .39
High = conservative
Distribution of scale scores: 0 = 13%; 1 = 16%; 2 = 19%; 3 = 11%; 4 = 4%
                        (9 = non-religious: 38%)

		% high
28.(53)	*Conformism to church rules*	
1.RN 240	Do you think that the rules of the church or of the religious community you belong to are too strict, are not strict enough, or are they just as they should be?	82(74)
2.RN 241	Are you of the opinion that you have to abide by all the rules of the church or religious community that you are a member of?	27
3.RN 244	Can a person be a believer without ever going to church?	8*

Response categories: item 2
      yes, it depends, no
Response categories: item 3
      yes, no
Scale characteristics:
Strong Mokken-scale; 3-items; H = .64
High = conformistic
Distribution of scale scores: 0 = 11%; 1 = 33%; 2 = 14%; 3 = 4%; (9 = non-religious: 38%)

---

* Item does not discriminate sufficiently

29.*(56)*   *Religious tolerance*   *% high*
1.MF 179 Suppose you had a daughter who wanted to marry some-
          one of another religion, would you have no objections,
          would you accept it albeit reluctantly, or would you oppose
          it?   78(10)
2.RN 242 Suppose you had a son or a daughter who chose a religion
          that was very different to yours, would you have no objec-
          tions, would you accept it albeit reluctantly, or would you
          oppose it?   40
3.RN 243 And if he or she decided to become an atheist, what then
          would be your point of view?   27

Scale characteristics:
Strong Mokken-scale; 3-items; H = .78
High = tolerant
Distribution of scale scores: 0 = 16%; 1 = 22%; 2 = 11%; 3 = 14% (9 = non-
          religious: 38%)

30.*(55)*   *Attitude to 'pillarization' ('confessionalism')*   *% high*
1.RN 245 Suppose you have a child of primary school age, what
          kind of school would you choose, a state school, a de-
          nominational school, or doesn't it make much difference?   84(26)
2.   Five different kinds of clubs/organizations are listed.
          Looking at each in turn, would you please tell me whether
          they should be based on religious principles or not?
          (items 2, 3, 5-7)
  RN 250 a youth club?   47(2)
3.RN 247 a broadcasting company?   32
4.RN 246 Some people think that religion and politics should be
          segregated, others do not. What is your opinion?
5.   251 a political party?   30
6.RN 249 a trade union?   29(3)
7.RN 248 a sports club?   15(2)
Response categories: 4
          segregated, depends, not segregated
Response categories: 2, 3, 5-7
          should be based on religious principles, not necessarily
          based on religious principles
Scales characteristics:
Strong Mokken-scale; 7-items; H = .58; Rep = .94; I = .59
High = positive attitude to 'pillarization'
Distribution of scale scores: 0 = 6%; 1 = 19%; 2 = 11%; 3 = 7%; 4 = 5%;
          5 = 5%; 6 = 5%; 7 = 4% (9 = non-religious: 38%)

31.*(28)*   *Attitude to change; general and brought about by govern-*
          ment interference   *% high*
1.PP 410 Do you want the existing society in our country on the
          whole to change rapidly, to change fairly rapidly, to
          change slowly or not to change at all?   48*

* rapidly + fairly rapidly

2.PP 409 Do you want the existing society in our country on the whole to remain as it is, to change a little or to change a great deal? 35†

3.PP 411 Do you think that the government should bring about much, little, or no change in Dutch society?

Scale characteristics:
Strong Mokken-scale; 3-items; H = .55‡
High = in favor of change
Distribution of scale scores: 0 = 5%; 1 = 40%; 2 = 28%; 3 = 26%

APPENDIX 4:
MEASUREMENT OF THE ABSTRACT-IDEOLOGICAL DIMENSIONS:

1. The CONSERVATISM-scale (cf. Table 6.1. and Table 5.1.)

(1) 3.2.1.1.	The customs and traditions of society are of indispensable value to mankind	C
	The customs and traditions of society often restrict people's freedom	P
(2) 3.2.1.2.	The maintenance of law and order is essential to the sound development of society	C
	It is essential to the sound development of society that all kinds of groups disturb law and order now and again, to demand reform	P
(3) 3.3.	When a social institution has been in existence over a long period of time, it is probably of value to mankind	C
	When a social institution has existed for a long time, it probably contains ideas that are for the greater part out of date	P
(4) 3.3.1.	By living according to the customs and traditions of society, man is best able to fully develop himself	C
	Man is best able to fully develop himself when he does not adjust to the customs and traditions of society	P
(5) 3.5. (4.2.)	The organization of society is far too complex to be improved upon by man and his ideas	C
	Society can be improved through ideas	P
(6) 3.5.1.	The origin of most social abuse like war and poverty mainly lies in human nature	C
	The origin of most social abuse like war and poverty mainly lies in the organization of society	P
(7) 4.3.1.	Social change should only be introduced when this has proven to be necessary	C
	Society should be changed as much as possible in order to realize certain ideals	P

† a great deal
‡ the first 2 items form a separate scale, of equal strength

(8) 4.3.6.   Social change should above all aim at restoring the past heritage some of which has got lost in modern times   C

Social change should above all aim at eradicating antiquated ideas that are still in existence today   P

(9) 4.3.7.   When implementing social change, one should above all be guided by the lessons of history   C

When implementing social change one should exclusively be guided by the goals set   P

(10) 6.1.2.   It is necessary that a small group of able men exercise authority in order to realize a sound society   C

In a sound society everybody must be able to have a say in matters that directly or indirectly concern him   P

(11) 6.4.2.   Complete democracy is impossible because people have such varying abilities   C

The fact that people have varying abilities does not mean that complete democracy would not be possible   P

(12) 7.4.2.   All social groups can live together in harmony without having to change social relations   C

If all social groups were to live in harmony together, the existing social relations would have to be drastically altered   P

(13) 9.3.2.   From an economic point of view, the existing social relations are inevitable   C

The existing social relations are created by an economic policy, which can be changed   P

Notes:

The 2 to 4 digit numbers indicate the number of the model-element from which the item has been derived (see Table 5.1.). The (C)onservative pole is always presented first (P = progressive opposite point of view).

All missing values (no opinion, no response) have been recoded to the middle-position: (dis)agree to the same extent with both statements. The total-sumscores (ranging from 0-78) have been recoded as follows: 0-7 = 0, 8-15 = 1, 16-23 = 2, 24-31 = 3, 32-39 = 4, 40-46 = 5, 47-54 = 6, 55-62 = 7, 63-70 = 8, 71-78 = 9. (High = conservative).

Percentages: 0 = 2%; 1 = 5%; 2 = 8%; 3 = 16%; 4 = 31%; 5 = 20%; 6 = 12%; 7 = 4%; 8 = 2%; 9 = 0%.

Scale characteristics: M = 4.14; S = 1.61.

In many cases, the scale has been trichotomized according to: 0-3 = 0, 4-5 = 1, 6-9 = 2 so that 51% is in the neutral category, 31% is 'progressive' and 18% is 'conservative'.

2. The SOCIALISM-scale

(1) 1.5.   The existing social differences between people are mainly caused by the unequal opportunities they get to develop themselves   P

The existing social differences between people are mainly caused by differences in inherited abilities   C

(2) 4.3.2.3.   A better society can only be realized through a radical

	change of the present social structure	P
	A better society is best realized by introducing gradual reform within present day society	C
(3) 6.1.1.	The freedom of many people is limited by existing authority	P
6.1.2.		
6.3.	The existing authority is best suited to the welfare of all	C
(4) 7.4.1.	The existence of social classes is unjust	P
	The existence of social classes is necessary for the welfare of all	C
(5) 7.4.2.	The most important social antithesis is still that between the social classes	P
	In present-day society, social classes no longer form an important social antithesis	C
(6) 9.3.3.	In a society based on private enterprise, insufficient attention is usually paid to the necessary public services	P
	In a society based on private enterprise, the welfare of all is best guaranteed	C

Notes: (See the note on the Conservatism-scale)
The total sumscores have been recoded as follows: 0-3 = 0, 4-7 = 1, 8-11 = 2, 12-14 = 3, 15-17 = 4, 18-20 = 5, 21-24 = 6, 25-28 = 7, 29-32 = 8, 33-36 = 9 (High = socialistic).
Percentages: 0 = 0%, 1 = 2%, 2 = 6%, 3 = 12%, 4 = 17%, 5 = 25%, 6 = 19%, 7 = 10%, 8 = 5%, 9 = 3%.
Scale characteristics: M = 4.96; S = 1.78.
In many cases the scale has been trichotomized with 0-3 = 0, 4-5 = 1 and 6-9 = 2, so that 42% is neutral, 20% is anti-socialist and 38% is socialist.

3. The LIBERALISM-scale

(1) 9.2.3.	A great deal of government interference can only lead to bureaucracy and economic stagnation	C
	A great deal of government interference leads to planning and therefore to a more efficient economy	P
(2) 9.3.3.	Private enterprise is essential to economic growth	C
	Economic growth can only be realized when the government restricts private enterprise	P
(3) 9.3.4.	If freedom of enterprise is restricted, other freedoms will also disappear	C
	Restricting freedom of enterprise does not endanger the loss of other freedoms	P
(4) 9.4.3.1.	Government care from the cradle to the grave leads to a slackened way of life	C
	Government care provides many with the feeling of security necessary to develop their potential	P

Notes:
See the note for the Conservatism-scale; note also that the classical liberal position is considered 'conservative' here.
The total sumscores from 0-24 have been recoded as follows: 0-2 = 0: 3-5 = 1,

6-7 = 2, 8-9 = 3, 10-11 = 4, 12-13 = 5, 14-15 = 6, 16-28 = 7, 19-21 = 8, 22-24 = 9 (High = liberal).
Percentages: 0 = 2%, 1 = 4%, 2 = 5%, 3 = 9%, 4 = 12%, 5 = 24%, 6 = 14%, 7 = 15%, 9 = 6%.
Scale characteristics: M = 5.27; S = 2.10
In many cases, the scale has been recoded to 4 levels as follows: 0-3 = 0, 4-5 = 1, 6-7 = 2, 8-9 = 3, so that 20% is strongly anti-liberal, 36% is moderately anti-liberal, 29% is moderately liberal and 16% is strongly liberal.

APPENDIX 5:
MEASUREMENT OF THE IDEOLOGICAL DIMENSIONS

1. The LIBERTARIANISM-TRADITIONALISM scale (LITR-dimension)

Introduction
The scale has been constructed from 15 subscales, including a total of 73 items, on the basis of double-weighed sum-scores. The first weighing-factor (a) was assigned on the basis of *factor-loading* (see Table 6.9.: the 'best solution': 2-factor structure). The second weighing factor was assigned on the basis of the *standard-deviation* of the sub-scale scores. Multiplication of both factors and rounding off to the nearest integer gives the total weighing-factor. The weights were given as follows:

Factor-loading	Weighing-factor 1	Standard deviation	Weighing-factor 2
.35-.44	1	.65-1.049	1.0
.45-.54	2	1.05-1.449	.75
.55-.64	3	1.50-1.85	.50
.65-.74	4		

Results

no. pos. (b) (c)	scale label (h)	no. items	factlo	WF 1	stdev	WF 2	WFTOT	Range (d)
1. 69	Governm. (non-directly econ.) welfare policy	3	-.36	1	.80	1.0	1	3-0
2. 62	Democratic attitudes	6	-.50	2	1.77	.50	1	6-0
3. 20	Political freedom of expression	6	-.60	3	1.69	.50	2	12-0(e)
4. 63	Aid to devel. countries	3	-.36	1	1.01	1.0	1	3-0
5. 23	Internationalism	5	-.70	4	1.42	.75	3	15-0
6. 70	Political tolerance	2	-.36	1	.81	1.0	1	2-0
7. 15	Tolerance controv TV pr.	2	-.40	1	.78	1.0	1	2-0
8. 13	Moral libertarianism	4	-.67	4	1.24	.75	3	12-0
9. 12	Family traditionalism	8	.61	3	1.79	.50	2	0-16(f)
10. 10	Auth. parent-child rel.	5	.70	4	1.29	.75	3	0-15
11. 11	Conventional male-fem. roles	4	.45	2	1.14	.75	2	0-8
12. 17	Tolerance reg. homosex.	4	-.59	3	1.18	.75	2	8-0

no. pos.	scale label	no.						Range
(b) (c)	(h)	items	factlo	WF 1	stdev	WF 2	WFTOT	(b)
13. 18	Premarit. sex. permissiv.	6	-.51	2	1.70	.50	1	6-0
14. 19	Extra marit. sex. permiss.	2	-.46	2	1.51	.50	1	4-0(g)
15. 1	CONSERVATISM	13	,49	2	1.61	.50	1	0-9

The total sum-scores have been recoded as follows: 0–12 = 0, 13–24 = 1, 25–36 = 2, 37–48 = 3, 49–60 = 4, 61–72 = 5, 73–84 = 6, 85–96 = 7, 97–108 = 8, 109–121 = 9.
Percentages: 0 = 2%, 1 = 6%, 2 = 8%, 3 = 15%, 4 = 19%, 5 = 21%, 6 = 19%, 7 = 9%, 8 = 2%, 9 = 0%.
Scale characteristics: M = 4.35; S = 1.80 (high = traditional).
The scale has often been recoded to 4 levels according to: 0–2, 3–4, 5–6, 7–9 so that strongly progressive is 16%, moderately progressive 34%, moderately traditional is 40% and strongly traditional 11%.

Notes:
(a) The weighing procedure has been carried out according to the procedures suggested by Wim van Nooten of the Mathematical Center, Amsterdam.
(b) No. according to the order in Table 6.9. The shortened classical F-scale has not been included in the LITR-dimension, although it loads highly in the 2-factor structure.
(c) Pos. indicates the position of the scales in the Analysis-set.
(d) Factlo is: factor-loading; WF = weighing factor; stdev = standard deviation; WFTOT is total weighing factor. Regarding the ranges, a range of 3-0 indicates that the scores have been reversed for negatively loading scales: 3 = 0, 2 = 1, 1 = 2, 0 = 3, etc.
(e) Scores are weighed 2 (rounded off from 1.5) according to: 0 = 12, 1 = 10, 2 = 8, 3 = 6, 4 = 4, 5 = 2, 6 = 0: first scores are reversed and subsequently multiplied by 2.
(f) Rounded off from 1.5 and scores not reversed.
(g) The only non-Mokken scale, so there is an unusually high standard deviation (due to an irregular patterns of marginals) and range.
(h) For the scales, see Appendix 3.

2. The LEFT-RIGHT scale (LERI-dimension)

Introduction
The scale was constructed from 12 subscales and 2 single items, comprising a total of 45 items, also selected on the basis of the 'best' 2-factor-solution in Table 6.9. Weighing-procedures have been similar to those for the LITR-dimension.

Results

	scale label	no. of						Range
no. pos	(a)	items	factlo	WF 1	stdev	WF 2	WFTOT	(d)
1. 25	Att. to equality of income, property, stat.	4	.63	3	1.28	.75	2	0-8(c)
2. 27	Governm. interf. for eq.	2	.59	3	.76	1.0	3	0-6
3. 64	Att. to soc. welfare laws	4	.36	1	1.26	.75	1	0-4

no.	pos.	scale label (a)	no. of items	factlo	WF1	stdev	WF2	WFTOT	Range (b)
4.	31	Government aid to educ.	4	.56	3	1.09	.75	2	0-8
5.	66	Governm. income policy	3	.68	4	.95	1.0	4	0-12
6.	67	Tax policy, high income	3	.51	2	1.04	1.0	2	0-6
7.	68	Tax policy, low incomes	3	.38	1	.94	1.0	1	0-3
8.	35	Governm. direct econ. int.	3	.56	3	.97	1.0	3	0-9
9.	69	Governm. (non-directly econom.) welfare policy	3	.37	1	.80	1.0	1	0-3
10.	38	Mil. trade-union policy	2	.45	2	.66	1.0	2	0-4
11.	62	Democratic attitudes	6	.47	2	1.77	.50	1	0-6
12.	78	Item: Governm. and eq. of opp.		.53	2	.88	1.0	2	0-8(d)
13.	80	Item: Governm. spending		.36	1	1.00	1.0	1	0-4
14.	2	SOCIALISM	6	.49	2	1.78	.50	1	0-9

The total sum-scores have been recoded as follows: 0-9 = 0, 10-18 = 1, 19-27 = 2, 28-36 = 3, 37-45 = 4, 46-54 = 5, 55-63 = 6, 64-72 = 7, 73-81 = 8, 82-90 = 9.

Percentages: 0 = 4%, 1 = 12%, 2 = 19%, 3 = 21%, 4 = 20%, 5 = 12%, 6 = 8%, 7 = 4%, 8 = 1%, 9 = 0% (high = right).

Scale characteristics: M = 3.37; S = 1.80 (distribution a bit skewed to the left).

The scale has often been recoded to 4 levels as follows: 0-1, 2-3, 4-5, 6-9 so that 16% are then strongly left-wing, 40% are moderately left-wing, 32% are moderately right-wing and 13% are strongly right-wing.

Notes:

(a) See Appendix 3 for details on the scales.
(b) See notes b, c and d above: the LITR-dimension.
(c) The sign of all loadings have been reversed.
(d) For the text of the items, see Table 6.9., notes d and e.

3. The AUTHORITARIANISM-scale (AUTH-dimension)

Introduction
The scale was constructed from 7 subscales, comprising 31 items, using the 'best 3-factor solution' in Table 6.9. Weighing-procedures were as usual.

Results

no.	pos.	scale label (a)	no. of items	factlo	WF1	stdev	WF2	WFTOT	Range (b)
1.	63	Aid to develop. countr.	3	-.47	2	1.01	1.0	2	6-0
2.	23	Internationalism	5	-.59	3	1.42	.75	2	10-0
3.	10	Auth. parent-child rel.	5	.54	2	1.29	.75	2	0-10
4.	11	Conv. male-fem. roles	4	.45	2	1.14	.75	1	0-4(c)
5.	16	Tolerance criminals	3	-.33	1	.90	1.0	1	3-0(d)
6.	17	Tolerance homosexuals	4	-.34	1	1.18	.75	1	4-0(e)
7.	8	Shortened classical F-scale	7	.64	3	1.82	.50	2	0-18(f)

The total sum-scores have been recoded as follows: 0-5 = 0, 6-11 = 1, 12-17 = 2, 18-22 = 3, 23-27 = 4, 28-32 = 5, 33-37 = 6, 38-43 = 7, 44-49 = 8, 50-55 = 9.

Percentages: 0 = 1%, 1 = 4%, 2 = 7%, 3 = 9%, 4 = 11%, 5 = 18%, 6 = 21%,

7 = 22%, 8 = 6%, 9 = 1% (high = authoritarian).
Scale characteristics: M = 5.17; S = 1.90.
The scale has often been recoded to 4 levels as follows: 0-2, 3-4, 5-6, 7-9 so that 12% are very non-authoritarian, 20% are moderately non-authoritarian, 39% are moderately authoritarian and 29% are very authoritarian.

Notes:
(a) See Appendix 3 for details on the scales.
(b) See notes above (on LITR).
(c) Total weighing-factor rounded down because both WF1 and WF2 were 'marginal' cases.
(d) This subscale was included for 'theoretical' reasons, although its loading was somewhat too low.
(e) idem.
(f) For the F-scale: see Appendix 6; the scale has been recoded to 10 points.

APPENDIX 6:
SETS OF (POTENTIALLY) SCALING ITEMS AND SINGLE ITEMS AS VARIABLES ROUNDING OUT THE TOTAL DESIGN

(Three-digit figures refer to the place of the item in the questionnaire; for letters indicating items incorporated from other studies: see Appendix 3: Introduction)

A. *PERSONALITY VARIABLES*

1. *Authoritarianism* (a)

1.1. Shortened F-scale items
1. 662 There are two sorts of people: the strong and the weak. (26).
2. 663 Most people fall short of your expectations when you get to know them better (Familiarity breeds contempt) (43)
3. 666 Young people often revolt against social situations that they find unjust; however, when they get older, they ought to become resigned to reality (21).
4. 671 Most of our social problems would be solved if we could somehow get rid of the immoral, crooked and feebleminded people (34).
5. 675 What we need are fewer laws and institutions and more courageous, tireless, devoted leaders whom people can trust (23).
6. 723 Ill-mannered people cannot expect decent people to want to mix with them (12).
7. 725 Nowadays more and more people are prying into matters that should remain personal and private (31).

1.2. Tolerance towards criminals (see Appendix 3; set 16A)
1. 665 Criminals should not be punished in the first instance, but one should attempt to change their ways.

2.   712 Sexual criminals should not be punished in the first instance, but one should attempt to cure them (25).

1.3. Other items

573 The most important thing that children should learn is total obedience to their parents' wishes (1)(b).

717 If somebody has a problem, it is better to give it due consideration rather than try to dismiss it by occupying oneself with more pleasant matters (9).

Notes:

(a) Figures in brackets refer to corresponding item numbers in the F-scale, forms 45 and 40 (Adorno et al., op cit.: 255-257). In some cases, the original item could be literally translated into Dutch. In others, a slightly different form had to be used. One item has not been taken from the classical scale (665), and some have been reversed (712, 717).

(b) This item loaded high on the authoritarianism-factor, but has been included in the scale on authoritarian parent-child relationships (Appendix 3, set 21).

Response categories: 1-7, 717

completely agree, agree in general, neither agree nor disagree, disagree but not wholeheartedly, completely disagree

Response categories: 573

strongly agree, agree, neither agree nor disagree, disagree, strongly disagree

Scale characteristics:

1.1. *Shortened F-scale*; scale based on factor loadings $\geq .40$

high = authoritarian (items 1-7)

Distribution of scale scores: $0 = 0\%, 1 = 3\%, 2 = 5\%, 3 = 11\%$
(recoded) $4 = 17\%, 5 = 17\%, 6 = 23\%, 7 = 16\%$
                             $8 = 6\%, 9 = 2\%$

$M = 5.16; S = 1.82$

2. Dogmatism

2.1. General dogmatism

1.Y2 664 A person who gets enthusiastic about too many things is likely to be a pretty wish-washy sort of person (33).

2.Y2 718 The present is all too often full of unhappiness. It is only the future that counts (19).

3.Y2 722 In the long run, the best way to live is to pick friends and associates whose tastes and beliefs are the same as one's own (16).

4.Y2 724 Of all the different philosophies which exist in this world, there is probably only one which is correct (32).

2.2. Militant dogmatism

5.   667 There are a number of people I have come to hate because of the things they stand for (29).

6.   719 Although the use of force is basically wrong, it is sometimes the only way to advance an ideal that one strongly believes in (27).

2.3. Submissive dogmatism
7.   676 It is often better to reserve judgement about what is going on until one has had the chance to listen to the opinions of those one respects (15).
8.   720 It is only when a person devotes himself to an ideal or a cause that life becomes meaningful (31).

2.4. Self-evaluation items
9.   570 At times I think I'm no good at all (55).
10.   578 I'm afraid of people who want to find out what I'm really like for fear they will be disappointed in me (56).

2.5 Single rest-items
11.   672 Most people really like each other after all (13).
12.   673 It is better to be dead hero than to be a live coward (53).

Note:
Figures in brackets refer to item-numbers in Rokeach, 1956: 7-10. Only one item (6) has been slightly amended; items 11 and 12 have been reversed.
Response categories: 1, 4-12
    completely agree, agree in general, neither agree nor disagree, disagree but not wholeheartedly, completely disagree
Response categories: 2, 3
    strongly agree, agree, neither agree nor disagree, disagree, strongly disagree
Scale characteristics:
1. *Militant dogmatism* (dogmatism) (items 1-6)
   Scale based on factor loadings $\geqslant$ .45
   High = dogmatic
   Distribution of scale scores: 0 = 2%, 1 = 9%, 2 = 12%, 3 = 15%
   (recoded)   4 = 18%, 5 = 18%, 6 = 13%, 7 = 10%
   M = 4.15; S = 1.99   8 = 3%, 9 = 1%
2. *Submissive dogmatism* (items, 1-4, 7, 8) (not used in subsequent analyses)
   Scale based on factor loadings $\geqslant$ .40
   High = dogmatic
   Distribution of scale scores: 0 = 1%, 1 = 2%, 2 = 5%, 3 = 9%
   (recoded)   4 = 15%, 5 = 20%, 6 = 21%, 7 = 19%
   M = 5.32; S = 1.82   8 = 7%, 9 = 2%
3. *Self-evaluation items* (see set 6 below)

3. Anomia and alienation

3.1. Anomia   % high
1.   713 There are so many different opinions about what is right and what is wrong that you hardly know where you stand   59(21)
2.Y2 714 Things can change so rapidly these days that often you hardly know what is right and what is wrong   59(17)
3.   716 To be successful in society one needs a lot of good luck   47
4.Y2 715 The future is so uncertain that it is best to live from day to day (3)   39(14)

5.   668   You hardly know who you can trust nowadays (2)   38

3.2. Political alienation

6.PN 145   Do you think that political parties usually keep their promises made during pre-election campaigns, do you think that this is not the case, or that this differs from party to party?

7.PN 146   It is said that there is little difference between the major political parties, considering the results of their governmental actions. Do you agree?

8.PN 147   Is there a political party in our country that really has you interests at heart?

3.3. Misanthropy

9.   672   Most people really like each other after all (from set 2.5. on dogmatism)

10.   674   One of the good things about today is that people often really communicate with each other.

11.   669   Most politicians are genuinely interested in the welfare of their fellow-countrymen (4)

3.4. Rest-items

Y2 142   Do you expect your future to be determined by your own efforts, or by circumstances beyond your control?

Y2 670   People like me have no influence at all on government policy

528   Do you ever have that peculiar feeling that you are not yourself anymore?

Note:

Figures in brackets refer to similar items in Scole's classical anomia-scale (Bonjean et al., 1967: 34).

Response categories: 1-5, 9-11, 670
    completely agree, agree in general, neither agree nor disagree, disagree but not wholeheartedly, completely disagree

Response categories: 7
    agree, disagree

Response categories: 8
    yes, no

Response categories: 528
    often, pretty often, not so often, hardly ever, never

Scale characteristics:

1. *Anomia*
    Medium Mokken-scale, 5 items, H = .43, Rep = .90, I = 43
    High = anomic
    Distribution of scale scores: 0 = 13%, 1 = 15%, 2 = 19%, 3 = 20%
    M = 2.57; S = 1.61   4 = 18%, 5 = 14%

2. *Political alienation*
    Scale based on factor loadings ≥ .60
    Distribution of scale scores: 0 = 1%, 1 = 7%, 2 = 12%, 3 = 19%
    M = 5.04; S = 1.93   4 = 25%, 5 = 12%, 6 = 24%

3. *Misanthropy*
    Scale based on factor loadings ≥ .60

Distribution of scale scores: 0 = 2%, 1 = 13%, 2 = 13%, 3 = 17%
(recoded)   4 = 18%, 5 = 13%, 6 = 10%, 7 = 6%
M = 3.90; S = 2.20   8 = 4%, 9 = 3%

4. Optimism-pessimism

4.1. Regarding the situation in the Year 2000

			% high
1.Y2	544	There will be more or less criminality than nowadays	42(34)
2.Y2	543	There will be more or less divorce than is now the case	29(22)
3.Y3	541	People will enjoy their work more or less than now	11
4.Y2	542	People will be kinder or less kind to each other than nowadays	9

4.2. General

5.PP	622	Do you expect that a better society can be established in our country?	85(22)
6.RN	143	In some peoples' opinion the morals and behavior in our country are degenerating more and more; others find that (on the contrary) they are improving. What is your opinion?	23

Response categories: 1-4
   more, as it is now, less
Response categories: 5
   certainly, probably, probably not, certainly not
Response categories: 6
   improving; some improvement, some degeneration, remain the same, degenerating
Scale characteristics:
1. *Optimism-pessimism Year 2000* (not included in subsequent analysis)
   Medium Mokken-scale, 4 items, H = .43, Rep = .96, I = .49
   High = optimistic
   Distribution of scale scores: 0 = 47%, 1 = 25%, 2 = 22%, 3 = 4%, 4 = 2%
   M = 9.1; S = 1.03
2. *Optimism-pessimism, general*
   Medium Mokken-scale, H = 43
   High = optimistic
   Distribution of scale scores: 0 = 22%, 1 = 58%, 2 = 20%
   M = .98; S = .64

5. General satisfaction (neuroticism)

			% high
1.	525	Do you often feel listless and weary without knowing why?	85(29)
2.	522	Are you irritable?	79(49)
3.	524	Are you often moody?	55
4.	523	Are you often dissatisfied and grumbly?	50
	527	Do you ever feel wretched without knowing why?	

Response categories:
   often, rather often, not so often, hardly ever, never
Scale characteristics:
Medium Mokken-scale, 4 items, H = .45, Rep = .94, I = .46

High = satisfied
Distribution of scale scores: 0 = 5%, 1 = 13%, 2 = 24%, 3 = 24%, 4 = 34%

6. Self-evaluation/anxiety

1. 526 Have you often been afraid of people or things that could not really do you any harm?
2. 577 I am often afraid of something or somebody
3. 616 Do you feel you have enough self-confidence?
4. 570 At times I think I'm no good at all (from set 2.4.: dogmatism)
5. 578 I'm afraid of people who want to find out what I'm really like for fear they will be disappointed in me (from set 2.4.: dogmatism)

Rest-items

6. 609 Compared to my acquaintances, I'm only afraid of a few things
7. 530 When you do things that interest you, are you then satisfied with the result?
8. 566 It is very important to me that people like me
9. 571 I believe that most people like me

Response categories: 1, 7
  often, rather often, not so often, hardly ever, never
Response categories: 2, 6, 8, 9
  strongly agree, agree, neither agree nor disagree, disagree, strongly disagree
Response categories: 4, 5
  completely agree, agree in general, neither agree nor disagree, disagree but not wholeheartedly, completely disagree
Response categories: 3
  sufficient, moderate, not so much, too little, definitely not enough
Scale characteristics:
5-item scale based on factor loadings $\geqslant$ .60
High = low self-evaluation, high anxiety
Distribution of scale scores: 0 = 8%, 1 = 14%, 2 = 23%, 3 = 22%
(recoded) 4 = 17%, 5 = 11%, 6 = 4%, 7 = 2%
M = 2.89; S = 1.71 8 = 1%, 9 = 0%

7. Social desirability

1. 515 As a child, did you always immediately do what you were told without grumbling?
2. 518 Do you always keep your promises, even if it is very inconvenient to do so?
3. 519 Can you remember if you ever pretended to be ill to avoid an unpleasant or difficult situation?
4. 520 Do you sometimes have thoughts that you would not like other people to know about?
5. 521 Do you ever talk about things you don't really know about?
   516 Would you always declare goods when going through customs, even if you knew that you definitely could not be caught?
   517 Have you ever told a lie?

Response categories:
   yes, no
Scale characteristics:
Cluster of Tau-coefficients, p = < .001 (items 1-5)
High = tendency to respond socially desirable
Distribution of scale scores: 0 = 8%, 1 = 20%, 2 = 27%
(recoded)   3 = 26%, 4 = 15%, 5 = 3%
M = 2.30; S = 1.27

B. BACKGROUND VARIABLES*

1.   126   What sort of *schooling* did you last have?
        1. primary school
        2. primary school + technical school, evening classes, etc.
        3. secondary modern school
        4. idem + technical training, evening classes
        5. grammar school, training college
        6. idem + technical training, evening classes
        7. university, technical college, specialized courses, e.g. accountancy
     130   Did you finish this school? (if not) Which school did you last finish? (var 127)
     128   Which school did the *head of the family* last finish? (if it is not the head of the family)
     129   Which school did *your father* last finish? (if father is not the head of the family)

2.   131   What is your *occupation*? What work do you do? (var. 132)
        1. free and academic professions, managers, teachers (grammar schools), higher employees and civil servants, higher and middle-grade technicians (8.7%)
        2. larger and middle-range shopkeepers and tradesmen, middle-grade civil servants, big farmers, teachers, 'agents' for firms (13.2%)
        3. smaller shopkeepers, lower employees and civil servants, office clerks, small farmers (20.7%)
        4. skilled workers (8.1%)
        5. unskilled and semi-skilled workers (5.9%)
        6. students (6.3%)
        7. without occupation (e.g. housewifes, etc.) (33.4%)
     133   What is the occupation of the *head of the family*? (if resp. is not the head). What work does he do? (var. 134)
     135   What is/was your father's (last) occupation? (if family head is not the father of resp.) What work does/did he do? (var. 136)

---

* Not all background-variables available will be presented here as some have not been used in the present study.

Note: Information from 131-132; 133-134; 135-136 has been combined and coded by the staff of Makrotest N.V. into one of the 7 categories mentioned above. These are just labels to indicate which type of occupations have been coded that way. Occupation has been noted down literally on the questionnaire-form.

3. 140 Interviewer-rating on the 'standard of living' (social class or status) of respondent (not used on an independent variable in subsequent analysis)
    1. well-to-do (upper class)
    2. middle class (tends to upper-middle)
    3. upper-lower class (tends to lower-middle)
    4. lower class

4. 732 This is about your *gross yearly income*, or, if applicable, the gross yearly income of the family.
    We would appreciate getting a rough impression of this.
    You can see that the table below contains wide categories.
    0. no income at all
    1. less than 6000 per year (e.g. 500 per month, 125 per week)
    2. between 6000 and 12,000 gross per year (e.g. 500-1000 per month, 125-250 per week)
    3. between 12,000 and 18,000 per year (e.g. 1000 and 1500 per month, 250-375 per week)
    4. between 18,000 and 24,000 per year
    5. between 24,000 and 30,000 per year
    6. over 30,000 per year
    7. refusal to participate

Note: In the questionnaire, this (last) question to be filled out by resp. was phrased in a more elaborate way. Figures refer to Dutch guilders.

5. INDEX *Social class*
    The index was constructed from variables 126, 131, 133, 140 and 732 as follows:
    (a) all variables were recoded to 4 levels
    (b) a basic 10-point index was constructed from variables 126, 131 and 732.
      —for students, housewives, etc., the occupational level of the head of the family was used; if this was coded 0, 6 or 7, information from variable 140 was used.
      —if variable 732 is coded 0 or 8 (no information), variable 140 is used instead.
      —for variable 732, code 7 (refusal) has been recoded to the highest income levels.*
    (c) The 10-point scale has been recoded in 2 ways to 4 levels. It depends to some extent on one's 'image of society' as to which recoding is

---

* It was expected that people with *high incomes* might refuse to answer the income-question. There is only slight evidence of this, however, so that it would have been better not to have used this information (like the codes 0 and 9: no income, no answer).

preferred. In the present study, a social class distribution has been worked with of (1) a small upper class (14.5%), a somewhat larger upper-middle class (19.7%), a large lower-middle or upper-lower class (43%) and a relatively small working class (22.8%). This distribution is similar to that for occupation, according to the coding scheme presented. The other distribution has also been used: here, by shifting one cutting point, a relatively small lower-middle class and a large working class was obtained. In numerous checks, results were very similar in correlational analysis.

6. INDEX *Inter-generation social mobility*

First, 2 sub-indices were constructed, based on educational level and occupation. All variables remain recoded on 4 levels (see note below).

(a) *sub-index* for educational level has basically been constructed from variables 126 and 129: a 7-point difference score was obtained. For *housewives*, the sub-index was based on variables 128 and 129, i.e. on the educational level of her husband; generally: the head of the family (widows and divorcees are themselves the head of the family).

For *students* or other children, the index has been based on variables 126 and 128.

(b) *sub-index* for occupation has been based on variables 131 and 135. A 7-point difference score was again obtained.

For housewives and children in the family, the sub-index was again based on 133 and 135, 131 and 133 respectively. If, however, 133 or 135 equals 0 or 7, a subscale score of 3 has been assigned (a middle-score for unclassifiable cases). In case 131 or 135 equals 6 (student), this value has been recoded to the highest occupational level.

(c) A TOTAL INDEX has been constructed by summing both 7-points scales and recoding them to form a 10-point scale. *After examination of frequencies*, this scale was recoded in 2 ways. First, to a 4-point index with values: strong upward mobility (at least one level difference on both occupation and education, 21.5%), weak upward mobility (one level difference on either education or occupation, 23.3%), constants (33.3%) and a downwardly mobile group (22.0%). There were very few that were upwardly mobile by more than 2 points (9.7%) or downwardly mobile by more than 1 point (6.8%). Still, in a second categorization, these categories were also distinguished. More than 70% of the sample did not manifest any, or only very moderate (plus or minus 1 point) mobility.

7. INDEX *Status inconsistency*

The index was based on education and income, first to simplify matters and second, since the correlation between educational level and income is somewhat lower (Tau = .37) than that between education and occupation (.50). So there would be more inconsistency of the former type than of the latter, e.g. with a low-level of education, it is more difficult to reach a higher level of occupation than a higher income (of course: within the classifications used in this study).

The index has been constructed from variables 126 and 732; if 732 equals 0 or 8, variable 140 has been used instead. The 7-point index has been recoded to a 4-level one: 21.9% lower income than educational level, 42.8% consistent, 21% weakly inconsistent (one point higher income than educational) and 14.3% strongly inconsistent by having higher incomes than their educational level 'warrants' by at least 2 points on the indicators used. Very few (4.9%) are strongly inconsistent in the sense that their educational level is much higher than their income would suggest.

Notes on Indices 5, 6, 7
Variables 126-135, 140 and 732 have been recoded to 4 levels as follows:
126, 128, 129: 1, 2 = 0; 3; 4 = 1; 5; 6 = 2; 7 = 3;   0 (NA) = 0
131, 133, 135: 1 = 3; 2 = 2; 3= 1; 4, 5 = 0   rest = 1
140   : 0 (no score) = 2; scoring reversed
732   : 1, 2 = 0; 3 = 1; 4, 5 = 2; 6, 7 = 3*

Subjective social class
8.   636   To which class do you consider (and/or your family) you belong? Resp. categories: working class, lower middle class, upper middle class, upper class.
INTRODUCTION: As you know, people are often considered as belonging to the working class, the lower middle class, the upper middle class and the upper class.

637   *Respondents not living at home*
And to which social class do you consider your parents or foster-parents belong? (personal history variable; see below). Resp. categories: as above.

9. INDEX *Subjective social mobility*
Index based on a 7-point difference score between 636-637. In case of missing data in either 636 or 637 (no answer, or people unwilling or unable to assign oneself to a class), a separate code was given. The 7-point scale was recoded to 3 levels: downward mobility (6.7%), no mobility (36.5%), upwards mobility (11.8%), rest 45%.

10.   826 *Age,* categorized: 10-points, subsequently recoded into 4 levels: 17-24 (23.2%), 25-39 (31%), 40-55 (26%), 56-69 (19.8%)

11.   125 *Sex*

12.   831 *Residence, degree of urbanization*
The municipalities were categorized according to official criteria from the Bureau of the Census (Centraal Bureau voor de Statistiek: Typologie van Nederlandse gemeenten naar urbanisatiegraad, Den Haag, 1960) into 7 classes: A1-4, B1-3, B4, C1, C2, C3, C4. They were classified into 4 categories as follows:
1. (A1-4, B1-2, C1) = the country (small villages and country towns of up to 20.000 inhabitants: 37.8%

2. (C2, C3): small towns of up to 100.000 inhabitants: 23.8%
3. (B3, C4, minus the 3 largest cities): larger cities, including suburban complexes and smaller towns near large cities, with most of their inhabitants working in the latter: 20.3%
4. The 3 largest cities: Amsterdam, Rotterdam, The Hague: 18%

13.   221   *Church membership*
Do you consider you belong to a religious community?
Response categories: no, roman catholic, Dutch reformed, Calvinist, other

14.   222   *Church attendance*
How often have you been to church lately (say, in the last 6 months)?
Response categories: once a week or more, once a fortnight, once a month, less than once a month, never

C. PERSONAL HISTORY VARIABLES*

1. Relationship to parents in youth

1.   529   Were you often severely punished by your parents (or foster-parents, or guardian)?
2.   534   How well did you get on with your mother when you were young?
3.   535   And with your father?
4.   536   In retrospect, did your parents or foster-parents keep too tight a grip on you, did they allow you too much freedom or do you think they steered a middle course?
5.   539   Were you always able to discuss matters that worried you with your parents?
6.   540   What is your opinion on your parents' marriage?
7.   531   Did (or do) your parents (or foster-parents) want you to achieve something in life that they were not given the opportunity to do when they were young?
8.   532   Can you remember that you often wanted to be like your father (foster-father) when you were young?
9.   533   And like your mother (foster-mother)?
10.   537   Did your parents have great hopes for you or not?
11.   539   Did your parents continually tell you to follow certain rules or didn't they?
Response categories, (somewhat categorized for x^2-computations): 1
often, not so often, rather often, hardly ever, never
Response categories: 7, 8, 9
yes, no
Response categories: 2, 3
very good, quite good, so so, not so good, bad

* Not all available variables are relevant to the present study, so are not mentioned here.

Response categories: 4
too tight, middle course but sometimes too tight, middle course but sometimes too lenient, too much freedom
Response categories: 5
yes, with both parents, only with mother, only with father, with neither parents
Response categories: 6
very happy, happy, quite happy, not so happy, unhappy
Response categories: 10
very high hopes, high hopes, not such high hopes, few hopes, no clear hopes at all
Response categories: 11
only definite rules, mostly definite rules, definite rules sometimes, no definite rules at all

Scale characteristics:
items 1-6: Socio-emotional relationship with parents
Scale characteristics: cluster x^2: p = <.0001
High = good socio-emotional relationship
Distribution of scale scores: o = 2%, 1 = 6%, 2 = 13%, 3 = 9%,
(recoded) 4 = 10%, 5 = 11%, 6 = 12%, 7 = 13%,
M = 5.15; S = 2.52 8 = 17%, 9 = 7%
items 7-11: Normative-instrumental relationship with parents
Scale characteristics: cluster x^2: p = <.0001
High = strongly normative-instrumental relationship
Distribution of scale scores: 0 = 8%, 1 = 11%, 2 = 12%, 3 = 15%,
(recoded) 4 = 13%, 5 = 17%, 6 = 7%, 7 = 9%,
M = 3.88; S = 2.43 8 = 3%, 9 = 5%

INTRODUCTION TO ITEMS 2-4
If you haven't been raised in a family from your 5th year on, indicate: inapplicable
INTRODUCTION TO ITEMS 5-11
Here are some questions about how it was at home when you were young, and the conditions in your family or in the foster-family you grew up in. Think of the period up till your 17-18th year, and of the family you lived with the longest (in case you lived with more than one family). If you have been living in an institution for some time, just concentrate on the period when you were with a family. If you left home before you were 17, think only of the period when you lived at home. For respondents living at their parents' home: think about the recent past when you answer these questions. If you haven't lived in a family since you were 5 years of age, indicate: 'not applicable'.

2. INDEX *Social class of parents, objective criteria*

This index has been taken from the original 10-point index on respondent's social class (see B5) and the 10-point index on inter-generation social mobility (see B6). The difference between one's social class position and the extent of upward or downward social mobility gives an indication of the parent's social class. The resulting 10-point scale has again been recoded in 2 ways. First, in a way that is comparable to the social class distribution used in the present study (see above): a small upper-class (17.7%), a somewhat larger upper-middle class

(23.8%), quite a large lower-middle class (31.8%) and a smaller working class (26.6%).

For practical reasons, the index has been derived *indirectly*. The index of social class has been based on education, occupation and *income*, the index of social mobility only on education and occupation. So the social class index of parents is partly *corrected* for income, which is assessed on the basis of the present income of respondents.

It was found, however, that for about 45% of the sample some degree of upward social mobility could be established. This is not reflected in the relationship between the social class distributions of respondents and their parents. Of the parents, 26.6% were assigned to the working class, as against 22.8% in the present sample. 31.8% of the parents were assigned to the lower middle class as against 43% in the sample and 23.8% to the upper-middle class as against 19.7% in the present sample. Finally, 17.7% of parents and only 14.5% of respondents were assigned to the upper class. The reason for the fact that the reported mobility rate cannot be found reflected in the 2 distributions is that for the parents' social class a similar distribution to the one decided on for the sample was aimed at. Therefore, perhaps a more realistic distribution could be the second recoding of parents' social class in the upper class as 9.5%, upper-middle 18.5%, lower-middle 27.6% and working class 44.3%.

A possible theory might be that, over the period of about one generation, the latter *classical* distribution of the social classes has been *modified* to that which exists today, with a much smaller working class, a much larger lower-middle class (lower employees and civil servants, etc.) and somewhat larger upper-middle and upper classes.

3.   637 *Subjective assessment of parents' social class*
           See above, section B, variable 8(637).

4.   137 *Degree of urbanization of residence in youth*
           Where for the most part did you spend your youth?
           Response categories: country, town, large city, other

5.   220 *A religious upbringing*
           Have you been brought up to follow a certain religion?
           Response categories: no, roman catholic, Dutch reformed, Calvinist, other religions

6.   278 *Political party-choice of father*
       279 For which party did your father mostly vote?
           Response categories:
           1. *VVD* = Volkspartij voor Vrijheid en Democratie (People's Party for Freedom and Democracy), classical, economic liberals
           2. *Christen-democratische partijen* (christian-democratic parties; at present united in the Christen-Democratisch Appel (Christian-Democratic 'Appeal'; CDA)
             a. KVP = Katholieke Volkspartij (Catholic People's Party)
             b. ARP = Anti-Revolutionaire Partij (Anti-Revolutionary Party)
             c. CHU = Christelijk-Historische Unie (Christian-Historical Union)
           3. *Progressieve partijen* (Progressive parties)
             a. PvdA = Partijd van de Arbeid (Labor Party)

     b. D'66 = Democraten '66 (Democrates '66); 'modern liberals' (a)

     c. PPR = Politieke Partij Radikalen (Radical Political Party)(b)

4. *Extreem-linkse partijen* (Extremely left-wing parties)

     a. PSP = Pacifistisch-Socialistische Partij (Pacifistic Socialist Party)(c)

     b. CPN = Communistische Partij van Nederland (Communist Party of the Netherlands)(d)

5. *Extreem-rechtse Partijen* (Extremely right-wing parties)

     a. BP = Boeren Partij (Farmers' Party)(e)

     b. BR = Binding Rechts (Rightist Bond)(f)

     c. GPV = Gereformeerd Politiek Verbond (Calvinist Political Bond)(g)

     d. SGP = Staatkundig-Gereformeerde Partij (Political-Calvinist Party)(g)

Note:

Another party, DS'70 (Democratisch Socialisten '70; Democratic Socialists '70) broke away from the Labor Party in 1970. It has not been relevant to the fathers' vote, but has been included elsewhere. For some very brief indications on the emergence of the Dutch party-system, see Chapter 4.

Notes:

(a) New party founded in 1966, at a time when there was a widespread feeling of 'alienation' from the system of the 'established' parties.

(b) Party broke away from the Roman-Catholic People's Party in 1968.

(c) Party broke away from the Labor Party in 1962.

(d) Party broke away from the forerunner of the Labor Party (the SDAP = Sociaal-Democratische Arbeiders Partij — Social-Democratic Workers Party) as early as 1913.

(e) Party founded in the early 1960's as a protest against government-regulation of farming and to focus attention on problems in farming. As a protest party, and seen in the context of Dutch politics, it had quite a lot of success, relatively speaking, in the 1963 and especially the 1966 elections; it cornered the farmers' votes and also received a considerable amount of support from the larger cities. At present (1977) it no longer plays a role in Dutch politics.

(f) Broke away from the Farmers' Party in the late 1960's. By 1975, it had ceased to exist.

(g) Both GPV and SGP are extremely orthodox right-wing protestant parties, which have never played any significant role in Dutch politics.

D. SITUATIONAL VARIABLES*

1. Social integration

1.   255 How many clubs do you belong to? (Please do not include a political party or trade union)

* See notes to section B and C above.

2. 256 For how many hours a week are you involved in club work (weekends included)?
3. 257 How often, on average, do you visit friends, acquaintances or relations or do they visit you?

    Response categories: 3
    nearly every day, 3-4 times a week, 1-2 times a week, 1-2 times a fortnight, 1-2 times a month, less than once a month

Scale characteristics:
Scale based on cluster; Chi-2 tests, $p < .05$
High = highly integrated
Distribution of scale scores: $0 = 8\%$, $1 = 7\%$, $2 = 20\%$, $3 = 25\%$,
(recoded) $4 = 10\%$, $5 = 8\%$, $6 = 10\%$, $7 = 7\%$,
$M = 3.51$; $S = 2.18$ $8 = 4\%$, $9 = 1\%$

2. Satisfaction with living conditions

1.PP 623 What about your (family) income? Are you:
2.PP 624 What about your housing conditions? Are you:
3.PP 626 What about your position on the social ladder? Are you:
4.PP 627 What about your possibilities of promotion? Are you:
5.PP 625 What about your health? Are you:
6.PP 621 What is your opinion of society today?
       628 *if not applicable*: What about your possibilities of promotion in your future job?

       Response categories: 1-5, 628
       very satisfied, satisfied, neither satisfied nor dissatisfied, quite dissatisfied, dissatisfied
       Response categories: 6
       favorable, fairly favorable, neither favorable nor unfavorable, quite unfavorable, unfavorable

Scale characteristics:
Scale based on cluster (items 1-4): $p < 10^{-10}$
High = satisfied
Distribution of scale scores: $1 = 1\%$, $2 = 3\%$, $3 = 8\%$, $4 = 8\%$,
(recoded) $5 = 9\%$, $6 = 16\%$, $7 = 36\%$, $8 = 14\%$, $9 = 5\%$

3. Religious involvement	% high
1.HS 235 I am indifferent towards the church	54
2.HS 233 I always set great store by the visit of a clergyman	42
3.HS 234 I am very interested in religious matters	42

Response categories:
completely agree, agree in general, no opinion, disagree but not wholeheartedly, disagree completely

Scale characteristics:
Medium Mokken-scale, 3 items, H = .45
High = involved
Distribution of scale scores: 0 = 5%, 1 = 10%, 2 = 15%, 3 = 31%
  9 = 38% (non-religious people)

4. Political interest   % high

1.PN 260 Have you ever watched a direct broadcast of a
          parliamentary debate?   66
2.PN 261 Do you ever watch other TV programs on politics?   61
3.PN 262 Do you ever read about politics in our country, e.g.
          in newspapers? If so, do you do this regularly, now 60 (regularly +
          and then, seldom or never?   now and
                                                                  then)

4.   263 Do you think of yourself as very interested in   35 (very +
          politics, or interested, moderately interested, not   normal)
          very or not at all interested?
Response categories: 1, 2
  yes, no
Scale characteristics:
Strong Mokken-scale, 4-items, H = .58, Rep. = .94, I = .63
High = interested; M = 2.23; S = 1.46
Distribution of scale scores: 0 = 19%, 1 1 = 15%, 2 = 18%, 3 = 22% 4 = 26%

5. Political information

1.   313 Can you give the names of a few ministers in the present govern-
          ment?
2.   314 Can you mention some of the countries that are members of the
          North Atlantic Treaty Organization (NATO)?
Response categories:
  1, 2, 3, 4, 5, 6, 7, 8, 9 or more names
  mentioned correctly
Scale characteristics:
Chi-2: p < 10^{-9}
High = much information
Distribution of scale scores: 0 = 8%, 1 = 9%, 2 = 7%, 3 = 8%,
(recoded)   4 = 11%, 5 = 6%, 6 = 14%, 7 = 12%,
M = 4.96; S = 2.87   8 = 11%, 9 = 13%

6. Awareness of a possible communist threat   % high

1.   618 And what about Chinese communism?   72(17)

2. 617 Do you think that Russian communism is a threat to
        Western Europe or do you think that there is no (longer
        any) danger at all?   31
        Response categories:
        a threat, no immediate threat, no (longer any) danger at all
Scale characteristics:
Strong Mokken-scale, 2 items, H = .90
High = perception of communist threat
Distribution of scale scores: 0 = 27%, 1 = 44%, 2 = 30%

7. *Political alienation*

(see set 3.2. above, in the anomia domain; this variable has, somewhat
arbitrarily, been considered 'situational' rather than 'personal' in subsequent
analysis).

E. *'CONSEQUENTIAL' VARIABLES**

Note: Whether variables are independent or intervening, or dependent as
regards ideological, attitudinal or value-oriented variables depends on theoretical considerations. Some situational variables mentioned above might also
be considered as 'consequential'.

1. 728 Do you consider yourself as a conservative or as more of a pro-
        gressive?
        Response categories:
        very conservative, moderately conservative, neither, moderately pro-
        gressive, very progressive
2. 730 Do you consider yourself 'left-wing' or 'right-wing'
        Response categories:
        very left-wing, moderately left-wing, neither, moderately right-wing,
        very right-wing
3. 267 Are you/have you been a member of a political party?†
        Response categories:
        yes; no, but was in the past; no, never have been; does not want to
        say.
3a. 276 Which party are you have you been a member of?
    277
Response categories:
    KVP, PvdA, VVD, ARP, CHU, D66, PPR, PSP, CPN, DS70, BP, Binding
    Rechts, SGP, GPV, PAK, CCP, other
Note: For an explanation of the labels, see above. PAK and CCP are not
political parties, but coalitions that appeared as a result of some elections.
PAK = Progressive coalition with PvdA, PPR, D66 and sometimes PSP;

---

* See notes on sections B and C above.
† Not used as separate variables.

CCP = Combination of christian-democratic parties KVP, ARP and CHU. (at present CDA.)

4.   265   *Vote intention for: if a general election were to take place now*
    Response categories:
    yes, perhaps, no

4a.   274   For which party would you then probably vote?
    275   Response categories:-
    see 3a. above

APPENDIX 7:

RELATIONSHIPS BETWEEN VARIABLES USED IN TYPE-2 ANALYSIS AND IDEOLOGICAL DIMENSIONS

Variables in Type-2 analysis LABELS	LERI	LITR	AUTH	(a)
A. PERSONALITY VARIABLES (b)				
1. Authoritarianism (short F-scale)	−.01	.36	.66	(d)
2. Dogmatism (short D-scale)	−.02	.32	.46	
3. Anomia (Srole-type scale)	−.07	.24	.43	
4. General optimism-pessimism (c)	.24	.22	.17	
5. Social desirability	.00	.17	.14	
6. General satisfaction (neuroticism)	.08	.08	.05	
7. Self-evaluation- anxiety	.03	.03	.02	
8. Misanthropy (trust in people)	−.06	−.13	−.13	
B. BACKGROUND VARIABLES (e)				
1. Social mobility (objective)	.02	−.13	−.17	
2. Social mobility (subjective)	−.03	−.08	−.11	
3. Social class (objective)	.19	−.22	−.30	
4. Social class (subjective)	.23	−.14	−.24	
5. Educational level	.08	−.33	−.40	
6. Income level	.16	−.17	−.24	
7. Occupational level	.17	−.20	−.28	
8. Status-inconsistency	−.13	−.13	−.13	
9. Age	.04	.28	.24	
10. Sex (0 = man)	.11	.11	.09	
11. Residence (urban. level)	−.03	−.17	−.13	
12. Religion: subj. belong to a certain church	.18	.27	.12	
13. Church-attendance (c)	.06	.22	.08	

Notes:
(a) All coefficients are Tau-beta's; the ideological dimensions have been recoded to 4 levels as indicated in Appendix 4.
(b) For the scales: see Appendix 6A. All variables have been recoded to 4 levels.
(c) Scores reversed.
(d) The correlation between the short F-scale and the AUTH-dimension is inflated because the former scale has been included in the latter dimension (see Appendix 4).
(e) See appendix 6B. The variables were recorded to 4 levels as much as was possible. For social mobility (obj.) there are 2 upwardly mobile categories. Social mobility (subj.) has 3 levels and 45% of the respondents were not assigned to a category because they were unable or unwilling to assign themselves and/or their parents to a social class. Subjective social class also has 3 levels because so few considered themselves as belonging to the upper class. 13% were unable or unwilling to consider themselves as belonging to any social class. There were 18% refusals for income and for occupation, 37% considered to be housewives and 6% to be students. (All these categories were not included.) For religion, 6% were not considered since they stated that they belonged to a church, but not to one of the 3 major ones. (Rank-order as in Appendix 6.)

	LERI	LITR	AUTH
C. PERSONAL HISTORY VARIABLES (a)			
1. Relation to parents in youth socio-emotional	.03	.09	.05
2. Relation to parents in youth: normative-instrumental	−.03	.04	.01
3. Residence in youth (urb. level) (i)	−.04	−.23	−.16
4. A religious upbringing (b)	.16	.17	.07
5. Political partisanship father (c)	.25	−.09	−.03
5″. Idem (d)	.14	−.23	−.10
6. Parents' social class (objective) (e)	.19	−.11	−.16
6″. idem (f)	.20	−.14	−.19
7. Parents' social class (subjective) (g)	.26	−.09	−.15
D. SITUATIONAL VARIABLES (h)			
1. Political interest	−.14	−.26	−.27
2. Political information	−.05	−.28	−.32
3. Satisfaction with living-condit.	.18	.11	.01
4. Awareness of a possible communist threat	.12	.26	.25
5. Religious involvement	.06	.22	
6. Social integration	.00	−.10	−.12
7. Political alienation (from the party-system)	.10	−.07	−.01

Notes:
(a) See Appendix 6C for further details on the variables, which as much as was possible have again been recoded to 4 levels.
(b) Other religions left out; rank-order like in Appendix 6.
(c) Rank-order of the party-combinations according to the position of voters and members along the left-right dimension (see Table 6.16A.): VVD, chr. dem. parties, progressives, extr. left-wing.
(d) Rank-ordering of the party combinations along the LITR-dimension (see again Table 6.16A.): chr. dem. parties, VVD, progressives, extreme left-wing.
(e) Distribution comparable to that of present social class: working class smaller than the lower-middle class.
(f) Distribution of the 'classical' type with a large working class and smaller lower-middle class.
(g) 42% were unable or unwilling to place their parents in a social class
(h) See Appendix D for further details. As far as possible, scale-scores have again been recoded to 4 levels.
(i) 'Other' has been classified 'town', i.e. the middle category.

APPENDIX 8:

INTERRELATIONSHIPS OF INDEPENDENT AND INTERVENING VARIABLES TO BE INCLUDED IN TYPE-2 ANALYSIS

A. *Intercorrelations of personality variables* (see Appendix 6A)

	2	3	4	5	6	7	8
1. Authoritarianism (shortened F-scale)	.46	.44	.13	.10	.01	.02	−.10
2. Dogmatism (shortened D-scale)		.46	−.05	.06	−.01	.11	−.12
3. Anomia			−.05	.00	−.08	.15	−.05
4. General optimism-pessimism				−.03	.02	−.04	−.08
5. Social desirability					−.19	−.19	−.03
6. General satisfaction (neuroticism)						−.26	−.07
7. Self-evaluation/anxiety							.04
8. Misanthropy-trust in people							

Comments:
There are clearly 2 clusters in the matrix: one is the strong authoritarianism-dogmatism-anomia cluster, and the other the weaker social-desirability-general satisfaction-self-evaluation/anxiety one. The 2 clusters are practically unrelated to each other, although the weak relationships between dogmatism and anomia and self-evaluation-anxiety constitute validating evidence. This is also true of the

relationship between authoritarianism and general pessimism. The misanthropy-scale seems invalidated by its *negative* relationships to authoritarianism and dogmatism. The clusters themselves of course validate the scales included.

B. *Intercorrelations of background variables* (see Appendix 6B) (a)

	1	2	3	4	5	6	7	8	9	10	11	12	13
1. Social mobility (objective)		26	27	20	30	27	41	06	−05	−04	02	01	03
2. Social mobility (subjective)			11	29	07	21	15	−09	05	01	04	00	03
3. Social class (objective)				52	61	65	52	−12	−07	−01	12	−03	07
4. Social class (subjective)					48	48	49	−04	−03	06	11	03	07
5. Educational level						37	50	37	−16	−12	16	−07	07
6. Income level							44	−47	10	−09	07	−01	08
7. Occupational level								06	04	−01	11	−01	05
8. Status-inconsistency									−13	−11	05	−04	−03
9. Age										01	04	04	−08
10. Sex											01	09	02
11. Residence (urban.)												−14	18
12. Religion													09
13. Church-attendance													

Note:
(a) See Appendix 7 for some information on recoding, missing data, rank-ordering, etc.

Comments:
Both social mobility measures (objective and subjective) are moderately related; both social class measures are strongly related and, of course, form a strong cluster with the 3 class-indicators (educational level, occupation and income). Both mobility measures are, as might be expected, positively related to social class and class indicators; and objective mobility more strongly so than subjective mobility, with the exception of the relationship to subjective social class. Likewise, objective social class is somewhat more strongly related to class-indicators than subjective social class. Status-incongruency is related to educational level and income, because the former index has been built upon the latter ones. As might have been predicted, social class is weakly related to the degree of urbanization of residence (especially education). The relationship of educational level to age is weakly negative, but the latter also has a weakly positive relation to income.

C. *Intercorrelations of personal history variables* (see Appendix 6C) (a)

	2	3	4	5	5″	6	7
1. Rel. to parents in youth (socio-emotional)	*18*	−06	01	−02	−00	04	02
2. Rel. to parents in youth (normative-instrumental)		−03	05	+01	−05	−01	03
3. Residence in youth (urbanizat. level)			−09	+03	*+19*	*+15*	+13
4. A religious upbringing				*+18*	*−25*	02	06
5. Political partisansh. fath. (LERI)						*+21*	*+40*
5″. Political partisansh. fath. (LITR)						−04	*−10*
6. Parents social class (obj.)							*38*
7. Parents social class (subj.)							

Note:
(a) See Appendix 7 for some information on recoding, rank-ordering, etc.

Comments:
There is a rather strong relationship between the political partisanship of the father and *subjective* social class of parents, and also with 'a religious upbringing'; somewhat weaker relationships exist for objective social class and residence.

The chi-2 value for 'residence in youth' vs. 'a religious upbringing' is highly significant (83.2, df = 8) which means that there is indeed a tendency that the upbringing is not for the most part, a religious one in large cities and that the country is predominantly roman catholic, Dutch reformed and especially Calvinist.

The parents' setting of norms and goals for their children (as later reported by the latter, of course) tends to go hand in hand with a good emotional relationship — but both variables are unrelated to any other 'personal history' variable.

D. *Intercorrelation of situational variables* (see Appendix 6D)

	1	2	3	4	5	6	7
1. Political interest		*.39*	−.01	−.05	.06	*.12*	.01
2. Political information			.04	−.09″	.03	*.15*	.02
3. Satisfaction with living conditions				.09	.05	.04	−.08
4. Awareness of a possible communist threat					*.12*	−.02	−.02
5. Religious involvement						.04	−.02
6. Social integration							−.05
7. Political alienation (from the party syst.)							

E. Intercorrelations: personality vs. background variables

Background variables:	Personality variables (a)							
	1	2	3	4	5	6	7	8
1. Social mobility (objective)	−13	−16	−15	02	−01	01	−03	06
2. Social mobility (subjective)	−09	−12	−12	03	−01	01	−04	03
3. Social class (objective)	−24	−24	−25	02	05	04	−05	05
4. Social class (subjective)	−21	−19	−24	07	−03	07	04	04
5. Educational level	−31	−29	−32	01	−07	04	−09	07
6. Income level	−19	−22	−25	04	−03	06	07	03
7. Occupational level	−23	−25	−23	10	−06	01	−02	07
8. Status-incongruency	−08	−07	−09	02	−01	−01	−03	06
9. Age	20	10	09	15	12	05	−05	−04
10. Sex	05	06	13	05	02	−04	21	−05
11. Residence (urbanization level)	09	−07	−06	04	−02	−00	−02	10
12. Religion	03	01	−06	16	−01	03	06	−08
13. Church-attendance	−03	−03	01	08	−05	−05	−03	00

Note:
(a) Personality variables:
1. Authoritarianism
2. Dogmatism
3. Anomia
4. General optimism-pessimism
5. Social desirability
6. General satisfaction (neuroticism)
7. Self-evaluation/anxiety
8. Misanthropy-trust in people

Comments:
The 3 'major' personality variables (authoritarianism, dogmatism and anomia) all seem to have a rather strong negative relation to social class, social class indicators and (somewhat weaker) to social mobility: the well known fact has been reestablished that on the conventional measuring instruments for these phenomena the upper classes tend to be less authoritarian, dogmatic and anomic than the lower classes. Social class seems unrelated to the other personality variables incorporated into the present design, however, The same seems mainly true of the relationships of the other background variables to personality variables, including religion and church-attendance: it might be a surprise that there are no relationships between residence- and religion-variables and the 3 major personality variables mentioned above.

There are some relationships between age and sex and some personality variables that increase confidence in the validity of the latter's measurement. Age, for example, is positively related to authoritarianism and pessimism. Women prove to be more anomic and to have a lower self-evaluation and more anxiety than men. Finally, religion proves to be negatively related to optimism: generally, Calvinists tend to be most pessimistic, and non-religious people least pessimistic. It may finally be noted that status-incongruency is virtually unrelated to any personality variable.

Chi-2's have also been computed for all tables. No clear or strongly curvilinear relationships could be observed, however.

E. Intercorrelations: personality vs. personal history variables

	Personal history variables (a)							
	1	2	3	4	5	5″	6	7
1. Authoritarianism	01	02	−09	01	−02	−04	−15	−15
2. Dogmatism	00	−02	−09	−00	−04	−05	−13	−08
3. Anomia	−04	−04	−08	−04	01	−02	−16	−12
4. General optimism-pessimism	00	02	05	−14	10	11	−01	−08
5. Social desirability	09	02	−01	00	00	−01	−05	−06
6. General satisfaction	17	06	01	04	−02	00	02	07
7. Self-evaluation/anxiety	−13	−03	−02	06	−05	−06	−03	04
8. Misanthropy-trust in people	−10	−03	+07	00	06	09	01	03

Note:
(a) Personal history variables:
1. Relation to parents in youth; socio-emotional
2. Idem; normative
3. Residence in youth; urb. level
4. A religious upbringing
5. Political partisanship father; left-right rank-ordered
5″. Idem, libertarianism-traditionalism rank-ordered
6. Parents social class (objective)
7. Parents social class (subjective)

Comments:
Validating evidence for at least 1 of the 2 'relation to parents' variables is provided by the moderate relationships between socio-emotional relationship to parents in youth and general satisfaction (neuroticism), self-evaluation/anxiety and misanthropy. The religious variable is again related to general optimism-pessimism? and the 3 major personality variables of authoritarianism, dogmatism and anomia are again related, though relatively weakly, to (parents') social class variables.

G. Intercorrelations: personality vs. situational variables

	Situational variables (a)						
	1	2	3	4	5	6	7
1. Authoritarianism	−18	−23	−01	20	03	−14	04
2. Dogmatism	−18	−25	−06	14	02	−12	02
3. Anomia	−22	−30	−09	13	−05	−12	05
4. General optimism-pessimism	−04	00	06	16	−11	−03	02
5. Social desirability	−05	−04	05	06	05	−02	−01
6. General satisfaction	00	05	15	02	04	04	−02
7. Self-evaluation/anxiety	−09	−13	−05	04	05	−07	−00
8. Misanthropy-trust in people	05	07	−07	−02	−01	01	08

Note:
(a) Situational variables:
1. Political interest
2. Political information
3. Satisfaction with living conditions
4. Awareness of a possible communist threat
5. Religious involvement
6. Social integration
7. Political alienation

Comments:
Authoritarianism, dogmatism and anomia are consistently and rather strongly related to political interest and information, awareness of a possible communist threat as well as, more weakly, to social integration. Note the strong negative relationship between anomia and political information, the positive one between authoritarianism and awareness of a possible communist threat. The latter is consistently related to general pessimism. Social desirability is unrelated to any situational variable. General satisfaction is consistently related to satisfaction with living conditions.

H. *Intercorrelations: personal history vs. background variables*

Personal history variables (a)

	1	2	3	4	5	5″	6	7
1. Social mobility (objective)	00	06	−05	−01	02	01	−13	01
2. Social mobility (subjective)	−04	01	04	−03	16	08	−06	−37
3. Social class (objective)	−03	02	18	−01	20	01	61	38
4. Social class (subjective)	−01	05	18	00	−29	−05	36	65
5. Education level	−00	06	23	−01	−18	02	39	38
6. Income level	−07	00	13	04	−16	−02	43	30
7. Occupational level	−03	04	17	−01	−17	−05	27	31
8. Status-inconsistency	03	04	06	02	−00	02	−14	01
9. Age	−04	−04	00	07	01	−02	−04	−06
10. Sex	−01	−02	00	03	−06	−05	02	10
11. Residence (urban. level)	06	07	47	06	01	17	−11	−10
12. Religion	06	06	−17	41	−13	−41	−02	01
13. Church-attendance	−06	−06	−18	−04	05	32	03	08

Note:
(a) Personal history variables:
1. Relation to parents in youth; socio-emotional
2. Relation to parents in youth; normative
3. Residence in youth; urbanization level
4. A religious upbringing
5. Political partisanship of father; left-right order
5″. Idem; libertarian-traditional
6. Parents' social class (objective)
7. Parents' social class (subjective)

Comments:
Relationship to parents in youth is unrelated to any background variable. Residence in youth is moderately related to both social class and religious variables. Whether one has had a religious upbringing, and in which religion, is related to residential and other religious variables. Political partisanship of father along the left-right dimension is related to social class variables; along the libertarianism-traditionalism dimension to residential and religious variables. Social class background of the respondents' parents is consistently related to social class variables: note the rather strong negative relationship between subjective mobility and subjective class of parents.

I. Intercorrelations situational vs. background variables

	Situational variables (a)						
	1	2	3	4	5	6	7
1. Social mobility (objective)	11	12	05	−03	−03	−01	02
2. Social mobility (subjective)	11	09	12	−08	02	03	03
3. Social class (objective)	15	25	15	−04	−06	11	−02
4. Social class (subjective)	14	22	20	00	−05	12	−01
5. Educational level	23	37	05	−09	−05	12	01
6. Income level	20	25	23	−02	−10	09	00
7. Occupational level	19	23	09	−04	03	07	−01
8. Status-inconsistency	07	12	−13	−03	04	03	01
9. Age	04	−05	09	18	18	−09	01
10. Sex	−21	−29	12	07	02	−10	−08
11. Residence (urban. level)	05	08	−09	−00	−10	−05	09
12. Religion	00	−04	11	16	16	00	−09
13. Church-attendance	03	02	−09	−03	−33	−01	02

Note:
(a) Situational variables:
1. Political interest
2. Political information
3. Satisfaction with living conditions
4. Awareness of a possible communist threat
5. Religious involvement
6. Social integration
7. Political alienation

Comments:
Political interest and information are most strongly related to social class variables (especially educational level) and, as might have been predicted, to sex (women have less interest in and information on politics). As also might have been predicted, satisfaction is related to social class variables, but most strongly so to income-level. Communist threat-awareness is moderately related to age and religion: older people and protestants do feel that there is a greater possibility of

a communist threat, which is consistent with their general pessimism (see Table E). Religious involvement is also related to religion (protestants tend to be more involved than catholics), age, residence and of course to church-attendance. The (weak) measure of social integration only shows weak relationships to some social class variables and an unexpected negative relation to sex. Political alienation is virtually unrelated to any other variable.

J. *Intercorrelations: personal history vs. situational variables*

	Situational variables (a)						
	1	2	3	4	5	6	7
1. Rel. to parents in youth (socio-emotional)	−03	00	*11*	01	01	04	−03
2. Rel. to parents in youth (normative)	04	03	05	04	*10*	04	−02
3. Residence in youth (urbanizat. level)	06	*12*	−07	−04	*−11*	−04	−07
4. A religious upbringing	03	00	07	*13*	*26*	−02	−03
5. Political partisanship father: left-right	01	02	11	06	02	01	00
5″. Political partisanship father: libert.-trad.	04	06	−04	−07	*−15*	03	03
6. Parents social class (objective)	08	*15*	*11*	−01	−03	09	−03
7. Parents social class (subjective)	09	*11*	*12*	01	02	*11*	−01

Note:
(a) Situational variables:
1. Political interest
2. Political information
3. Satisfaction with living conditions
4. Awareness of a possible communist threat
5. Religious involvement
6. Social integration
7. Political alienation

Comments:
Some weak evidence of the validity of the 'normative relationship to parents in youth' scale is found in its positive relationship to religious involvement. Religious involvement is also consistently related to place of residence in youth, being raised as protestant (especially Calvinist) vs. roman-catholic and political partisanship along the libertarian-traditional dimension. Parents social class is consistently, though not strongly, related to both political information and satisfaction with living conditions. The positive relationship of the latter variable to socio-emotional relations to parents in youth is also partly validating as regards the latter variable.

Author Index*

* This index does not include references to Chapter 3, where a survey of the research literature has been given.

Subject Index